KT-526-095

J2ME™
IN A NUTSHELL

A Desktop Quick Reference

PARK LEARNING CENTRE
UNIVERSITY OF GLOUCESTERSHIRE
P.O. Box 220, The Park
Cheltenham GL50 2RH
Tel: 01242 532721

Kim Topley

O'REILLY®

Beijing • Cambridge • Farnham • Köln • Paris • Sebastopol • Taipei • Tokyo

J2ME™ in a Nutshell

by Kim Topley

Copyright © 2002 O'Reilly & Associates, Inc. All rights reserved.
Printed in the United States of America.

Published by O'Reilly & Associates, Inc., 1005 Gravenstein Highway North,
Sebastopol, CA 95472.

O'Reilly & Associates books may be purchased for educational, business, or sales
promotional use. Online editions are also available for most titles
(*safari.oreilly.com*). For more information contact our corporate/institutional sales
department: 800-998-9938 or *corporate@oreilly.com*.

Editor: Robert Eckstein

Production Editor: Leanne Clarke Soylemez

Cover Designer: Ellie Volckhausen

Printing History:

March 2002:   First Edition.

Nutshell Handbook, the Nutshell Handbook logo, and the O'Reilly logo are
registered trademarks of O'Reilly & Associates, Inc. The association of the image of
a galago and the topic of J2ME is a trademark of O'Reilly & Associates, Inc. Java and
all Java-based trademarks and logos are trademarks or registered trademarks of Sun
Microsystems, Inc., in the United States and other countries. O'Reilly & Associates,
Inc., is independent of Sun Microsystems.

Many of the designations used by manufacturers and sellers to distinguish their
products are claimed as trademarks. Where those designations appear in this book,
and O'Reilly & Associates, Inc., was aware of a trademark claim, the designations
have been printed in caps or initial caps.

While every precaution has been taken in the preparation of this book, the publisher
and the author assume no responsibility for errors or omissions, or for damages
resulting from the use of the information contained herein.

0-596-00253-X
[M]

Table of Contents

Preface

This book is a desktop quick reference for the Java™ 2 Micro Edition (J2ME™). It is intended for Java programmers writing applications for devices with limited memory resources and processor power, such as cell phones, Personal Data Assistants (PDAs), and set-top boxes. The first part of this book provides a fast-paced introduction to the two different configurations that make up the J2ME platform—the Connected Limited Device Configuration (CLDC) and the Connected Device Configuration (CDC), along with the profiles that are based on them, such as the Mobile Information Device Profile (MIDP), which provides the APIs for programming cell phones and similar devices. These chapters are followed by a quick-reference section that details each class of the CLDC and MIDP APIs, along with tables that show which Java packages and classes are available in each configuration and profile.

This book is intended to be used in conjunction with the best-selling *Java in a Nutshell*, by David Flanagan, and *Java Enterprise in a Nutshell*, by Jim Farley, David Flanagan, and William Crawford (both published by O'Reilly). *Java in a Nutshell* introduces the Java programming language itself and provides an API quick reference for the core packages and classes of the Java 2 Standard Edition (J2SE) platform. *Java Enterprise in a Nutshell* does the same for the APIs in the Java 2 Enterprise Edition (J2EE). The CDC and its profiles are actually large subsets of the J2SE API, and, therefore, this book does not replicate their API quick reference material, which you can find in *Java in a Nutshell* and, in the case of the RMI profile, in *Java Enterprise in a Nutshell*.

Contents of This Book

The first nine chapters of this book describe the J2ME platform, the command-line tools that are provided with Sun's J2ME reference implementations, and some of the visual development environments that you can use when writing J2ME applications:

Chapter 1, *Introduction*

This chapter introduces the J2ME platform and the concepts of configuration and profile, and it compares J2ME to a number of other Java platforms for small devices.

Chapter 2, *The Connected Limited Device Configuration*

This chapter covers the Connected Limited Device Configuration (CLDC), which is the basic building block for the J2ME profiles for wireless devices and PDAs. It begins by outlining the differences between CLDC and the core libraries of the J2SE platform. Then it takes a close look at KVM, the small-footprint virtual machine that is used in Sun's reference implementation of CLDC.

Chapter 3, *The Mobile Information Device Profile and MIDlets*

This chapter introduces *MIDlets*, the wireless Java equivalent of applets. MIDlets are part of the Mobile Information Device Profile (MIDP), which is the subject of this and the following three chapters. This chapter looks at the lifecycle of a MIDlet and illustrates it with a simple example. It concludes with a discussion of the facilities that a typical mobile device would provide to allow the user to download, install, manage, and remove MIDlets.

Chapter 4, *MIDlet User Interfaces*

The devices that MIDlets run on range from cell phones with a small two-color display and room for only a few lines of text to PDAs with larger, multi-color screens. In order to isolate MIDlets from the specifics of the devices on which they are running, MIDP includes a high-level API that provides simple input and output controls and the ability to combine these controls to create form-like screens. This chapter takes a detailed look at the high-level API and provides sample MIDlets that can be run on cell phones or PDAs.

Chapter 5, *The Low-Level MIDlet User Interface API*

This chapter looks at an alternative user interface API that provides lower-level access to a mobile device's screen and input devices. This chapter looks at the details of this API and shows how to avoid writing code that may not be portable between devices with different user interface capabilities.

Chapter 6, *Wireless Java: Networking and Persistent Storage*

Networking is a key feature of a mobile device. The first part of this chapter looks at the Generic Connection Framework (GCF), which provides the basis for access to various networking APIs, including optional protocols (such as sockets and datagrams) and HTTP, which all MIDP implementations are required to support. A simple example that involves fetching information from a web site is used to illustrate the use of HTTP on a mobile device and shows how to avoid problems that arise when working in an environment with limited memory. The second part of this chapter looks at the facilities available for storing information on a mobile device and illustrates them by extending the HTTP example to include persistence of information retrieved from the web site.

Chapter 7, *The Connected Device Configuration and Its Profiles*

This chapter looks at the Connected Device Configuration (CDC) and its profiles, which are designed for use on devices that have more than 2 MB of memory to devote to the Java platform. It begins by looking at Sun's reference implementation of CDC and the CVM, the virtual machine for CDC devices, then briefly covers the content of the CDC-based profiles that are currently defined.

Chapter 8, *J2ME Command-Line Tools*

This chapter contains reference material for the command-line tools that are provided with the CLDC and CDC reference implementations and the MIDP for the PalmOS product.

Chapter 9, *J2ME Programming Environments*

This chapter covers the J2ME wireless toolkit, a development environment provided by Sun that allows you to create and test MIDlets using a cell-phone emulator that can be customized to resemble a number of different cell phones and PalmOS-based handhelds. It also looks at how to use the wireless toolkit in conjunction with Sun's Forte for Java IDE to create a complete development environment, and it investigates a number of alternative third-party products that provide similar functionality.

These first nine chapters provide a tutorial introduction to J2ME, with particular emphasis on wireless devices, which are currently the most popular application of J2ME technology. The core of this book, however, is the API quick reference, Chapters 10 through 18, which is a succinct but detailed API reference formatted for optimum ease of use. Please be sure to read "How To Use This Quick Reference," which appears at the beginning of the reference section; it explains how to get the most out of this section.

Related Books

O'Reilly & Associates, Inc., publishes an entire series of books on Java programming. These books include *Java in a Nutshell* and *Java Enterprise in a Nutshell*, which, as mentioned earlier, are companions to this book.

You can find a complete list of Java books from O'Reilly at *http://java.oreilly.com*. Books that are of particular interest to J2ME programmers include:

Java in a Nutshell, by David Flanagan

A Java language tutorial and complete API reference for the core Java classes. This book is of particular interest if you intend to work with the CDC-based profiles, since the APIs very closely match those of J2SE.

Java Enterprise in a Nutshell, by Jim Farley and William Crawford, with David Flanagan

A tutorial and API reference for Java's enterprise APIs, including Remote Method Invocation (RMI). This book will be of interest to you if you intend to use the RMI profile.

Java Network Programming, by Elliotte Rusty Harold

A book that describes the J2SE networking APIs.

Java I/O, by Elliotte Rusty Harold

A book that describes the input/output architecture of the Java platform, a proper understanding of which is essential if you intend to use the networking and persistent storage features of MIDP.

Java Threads, by Scott Oaks and Henry Wong
> A book that describes how to make use of Java's built-in multithreading features, which are also available in the J2ME platform.

Learning Wireless Java, by Qusay Mahmoud
> An introduction to Wireless Java, this book also shows how to install MIDlets in some of the Java-enabled cell phones that are currently available.

J2ME Programming Resources Online

This book is a quick reference designed for speedy access to frequently needed information. It does not, and cannot, tell you everything you need to know about J2ME. In addition to the books listed earlier, there are several valuable (and free) electronic sources of information about J2ME.

Sun's web site for all things related to Java is *http://java.sun.com*. This web site includes home pages for many of the products that make up the J2ME platform, including the following:

http://java.sun.com/j2me/
> General information on the J2ME platform

http://java.sun.com/products/cldc/
> The CLDC specification and to download the reference implementation

http://java.sun.com/products/midp/
> The MIDP specification

http://java.sun.com/projects/cdc/
> The specification and reference implementation of the CDC

The following page is useful as a starting point for finding the latest documentation:

> *http://java.sun.com/j2me/docs/*

The web site specifically for Java developers is *http://developer.java.sun.com*. Much of the content on this developer site is password-protected, and access to it requires (free) registration. This site includes a forum for the K Virtual Machine (KVM), which also discusses wider issues related to wireless development and J2ME in general. Once you have registered, you can reach this forum at the following URL:

> *http://forum.java.sun.com/forum.jsp?forum=50*

Sun also has a web site dedicated to Wireless Java development:

> *http://wireless.java.sun.com*

There is also a mailing list for discussion of KVM and MIDP; you can subscribe to it or just browse the archives at:

> *http://archives.java.sun.com/archives/kvm-interest.html*

Bill Day's J2ME site is very useful for up-to-date documentation and for links to other sources of J2ME-related information and development tools:

> *http://www.billday.com/j2me/*

J2ME implementations currently do not have XML or cryptography support included. In many applications, one or both of these is vital. You can find an open-source XML product suitable for J2ME at *http://www.kxml.org* and an open-source, lightweight crytography product at *http://www.bouncycastle.org.*

Information on cell phones and PDAs that support J2ME can be obtained from:

http://www.javamobiles.com

Examples Online

The examples in this book are available online and can be downloaded from the home page for the book at *http://www.oreilly.com/catalog/j2meanut/.* You may also want to visit this site to see if any important notes or errata about the book have been published there.

The example code is held in two separate directory structures, which contain exactly the same source code, but organized differently. The directory *src* has the source code arranged in a hierarchy that is convenient if you intend to build and run the examples using an integrated development environment such as Sun's Forte for Java. If, on the other hand, you plan to use the J2ME Wireless Toolkit, which expects its source files to be arranged differently, you should use the examples in the *wtksrc* directory. The J2ME Wireless Toolkit is available for free download from Sun's web site at *http://java.sun.com/products/j2mewtoolkit/.*

Some of the descriptions of the examples in this book assume that you are using the J2ME Wireless Toolkit. You'll find information on how to use the example source code with the wireless toolkit in Chapter 3 and how to use it with Forte for Java in Chapter 9.

Conventions Used in This Book

The following font conventions are used in this book:

Italic
> Used for emphasis and to signify the first use of a term. Italic is also used for commands, email addresses, URLs, FTP sites, file and directory names, and newsgroups.

`Constant width`
> Used in all Java code and generally for anything that you would type literally when programming, including keywords, data types, constants, method names, variables, class names, and interface names.

`Constant width italic`
> Used for the names of function arguments and generally as a placeholder to indicate an item that should be replaced with an actual value in your program.

 Used to indicate a general note or tip.

Used to indicate a warning.

Request for Comments

Please address comments and questions concerning this book to the publisher:

O'Reilly & Associates, Inc.
1005 Gravenstein Highway North
Sebastopol, CA 95472
(800) 998-9938 (in the United States or Canada)
(707) 829-0515 (international/local)
(707) 829-0104 (fax)

There is a web page for this book, which lists errata, examples, or any additional information. You can access this page at:

http://www.oreilly.com/catalog/j2meanut/

To comment or ask technical questions about this book, send email to:

bookquestions@oreilly.com

For more information about books, conferences, Resource Centers, and the O'Reilly Network, see the O'Reilly web site at:

http://www.oreilly.com

Acknowledgments

This book is based on the style of the bestselling *Java in a Nutshell*, which is one of the two books that made it possible for me to make my living in the Java world. First and foremost, therefore, I would like to express my thanks to David Flanagan, the author of *Java in a Nutshell*, both for his part in getting me started down this path and for his help and advice during the creation of reference material for *J2ME in a Nutshell*.

Thanks are also due Mike Loukides and Bob Eckstein, who gave me the opportunity to write this book based on a very sketchy proposal and realize my longstanding ambition to write for O'Reilly. Bob was also this book's editor and provided excellent feedback on each chapter as it was completed. He and the rest of the O'Reilly production team, whose names appear in the colophon, also converted my final draft into the more polished form in which it now appears. Special thanks to Leanne Soylemez for arranging the production schedule to fit my holiday plans, to Robert Romano for making the diagrams in the book look like they were produced by a professional, and to the book's technical reviewers, Marc Loy (coauthor of O'Reilly's *Java Swing*, along with Bob Eckstein) and Tom Keihl, for their helpful and constructive comments.

The final couple of chapters and the reference material for this book were completed over the Christmas and New Year 2000–2001 holiday period, when I should really have been spending more time with my family eating turkey and Christmas pudding and drinking the beer my son thoughtfully gave me as a present. Thanks to Berys, Andrew, and Katie for allowing me to retreat to my study for most of every day (and night) during that hectic period, and for allowing me to come out and rejoin the family when the book was finished!

PART I

Introduction to the Java 2 Micro Edition Platform API

Part I is an introduction to the Java 2 Micro Edition platform. These chapters provide enough information for you to get started using the J2ME APIs right away.

Chapter 1, *Introduction*

Chapter 2, *The Connected Limited Device Configuration*

Chapter 3, *The Mobile Information Device Profile and MIDlets*

Chapter 4, *MIDlet User Interfaces*

Chapter 5, *The Low-Level MIDlet User Interface API*

Chapter 6, *Wireless Java: Networking and Persistent Storage*

Chapter 7, *The Connected Device Configuration and Its Profiles*

Chapter 8, *J2ME Command-Line Tools*

Chapter 9, *J2ME Programming Environments*

CHAPTER 1

Introduction

This book is an introduction to and a quick reference for the Java 2 Micro Edition (J2ME) APIs. J2ME is a family of specifications that defines various downsized versions of the standard Java 2 platform; these downsized versions can be used to program consumer electronic devices ranging from cell phones to highly capable Personal Data Assistants (PDAs), smart phones, and set-top boxes. Diverse as they are in both form and function, these devices have in common the fact that they either do not have the memory and/or processing power or do not need to support J2SE, the standard Java platform used on desktop and server systems. This chapter introduces J2ME and compares it to other platforms that target the same range of hardware.

What Is the J2ME Platform?

In the early 1990s, Sun Microsystems created a new programming language called Oak as part of a research project to build consumer electronics products that relied heavily on software. The first prototype for Oak was a portable home controller called Star7, a small handheld device with an LCD touchscreen and built-in wireless networking and infrared communications. It could be used as remote control for a television or VCR and as an electronic program guide, and it also had some of the functions that are now associated with PDAs, such as appointment scheduling. Software for this type of device needs to be extremely reliable and must not make excessive demands on memory or require an extremely powerful (and therefore expensive) processor. Oak was developed as a result of the development team's experiences with C++, which, despite having many powerful features, proved to be prone to programmer errors that affected software reliability. Oak was designed to remove or reduce the ability for programmers to create problems for themselves by detecting more errors at compile time and by removing some of the features of the C++ language (such as pointers and programmer-controlled memory management) that seemed to be most closely associated with the reliability problems. Unfortunately, the market for the type of devices that the new language was intended for did not develop as Sun hoped, and no Oak-based devices were ever sold to consumers. However, at around the same time, the beginnings of public awareness of the Internet created a market for Internet browsing software. In response to this, Sun renamed the Oak programming language Java and used it to build a cross-platform browser called HotJava. It also licensed Java to Netscape, which incorporated it into its own popular browser, at the time the undisputed market leader. Thus, the world was introduced to Java applets.

Within a couple of years, the cross-platform capabilities of the Java programming language and its potential as a development platform for free-standing applications that could be written once and then run on both Windows and Unix-based systems had sparked the interest of commercial end users as a way of reducing software development costs. In order to meet the needs of seasoned Windows and Motif/X-Windows developers working to create applications for sophisticated end users accustomed to using rich user interfaces, Sun rapidly expanded the scope (and size) of the Java platform. This expanded platform included a much more complex set of user interface libraries than those used to build the original applets, together with an array of features for distributed computing and improved security.

By the time Sun released the first customer shipment of the Java 2 platform, it had become necessary to split it into several pieces. The core functionality, regarded as the minimum support required for any Java environment, is packaged as the Java 2 Standard Edition (J2SE). Several optional packages can be added to J2SE to satisfy specific requirements for particular application domains, such as a secure sockets extension to enable electronic commerce. Sun also responded to an increasing interest in using Java for enterprise-level development and in application server environments with the Java 2 Enterprise Edition (J2EE), which incorporates new technology such as servlets, Enterprise JavaBeans, and JavaServer pages.

As with most software, Java's resource requirements have increased with each release. Although it has its roots in software for consumer electronics products, J2SE requires far too much memory and processor power to be a viable solution in that marketplace. Ironically, while Sun was developing Java for the Internet and commercial programming, demand began to grow for Java on smaller devices and even on smart cards, thus returning Java to its roots. Sun responded by creating several reduced-functionality Java platforms, each tailored to a specific vertical market segment, some of which will be covered briefly at the end of this chapter. These platforms are all based on JDK 1.1, the predecessor of the Java 2 platform, and they take different approaches to the problem of reducing the platform to fit the available resources. In a sense, therefore, each of these reduced-functionality platforms represents an ad-hoc solution to this problem, a solution that has evolved over time to meet the needs of its own particular markets.

J2ME is a platform for small devices that is intended eventually to replace the various JDK 1.1–based products with a more unified solution based on Java 2. Unlike the desktop and server worlds targeted by J2SE and J2EE, the micro-world includes such a wide range of devices with vastly different capabilities that it is not possible to create a single software product to suit all of them. Instead of being a single entity, therefore, J2ME is a collection of specifications that define a set of a platforms, each of which is suitable for a subset of the total collection of consumer devices that that fall within its scope. The subset of the full Java programming environment for a particular device is defined by one or more *profiles*, which extend the basic capabilities of a *configuration*. The configuration and profile or profiles that are appropriate for a device depend both on the nature of its hardware and the market to which it is targeted.

Configurations

A configuration is a specification that defines the software environment for a range of devices defined by a set of characteristics that the specification relies on, usually such things as:

- The types and amount of memory available
- The processor type and speed
- The type of network connection available to the device

A configuration is supposed to represent the minimum platform for its target device and is not permitted to define optional features. Vendors are required to implement the specification fully so that developers can rely on a consistent programming environment and, therefore, create applications that are as device-independent as possible.

J2ME currently defines two configurations:

Connected Limited Device Configuration (CLDC)
CLDC is aimed at the low end of the consumer electronics range. A typical CLDC platform is a cell phone or PDA with around 512 KB of available memory. For this reason, CLDC is closely associated with wireless Java, which is concerned with allowing cell phone users to purchase and download small Java applications known as *MIDlets* to their handsets. A large and growing number of cell phone vendors have signed agreements with Sun Microsystems that will allow them to begin using this technology, so the number of handsets with the capability to be programmed in Java will probably grow rapidly in the next few years.

Connected Device Configuration (CDC)
CDC addresses the needs of devices that lie between those addressed by CLDC and the full desktop systems running J2SE. These devices have more memory (typically 2 MB or more) and more capable processors, and they can, therefore, support a much more complete Java software environment. CDC might be found on high-end PDAs and in smart phones, web telephones, residential gateways, and set-top boxes.

Each configuration consists of a Java virtual machine and a core collection of Java classes that provide the programming environment for application software. Processor and memory limitations, particularly in low-end devices, can make it impossible for a J2ME virtual machine to support all of the Java language features or instruction byte codes and software optimizations provided by a J2SE VM. Therefore, J2ME VMs are usually defined in terms of those parts of the Java Virtual Machine Specification and the Java Language Specification that they are *not* obliged to implement. As an example of this, devices targeted by CLDC often do not have floating point hardware, and a CLDC VM is therefore not required to support the Java language types float and double or any of the classes and methods that require these types or involve floating-point operations.

It is important to note that configuration specifications do not require implementations to use any specific virtual machine. Vendors are free to create their own VM or license a third-party VM, provided that it meets the minimum requirements of the specification. Sun provides reference implementations of both configurations, each of which includes a conforming virtual machine:

- The CLDC reference implementation is a source code and binary product for the Windows, Solaris and Linux platforms. It includes the Kilobyte Virtual Machine (KVM), a reduced-functionality VM that has a very small memory footprint and incorporates a garbage collector that is optimized for a memory-constrained environment. KVM, which is discussed in Chapter 2, is likely to be used as the basis for most CLDC implementations in the near future, but there are other VMs that could be used instead, such as the J9 VM from IBM.

- The CDC reference implementation is a source code–only product for Linux and the Wind River VxWorks real-time operating system. The VM included with this product, called CVM (see Chapter 7), implements the full range of J2SE VM features as required by the CDC specification. However, it does not include the HotSpot technology found in the J2SE Version 1.3 VM or even a just-in-time compiler (JIT) as found in earlier J2SE releases. Several third-party vendors, including Insignia Solutions and IBM, have plans to release their own CDC implementations that include different virtual machines.

A configuration also includes a core set of Java language classes. The core class libraries defined for a configuration (and for profiles) are required to be based on those of the Java 2 platform. This promotes as much compatability as possible between applications written for different J2ME platforms and those written with J2SE, and it also reduces the learning curve for J2ME developers. Broadly speaking, this means that developers can rely on the following:

- Where possible, J2ME must reuse J2SE classes and packages. This means that, for example, it would not be acceptable for a J2ME configuration or profile to eschew the java.util.Date class and introduce one of its own.* As a result, everything that you know about J2SE can be carried forward to J2ME, provided you know the exceptions that apply to the configuration and profiles you are working with. That information is available in the reference section of this book.

- When a J2SE class is incorporated into J2ME, new methods and fields may not be added to it. Similarly, new classes cannot be added to a coopted J2SE package. These rules ensure that code written for J2ME that uses only those classes it shares with J2SE will compile and work on J2SE, thus making it possible to share code between these platforms.

---

* It could be argued that CLDC breaks this rule with its networking classes, because there is no usable subset of the java.net package that would fit into the restricted memory available to a CLDC-based device. This problem is solved by creating a new package that contains a more lightweight set of networking classes. See Chapter 6 for details.

You'll find detailed coverage of CLDC and KVM in Chapter 2 and coverage of CDC and CVM in Chapter 7.

Profiles

A profile complements a configuration by adding additional classes that provide features appropriate to a particular type of device or to a specific vertical market segment. Both J2ME configurations have one or more associated profiles, some of which may themselves rely on other profiles. Figure 1-1 shows the profiles that are currently defined or in the process of being defined and the configurations they are dependent upon. These processes are described in the following list:

Mobile Information Device Profile (MIDP)
This profile adds networking, user interface components, and local storage to CLDC. This profile is primarily aimed at the limited display and storage facilities of mobile phones, and it therefore provides a relatively simple user interface and basic networking based on HTTP 1.1. MIDP is the best known of the J2ME profiles because it is the basis for Wireless Java and is currently the only profile available for PalmOS-based handhelds.

PDA Profile (PDAP)
The PDA Profile is similar to MIDP, but it is aimed at PDAs that have better screens and more memory than cell phones. The PDA profile, which is not complete at the time of writing, will offer a more sophisticated user interface library and a Java-based API for accessing useful features of the host operating system. When this profile becomes available, it is likely to take over from MIDP as the J2ME platform for small handheld computers such as those from Palm and Handspring.

Foundation Profile
The Foundation Profile extends the CDC to include almost all of the core Java 2 Version 1.3 core libraries. As its name suggests, it is intended to be used as the basis for most of the other CDC profiles.

Personal Basis and Personal Profiles
The Personal Basis Profile adds basic user interface functionality to the Foundation Profile. It is intended to be used on devices that have an unsophisticated user interface capability, and it therefore does not allow more than one window to be active at any time. Platforms that can support a more complex user interface will use the Personal Profile instead. At the time of writing, both these profiles are in the process of being specified.

RMI Profile
The RMI Profile adds the J2SE Remote Method Invocation libraries to the Foundation Profile. Only the client side of this API is supported.

Game Profile
The Game Profile, which is still in the process of being defined, will provide a platform for writing games software on CDC devices. At the time of writing, it is not certain whether this profile will be derived from the Foundation Profile or based directly on CDC.

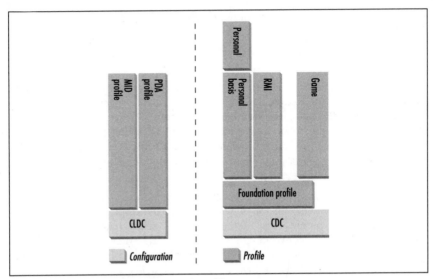

Figure 1-1: J2ME configurations and profiles

J2ME Specifications

All of the J2ME configurations and profiles have been developed as part of the Java Community Process (JCP). The JCP brings together leading players in the relevant industries with the aim of agreeing on a common specification to which they can all design their products. Each configuration or profile started out as a Java Specification Request (JSR), which describes the scope of the work to be done and an outline of the areas to be covered. An expert group is assembled to create the specification, which is then subject to an internal ballot and revision before being made available for public review. Following public review and a possible last revision, the final draft is produced, and the JSR is completed.

The current list of JSRs, including those that have been completed, can be found on the JCP web site at *http://jcp.org/jsr/all/*. The JSRs that define the current J2ME configurations and profiles are as follows:

Number	Scope
JSR 30	J2ME Connected Limited Device Configuration (CLDC)
JSR 37	Mobile Information Device Profile for the J2ME Platform (MIDP)
JSR 75	PDA Profile for the J2ME Platform
JSR 36	J2ME Connected Device Configuration (CDC)
JSR 46	J2ME Foundation Profile
JSR 129	Personal Basis Profile Specification
JSR 62	Personal Profile Specification
JSR 66	J2ME RMI Profile
JSR 134	Java Game Profile

There is also work in progress that is not directly related to any configuration or profile:

Number	Scope
JSR 82	Java APIs for Bluetooth
JSR 120	Wireless Telephony Communication APIs (WTCA)
JSR 135	J2ME Multimedia API

Finally, even though some of the current profiles have not yet been fully defined, work is already underway to define the next generation of the J2ME platform. At the time of writing, nothing is available for public review, but it would be worth keeping an eye on the following JSRs:

Number	Scope
JSR 68	J2ME Platform Specification
JSR 118	Mobile Information Device Next Generation
JSR 139	Connected Limited Device Configuration Next Generation

J2ME and Other Java Platforms

J2ME is intended to be the way ahead for Java on small devices, but, as noted at the beginning of this chapter, there are other Java platforms already in existence (and in use) that have similar scope. The following sections briefly summarize these alternative platforms and compare them to J2ME.

JavaCard

JavaCard is a platform aimed at smart card technology. Smart cards are the smallest environment for which a Java platform exists. The constraints of these devices are such that the JavaCard virtual machine and the small set of Java class libraries that it supports require only around 16 KB of non-volatile memory and 512 bytes of volatile memory. The scope of J2ME does not extend to platforms with this little resource, so there is no J2ME configuration that is suitable for the current generation of smart cards. You can find more information about JavaCard at *http://java. sun.com/products/javacard/*.

EmbeddedJava

EmbeddedJava is a JDK 1.1–based platform that is used to create software for embedded devices. These devices typically have a 32-bit processor with 512 KB of ROM and 512 KB of RAM available for the VM, class libraries, and embedded application. Since embedded devices generally serve only one purpose, it is unnecessary to include parts of the Java platform that the application does not require. In fact, EmbeddedJava allows the implementor to remove any package or class—or even a method within a class—that is not required, in order to fit the final product into the memory available. The EmbeddedJava specification, which can be found at *http://java.sun.com/products/embeddedjava/*, defines only the maximum possible content of the platform, rather than a minimum (as is the case with J2ME specifications).

EmbeddedJava is currently undergoing its end-of-life cycle, which means that it will no longer be supported as of January 1, 2003. In the future, developers in embedded environments will probably migrate to CDLC and one of its profiles, which are targeted to devices with similar resources.

PersonalJava

PersonalJava is intended for a much more general application environment than EmbeddedJava. The target devices for Personal Java have up to 2 MB of ROM and at least 1 MB of RAM available for the Java platform itself, with more required for application software. Some of the larger PDAs and communicator devices, such as the Compaq iPAQ and the Nokia 9210 cell phone, are currently using the PersonalJava environment.

PersonalJava is based on JDK 1.1.8 and includes a fully featured Java VM. The specification, available at *http://java.sun.com/products/personaljava/*, designates each of the core JDK 1.1.8 packages as required, modified, or optional. Similar designations may also be applied to individual classes and methods. A required package must contain all of the classes from its JDK 1.1.8 counterpart, and each class must be a full implementation. An optional package may or may not be present, but if it is present, it must be complete. A modified package must be present, but its content may differ from its JDK 1.1.8 equivalent according to rules laid down in the specification. PersonalJava includes user interface components in the form of a modified `java.awt` package, and it also has optional support for RMI.

PersonalJava developers are expected to use CDC as a migration path to the Java 2 platform. Since PersonalJava includes user interface components, it will be necessary to wait for the Personal Basis and Personal Profiles to become available before migration can be started. PersonalJava applications that use RMI will also need to use the CDC RMI profile.

CHAPTER 2

The Connected Limited Device Configuration

The Connected Limited Device Configuration (CLDC) is the basic building block on which the J2ME profiles for small devices, such as cell phones, pagers, and low-end PDAs, are built. These devices are characterized by their limited memory resources and processing power, which make it impossible for them to host a fully featured Java platform. CLDC specifies a minimal set of Java packages and classes and a reduced functionality Java virtual machine that can be implemented within the resource constraints imposed by such small devices.

The first part of this chapter describes the features that a Java virtual machine capable of supporting CLDC must provide, and it explains how such a VM differs from the standard one required by J2SE. As part of this discussion, we'll make use of Sun's reference implementation of the CLDC specification and the Kilobyte Virtual Machine, or KVM, around which it is based. The second part of the chapter covers the Java packages and classes that a CLDC implementation must provide, which are a small subset of the core packages found in J2SE. The chapter concludes with a discussion of the debugging facilities provided by the KVM and a couple of advanced features—using native code and preloading Java classes—that will be of interest to readers who want to work with the KVM at the source code level.

The CLDC Java Virtual Machine

The hardware and software limitations imposed by the devices at which CLDC is targeted make it impractical to support either a full Java virtual machine or a complete set of J2SE core classes. Running a simple "Hello, world" application on the Windows platform requires around 16 MB of memory to be allocated. Contrast this with the minimum platform requirements for CLDC, which call for:

- 128 KB of ROM, flash or battery-backed memory for persistent storage of the Java VM and the class libraries that make up the CLDC platform.

11

- 32 KB (or more) of volatile memory to be available for runtime allocation. This memory is used to satisfy the dynamic requirements of Java applications, which include class loading and the allocation of heap space for objects and the stack.

In order to support a Java runtime environment with such limited resources, CLDC defines reduced requirements for the virtual machine, the language itself, and the core libraries, details of which we'll describe in the following sections.

Other than the memory requirements, CLDC makes few assumptions about its host platform. It does not, for example, assume that the device will have any kind of display or user input mechanism such as a keyboard or a mouse, and it does not require any kind of local storage for application data. These issues are all assumed to be addressed individually by each device vendor. J2ME profiles, of course, place additional requirements that are suitable for the more limited range of devices they are intended for, as you'll see in Chapters 3 and 7. For CLDC, the number of requirements is minimized in order to maximize the number of platforms on which it can be implemented.

As far as the software environment is concerned, CLDC assumes only that the host device has some kind of operating system that can execute and manage the virtual machine. Although Java is a multithreaded programming environment, it is not necessary for the operating system to have the concept of threads or even to be able to schedule more than one process at any given time. Instead, the virtual machine is required to provide the illusion of a multithreaded environment using whatever native functionality is available to it.

The full specification of CLDC, which was developed under the Java Community Process, can be downloaded from *http://jcp.org/jsr/detail/30.jsp*.

Virtual Machine and Language Features

The CLDC specification defines the features that a VM must have by describing the parts of the full Java Virtual Machine Specification and the Java Language Specification that it is *not* required to support and the parts to which limitations and qualifications are applied. Sun provides a reference implementation of the CLDC specification that is based on the KVM, a small-footprint VM that satisfies the CLDC requirements. Manufacturers of devices that support CLDC and its profiles are not, however, required to base their products around KVM. Any virtual machine that has the features required by the specification and can work within the resource restrictions of the CLDC environment can be used. In this book, I will often refer to features of KVM, but, unless I explicitly state the contrary, everything I say also applies to any conforming virtual machine.[*]

The following sections describe the virtual machine and language features that are not supported in a CLDC environment or in which the CLDC behavior is different from that in J2SE.

---

[*] The IBM J9 virtual machine is another example of a VM that conforms to the CLDC specification. See *http://www.embedded.oti.com* for further information.

Floating point support

Since many of the processors used in the target platforms for CLDC do not have floating point hardware, the virtual machine is not required to support floating point operations.* In terms of the virtual machine, this means that the byte code operations listed in Table 2-1 are not implemented.

Table 2-1: Floating-Point Byte Codes Not Implemented by a CLDC VM

dadd	dload	dsub	fcmpl	frem	i2d
daload	dload_x	d2f	fconst_0	freturn	i2f
dastore	dmul	d2i	fconst_1	fstore	l2d
dcmpg	dneg	d2l	fdiv	fstore_x	l2f
dcmpl	drem	fadd	fload	fsub	newarray (double)
dconst_0	dreturn	faload	fload_x	f2d	newarray (float)
dconst_1	dstore	fastore	fmul	f2i	
ddiv	dstore_x	fcmpg	fneg	f2l	

CLDC

This leads to the following coding restrictions:

- Variables of type float and double and arrays of these types cannot be declared or used.
- Constants of type float and double (i.e., 1.0, 2.0F) cannot be used.
- Method arguments may not be of type float or double.
- Methods may not return double or float values.
- Objects of type Float and Double cannot be created (and, in fact, these classes do not exist in CLDC—see the later section "The CLDC Class Libraries" for further details).

Sun does not supply a different version of its Java compiler for use when developing CLDC applications, so it is possible, using a J2SE compiler, to create Java class files that use floating point types and, therefore, violate these rules. However, these class files will be rejected when they are loaded into the CLDC virtual machine during class file verification (see the later section "Security Features" for a discussion of class file verification).

Language omissions

Aside from the floating point restrictions, there are a few other Java language features that are not available to CLDC applications:

Reflection

The java.lang.reflect package and all of the features of java.lang. Class that are connected with reflection are not available. This restriction is

---

* Nothing prevents a VM from emulating floating point instructions in software, but the memory resources required for this are too great for this to be a general requirement for all platforms.

applied partly to save memory, but it also saves having to determine whether application code has the privilege to access these features.

Weak references
Weak references and the `java.lang.ref` package are not provided because of the memory required to implement them.

Object finalization
Object finalization causes great complexity in the VM for relatively little benefit. Therefore, finalization is not implemented, and the CLDC `java.lang.Object` class does not have a `finalize()` method.

Threading features
CLDC provides threads, but it does not allow the creation of a daemon thread (a thread that is automatically terminated when all non-daemon threads in the VM terminate) or thread groups.

Errors and exceptions
J2SE has a large number of classes that represent error and exception conditions. Since Java applications are not, in general, expected to recover from errors (meaning thrown exceptions derived from the class `java.lang.Error`), most of the classes representing them are not included in the CLDC platform. When such an error occurs, the device is responsible for taking appropriate action instead of reporting it to application code. For further details, see the later section "The CLDC Class Libraries."

Java Native Interface
CLDC does not provide the J2SE JNI feature, which allows native code to be called from Java classes. JNI is omitted partly because it is memory-intensive to implement and partly in order to protect CLDC devices against security problems caused by malicious application code. Further discussion of this issue will be found in the later section "Security Features."

Class loading

Class loading in J2SE is performed by class loaders, including application-defined class loaders that can implement an open-ended set of mechanisms for locating and loading Java classes. By contrast, the CLDC specification requires implementations to provide their own class loading mechanism that cannot be overridden or extended by application code. Doing so removes the security implications of allowing classes to be loaded from untrusted sources.

CLDC specifies that all VM implementations must be able to load applications packaged in compressed JAR files. It does not, however, rule out additional, device-dependent means of representing or accessing application code, and it does not prescribe any particular means whereby the device would locate and fetch the packaged code. These tasks are delegated to a piece of device-dependent application management software, the nature of which is outside the scope of the specification. Sun's CLDC reference implementation includes an example implementation of this functionality, which it refers to as a Java Application Manager (JAM).

A device is allowed to transform applications presented in any supported external format into an internal format that is more suitable or more efficient for that device. For example, the MIDP for PalmOS product, which includes an implementation of CLDC for the PalmOS platform, accepts applications in the form of a JAR file and converts them to the internal PRC format used by PalmOS for storage on the device. See "MIDP for PalmOS" in Chapter 9 for further details.

Security Features

In J2SE, the security model is powerful enough to allow code originating from different sources to have different levels of privilege and therefore different levels of access to system resources. At one end of the scale, applications installed on a user's system have, by default, unrestricted access. An applet downloaded from an untrusted web site, however, operates in an extremely restricted environment that permits no access to local resources, such as the user's filestore, and only limited access to the network. Between these extremes, the security model allows privileges to be individually assigned or denied to an application or applet based on the level of trust that the user has for its originator. Code to be trusted can be delivered with a certificate that provides assurance that the code comes from its claimed point of origin. It can also be cryptographically signed so that the receiver can be sure that it has not been modified while being transported from its source.

A CLDC VM could be used in a device that does not allow code to be installed by the user, and which, therefore, has much less need of security features. It could also be used at the heart of a cell phone connected to a network that allows applications to be downloaded, possibly from untrusted sources; the network should be subject to the same type of security constraints that apply to J2SE applets. It would also be useful to have intermediate security levels for code that is known to be trusted. Unfortunately, this is not practical in the general case, because the memory and processing power required to implement the fine-grained security model of J2SE, verify cryptographic signatures, and check certificates are too great for the devices targeted by the CLDC specification. Therefore, a CLDC VM runs application code in a "sandbox" environment that ensures it cannot maliciously damage the device on which it is executing. The following sections summarize the constraints that the VM applies to create the sandbox.

Class loading controls

Each CLDC implementation has its own class loader that can load classes from whatever location or locations the host device can support, typically over a network or from device local storage, if there is any. Unlike J2SE, application code is not permitted to create its own class loaders and cannot affect in any way the process that the system's own class loader uses to search for and locate classes. (In other words, there is no way to change the system's effective CLASSPATH or its equivalent.)

An important consequence of this restriction is that application code cannot attempt to substitute its own versions of core classes in the java and javax. microedition package hierarchies. If this were allowed, it could compromise the security of the Java runtime environment. The system class loader always ignores classes that claim to be part of these packages if they are included in application code.

Access to native code

CLDC does not include an implementation of JNI, and therefore it is not possible to link dynamically to native code at runtime, even if such code could be installed as part of an application. As a side effect, this also prevents direct access to functionality provided by the host device's native operating system, unless a specific Java interface for it is provided by CLDC or one of its profiles. This restriction prevents application code from reading or modifying information to which the user might not want it to have access.

However, it is possible to extend the API available to Java applications by *prelinking* extra native code with the VM, but this facility is available only to applications that are installed with a custom-built VM and is therefore not a general security risk. See the later section "Interfacing with Native Code" for details of this mechanism.

Class verification

J2SE has always provided a byte-code verifier that can check the integrity of Java class files. It ensures that the class files do not pose a risk to system security by failing to uphold rules of the Java language that are normally checked and enforced by the Java compiler, such as the following:

- All local variables must be initialized before use.

- Following creation of an object, its constructor must be called before it is used further.

- Each constructor must begin with an invocation of a constructor of its superclass (with the exception of the constructor of `java.lang.Object`).

- Local variables and instance and static members declared to contain a reference to an object of a particular type must always hold a reference to an object of that type or one that is legally assignable to it. It is not legal, for example, to define a variable of type `TimerTask` and then assign a reference to a `Timer` to it.

By default, the J2SE VM runs the byte-code verifier over all classes loaded from an external source (such as over a network) but not to classes loaded from a local filesystem. In the mobile environment, it is generally advisable to apply these checks to all application code. However, the algorithms necessary to perform the checks are very processor-intensive and may require large amounts of memory, and, therefore, they cannot feasibly be carried out at runtime on the small devices for which CLDC is primarily intended. For this reason, class file verification is performed in two stages:

1. Preverification is performed on class files before they are installed on the target device. This process involves most of the complex and time-consuming parts of the byte-code verification algorithm and is typically performed as part of or immediately followimg source code compilation. The results of the preverification step are recorded in the class file, where they can be accessed at runtime.

2. Runtime verification is performed on the device itself. Depending on the nature of the device, it may be done when a class is loaded or as part of the

application installation process, provided that installed code cannot subsequently be modified. This step uses the information stored by preverification in conjunction with a linear sweep through the byte codes of the class to ensure that all the language rules are followed. It is much quicker than preverification and requires far less memory.

You don't need to know much about preverification and runtime verification in order to compile and run CLDC applications, but brave souls can find the details in the CLDC Specification.

Compiling and Running Code with the KVM

In order to compile and run applications using the KVM, you need to download and install the following software:

- The Java 2 SDK or a development environment that has a command-line Java compiler

- Sun's CLDC reference implementation

If you don't already have a suitable Java 2 SDK installed, you can download one from *http://java.sun/com/j2se/*.

The CLDC reference implementation contains source code and documentation for Sun's CLDC implementation, which runs on Microsoft Windows, Linux, and Solaris, and it also contains the KVM and its associated tools in executable form. It can be obtained from *http://java.sun.com/products/cldc/*.

The reference implementation is provided in the form of an archive suitable for your target platform, which you should unpack into a convenient directory. In the rest of this section, we'll use the following variables to refer to the installation directories for both the Java 2 SDK and the CLDC reference implementation:

%JAVA_HOME% (Windows) or $JAVA_HOME (Linux/Solaris)
> The base installation directory for the Java 2 SDK. For Windows, this is typically *c:\jdk1.3.1*.

%CLDC_HOME% (Windows) or $CLDC_HOME (Linux/Solaris)
> The base installation directory for the CLDC reference implementation, such as *c:\CLDC*. The archive unpacks itself into a directory called *j2me_cldc* beneath this location.

%CLDC_PATH% (Windows) or $CLDC_PATH (Linux/Solaris)
> The *bin* directory beneath the CLDC installation directory. Equal to *%CLDC_HOME%\j2me_cldc\bin* for Windows and *$CLDC_HOME/j2me_cldc/bin* for Linux and Solaris.

The source code for this book includes a trivial example that we'll use to demonstrate how to compile and run code for the KVM. We'll use the variable *%EXAMPLES%* (or *$EXAMPLES*) to refer to the location at which the example source code is installed. Based on this variable, the source file for the example that we're going to use is contained in the file *%EXAMPLES%\src\ora\ch2\HelloWorld.java* and shown in Example 2-1.

Example 2-1: A Trivial KVM Application

```
package ora.ch2;

public class HelloWorld {
    public static void main(String[] args) {
        System.out.println("Hello, KVM world");
    }
}
```

The first step is to open a command window (or a shell if you're using Linux or Solaris) and set the *PATH* variable to include the executable files for both the Java 2 SDK and the CLDC reference implementation. For Windows, the following command should be used:

```
PATH=%JAVA_HOME%\bin;%CLDC_PATH%\win32;%PATH%
```

If you are using Linux or Solaris, you'll need to use the appropriate command for your chosen shell and also make sure that you pick the correct directory for the CLDC executables, which is *$CLDC_PATH/linux* or *$CLDC_PATH/solaris*.

The second step is to compile the example source code to produce a class file. In order to simplify the following commands, change your working directory to *%EXAMPLES%\src*, the directory in which the example source code is installed, and then type the following commands:

```
mkdir tmpclasses
javac -bootclasspath %CLDC_PATH%\common\api\classes -d tmpclasses
        ora\ch2\HelloWorld.java
```

These commands compile the source file *ora\ch2\HelloWorld.java*, creating a single class file called *tmpclasses\ora\ch2\HelloWorld.class*. A couple of points are worth noting:

- We used the *-d* command line option to direct the compiler to put the class file into a directory under the newly created *tmpclasses* directory instead of in the same directory as the source file, which is the default. This is because all class files to be loaded into the KVM have to be preverified (see the earlier section "Class verification") before they can be used, which involves creating a modified class file. We'll use the class file under *tmpclasses* as input to the pre-verification process and write the output class file to the source file directory.

- When running the Java compiler, we used the *–bootclasspath* option to change the location from which the core classes are loaded during compilation. As you'll see in the later section "The CLDC Class Libraries," CLDC does not include all the packages and classes available to a J2SE application, so we need to be sure that the compiler picks up the CLDC core libraries instead of those for J2SE, which it would use by default. If we had not done this, it would be possible to compile code that referenced J2SE APIs that are not available in CLDC. This would produce a legal class file that would subsequently fail to load into the KVM.

Before you can use the class file with the KVM, it has to be preverified using the *preverify* command that is included in the CLDC reference implementation. To

---

preverify the class file and write the preverified version to the same directory as the original source code, use the following command:

```
preverify -classpath %CLDC_PATH%\common\api\classes;tmpclasses -d .
    ora.ch2.HelloWorld
```

The *–classpath* command-line option indicates the directories in which the *preverify* command should look for class files, both the core Java libraries and the class file to be preverified, while the *–d* option is used to control where the preverified class file will be written. The directory names supplied with the *–classpath* option should be separated by semicolons on the Windows platform, colons in the case of Linux or Solaris. Notice that the compiler requires a source filename, but *preverify* needs a fully qualified Java class name (with its parts separated by periods) instead.

In the case of an application that consists of more than one class file, all class files must be preverified, although not necessarily at the same time. There are two ways to arrange for *preverify* to operate on more than one class file at a time. The most obvious way is to list all of the classes on the command line:

```
preverify -classpath %CLDC_PATH%\common\api\classes;tmpclasses -d .
    ora.ch2.HelloWorld ora.ch2.Help
```

Alternatively, if you supply one or more directory names on the command line, *preverify* recursively searches them and processes every class file and each ZIP and JAR file that it finds:

```
preverify -classpath %CLDC_PATH%\common\api\classes -d . tmpclasses
```

Notice that in this case, there was no need to include *tmpclasses* in the *–classpath* argument because its presence is inferred from the fact that it is the directory to be searched.

The complete set of command-line options recognized by the *preverify* command can be found in Chapter 8.

Finally, you can run the example using the *kvm* command:

```
kvm -classpath . ora.ch2.HelloWorld
```

which produces some very familiar output:

```
Hello, KVM world
```

Notice that the *–classpath* option identified only the directory search path needed to find the class file for `ora.ch2.HelloWorld`. There is no need to specify where the core libraries are located, because the KVM knows where to find them.[*]

The CLDC Class Libraries

CLDC addresses a wide range of platforms that do not have sufficient memory resources to support the full range of packages and classes provided by J2SE. Because CLDC is a configuration rather than a profile, it cannot have any optional

---

[*] In fact, the core libraries are built into the KVM using a technique known as "ROMizing," which will be covered in "Preloading Java Classes," later in this chapter.

features. Therefore, the packages and classes that it specifies must have a small enough footprint that they can be hosted by devices that meet only the minimum requirements of the CLDC specification. The CLDC class library is very small—it is composed of a package containing functionality that is specific to J2ME (called `javax.microedition.io`), along with a selection of classes from the following packages in the core J2SE platform:[*]

- `java.io`
- `java.lang`
- `java.util`

All J2ME configurations and profiles include packages or classes from J2SE. When J2ME incorporates software interfaces from J2SE, it must follow several rules:

- The names of the packages or classes must be the same, wherever possible. It would not be acceptable, for example, to completely reimplement the `java.lang` package in a package called `javax.microedition.lang` if the API in the `java.lang` package can be used.

- The semantics of classes and methods that are carried over into J2ME must be identical to those with the same name in J2SE.

- It is not possible to add public or protected fields or methods to a class that is shared between J2SE and J2ME.

Because of these rules, J2ME packages and classes will always be a subset of the packages and classes of the same name in J2SE, and the J2ME behavior will not be surprising to developers familiar with J2SE. Furthermore, J2ME configurations and profiles are not allowed to add extra functionality in packages and classes that they share with J2SE, so upward compatibility from J2ME to J2SE is preserved. However, it is permissible to exclude from J2ME those fields, methods, and classes that are deprecated in J2SE and this has been done by the Java Community Process expert group responsible for the CLDC specification.

You'll find complete information on which classes from J2SE are included in CLDC and how this set compares to other J2ME configurations and profiles in Chapter 10. Detailed information on the individual classes in the reference chapters can be found in Part II of this book. The following sections describe the most important aspects of each of the CLDC packages that distinguish them from their counterparts in J2SE.

The java.lang Package

The CLDC `java.lang` package has only half of the classes of its J2SE counterpart and some classes that are included are not complete implementations. The major points of interest are covered in the following sections.

---

[*] Among other things that have been omitted due to resource constraints, CLDC does not include any support for internationalization of applications and the formatting of dates and numbers according to locale-specific conventions. If you need to write an application that is locale-sensitive, you will need to do all the hard work yourself.

The Object class

The CLDC `java.lang.Object` class has no `finalize()` method because CLDC virtual machines do not implement finalization. Furthermore, the `clone()` method has been removed along with the `java.lang.Cloneable` interface. There is, therefore, no generic way to clone an object in a CLDC VM.

Number-related classes

As noted earlier, floating point operations are not supported by the CLDC VM and, as a consequence, the J2SE `java.lang.Float` and `java.lang.Double` classes, are not part of the core library set. The other number classes (`Byte`, `Integer`, `Long`, and `Short`) are provided, but their J2SE base class, `java.lang.Number`, is not included. The numeric classes are, therefore, derived from `Object` instead of `Number`. Another difference worthy of note is that the `java.lang.Comparable` interface does not exist in CLDC, so CLDC numbers cannot be directly compared in the same way that their J2SE counterparts are.

Reflective features

The exclusion of all VM support for reflection means that all methods in `java.lang.Class` that are connected with this feature have been removed. It is still possible, however, to perform limited operations on classes whose types are not known at compile time by using the `forName()` and `newInstance()` methods.

System properties

The CLDC profile defines only a very small set of system properties that does not include any of those available with J2SE. The properties that an implementation is required to provide are listed in Table 2-2.*

Table 2-2: System Properties Defined by CLDC

Property Name	Meaning	Example
microedition. configuration	The name of the J2ME configuration that the platform supports, together with its version number.	CLDC-1.0
microedition. encoding	The default character encoding that the device supports. Devices are not required to provide any extra encodings, but vendors are free to do so. There is, however, no way to find out which encodings are available.	ISO8859_1
microedition. platform	The name of the platform or device. The default KVM implementation returns the value `null` for this property.	J2ME
microedition. profiles	The J2ME profiles that the device supports, separated by spaces. Since the KVM does not provide any profiles, the reference implementation returns `null` for this property.	MIDP-1.0

---

* Note that, at the time of writing, there is no consistency in the way that the default encoding is represented. The KVM returns the default encoding as `ISO8859_1`, which is the value required in the CLDC specification document, whereas the MIDP reference implementation returns `ISO-8859-1`.

The value of a specific property can be obtained by using the `getProperty()` method in the `java.lang.System` class:

```
String configuration = System.getProperty("microedition.configuration");
```

Since the CLDC `java.util` package does not include the J2SE `Properties` class, the `System` class does not include the `getProperties()` method, and it is not possible to get a list of all of the available properties programmatically. Vendors are free to add their own implementation-specific properties, but it is not possible for application code to define its own, because there is no `setProperty()` method. A device that supports one or more J2ME profiles must include them in the `microedition.profiles` property, and profiles typically define their own properties in addition to those listed in Table 2-2.

The System and Runtime classes

The `System` and `Runtime` classes in J2SE contain a collection of methods that perform relatively low-level operations. These operations often involve the underlying host platform, such as starting the execution of a native-language executable from within a Java application. Because of the platform-dependent nature of these operations, and because of other restrictions imposed by the virtual machine, many features supported by these classes have been removed, including the following:

- Direct access to system properties using the `getProperties()`, `setProperty()`, and `setProperties()` methods
- Methods that allow the source and destinations for the standard input, output, and error streams to be changed
- Methods that provide access to native code libraries, which are not required because JNI is not supported
- The ability to get a reference to and change the active `SecurityManager`

Threads

CLDC virtual machines are required to provide a multithreaded programming environment even if the underlying platform does not. The Java programming interfaces used in J2SE to support multithreading—the `synchronized` keyword, the `Object wait()`, `notify()`, and `notifyAll()` methods, and the `Thread` class—are all included in the CLDC specification. However, CLDC does not provide thread groups or the `ThreadGroup` class, and several features of the J2SE `Thread` class are omitted, including the following:

- All constructors and methods relating to `ThreadGroups` have been removed.
- Threads do not have application-settable names, so the `getName()` and `setName()` methods are not required and have been removed.
- The `resume()`, `suspend()`, and `stop()` methods have been removed. These methods are, in any case, deprecated in J2SE, because they are inherently unsafe with respect to locking in a multithreaded environment.
- The `destroy()`, `interrupt()`, and `isInterrupted()` methods do not exist. Consequently, the only way to cause a thread to terminate is to signal it

to do so by changing the value of an instance variable that the thread periodically inspects, using a construction like the following:

```
public void run() {
    while (!requestedToStop) {
        // Do whatever is required
    }
}
```

- The dumpStack() method has been removed. The only way to get a stack backtrace for debugging purposes (other than to run your code under the control of a debugger) is to throw an exception, as described in the next section.

Exceptions and errors

As discussed in the earlier section "Language omissions," CLDC includes the majority of the exceptions defined by the J2SE java.lang package, but most of the error classes have been removed, leaving only the following:

- java.lang.Error
- java.lang.OutOfMemoryError
- java.lang.VirtualMachineError

The Throwable method printStackTrace() is part of the CLDC specification (although the overloaded version that directs the stack trace to somewhere other than the standard error stream is not). However, the format of the output from this method is implementation-dependent; more importantly, in the KVM reference implementation, this method simply prints the name of the exception. To get a stack backtrace, it is necessary either to recompile the virtual machine with the symbol PRINT_BACKTRACE defined and nonzero or to use the debug version of the VM in the directory *j2me_cldc\bin\win32\debug* (for the Windows platform), which is compiled in this way.

As noted in the previous section, the Thread method dumpStack() is not available, so the following code, which is commonly used in J2SE, does not even compile in a CLDC environment:

```
Thread.currentThread().dumpStack();
```

Unfortunately, an attempt to work around this by creating an exception like the following also fails:

```
new Exception().printStackTrace();
```

This works for J2SE, but it fails in CLDC because the VM is not required to fill in the stack trace in the exception when it is created. The KVM fills in the stack trace only when the exception is actually thrown, so the only way to get a stack trace is to use the debug version of the KVM and include the following code:

```
try {
    throw new Exception();
} catch (Exception ex) {
    ex.printStackTrace();
}
```

Of course, this technique is not available when working with production CLDC platforms, such as cell phones, where debugging is not compiled in. Fortunately, most problems can be diagnosed by running your code in an emulated environment where a debugger or a debug version of the VM is available.

The java.util Package

The CLDC java.util package contains collection classes and classes that are related to date and time handling.

Collection classes

CLDC includes the following collection-related classes:

- Hashtable
- Stack
- Vector
- Enumeration

This is a subset of the collections that were available in JDK 1.1, excluding Dictionary, Properties, and the pseudo-collection BitSet. Unfortunately, due to resource constraints, none of the Java 2 collection framework is available to CLDC applications, and, therefore, methods that were added to the Hashtable and Vector classes that make them more compatible with the Java 2 collection framework (such as keySet() and entrySet()) have also been removed. As noted earlier in this chapter, the lack of the Properties class has the side effect that it is not possible to get access to or change the complete set of system properties.

The Date class

The J2SE Date class has a lot of functionality that was originally introduced by JDK 1.0 and subsequently deprecated, such as the ability to construct a Date given a date and time specified as day, month, year, hours, minutes, and seconds and the ability to extract those values from an existing Date. In JDK 1.1, those functions became the responsibility of the Calendar and GregorianCalendar classes. In line with the policy of cleaning up deprecated functionality, the CLDC Date class does not have any of the constructors or methods that deal with this functionality. Instead, a Date is simply a wrapper around a long value that represents a date and time as its offset from 00:00 GMT on January 1, 1970. It only has constructors that create a Date object representing the current time or a time given by its offset, a pair of methods that allow the time offset to be set or retrieved, and an equals() method that compares one Date with another. To convert between Dates and externally meaningful date and time representations, you have to use the Calendar class, described a little later.*

---

* A useful feature of the J2SE Date class was the fact that its toString() method produced a reasonable representation of the corresponding date and time, such as "Tue Nov 20 20:05:00 GMT 2001". The CLDC Date class does not override the Object toString() method and therefore does not return anything as useful as this. The only way to get a formatted date from a CLDC Date object is to use the Calendar class.

The TimeZone class

A `TimeZone` object represents the offset of a time zone from GMT. Because all dates in Java are represented in terms of an offset from 00:00 GMT on January 1, 1970, you need to know its time offset from GMT to format the corresponding time correctly for your location. This offest is encapsulated in the default `TimeZone` object for the platform on which the Java VM is running. J2SE has full support for time zones specified with familiar time-zone names (such as PST, CDT, etc., although these are deprecated), those using more complete specifications (such as `America/Los_Angeles`), or those specified as an offset from GMT (e.g., `GMT-5` for EST).

The CLDC `TimeZone` class is somewhat more restricted; implementations are required to support only GMT, and, in fact, the CLDC reference implementation provides only GMT and UTC (which is, to all intents and purposes, identical).

The Calendar class

The CLDC `Calendar` class is a simplified version of its J2SE counterpart, whose primary use is to convert back and forth between an instant in time given as a `Date` and the corresponding day, month, year, hours, minutes, and seconds values. The details of this conversion depend on two things:

- The time zone for which the operation is performed
- The calendar rules used in the user's locale

`Calendar` takes account of the first of these by virtue of the fact that it is associated with an appropriate `TimeZone` object. As noted in the previous section, however, the range of time zones that a given host environment supports may be limited. The second issue is slightly more complex. `Calendar` is actually an abstract class; to obtain an instance of it, you must use the static `getInstance()` methods, which can be parameterized with a `TimeZone` object if necessary. These methods are supposed to return a subclass of `Calendar` that implements appropriate rules for the environment in which the host device operates. In most cases, this would be an object that operated with the same rules as the J2SE `GregorianCalendar` class (which is not included in the CLDC specification), although some locales, such as Japan, might require different rules to be applied. Implementations of CLDC that are intended to operate in regions where there are requirements of this kind are expected to return an appropriate `Calendar` subclass.

Once you have a `Calendar` object, you can use the `setTime()` method to install a time and date value, then the `get()` method to extract the values of the various fields that represent that value in a more user-friendly form. The following code, for example, gets the current day and month:

```
Calendar cal = Calendar.getInstance();
Date date = new Date();
cal.setTime(date);
int month = cal.get(Calendar.MONTH);
int day = cal.get(Calendar.DAY_OF_MONTH);
```

On March 23, 2002, for example, this code would set day to 23 and month to 2 (month numbers count from 0). (You can find the complete list of constant values that can be passed to the get() method in the reference materials in Part II.) You can also use the Calendar object to perform the reverse process by setting individual fields using the get() method and then calling getTime() to get the corresponding Date object. Unlike its J2SE counterpart, Calendar does not have any explicit methods that perform date arithemetic, but you can easily implement this yourself using the Calendar and Date classes together. The following code, for example, determines the day and month 20 days from today:

```
// Get a Calendar and get the millisecond value of today's date
Calendar cal = Calendar.getInstance();
Date date = new Date();
long offset = date.getTime();

// Add 20 days to the date
final long MILLIS_PER_DAY = 24 * 60 * 60 * 1000L;
offset += 20 * MILLIS_PER_DAY;
date.setTime(offset);

// Install the new date in the Calendar offset
cal.setTime(date);

// Now get the adjusted date
month = cal.get(Calendar.MONTH);
day = cal.get(Calendar.DAY_OF_MONTH);
```

This code uses the Date class to get the current date and time in milliseconds; adds the required offset, also in milliseconds; stores it in the Date object; and then installs the Date object in the Calendar so that the day and month can be extracted. Unfortunately, there are no useful definitions for things like the number of milliseconds in a day, so you have to create them yourself.

It is worth noting that setting an individual field does not affect other fields, even if it appears that it should. As an example of this, consider the following code, which also attempts to add 20 days to the current date:

```
// Get the day and month for today
Calendar cal = Calendar.getInstance();
Date date = new Date();
cal.setTime(date);
int month = cal.get(Calendar.MONTH);
int day = cal.get(Calendar.DAY_OF_MONTH);

// Add 20 days to the day and change the Calendar
cal.set(Calendar.DAY_OF_MONTH, day + 20);

// Now get the adjusted date -- THIS DOES NOT WORK!
month = cal.get(Calendar.MONTH);
day = cal.get(Calendar.DAY_OF_MONTH);
```

Suppose this code were executed on March 20, 2002. The day and month values would initially be set to 20 and 2, respectively. Adding 20 to the day and storing it back would set it to 40, which is illegal for March, so it would be adjusted to 9 (i.e., 40 minus the number of days in March). You might expect this operation to increment the month field to April, but it does not, so the result is March 9, 2002, not April 9, 2002.

The `Calendar` class does not return string values for the days of the week and the months of the year, and, because the J2SE `java.text` package is not included in the CLDC specification, there is no way to get these strings from the system in a convenient form. The only way to get day and month strings without creating them yourself is to call the `Calendar toString()` method, which formats the date in readable terms:

```
Tue, 9 Apr 2002 12:00:00 UTC
```

This is only a feature of the reference implementation, however, and not part of the official specification. Device vendors might implement this method to return a string suitable for the locale in which their device is operating, or they may not.

The java.io Package

CLDC provides only a limited subset of the extensive J2SE `java.io` package. The only input and output streams that you can connect to a real data source or sink are `ByteArrayInputStream` and `ByteArrayOutputStream`. These streams can be used to read from or write into a byte array directly, or, wrapped with a `DataInputStream` or `DataOutputStream`, they provide a way of storing or transmitting primitive Java data types. Access to all other data sources is provided by private `InputStream` and `OutputStream` implementations that are obtained by calling methods on other classes. The most important examples of this pattern are the `openInputStream()` and `openOutputStream()` methods of the `StreamConnection` interface, which is part of a generic framework that is used to access external data sources. This is described in detail in "A Networking Architecture for Small Devices" in Chapter 6.

The CLDC `java.io` package also retains support for character input and output by wrapping byte streams with an `InputStreamReader` or `OutputStreamWriter`. However, the set of character encodings that can be used with these classes is implementation-dependent and is required to extend only to the device's default encoding. Self-contained `Reader` and `Writer` classes like `FileReader` and `StringWriter` are not part of the CLDC specification.

The javax.microedition.io Package

This package, which is not inherited from J2SE, contains a collection of interfaces that define the *Generic Connection Framework*. This framework is intended to be used by CLDC-based profiles to provide a common mechanism for accessing network resources and other resources that can be addressed by name and that can send and receive data via an `InputStream` and an `OutputStream`. A typical example of such a resource is an HTML page or a Java servlet, which can be identified by its Uniform Resource Locator (URL).

Although the CLDC specification defines the interfaces and methods of the framework and suggests how it might be used to allow applications to open connections to various types of resources, including network servers and serial ports, the specification does not require any actual implementations to be provided. However, by specifying common methods needed to open, close, and get data from any of these resources, the framework makes it a lot easier for developers to write applications that can connect to data sources using different communication mechanisms, such as sockets, datagrams, or HTTP, because there is only one coding pattern to follow. (In J2SE, socket communication and HTTP communication involve using different classes and different coding patterns.) Further discussion of this topic and a full description of the Generic Connection Framework and the `javax.microedition.io` package are found in Chapter 6.

KVM Debugging

In order to provide Java-level debugging facilities, hooks must be supplied by the Java VM so that a debugger can perform tasks such as placing breakpoints, inspecting and modifying objects, and arranging to be notified when a debugging-related event occurs within the VM. The Java 2 platform includes an architecture, called the Java Platform Debugger Archicture (JPDA), that defines the debugging features that must be provided by a VM and the way in which they can be accessed by a debugger. Figure 2-1 shows the logical software components defined by the JPDA.

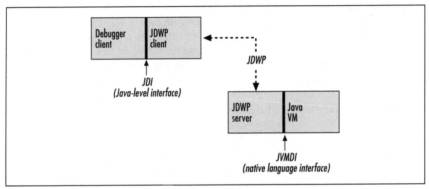

Figure 2-1: The Java 2 Platform Debugger Architecture

The JPDA

In the JPDA, the debugger interacts with the Java VM using a well-defined protocol called the *Java Debug Wire Protocol* (JDWP). This protocol specifies messages that are passed from a JDWP client to a JDWP server to request that operations be performed on the target VM, corresponding to debugging commands issued by the user. It also defines events that can be transmitted in the opposite direction to notify the debugger of state changes within the VM.

The architecture separates the debugger and the JVM from the details of the wire-level protocol by inserting an insulating layer on each side of the JDWP; this layer takes care of mapping the protocol messages to and from the programming inter-faces required by the debugger and provided by the VM. In order to make it possible to accomodate different VM or debugger implementations without requiring each of them to provide their own JDWP implementation, two internal APIs are defined:

The Java Debug Interface (JDI)
> The JDI is a Java-level interface that exposes the services of a JDWP client to a debugger. Typically, the debugger is a GUI program written by a third party

vendor, but it could provide a command-line interface (such as that provided by the jdb command in the SDK). Debuggers using this interface can be assured that they will work with any JVM written to conform to the JPDA.

The Java Virtual Machine Debug Interface (JVMDI)

JVMDI is the interface exposed by the JVM itself to allow operations received by the JDWP to be performed and to report VM state changes to the JDWP server. Unlike JDI, JVMDI is a native language interface because it requires low-level access to the virtual machine.

The only absolute requirement of the JPDA is that the VM must support the use of the JDWP as the means for the debugger to communicate with it.* As a consequence, there is no requirement for a VM actually to implement the JVMDI; it could, instead, directly provide the JDWP server interface and dispense with JVMDI. As long as the VM responds correctly to messages delivered by the JDWP, a debugger need not be aware of the implementation details. Similarly, although a debugger may be written to interface to the JWDP using the JDI (and a reference implementation of the JDI is part of the Java 2 SDK), it is not required to do so and could instead include its own JDWP client implementation.

The KVM Implementation of the JPDA

The CLDC specification does not place any requirements for debugging support within the VM, but a practical VM implementation needs to provide some kind of debugging capability. The KVM has debugging support, but resource constraints make it impossible to fully implement the server side of the JDWP protocol and the hooks within the KVM itself. Instead, this functionality is divided between the VM and another process called the *KVM debug proxy* (or KDP), as shown in Figure 2-2.

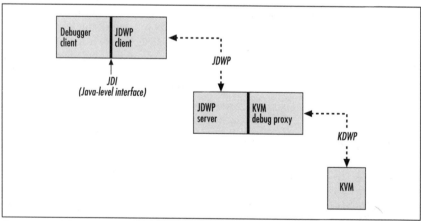

Figure 2-2: The KVM implementation of the JPDA

---

* The architecture does not specify how JWDP messages should be carried between the debugger and the VM, but typically either a socket (for remote debugging) or shared memory (for colocated debugger and VM) is used.

The function of the debug proxy is to implement features of the JDWP that are too resource-intensive to be placed within the KVM process itself. Normally, the debug proxy is not run on the same device as the KVM itself, so it does not require device resources. Instead, the debug proxy might be executed on a desktop system and communicate with the KVM using a specially designed variant of JDWP called the KVM Debug Wire Protocol (KDWP), carried over a socket connection. The definition of the KDWP can be found in the *KVM Debug Wire Protocol Specification*, which is included with the CLDC reference implementation.

From the viewpoint of the debugger, the debug agent appears to support the JDWP, and it can therefore be accessed either directly or through the JDI. A debugger does not need to be aware that it is communicating with the debug proxy instead of the KVM itself and that it might not be on the same machine as the debug proxy.

Debugging a KVM Application

In the earlier section "Compiling and Running Code with the KVM," you saw how to run a simple CLDC application. In this section, you'll see how to modify the procedure used earlier in order to run an application under the control of a debugger. As before, the commands shown are for the Windows platform; if you are using Solaris or Linux, you should adjust them appropriately. The source for the application that we are going to use in this section is in the file *ora\ch2\ KVMProperties.java*, which can be found in the example source code for this book. The application consists of a loop that prints the values of the system properties as listed in Table 2-2.

Begin by opening a DOS window and setting the shell variable *EXAMPLES* to point to the directory in which the example source code is installed. Then change your working directory to *%EXAMPLES%\src* and create a directory called *tmpclasses*, if you do not already have one. As before, we need to first compile the source code for the application that we're going to run under the control of the debugger and preverify it. With the shell variable *CLDC_PATH* set to the *bin* directory beneath the installation directory of the CLDC reference implementation and *JAVA_HOME* set to the directory in which the J2SE SDK is installed (such as *c:\ jdk1.3.1*), set up the DOS *PATH* variable as follows:*

```
PATH=%JAVA_HOME%\bin;%CLDC_PATH%\win32;%PATH%
PATH=%CLDC_PATH%\win32\debug;%PATH%
```

Now use the following commands to compile and preverify the example source code:

```
javac -g -bootclasspath %CLDC_PATH%\common\api\classes -d tmpclasses
    ora\ch2\KVMProperties.java
preverify -classpath %CLDC_PATH%\common\api\classes;tmpclasses -d .
    ora.ch2.KVMProperties
```

---

* Refer to the earlier section "Compiling and Running Code with the KVM" for a full description of these shell variables.

An important difference between these commands and those used in our earlier example is that in this case we include the –g argument to the Java compiler. This argument causes debugging information to be written to the class file; be sure to use this argument when creating class files for debugging purposes.

The next step is to start the KVM to run the example code. The standard KVM is built without debugging support to minimize its memory footprint, but the CLDC reference implementation contains a second copy of the KVM (called *kvm_g*) in the directory *%CLDC_PATH%\win32\debug* that can be used for debugging. You will notice that this directory is one of those included in the *PATH* variable set above. The following command starts the VM and prepares it for debugging:

```
kvm_g -classpath . -debugger -port 2000 ora.ch2.KVMProperties
```

The *–debugger* argument causes the VM to load the specified class and suspend execution to wait for the debug proxy to connect to it. The *–port* argument specifies the TCP/IP port number on which the KVM will listen for a connection from the debug proxy; in this case, port 2000 has been chosen, but any other free port could be used instead. Suspending execution of the application is the default and usually the correct thing to do, because you normally do not want to allow execution to proceed until you have set a breakpoint from the debugger. You can explicitly request suspension by supplying the *–suspend* argument, or you can allow execution to proceed without waiting for the debugger with the *–nosuspend* argument:

```
kvm_g -classpath . -debugger -nosuspend  -port 2000 ora.ch2.KVMProperties
```

Now open another DOS window and set up the shell variables *EXAMPLES, CLDC_ PATH* and *PATH* as before. We'll use this window to start the debug proxy process and connect it to the KVM listening on port 2000. The debug proxy is a Java application that is included in the CLDC reference implementation; its class files are located in the directory *%CLDC_PATH%\common\tools\kdp\classes*. For convenience, you should set up two more shell variables as follows:

```
set KDPCLASSPATH=%CLDC_PATH%\common\tools\kdp\classes
set CP=%CLDC_PATH%\common\api\classes;%EXAMPLES%\src
```

KDPCLASSPATH points to the class files for the debug proxy itself, and the *CP* variable points to the class files for the CLDC core libraries and the compiled classes for this book's example source code. Using these variable definitions, the debug proxy can be started using the following command:

```
java -classpath %KDPCLASSPATH% kdp.KVMDebugProxy -l  3000 -p
   -r localhost 2000 -cp %CP%
```

The arguments passed to the debug proxy are as follows:

–l 3000

The port number on which the debug proxy listens for incoming connections from the debugger. This can be any free port number to which you have access (i.e., on Solaris or Linux, it must be greater than 1023 unless you are logged in as *root*).

–r localhost 2000

The host and port number for the KVM to be debugged, which must match the value of the KVM *–port* argument. Here we assume that the debug proxy and the KVM are on the same machine, but this is not a requirement; if you run them on different machines, the name of the machine on which the KVM is running should be supplied in place of localhost.

–cp %CP%

The class path used to locate the CLDC core libraries and the classes for the application being run in the debugger. Of course, the application classes should have been compiled with the *–g* compiler option so that they have debugging information available. If you are running the debug proxy and the KVM on different machines, you will need to take a local copy of the class files or make them available on a network drive.

You'll find a description of the complete set of arguments supported by the debug proxy in Chapter 8.

As soon as it is started, the debug proxy connects to the KVM and then waits for a debugger to connect on its socket port. You can use any debugger that supports JPDA, such as the ones that are provided with Borland JBuilder* or with Sun's free Forte for Java IDE, which we'll use here.

To connect a debugger to the debug proxy, follow these steps:

1. Start Forte for Java and create a new project, supplying *%EXAMPLES%\src* as the source directory to be initially mounted.

2. In the filesystem window, open the nodes for the example source code and double-click the KVMProperties class so that it is opened in the editor window.

3. Right-click on the first line of the for loop in the main() method and apply a breakpoint using the Add/Remove Breakpoint command in the popup menu.

4. From the main menu, select Debug and then Attach to VM. In the dialog that appears, ensure that the debugger type is set to JPDA and the connector type is sockets. Then fill in the debug proxy host and port names, typically localhost and 3000, respectively.

5. Press OK to start the debugger.

At this point, Forte connects to the debug agent and resumes the application in the KVM, which quickly reaches a breakpoint and stops, causing Forte to highlight the source line in the editor window, as shown in Figure 2-3.

With the debugger stopped at a breakpoint, you can now open the debug window (from View on the main menu) and examine variables, look at the stack back-traces for the threads in the KVM (as in Figure 2-4) or use any of the other features provided by the debugger, including stepping through the code line by line. More information on Forte for Java and the facilities it provides for building and debugging code, especially code written for MIDP, can be found in Chapter 9. Further information on the debug proxy and KVM debugging in general can be found in the *KVM Porting Guide* and the *KVM Debug Wire Protocol Specification*, both of which are supplied with the CLDC reference implementation.

---

* JBuilder 5 provides JPDA support for remote debugging in the Professional and Enterprise editions only; it is not available in the Personal edition (or the Foundation edition for JBuilder 4).

```
Source Editor [KVMProperties]                              _ □ X
 1  package ora.ch2;
 2
 3  public class KVMProperties {
 4
 5      private static final String[] properties = {
 6          "microedition.configuration",
 7          "microedition.encoding",
 8          "microedition.platform",
 9          "microedition.profiles"
10      };
11
12      public static void main(String[] args) {
13          for (int i = 0; i < properties.length; i++) {
14              System.out.println(properties[i] + " = " +
15                              System.getProperty(properties[i]))
16          }
17      }
18  }
```

```
13:19   INS
```

Figure 2-3: Reaching a breakpoint in Forte for Java

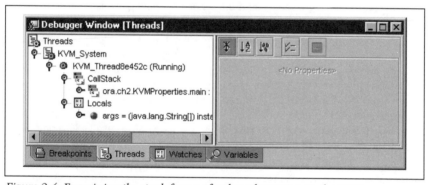

```
Debugger Window [Threads]                                  _ □ X
Threads
  KVM_System
    KVM_Thread8e452c (Running)              *  |A↓ |A↓  ½=   ■
      CallStack                                  <No Properties>
        ora.ch2.KVMProperties.main :
      Locals
        args = (java.lang.String[]) insta
◄                                    ►
 Breakpoints  Threads  Watches  Variables
```

Figure 2-4: Examining the stack frame of a thread running in the KVM

Advanced KVM Topics

To close this chapter, we look at a couple of advanced techniques you can use
with the KVM. If your focus is on developing applications for mass market wireless devices, the techniques shown in this section will be of little relevance,
because they require you to be able to build your own copy of the VM from its
source code and ship it along with your application. This is an option that is likely
to be open to you only if you are using the KVM in a specialist application of
some kind or if you are working for a device vendor incorporating the KVM into a
new product.

In order to build the KVM, you need to download a copy of the CLDC reference implementation and acquire a suitable compiler and build tools. The details of the build process and the development tools with which it has been tested can be found in the *KVM Porting Guide*, which is one of documents included with the reference implementation. Since describing how to compile the VM is beyond the scope of this book, the rest of this section assumes you have set up an environment within which you can compile and link the VM using the *Makefiles* supplied by Sun.

Preloading Java Classes

In a J2SE system, the core class libraries are stored in the file *rt.jar* and are dynamically loaded and linked on demand from the point at which the VM starts up. This has two consequences, both of which are not ideal in the kind of limited-resource environment toward which the KVM is targeted:

- The process of loading a class and locating and linking it to other classes that it depends upon takes a certain amount of time. This time is relatively small for each individual class, but it becomes noticable when a large number of classes have to be loaded at the same time, which is typically what happens when an application starts executing. This effect would be much worse on the processors that the KVM runs on. These processors are slower than those used in desktop systems, but they are used in devices, such as cell phones, where the user will probably be prepared to wait only a very short time between requesting a service and the service becoming available.

- In a desktop system, classes are loaded from the *rt.jar* file on disk into memory. KVM-based systems, however, typically don't have disks; instead, they just have a small amount of memory. In a typical device, the KVM and its class libraries are held in nonvolatile memory (ROM). If the KVM used the same technique as J2SE, these classes would have to be (at least partly) copied from ROM into RAM during the loading and linking process, causing an unacceptable overhead both in time and memory usage. (This is because the CLDC specification requires that only 32 KB of RAM be available, compared to a minimum of 128 KB of ROM.)

To address both these problems, the KVM uses a technique called *prelinking* or *ROMizing*, which involves preprocessing all the core classes into a compact image form in which they appear to have been loaded and linked already. This image is then burned into the device ROM along with the KVM itself. Thus, when the VM starts up, all the core classes appear to have been loaded already, thus avoiding the memory overhead of copying the classes and the time overhead of linking them. The ROMizing process is performed during the KVM build process by a tool called *JavaCodeCompact*, which is itself built when the KVM is compiled.[*]

You can arrange to have your own classes included in the ROMizing process, so that they appear to be preloaded when the KVM starts up. If you are building a device that has the KVM in ROM, you would use this technique to ensure that

---

[*] ROMizing is optional. You can build a KVM that does not have any classes preloaded by defining the build-time constant *ROMIZING* to have the value false.

your application is available as soon as the device starts up. In order to do this, you have to understand how the KVM build process works. The steps of the process that are relevant to ROMizing are as follows, where the pathnames are relative to the directory in which the CLDC reference implementation is installed:

1. The core class libraries are compiled and built into a ZIP file called *classes.zip* in the directory *j2me_cldc\api*.

2. The *Makefile* in the directory *j2me_cldc\tools\jcc* extracts all of the files from *classes.zip*, removes any that are not required on the platform for which the KVM is being built, and builds a new ZIP file consisting of the files that remain. For the Windows platform, for example, this file would be called *classesWin.zip*.

3. The new ZIP file is processed by *JavaCodeCompact* to produce the ROMized image for the corresponding platform in the form of a C-language source file. For the Windows platform, this file would be called *ROMJavaWin.c*. This file is then compiled and linked into the KVM.

To include your own classes among those preloaded into the KVM, you can do one of two things:

- Create your own directory containing your source code and the *Makefiles* to compile it into Java class files, and modify *j2me_cldc\tools\jcc\Makefile* so that it includes your class files when building *classesWin.zip*.

- Include your source code below the directory *j2me_cldc\api\src*, which contains the source for the CLDC class libraries. All Java source files below this directory will be compiled and included in *classes.zip* without the need to modify any *Makefiles*.

The first of these is the better solution and the one recommended for serious development. However, for simplicity, we'll use the second alternative to demonstrate the ROMizing process. In the next section, you'll see an example that uses the first technique.

To create a KVM with an additional preloaded class, do the following:

1. Copy the file *ora\ch2\KVMProperties.java* in the source code examples for this book to *j2me_cldc\api\src\ora\ch2\KVMProperties.java*.

2. Make *j2me_cldc\build\win32* your current directory.

3. Use *make* (or *gnumake*) to build the KVM as normal, as described in the *KVM Porting Guide*.

The KVM that this process creates will be in the directory *j2me_cldc\kvm\ VmWin\build*. If you make that directory your working directory and type the command:

```
.\kvm ora.ch2.KVMProperties
```

you'll see that the values of the four CLDC system properties are printed on the standard output stream, indicating that the **KVMProperties** class has been preloaded into the KVM.

Interfacing with Native Code

Since the KVM does not support the Java Native Interface, it is not possible to write an application that consists of a mixture of Java and native code and simply load the native code into the VM on demand at runtime. The only way to make native code available to Java applications running on the KVM is to include it in the VM build process. Like class preloading, this is a technique that you can use only when you have full control over the VM, and it is therefore not of any use when writing mass-market cell phone or PDA applications.

The *KVM Porting Guide* describes the environment that the KVM provides for native code programming. A discussion of the details of native code programming is beyond the scope of this book, but, before embarking on writing your own native code, you should read the relevant chapters of the porting guide to ensure that you understand how to handle interaction with the garbage collector and how to interface with Java code. This section concentrates on getting you started with KVM native programming by showing you how to get your code built and linked into the VM and what you need to do to create the linkage between the VM and your Java code.

Writing the Java code

The first step when writing native code is to decide which methods of your Java classes will be implemented as native methods. When you have done this, you simply declare them in the same way as you would with a standard JVM. For the purposes of discussion, in this section we'll use the class KVMNative, which you'll find in the directory *ora\ch2* in the source code examples for this book. This class has a single native method, declared using the Java language native keyword, as shown in Example 2-2.

Example 2-2: A Java Class Containing a Native Method

```
package ora.ch2;

public class KVMNative {

    public native void printMessage(String message);

    public static void main(String[] args) {
        String msg = args.length > 0 ? args[0] : "";
        for (int i = 1; i < args.length; i++) {
            msg += " " + args[i];
        }
        new KVMNative().printMessage(msg);
    }
}
```

The intent of this simple application is to use native code to print on the standard output a message constructed by concatenating all of the application's command-line arguments. Once you've written the Java code, compile and preverify it in the usual way, then wrap it in a JAR file:

```
javac -bootclasspath %CLDC_PATH%\common\api\classes -d tmpclasses
    ora\ch2\KVMNative.java
preverify -classpath %CLDC_PATH%\common\api\classes -d . tmpclasses
jar cvfM0 native.jar ora\ch2\KVMNative.class
```

If you have several classes that need access to native code, it is easier to integrate them with the KVM build process if they are in a JAR file, so we opt to create a JAR file in this example—even though we have only a single class—to demonstrate the most general case. Note that the JAR file does not need a manifest (hence the *M* option), and it must not be compressed, which explains the use of the *0* option (note that this is the digit 0, not the uppercase letter O).

Determining the name of the native function

The second step is to write the native code. Native code is written in the C programming language. The first problem to be tackled when writing a C-language function that implements a native method is naming the function. The KVM uses the same naming convention as the JNI; that is, the native function name is constructed as follows:

1. It starts with the string "Java_".

2. The fully qualified name of the class is appended, replacing periods with underscore characters.

3. The method name is appended, separated from the class name by another underscore.

4. If the method is overloaded, then the method signature is appended, preceded by two underscores.

In the case of the native method shown in Example 2-2, the correct native function name would be `Java_ora_ch2_KVMNative_printMessage()`. Since it is not overloaded, there is no need to include the argument types in the name. However, if we declared a pair of methods like this:

```
public native void printMessage(String str);
public native void printMessage(String intro, String str);
```

the native function names would have to include the method signature in order to disambiguate them. The easiest way to obtain the method signatures is to compile the Java class and then examine its content using *javap*, specifying argument *-s*:

```
javap -s ora.ch2.KVMNative
```

If the two definitions of **printMessage()** shown previously had been included in this class, then the output from this command would look like this:

```
public class KVMNative extends java.lang.Object {
    public KVMNative();
        /*   ()V   */
    public native void printMessage(java.lang.String);
        /*   (Ljava/lang/String;)V   */
    public native void printMessage(java.lang.String, java.lang.String);
        /*   (Ljava/lang/String;Ljava/lang/String;)V   */
}
```

The method signatures are shown in brackets. To build the complete native method name, the signature is modified and added to the part constructed from the package and class name. The signature is modifed as follows:

- The part within the brackets, which specifies the arguments, is extracted.
- Any "/" characters are replaced with "_".
- Any "_" characters are replaced with "_1".
- Any ";" characters are replaced with "_2".
- Any "[" characters are replaced with "_3".

For your convenience, a utility program that prints the name of the native function, given the class name, method name, and signature, is included in the example source code for this book. To get the signature for a method that is not overloaded, you need to specify only the class and method names, being careful to use "/" as the separator within the class name. For example, the command:

```
java ora.ch2.KVMPrintNativeMethodName ora/ch2/KVMNative printMessage
```

produces the output:

```
Java_ora_ch2_KVMNative_printMessage
```

For overloaded methods, include the signature as displayed by *javap* as the third argument, like this:

```
java ora.ch2.KVMPrintNativeMethodName ora/ch2/KVMNative printMessage
(Ljava/lang/String;)V
```

which gives the following output:

```
Java_ora_ch2_KVMNative_printMessage__Ljava_lang_String_2
```

The result for the two-argument variant of `printMessage()` would be:

```
Java_ora_ch2_KVMNative_printMessage__Ljava_lang_String_2Ljava_lang_
String_2
```

Writing the native code

Having determined what the native code function will be called, all that remains is to write it. Native code needs to make use of utility methods provided by the KVM. Some of the more useful KVM functions used by native code are described in the KVM porting guide, but, in general, you will need to examine the KVM source code to work out what is available to you and how to use it. In this case, we simply need to get hold of the Java string passed to the method and print it on standard output. Example 2-3 shows a possible implementation of this method, which you can find in the source file *KVMNativeExample.c* in the directory *ora\ch2* of the example source code.

Example 2-3: An Example of Native Code for the KVM

```
#include <global.h>

void Java_ora_ch2_KVMNative_printMessage()
{
    STRING_INSTANCE stringInstance = popStackAsType(STRING_INSTANCE);
```

Example 2-3: An Example of Native Code for the KVM (continued)

```
INSTANCE thisPtr = popStackAsType(INSTANCE);
char *string = getStringContents(stringInstance);
if (string != (char *)0 && *string != (char)0) {
    printf("Message is %s\n", string);
} else {
    printf("No message\n");
}
}
```

Although it is beyond the scope of this book to cover the details of native language programming for the KVM, it is worth reviewing a few details of this code:

- The source code starts by including the header file *global.h*. This file contains definitions of constants and functions that native code will need to reference. You'll find this file in the directory *j2me_cldc\kvm\VmCommon\h* within the CLDC reference implementation.

- The function name matches that described above. Note, however, that it is declared to have no arguments, even though the corresponding Java method has an argument of type String.

- Instead of being passed to the function in the usual way, Java language arguments are pushed onto a stack, along with the value of the this pointer for the object on which the method was invoked (except in the case of a static method). The item at the top of the stack is the rightmost argument in the argument list.

- To access the arguments, you use macros defined in the file *global.h*. Here, the macro popStackAsType() is used to pop first the pointer to the string argument and then the value of the this pointer. Other macros can be used for removing primitive types such as integers and longs, and there are also a small number of reference types (or INSTANCE types) defined for use with the popStackAsType() macro. Refer to *global.h* for further information on these definitions.

- It is important that all arguments and the this pointer (if it is present) be popped off the stack before the function returns. If this is not done, the likely result is that the KVM will crash.

- The string reference obtained from the stack is not a pointer that can be directly used by C-language code. References to Java objects are passed to native code in the form of opaque objects known as *handles*; handles cannot be used directly but must be passed to KVM methods to access the real data. In this case, the string reference is used as an argument to the getStringContents() method, which returns a pointer to an array of characters that can be used directly by the C code. From here, the string's value is printed directly to the standard output using the printf function in the usual way. Note that getStringContents() copies the string into a global buffer, so there is no need to worry about freeing the memory that it occupies.

- This particular method does not return a value to the Java code that calls it. To return a value, you must push it onto the stack using one of the macros such as pushStack(), pushLong() or pushStackAsType(), defined in *global.h*.

Arranging for the native code to be compiled and included in the KVM

Once you have written your native code functions, you need to arrange for them to be compiled and linked with the KVM. The simplest way to achieve this is to include them with the source files for the KVM itself and to modify its *Makefiles* so that they are included in the build process. The following steps arrange for the native code created above to be linked into the KVM:

- Create a new directory called *j2me_cldc\Native\src* in the source distribution included with the CLDC reference implementation.

- Copy the file *KVMNativeExample.c* from the *ora\cb2* directory to *j2me_cldc\ Native\src*.

- Modify the KVM build *Makefile* to include the new source code in the build.

The *Makefile* to be modified in the last step depends on the platform for which the KVM is to be built. For Windows, this Makefile can be found at *j2me_cldc\kvm\ VmWin\build\Makefile*, while for Linux and Solaris it is *j2me_cldc\kvm\VmUnix\ build\Makefile*. Add the following lines (shown in bold) to include *KVMNativeExample.c* in the list of source files to be compiled:

```
ifeq ($(ROMIZING), false)
   ROMFLAGS = -DROMIZING=0
else
   SRCFILES += ROMjavaWin.c
endif

# Include the example native code
SRCFILES += KVMNativeExample.c
```

The directory in which the native code file is included also needs to be added to the list of those searched for source files by adding it to the existing list:

```
# Add last entry to include native code directory
vpath %.c  $(TOP)/kvm/VmCommon/src/ $(TOP)/kvm/VmWin/src/ \
           $(TOP)/kvm/VmExtra/src/  $(TOP)/tools/jcc/ \
           $(TOP)/jam/src/     $(TOP)/Native/src
```

With these changes, when the KVM is next built, the native code in *KVMNativeExample.c* will be built and linked into it.

Connecting the Java code to the native code

The final step is to connect the native code in the KVM to the Java code that will invoke it. Because the KVM does not support JNI, there has to be a different mechanism that maps at runtime a native Java method call to the corresponding native function that implements it. The details of how this is done depends on whether the KVM is built with ROMizing enabled. Before looking at this in more detail, here are the steps that you need to follow to arrange for the KVM build process to link the Java code and native code:

- Copy the file *native.jar* that contains the compiled Java classes created earlier (see the earlier section "Writing the native code") to the directory *j2me_cldc\ tools\jcc*.

- Delete the files *nativeFunctionTableWin.c* and *ROMjavaWin.c* (or *nativeFunctionTableUnix.c* and *ROMjavaUnix.c* for Linux and Solaris), if they exist, to force them to be rebuilt.

- Edit the file *j2me_cldc\tools\jcc\Makefile* as shown later.

In the *Makefile*, you will find two targets called *ROMjava%.c*. Modify the first of these targets and the *nativeFunctionTable%.c* target that follows it by making them depend on the file *native.jar*:

```
ROMjava%.c: classes%.zip native.jar tools
        @cp -f src/*.properties classes
        @$(MAKE) $@ JCC_PASS_TWO=true

nativeFunctionTable%.c: classes%.zip native.jar tools
        @cp -f src/*.properties classes
        @$(MAKE) $@ JCC_PASS_TWO=true
```

These changes ensure that if you change your Java source code and rebuild the *native.jar* file, the appropriate parts of the KVM will also be rebuilt.

Further down the *Makefile*, you will find a second set of the same targets. Modify these so that they also depend on *native.jar* and to ensure that the files in *native. jar* are included in the build process:

```
ROMjava%.c: classes%.zip native.jar
        echo ... $@
        echo Arch $($(patsubst classes%.zip,%Arch,$<))
        $(JAVA) -classpath classes JavaCodeCompact \
                -nq -arch $($(patsubst classes%.zip,%Arch,$<)) -o $@ $^

nativeFunctionTable%.c: classes%.zip native.jar
        echo ... $@
        echo ... $^
        cp -f src/*.properties classes
        $(JAVA) -classpath classes JavaCodeCompact \
                -nq -arch KVM_Native -o $@ $^
```

Note that the $< on last line of each target has been changed to $^. This causes *JavaCodeCompact* to include the class files in both *classesWin.zip* (or *classesUnix. zip*) and *native.jar*. With these changes in place, you can rebuild the KVM. The new VM can be found in the directory *j2me_cldc\kvm\VmWin\build* for the Windows platform or *j2me_cldc\kvm\VmWin\build* for Linux and Solaris. If you use it to run the example code written earlier, you should see any words you supply as command line arguments written to the standard output by the native function in the *KVMNativeExample.c* file:

```
> kvm ora.ch2.KVMNative Hello, Native World
Message is Hello, Native World
```

Now let's look a little more closely at how this works. There are slightly different explanations depending on whether ROMizing is in use or not.

When ROMizing is enabled, *JavaCodeCompact* creates the linkage between the Java code and the native code at build time. In this case, any Java code that needs to access native methods *must* be included as part of the KVM build. This is why the *native.jar* file is one of the files included as a target for the *ROMjava%.c* target in the *Makefile*. At build time, this target builds a file in the directory *j2me_cldc\ tools\jcc* called *ROMjavaWin.c* or *ROMJavaUnix.c*, which contains the ROMized image of the CLDC core libraries and any application preloaded classes. When we run the KVM and load the class ora.ch2.KVMNative, we are actually using the copy of this class that was preloaded into the KVM and linked to the native code at build time. If we had linked the native code into the KVM but *not* preloaded the class ora.ch2.KVMNative, we would see an error message saying that the native method could not be found when we attempt to run the example, even though the native code has been built into the KVM.

When ROMizing is not enabled, the core libraries and all application code is loaded into the KVM on demand, from the class path supplied using its *–classpath* argument. In this case, there is no build-time linkage created between the Java code and its corresponding native methods. Instead, the *nativeFunctionTable%.c* target of the *Makefile* causes *JavaCodeCompact* to generate a file called *nativeFunctionTableWin.c* or *nativeFunctionTableUnix.c* that maps from the name of a Java native method to a pointer to the native function that implements it. *JavaCodeCompact* generates the code in this file automatically by scanning all the Java classes passed to it on the command line (in ZIP files, JAR files, or individually named class files) looking for native methods. The generated source file contains native method information for each class that contains a native method, as well as a master index for all packages that have classes with native methods. Since this file is generated automatically, you do not need to concern yourself with all the details, but it is still instructive to examine the file's content. For the class ora.ch2.KVMNative, for example, the following code is generated:

```
const NativeImplementationType ora_ch2_KVMNative_natives[] = {
    { "printMessage",         NULL, Java_ora_ch2_KVMNative_printMessage},
      NATIVE_END_OF_LIST
};
```

This shows that this class has one native method called printMessage(), which is implemented by the function Java_ora_ch2_KVMNative_printMessage(). The NULL that appears before the function reference is used to indicate the method signature in cases of method overloading. Since there is only one printMessage() method in this class, there is no need to specify a signature. Compare this with the entries for the native methods in the core library class java.lang.String:

```
const NativeImplementationType java_lang_String_natives[] = {
    { "charAt",             NULL, Java_java_lang_String_charAt},
    { "equals",             NULL, Java_java_lang_String_equals},
    { "indexOf",            "(I)I", Java_java_lang_String_indexOf__I},
    { "indexOf",            "(II)I", Java_java_lang_String_indexOf__II},
      NATIVE_END_OF_LIST
};
```

Here, the entries for the indexOf method have to include the signature field because there are two overloaded variants:

```
public int indexOf(int ch);
public int indexOf(int ch, int fromIndex);
```

You can see that the function names also include the method signature parts.

There is also a master index that is used to map from a class name to the native methods for that class. Here is an extract from that index, which clearly shows how it works:

```
const ClassNativeImplementationType nativeImplementations[] = {
    { "java/lang",              "Object",              java_lang_
Object_natives },
    { "java/lang",              "Throwable",           java_lang_
Throwable_natives },
    { "ora/ch2",                "KVMNative",           ora_ch2_
KVMNative_natives },
    // MORE ENTRIES - NOT SHOWN
NATIVE_END_OF_LIST
    };
```

Note that this file is generated even if ROMizing is enabled, but its content is not used.

CHAPTER 3

The Mobile Information Device Profile and MIDlets

The Connected Limited Device Configuration provides the basis for running Java on devices that have insufficient resources to support a complete virtual machine together with a full version of the J2SE core packages. However, if you are an application developer, it is extremely unlikely that you will ever need to write software that works solely with the APIs provided by CLDC, because it contains nothing that allows for interaction with users, storage devices, or a network. CLDC is intended to be a base layer on top of which a range of profiles that provide the missing facilities can be provided, in a form suitable for the class of device for which each profile is designed. The *Mobile Information Device Profile*, or MIDP for short, is one such profile, intended for use on small footprint devices with a limited user interface in the form of a small screen with some kind of input capability. This chapter introduces MIDP; in the following two chapters, we'll look in more detail at how it supports user interfaces, networking, and persistent storage of information.

MIDP Overview

MIDP is a version of the Java platform based on CLDC and KVM that is aimed at small footprint devices, principally cell phones and two-way pagers. It is also suitable for running on PDAs, and an implementation is available for PalmOS Version 3.5 and higher. (In the longer term, it is intended that these devices use the PDA profile, which is also hosted by CLDC.) The MIDP specification was developed under the Java Community Process and is available for download from *http://jcp. org/jsr/detail/37.jsp*.

The logical position of MIDP within the software architecture of a device that implements it is shown in Figure 3-1. The software that implements MIDP runs in the KVM supplied by CLDC and provides additional services for the benefit of application code written using MIDP APIs. MIDP applications are called *MIDlets*. As Figure 3-1 shows, MIDlets can directly use both MIDP facilities and the APIs described in Chapter 2 that MIDP inherits from CLDC itself. MIDlets do not access the host platform's underlying operating system and cannot do so without becoming nonportable. Because the KVM does not support JNI, the only way for a MIDP application to access native platform facilities directly is by linking native code into a customized version of the virtual machine.

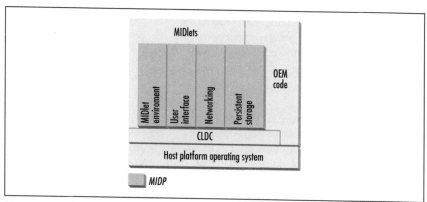

Figure 3-1: The Mobile Information Device Profile

Sun provides a reference implementation of MIDP that can be used on Windows; the Wireless Toolkit, which contains versions of MIDP for Windows, Solaris and Linux; and a separate MIDP product for use on PalmOS-based PDAs. Device manufacturers typically use the Sun reference implementation as the basis for their own products. They usually integrate additional code as part of their MIDP implementation to provide management features such as installation, removal, and management of MIDlets that are not portable between devices and hence not part of the reference software. As shown in Figure 3-1, this code (labeled "OEM Code") may use some combination of MIDP and CLDC services and will also depend on the host platform's operating system. Some parts of the core MIDP software are themselves device-dependent and thus are also supplied by the manufacturer. These typically include parts of the networking support, the user interface components, and the code that provides persistent storage.

MIDP Hardware Requirements

As mentioned earlier, MIDP is intended for small devices with limited memory, CPU, and display capabilities. The minimum hardware requirements are described in the following sections.

Memory

As you'll see over the next few chapters, MIDP includes quite a lot of software that is not part of the core Java platform and therefore requires more memory than the minimal CLDC environment is obliged to supply. The MIDP specification requires at least 128 KB of RAM be available to store the MIDP implementation itself, over and above whatever is needed by CLDC. In addition to this, there must be at least 32 KB available for the Java heap. In practice, a 32 KB heap is very limiting and demands that the developer exercise great care when allocating objects and take all possible steps to avoid holding references to objects longer than necessary, in order to allow the garbage collector to reclaim heap space as quickly as possible. As well as the RAM requirement, MIDP devices must also supply at least 8 KB of nonvolatile memory to be used as persistent storage so that MIDlets can save information in such a way that it is not lost when the device is switched off. The content of this storage is not guaranteed to be preserved over battery changes, however, and there is a general expectation that the device also provides some way (such as the PDA "hot sync" mechanism) to back up its content to a more permanent location.

Display

MIDP devices are characterized by small displays. The specification requires that the screen should be at least 96 pixels wide and 54 pixels high and that each pixel be (approximately) square. The screen must support at least two colors, and many cell phones are capable of no more than this. At the top of the range, PDAs typically have screens with 160 pixels in each direction and support as many as 65,536 different colors. This wide disparity in capability provides the developer who wants to write a fully portable MIDlet with some interesting challenges, and it has led to some trade-offs in the MIDP user interface library, as we'll see in Chapters 4 and 5.

Input device

As with displays, there are several different types of input device that might be found on a MIDP platform. At one end of the spectrum, the more sophisticated devices, like the RIM wireless handheld, have a complete alphanumeric keyboard, as shown on the left of Figure 3-2. Similarly, PalmOS-based handhelds allow the user to "write" on a special area of the screen using a form of shorthand known as Graffiti; they also provide a simulated onscreen keyboard for users who prefer a more traditional approach. The screenshot on the right side of Figure 3-2 shows the Graffiti area of a Palm handheld.

Figure 3-2: Handheld input devices

Contrast these highly functional keyboards (or keyboard substitutes) with the more basic one that you'll find on most cell phones, an example of which is shown in Figure 3-3. Keyboards like this provide relatively easy numeric input, but they require slightly more work on the part of the user to type alphabetic characters, and there are almost no special characters available.

The minimum assumption made by the MIDP specification is that the device has the equivalent of a keypad that allows the user to type the numbers 0 through 9, together with the equivalent of arrow keys and a select button as shown in the diamond-shaped arrangement at the top of Figure 3-3, where the select button is the white circle between the arrows. These requirements are directly met by cell phones and may be satisfied in various ways on other devices. On the Palm, for example, there are buttons that may be programmed to act as directional arrows, while the select operation can be performed by tapping the screen with the stylus. As we'll see in Chapter 5, this cut-down representation of the input device is reflected in the APIs that handle the user interface, and it requires the developer to be careful when handling events from whatever passes for the keyboard on the device on which a MIDlet is running.

Figure 3-3: A typical cell phone keypad

Connectivity

Mobile information devices have some kind of network access, whether it's the built-in wireless connection in a cell phone or pager, or a separate modem attached to a PDA. MIDP does not assume that devices are permanently attached to a network or that the network directly supports TCP/IP. It does, however, require that the device vendor provide at least the illusion that the device supports HTTP 1.1, either directly over an Internet protocol stack, as would be the case for a Palm handheld connected to a modem, or by bridging a wireless connection to the Internet via a WAP gateway. This provision allows developers to write network-aware MIDlets that work equally well (other than performance differences due to differing network bandwidth) across all supported platforms.

MIDP Software Requirements

Sun's reference version of MIDP is not a commercial product. Device vendors are expected to port the reference implementation to their own hardware and software by implementing code that bridges the gap between the expectations of Sun's reference code and the vendor's hardware and operating system software. As with the hardware described previously, the reference implementation makes the following assumptions about the capabilities offered by the software base on which it will be hosted (shown as "Host Platform Operating System" in Figure 3-1:

- The operating system must provide a protected execution environment in which the JVM can run. Because CLDC supports the threading capabilities of J2SE, the host platform ideally supports multithreading, and, if it does, the KVM can make direct use of it. However, MIDP implementations are required to provide the illusion of multithreading even when this is not available from the native operating system. They do this by sharing the single available thread between the Java threads that belong to application code and those used within the VM and the MIDP and core libraries.

- Networking support is required in some form. On some platforms, such as PalmOS, a socket-level API is available, over which the mandatory MIDP HTTP support can be implemented. In the case of devices that do not offer such a convenient interface, including those that do not have direct connectivity to an IP-based network, the vendor is required to provide a means for HTTP to be bridged from the device's own network to the Internet. The networking aspects of MIDP are discussed in detail in Chapter 6.

- The software must provide access to the system's keyboard or keypad (or equivalent) and a pointing device, if it is available. The software must be able to deliver events when keys are pressed and released and when the pointing device is moved or activated. (For example, for a handheld with a stylus, the software must deliver an event when the stylus touches the screen, when it is lifted off the screen, and when it moves over the screen.) The vendor is required to map whatever codes are delivered by the user's keystrokes to a standard set of values so that similar keystrokes lead to the same results across different hardware platforms. This issue is discussed further in Chapter 5.

- It must be possible to access the device's screen. MIDP allows MIDlets to treat the screen as a rectangular array of pixels, each of which may be independently set to one of the colors supported by the device. Therefore, it is required that the software provide access to the screen as if it were a bit-mapped graphics device. MIDP user interfaces and graphics are covered in detail in Chapters 4 and 5.

- The platform must provide some form of persistent storage that does not lose its state when the device is switched off (that is, when it is in its minimum power mode, but not necessarily when it has no power at all). MIDP provides record-level access to this storage and therefore requires that the host software supply some kind of programmatic interface to its persistent storage mechanism. The MIDP storage APIs are described in Chapter 6.

The MIDP Java Platform

The Java platform available to MIDlets is that provided by CLDC as described in Chapter 2, together with a collection of MIDP-specific packages arranged under the `javax.microedition` package hierarchy. The core libraries themselves are almost unaffected by the MIDP specification; the only change is the addition of the

J2SE 1.3 timer facility in the `java.util` package, which will be covered in the later section "Timers and TimerTasks." The MIDP specification also places the following requirements on the core libraries:

- Like applets, MIDlets are managed in an execution environment that is slightly different from that of a Java application. As you'll see shortly, the initial entry point to a MIDlet is not the `main()` method of its MIDlet class, and the MIDlet is not allowed to cause the termination of the Java VM. In order to enforce this restriction, the `exit()` methods in both the `System` and `Runtime` classes are required to throw a `SecurityException` if they are invoked.

- In addition to the system properties defined by CLDC, MIDP devices must set the `microedition.locale` property to reflect the locale in which the device is operating. The locale names are formed in a slightly different way from those used by J2SE, because the language and country components are separated by a hyphen instead of an underscore character. A typical value for this property would be `en-US` on a MIDP device, whereas a J2SE developer would expect the locale name in the form `en_US`. Since both MIDP and CLDC provide almost no support for localization, however, the precise format of this property is of little direct interest to MIDlets. Instead, it is intended to be used when installing MIDlets from external sources, to allow the selection of a version of the MIDlet suitable for the device owner's locale. The property must therefore be properly interpreted by the agent (perhaps a servlet running in a web server) that supplies the software.

- The system property `microedition.profiles` must contain at least the value `MIDP-1.0`. In the future, as new versions of the MIDP specification are released and implemented, devices that support multiple profiles may list them all in this profile, using spaces to separate the names.

In summary, the values of the system properties that are introduced by or changed by MIDP relative to the requirements placed by CLDC, are shown in Table 3-1.

Table 3-1: MIDP System Properties

Property	Meaning	Value
microedition. locale	The current locale of the device	e.g., en-US
microedition. profiles	Blank-separated list of supported profiles	MIDP-1.0

MIDlets and MIDlet Suites

Java applications that run on MIDP devices are known as MIDlets. A MIDlet consists of at least one Java class that must be derived from the MIDP-defined abstract class `javax.microedition.midlet.MIDlet`. MIDlets run in an execution environment within the Java VM that provides a well-defined lifecycle controlled via methods of the `MIDlet` class that each MIDlet must implement. A MIDlet can also use methods in the MIDlet class to obtain services from its environment, and it must use only the APIs defined in the MIDP specification if it is to be device-portable.

A group of related MIDlets may be collected into a *MIDlet suite*. All of the MIDlets in a suite are packaged and installed onto a device as a single entity, and they can be uninstalled and removed only as a group. The MIDlets in a suite share both static and runtime resources of their host environment, as follows:

- At runtime, if the device supports concurrent running of more than one MIDlet, all active MIDlets from a MIDlet suite run in the same Java VM. All MIDlets in the same suite therefore share the same instances of all Java classes and other resources loaded into the Java VM. Among other things, this means that data can be shared between MIDlets, and the usual Java synchronization primitives can be used to protect against concurrent access not only within a single MIDlet, but also between concurrently executing MIDlets from the same suite.

- Persistent storage on the device is managed at the MIDlet suite level. MIDlets can access their own persistent data and that of other MIDlets in the same suite. However, it is not possible for a MIDlet to gain access to persistent storage owned by another suite, because the naming mechanism used to identify the data implicitly includes the MIDlet suite. This is partly to avoid unintended name clashes between MIDlets obtained from unrelated sources, and partly as a security measure so that a MIDlet's data cannot be read or corrupted by malicious code imported from an unreliable source.

As an example of the sharing of classes and data between MIDlets, suppose a MIDlet suite contains a class called `Counter`, intended to keep count of the number of instances of MIDlets from that suite are running at any given time.

```
public class Counter {
    private static int instances;

    public static synchronized void increment() {
        instances++;
    }

    public static synchronized void decrement() {
        instances--;
    }

    public static int getInstances() {
        return instances;
    }
}
```

Only a single instance of this class will be loaded in the Java VM, no matter how many MIDlets from the suite that supplies it are running in that VM. This means that the same static variable `instances` is used by all of these MIDlets, and, therefore the `increment` and `decrement` methods all affect the same counter. The fact that these methods are synchronized protects the `instances` variable from concurrent access by any threads in all of the MIDlets.

MIDlet Security

For the developer, dealing with MIDlet security is a very simple issue, because there isn't any! The Java security model used in J2SE is both powerful and flexible, but it is expensive in terms of memory resources, and it requires a certain amount of administration that may be beyond the knowledge expected of a mobile device user. Therefore, neither CLDC nor MIDP includes any of the security checking of API calls that is available in J2SE, with the exception of the Runtime and System exit() methods, which can never be used by a MIDlet.

For the mobile device owner, this means that a MIDlet appears to be more of a potential threat than an applet would to a browser user, because the MIDlet is not constrained by the Java applet "sandbox" that the browser imposes via a SecurityManager. A mobile device owner needs to be careful when installing MIDlets and, preferably, he should accept software only from trusted sources. Unfortunately, at the time of writing, there is no way for the user to be completely sure who is actually providing a MIDlet or that the MIDlet code has not been interfered with en route to the device; the authentication mechanisms that provide this for the J2SE platform (i.e., public key cryptography and certificates) are not a standard part of the MIDP specification. The secure version of the HTTP protocol (HTTPS), which will help to alleviate this problem, is under consideration for inclusion in a future version of MIDP. In the meantime, there is limited security against malicious MIDlets. There are no MIDlet APIs that allow access to information already on the device, such as address and telephone number lists or calendars, and it is not possible for a MIDlet to directly control the device. As you'll see in Chapter 6, a MIDlet can store information on a device, but that storage is private to that MIDlet and its suite, so the MIDlet can harm only its own data.

MIDlet Packaging

MIDlets need to be properly packaged before they can be delivered to a device for installation. The MIDlet subclass that acts as the main entry point for the MIDlet, together with any other classes that it requires (apart from those provided by MIDP itself) and any images or other files to which it needs access at runtime, must be built into a single JAR file. Packaging information that tells the device what is in the JAR must be supplied in the JAR's manifest file. Similar packaging information is also provided in another file called the *Java application descriptor* (or JAD file for short), which is held separately from the JAR. A JAR may contain more than one MIDlet, in which case all the MIDlets are deemed to be in the same MIDlet suite. To put the same thing another way, all MIDlets that are in the same MIDlet suite *must* be packaged in the same JAR.

Both the manifest file and the JAD file are simple text files in which each line has the form:

```
attribute-name: attribute-value
```

The name and value are separated by a colon and optional whitespace. All the attributes that are of relevance to the installation of MIDlets have names with the prefix "MIDlet-". A complete list of these attributes, together with a short description of their associated values, can be found in Table 3-2. The values in the JAR and JAD columns indicate whether the attribute is mandatory (M), optional (O) or ignored (I) in the file corresponding to that column.

Table 3-2: MIDlet Packaging Attributes

Attribute Name	JAR	JAD	Value and Meaning
MIDlet-Name	M	M	The name of the MIDlet suite packaged in the JAR file. This name may be displayed to the user.
MIDlet-Version	M	M	The version number of the MIDlet suite packaged in the JAR file. Version numbers take the form a.b.c (for example 1.2.3), where larger values in each field indicate a newer version, with the leftmost field taking precedence. For example, version 1.2.5 is taken to be more recent than version 1.2.3, and, similarly, version 2.1.5 is newer than 1.3.7.
MIDlet-Vendor	M	M	The name of the MIDlet suite provider. This is free-form text that is intended for display to the user.
MIDlet-*n*	M	I	Attributes that describe the MIDlet in the MIDlet suite. The value *n* is replaced by a numeric value starting from 1 to identify individual MIDlets. The format of the value associated with this attribute is described in the text.
MicroEdition-Profile	M	I	The version or versions of the MIDP specification that the MIDlets in this suite can work with. Where more than one version appears, they must be separated by spaces. The versions specified are compared to those listed in the `microedition.profiles` property of the target device to determine whether the MIDlets are compatible with them. `MIDP-1.0` is a typical value for this attribute.
MicroEdition-Configuration	M	I	The J2ME configuration required by the MIDlets in this suite. This value is compared to the target device's `microedition.configuration` property to determine compatibility.
MIDlet-Description	O	O	A description of the MIDlet suite intended to be displayed to the user.
MIDlet-Icon	O	O	An icon that may be used to represent the MIDlet suite during or following installation. The icon must be a Portable Network Graphics (PNG) file.
MIDlet-Info-URL	O	O	The URL of a file that contains further information describing the MIDlet suite. The content of this file may be displayed to the user to allow the user to decide whether to install the MIDlet suite.
MIDlet-Data-Size	O	O	The minimum amount of persistent storage that this MIDlet suite requires. This refers to space used for the long-term storage of data used by the MIDlet suite, not the space required to install and manage the MIDlet suite itself. It is specified in bytes. If this attribute is not supplied, it is assumed that the MIDlet suite does not require persistent storage. Whether or not MIDlets can use more persistent storage space than they initially request is device-dependent.

Table 3-2: MIDlet Packaging Attributes (continued)

Attribute Name	JAR	JAD	Value and Meaning
MIDlet-Jar-URL	I	M	The URL of the JAR file that contains the MIDlet or MIDlet suite described by these attributes. This attribute is used only in the application descriptor.
MIDlet-Jar-Size	I	M	The size of the MIDlet JAR file in bytes. This attribute is used only in the application descriptor.
MIDlet-Install-Notify	I	O	A URL used to report the success or failure of MIDlet installation performed from a remote server. This attribute is not included in the current MIDP specification, but it is supported by the Wireless Toolkit. See the later section "Delivery and Installation of MIDlets" for further details.
MIDlet-Delete-Confirm	I	O	A message to be displayed to the user before the MIDlets are deleted from the device on which they are installed. Like MIDlet-Install-Notify, this attribute is not currently included in the formal specification.
MIDlet-specific attributes	O	O	MIDlet developers can provide limited configurability for MIDlets by including attributes that can be retrieved at runtime.

As you can see, many of the attributes must be supplied in both the manifest file, which resides in the JAR, and in the JAD file, which does not. To see why, it is necessary to understand why two files are used.

The job of the manifest file is to indicate to the device the name and version of the MIDlet suite in the JAR and to specify which of the class files it contains correspond to the individual MIDlets. In order to make use of this information, however, the device must download the JAR and extract the manifest. Having done this, it can then display the values associated with the MIDlet-Name, MIDlet-Version, and MIDlet-Vendor attributes and the optional MIDlet-Description and MIDlet-Icon attributes. These attributes allow the user to decide whether the MIDlets should be installed. However, the JAR for a MIDlet suite might be quite large and may take some time to retrieve over the relatively slow networks to which mobile devices typically have access. If the only useful description of its content were in the JAR itself, a lot of time might be wasted transferring large files that are immediately rejected as uninteresting.

To solve this problem, some of the attributes from the manifest file, together with extra information, is duplicated in the JAD file. Instead of downloading the whole JAR, a MIDP device first fetches its JAD file, which is much smaller than the JAR and can be transferred quickly. The device then displays the JAD file's contents to the user so that she can decide whether to fetch the JAR file. The JAD contains some attributes that come from the manifest file and others that do not appear in the manifest. The common attributes are as follows:

    MIDlet-Name
    MIDlet-Vendor
    MIDlet-Version

```
MIDlet-Description
MIDlet-Icon
MIDlet-Info-URL
MIDlet-Data-Size
```

These attributes (with the possible exception of the last one) can all be presented to the user as an aid to deciding whether the content of the corresponding JAR file is interesting enough to download. The first three of these attributes are mandatory in both JAR and JAD files, and the MIDP specification requires that their values be identical. The remaining attributes are all optional. If they appear in both the manifest and the JAD file, the value in the JAD file takes precedence over that in the manifest (and at this stage, the device can see only the value in the JAD file).

The JAD file also contains two other attributes that are not present in the manifest file:

```
MIDlet-Jar-Size
MIDlet-Jar-URL
```

The `MIDlet-Jar-Size` attribute can be displayed to the user to help determine how long it will take to fetch the JAR; it also enables the user to guess whether the device has enough free space to install the JAR. Assuming the user decides to install the MIDlet suite, the next step is to fetch the JAR itself, which can be found by using the value of the `MIDlet-Jar-URL` attribute.

Suppose a company called "Wireless Java Inc." creates a suite of MIDlets called `WirelessTrader` that allow a user to do online stock trading from a MIDP device. The suite contains two MIDlets, one for trading, the other for simply browsing through stock prices. The main classes for these two MIDlets are called `com.wireless.TradeMIDlet` and `com.wireless.BrowseMIDlet`, and they make use of common code in the `com.wireless.Utils` class. The manifest for this suite would look something like this:

```
MIDlet-Name: WirelessTrader
MIDlet-Vendor: Wireless Java Inc.
MIDlet-Version: 1.0.1
MIDlet-Description: A set of MIDlets for online trading.
MIDlet-Icon: /com/wireless/icons/wireless.png
MIDlet-Info-URL: http://www.wireless.com/trader/info.html
MIDlet-Data-Size: 512
MicroEdition-Profile: MIDP-1.0
MicroEdition-Configuration: CLDC
MIDlet-1: StockTrader,/com/wireless/icons/trader.png,com.wireless.
TradeMIDlet
MIDlet-2: StockBrowser,/com/wireless/icons/browser.png,com.
wirelessBrowseMIDlet
```

In the JAR, this file would appear as `META-INF/MANIFEST.mf`. The JAR would also include the following files:

/com/wireless/BrowseMIDlet.class
/com/wireless/TradeMIDlet.class
/com/wireless/Utils.class

/com/wireless/icons/browser.png
/com/wireless/icons/trader.png
/com/wireless/icons/wireless.png

Note the following about the attributes in the manifest file and the content of the JAR:

- The JAR contains the two MIDlet class files and the class file for `com.wireless.Utils`, which contains code that is used by both MIDlets. This latter file, however, does not need to be referenced from the manifest file. The JAR also contains the three icons that are referred to from the manifest file.

- The `MIDlet-Icon` attribute contains the absolute path of the icon file for the MIDlet suite, relative to the JAR file itself.

- Each MIDlet has an attribute that describes it; the attribute's name is of the form `MIDlet-n`, where `n` is an integer. The value of this attribute has the following form:

  ```
  name,icon,class
  ```

  `name` is the name of the MIDlet within the MIDlet suite. `icon` is the full path of the icon that the device may use along with the MIDlet name when displaying the content of the MIDlet suite to the user. `class` is the name of the MIDlet's main class. The icon is optional; if no icon is required, it should be omitted:

  ```
  MIDlet-2: StockBrowser,,com.wireless.BrowseMIDlet
  ```

  Note that even if an icon is specified, the device is not obliged to display it. The same applies to the MIDlet suite icon defined by the optional `MIDlet-Icon` attribute.

The JAD file for this suite can be constructed like this:

```
MIDlet-Name: WirelessTrader
MIDlet-Vendor: Wireless Java Inc.
MIDlet-Version: 1.0.1
MIDlet-Description: A set of MIDlets for online trading.
MIDlet-Info-URL: http://www.wireless.com/trader/info.html
MIDlet-Data-Size: 512
MIDlet-Jar-Size: 10312
MIDlet-Jar-URL: http://www.wireless.com/trader/Midlets.jar
```

This file contains the information that the device displays to the user, together with the URL of the MIDlet suite JAR. In this case, the common attributes have the same values in the manifest and the JAR, but it is possible to override the `MIDlet-Description`, `MIDlet-Icon`, `MIDlet-Info-URL`, and `MIDlet-Data-Size` attributes by specifying different values in the JAD file.

In order to be fully portable, the JAD file should be encoded using ISO-8859-1, because all MIDP implementations are required to support this character encoding. The successful use of any other encoding depends on the target device, which may not support the encoding, and the way in which the JAD file is transported to the device. If, for example, the file is fetched using HTTP, the Content-Type header can be used to specify the encoding as described in the later section "Delivery and Installation of MIDlets." In some cases, it is useful to be able to include in the JAD file Unicode characters that are not available in the ISO-8859-1 encoding or that are not easy to access from a standard keyboard. The MIDP reference implementation allows you to use Unicode escape sequences of the form \uxxxx to overcome encoding limitations. For example, the following line includes the copyright character (Unicode value 00A9) in the MIDlet suite description:

```
MIDlet-Description: A set of MIDlets for online trading. \u00A9 Wireless
Java Inc.
```

Although this feature is available in the MIDP reference implementation, it is not mentioned in the MIDP specification, so there is no guarantee that real devices will actually support it.

At runtime, a MIDlet can access files from its JAR using the getResourceAsStream() method of java.lang.Class. Any file in the JAR, apart from class files, can be accessed this way. This is typically how you would include images or text files that should be displayed in the user interface, an example of which will be shown in Chapter 4. A MIDlet can also define its own private attributes in the manifest file and the JAD and retrieve them at runtime, as you'll see in "Developing MIDlets," later in this chapter.

MIDlet Execution Environment and Lifecycle

All MIDlets are derived from the abstract base class javax.microedition. midlet.MIDlet, which contains methods that the MIDP platform calls to control the MIDlet's lifecycle, as well as methods that the MIDlet itself can use to request a change in its state. A MIDlet must have a public default constructor (that is, a constructor that requires no arguments), which may be one supplied by the developer if there is any initialization to perform or, when there are no explicit constructors, the empty default constructor inserted by the Java compiler. This is what a skeleton MIDlet class might look like:

```
public class MyMIDlet extends MIDlet {

    // Optional constructor
    MyMIDlet() {
    }

    protected void startApp() throws MIDletStateChangedException {
    }

    protected void pauseApp() {
    }

    protected void destroyApp(boolean unconditional)
                            throws MIDletStateChangedException {
    }
}
```

At any given time, a MIDlet is in one of three states: Paused, Active, or Destroyed. A state diagram that shows how these states are related and the legal state transitions is shown in Figure 3-4.

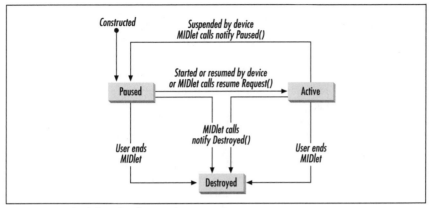

Figure 3-4: The lifecycle of a MIDlet

When a MIDlet is loaded, it is initially in the Paused state. The usual class and instance initialization is then performed—that is, static initializers are called the first time the MIDlet class is loaded, all instance initializers are invoked when the MIDlet instance is created, and its public, no-argument constructor is then invoked. If the MIDlet throws an exception during the execution of its constructor, the MIDlet is destroyed. If the MIDlet does not throw an exception, it is scheduled for execution at some later time. Its state is changed from Paused to Active, and its `startApp()` method is called. The MIDlet class declares this method as follows:

```
protected void startApp() throws MIDletStateChangeException;
```

That this method is abstract means that you must implement it in your MIDlet, and that it is protected implies that it will be called either from the MIDlet class itself or from another class in the `javax.microedition.midlet` package. In the reference implementation, the MIDlet lifecycle methods are called from a class in this package called `Scheduler`, but there is nothing in the MIDP specification that requires this class be used. Licensees may provide their own scheduler implementations, provided that it supports the MIDlet lifecycle as described in this section. It is very common for MIDlet developers to redefine the `startApp()` method as public, which is certainly a safe option, but this should not be necessary because vendor implementations must continue to work even if these methods are declared as protected.

The `startApp()` method may complete normally, in which case the MIDlet is allowed to run, or it may inform the MIDP platform that the MIDlet does not want to run at this point. There are several ways to achieve the latter:

- If the `startApp()` method detects an error condition that stops it from completing, but which might not exist later (i.e., a transient error condition), it should throw a `MIDletStateChangeException`. This moves the MIDlet back to the Paused state, so that another attempt to start it can be made later.

- If the `startApp()` method detects an error condition from which recovery is likely never to be possible (a nontransient error condition), it should call its `notifyDestroyed()` method, which is described a little later.

- Finally, the MIDlet may throw an exception other than `MIDletStateChangeException`, either deliberately or because a method that it invokes throws the exception, and the `startApp()` method does not catch it. In this case, it is assumed that a fatal error has occurred, and the MIDlet is destroyed by calling its `destroyApp()` method (described later).

If the MIDlet does none of these things, it is in the Active state and will be allowed to run until it is either paused or destroyed. A MIDlet returns after completing its `startApp()` method, and it does not have a method that contains the main logic to which control could be passed, so where is the MIDlet's code placed? Usually, a MIDlet has a user interface and executes code as a result of events generated by key presses or pointer movements. MIDlets can also start separate background threads to run code that does not depend on the user interface, or they can use a timer to schedule work periodically, as will be shown later. If you take these approaches, it is important to manage the background threads and/or timers appropriately when the MIDlet itself is paused or destroyed.

At any time, the MIDP platform can put a MIDlet into the Paused state. On a cell phone, for example, this might happen when the host software detects an incoming call and needs to release the phone's display so the user can answer the call. When a MIDlet is paused, its `pauseApp()` method is called:

```
protected abstract void pauseApp();
```

As with `startApp()`, a MIDlet is required to provide an implementation for this method. The appropriate response to this state change depends on the MIDlet itself, but, in general, it should release any resources it is holding and save the current state so it can restore itself when it is reactivated later.

The main consequence of being moved to the Paused state is that the MIDlet no longer has access to the screen; any threads that it created are not automatically terminated, and timers remain active. A MIDlet may choose to terminate any open network connections or background threads and cancel active timers when told to pause, but it is not obliged to do so.

If the host platform decides to resume a paused MIDlet, because the incoming call has terminated, for example, the MIDlet's `startApp()` method is invoked again to notify the MIDlet that it has access to the screen. As a consequence, a MIDlet's `startApp()` method should be written carefully to distinguish, if necessary, between the first time that it is called, which signifies that the MIDlet is being started for the first time, and subsequent calls notifying resumption from the Paused state, to prevent resources from being allocated multiple times. Of course, if a MIDlet reacts to being moved to the Paused state by releasing all of its resources, it would probably be appropriate to execute the same initialization code in `startApp()` to reallocate the resources upon resumption. However, a properly written MIDlet would still take special action in the `startApp()` method to restore the user interface and its internal state to the way it was before it was paused, rather than show the initial screen again.

The fact that the `startApp()` method can be invoked more than once in the lifetime of a MIDlet raises the question of whether initialization should be performed here or in the MIDlet's constructor. The developer is free to choose the more convenient location to allocate resources and prepare the MIDlet's state. In general, resources that will be released in **pauseApp**() should be allocated in startApp(). Other resources can be allocated in either startApp() or the constructor, with care being taken to ensure that allocations performed in startApp() are not repeated following resumption from the Paused state.

An important difference between the startApp() method and the constructor is that, according to the MIDP specification, the MIDlet is guaranteed to be able to access the Display object that corresponds to the screen (see Chapter 4) only from the point at which startApp() is invoked for the first time. Under a strict interpretation of the specification, therefore, initialization that involves a Display object cannot be performed in the constructor. Of course, actual MIDP implementations may not enforce this apparent restriction, but portability may be compromised if the MIDlet accesses the Display object in its constructor.

A MIDlet may refuse a request to be resumed from the Paused state by throwing a MIDletStateChangeException when its startApp() method is called, as described earlier.

When the host platform needs to terminate a MIDlet, it calls the MIDlet's destroyApp() method:

```
public abstract void destroyApp(boolean unconditional) throws
    MIDletStateChangeException;
```

In the destroyApp() method, the MIDlet should release all the resources that it has allocated, terminate any background threads, and stop any active timers. When the MIDlet is terminated this way, the unconditional argument has the value true, to indicate that the MIDlet cannot prevent the process from continuing. Under some circumstances, however, it is useful to give the MIDlet the option to not terminate, perhaps because it has data that it needs to save. In this case, the destroyApp() method can be invoked with the argument false, in which case the MIDlet can indicate that it wants to continue by throwing a MIDletStateChangeException. The following code illustrates how this technique can be used to implement the conditional shutdown of a MIDlet:

```
try {
    // Call destroyApp to release resources
    destroyApp(false);

    // Arrange for the MIDlet to be destroyed
    notifyDestroyed();
} catch (MIDletStateChangeException ex) {
    // MIDlet does not want to close
}
```

This code might be used to respond to an Exit button in the MIDlet's user interface. It begins by directly invoking the MIDlet's own destroyApp() method so that resources are released. If the MIDlet is not in an appropriate state to terminate, and destroyApp() is called with argument false, the MIDlet should throw a MIDletStateChangeException. The calling code should catch this exception and do nothing, as shown here. On the other hand, if the MIDlet is prepared to be terminate, it should complete the destroyApp() method normally, in which case the calling code uses the MIDlet notifyDestroyed() method to tell the MIDP platform that the MIDlet wants to be terminated.

This example also illustrates the use of the notifyDestroyed() method, which is used by a MIDlet to voluntarily terminate. It is important to understand the relationship between the destroyApp() and notifyDestroyed() methods and when they are used:

- When the MIDlet is being destroyed by the platform, most likely because the user has requested it, the MIDlet's destroyApp() method is called with the argument true, and the MIDlet is destroyed when this method completes. It is not necessary in this case for the MIDlet to invoke its notifyDestroyed() method.

- When the MIDlet itself wants to terminate, typically because it has no more useful work to do or the user has pressed an Exit button, it can do so by invoking its notifyDestroyed() method, which tells the platform that it should be destroyed. In this case, the platform does not call the MIDlet's destroyApp() method; it assumes that the MIDlet is already prepared to be terminated. Most MIDlets invoke their own destroyApp() method to perform the usual tidy up before calling notifyDestroyed(), as shown earlier.

Note that calling notifyDestroyed() is the only way for a MIDlet to terminate voluntarily. MIDlets cannot terminate by calling the System or Runtime exit() methods, because these throw a SecurityException.

There are two other methods that a MIDlet may invoke to influence its own lifecycle:

```
public final void notifyPaused();
public final void resumeRequest();
```

The notifyPaused() method informs the platform that the MIDlet wishes to be moved to the Paused state; this has the same effect as if the platform had invoked the MIDlet's pauseApp() method. When the MIDlet calls notifyPaused(), the platform does *not* invoke its pauseApp() method, in the same way that it does not call destroyApp() in response to notifyDestroyed(), because it assumes that the MIDlet has prepared itself to be paused. A MIDlet often, therefore, precedes an invocation of notifyPaused() with a call to pauseApp() so that the appropriate steps are taken before the MIDlet is suspended.

The resumeRequest() method is the reverse of notifyPaused(); it tells the platform that a MIDlet in the Paused state wishes to return to the Active state. At some future time, the platform may resume the MIDlet by calling its startApp() method. The resumeRequest() method typically is called by a background thread or from a timer that the MIDlet left active while it was paused, an example of which is shown in the next section.

Developing MIDlets

To illustrate the MIDlet lifecycle and how it can be controlled, we'll create a very simple MIDlet that does the following:

- Prints a message when its constructor is called.

- Creates a timer that fires from time to time, putting the MIDlet in the paused state if it is active and returning it to the active state if it is paused. When the timer has been through this cycle twice, it terminates the MIDlet.

- Creates a background thread when it is started that simply prints a message every second. This thread is allowed to run only when the MIDlet is active.

Since you haven't yet seen how to create user interfaces, this example MIDlet communicates by writing messages to its standard output stream. On a real device, you can't see what is written to standard output or standard error (unless you are using debug facilities provided by the device vendor), but most device emulators provide a way to monitor the content of these streams. There are several products available that allow you to build and test MIDlets either in an emulated environment or on the real device; some of these products are described in Chapter 9. Here, we'll use the Wireless Toolkit, which is available free of charge from Sun.

Building a MIDlet with the Wireless Toolkit

The Wireless Toolkit provides an implementation of MIDP together with an emulator that can be customized to look and behave somewhat like a number of real cell phones. It can also be used in conjunction with a third-party emulator that allows you to see how your MIDlets would behave on handhelds that are based on PalmOS. It is not, however, a complete development enviroment, because it does not provide an integrated editor to allow you to create, view, and modify source code. Consequently, if you want to use the Wireless Toolkit as part of a complete development cycle, you will need a text editor or IDE to manage the source code. At the time of writing, the Wireless Toolkit can be installed to integrate with Forte for Java, which is available for download from Sun's web site, and Borland JBuilder, but any IDE will do.

The first step when using the Wireless Toolkit is to create a project, which manages the source code, classes, and resources corresponding to a MIDlet suite. To do this, start the `KToolbar` and press the New Project button to open the New Project dialog, which is shown in Figure 3-5. For this example, the name of the MIDlet's main class should be `ora.ch3.ExampleMIDlet`, and the project name can be anything you like.

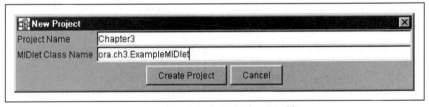

Figure 3-5: Creating a new project with the Wireless Toolkit

When you press the Create Project button in the dialog, the Wireless Toolkit opens another window, shown in Figure 3-6; it contains a set of tabs that allow you to provide the attributes used to generate the manifest for the MIDlet's JAR and the JAD file. You can edit these attributes by clicking the cell that you want to change and typing the new value. The fields on the Required tab contain the attributes shown in Table 3-2 that are marked as mandatory. Most of the values supplied by default can be used without modification. For example, the `MIDlet-Name` field (which is actually the name that will be used for the MIDlet suite, not for any individual MIDlet) matches the project name, and the name of the JAR that will be created is also derived from the project name. The only field you might want to change on this tab is MIDlet-Vendor, which is initially set to Sun Microsystems by default.

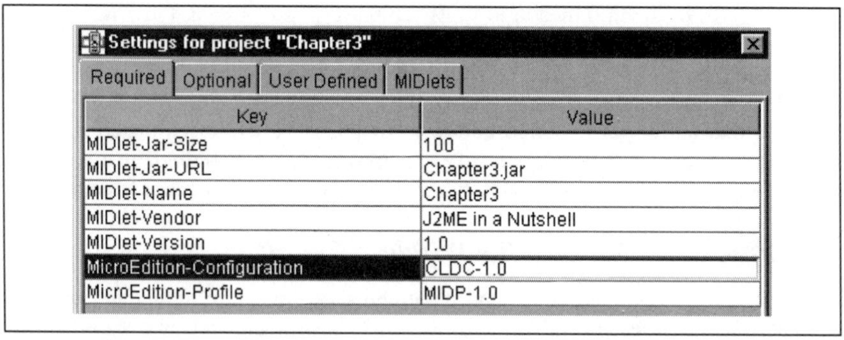

Figure 3-6: Setting required attributes for a MIDlet suite

To define the MIDlets that should be included in the MIDlet suite, select the MIDlets tab. Initially, this contains a single row whose content is constructed from the name of the project. In this example, the suite contains a single MIDlet called ExampleMIDlet in the package ora.ch3, so you should press the Edit button and edit the values for the MIDlet-1 attribute on this tab so that it looks like this:

Key	Name	Icon	Class
MIDlet-1	ExampleMIDlet	/ora/ch3/icon.png	ora.ch3.ExampleMIDlet

In this example, the name assigned to the MIDlet matches the class name (ignoring the package prefix), but this need not be the case. Notice also that although the class name is specified in the usual way, with the parts of the name separated by periods, the location of the icon is specified as a filename, in which the path components are separated by a "/" character. If an icon is present, an absolute pathname must be provided here. If the MIDlet does not have an associated icon, this field should be left blank.

For a MIDlet suite with more than one MIDlet, you add an extra line for each MIDlet. It is important that consecutive numbers are used in the key field, so the next MIDlet to be added in this example would need to have the key MIDlet-2. Other required class files must be included in the JAR, but they should not be included in the MIDlets list.

For this example, we are also going to use a user-defined attribute. A user-defined attribute is a private attribute that can be set in the manifest and/or the JAD; its value can be retrieved at runtime by any MIDlet in the MIDlet suite. These attributes provide a mechanism similar to the setting of system properties in J2SE and allow the operation of the MIDlet to be customized without the need to recompile source code. In this example, we'll use a user-defined attribute to specify the length of a timer. To set the value of the attribute, select the User Defined tab and press the Add button. In the dialog box that appears, supply the property name as Timer-Interval and press OK. This creates a new entry in the table on the User Defined tab. Click in the Value cell, and type the required value, which, in this case, should be 3000. The property name is case-sensitive and, to avoid confusion with reserved attribute names, should not begin with "MIDlet-". The property value is always a string that is interpreted by the MIDlet. In this case, it represents the timer interval in milliseconds, so the value given here results in a timer that has a three-second interval. You'll see shortly how the MIDlet retrieves the values of user-defined attributes.

This completes the setting of the MIDlet's attributes. To save them, press the OK button at the bottom of the dialog. You can change these settings (perhaps to add extra MIDlets) at any time by pressing the Settings . . . button on the main KToolbar window, which is shown in Figure 3-7.

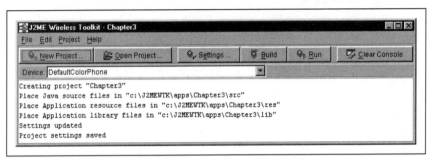

Figure 3-7: The main window of the Wireless Toolkit KToolbar

The next step is to place the source code and the icon for the MIDlet where the Wireless Toolkit can get access to them. Most IDEs allow you to choose where your project source files are kept, but the Wireless Toolkit uses a fixed filesystem layout for each project, based beneath the directory in which the Toolkit was originally installed. The name of the top-level directory for a project is derived from the name given to the project when it was created. If, for example, you installed the Windows Toolkit in the directory *c:\J2MEWTK*, all the files for the Chapter3 project need to be placed below the directory *c:\J2MEWTK\apps\Chapter3*. When the Chapter3 project was created, the toolkit created the following four directories below the main directory for the project:

src
    Holds the source code for the MIDlets and any shared classes

res
    Holds any resources required by the MIDlets, such as icons

lib
    Holds JAR or ZIP files for third-party libraries that the MIDlets need

bin
    Holds the JAR, JAD and manifest files

Before building the project, you need to place the appropriate files in the *src, res* and *lib* subdirectories. This example has one source file and a single icon, which can both be found in the directory *ora\ch3* of the source code for this book. The package structure used by the MIDlet must be reflected in the directory layout as seen by the Wireless Toolkit, as it would be by an IDE. Therefore, to install the files where the Wireless Toolkit can use them, you should copy them as follows, creating the *ora\ch3* subdirectory beneath both the *src* and *res* directories while doing so:

Source	Destination
ora\ch3\ExampleMIDlet.java	*c:\J2MEWTK\apps\Chapter3\src\ora\ch3\ ExampleMIDlet.java*
ora\ch3\icon.png	*c:\J2MEWTK\apps\Chapter3\res\ora\ch3\icon.png*

Once the files have been placed in the correct directories, the next step is to build the project by pressing the Build button on the KToolbar main window. The build process performs the following steps:

- Creates a *tmpclasses* directory below the main directory, compiles all the source files below the *src* directory, and places the class files beneath *tmpclasses*, having regard to the package hierarchy. Thus, for example, the class files for the MIDlet `ora.ch3.ExampleMIDlet` would be placed in the directory *c:\J2MEWTK\apps\Chapter3\tmpclasses\ora\ch3*.

- Creates a *classes* directory below the main directory and runs the preverifier on all of the classes found below *tmpclasses*, placing the verified class files below the *classes* directory in a directory layout that again reflects the package hierarchy. The verified *ExampleMIDlet* classes would, therefore, end up in *c:\J2MEWTK\apps\Chapter3\classes\ora\ch3*.

- Creates the manifest file and the JAD file and places them in the *bin* directory.

 The source code for this book is actually stored in two different directory hierarchies, one for standard IDEs, the other for the J2ME Wireless Toolkit. This example showed you how to create a project from scratch using existing source files. A quicker way to use the book's source code is to copy the content of the directory *wtksrc* into *c:\J2MEWTK\apps*. This will give you subdirectories called *Chapter3*, *Chapter4*, etc., that contain all the source code and resources for each chapter's examples in the format expected by the J2ME Wireless Toolkit. To use each set of examples, select Open Project on the KToolBar main screen instead of Create Project, and then select the project from the dialog box that appears.

Running a MIDlet

At this stage, the JAR file has not been created, but you can nevertheless test the MIDlet suite by selecting an appropriate target device on the KToolbar main window and pressing the Run button. This loads the MIDlet classes, its resources, and any associated libraries from the *classes*, *res*, and *lib* subdirectories. If you select the default gray phone and press the Run button, the emulator starts and displays the list of MIDlets in this suite, as shown in Figure 3-8.

When the MIDlet suite is loaded, the device's application management software displays a list of the MIDlets that it contains and allows you to select the one you

Figure 3-8: The Wireless Toolkit emulator

want to run. In this case, even though the suite contains only one MIDlet, the list is still displayed, as shown in Figure 3-8. Given the current lack of security for MIDlets imported from external sources, it would be dangerous for the device to run a MIDlet automatically, and, by giving the device user the chance to choose a MIDlet, it allows him the opportunity to decide not to run any of the MIDlets if, for any reason, they are thought to be a security risk or otherwise unsuitable. It is not obvious, though, on what basis such a decision would be made, since the user will see only the MIDlet names at this stage, but requiring the user to confirm that a MIDlet should be run transfers the ultimate responsibility to the user. In this case, the device displays the MIDlet name and its icon (the exclamation mark) as taken from the `MIDlet-1` attribute in the manifest file. The device is not obliged to display an icon, and it may use its own icon in preference to the one specified in the manifest.

When you run the MIDlet suite this way, the Wireless Toolkit compiles the source code with the option set to save debugging information in the class files, and it does not create a JAR file. If you want to create a JAR, you can do so by selecting the Package item from the Project menu. This rebuilds all the class files without debugging enabled, which reduces the size of the class files, a measure intended to keep the time required to download the JAR to a cell phone or PDA as small as possible. It also extracts the content of any JARs or ZIP files it finds in the *lib* subdirectory and includes them in the MIDlet JAR, after running the preverifier over any class files that it finds in these archives. The JAR can be used, along with the JAD file, to distribute the MIDlet suite for installation into a device over a network, as will be shown in the later section "Delivery and Installation of MIDlets."

Further information on the Wireless Toolkit and other MIDlet development environments can be found in Chapter 9.

A Simple MIDlet

Now let's look at the implementation of the **ExampleMIDlet** class you have just built and packaged with the Wireless Toolkit. This simple MIDlet demonstrates the lifecycle methods that were described in the earlier section "MIDlet Execution Environment and Lifecycle," and it also illustrates how the MIDlet's foreground activity interacts with background threads, as well as how to create and use timers. The code for this example in shown in Example 3-1. For clarity, the timer-related code has not been included in the code listing; you'll see how that works when timers are discussed later in this chapter.

Example 3-1: A Simple MIDlet

```
package ora.ch3;

import java.util.Timer;
import java.util.TimerTask;
import javax.microedition.midlet.MIDlet;
import javax.microedition.midlet.MIDletStateChangeException;

public class ExampleMIDlet extends MIDlet {

    // Flag to indicate first call to startApp
    private boolean started = false;

    // Background thread
    private Thread thread;

    // Timer interval
    private int timerInterval;

    // Timer
    private Timer timer;

    // Task to run via the timer
    private TimerTask task;

    // Required public constructor. Can be omitted if nothing to do and no
    // other constructors are created.
    public ExampleMIDlet() {
        System.out.println("Constructor executed");

        // Get the timer interval from the manifest or JAD file.
        String interval = getAppProperty("Timer-Interval");
        timerInterval = Integer.parseInt(interval);
        System.out.println("Timer interval is " + interval);
    }

    protected void startApp() throws MIDletStateChangeException {
        if (!started) {
            // First invocation. Create and start a timer.
            started = true;
            System.out.println("startApp called for the first time");
            startTimer();
```

Example 3-1: A Simple MIDlet (continued)

```
    } else {
        // Resumed after pausing.
        System.out.println("startApp called following pause");
    }

    // In all cases, start a background thread.
    synchronized (this) {
        if (thread == null) {
            thread = new Thread() {
                public void run() {
                    System.out.println("Thread running");
                    while (thread == this) {
                        try {
                            Thread.sleep(1000);
                            System.out.println("Thread still active");
                        } catch (InterruptedException ex) {
                        }
                    }
                    System.out.println("Thread terminating");
                }
            };
        }
    };
     thread.start()
}

protected void pauseApp() {
    // Called from the timer task to do whatever is necessary to pause
    // the MIDlet.
    // Tell the background thread to stop.
    System.out.println("pauseApp called.");
    synchronized (this) {
        if (thread != null) {
            thread = null;
        }
    }
}

protected void destroyApp(boolean unconditional)
                    throws MIDletStateChangeException {
    // Called to destroy the MIDlet.
    System.out.println("destroyApp called - unconditional = "
                    + unconditional);
    if (thread != null) {
        Thread bgThread = thread;
        thread = null;        // Signal thread to die
        try {
            bgThread.join();
        } catch (InterruptedException ex) {
        }
    }
    stopTimer();
```

Example 3-1: A Simple MIDlet (continued)

```
    }

    // Timer code not shown here
}
```

This simple MIDlet does two things:

- Starts a background thread that writes a message to standard output every second so that you can see that the MIDlet is active

- Starts a timer that periodically pauses the MIDlet if it is active and makes it active again if it is paused

The code listing shows the implementation of the MIDlet's constructor and its `startApp()`, `pauseApp()` and `destroyApp()` methods. A MIDlet is not required to do anything in its constructor and may instead defer initialization until the `startApp()` method is executed. In this example, the constructor prints a message so that you can see when it is being executed. It also performs the more useful function of getting the interval for the timer that will be used to change the MIDlet's state. It is appropriate to put this code in the constructor because this value needs to be set only once. The timer value is obtained from the `Timer-Interval` attribute that was specified in the settings dialog of the Wireless Toolkit and subsequently written to the JAD file. Here is what the JAD file created for this MIDlet suite actually looks like:

```
MIDlet-1: ExampleMIDlet, /ora/ch3/icon.png, ora.ch3.ExampleMIDlet
MIDlet-Jar-Size: 100
MIDlet-Jar-URL: Chapter3.jar
MIDlet-Name: Chapter3
MIDlet-Vendor: J2ME in a Nutshell
MIDlet-Version: 1.0
Timer-Interval: 3000
```

A MIDlet can read the values of its attributes using the following method from the `MIDlet` class:

```
public final String getAppProperty(String name);
```

This method looks for an attribute with the given name; it looks first in the JAD file, and then, if it was not found there, in the manifest file. Attributes names are case-sensitive and scoped to the MIDlet suite, so every MIDlet in the suite has access to the same set of attributes. The `getAppProperty()` method can be used to retrieve any attributes in the JAD file or the manifest, so the following line of code returns the name of the MIDlet's suite, in this case `Chapter3`:

```
String suiteName = geAppProperty("MIDlet-Name");
```

The timer interval for this MIDlet is obtained as follows:

```
String interval = getAppProperty("Timer-Interval");
timerInterval = Integer.parseInt(interval);
```

Once the value in the form of a string has been retrieved, the next step is to convert it to an integer by calling the `Integer parseInt()` method. If the `Timer-Interval` attribute is not included in the JAD file or manifest (or if its name is misspelled), `getAppProperty()` returns `null`, and the `parseInt()`

method throws an exception. A similar thing happens if the attribute value is not a valid integer. Notice that the constructor does not bother to catch either of these exceptions. The main reason for catching an exception is to display some meaningful information to the user and possibly allow recovery, but, strictly speaking, the MIDlet is not allowed to use the user interface in the constructor, so attempting to post a message would not necessarily work. The most appropriate thing to do in a real MIDlet is to install a default value for the timer interval and arrange to notify the user from the startApp() method, when access to the user interface is possible. In this simple example, we allow the exception to be thrown out of the constructor, which causes the MIDlet to be destroyed. Additionally, the version of MIDP in the Wireless Toolkit does, in fact, display the exception on the screen, but vendor implementations are not bound to do so.

Once the constructor has completed execution, the device eventually calls the MIDlet's startApp() method, which allocates any resources that the MIDlet needs. The startApp() method is also called when the MIDlet is resumed after being in the Paused state. In that case, however, it should allocate only the resources that were released by pauseApp(). A boolean variable called started, which is false only when startApp() is entered for the first time, is used to distinguish these two cases:

- When started is false, startApp() creates and starts the MIDlet timer and the MIDlet's background thread.

- When started is true, startApp() does not need to concern itself with the timer, because it is not canceled by the pauseApp() method. It does, however, create a new background thread, because the original thread will be stopped when the MIDlet is paused.

Since the timer is going to be active throughout the lifetime of the MIDlet, it could have been allocated in the constructor. We deferred creating the timer until startApp() executes for the first time, however, because it isn't actually needed until that point; it is better, in an environment with such limited memory, to delay allocating resources until they are needed. The decision whether to commit resources in the constructor or in the startApp() method depends on the MIDlet and must therefore be made on a case-by-case basis.

The pauseApp() method is relatively simple. Its job is to release any resources that the MIDlet does not need while it is not in the Active state. The MIDlet is making use of only two resources:

- A background thread printing a message every second

- A timer responsible for pausing and resuming the MIDlet periodically

Clearly, we can't stop the timer when the MIDlet is paused, because the timer is responsible for resuming it later. Therefore, the only resource the pauseApp() method can release is the background thread, by arranging for it to stop execution.

How is the pauseApp() method going to stop the background thread? The J2SE Thread class has two methods that might help: stop() and interrupt(). Neither of these methods is available in the CLDC version of Thread, however, so it is not possible to act directly on the background thread to stop it. Instead, we use a common mechanism, a shared variable that the thread inspects from time to time to find out whether it has been asked to stop. In this case, the MIDlet class keeps a reference to the Thread instance in a variable called thread. In order to stop the thread, the pauseApp() method sets this variable to null, while the main loop of the background thread checks its value on each pass:

```
public void run() {
    System.out.println("Thread running");
    while (thread == this) {
        try {
            Thread.sleep(1000);
            System.out.println("Thread still active");
        } catch (InterruptedException ex) {
        }
    }
    System.out.println("Thread terminating");
}
```

You'll notice that this code actually checks not whether the thread variable is null, but whether it is pointing to the background thread itself. This prevents a race condition in which the pauseApp() method clears thread to null, and the timer thread resumes the MIDlet before the background thread restarts following the sleep() call and checks its value. In this case, the startApp() method has started a new thread and stored its reference in thread, which therefore will not be null when the previous code checks it.

Finally, the destroyApp() method needs to stop the background thread and stop and release the timer. The thread can be stopped just as it is in the pauseApp() method. However, destroyApp() also waits for the thread to terminate so that it can guarantee that the MIDlet is not using any resources when it returns. It does this by calling the Thread.join() method, which blocks until the thread terminates (and returns immediately if it has already terminated). The stopTimer() method, which destroyApp() calls to stop and release the timer, is described in the next section.

If you now launch the MIDlet from the emulator, you'll see the results in the Wireless Toolkit's console window, an extract of which follows:

```
Constructor executed
Timer interval is 3000
startApp called for the first time
Timer started.
Thread running
Thread still active
Thread still active
Timer scheduled
>> Pausing MIDlet
pauseApp called.
Thread still active
Thread terminating
Timer scheduled
>> Resuming MIDlet
startApp called following pause
Thread running
```

As you can see, the constructor is executed first; it reads the value of the timer interval from the JAD file. Then startApp() is called, and it detects that it is being called for the first time and starts both the timer and the background thread. The "Thread running" and "Thread active" messages are printed by the background thread itself and show that the thread executes its loop twice before the timer fires. The code that executes when the timer expires, which will be shown in the next section, alternately pauses and resumes the MIDlet. In this case, as you can see, pauseApp() is called, which signals the background thread to stop running; the "Thread terminating" message indicates that the thread detects that it has been told to stop. Three seconds later, the timer expires again and resumes the MIDlet, causing its startApp() method to be invoked again to recreate the background thread. This process continues through two cycles, at which point the timer code destroys the MIDlet.

Timers and TimerTasks

Code to be executed when a timer expires should be implemented as a TimerTask and scheduled by a Timer. The Timer class provides the ability to execute sequentially one or more TimerTasks in a dedicated background thread. Usually, a MIDlet creates a single Timer to schedule all its TimerTasks, but it is possible to have more than one Timer active, each running its assigned TimerTasks in its own thread.

TimerTask is an abstract class with three methods:

```
public abstract void run();
public boolean cancel();
public long scheduledExecutionTime();
```

You create a unit of work to be scheduled by a Timer by subclassing TimerTask and implementing the run() method. You can schedule the run() method to be executed just once or to be executed repeatedly at either a fixed interval or a fixed rate. You can use the TimerTask cancel() method to stop future execution of a specific TimerTask. You may invoke it from the run() method, in which case the current execution of the task is allowed to complete, or you make invoke it from somewhere else. This method returns true if the task was scheduled to run either once or repeatedly and has been canceled; it returns false if the task was not associated with a Timer or if it had had been scheduled to be run once and has already run. The scheduledExecutionTime() method gets the time at which the task was most recently executed by its associated Timer. If called from within the run() method, it returns the time at which the run() method began execution. The value returned by this method is the number of milliseconds since midnight, January 1, 1970, which is the same as that returned by the System currentTimeMillis() method. If this method is called before the task is scheduled for the first time, its return value is undefined.

The Timer class has two methods that can be used to arrange for a task to be run exactly once:

```
public void schedule(TimerTask task, Date time);
public void schedule(TimerTask task, long delay);
```

The first of these methods schedules the task at the given time or as soon as possible afterwards; the second runs the task when a given time interval, specified in milliseconds, has passed. There are four methods that schedule a task for repeated execution:

```
public void schedule(TimerTask task, Date time, long period);
public void schedule(TimerTask task, long delay, long period);
public void scheduleAtFixedRate(TimerTask task, Date time, long period);
public void scheduleAtFixedRate(TimerTask task, long delay,
       long period);
```

The difference between these methods is that the first two apply a fixed delay between successive executions of the task, and the last two attempt to execute the task at a fixed rate. In both cases, the desired interval between task executions is given by the `period` parameter. Figure 3-9 shows how fixed-delay and fixed-rate scheduling differ.

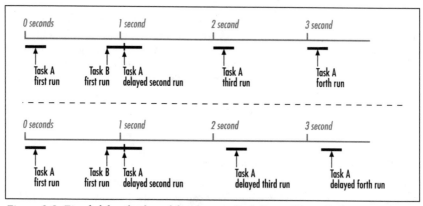

Figure 3-9: Fixed-delay (top) and fixed-rate scheduling of TimerTasks

In this example, task A is scheduled to run once every second; task B runs once, starting 900 milliseconds along the time line shown in the diagram. Task A first runs at T+0, followed by task B, which begins its execution at T+900ms. Task B takes 200 milliseconds to complete, however, which means that it is still running at T+1 second, when task A is supposed to run for the second time. Since a `Timer` can schedule only one `TimerTask` at a time, the execution of task A is delayed until task B finishes. Task A's second run begins, therefore, at T+1100ms. The difference between fixed-delay and fixed-rate scheduling is what happens as a result of this delay:

- In fixed-rate scheduling, the next execution of task A is scheduled relative to the time its previous execution should have started. In this case, task A should have begun execution at T+1 second. Under fixed rate scheduling, it will next run at T+2 seconds, as it would have had task B not delayed it.

- With fixed-delay scheduling, the next execution of task A is timed relative to the time its previous execution actually took place. Since task A last ran at T+1100ms, it will next run at T+2100ms, then at T+3100ms, and so on.

With fixed-delay scheduling, therefore, any delay affects all future executions of the task. With fixed-rate scheduling, however, an attempt is made to "ignore" the delay and schedule the task again where it would have run had there been no delay.

In some cases, additional executions of a fixed-rate task may be required to ensure that it runs the correct number of times when viewed over a long period. When this is necessary, the task may be run two or more times in succession to catch up with the number of times that it should have been run. For example, fixed-rate scheduling would be appropriate if you were using a timer to trigger redrawing the second hand of a clock displayed on the screen. Delayed execution of the redrawing task would cause the second hand to move more slowly, but the extra executions would ensure that it eventually moved forward to catch up with the real time. By contrast, using fixed delay execution in this case would result in the clock losing time that it would never make up, because execution delays are never corrected.

You may be able to reduce timing delays by using more than one Timer and dividing tasks among the Timers, because each Timer uses its own Thread. This only works, however, if the platform has more than one processor (which is unlikely in a J2ME environment), or if it has preemptive thread scheduling and chooses to suspend the thread of the Timer scheduling the long-running task B in favor of the thread for task A's Timer. The most reliable way to obtain predictable timer scheduling, however, is to ensure that code to be executed by a TimerTask executes as quickly as possible and does not block.

Like TimerTask, the Timer class has a cancel() method:

```
public void cancel();
```

This method cancels all the TimerTasks associated with the Timer. The Timer's thread stops executing when it has no more TimerTasks to be scheduled and there are no live references to it.

Example 3-2 shows the timer-related code for our example MIDlet.

Example 3-2: Using a MIDlet Timer

```
// Starts a timer to run a simple task
private void startTimer() {

    // Create a task to be run
    task = new TimerTask() {
        private boolean isPaused;
        private int count;

        public void run() {
            // Pause or resume the MIDlet.
            System.out.println("Timer scheduled");
            if (count++ == 4) {
                // Terminate the MIDlet
                try {
                    ExampleMIDlet.this.destroyApp(true);
                } catch (MIDletStateChangeException ex) {
```

Example 3-2: Using a MIDlet Timer (continued)

```
                    // Ignore pleas for mercy!
                }
                ExampleMIDlet.this.notifyDestroyed();
                return;
            }
            if (isPaused) {
                System.out.println(">> Resuming MIDlet");
                ExampleMIDlet.this.resumeRequest();
                isPaused = false;
            } else {
                System.out.println(">> Pausing MIDlet");
                isPaused = true;
                ExampleMIDlet.this.pauseApp();
                ExampleMIDlet.this.notifyPaused();
            }
        }
    };

    // Create a timer and schedule it to run
    timer = new Timer();
    timer.schedule(task, timerInterval, timerInterval);
    System.out.println("Timer started.");
}

// Stops the timer
private void stopTimer() {
    if (timer != null) {
        System.out.println("Stopping the timer");
        timer.cancel();
    }
}
```

The `startTimer()` method, which is called during the first invocation of `startApp()`, creates a `TimerTask` and schedules it to be run by a `Timer` object with the initial delay and repeat period given by the `Timer-Interval` attribute obtained from the application descriptor. The `stopTimer()` method is called from `destroyApp()`. It cancels the `TimerTask` and the `Timer` by calling the `Timer`'s `cancel()` method.

The code that is executed when the timer expires is worth looking at because it demonstrates how to control the lifecycle of a MIDlet. The intent of this code is to pause the MIDlet if it is active when the timer expires and resume if it is paused. However, there is no method that allows a MIDlet to find out whether it is in the Paused state, so the timer code has to retain this state for itself using an instance variable called `isPaused`. The code used to suspend the MIDlet looks like this:

```
isPaused = true;
ExampleMIDlet.this.pauseApp();
ExampleMIDlet.this.notifyPaused();
```

The `notifyPaused()` method tells the MIDlet scheduler that the MIDlet wants to be moved into the Paused state. As stated earlier, when the MIDlet calls this method, it is assumed that it is ready to be suspended, so its `pauseApp()` method is not called to give it a chance to release resources. For this reason, the timer code calls the MIDlet's `pauseApp()` method directly before suspending it. Moving a MIDlet to the Paused state simply means that it no longer has access to the screen and so does not receive user interface events in response to key presses or pointer movements. Timers and background threads belonging to a suspended MIDlet continue to be scheduled, provided that they are not stopped by the MIDlet itself in its `pauseApp()` method.

Moving the MIDlet from the Paused state to the Active state is a little easier:

```
ExampleMIDlet.this.resumeRequest();
isPaused = false;
```

The `resumeRequest()` call notifies the scheduler that the MIDlet would like to be made Active. In response to this, the MIDlet's `startApp()` method will be called at some future time to allow it to reallocate resources that were released when it was paused. If another MIDlet is currently in the foreground, the resumed MIDlet has to wait until the foreground MIDlet is paused or terminates before it becomes eligible to become the foreground MIDlet and recover use of the screen and input devices.

Finally, after two suspend/resume cycles are completed, the timer code destroys the MIDlet by calling `notifyDestroyed()`:

```
// Terminate the MIDlet
  try {
      ExampleMIDlet.this.destroyApp(true);
  } catch (MIDletStateChangeException ex) {
      // Ignore pleas for mercy!
  }
  ExampleMIDlet.this.notifyDestroyed();
```

As is the case with `notifyPaused()`, the MIDlet's `destroyApp()` method is not invoked as a result of a call to `notifyDestroyed()`, so the timer code explicitly invokes it in order to allow the MIDlet to release its resources. Because this is an involuntary termination, the `destroyApp()` method is called with its `unconditional` argument set to `true`. However, care is taken to catch a `MIDletStateChangeException` in case the `destroyApp()` method ignores this argument. It is important to note that `notifyDestroyed()` does not actually terminate the MIDlet or any of its threads; it simply arranges for the MIDlet never to be scheduled as the foreground MIDlet and removes it from the list of active MIDlets. It is the MIDlet's responsibility to stop its active threads and timers in its `destroyApp()` method. Failure to do this may cause the Java VM to continue running and consuming memory when it has no useful work to do, which is unacceptable given the resource constraints of the typical MIDP device.

Delivery and Installation of MIDlets

The MIDP specification creates the concept of a MIDlet, defines its lifecycle and its execution environment, and specifies the programming interfaces that a MIDlet can expect to be present on any conforming device. However, it currently does not address in any detail how the user should locate MIDlet suites, how MIDlet suites will be installed on a cell phone or a PDA, and what facilities are to be provided to allow the user to select and launch an installed MIDlet or to remove

MIDlet suites from the device. These features are not covered in detail in the MIDP specification because they are largely device-specific. Instead, it refers loosely to software that is intended for application delivery and management. The term *Application Management Software* (AMS) is generally used to describe the software components that take on this responsibility.* The MIDP reference implementation provides an example AMS for the benefit of vendors porting the software to their own devices, and both the Wireless Toolkit and the MIDP for PalmOS product have their own AMS implementations, which allow software to be installed from two different sources:

From a local host computer via a dedicated, relatively high speed connection
> This mode of operation is particularly suitable for PDAs, which are typically associated with a desktop or laptop computer with which they periodically synchronize. Synchronizing backs up the user's data from the handheld onto the larger system and copies software and data in the other direction, as well. The MIDP for PalmOS implementation is a good example of this, because its AMS allows MIDlet suites to be installed from a host PC during the synchronization process. Once the MIDlets are installed, they can be launched on the PDA in the same way as its native applications. The same application management features are supported for MIDlets, so they appear to be almost the same as native applications.

Over a network to which the device is connected
> This is the most common way in which MIDlets are downloaded to cell phones and similar wireless devices, although it is also applicable to network-connected PDAs. The process of deploying MIDlet suites over a network is referred to as *over-the-air provisioning*, or *OTA provisioning* for short. OTA provisioning is not part of the MIDP specification, but it is likely to be the dominant mechanism for distributing MIDlets, and it will doubtless be included in the formal specification in the near future. An AMS that supports installation of MIDlets from an HTTP server is included in the Wireless Toolkit.

Over-the-Air Provisioning

With OTA provisioning, MIDlet providers install their MIDlet suites on web servers and provide hypertext links to them. A user activates the links to download the MIDlets to a cell phone via a WAP or Internet microbrowser. Figure 3-10 shows the steps involved in a typical MIDlet installation.

 OTA provisioning as described in this section is not formally a part of the MIDP specification at the time of writing, but it is likely to be included in the next version of the specification. Meanwhile, it has the status of best-practice recommendation.

---

* The term *Java Application Manager* (or JAM) was originally used to describe the MIDP application management software. However, this resulted in confusion with the Java Application Manager software that is part of the CLDC reference implementation, which performs similar functions but with which it is incompatible.

The process begins when the user fetches a page from the corporate web site of the (fictional) corporation ACME, Inc. The page includes a link to a suite of MIDlets that allow the user to browse ACME's product catalog and place orders directly from a Java-enabled cell phone. Intrigued by this prospect, the user activates the link, which causes a request for the target to be sent to ACME's web server. The link in question would look something like this:

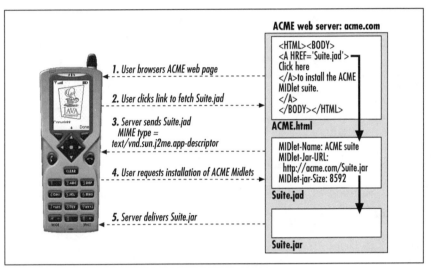

Figure 3-10: Installing MIDlets using OTA provisioning

```
<A HREF="Suite.jad">Click here</A> to install the ACME MIDlet suite
```

As you can see, this link points to the JAD file for the ACME MIDlet suite. The request to retrieve this file is sent by the cell phone's browser (see step 2 in Figure 3-10), but it will be passed to and handled by the phone's application management software. To enable browsers to easily identify JAD files, the web server is configured to return them with the following MIME type:

```
text/vnd.sun.j2me.app-descriptor
```

On receipt of data with this content type, the phone's AMS activates and displays the content of the application descriptor, so that the user can decide whether or not to install the MIDlet suite. At this stage, the user has waited only a relatively short time for the download of the small JAD file. Since this file contains an attribute that corresponds to the size of the JAR file that contains the MIDlets as well as a textual description of the services they provide, the user should be able to choose whether to install them. This is the advantage of providing MIDlet information in both the JAD file and the JAR file manifest.

Should the user decide to install the MIDlets, the AMS looks for the `MIDlet-Jar-URL` attribute in the JAD file and sends a request to that URL for the JAR, which the server should return tagged with the MIME type `application/java-archive`.

At this point, the MIDlet suite is installed, and the user can select and run the individual MIDlets. Following installation, the AMS may be required to deliver a status report to the provisioning server indicating whether the suite was successfully installed and identifying the reason for failure if it was not. This report takes the form of a status code and a status message that is sent using an HTTP POST request to the URL given by the MIDlet-Install-Notify attribute in the JAD file. If this attribute is not present, no installation report is sent. Of course, the server must be configured to expect an installation report at the given URL. The server typically uses a servlet or CGI script to save the report along with details of the originator for later use.

 If you are not familiar with the HTTP protocol, you'll find a discussion of those parts of it that are supported by MIDP devices, including the POST request, in Chapter 6. More complete coverage of HTTP can be found in *Java Network Programming* by Elliotte Rusty Harold (O'Reilly & Associates, Inc.).

The status codes and their meanings are listed in Table 3-3.

Table 3-3: Status Codes Used to Report Success or Failure of MIDlet Installation

Status Code	Meaning
900	Success
901	Insufficient memory
902	Canceled by the user
903	Loss of network service (because of the network service loss, this report may never get delivered to the server)
904	JAR size mismatch
905	Attribute mismatch
906	Invalid descriptor

As well as implementing the MIDlet discovery and installation service as just described, the AMS software is required to provide the following functionality:

MIDlet suite updates

MIDlet updates are delivered just as the original MIDlet suite is: the user returns to the original server and requests the software as if an installation were being performed. Because the JAD file contains the version number of the associated MIDlet suite, the AMS can determine whether the software already installed is older than that on the server; if it is, the AMS can perform an upgrade, with permission from the user. Equally important, it can avoid downloading the JAR file if the newest version is already installed.

MIDlet selection and execution

The AMS provides the user with a means of selecting an installed MIDlet to run. The exact means by which this is achieved is device-dependent. On a cell phone, a menu item might give the user the ability to launch the AMS, or individual MIDlet suites may be included in the menu itself. On a PDA, MIDlet suites might be available in exactly the same way as native applications.

MIDlet removal

The Java application management software is responsible for removing MIDlet suites from the device on user request. MIDlets cannot be removed individually. Following successful removal, the application manager must also delete any persistent storage resources that were allocated to the MIDlet suite (see "Persistent Storage" in Chapter 6 for further details). Because MIDlet removal causes loss of persistent data and is therefore almost certainly an irreversible process, the AMS will normally prompt the user for confirmation. The MIDlet suite vendor can use the `MIDlet-Delete-Confirm` attribute in the JAD file to include a message that should be displayed to the user before removal. This message can be used to warn the user of the consequences, if any, of removing the MIDlet suite.

The Wireless Toolkit Application Management Software

To prepare a MIDlet suite for remote installation, take the following steps:

1. Install the MIDlet suite JAR file on your web server.

2. Edit the JAD file so that its `MIDlet-Jar-URL` attribute points to the JAR file. Note that the specification requires that an *absolute* URL is required in the JAD file; relative URLs are not guaranteed to work. The Wireless Toolkit does not generate a JAD file containing an absolute URL, so you will need to edit it manually.

3. Place the JAD file on the web server.

4. Create an HTML or WML page with a hypertext link to the JAD file. The hypertext link must use an absolute URL, since application managers are not required to support relative URLs.

5. Configure the web server so that JAD files are returned with MIME type `text/vnd.sun.j2me.app-descriptor` and JAR files with MIME type `application/java-archive`.

The Wireless Toolkit contains a graphical AMS that can be used to test the OTA provisioning of MIDlet suites as well as to provide developers and vendors with a demonstration of typical application management and removal features. To use it, run the emulator provided with the Toolkit from the command line and pass it the argument *–Xjam*. Assuming you have installed the Wireless Toolkit in the directory *c:\j2mewtk*, issuing the following command in DOS starts the emulator and activates the AMS:

```
c:\j2mewtk\bin\emulator.exe -Xjam
```

When started, the application manager displays the Java logo and a copyright message. Press the Done button to show the application manager's main screen, which is shown on the left of Figure 3-11.

Pressing the Install button opens another screen that allows you to supply the URL of an HTML page that contains links to MIDlet suites, as shown on the right of Figure 3-11. This should be the URL of the HTML page set up previously, in step 4. The directory *ora\ch3* in this book's example source code contains a sample

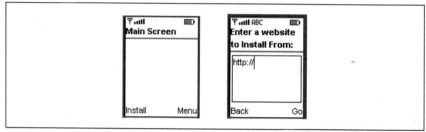

Figure 3-11: The Wireless Toolkit application management software

HTML file called *MIDlet.html* that you can use for testing purposes. You should compile and package the MIDlet in this directory in the usual way and copy the files *MIDlet.html, Chapter3.jad* and *Chapter3.jar* onto your web server. Open *Chapter3.jad* and change the MIDlet-Jar-URL attribute to the absolute URL that corresponds to the location of the JAR file. Also edit the *MIDlet.html* file so that the HREF attribute in the <A> tag is the absolute URL of the JAD file.

Press the Go button to start the process. At this point, the AMS loads the HTML page and scans it for links that point to JAD files. A commercial application manager distinguishes these links from other links by making a request to the server for the target of the link and looking for a returned MIME type of text/ vnd.sun.j2me.app-descriptor. However, the Wireless Toolkit AMS appears to take a shortcut and simply looks for links for which the target URL ends with *.jad*. If the target page does not contain any links that correspond to MIDlet suites, the error message shown on the left of Figure 3-12 appears.

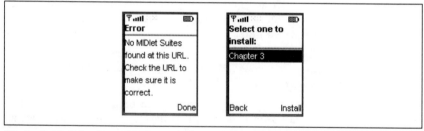

Figure 3-12: Selecting a MIDlet suite for installation

If you experience problems with this example, check that the server is properly configured and that the JAR and JAD files are consistent:

*   The URL that you supply to the AMS must point to an HTML file that contains *absolute* hypertext links to one or more JAD files. The HTML file for this example looks like this:

```
<HTML>
    <HEAD>
        <TITLE>
        J2ME in a Nutshell Example MIDlet Download Page
        </TITLE>
    </HEAD>
    <BODY>
```

```
    Install the example MIDlet suite for
    <A HREF="http://localhost:8080/Chapter3.jad">Chapter 3</A> of
"J2ME in a Nutshell".
    </BODY>
</HTML>
```

- The web server must be configured to return JAD files with MIME type `text/vnd.sun.j2me.app-descriptor`.

- The `MIDlet-Jar-URL` attribute in the JAD file must be an absolute URL pointing to the JAR file.

- The JAD file must contain the mandatory attributes listed in Table 3-2.

If the AMS locates any JAD files, it displays a list of the links that point to them, using the text within the `<A></A>` tag pair to identify each MIDlet suite, as shown on the right side of Figure 3-12. This implementation does not display the MIDlet suite name or the JAR file size from the JAD file because it hasn't fetched it yet. To continue with the installation process, press the Install button.

At this point, the Wireless Toolkit AMS reads the JAD file from the server and uses the `MIDlet-Jar-URL` attribute to locate and fetch the JAR file. If this process succeeds, a confirmation message appears as shown on the left side of Figure 3-13. After a short pause, the application manager switches back to its main screen, shown in the center of Figure 3-13. If you compare this to Figure 3-11, you'll see that the main screen now contains the name of the MIDlet suite that was just installed. The list of installed MIDlets is saved on the device, so this list will reappear when you next run the emulator. In the case of a MIDlet suite containing more than one MIDlet, the list in the main screen displays each suite together with the MIDlets that it contains. An example of this is shown on the right-hand side of Figure 3-13, in which a MIDlet suite called `Chapter5` containing individual MIDlets called `Socket`, `Time`, `Ranking` and others that are not visible in the screen shot, has been installed.

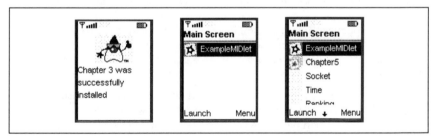

Figure 3-13: Installing a MIDlet suite

The main screen also includes an option that lets you launch MIDlets. If you select a MIDlet suite and choose this option, the usual MIDlet selector lets you pick the actual MIDlet to be run (see Figure 3-8). For a suite with multiple MIDlets, you can also choose an individual MIDlet from the main screen and launch it directly.

The Menu option provides access to the other application management features of the Wireless Toolkit AMS, presented in the form of a list, as shown in Figure 3-14.

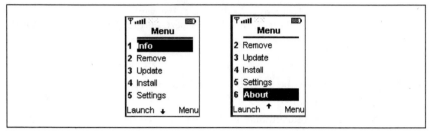

Figure 3-14: The Wireless Toolkit AMS application management menu

Of these menu items, only the first three are worth discussing here. Each of these items operates on a MIDlet suite, so selecting any of them brings up another copy of the MIDlet selection screen so that you can choose the suite to which the command should apply.

The Info command displays the content of the JAD file that was fetched when the MIDlet suite was installed. Ideally, this information would be displayed to the user before the installation process starts, but, as noted previously, the Wireless Toolkit AMS does not implement this feature. Figure 3-15 shows the information displayed for the Chapter3 MIDlet suite.

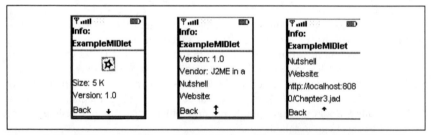

Figure 3-15: MIDlet suite information as displayed by the Windows Tooklit AMS

The Update command reinstalls the MIDlet suite from its original source. As noted earlier, the AMS can compare the MIDlet version in its installed JAD file and the one it acquires from the server to determine if it already has the latest version of a MIDlet suite.

The Remove option deletes a MIDlet suite and all its associated persistent storage from the device. The Wireless Toolkit AMS displays a warning message and asks the user for confirmation before performing this operation (see Figure 3-16).

The Wireless Toolkit AMS can be controlled from the command line as well as through its user interface. For example, you can install a MIDlet suite directly from a web server using the command:

```
c:\j2mewtk\bin\emulator.exe -Xjam:install=http://www.yourserver.com/
     SOMETHING/Chapter3.jad
```

A complete description of the command-line arguments recognized by the Wireless Toolkit emulator can be found in Chapter 8.

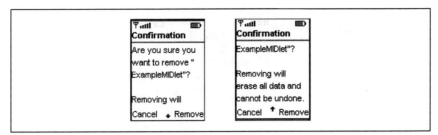

Figure 3-16: Deleting a MIDlet suite using the Wireless Toolkit AMS

CHAPTER 4

MIDlet User Interfaces

MIDlets are intended to be portable to a range of devices with widely varying input and display capabilities, ranging from the very small, mainly two-color screens and restricted keypads on pagers and cell phones to the larger, often multicolor displays and more sophisticated keyboards or handwriting recognizers available on PDAs. Creating a set of user interface components suitable for such a wide range of devices is not a simple task. One option available to the MIDP designers was to use a subset of the Abstract Windows Toolkit (AWT) or Swing components from J2SE. However, this is not really a viable solution. Resource constraints rule out the adoption of Swing, while the basic user interface model around which the AWT is based is far too complex to be used on small devices.

Both AWT and Swing are based on giving the developer maximum freedom to create a rich and complex GUI in a multiwindowed environment, in which the user might be interacting with several applications at the same time. By contrast, because of the limited screen size, cell phone users do not expect to be able to work with more than one window or even more than one MIDlet at any given time. Instead of trying to find a subset of the AWT that would be appropriate for this restricted environment, the MIDP expert group chose to introduce a much simpler set of components and a lighter, screen-based programming model. In this model, the MIDlet developer focuses more on the business logic of the application rather than on the minute details of the user interface itself. The result is a class library that is much smaller and easier to use and also less demanding of memory and processor resources than either Swing or AWT.

The price to be paid for this simplicity is that developers using this "high-level" API are much less able to control the exact look and feel of their MIDlets; the programming interface does not include features that would allow customization of colors, fonts, or even component layout. The high-level API is covered in the second half of this chapter, but it does not represent the entire scope of the MIDlet user interface support. Recognizing that some application types, such as games (which are likely to form a large part of the software market for cell phones) require a much greater level of control, MIDP also includes a "low-level" user interface API. This API gives the developer exactly the opposite of the high-level API, namely complete control over (a part of) the screen and access to the keypad and whatever pointing device might be available. The trade-off for this greater control is greater responsibility: using the low-level API means writing code to draw everything that appears on the user's screen and interpreting every input keystroke and pointer movement to decipher what the user wants to do. J2SE developers with experience creating custom components for AWT and Swing applications will probably feel very much at home with the low-level API, which is covered in the next chapter.

User Interface Overview

The user interface model for MIDP devices is very simple. J2SE applications often consist of several simultaneously visible windows between which the user can move the input focus simply by clicking with the mouse. A MIDP device, on the other hand, is required to display only a single "window" at a time, and the ability to move from one window to another depends on whether the MIDlet developer includes UI components that allow the user to do so. Furthermore, if there is more than one MIDlet running in a device at the same time, only one of them can have access to the screen, and the device may or may not provide a way for the user to select which MIDlet should be given the screen at any particular time. The MIDlet user interface library, which is implemented in the `javax.microedition.lcdui` package, includes several classes that represent the device's screen and provide the basic top-level windows. Developers can use these as the basis for building form-based MIDlets or more graphically sophisticated MIDlets, such as games.

The Display and Displayable Classes

The `Display` class represents a logical device screen on which a MIDlet can display its user interface. Each MIDlet has access to a single instance of this class; you can obtain a reference to it by using the static `getDisplay()` method:

```
public static Display getDisplay(MIDlet midlet);
```

A MIDlet usually invokes `getDisplay()` when its `startApp()` method is called for the first time and then uses the returned `Display` object to display the first screen of its user interface. You can safely call this method at any time from the start of the initial invocation of the `startApp()` method, up to the time when the MIDlet returns from `destroyApp()` or `notifyDestroyed()`, whichever happens first. Each MIDlet has its own, unique and dedicated instance of `Display`, so `getDisplay()` returns the same value every time it is called. A MIDlet will, therefore, usually save a reference to its `Display` object in an instance variable rather than repeatedly call `getDisplay()`.

Every screen that a MIDlet needs to display is constructed by mounting user interface components (which are called *items* in MIDP terminology) or drawing shapes onto a top-level window derived from the abstract class `Displayable`, which will be discussed later. A `Displayable` is not visible to the user until it is associated with the MIDlet's `Display` object using the `Display`'s `setCurrent()` method:

```
public void setCurrent(Displayable displayable)
```

Similarly, the Displayable currently associated with a Display can be retrieved by calling getCurrent():

```
public Displayable getCurrent()
```

Since a Display can show only one screen at a time, calling the setCurrent() method causes the previously displayed screen, if any, to be removed and replaced with the new one. However, the effect of calling setCurrent() is not guaranteed to be immediate; the device is allowed to defer the change to a more convenient time. This has the following consequences:

- Code such as the following:

```
Form newForm = new Form("New Form");
display.setCurrent(newForm);
Form currentForm = display.getCurrent();
System.out.println(newForm == currentForm);
```

  (where Form is a kind of Displayable that will be introduced shortly) does not necessarily print "true" because getCurrent() may return the Displayable that was installed before setCurrent() was called.

- Installing a new Displayable and then blocking to perform a slow operation, such as making a network connection, is likely to result in the MIDlet appearing to stop with the previous screen on display. If you want to display a "Please wait..." message to make it clear to the user that a long-lasting operation is in progress, it is best to call setCurrent() to install a new Form containing the message and initiate the operation in a separate thread. The original thread can then continue unblocked and eventually display the message.

The Display object does not correspond directly to the device's screen. Instead, it acts as a virtual screen that the MIDlet can use to control what it would like to display. If there is more than one active MIDlet, only one of them can control the real screen at any given time. The MIDlet that has direct access to the screen is said to be in the foreground, and other MIDlets are in the background. The MIDP device's AMS is responsible for selecting which MIDlet is in the foreground at any given time. When a MIDlet is moved to the foreground, the Displayable selected in its Display object is switched into the screen, and the MIDlet's startApp() method is called, as described in "MIDlet Execution Environment and Lifecycle" in Chapter 3. Figure 4-1 shows the relationship between the device screen and the Display and current Displayable of foreground and background MIDlets.

Once a MIDlet has the foreground, it retains it until it does one of the following things:

- Invokes its notifyPaused() method to request a temporary move to the background state

- Invokes its notifyDestroyed() method to indicate that it no longer wants to be scheduled into the foreground

Although a MIDlet would normally call these methods as part of its event handling in response to user commands, a background thread running in the same MIDlet (or even in another MIDlet) may also invoke them to move the MIDlet out of the foreground.

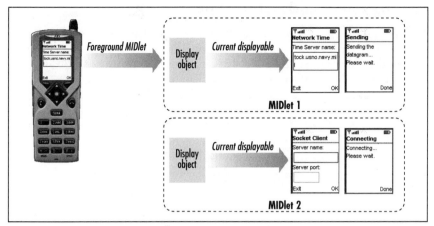

Figure 4-1: Foreground MIDlet and the Display object

Since the current `Displayable` is an attribute of the `Display` object, a background MIDlet also has a current `Displayable`, which it may change by calling the `setCurrent()` method if it has threads or timers running while it is not in the foreground. These changes have no effect on what the user sees until the MIDlet returns to the foreground.

A MIDlet can determine whether a given `Displayable` is visible to the user by calling `isShown()`, which is one of the four methods of the `Displayable` class:

```
public abstract class Displayable {
        public boolean isShown();
        public void addCommand(Command cmd);
        public void removeCommand(Command cmd);
        public void setCommandListener(CommandListener l);
}
```

The `isShown()` method returns `true` only when the `Displayable` can actually be seen by the user, which requires that it be the current `Displayable` of the MIDlet's `Display` and that the MIDlet be in the foreground. However, this condition is not sufficient, as the following code illustrates:

```
Form newForm = new Form("New Form");
display.setCurrent(newForm);
System.out.println("New form is shown? " + newForm.isShown());
```

In this case, `newForm` may not yet be visible, because the effect of `setCurrent()` is not required to be immediate.

The other three methods of the `Displayable` class deal with the addition and removal of `Command` objects and the registration of a listener to receive events from `Commands`. As the name suggests, `Commands` allow the user to request that an action be performed, such as opening a network connection, switching to another screen, or terminating the MIDlet. `Commands` are discussed in detail later in the section "Commands."

The High- and Low-Level User Interface APIs

`Displayable` is the base class for all MIDlet user interfaces, but it doesn't provide enough functionality to be useful in its own right. There is a set of more useful classes, derived from `Displayable`, that can be used as the basis for building real user interfaces. The class hierarchy for these classes is shown in Figure 4-2.

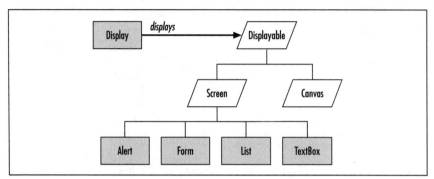

Figure 4-2: Top-level user interface classes

As you can see, there are two direct subclasses of `Displayable`, both of which are also abstract. These two subclasses are the starting points for the two different styles of user interface programming supported by the `javax.microedition.lcdui` package.

Canvas

The `Canvas` class is the cornerstone of the low-level GUI API. `Canvas` acts like a blank sheet of paper that covers most of the user's screen. In order to create a user interface using the low-level API, you subclass `Canvas` and implement the `paint()` method to draw directly on the screen. You can also respond to user input by overriding methods that are called as a result of key presses or pointer movements. The low-level API does not provide any individual components to handle text input, display lists, offer choices, and so on, although it does include the ability to use `Commands`, which `Canvas` inherits from `Displayable`. The low-level API is well suited for writing graphical games or displaying data in chart form and is described in detail in Chapter 5.

Screen

`Screen` is the basic class from which the top-level windows of the high-level API are derived. Like `Canvas`, `Screen` is an abstract class, but, unlike `Canvas`, developers are not expected to subclass it in order to implement a MIDlet user interface. `Screen` adds to `Displayable` the ability to include an optional title string and an optional ticker, which displays a continuously scrolling text message. The most commonly used concrete subclass of `Screen` is `Form`, which allows you to build a user interface by adding standard components (referred to as `Items`) to it, much like you add `Components` to a `Container` in the AWT. `List`, `TextBox`, and `Alert`, which is the MIDP equivalent of a dialog, are other subclasses of `Screen`. Unlike the low-level API, the high-level API does not allow the developer to draw directly to the screen or to handle events from the keyboard or the pointer. Instead, these events are handled internally and, where appropriate, are converted to higher-level events that originate from the Items that appear on the user's screen.

Although the low- and high-level APIs are very different in style, they can be used together within a MIDlet. A typical example of this might be using the high-level API to create a form that allows the user to specify the location of some data, then switching to a Canvas on which the data is presented as a chart. You cannot, of course, use the high- and low-level APIs on the same screen.

The High-Level User Interface API

A MIDlet written using the high-level API typically consists of one or more screens built using the Form, List, or TextBox classes, together with a set of Commands that allow the user to tell the MIDlet what actions to perform and how to navigate from screen to screen. Let's start our examination of the high-level API by creating a simple MIDlet with a single screen containing a TextBox.

A TextBox Example

TextBox is a component used to display and modify text. Since it is derived from Screen, TextBox occupies the entire screen of the device and therefore can accomodate relatively large amounts of text spread over several lines. Most of the API provided by TextBox is identical to that of a similar component called TextField, which is covered in detail in "TextFields and TextBoxes," later in this chapter. In this example, we use only the features that TextBox inherits from Screen (and which are not available to TextField, because it is not derived from Screen). The code for this example is shown in Example 4-1.

Example 4-1: Creating and Using a TextBox

```
package ora.ch4;

import java.io.InputStream;
import java.io.InputStreamReader;
import java.io.IOException;
import javax.microedition.lcdui.Display;
import javax.microedition.lcdui.TextBox;
import javax.microedition.lcdui.TextField;
import javax.microedition.lcdui.Ticker;
import javax.microedition.midlet.MIDlet;

public class TextBoxMIDlet extends MIDlet {

    // Maximum size of the text in the TextBox
    private static final int MAX_TEXT_SIZE = 64;

    // The TextBox
    protected TextBox textBox;

    // The MIDlet's Display object
    protected Display display;
```

Example 4-1: Creating and Using a TextBox (continued)

```java
    // Flag indicating first call of startApp
    protected boolean started;

    protected void startApp() {
        if (!started) {
            // First time through - initialize
            // Get the text to be displayed
            String str = null;
            try {
                InputStream is = getClass().getResourceAsStream(
                    "resources/text.txt");
                InputStreamReader r = new InputStreamReader(is);
                char[] buffer = new char[32];
                StringBuffer sb = new StringBuffer();
                int count;
                while ((count = r.read(buffer, 0, buffer.length)) > -1) {
                    sb.append(buffer, 0, count);
                }
                str = sb.toString();
            } catch (IOException ex) {
                str = "Failed to load text";
            }

            // Create the TextBox
            textBox = new TextBox("TextBox Example", str,
                                MAX_TEXT_SIZE, TextField.ANY);

            // Create a ticker and install it
            Ticker ticker = new Ticker("This is a ticker...");
            textBox.setTicker(ticker);

            // Install the TextBox as the current screen
            display = Display.getDisplay(this);
            display.setCurrent(textBox);

            started = true;
        }
    }

    protected void pauseApp() {
    }

    protected void destroyApp(boolean unconditional) {
    }
}
```

In this simple MIDlet, all of the code is in the startApp() method, which simply reads some text from a file, installs it in a TextBox, and arranges for the TextBox to appear on the screen. Since the startApp() method could be called more than once during the lifetime of a MIDlet, this initialization code is protected by a boolean flag that ensures that it is performed only on the first invocation of startApp().

Skipping for a moment the code that obtains the actual text, let's look at how the user interface is created. The TextBox is created using its only constructor:

```
public TextBox(String title, String text, int maxSize, int constraints)
```

The title argument sets the title that appears above the TextBox; you can set it to null if no title is required. The second argument specifies the text that will initially be displayed in the TextBox, and the final two arguments allow you to exercise some control over what the TextBox is allowed to contain, as follows:

maxSize

Specifies the maximum number of characters that the TextBox can contain at any time. Once the TextBox contains the maximum number of characters, the user will not be allowed to enter any more. The same restriction also applies to the text supplied to the constructor and to all the other methods that allow you to change programmatically the content of the TextBox, which you'll see later when we look at the TextField component. There is no way to avoid specifying an upper bound on the number of characters that the TextBox can hold; specifying 0, for example, creates a TextBox that cannot contain any text at all! Furthermore, the implementation is permitted to apply a smaller upper bound than the one you specify, so trying to avoid this constraint by setting a large maximum size is unlikely to work. You can find out the actual maximum size that applies to a TextBox by calling its getMaxSize() method.

constraints

Specifies the type of content that should be allowed in the TextBox. Using this argument, you can, for example, restrict the user to entering only numbers or more complex things such as phone numbers or URLs without having to write the code to validate the content yourself. Since this is another feature that TextBox shares with TextField, we'll defer further discussion of it until later in the chapter. In this example, the constraint has the value TextField. ANY, which places no restriction on what the TextBox can contain.

TextBox inherits the ability to display a title from its superclass (Screen). Here is how Screen itself is defined:

```
public abstract class Screen extends Displayable {
    public Ticker getTicker();
    public String getTitle();
    public void setTicker(Ticker ticker);
    public void setTitle(String title);
}
```

You can change the title associated with the TextBox at any time by calling the setTitle() method, and you can also use the setTicker() method to add a Ticker to the screen. Ticker is a very simple class that displays a string that continuously scrolls across the screen area allocated to it, which is usually at the top. Here's the definition of this class:

```
public class Ticker {
    public Ticker(String str);
    public String getString();
    public void setString(String str);
}
```

You'll notice that there is no way to explicitly start or stop the ticker or to control the direction or rate at which it scrolls its content; these aspects are all controlled by the MIDP implementation itself. This lack of direct control is a deliberate design feature of the high-level API, which emphasizes simplicity, partly to minimize the size of the API and partly to make it possible to port both the platform itself and the MIDlets that rely on it to devices with varying user interface capabilities. In this example, we add a `Ticker` to the `TextBox` so that you can see how it works and where it is placed:

```
Ticker ticker = new Ticker("This is a ticker...")
textBox.setTicker(ticker);
```

It is worth noting that a single `Ticker` can be associated with any number of screens at the same time. This is a very useful feature, not only because it potentially saves resources, but also because any changes made to the `Ticker` by calling its `setString()` method (e.g., updating stock prices) takes effect immediately for all the screens on which the `Ticker` appears.

To run this example, you can use the Run MIDP Application utility that comes with the Wireless Toolkit. Point it at the file *ora\ch4\Chapter4.jad* in the example source code for this book and select `TextBoxMIDlet`. The MIDlet's user interface, as seen on the default color phone, is shown in Figure 4-3.

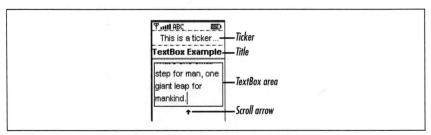

Figure 4-3: A TextBox with a ticker and screen title

This phone arranges the three parts of the screen so that the `Ticker` is placed at the top with the title below it and the content of the `TextBox` itself at the bottom. Other devices might take a different approach. For example, if you run this code on a PalmOS-based handheld, the result looks like Figure 4-4, where the title and ticker are placed side by side. Notice also that because less space is allocated for the title on the PalmOS platform, the text is truncated..

Chap...:TextBox...   This is a ticker.
That's one small step for man, one
giant leap for mankind.

Figure 4-4: Title and Ticker as shown on a PalmOS-based handheld

Although the text used in this example is fairly short due to the small size of the phone's screen and the space taken up by the title and ticker, it isn't possible for the TextBox to show all of the text at once. When this happens, the TextBox allows the user to scroll its content using the up and down arrow keys on the keypad and draws a scroll arrow on the screen to indicate that there is more text to be seen. On other devices, such as handhelds with pointing devices, a scrollbar that could be dragged using the pointer might be provided. The presence and nature of these visual cues and the way in which they work is transparent to the MIDlet, which doesn't need to include any code to deal with them or even be concerned about whether they are required.

Since TextBox provides editing facilities, you can use the keys on the emulated phone's keyboard to change the text or add extra characters. If you try to add more than 6 characters, however, you will fail, because this TextBox has a capacity of only 64 characters, and the initial text is 58 characters long. Using the arrow keys, you can move the insertion point around within the TextBox and insert or delete characters anywhere you like, provided you don't exceed the 64-character limit.

The emulated devices provided by the Wireless Toolkit attempt to mimic the input mechanisms of the real devices. In the case of a cell phone, the small number of keys available means that most of the keys are overloaded to perform several functions. Most of the keys give numbers when pressed, but if you press them repeatedly, they yield other characters. On the default color phone, for example, the 2 key can be used to input the number 2 or the letters A, B, or C, provided you press the key quickly enough. You can use the MODE key to shift into a separate mode to make the input of alphabetics quicker or to force each key to represent only the number on its face. You can also use the MODE key to select a screen that contains special symbols. The RIM wireless handheld, on the other hand, has a larger set of keys that include alphabetics, with numbers and special characters accessible via a mode shift. When you use the TextBox or TextField components, you don't need to concern yourself with the details of the keypad or keyboard, because the mapping from key strokes to Unicode characters is handled for you in a manner appropriate to the device that your MIDlet is running on.

When you are using the cell phone emulator, you will probably find it tedious and quite time-consuming to use the phone's keypad to enter text. In the real world, this would not be quite so difficult, because you are probably used to using the real keypad of your own phone, but it is inconvenient to use such a slow approach when developing MIDlets. To alleviate this problem, the emulators allow you use your PC's keyboard to edit the content of the TextBox instead of having to resort to the mouse. The quickest way to enter this mode is to press the Return key on your keyboard. This replaces the MIDlet's screen with a full-screen editor that accepts keystrokes from your keyboard, as shown in Figure 4-5. When you have finished editing, you can return to normal mode by pressing Return again. You can also abandon any changes you have made by pressing the Escape key. Another way to enter and leave full-screen editing mode is to use the mouse to "press" the key that corresponds to the SELECT action on the emulator's keypad. In the case of the default color phone, this is the round white button just below the screen, as shown in Figure 4-5. The full-screen editing facility is, of course, not available on real devices, and you should perform some testing without using this facility before deciding that your MIDlets are error-free.

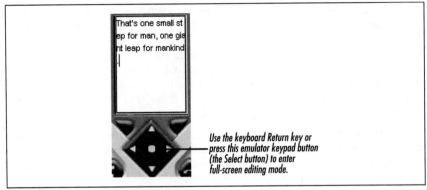

Use the keyboard Return key or press this emulator keypad button (the Select button) to enter full-screen editing mode.

Figure 4-5: Using the emulator's full-screen editor to enter text into a TextBox

Displaying the TextBox

Once you've created the TextBox, the next step is to make it visible to the user, which requires two lines of code:

```
display = Display.getDisplay(this);
display.setCurrent(textBox);
```

The static getDisplay() method of Display gets the Display object for the MIDlet passed as its only argument. Since this call is made directly from the MIDlet's startApp() method, it is appropriate to use this as the MIDlet reference. It is necessary to call getDisplay() only once in the lifetime of a MIDlet, because the returned reference is valid until the MIDlet is destroyed. Most MIDlets, therefore, simply store the reference in an instance variable, as shown in this example. To make the TextBox visible, the Display setCurrent() method is used with the TextBox reference supplied as the argument. The TextBox will appear on the user's screen sometime shortly after the setCurrent() method returns.

Accessing Resources in the MIDlet JAR File

For this example, instead of hard-coding the text to be displayed in the TextBox, I put it into a text file that is included in the MIDlet JAR file. Separating text from code is a useful technique that can be used to allow tailoring of a MIDlet suite to meet locale- or customer-specific requirements, such as the need to translate text in the user interface into other languages. The only problem with this approach is getting access to the file while the MIDlet is executing.

To solve this problem, the CLDC version of the class java.lang.Class provides an implementation of the J2SE method getResourceAsStream():

```
public InputStream getResourceAsStream(String name);
```

Given the name of a resource, this method returns an InputStream that can be used to read its content. To use this method, however, you need to have a Class object on which to invoke it and a properly formed resource name.

CLDC/MIDP does not provide an implementation of the other J2SE method that is commonly used to access resources in JAR files:

```
public URL getResource(String name)
```

Supporting this method would require the URL class, which is not part of either CLDC or MIDP. Another reason for not providing it is that it is of limited use even in J2SE, because some web browsers did not support it for applets but did implement getResourceAsStream(). Therefore, probably much less existing code uses getResource() than getResourceAsStream().

There are two different ways to specify the resource: with a relative name or an absolute name. To see how the resource name is constructed, you need to keep in mind how the JAR file is logically arranged. The simplest way to understand the layout is simply to imagine the JAR file expanded out into a filesystem hierarchy. This is usually very easy to do, because most JAR files are constructed from a filesystem anyway. In this example, the MIDlet class file is in a package called *ora\ch4* and, therefore, in terms of a filesystem layout, the class file would be called *ora\ch4\TextBoxMIDlet.class*. The text file is called *text.txt* and was placed in a package called *ora\ch4\resources*. Therefore, the filesystem pathnames for these two files would be:

ora\ch4\TextBoxMIDlet.class
ora\ch4\resources\text.txt

For the purposes of this example, we want to access the latter of these files while executing the code of the former. The simplest way to do this is to use an absolute resource name for the text file, which can be created by taking the logical pathname of the file, replacing all the "\" characters with "/", and prefixing the result with a "/" to form an absolute pathname:

/ora/ch4/resources/text.txt

When you use an absolute resource name, you can invoke the getResourceAsStream() method of any class in the same JAR file to get an InputStream for the resource. In this example, the simplest approach to take is to use the Class object of the MIDlet itself. Hence, one way to locate the text file is to write the following:

```
InputStream is = getClass().getResourceAsStream(
    "/ora/ch4/resources/text.txt");
```

Alternatively, you can use a relative resource name. Normally, you use a resource name that is relative to the class whose code is using it, so in this case you need a resource name relative to *ora\ch4\TextBoxMIDlet.class*. If you view the JAR as a filesystem, it is easy to see that the appropriate relative resource name would be *resources/text.txt*. Note that relative resource names do not begin with a "/" character. Because this name is relative to TextBoxMIDlet.class, you need to use the Class object of that class (or, in fact, any other class in the same package, since all such classes are in the same directory in a filesystem representation of the

JAR file structure). Hence, to use a relative pathname, you would code the following:

```
InputStream is = getClass().getResourceAsStream("resources/text.txt");
```

Relative resource names are a little more flexible than absolute names because they are unaffected by package name changes, provided that you keep the relative locations of the class file and the target file unchanged. Hence, if the MIDlet were moved from the package `ora.ch4` into a different package called `ora.ch8`, the relative resource name would continue to work, provided that the text file is moved to *ora/ch8/resources*. No code changes would need to be made, other than to change the package line at the top of the source file and recompile. If you use absolute resource names, changing the package hierarchy requires that you search for and change all affected instances of **getResourceAsStream()**.

Once you have an **InputStream** for the resource, you can use the usual mechanisms to load its content. Here, we simply wrap the **InputStream** with an **InputStreamReader** to convert the content of the file into Unicode characters and read it into a **StringBuffer** a piece at a time.

The MIDP specification allows you to use **getResourceAsStream()** to access anything in the JAR file apart from the class files. This includes the JAR's manifest file, which can be obtained as follows:

```
InputStream is = getClass().getResourceAsStream("/META-INF/MANIFEST.MF");
```

Commands

The **TextBoxMIDlet** example allows you to view and edit text, but there is no way to tell the MIDlet to save your changes in persistent storage, and it is not possible to terminate the MIDlet in an orderly manner. To provide this functionality, you need to use Commands. Commands are a feature of the **Displayable** class, so you can add them to any user interface, even those created using the low-level API.

Creating Commands

The **Command** class has a single constructor:

```
public Command(String label, int type, int priority);
```

The **label** argument supplies the text that will be used to represent the **Command** in the user interface, and the **type** and **priority** arguments are hints that the MIDP implementation can use when deciding where the **Command** will be placed. The **type** and **priority** arguments are required because of the diversity of the devices on which MIDP is intended to be used. Following construction, you cannot change the **label**, **type** and **priority** attributes of a **Command**.

If you were writing a J2SE application using AWT or Swing, you would add a command action to the user interface by creating a button or a menu item and connecting to it a listener that would perform the action associated with the command upon activation by the user. The limited capabilities of most MIDP devices make it impossible to rely on the general availability of anything that resembles a menu, nor do you have the screen space to display more than a couple of buttons. Cell phones, for example, typically have only two soft keys to which application actions can be assigned. PalmOS applications are more fortunate: they have access to a traditional pull-down menu system and a larger number of buttons that can be drawn on the screen.

Clearly, a portable MIDlet cannot be coded in such a way as to assign command actions explicitly to individual menus or buttons, because these may not be available on any given device. On the other hand, forcing all MIDlets to work to the lowest common denominator (i.e., two soft keys) would be overly restrictive, especially for PDAs. For this reason, the responsibility for mapping Commands to GUI resources rests with the MIDP implementation, which is specific to each platform and, therefore, aware of what is available. MIDlets can use the type and priority constructor arguments to supply hints to the MIDP implementation regarding the semantic meanings of Commands and their relative importance, so that those likely to be most frequently used can be made most easily accessible to the user.

The type argument is used to convey the meaning of a Command in terms of a small set of commonly required application operations. The possible values for this argument and their interpretations are given in Table 4-1.

Table 4-1: The Command type Parameter

type Paramter Value	Meaning
OK	Implies agreement by the user for some operation to be performed. Commands of this type would normally be placed to be easily accessible to the user.
BACK	Replaces the currently displayed screen with the one that preceded it.
CANCEL	Abandons an operation before it has been initiated. This command, along with the OK command, is typically made available while setting up the parameters for the operation. It might also be available on an Alert screen used to explicitly prompt the user for confirmation of an operation that might not easily be reversible.
STOP	Stops an operation that is already in progress.
EXIT	Requests that the MIDlet stop all outstanding operations and terminate in an orderly manner.
HELP	Requests general or context-sensitive help.
SCREEN	Relates to the function of the current screen, but does not fit into one of the specific categories listed previously. Most application-specific actions are of this type.
ITEM	Indicates a command that is associated with a particular user interface component.

Adding Commands to the user interface

Once you have created a Command object, the next step is to arrange for it to appear in the user interface. This is achieved by calling the addCommand() method of Displayable:

```
public void addCommand(Command cmd);
```

MIDP platforms are allowed to follow their own rules when determining how to represent Commands in the user interface. In general, however, the choice is made first based on the Command type and then on the priority, where lower priority values tend to result in a more favorable placement. The order in which Commands are added to a Displayable is not usually of any significance in the determination of placement, and the label text is not used at all, because the semantic meaning of the command is supposed to be conveyed via the type attribute.

On a cell phone, for example, the type might be used to favor well-known operations (such as OK, CANCEL, BACK, etc.) that the user would normally expect to be able to access via a soft key. Where the number of these Commands exceeds the number of soft keys available, the phone might use the priority to determine which Commands should be installed on the soft keys, with lower values increasing the likelihood of assignment to a soft key. The remaining Commands would then be placed on a menu that would itself be accessible via a soft key. When the number of Commands does not exceed the number of soft keys, they can all be allocated a soft key. When a platform has both soft keys and pull-down menus, it may choose to place Commands on menus as well as, or instead of, on soft keys, with the choice again being made usually based on the type and priority attributes.

Some commands, such as EXIT, might need to appear on more than one application screen. When this is the case, it is not necessary to create a dedicated instance for each screen, because a single Command can be added to any number of screens:

```
Command exitCommand = new Command("Exit", Command.EXIT, 0);
form1.addCommand(exitCommand);
form2.addCommand(exitCommand);
```

Responding to user activation of Commands

In order to be notified when the user activates a Command, you have to register a CommandListener with the Displayable to which the Command was added. You do this by invoking its setCommandListener() method:

```
public void setCommandListener(CommandListener l);
```

CommandListener is an interface with a single method:

```
public void commandAction(Command c, Displayable d)
```

The commandAction() method is called when any Command on the Displayable is activated. The first argument is the more useful, because it allows you to determine which operation the user wants to perform. The Displayable argument is useful if you add the same Command to more than one screen, and the resulting action is dependent on the current screen. It can also be useful if the action needs a reference to the screen in order to perform its assigned function.

Note that the setCommandListener() method allows only a single CommandListener to be registered at a time. Calling this method again replaces any existing listener with the new one, and calling it with a null argument removes the previous listener. This is very different from J2SE event handling, which normally allows you to add as many listeners as you like and requires you to register with the component itself rather than an enclosing container. Although it is very flexible, the J2SE model tends to result in the creation of lots of small event handler classes, which is very expensive in terms of memory and class-loading time; it is therefore not suitable for small-memory devices. MIDlets can get away with only one listener per screen and, if the MIDlet itself implements the CommandListener interface, this won't even entail creating a new class. If a MIDlet has several screens, it can choose to create a single listener class for each, or it can save even that overhead by subclassing the screen class to implement CommandListener, as follows:

```
public class MyTextBox extends TextBox implements CommandListener {
    public MyTextBox(String title, String text, int maxSize,
        int constraints) {
        super(title, text, maxSize, constraints);
        setCommandListener(this);
        // Add Commands (not shown)
    }

    // Handle command actions
    public void commandAction(Command c, Displayable d) {
        // Code not shown
    }
}
```

A Command example

We can easily illustrate the use of Commands by extending the TextBoxMIDlet example to include four operations:

- An Exit command that terminates the MIDlet.

- An OK command that prints a message to standard output. (In a real MIDlet, this would obviously do something a little more useful!)

- A Clear command that removes all of the text from the TextBox.

- A Reverse command that reverses the text in the TextBox.

The implementation of this modified example is shown in Example 4-2.

Example 4-2: Adding Commands to the TextBoxMIDlet Example

```
package ora.ch4;

import javax.microedition.lcdui.Command;
import javax.microedition.lcdui.CommandListener;
import javax.microedition.lcdui.Displayable;

import javax.microedition.lcdui.*;

public class TextBox2MIDlet extends TextBoxMIDlet implements CommandListener
{

    // Exit command
    private static final Command EXIT_COMMAND =
                    new Command("Exit", Command.EXIT, 0);

    // OK command
    private static final Command OK_COMMAND =
                    new Command("OK", Command.OK, 0);
```

Example 4-2: Adding Commands to the TextBoxMIDlet Example (continued)

```
// Clear text box content
private static final Command CLEAR_COMMAND =
                    new Command("Clear", Command.SCREEN, 1);

// Reverse the content of the text box
private static final Command REVERSE_COMMAND =
                    new Command("Reverse", Command.SCREEN, 1);

protected void startApp() {
    boolean firstTime = !started;
    super.startApp();

    // If this is the first execution of startApp, install commands
    if (firstTime) {
        textBox.addCommand(OK_COMMAND);
        textBox.addCommand(EXIT_COMMAND);
        textBox.addCommand(CLEAR_COMMAND);
        textBox.addCommand(REVERSE_COMMAND);
        textBox.setCommandListener(this);
    }
}

// Command implementations.
public void commandAction(Command c, Displayable d) {
    if (c == EXIT_COMMAND) {
        destroyApp(true);
        notifyDestroyed();
    } else if (c == OK_COMMAND) {
        System.out.println("OK pressed");
    } else if (c == CLEAR_COMMAND) {
        textBox.setString(null);
    } else if (c == REVERSE_COMMAND) {
        String str = textBox.getString();
        if (str != null) {
            StringBuffer sb = new StringBuffer(str);
            textBox.setString(sb.reverse().toString());
        }
    }
}
}
```

Notice that this example is implemented by deriving it directly from the
TextBoxMIDlet class from the previous example. Of course, you wouldn't
normally have to do this in the real world, but here it serves to show how easy it
is to add command handling to an existing class, and you don't need to replicate
code that you saw earlier!

The four Commands are defined as static class members, for example:

```
private static final Command EXIT_COMMAND = new Command("Exit",
    Command.EXIT, 0);
```

Since Commands are simply constant-valued objects, you can usually define them
in this way and then reuse them wherever you need to, which would include

adding the same instance to more than one screen, if necessary. You can see from Example 4-2 that the EXIT and OK commands use the standard types `Command.EXIT` and `Command.OK`, respectively, which allows the device on which the MIDlet will be run to represent them in whatever way it would normally present EXIT and OK actions. By contrast, the other two commands are of type `Command.SCREEN`, because they are application-defined actions that have no generic meaning. Notice that the OK and EXIT actions have priority 0, whereas the other two have priority 1. This hints to the device that if it has no built-in preferences, we would rather have the OK and EXIT actions more quickly accessible to the user than Clear and Reverse. However, there is no guarantee that the device will take this hint.

Making these operations available from the user interface is a simple matter of adding the `Command` instances to the `TextBox` and registering the MIDlet class itself as the `CommandListener`:

```
textBox.addCommand(OK_COMMAND);
textBox.addCommand(EXIT_COMMAND);
textBox.addCommand(CLEAR_COMMAND);
textBox.addCommand(REVERSE_COMMAND);
textBox.setCommandListener(this);
```

The last step is to implement the `CommandListener` interface by providing a `commandAction` method, which is responsible for carrying out the operations associated with the `Commands`. The `commandAction` method shown in Example 4-2 is typical of most event handling in MIDlets. Because there is only a single command handler for each screen, its first task is to determine which operation the user wants to perform. To do this, it examines the first method argument to see which Command has been activated. The neatest way to do this is with a `switch` statement, but this is not possible because `Command` is not an integral value. Instead, MIDlet event handlers tend to consist of `if` statements that compare the first method argument with each of the possible `Commands`. Once the correct operation is found, the code that performs the required function is trivial.

You can try this example by selecting `TextBox2MIDlet` from the MIDlet suite for this chapter. On the default color phone, the result is shown in Figure 4-6.

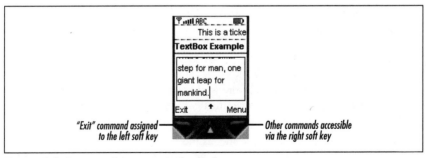

Figure 4-6: Commands on a typical cell phone

Command placement

The default color phone, like most cell phones, has two soft keys to which `Commands` can be assigned, but the `TextBox` used in this example has four

---

Commands. As a result, the Exit command has been mapped to the left soft key, and the right key provides access to a menu of the remaining three Commands, as shown in Figure 4-7. The fact that the Exit command has been given its own key in preference to the OK command is a feature of this particular MIDP implementation. The result might not be the same on other devices, and the menu might also not look the same as it does in Figure 4-7. The MIDlet developer, of course, has no real control over these decisions and can only provide hints in the form of the type and priority arguments to the Command constructor.

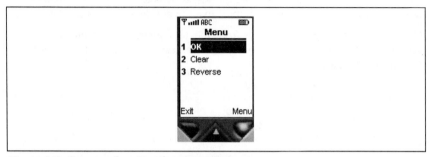

Figure 4-7: Command assigned to a separate menu

Command placement on a PalmOS device

The same MIDlet looks slightly different when run on a PalmOS platform, where the larger screen space means that more Commands can be assigned to buttons that are always visible to the user. Figure 4-8 shows two views of this MIDlet running on a PalmOS-based handheld. In this case, three of the four Commands have been assigned to buttons below the TextBox. Commands are assigned to buttons based on their types, as listed here in descending order of preference:

- Command.BACK
- Command.OK
- Command.CANCEL
- Command.STOP
- Command.SCREEN
- Command.CANCEL

If the number of commands exceeds the number of buttons that can be created in the button area, the command priority is also taken into account when assigning commands to buttons. Note, however, that commands of type Command.EXIT and Command.HELP are never mapped to buttons.

PalmOS also has pull-down menus, and, as these two views show, the application-specific Commands have been assigned to the Actions menu, while the OK and Exit commands appear on a menu labeled Go. In this implementation, the Actions menu is used to hold application-specific commands of type Command.SCREEN or Command.ITEM. If both types of Command are installed in the same screen, they all appear on the same menu, with Commands of the same type grouped together, and the two groups separated by a horizontal line, as shown in Figure 4-9. Commands

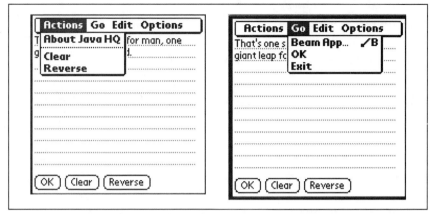

Figure 4-8: Commands on a PalmOS device

of type `Command.BACK`, `Command.OK`, `Command.CANCEL`, `Command.STOP`, and `Command.EXIT` are placed on the Go menu, and `Command.HELP` appears in the Option menu.

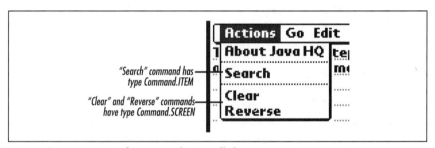

Figure 4-9: Grouping of commands on pull-down menus

Forms and Items

`Form` is a subclass of `Screen` that can be used to construct a user interface from simpler elements such as text fields, strings, and labels. Like `TextBox`, `Form` covers the entire screen and inherits from its superclasses the ability to have a title, display a `Ticker`, and be associated with `Commands`. The elements that you can add to a `Form` are all derived from the abstract class `Item`:

```
public abstract class Item {
    public String getLabel();
    public void setLabel(String label);
}
```

On its own, `Item` provides only the ability to store and retrieve a text label, but because each component that can be added to a `Form` is derived from `Item`, it follows that all of them can have an associated label. The implementation displays this somewhere near the component in such a way as to make the association between the label and the component clear. The components that MIDP provides are described briefly in Table 4-2; each of them will be discussed in greater detail in later sections of this chapter.

Table 4-2: Items That Can Be Added to a Form

Item	Description
StringItem	An item that allows a text string to be placed in the user interface
TextField	A single-line input field much like the full-screen TextBox
DateField	A version of TextField that is specialized for the input of dates; it includes a visual helper that simplifies the process of choosing a date
Gauge	A component that can be used to show the progress of an ongoing operation or allow selection of a value from a contiguous range of values
ChoiceGroup	A component that provides a set of choices that may or may not be mutually exclusive and therefore may operate either as a collection of checkboxes or radio buttons
ImageItem	A holder that allows graphic images to be placed in the user interface

The Form class has two constructors:

```
public Form(String title);
public Form(String title, Item[] items);
```

The first constructor creates an empty Form with a given title, which may be null in the unlikely event that no title is required; the second constructor can be used to install an initial set of Items on the Form. The Items that are associated with the Form are held in an internal list, the order of which determines how they are placed on the form. Form has three methods that allow items to be added to the end of this internal list, which causes them to appear on the Form itself:

```
public void append(Item item);
public void append(Image image);
public void append(String string);
```

The second and third methods provide a quick and convenient way to include an image or string on the Form: just create and append an ImageItem containing a supplied Image or a StringItem containing the given string.

Unlike an AWT container, Form does not have the concept of a separate layout manager that you can select to control how items are arranged on the screen. Instead, Form has a few simple rules that determine how items are arranged:

- Items that involve user input (that is, TextField, DateField, Gauge, and ChoiceGroup) are laid out vertically, with the first item in the Form's internal list at the top of the screen, the second one directly below it, and so on.

- Adjacent StringItems and ImageItems that have a null or empty label are laid out horizontally. If there is insufficient space to fit a complete StringItem in the horizontal space remaining in a row, the text is wrapped to the next line, and the implementation breaks at whitespace where possible. If there is insufficient space to fit an entire ImageItem, the image is simply clipped.

- StringItems and ImageItems with a nonempty label cause a line break before the label is rendered.

- Newlines in StringItems cause a line break. A similar effect can be obtained using layout directives of the ImageItem class, as described in the section "ImageItems," later in this chapter.

- The width of the Form is always the same as that of the screen. The Form may, however, be taller than the screen. If so, the implementation provides a means for the user to scroll the Form vertically. Horizontal scrolling is not provided.

- Where it is necessary to scroll vertically, the implementation attempts to ensure that scrolling never obscures the label associated with a visible item, if the item has one.

To clarify how these rules work in practice, let's look at a simple example that places strings and TextFields on a Form. The code that builds the Form is shown in Example 4-3. You can run it by selecting FormExampleMIDlet from the MIDlet suite in *Chapter4.jad*.

Example 4-3: A Demonstration of Form Layout Rules

```
Form form = new Form("Item Layout");

form.append("Hello");
form.append("World");

form.append("\nLet's start\na new line\n");
form.append("This is quite a long string that may not fit on one line");

form.append(new TextField("Name", "J. Doe", 32, TextField.ANY));
form.append("Address");
form.append(new TextField(null, null, 32, TextField.ANY));
```

The first four append() calls add text strings to the Form, the results of which can be seen in the leftmost two screenshots in Figure 4-10. These screenshots show the MIDlet running on the relatively small screen of the default color phone emulator from the Wireless Toolkit. The top line of the screen holds the two separate items "Hello" and "World", which have been laid out horizontally because they are string items. Note that, even though they were added separately, no space has been left between them.

The next item to be added begins and ends with newline characters; you can see that it is placed vertically below the first two items because of the leading newline, and the trailing newline also causes a line break. Notice that in this string, and in the next, rather longer, one, the text is automatically wrapped, and line breaks are placed between words.

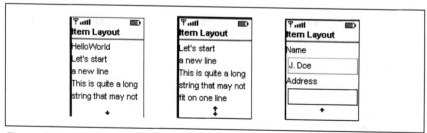

Figure 4-10: Form layout on a cell phone

Since the `Form` is too large to fit on the screen, the implementation draws an arrow at the bottom to indicate that the screen can be scrolled vertically, as has been done in the middle and right views.

Following the text strings, a `TextField` is added:

```
form.append(new TextField("Name", "J. Doe", 32, TextField.ANY))
```

The constructor supplies both the `Item` label ("Name") and the initial content of the field itself ("J. Doe"). As you can see, the label has been placed below the previous text string, even though the string did not end with a newline, but above the input field itself. If you scroll the screen up and down, you'll find that it is impossible to arrange for the label to be visible without the text field, and vice versa.

The last two items are the text string "Address" and another `TextField`. Because this device's screen is so narrow, it would be difficult to see the difference between the effect of the code used here:

```
form.append("Address");
form.append(new TextField(null, null, 32, TextField.ANY));
```

and the apparently similar:

```
form.append(new TextField("Address", null, 32, TextField.ANY));
```

which includes the string "Address" as the item's label. To see the difference, you need to run this example using the PalmOS emulator. Because this emulator has a much larger screen, it can lay out the items differently, as shown in Figure 4-11.

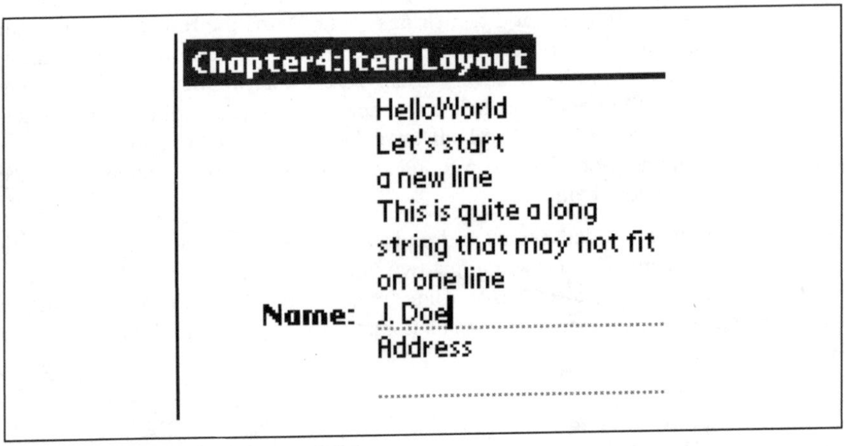

Figure 4-11: Form layout on a PDA

Most of the items are shifted over to the right side of the screen, leaving mostly blank space to the left. This is because the MIDP for PalmOS implementation allocates the left side of the screen to the label part of each `Item` and places the active part of the `Item` to the right. Hence, all the strings (which are actually `StringItems` with no label) appear on the right side of the screen. The only `Item` with a real label is the first `TextField`, and its label has been placed on the left of the input field itself, rendered in a bold font, and been appended with a colon.

Compare this to the next `TextField`: the "Address" string was added as a separate string and not installed as the `Item` label, and it therefore appears above the input field itself. Although the difference between using a label and using a separate text string was hard to detect with the cell phone emulator, here it becomes very obvious and underlines the fact that the `Item` label should be used instead of installing a separate a text string to describe the following input field. Another important reason to take advantage of the `Item` label is the automatic font highlighting provided for the label. You cannot achieve this in any other way, because the high-level API does not allow you to select fonts or colors.

`Form` has a small number of other methods, in addition to the three variants of `append()`, that allow the list of `Item`s it contains to be manipulated:

```
public void delete(int index);
public Item get(int index);
public void insert(int index, Item item);
public void set(int index, Item item);
public int size();
```

Most of these methods use an index argument to specify the list position to be operated on, where the first item has index 0. The `delete()` method removes the `Item` at the given index; like all the other methods that change the `Item` list, it causes the screen layout to be updated immediately to reflect the change. The `get()` method returns the `Item` at the given index without modifying the list at all. The `insert()` method places a new `Item` at the given index within the list, moving the `Item` at that index and greater indices down by one position. The `set()` method, by contrast, replaces the `Item` at the index supplied as its first argument and does not affect any other `Item` in the `Form`. Finally, the `size()` method returns the number of `Item`s on the `Form`.

A single `Command` or `Ticker` instance can be shared between multiple screens simply by adding it to each screen in turn. However, an `Item` is allowed to be on only one `Form` at any given time. If you try to add the same `Item` to another `Form` without first removing it from the original, an `IllegalStateException` is thrown.

Item State Changes

Since `Form` is subclassed indirectly from `Displayable`, it is possible to add a `Command` to a `Form` to allow the user to request that values entered into it be processed. The logic for this processing is implemented in the `commandAction` method of a `CommandListener` attached to the `Form`, as illustrated in Example 4-2. Sometimes, however, it is necessary to take action as soon as the value in an input field is changed. Changes in the state of `Item`s that accept user input are notified to an `ItemStateListener` registered with the `Form`. `ItemStateListener` is an interface with a single method, which is called when any `Item` on the `Form` has a state change to report:

```
public void itemStateChanged(Item item);
```

An `ItemStateListener` is registered using the following `Form` method:

```
public void setItemStateListener(ItemStateListener l);
```

As was the case with `CommandListeners`, only one `ItemStateListener` can be associated with a `Form` at any time and calling `setItemStateListener()` removes any listener that was previously installed. Calling this method with the argument `null` removes any existing listener.

The conditions under which the `ItemStateListener` is notified of a state change are specific to each individual type of `Item`; these conditions are described in the sections that follow. It is important to note, however, that only user actions result in the listener's `itemStateChanged` method being called. Changing the state of an `Item` programmatically does *not* cause notification to the listener.

High-Level API User Interface Components

In the rest of this section, we take a closer look at each of the `Items` you can use with the `Form` class, together with the `TextBox` and `List` components. `TextBox` and `List` are derived from `Screen`, so they are not suitable for use with `Forms`, but they have `Form`-based counterparts that are sufficiently similar that they are best described together.

The examples used in this section are all part of a single MIDlet called `ItemMIDlet`. You can run it with the Wireless Toolkit by opening the project called `Chapter4` and pressing the Run button, then selecting `ItemMIDlet`. This displays a screen (actually a `List`) that has an entry that runs the example for each of the following sections. To run the example code for these sections, simply highlight the appropriate entry in the list and press the SELECT button on the emulated phone's keypad, as shown in Figure 4-5.*

StringItems

`StringItem`, the simplest of the MIDP user interface components, provides the ability to place a string or pair of strings on a `Form`. Initial values for both strings may be supplied to the constructor:

```
public StringItem(String label, String text)
```

The label part is the label that is inherited by all `Items` from their base class; its value can be retrieved or changed using the `Item getLabel()` and `setLabel()` methods. `StringItem` provides similar methods for its own text attribute:

```
public String getText()
public void setText(String text)
```

Either or both of the label and text string may be `null`.

---

* A small number of examples in this section produce output on the MIDlet's standard output stream. When using the Wireless Toolkit, this stream usually directs its output to the Wireless Toolkit console. However, if you use the PalmOS device emulator, this information is written to a separate file instead. To examine the file content, you must stop the emulator. For further details, see Chapter 9.

A technique often used when adding text to a `Form` is simply to use the variant of the `append` method that accepts a `String` argument:

```
form.append("Name");
```

This code, in fact, amounts to the use of a `StringItem` with a `null` label and so could also be written like this:

```
form.append(new StringItem(null, "Name"));
```

It might seem strange to provide a component that displays two text strings, when the same effect could apparently be achieved by creating a component that supports only one string and the ability to place two of them next to each other. In fact, this would not lead to the same result, because the label and text string parts of a `StringItem` are not equivalent. The difference between the label and the text is the same for `StringItem` as it is for the label and content of any `Item`, namely:

- The layout management code of the MIDP platform should attempt to display the label close to the text and ensure that they are either both visible or both not visible when scrolling takes place.*

- The platform may choose to render the label differently from the content to make clear the distinction between them.

As described in the earlier section "Forms and Items," the layout policy for `StringItems` required by the MIDP specification results in a horizontal arrangement, unless a line break is forced by the use of newline characters within the label or text, or if there is insufficient space to fit the entire `StringItem` in the current line. Additionally, the Sun reference implementations force a line break before a `StringItem` that has a non-`null` label.

A typical example in which it would be advantageous to use both the label and text attributes of a `StringItem` is a labeled item in which the content can be updated by the MIDlet but must not by the user. Such a `StringItem` might be used to show the state of a connection to a web server:

```
StringItem status = new StringItem("Status ", "Not connected");
status.setText("Connecting");  // Change the state
```

In Example 4-3, you've already seen several examples of the use of `StringItem` created indirectly by appending a `String` to a `Form`. `ItemMIDlet` includes a screen that has a few more `StringItem` examples. The code that creates this `Form` is shown in Example 4-4.

Example 4-4: Using StringItem

```
Form form = new Form("StringItem");
form.append(new StringItem("State ", "OK"));
form.append(new StringItem(null, "No label\n"));
form.append(new StringItem(null, "Line\nbreak"));
form.append(new StringItem("Label", "Text."));
form.append(new StringItem("Label2 ", "Text2."));
```

---

* Unfortunately, at the time of writing, the MIDP implementation used in the Wireless Toolkit does not do this.

The results of running this example on both the default color phone and on the PalmOS device are shown in Figure 4-12. The first `StringItem` uses both the label and text attributes. Notice that the color phone doesn't distinguish between the label and the text in any way, whereas the PalmOS MIDP implementation uses a bold font to represent the label, adds a colon, and places all the labels in a dedicated area on the left side of the screen. The second `StringItem` contains only the text and is placed immediately after the text of the first `StringItem`, with no line break. Because the text ends with a newline character, however, it is followed by a line break.

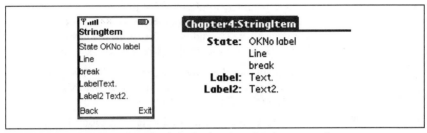

Figure 4-12: StringItems on the default phone and PalmOS emulators

The third example shows the effect of embedding a newline in the text, which results in a line break on the screen. Although it isn't illustrated here, you can also include a newline in the label part, and the effect is the same. The final two examples illustrate an important difference in the handling of labels between the PalmOS platform and the cell phone version. In the first case, the label and text are set up as follows:

```
form.append(new StringItem("Label", "Text."));
```

As you can see, the color phone does not interpose any whitespace between the label and text, whereas the PalmOS version displays them with a clear gap, owing to its special handling for labels. In most cases, you want to clearly separate the label from the text; you can do this by adding a space at the end of the label:

```
form.append(new StringItem("Label2 ", "Text2."));
```

This produces the desired effect on the color phone and also works on the PalmOS platform, which strips out trailing whitespace before appending the colon that marks the end of the label, as you can see on the right side of Figure 4-12.

TextFields and TextBoxes

`TextField` and `TextBox` are two very similar components that have almost the same programming interface. The differences between them are as follows:

- `TextBox` is derived from `Screen` and therefore occupies the entire display. `TextField` is an `Item` that occupies space on a `Form`. Usually, a `TextField` appears as a single-line input field, but some implementations spread its content over extra lines if a single line is not sufficient.

- `TextBox` does not have a way to report changes in its content to a listener, but modifications to a `TextField` are reported to the `ItemStateListener` associated with the `Form` on which the `TextField` is displayed.

Since the specifics of TextBox have already been covered, the rest of this section focuses on the common features of these two components and illustrates them with TextFields.

Construction

TextField has only one constructor:

```
public TextField(String label, String text, int maxSize,
    int constraints);
```

The label and text arguments specify, respectively, the Item label to be placed near the component and the string to be placed initially in the TextField; either or both of these arguments may be null. The constraints argument can be used to limit the type of data that can be entered into the TextField. See "Constraints," later in this chapter, for details.

The maxSize argument determines the maximum number of characters that the TextField can hold. The MIDP implementation is allowed to place an upper limit on the allowed values of maxSize and may therefore impose a lower limit than the one specified in the constructor. The actual limit applied to a particular TextField can be obtained by calling the getMaxSize() method. The maximum size is applied whenever the field content is changed, that is:

- When the initial value is set at construction time

- When a new value is supplied by calling the setString() method

- When some or all of the field content is modified using the insert or setChars methods

- As the user amends the content of the TextField by adding characters anywhere in the string

In the first three cases, the result of attempting to install a value whose length exceeds the capacity of the TextField is an IllegalArgumentException. If the user tries to type more characters than the field can hold, the extra characters are ignored, and the device may supply audible feedback.

The capacity of the TextField can be changed by calling the setMaxSize() method. If the number of characters in the TextField exceeds the new capacity, it is truncated to the maximum size.

Field content changes and listener notification

If the Form that contains the TextField has an ItemStateListener installed, it will be notified of changes made by the user to its content. You can get the value held in the TextField by calling its getString() or getChars() methods, which return a String or an array of characters, respectively:

```
public String getString()
public int getChars(char[] chars)
```

To use the getChars() method, you have to allocate the character array to be filled. The return value of this method is the number of characters of the array that were used. If the array is too short to hold the content of the TextField, an ArrayIndexOutOfBoundsException is thrown. You can avoid this by using the size() method to get the number of characters that are currently in the TextField:

```
char[] chars = new char[textField.size()];
int copied = textField.getChars(chars);
```

The following code extract shows how a listener might use getString() to retrieve the last value that the user entered as a String:

```
public void itemStateChanged(Item item) {
    if (item instanceof TextField) {
        System.out.println("Text field content: <" +
                        ((TextField)item).getString() + ">");
    }
}
```

The point at which the ItemStateListener is called following a change in the content of the TextField is implementation-dependent. The MIDP specification requires only that this should happen no later than when the user moves the input focus away from the TextField or activates a command on the Form. The reference implementation provides notification when the user completes an editing operation in the TextField; the MIDP for PalmOS version does it after any character has been inserted or deleted.

The TextField (and TextBox) API contains several methods that allow programmatic changes to its content.* All of these methods throw an IllegalArgumentException and leave the TextField content unchanged if the result of performing the requested operation would make the content inconsistent with the constraint, if any, applied to the TextField. This means, for example, that an exception would be thrown if an attempt were made to insert non-numeric characters into a TextField to which the TextField.NUMERIC constraint has been applied. Constraints are described in the later section "Constraints."

The following are the methods that enable programmatic changes to TextField and TextBoxes:

public void delete(int offset, int length)
> Removes length characters from the TextField, starting with the character at position offset.

public void insert(char[] chars, int offset, int length, int position)
> Inserts the characters from chars[offset] through chars[offset + length - 1] into the TextField, starting at the given position. The characters that originally occupied offsets position and higher are moved to the right to make room for the new characters. An IllegalArgumentException is thrown if this operation would make the content of the TextField exceed its maximum size.

---

* As noted earlier, TextBox does not have any way of notifying application code that its content has changed because it is not an Item and therefore cannot be associated with an ItemStateListener. Application code normally retrieves the content of a TextBox (using getString() or getChars()) only when prompted to do so by the activation of a Command attached to the TextBox.

```
public void insert(String src, int position)
```
Inserts the characters that make up the given String into the TextField, starting at the given position. The characters that originally occupied offsets position and higher are moved to the right to make room for the new characters. An IllegalArgumentException is thrown if this operation would make the content of the TextField exceed its maximum size.

```
public void setChars(char[] chars, int offset, int length)
```
Replaces the content of the TextField with chars[offset] through chars[offset + length - 1] of the given character array. An IllegalArgumentException is thrown if this operation would make the content of the TextField exceed its maximum size.

```
public void setString(String src)
```
Replaces the content of the TextField with the characters from the given String. An IllegalArgumentException is thrown if this operation would make the content of the TextField exceed its maximum size.

Note that programmatic changes are *not* notified to ItemStateListeners.

In general, application code that modifies the content of a TextField uses either the setString() or setChars() methods to replace its entire content. Less frequently, it is necessary to insert content starting at the location of the TextField's insertion point, which is indicated on the screen by a cursor, otherwise known as a *caret*. You can get the offset of the cursor within the TextField using the following method:

```
public int getCaretPosition();
```

The following code could be used to insert three characters starting at the cursor position:

```
textField.insert("ABC", textField.getCaretPosition());
```

Constraints

The constraints argument of the constructor or the setConstraints method can be used to limit the characters that the user can type into a TextField. The effect of each constraint may be device-dependent. Table 4-3 describes what these constraints do in the MIDP reference implementation.

Table 4-3: TextField Input Constraints

Constraint Value	Effect
TextField.ANY	Allows any characters to be typed into the input field.
TextField.EMAILADDR	Limits the user's input to a legal email address. The format of a valid email address may vary from device to device, so vendors are expected to implement this in a manner appropriate to the network to which their device will be connected. In the reference implementation, the constraint has no effect.
TextField.NUMERIC	Limits input to integer values. The first character may be a minus sign, and the other characters must be digits 0 through 9. On a cell phone, the implementation typically forces the keypad into a mode where it assumes that each key press represents the number on the face of the key when this constraint is applied.

Table 4-3: TextField Input Constraints (continued)

Constraint Value	Effect
TextField.PHONENUMBER	Specifies that the field should contain a phone number. The format of a valid phone number may vary from device to device and network to network. The reference implementation provides a default implementation of this constraint that is described later in this section.
TextField.URL	Although this constraint signifies that the input field should only be allowed to hold a valid URL, it has no effect in the reference implementation.
TextField.PASSWORD	This constraint may be specified in conjunction with `TextField.ANY` or `TextField.NUMERIC` to convert the `TextField` into a field intended to hold a password, for example:
	`TextField.PASSWORD` | `TextField.ANY`
	The implementation usually displays the content of a password field differently from that of a plain `TextField`. Typically, the characters are displayed as asterisks for security reasons.

When input is constrained, the user cannot type any characters that would result in the field content becoming inconsistent with the constraint. Calling a method to change the field content results in an `IllegalArgumentException` if the result would not match the constraint.

You can change the constraint associated with a `TextField` or `TextBox` at any time by calling the `setConstraints()` method:

```
public void setConstraints(int constraints);
```

When this method is called, the current content of the control is checked to ensure that it is consistent with the new constraints; if not, the field is cleared.

The effect of some of the constraint values can be seen by launching the `ItemMIDlet` and selecting the `TextField` example. This example contains four `TextFields` with different constraints, as shown in Figure 4-13.

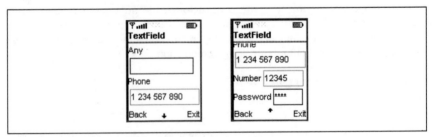

Figure 4-13: TextFields with various input constraints

The first field, shown at the top on the left side of Figure 4-13, has constraint `TextField.ANY`, which permits any characters to be entered. If you start typing into this field, either by clicking with the mouse on the emulator's onscreen keypad or using your PC keyboard, the display switches to a full-screen `TextBox` that you can use to type and edit the value that you want, as shown in Figure 4-14. To enter the displayed value into the `TextField`, press the Save soft key, or press Back to abandon editing and leave the field content unchanged.

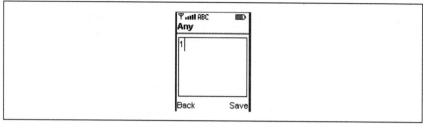

Figure 4-14: Full-screen TextBox for entering or editing a value

The second `TextField` has the `TextField.PHONENUMBER` constraint. In the reference implementation, this constraint limits the characters that can be typed to the digits 0 through 9 and the characters +, *, and #. This constraint also causes the content of the `TextField` to be displayed so that it looks like a telephone number by separating the digits into groups separated by space characters. The appropriate grouping depends entirely on the part of the world in which the cell phone or PDA is being used, since different conventions apply in different countries. The reference implementation uses the following rules:

- If the first digit is zero, the number is assumed to be for international dialing and is represented in the form "0xx xxx xxxx . . . ".
- If the first digit is 1, the number is formatted as "1 xxx xxx xxxx . . . ".
- In all other cases, the number is displayed as "xxx xxx xxx . . . ".

Note that the spaces used to separate the number groups are purely visual and do not appear in the `TextField` content. For example, if the `TextField` displayed "044 171 1234567", the result of calling the `getString()` method would be "0441711234567". Similarly, an attempt to store a value containing spaces would result in an `IllegalArgumentException`. If you run this example using the Wireless Toolkit, you can observe the results of typing different values into this field or any of the other fields by looking at the Wireless Toolkit console, to which a message is written whenever any of the fields calls the `ItemStateListener` registered with this screen.

The third field has the constraint `TextField.NUMERIC` applied to it. As you can verify for yourself, this field will allow you to type only positive and negative integer values and zero.

The final field is set up with the constraint `TextField.PASSWORD|TextField.NUMERIC`, which limits the user to numeric values but also displays each character that is typed as an asterisk, as shown on the right side of Figure 4-13. On PalmOS, a field that includes the constraint `TextField.PASSWORD` is handled slightly differently. When the field is empty, its content is shown as "-Prompt-", as shown on the left side of Figure 4-15. When an attempt is made to enter a value, a separate window opens up to allow you to type the required password. As you can see from the screen shot in Figure 4-15, this window displays the actual password value instead of disguising it. Once a password has been entered, the `TextField` displays "-Assigned-", as shown at the right side of the figure.

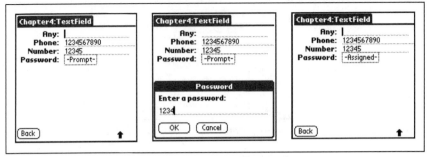

Figure 4-15: Password fields on the PalmOS platform

DateFields

DateField is a component that allows you to display and edit the value of an object of type Date. The DateField class has two constructors:

```
public DateField(String label, int mode)
public DateField(String label, int mode, TimeZone timeZone)
```

The date and time value held in a Date object is always relative to midnight UTC on January 1, 1970. When displaying the time, a correction needs to be made for the time zone in which the user is working. On the east coast of the United States, for example, a Date value that corresponds to 9:00 P.M. on January 31, 2002 (UTC), would need to be displayed as 4:00 P.M., January 31, 2002, and in Tokyo, it would need to be shown as 6:00 A.M., February 1, 2002. You can use the timeZone argument to supply a TimeZone object that can be used to determine how to display the date and time for a specific location in the world. If this argument is not supplied (or is null), the device's default TimeZone is used, which should properly display local time. Therefore, it should be necessary to supply a TimeZone value only when the date and time for a different time zone are to be displayed.

 The DateField component works with any valid TimeZone object and therefore should be able to properly display the date and time anywhere in the world. However, the CLDC specification requires only that the time zone for GMT be supported. Practical considerations dictate that a device also support the time zone in which it normally operates, but there is no guarantee that other time zones will be available.

The mode argument determines what the DateField will display and takes one of the following values:

DateField.TIME
> The DateField should display only the time.

DateField.DATE
> The DateField should display only the date.

DateField.DATE_TIME
> The DateField should display both the date and time.

An example of a DateField in each of these three modes can be seen by running the ItemMIDlet and selecting the DateField screen. The result is shown in Figure 4-16. The left side of this figure shows DateFields configured with mode DateField.TIME at the top and DateField.DATE at the bottom, while the bottom DateField on the right side has mode DateField.DATE_TIME.

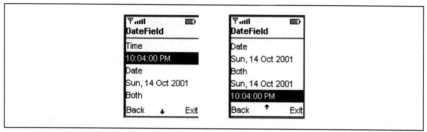

Figure 4-16: DateFields on the default color phone

DateField allows the user to edit the date and/or time that it displays. In the reference implementation, if you start pressing keys or press the SELECT button on the emulator keypad while a DateField has the input focus, a full-screen editor appears. There are separate editors for dates and times, as shown in Figure 4-17.

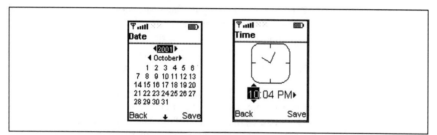

Figure 4-17: DateField date and time editing helper components on the default color phone emulator

Note that DateField is derived from Item and not from TextField, so it is not possible to gain access to the characters displayed on the screen as would be the case with TextField.

Like all Items, when the user changes the date and/or time displayed by a DateField, the change is reported to the ItemStateListener, if any, registered with the Form that the DateField is displayed on. The value of the Date object associated with the DateField can be obtained or changed using the following methods:

```
public void setDate(Date date);
public Date getDate();
```

When the setDate method is called, the DateField does not store a reference to the Date that is passed to it. Instead, it copies the value so that changes made within the DateField component are not reflected in the Date object supplied. Similarly, the value returned by getDate() is a newly created object that reflects the date and/or time in the DateField at the time of the method call.

The setDate method may be called with argument null. In this case, the DateField is considered to be in an uninitialized state and does not display a valid value. The DateField is also in this state following construction and until setDate() is called with a valid Date. The getDate method returns null when the DateField is in this state, and, in the reference implementation, the time part displays the string <time> while the date part displays <date>.

DateField has a very simple programming interface, but there are some traps waiting for the unwary. The nature of these traps depends on the mode in which the DateField is operating.

DateField in DATE_TIME mode

This is the simplest case to handle. The only possible problem here arises from the fact that the DateField does not preserve the seconds and milliseconds value of the Date object that is passed to it. As a consequence of this, for example, if the setDate() method is called with a Date object for 10:04:03 P.M. on January 31, 2002, and no changes are made by the user, the value returned by the getDate() method corresponds to 10:04 P.M. on the same date.

DateField in DATE mode

In this mode, the DateField works only with the year, month, and date parts of the time and does not preserve the time elements. Therefore, the value returned by getDate() in this mode reports zero values for the time.

DateField in TIME mode

TIME mode causes the greatest inconvenience. According to the specification, in this mode, the Date passed to the setDate() method *must* have the date parts initialized to the "epoch" date, January 1, 1970, and the Date returned by getDate() contains this same date. The problem with this is that code like the following does not necessarily work as you might want it to:

```
Date now = new Date();    // Current date and time
dateField.setDate(now);   // We want to display only the time
```

Ideally, the setDate method would ignore the date and display only the time. Unfortunately, the specification excludes this possibility. For predictable results, you have to pass in a Date value with the date parts set to those for the epoch. In the reference inplementation, if you fail to do this, the DateField considers its content to be invalid and puts itself into the uninitialized state, as if setDate(null) had been called. The following code extract can be used to create a Date object that contains the current time and the year, month, and day values for the epoch, without assuming what the epoch date is:

```
// Get Calendar for the epoch date and time
Calendar baseCal = Calendar.getInstance();
Date baseDate = new Date(0);
baseCal.setTime(baseDate);

// Get Calendar for now and use the epoch
// values to reset the date to the epoch.
```

```
Calendar cal = Calendar.getInstance();
Date now = new Date();
cal.setTime(now);

// Set the year, month and day in month from the epoch
cal.set(Calendar.YEAR, baseCal.get(Calendar.YEAR));
cal.set(Calendar.MONTH, baseCal.get(Calendar.MONTH));
cal.set(Calendar.DATE, baseCal.get(Calendar.DATE));
```

Changing the DateField mode

Under most circumstances, the `DateField` mode would not be changed following construction. If required, however, the mode can be changed using the `setInputMode()` method:

```
public void setInputMode(int mode);
```

where the mode argument is `DateField.DATE`, `DateField.TIME`, or `DateField.DATE_TIME`. Changing the mode affects the visual appearance of the component and may also affect the `Date` value that it contains, as follows:

Changing to DateField.DATE mode
The time part is reset to 00:00 A.M. on the date contained in the `DateField`.

Changing to DateField.TIME mode
The date part is reset to the epoch date, January 1, 1970.

ImageItems

`ImageItem` lets you place an image on a `Form` with some limited control over how it is placed relative to other Items. The `ImageItem` class has a single constructor:

```
public ImageItem(String label, Image image, int layout, String altText)
```

Adding an `ImageItem` to a `Form` causes the optional label and the image to be placed subject to the constraints specified by the `layout` argument. The device is free to ignore the `layout` argument and apply its own layout rules. It may also use the text supplied by the `altText` argument in place of the image when, in the words of the MIDP specification, "the image exceeds the capability of the device to display it."

The image is supplied in the form of an `Image` object, which will be described in detail when we discuss the low-level API in Chapter 5. There are several ways to create an `Image`, including loading data over a network connection, using graphics primitives to compose the `Image` from lines, points, curves and solid shapes, and loading encoded data from a file. For the purposes of illustration, we will use the last of these methods in this chapter because it is easy to demonstrate and creates an immutable image, which is a requirement for `ImageItem`.*

---

* An immutable image is one that cannot be changed in situ. Some methods of building an `Image` produce an immutable `Image`, while others result in one that is mutable. As you'll see in Chapter 5, an immutable `Image` can always be obtained from a mutable one, so any `Image` you create can be used in conjunction with an `ImageItem`, either directly or after being made immutable.

To load an image from a file, use the following static method of the `Image` class:

```
public static Image createImage(String name) throws IOException
```

`name` is a resource name that corresponds to the location of the file in the MIDlet suite's JAR file. The `name` parameter is used as the argument to the `getResourceAsStream()` method that was described in "Accessing Resources in the MIDlet JAR File," earlier in this chapter. Although `getResourceAsStream()` can be given either an absolute or relative resource name, the `name` parameter should always be absolute in this case, because a relative name would not be interpreted as being relative to your MIDlet's class (and, in fact, the class relative to which a relative resource name would be interpreted is implementation-dependent). The indicated file must contain an image encoded in Portable Network Graphics (PNG) format, since this is the only graphics file format that MIDP devices are required to support. Most of the commonly used utilities that allow you to design graphics or manipulate images provide the option to save in PNG format.

The `layout` parameter is a bitmask made up from legal combinations of the following values:

ImageItem.LAYOUT_DEFAULT
> The image should be placed according to the platform's default layout policy.

ImageItem.LAYOUT_LEFT
> The image should be left-justified in the space available to it.

ImageItem.LAYOUT_RIGHT
> The image should be right-justified in the space available to it.

ImageItem.LAYOUT_CENTER
> The image should be centered in the space available to it.

ImageItem.LAYOUT_NEWLINE_BEFORE
> A line break should occur before the image is drawn.

ImageItem.LAYOUT_NEWLINE_AFTER
> A line break should occur after the image is drawn.

When `LAYOUT_DEFAULT` is used, the device places the image according to implementation-dependent rules. In the reference implementation, this value causes the `ImageItem` to be handled in the same way as `StringItem`—that is, it is placed on the same horizontal line as the `Item` that precedes it, providing that both of the following conditions are met:

- The `ImageItem` does not contain a nonempty label, because this always forces a line break.

- The space remaining in the current line is not less than the width of the image.

If these conditions are not met, a line break occurs before the optional label and image are drawn. The remaining layout constraints may be mixed together subject to the following rules:

- `LAYOUT_LEFT`, `LAYOUT_RIGHT`, and `LAYOUT_CENTER` are mutually exclusive. They determine how the image is placed within the remaining space on the current line.

- LAYOUT_NEWLINE_BEFORE and LAYOUT_NEWLINE_AFTER can be used separately or together; they may also be used in conjunction with either LAYOUT_DEFAULT or one of LAYOUT_LEFT, LAYOUT_RIGHT, or LAYOUT_CENTER. Because LAYOUT_DEFAULT has value 0, a layout value of LAYOUT_NEWLINE_BEFORE is equivalent to LAYOUT_NEWLINE_BEFORE | LAYOUT_DEFAULT.

As a shorthand, you can add an image to a Form using the following Form method:

```
public void append(Image image);
```

This is equivalent to creating and appending an ImageItem with layout LAYOUT_DEFAULT and no label, that is:

```
form.append(new ImageItem(null, image, ImageItem.LAYOUT_DEFAULT, null));
```

You can see some examples of ImageItems by selecting the ImageItem entry from the list presented by ItemMIDlet. The result of running this example on the default color phone is shown in Figure 4-18 and on the PalmOS platform in Figure 4-19.

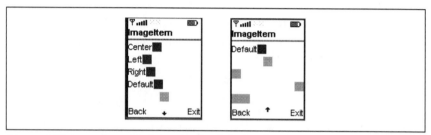

Figure 4-18: ImageItems as shown by the default color phone emulator

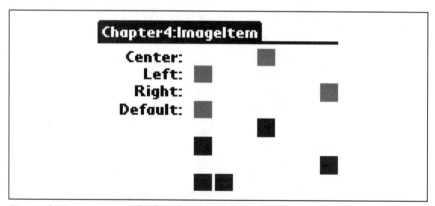

Figure 4-19: ImageItems displayed by MIDP for PalmOS

The top four lines all contain ImageItems that have both an image and a label. These components were created as follows:

```
Image red = Image.createImage("/ora/ch4/resources/red.png");
Image blue = Image.createImage("/ora/ch4/resources/blue.png");

// ImageItems with labels
```

```
form.append(new ImageItem("Center", red, ImageItem.LAYOUT_CENTER, null));
form.append(new ImageItem("Left", red, ImageItem.LAYOUT_LEFT, null));
form.append(new ImageItem("Right", red, ImageItem.LAYOUT_RIGHT, null));
form.append(new ImageItem("Default", red, ImageItem.LAYOUT_DEFAULT,
    null));
```

The `layout` arguments used here do not include `LAYOUT_NEWLINE_BEFORE`, so the images directly follow their labels. However, each `ImageItem` is placed on a line of its own even though `LAYOUT_NEWLINE_AFTER` is not specified, because each has a label, which forces a line break.

If you compare Figure 4-18 and Figure 4-19, you'll notice that the image placements on the default color phone do not correspond to those requested by the `layout` argument: they all appear to be left-aligned, whereas the PalmOS implementation places them properly. This is not inconsistent with the MIDP specification, which allows a device to treat the `layout` parameter as a hint. It serves to illustrate that you cannot rely on having images placed exactly where you want them.

The last five `ImageItems` differ from the first four in two respects:

- They do not have labels.

- Three of them have `layout` values that include both `LAYOUT_NEWLINE_ BEFORE` and `LAYOUT_NEWLINE_AFTER`.

The code used to add these components is as follows:

```
form.append(new ImageItem(null, blue, ageItem.LAYOUT_NEWLINE_BEFORE |
    ImageItem.LAYOUT_CENTER |ImageItem.LAYOUT_NEWLINE_AFTER, null));
form.append(new ImageItem(null, blue, mageItem.LAYOUT_NEWLINE_BEFORE |
    ImageItem.LAYOUT_DEFAULT | ImageItem.LAYOUT_NEWLINE_AFTER, null));
form.append(new ImageItem(null, blue, ImageItem.LAYOUT_NEWLINE_BEFORE |
    ImageItem.LAYOUT_RIGHT | ImageItem.LAYOUT_NEWLINE_AFTER, null));
form.append(new ImageItem(null, blue, ImageItem.LAYOUT_DEFAULT, null));
form.append(new ImageItem(null, blue, ImageItem.LAYOUT_DEFAULT, null));
```

Because these `ImageItems` do not include labels, they would normally be laid out on a single line with no line breaks. The `LAYOUT_NEWLINE_BEFORE` and `LAYOUT_ NEWLINE_AFTER` values cause each image to be preceded and followed by a line break. Note that only a single line break is used between each pair of images, even though it might appear that two newlines have been requested (i.e., one after each image and one before the image that follows it). The last two `ImageItems` are created with the `layout` argument set to `LAYOUT_DEFAULT` only. As a result, no line breaks are added, and, as you can see, they appear on the same line. The line break before the first `ImageItem` is due to the `LAYOUT_ NEWLINE_AFTER` part of the `layout` attribute of the `ImageItem` on the line above.

Notice that the default color phone has obeyed the positioning constraints when placing these `ImageItems`, as you can see from the right side of Figure 4-18. At the time of writing, the MIDP reference implementation honors the `LAYOUT_RIGHT` and `LAYOUT_CENTER` constraints only if the layout attribute also includes both `LAYOUT_NEWLINE_BEFORE` and `LAYOUT_NEWLINE_AFTER`.

Gauges

A Gauge provides a way to represent a single selected value from a contiguous range of integers starting from 0 and ranging up to an application-supplied maximum. The Gauge class has a single constructor:

```
public Gauge(String label, boolean interactive, int maxValue,
    int initialValue);
```

The maxValue and initialValue arguments specify, respectively, the largest value of the range covered by the gauge and the value that will be displayed initially. The minimum value is always implicitly zero, and the current value must always be positive and not greater than the maximum.

The interactive argument determines whether the user can adjust the value in the gauge. To use a gauge as a slider, you should set this argument to true. Adjustments made by the user are reported to the ItemStateListener attached to the Form on which the gauge is displayed. If interactive is false, the value of the gauge can be adjusted only under application control. In this mode, the gauge acts more like a progress bar.

The current value of a gauge can be obtained or changed using the following methods:

```
public int getValue();
public void setValue(int value);
```

The value passed to the setValue() method must be nonnegative and less than or equal to the maximum value. The maximum value can itself be manipulated using similar methods:

```
public int getMaxValue();
public void setMaxValue(int value);
```

The value passed to setMaxValue() must be greater than 0. If the new maximum value is less than the current value, the current value is reduced to the new maximum. Note that, as with all programmatic changes, this change in the current value is not reported to ItemStateListeners.

There is also a method that allows you to determine whether a gauge is interactive:

```
public boolean isInteractive();
```

However, you cannot change this attribute: a gauge is either always interactive or always not interactive.

If you run the ItemMIDlet and select the Gauge example, you'll see a screen displaying three gauges, all of which have a maximum value of 100, as shown in Figure 4-20. The code used to create this Form is as follows:

```
Form form = new Form("Gauge");
form.append(new Gauge(null, true, 100, 50));
form.append(new Gauge(null, true, 100, 25));
form.append(new Gauge(null, false, 100, 50));
```

The top two gauges are interactive, and the bottom one is not. Notice first that the Gauge that has the focus is distinguished from the the others in that its bars are fully drawn, while those of the other two are not. Also, the two interactive gauges

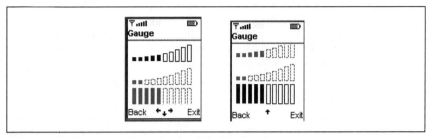

Figure 4-20: Gauges as shown by the default color phone

have bars that increase in size from left to right, but the noninteractive one has bars of constant height.

These gauges represent their complete range using 10 bars, so that each bar corresponds to a range of 10 values. For a larger value range, each bar would correspond to a wider range of values. On the default color phone, the number of filled bars gives a guide to the current value of the gauge, but the user can see only an approximation of the real value, because each bar represents more than one possible value (a range of 10 possible values, in this case). On other devices, the gauge might use a different total number of bars to represent the same total value range, or it might not use bars at all. On the PalmOS platform, for example, both interactive and noninteractive gauges are represented quite differently from those on the default color phone, as shown in Figure 4-21.

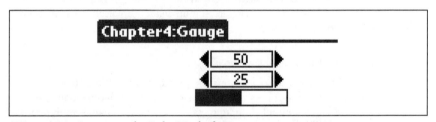

Figure 4-21: Gauges on the PalmOS platform

On the default color phone, you can use the up and down arrow keys to move the input focus from gauge to gauge. When an interactive gauge has the focus, you can use the left and right arrow keys to adjust the current value up or down; horizontal arrows are drawn on the screen as a visual cue, as you can see at the bottom of the left screenshot in Figure 4-20. When the gauge is at its maximum value, the right-pointing arrow is not shown, and the right arrow key has no effect; the left arrow and key show similar behavior when the gauge is at its minimum value. No visual cues are shown when the input focus is assigned to a noninteractive gauge, as is the case in the right screen shot in Figure 4-20, because the user cannot change the value of this gauge.

If you change the value of either of the top two gauges with the arrow keys, you'll notice that a message is written to the Wireless Toolkit console window to reflect every value change. This value is obtained by calling the `Gauge.getValue()` method from the Form's `itemStateChanged()` method:

```
public void itemStateChanged(Item item) {
    if (item instanceof Gauge) {
        int value = ((Gauge)item).getValue();
        System.out.println("Gauge value set to " + value);
    } else {
        // Other code not shown here
    }
}
```

You have to click the right or left arrow key 10 times to affect the visual representation of the gauge, but the `ItemStateListener` is notified of each individual change.

An interactive gauge generally is used to allow the user to select one of a range of values, and the MIDlet usually interacts with it only when the user changes the value or when it is necessary to set a new value programmatically. By contrast, when the gauge is used as a progress bar, the MIDlet updates it regularly to reflect the state of an operation that it is performing.

ChoiceGroups and Lists

ChoiceGroup and List are two similar components that present the user with a set of choices and allow one or more them to be selected. The relationship between them is similar to that between `TextField` and `TextBox`: ChoiceGroup is an `Item` to be used as part of a `Form`, while List is derived from `Screen` and is therefore a freestanding component that occupies the entire screen. Most of the programming interface is common and is described by an interface called `Choice`. For simplicity, we'll cover the common features by examining ChoiceGroup and then look at how List differs from it.

Creating a ChoiceGroup

There are two types of ChoiceGroup, distinguished by the number of items within the group that can be selected at the same time. The choice between these two types is made when the ChoiceGroup is created with one of its two constructors:

```
public ChoiceGroup(String label, int choiceType);
public ChoiceGroup(String label, int choiceType, String[] strings,
    Image[] images);
```

The `choiceGroup` parameter takes one of the following values, defined in the interface `Choice`, which ChoiceGroup implements:

Choice.EXCLUSIVE

Creates an exclusive ChoiceGroup in which only one item can be selected and which, therefore, acts like a collection of radio buttons

Choice.MULTIPLE

Creates a multiple-selection ChoiceGroup, which is like a set of check boxes, in which any number of items can be selected.

You can see examples of both types of ChoiceGroup by running the `ItemMIDlet` and choosing the ChoiceGroup entry. The result of running this on the default color phone is shown in Figure 4-22, with an `EXCLUSIVE` ChoiceGroup on the left and a `MULTIPLE` ChoiceGroup on the right.

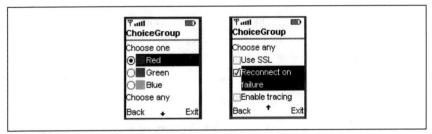

Figure 4-22: ChoiceGroups on the default color phone

There are two ways to initialize a ChoiceGroup: the selections can be added using the second of the constructors shown above, or they can be added following construction. The left ChoiceGroup in Figure 4-22 was initialized at construction time:

```
Image red = Image.createImage("/ora/ch4/resources/red.png");
Image green = Image.createImage("/ora/ch4/resources/green.png");
Image blue = Image.createImage("/ora/ch4/resources/blue.png");

// Exclusive choice group
String[] strings = new String[] { "Red", "Green", "Blue" };
Image[] images = new Image[] { red, green, blue };
ChoiceGroup exGroup = new ChoiceGroup("Choose one",
    ChoiceGroup.EXCLUSIVE, strings, images);
```

Each element of a ChoiceGroup consists of a string and an optional Image that the device may display near the string, although it is not obliged to display the Image at all. When using the constructor to initialize a ChoiceGroup, the following rules must be followed:

- The strings argument must not be null and no element of the strings array can be null. This restriction implies that image-only entries are not supported.

- The images argument may be null if images are not required.

- If the images argument is not null, it must have the same number of elements as the strings array. The image at index N of the images array corresponds to the string at element N of the strings array. Images must be immutable. Any element in the images array may be null if an image is not required for that entry of the ChoiceGroup.

The device is responsible for rendering the ChoiceGroup in such a way as to visually distinguish an EXCLUSIVE ChoiceGroup from a MULTIPLE one. As shown in Figure 4-22, the default color phone achieves this by following the common convention of using a circle to represent a radio button in the EXCLUSIVE group and a square for a check box in the MULTIPLE group. This is not the only way to achieve this differentiation, however, as you can see in Figure 4-23, later in this chapter, which shows the same ChoiceGroups as those in Figure 4-22 as they appear on the PalmOS platform. Note that the EXCLUSIVE ChoiceGroup is represented in the form of a popup menu, which shows only the selected item when the menu is not visible. This figure also illustrates that a platform is not obliged to use Images even if they are supplied.

An alternative way to initialize a ChoiceGroup is to add entries after construction. This is how the multiple-choice group shown on the right side of Figure 4-22 was created:

```
ChoiceGroup multiGroup = new ChoiceGroup("Choose any",
    ChoiceGroup.MULTIPLE);
multiGroup.append("Use SSL", null);
multiGroup.append("Reconnect on failure", null);
multiGroup.append("Enable tracing", null);
```

The append() method supplies both the string and the optional image, in that order:

```
public int append(String string, Image image);
```

This method requires that the string argument is not null. The image argument may be null if no image is required; if it is not null, the Image that it refers to must be immutable. The value returned by this method is the index of the entry created within the ChoiceGroup, so the first call in the code example would return 0, the second would return 1, and so on. The append() method is one of several methods from the Choice interface that can be used to change the content of the ChoiceGroup at any time. The other methods are described in Example 4-5, a little later in the chapter.

Handling selection

When a ChoiceGroup has the input focus, the user can navigate from item to item within it with the up and down arrow keys (or their equivalents) on the phone keypad. These internal navigation operations are not visible to application code. To change the selected state of an entry, the user must press the device's SELECT button. The location of the SELECT button on the default color phone is shown in Figure 4-5. The effect that this has depends on the ChoiceGroup type:

MULTIPLE ChoiceGroup

Pressing the SELECT button when an element that is not currently selected has the focus results in that element being selected, but it does not affect the state of any other item. Pressing the SELECT button for an item that is already selected has the effect of deselecting it.

EXCLUSIVE ChoiceGroup:

Because only one item in an exclusive group may be selected at any time, selecting an element clears the previous selection. Attempting to select an element that is already selected has no effect. (It does not deselect the entry; this would result in no element being selected, which is not allowed.)

Changes in the selection state of an element within a ChoiceGroup are reported to the ItemStateListener of the Form on which the ChoiceGroup is displayed. In the case of a multiple-selection group, notification occurs whenever an element is selected or deselected. For an exclusive group, selecting one element implicitly deselects another element, but only one notification takes place.

Handling state changes using an ItemStateListener is appropriate for applications where an immediate response is required, perhaps to update some other part of the user interface to reflect the user's selection. On the other hand, the ChoiceGroup might be part of a larger input form whose contents will be processed as a single unit when all fields have been filled in. In this case, you add a Command (typically Command.OK) to the Form and implement the logic of the Form in its commandAction() method. Whichever approach you take, you need to be able to find out which elements of the ChoiceGroup are selected. ChoiceGroup has three methods that can be used to get the current selection state:

```
public boolean isSelected(int index);
public int getSelectedIndex();
public int getSelectedFlags(boolean[] flags);
```

The isSelected() method returns true if the element with the given index is selected, false if it is not. This method is most often used with multiple-selection ChoiceGroups where each check box represents a different program action that is likely to be independent of the others. Typical code for this case might look like this:

```
public static final int USE_SSL = 0;
public static final int RECONNECT_ON_FAILURE = 1;
public static final int TRACING_ENABLED = 2;
....
do {
    if (multiGroup.isSelected(USE_SSL)) {
        // Connect using SSL
    } else {
        // Connect using vanilla sockets
    }
    if (failed && multiGroup.isSelected(TRACING_ENABLED)) {
        // Log failure
    }
} while (failed && multiGroup.isSelected(RECONNECT_ON_FAILURE));
```

In the case of an EXCLUSIVE ChoiceGroup, since only one element can be selected, the getSelectedIndex() method can be used to determine its index:

```
public static final int RED = 0;
public static final int GREEN = 1;
public static final int BLUE = 2;
....
int index = exGroup.getSelectedIndex();
if (index == RED) {
    // Act on red selection
}
```

This method always returns –1 if it is called for a multiple-choice ChoiceGroup because there could be more than one selected element. It also returns –1 if the ChoiceGroup has no elements at all (which is unlikely in practice).

If you need to get the selection state of every element in the ChoiceGroup, the getSelectedFlags() method should be used. This method requires an array of booleans that has at least as many elements as there are items in the ChoiceGroup; it sets each entry in the array to true or false depending on whether the corresponding entry is selected. The return value is the number of items that are selected. Before invoking this method, you need to allocate a boolean array of the appropriate size. If the number of elements in the

ChoiceGroup is not constant, you can use the size() method to find out how many there are:

```
boolean[] flags = new boolean[multiGroup.size()];
int count = multiGroup.getSelectedFlags(flags);
do {
    if (flags[USE_SSL]) {
            // Connect using SSL
        } else {
            // Connect using vanilla sockets
        }
    if (failed && flags[TRACING_ENABLED]) {
        // Log failure
    }
} while (failed && flags[RECONNECT_ON_FAILURE]);
```

This technique works for both types of ChoiceGroup.

Finally, to get the value of an element within the ChoiceGroup, use the getString() method:

```
public String getString(int index);
```

The following code extract returns either "Red", "Green", or "Blue":

```
String color = exGroup.getString(exGroup.getSelectedIndex());
```

The code that handles selection changes for the ChoiceGroups used in the ItemMIDlet is shown in Example 4-5.

Example 4-5: Handling Selection Changes in a ChoiceGroup or List Component

```
// Handles the selection for a Choice
private void handleChoiceSelection(Choice choice) {
    int count = choice.size();
    boolean[] states = new boolean[count];
    int selCount = choice.getSelectedFlags(states);
    if (selCount > 0) {
        System.out.println("Selected items:");
        for (int i = 0; i < count; i++) {
            if (states[i]) {
                System.out.println("\t" + choice.getString(i));
            }
        }
    } else {
        System.out.println("No selected items.");
    }
    int selectedIndex = choice.getSelectedIndex();
    System.out.println("Selected index is " + selectedIndex);
}
```

This method, which is called from the ItemStateListener attached to the Form in which the ChoiceGroups are contained, is given an argument of type Choice instead of ChoiceGroup. When it is invoked, however, the calling code passes a reference to the ChoiceGroup. This is acceptable, because ChoiceGroup implements the Choice interface. The benefit of requiring an argument of type Choice instead of ChoiceGroup is that this same code can also be used to handle selection changes for the List component, which also implements Choice.

The aim of this code is simply to demonstrate a couple of ways of handling selection changes. The first part of this code uses the getSelectedFlags() method to get an array of booleans that shows which elements are selected. The code then loops over the returned array, gets the strings corresponding to selected entries, and prints them. The second part of the method uses the getSelectedIndex() method to access directly the index of the selected item, which, as noted above, returns a meaningful result only for an EXCLUSIVE ChoiceGroup. Selecting the Green item in the ChoiceGroup example and pressing the SELECT button results in the following output in the Wireless Toolkit console:

```
Selected items:
        Green
Selected index is 1
```

Because this is an EXCLUSIVE ChoiceGroup, only one item can ever be selected, so the getSelectedIndex() method is able to return its index. Selecting Use SSL in the multiple-choice ChoiceGroup gives this result:

```
Selected items:
        Use SSL
Selected index is -1
```

Here, getSelectedIndex() has returned −1 because the type is MULTIPLE. Selecting another entry in the same ChoiceGroup results in the following:

```
Selected items:
        Use SSL
        Enable tracing
Selected index is -1
```

As you can see, the getSelectedFlags() method returns all the selected items.

Setting and changing the selection

The selection state of the elements within a ChoiceGroup can be changed programmatically using the following methods:

```
public void setSelectedIndex(int index, boolean selected);
public void setSelectedFlags(boolean[] flags);
```

The effect of the setSelectedIndex() method depends on the ChoiceGroup type. In the multiple-choice case, this method selects or deselects the element at the given index, depending on the value of the selected argument. In an exclusive ChoiceGroup, however, this method has an effect only if the selected argument has value true. In this case, it selects the element at index and deselects the element that was previously selected. If selected is false, the call is ignored. This happens because an exclusive ChoiceGroup must always have one selected element, so it is not possible simply to deselect the element that is currently selected without selecting another element at the same time.

You can set the selected state of all the elements in a ChoiceGroup by calling the setSelectedFlags() method, passing it an array of booleans containing true for those elements that are to be selected and `false` for those that are not. The `boolean` array must contain an entry for each element in the `ChoiceGroup`:

```
public boolean[] initialStates = new boolean[3];
initialStates[RECONNECT_ON_FAILURE] = true;  // Select just this element
multiGroup.setSelectedFlags(initialStates);
```

In the multiple-choice case, any number of entries in the array can be `true`. Since exclusive `ChoiceGroups` can have only one element selected, in this case the `boolean` array must have exactly one entry with value `true`. If this is not the case, the following selection rules apply:

- If the array has no entries set to `true`, the first entry in the `ChoiceGroup` is selected.

- If the array has more than one entry set to `true`, the element in the `ChoiceGroup` corresponding to the first `true` entry is selected.

Note that changing the selection using these methods does not result in notification to the `Form`'s `ItemStateListener`.

Changing the content of a ChoiceGroup

The content of a ChoiceGroup can be changed at any time using the following methods:

```
public int append(String string, Image image);
public void insert(int index, String string, Image image);
public void set(int index, String string, Image image);
public void delete(int index);
```

The `append()` method, which has already been discussed, adds a new element to the end of the `ChoiceGroup`. The `insert()` method is similar, except that it places the new entry at the given index, moving the element at that index and all higher indexes down to make room for the new one. This method can also be used to add an element at the end of the `ChoiceGroup` by supplying the size of the `ChoiceGroup` as the insertion index:

```
multiGroup.insert(multiGroup.size(), "New Entry", null);
```

Insertion indexes greater than `size()` are invalid and cause an `IndexOutOfBoundsException` to be thrown.

The `set()` method replaces the content of an existing element with new values. Both the string and image parts of the element are changed: it is not possible to change only one of these attributes by supplying `null` for the other. For all of these methods, the `image` argument may be `null` if no image is required, but the `string` argument must not be `null`. If an image is supplied, it must be immutable.

Finally, an element can be removed from the `ChoiceGroup` using the `delete()` method:

```
public void delete(int index);
```

Changing the content of a ChoiceGroup may have an effect on its selection state. The rules that apply are as follows:

- Adding an item using the append() method has no effect on the selection. The only exception to this is an EXCLUSIVE ChoiceGroup that was previously empty. In this case, the newly added element is selected.

- Inserting an element using the insert() method preserves the selected state of each existing item in the list, but, of course, the indexes of the selected items may change. As an example of this, if elements 2 and 3 are selected and a new element is inserted at index 2, the selected item indexes change to 3 and 4. As a special case, as with the append() method, if an EXCLUSIVE ChoiceGroup was previously empty, the new element is selected.

- Replacing an item using the set() method gives the new item the same selected state as the item that it replaced.

Deleting an item has no effect on the selection state of other items, except when the selected element in an EXCLUSIVE ChoiceGroup is deleted. In this case, if the deleted item is not at the end of the list, the item that replaces it is selected (that is, the selected index remains the same). If the selected item is the last item, then the element that becomes the last item is selected instead.

The List component

List is a full-screen version of ChoiceGroup that shares most of its programming interface. The common functionality is grouped into an interface called Choice, which has the following methods:

```
public int append(String string, Image image);
public void delete(int index);
public Image getImage(int index);
public int getSelectedFlags(boolean[] flags);
public int getSelectedIndex();
public String getString(int index);
public void insert(int index, String string, Image image);
public boolean isSelected(int index);
public void set(int index, String string, Image image);
public void setSelectedFlags(boolean[] flags);
public void setSelectedIndex(int index, boolean selected);
public int size();
```

List has two constructors that mirror those of ChoiceGroup and work in exactly the same way:

```
public List(String title, int type);
public List(String title, int type, String[] strings, Image[] images);
```

The only difference is that the first parameter is used to set the title of the List's screen, whereas it is used as the label for a ChoiceGroup.

As well as supporting the EXCLUSIVE and MULTIPLE modes of operation, List has a third mode, selected by setting the type to Choice.IMPLICIT, which cannot be used with ChoiceGroup. IMPLICIT mode creates a List that behaves somewhat like a standard list (e.g., the Swing JList component), with the restriction that only one element can be selected at a time. This mode is often used to create a menu, and, in fact, this is how the list of MIDlets in a MIDlet suite is presented when you launch the Java VM (see Figure 3-8). If you select the `List` item from the menu presented by `ItemMIDlet`, you'll see an `IMPLICIT` `List`, as shown on the left side of Figure 4-23. The code used to create this list is very similar to the corresponding `ChoiceGroup` code:

```
List list = new List("List", List.IMPLICIT);
Image red = Image.createImage("/ora/ch4/resources/red.png");
Image green = Image.createImage("/ora/ch4/resources/green.png");
Image blue = Image.createImage("/ora/ch4/resources/blue.png");

list.append("Red", red);
list.append("Green", green);
list.append("Blue", blue);
```

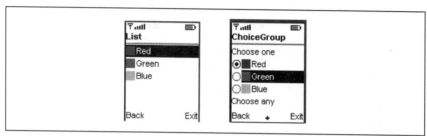

Figure 4-23: List component on the default color phone

MIDlet User Interfaces

The same `List` as displayed on the PalmOS platform is shown in Figure 4-24. As you can see, the cell phone emulator displays both the string and the image associated with each element in the list, whereas the PalmOS implementation ignores the image, as it did in the case of the `ChoiceGroup`.

Figure 4-24: List component on the PalmOS platform

The `IMPLICIT` and `EXCLUSIVE` modes are very similar, in that both require exactly one element of the list to be selected at any time. In fact, all previous comments regarding `EXCLUSIVE` mode made in connection with `ChoiceGroup` also apply to the `IMPLICIT` mode of `List`. The difference between these modes can be seen by comparing the `IMPLICIT` `List` on the left side of Figure 4-23 with the `EXCLUSIVE` `ChoiceGroup` on the right. As you can see, the `ChoiceGroup` has a separate radio button that indicates which element is selected, whereas the `List` does not. This means that the highlighted element in the `ChoiceGroup` (Green) need not be the same as the selected element (Red). In the case of an `IMPLICIT` list, however, the highlighted element is *implicitly* considered to be the selected element, which is why this is referred to as `IMPLICIT` mode.

Since List is not an Item, changes in its selection state cannot be notified to application code via an ItemStateListener. In fact, there is no way to detect when the selected element of a List changes, in any of its modes, until the user activates a Command installed on the List that would prompt application code to examine its selection state.* In the case of an IMPLICIT List, however, if the user presses the SELECT key on the cell phone keypad or presses the arrow to the left of each item on the PalmOS platform (refer to Figure 4-24), the List's CommandListener, if there is one, is notified of a selection change. Usually, when the commandAction() method of the CommandListener is called, it is passed a reference to the application-supplied Command that was activated and the Displayable to which the Command was attached. In this case, however, there is no application Command associated with the selection action, so the List provides a private Command called List.SELECT_COMMAND, which indicates that the commandAction() method has been called as a result of an IMPLICIT List selection. The Displayable argument passed to commandAction() refers to the List itself.

To associate a CommandListener with a List, you use the setCommandListener() method inherited from Displayable:

```
List list = new List("List", Choice.IMPLICIT);
list.setCommandListener(new CommandListener() {
    public void commandAction(Command c, Displayable d) {
        // Handle notification from the List
    }
});
```

The ItemMIDlet commandAction() method includes a case that detects the List selection change:

```
public void commandAction(Command c, Displayable d) {
    if (c == List.SELECT_COMMAND) {
        // Selection made in the IMPLICIT LIST
        handleChoiceSelection((Choice)d);
    } else {
        // Other cases not shown
    }
}
```

Because List implements the Choice interface, you can use the same methods to handle the selection as those shown in connection with ChoiceGroup. In fact, the previous code uses the same handleChoiceSelection() method as was used to handle the ChoiceGroup selection in Example 4-5. Notice that a reference to the List is obtained by casting the Displayable to an object of type Choice. This is correct because the notification comes from the List (the Displayable), which implements Choice.

---

* Strictly speaking, this is not true, because you could periodically examine the selection state from a background thread or on expiration of a Timer, but such tactics are not likely to be useful in a real application!

Note carefully that this discussion applies only to Lists created with type IMPLICIT. The CommandListener will *not* be notified of any selection change for Lists of type MULTIPLE or EXCLUSIVE. For these types, it is necessary to attach to the List a Command that notifies application code that the List selection should be checked.

The behavior of the Choice methods concerned with selection handling in the IMPLICIT mode is the same as that for EXCLUSIVE mode, as described in the earlier sections "Handling selection" and "Setting and changing the selection."

Alerts

Alert is a subclass of Screen that behaves much like a dialog, albeit with very limited functionality. When an Alert is displayed by calling the Display setCurrent() method, it covers some or all of the device screen and receives all key and pointer events generated by user action while it is visible. An Alert may be *modal* or *nonmodal*. In this context, an Alert is modal if it remains displayed until the user explicitly dismisses it. A nonmodal dialog, by contrast, is displayed for a limited maximum time period before being closed automatically.

Alert has several attributes that determine its appearance and behavior:

Title

This attribute is inherited from Screen. An Alert is not required to have a title.

String

This attribute contains the message that the Alert displays to the user. Line breaks may be created within the message by including newline characters.

Image

An optional image may be provided to be displayed along with the message. The way in which the image is displayed, and whether it is displayed at all, is device-dependent.

Timeout

Specifies how long the Alert is displayed. A default timeout is applied if no explicit timeout value is set. The distinguished value Alert.FOREVER is used to indicate that the Alert should be displayed until the user dismisses it. There is no requirement for the device to provide a means for the user to remove an Alert with a finite timeout value before the timeout expires. This feature should be used with care to ensure that the user does not have to wait an unduly long period for a simple confirmation message to time out and dismiss itself.

Type

This attribute, which is of type AlertType, conveys the intent of the Alert to the platform. The platform may use this attribute to tailor the alert's visual appearance to help the user distinguish between errors, warnings, and informational messages. The platform may also generate an appropriate sound to draw the user's attention to the alert. An Alert is not required to have an

MIDlet User Interfaces

AlertType, and the platform is not required to act upon it even if it does. The available types are:

> AlertType.ALARM
> AlertType.CONFIRMATION
> AlertType.ERROR
> AlertType.INFO
> AlertType.WARNNG

Note that the CONFIRMATION type is intended to confirm to the user that an action previously requested has been completed, not to solicit something like a Yes, No, or Cancel response before an action is performed. In fact, it is not possible to construct an Alert that accepts any input. If you want to get confirmation from a user before performing an action, you must construct and display a Form containing the appropriate Commands to allow the user to approve or cancel the proposed action.

You can see all the available Alert types and how the timeout works by selecting the Alert example from the ItemMIDlet. This example lets you configure the attributes of an Alert and display the result. When the example starts, you see a Form containing two ChoiceGroups. Figure 4-25 shows how this looks on the default color phone, where you need to scroll to see all of the Form.

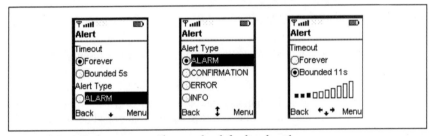

Figure 4-25: Configuring an Alert on the default color phone

The first ChoiceGroup, shown on the left side of Figure 4-25, lets you select the timeout for the Alert, which can be either Alert.FOREVER or a value specified in seconds. If you select the second item in the ChoiceGroup, a Gauge appears so that you can adjust the timeout value, as shown on the right side of the figure. The second ChoiceGroup allows you to choose the AlertType. On the PalmOS platform, this Form has a more compact representation, shown in Figure 4-26, but the functionaility is the same.

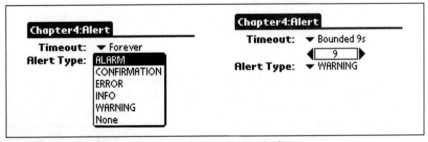

Figure 4-26: Configuring an Alert on the PalmOS platform

Once you've configured the `Alert`, you can use the OK command to display it. On the PalmOS platform, this is available as a button on the `Form`, but on other devices you might need to access a soft-key menu to locate it. Pressing the OK button displays the `Alert`, and, on some devices, a sound plays (the specific sound may depend on the `AlertType`). If you experiment with different types, you'll notice that, with the exception of the text message (which is constructed by `ItemMIDlet` to remind you of the parameters that you selected), there is no difference in appearance on the default color phone. The alerts all look like the one shown on the upper left side of Figure 4-27. The exception is when you select a timeout of `Alert.FOREVER`: you get a command button labeled Done that allows you to dismiss the `Alert` at any time.

On the PalmOS platform, however, the `Alert`s use different icons to indicate the `AlertType`. Furthermore, as you can see from Figure 4-27, when a finite timeout is selected, the time remaining until the `Alert` is dismissed counts down in a small circle in its bottom left. When the timeout value is set to `Alert.FOREVER`, there is a Done button in this area instead.

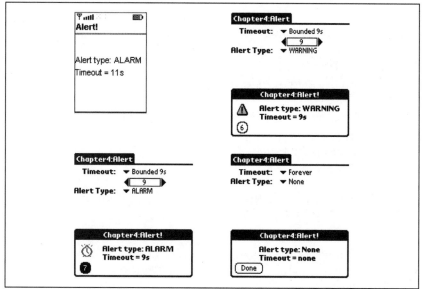

Figure 4-27: Various Alerts on the default color phone and the PalmOS platform

 Only `Alert`s with the timeout set to `Alert.FOREVER` can be dismissed by the user; the others remain displayed until their timeout expires. You can't get around this by trying to add your own Done button, because `Alert` overrides the `addCommand` and `setCommandListener` methods of `Displayable` and throws an `IllegalStateException` if you try to add a `Command` or install a `CommandListener`.

The code used to create and display an `Alert` is simple:

```
Alert alert = new Alert("Alert Title", "This is an Alarm", alarmImage,
    AlertType.ALARM);
Display.getDisplay(this).setCurrent(alert);
```

As you can see, you use the `Display` `setCurrent()` method to display an `Alert`, just as you would any other type of `Displayable`. The `Alert` partially or completely covers the screen that was active when the `setCurrent()` method is called. When the `Alert` is dismissed, the original screen is redisplayed. In some cases, though, it might be appropriate to show a different screen once the `Alert` has closed. You can arrange for this to happen by using a different form of `setCurrent()`:

```
public void setCurrent(Alert alert, Displayable displayable);
```

This method first displays the given `Alert`; when it closes, the `Displayable` given as the second argument appears instead of the screen that was originally displayed. As a special case, passing `null` for the `Displayable` reverts to the original screen—that is, it behaves just like the single-argument variant of `setCurrent()`.

`Alert` has several methods that you can use to customize it after creation or to get some of its attributes. The `AlertType` can be obtained or changed using the following methods:

```
public void setAlertType(AlertType alertType);
public AlertType getAlertType();
```

You can get or change the text string and image using similar methods:

```
public void setString(String string);
public String getString();
public void setImage(Image image);
public Image getImage();
```

When an `Alert` is created, a default timeout is applied, which you can get using the `getDefaultTimeout()` method:

```
public int getDefaultTimeout();
```

Note that this is not a static method, so you have to create an `Alert` before you can use it. There is no method to change the default timeout. The returned value is in milliseconds.

Finally, you can get or change the actual timeout for a specific `Alert` using the following methods, where the time is again measured in milliseconds:

```
public int getTimeout();
public void setTimeout(int timeOut);
```

If you call `setTimeout()` with the argument `Alert.FOREVER`, then the `Alert` will be modal.

An `Alert` with timeout set to `Alert.FOREVER` is described in the MIDP specification as a modal dialog, but it is not modal in the same sense that a J2SE `Dialog` or `JDialog` is. In particular, when you display a J2SE modal dialog by calling its `show()` or `setVisible()` method, control is not returned until the dialog is dismissed. The same is not true of `Alert`. That is, in the following code the `setCurrent()` method returns control immediately; it does not wait for the `Alert` to be dismissed:

```
Alert alert = new Alert("Modal", "Modal Alert", null,
AlertType.ALARM);
alert.setTimeout(Alert.FOREVER); // Make the Alert
"modal"
Display.getDisplay(this).setCurrent(alert)
// Returns IMMEDIATELY
```

In fact, the `Alert` may not actually have been displayed when it returns, as discussed in "The Display and Displayable Classes," earlier in this chapter.

Playing Sounds

MIDP does not currently have an API for playing arbitrary sounds, but it is possible to create a small set of sounds on devices that support it by using the `AlertType` method on its own. The `AlertType` method has a public method that plays its associated sound:

```
public boolean playSound(Display display);
```

where `display` is the `Display` object associated with the MIDlet. The following code extract requests that the device play the sound associated with an `ALARM`:

```
AlertType.ALARM.playSound(Display.getDisplay(this));
```

The device is not obliged to play any sounds or to generate a different sound for each `AlertType`. If the `playSound()` method actually plays a sound, it returns `true`. You can experiment with the various sounds by selecting the `Sounds` example from `ItemMIDlet`, choosing each sound in turn from the `List` component that the MIDlet displays, and using the SELECT key (or its equivalent) to play it. The return value of the `playSound()` method is written to the Wireless Toolkit console. If you are running this example on a PalmOS device, and you don't hear any sounds, be sure to enable System Sounds using the Prefs applet from the main screen.

CHAPTER 5

The Low-Level MIDlet User Interface API

The high-level API provides enough functionality for you to create, with relatively little effort, MIDlets with user interfaces that work unchanged across a wide range of devices. The price to be paid for this, however, is that you are restricted to using the components provided in the `javax.microedition.lcdui` package, and you have very little control over the appearance of your MIDlet.

The low-level API gives you almost exactly the opposite situation. To use it, you need to put much more effort into creating the user interface, but in return you get pixel-level access to the screen, you have control over colors (or shades of gray) and fonts; and you can respond directly to the user's key presses or pointer actions. This section takes a detailed look at the low-level API, which is useful for writing simple games or drawing charts. It may be used on its own or mixed with screens built using Form and the other classes covered in the previous chapter.

The Canvas Class

Canvas is the basic building block of the low-level API. Because it is derived directly from Displayable, it inherits the ability to have associated Commands, but it does not provide a title or the ability to contain other components. Canvas gives you direct access to the screen of a MIDP device, apart from the area used to draw Command buttons or labels, as shown in Figure 5-1. In the figure, the black area is the part of the screen occupied by the Canvas itself.

Unlike the user interface components that we have seen so far, Canvas is an abstract class. To use Canvas, you have to subclass it and implement the paint method to draw whatever you want to appear on the screen. This method is called with a single argument, which is an instance of another low-level API class called Graphics. This class provides methods that allow you to draw lines, rectangles, and arcs, fill areas with a solid color, and render text onto the device's screen. The Canvas class also has methods—which you can override—to receive notification of key presses and use of the pointer (on those devices that have one).

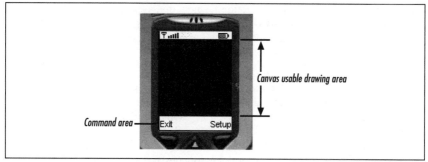

Command area —

Canvas usable drawing area

Exit   Setup

Figure 5-1: The Canvas class

Screen Attributes

The low-level API is intended to give you much greater control over the screen and keypad of a MIDP device than the high-level API does. In doing so, however, it makes it more likely that you will inadvertently create a MIDlet that is device-dependent because it relies on the dimensions of the screen or on a feature that is not universally available. To make it easier to write code that adapts itself to its environment, the Canvas and Display classes provide methods, described in the following sections, to allow you to query the attributes that distinguish one device from another.

Display methods

The Display class provides the following methods:

public boolean isColor()
>This method returns true if the device has a color display, false if not.

public int numColors()
>If the isColor() method returns true, numColors() can be used to get the number of different colors the device supports. When isColor() returns false, numColors() returns the number of shades of gray that the device's display can provide. As you'll see later, you can treat a grayscale device as if it supported color, and the color values you use will be converted to a shade of gray that approximates the brightness of the original color. However, you might be able to obtain better results in some cases by coding your MIDlet to work in grayscale if the device does not support color.

Canvas methods

The Canvas class provides the following methods:

public int getWidth()
public int getHeight()
>These methods return the width and height of the Canvas, which corresponds to the usable part of the device's screen.

public boolean hasRepeatEvents()
>While all MIDP platforms provide keyboard input, some (especially cell phones) do not support the concept of repeated keys. If this method returns

true, your MIDlet will be notified when the user holds down a key long enough for the device to consider it a repeated key. Key handling and the mechanism by which the MIDlet is informed of repeated keys are covered in Example 5-7, later in this chapter.

public boolean hasPointerEvents()
public boolean hasPointerMotionEvents()

Cell phones are usually limited to input via the keypad, but more functional devices, such as PDAs, usually also have some kind of pointing device (such as a stylus) used in conjunction with a touch screen. If such a pointer is available, the `hasPointerEvents()` method returns true, and the MIDlet can expect to be notified when the user touches the screen with the pointer or lifts the pointer away from the screen. Additionally, if the `hasPointerMotionEvents()` method returns true, the platform might periodically deliver notifications to the MIDlet if the user drags the pointer while it is in contact with the screen. For maximum portability, MIDlets should not rely on the availability of a pointer and should not assume, even if a pointer is available, that pointer motion events will be available.

public boolean isDoubleBuffered()

This method returns true if the MIDP implementation provides double buffering, so that graphics operations performed in the Canvas `paint()` method are applied to an offscreen buffer instead of directly to the screen. The advantage of double buffering is that it can make screen updates look much smoother because the user never sees partially updated frames that can result in display flashing or temporary inconsistencies while the display is being redrawn. If `isDoubleBuffered()` returns false, a MIDlet can still attempt to alleviate display problems of this type by performing its own double buffering. The disadvantage of this, however, is that allocating an off-screen buffer may require more memory than the platfom can make available to the MIDlet.

You can obtain the values of these attributes for the emulated devices supported by the Wireless Toolkit by building and running the Chapter5 project from this book's example source code. Select the MIDlet called AttributesMIDlet, which uses the high-level API to show these attributes; it creates (but does not display) a Canvas from which the attribute values are obtained, as shown in Example 5-1.

Example 5-1: Getting Display and Canvas Attributes for a Device

```
package ora.ch5;

import javax.microedition.lcdui.Canvas;
import javax.microedition.lcdui.Command;
import javax.microedition.lcdui.CommandListener;
import javax.microedition.lcdui.Display;
import javax.microedition.lcdui.Displayable;
import javax.microedition.lcdui.Form;
import javax.microedition.lcdui.Graphics;
import javax.microedition.lcdui.StringItem;
import javax.microedition.midlet.MIDlet;
```

```
public class AttributesMIDlet extends MIDlet  implements CommandListener {

    // The MIDlet's Display object
    private Display display;

    // Flag indicating first call of startApp
    protected boolean started;

    // Exit command
    private Command exitCommand;

    protected void startApp() {
        if (!started) {
            display = Display.getDisplay(this);
            Canvas canvas = new DummyCanvas();

            // Build a Form displaying the Display and Canvas attributes.
            Form form = new Form("Attributes");
            exitCommand = new Command("Exit", Command.EXIT, 0);
            form.addCommand(exitCommand);

            boolean isColor = display.isColor();
            form.append(new StringItem(isColor ? "Colors: " : "Grays: ",
                String.valueOf(display.numColors())));
            form.append(new StringItem("Width: ", String.valueOf
                (canvas.getWidth())));
            form.append(new StringItem("Height: ", String.valueOf
                (canvas.getHeight())));
            form.append(new StringItem("Pointer? ",  String.valueOf
                (canvas.hasPointerEvents())));
            form.append(new StringItem("Motion? ", String.valueOf
                (canvas.hasPointerMotionEvents())));
            form.append(new StringItem("Repeat? ", String.valueOf
                (canvas.hasRepeatEvents())));
            form.append(new StringItem("Buffered? ", String.valueOf
                (canvas.isDoubleBuffered())));

            form.setCommandListener(this);

            display.setCurrent(form);

            started = true;
        }
    }

    protected void pauseApp() {
    }

    protected void destroyApp(boolean unconditional) {
    }
```

```
public void commandAction(Command c, Displayable d) {
    if (c == exitCommand) {
        // Exit. No need to call destroyApp
        // because it is empty.
        notifyDestroyed();
    }
}

// A Canvas that has no painting logic
static class DummyCanvas extends Canvas {
    protected void paint(Graphics g) {
        // Do nothing
    }
}
}
```

The results of running this MIDlet on the default color phone and a color PalmOS platform are shown in Figure 5-2. Notice that, as expected, the cell phone does not provide pointer events, but the PalmOS device does. The cell phone also has far fewer colors available than this particular PDA. On the other hand, the cell phone implementation of MIDP provides automatic screen double-buffering, whereas that on the PDA does not. Finally, note that the PDA screen size is reported as 160 pixels wide and 142 pixels high, although the physical screen of this device is actually 160 pixels in each direction. The missing 18 pixels on the vertical axis are not available to MIDlets because they are reserved for Command buttons.

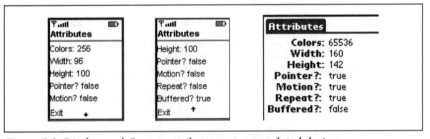

Figure 5-2: Display and Canvas attributes on two emulated devices

Painting and the Graphics Class

When the platform determines that the content of a Canvas needs to be drawn onto the screen, it calls the paint() method, which the MIDlet developer is required to implement:

```
protected void paint(Graphics g)
```

This method is called at the following times:

- When the Canvas becomes visible as a result of the Display setCurrent() method being invoked

---

- When some or all of the Canvas reappears after being partly or wholly obscured by an Alert or a system screen, such as a menu of Commands opened from a soft button

- As a result of application code requesting that the screen be repainted following a change in the data that it is rendering

The Graphics object passed to the paint() method provides methods that allow graphics operations, such as line and text rendering and color filling, to be performed on its target. The target is either the screen itself or, in the case of a platform that supports double buffering, an off-screen image that will be copied to the screen when the paint() method returns. Implementing this method is the only way to get a Graphics object that can access the screen; unlike the J2SE Component class, Canvas does not have a getGraphics() method that can be used to get access on demand to the screen space that it occupies. Therefore, all screen updates must be performed in the paint() method. The MIDP specification prohibits holding a reference to the Graphics object passed to paint() for use elsewhere.*

When the visibility of a Canvas changes, the following methods are called:

```
protected void showNotify()
protected void hideNotify()
```

The MIDP specification guarantees that the paint() method will not be invoked before showNotify() is called and, following return from hideNotify(), any further calls to the paint() method will be preceded by another call to showNotify(). This essentially amounts to the statement that paint() is called only when the Canvas is visible. The default implementations of these methods do nothing. Subclasses may override the showNotify() method to perform any initialization required prior to the Canvas being displayed, while hideNotify() typically reverses the steps taken by showNotify().

As an example of typical use of these methods, a "Space Invaders"-type game might use the showNotify() method to start a timer to control the regular movement of the aliens across the screen and hideNotify() to stop the timer. This would ensure that resources are not wasted moving aliens while the game is not in use. This technique is used in an example shown later in this chapter (see Figure 5-13).

Graphics Attributes

The Graphics class provides operations that let you do the following:

- Draw straight lines, arcs, and rectangles

- Fill the space occupied by an arc or a rectangle

- Render images

- Draw text presented in the form of a String or as character data

---

* It is also possible to get a Graphics object that allows you to draw onto a mutable Image. Graphics objects obtained in this way are valid for use at any time, and a persistent reference to one can be kept. For further discussion on this topic, refer to Figure 5-17.

All these operations use a coordinate system to indicate at least their starting point, and most of them also use one or more attributes of the Graphics object that act as implicit parameters. When the paint() method is called, the attributes of the Graphics object that is passed to it have well-defined values that can be modified if necessary. The attributes and their initial values are listed in Table 5-1. A more detailed description of each attribute and the way in which it is used are found in later sections.

Table 5-1: Graphics Attributes

Attribute	Use	Initial Value
Clip	The clip sets the region of the Canvas within which graphics operations have any effect. The clip is discussed in "The Graphics Clip."	Depends on the reason paint() was invoked
Color	The color that will be used when drawing or filling shapes or rendering text. See "Colors and Grayscale" for further details.	Black
Font	The font used when rendering text. Fonts are discussed in "Rendering Text."	Set to the platform's default font
Stroke Style	Determines whether lines, rectangles, and arcs are drawn using solid or dotted strokes, as described in "Lines and Rectangles."	Set to draw a solid line
Origin	The position of the coordinate point (0, 0) relative to the top left of the Canvas.	The top left corner of the Canvas

The Coordinate System

The Graphics class uses a coordinate system in which the origin is situated at the top left corner of the Canvas. Along the x-axis, coordinates increase from 0 on the left side of the Canvas to their maximum value on the right. Similarly, the value of the y coordinate increases toward the bottom of the Canvas, as shown on the left side of Figure 5-3.

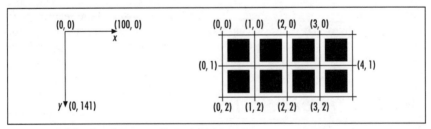

Figure 5-3: The Graphics coordinate syatem

It is important to note that the coordinates do not refer to the locations of the pixels themselves but to the intersection points of an imaginary grid that occupies the space between the pixels, as shown on the right in Figure 5-3. In the figure, the pixels themselves are shown as filled squares. The coordinate location (0, 0), corresponding to the origin, does not strictly refer to the pixel at the top left corner of the grid, but to the grid intersection point just to the left of and above it. Similarly, (1, 0) refers to the grid intersection point just to the top right of that pixel, which is also at the top-left of the pixel to its right. Although this might seem a trivial and rather technical distinction, it becomes important when describing how line drawing and color fill operations work, as will be seen in the later section "Drawing Lines and Arcs." For the sake of clarity, and notwithstanding the fact that it is slightly innacurate to do so, this book usually refers to "the pixel at (0, 0)" when what is really meant is "the pixel whose top left corner is at (0, 0)."

The MIDP specification requires that pixels be approximately square, as shown in Figure 5-3. In reality, a device need not have square pixels. If it does not, the MIDP platform or the host operating system is expected to group device pixels logically so that they appear square to a MIDlet. If, for example, a particular device has pixels that are four times as long as they are tall, the software is required to map a request from a MIDlet to set the color of the pixel at (0, 0) into hardware operations that set the color of that hardware pixel and the three below it to the requested color. Furthermore, the screen size as reported by the `Canvas getWidth()` and `getHeight()` methods are expressed in terms of logical, square pixels, so a MIDlet does not need to be concerned about any mapping that is taking place.

Colors and Grayscale

The `Graphics` operations that draw and fill shapes, lines, and text use the color attribute as an implicit parameter to determine the color to be used for each affected pixel. This attribute can be set using one of the following `Graphics` methods, of which the second is the one most commonly used:

```
public void setColor(int color)
public void setColor(int red, int green, int blue)
public void setGrayScale(int value)
```

The color model specified by MIDP represents a color as an RGB value with 8 bits to represent each of the red, green, and blue components. Numerically lower values represent less of the corresponding color and therefore produce a darker effect. The second `setColor()` method lets you set the color by specifying these component values individually, so that the following setting gives a pure, bright red:

```
setColor(255, 0, 0)
```

This setting is a combination of red and green that produces yellow:

```
setColor(255, 255, 0)
```

The other `setColor()` method uses its integer argument to encode the color components as follows:

```
00 RR GG BB
```

Using this encoding, the bright red with RGB components (255, 0, 0) is represented as 0x00FF0000, yellow is 0x00FFFF00, black is 0, and white is 0x00FFFFFF. The current MIDP specification does not support transparency, so colors are always opaque, and there is no alpha value to encode.*

---

* In J2SE, the alpha channel represents the transparency of a color; it is usually held in the top 8 bits of a color when encoded as an integer. An opaque red pixel, for example, would actually be encoded as 0xFFFF0000, while 0x00FF0000 would be a transparent red that would be invisible! Note also that MIDP does not have a `Color` class: colors are always represented as integers or integer triplets.

The availability of 24 bits to encode a color means that a total of 16,581,375 colors can be represented. Most MIDP devices cannot display anywhere near that number of colors, and some cannot display color at all. When a pixel is drawn, the color value is mapped to the nearest available color that the device can actually represent. This mapping is not visible to the MIDlet, which does not have direct access to the actual pixel data.

On a device that uses grayscale instead of color (that is, one for which the Display isColor() method returns false), the pixel value is converted to a gray value that approximates the brightness of the actual color. This automatic conversion means that a MIDlet originally intended for a color device can also be used on one that does not support color. Grayscale values are encoded using integer values 0 to 255 inclusive, where 0 is the darkest (black) and 255 the brightest (white). A MIDlet that can work directly with grayscale values can use the setGrayScale() method instead of setColor() to set the Graphics color attribute.

There are several Graphics methods that retrieve the value of the color attribute:

```
public int getColor()
public int getRedComponent()
public int getGreenComponent()
public int getBlueComponent()
public int getGrayScale()
```

The getColor() method returns the color attribute in the same integer encoding as that used by setColor(). The getRedComponent(), getGreenComponent(), and getBlueComponent() methods return the individual red, green, and blue parts of the color. The getGrayScale() method returns a grayscale value in the range 0–255 that approximates the brightness of the current color.

If the color attribute was actually set using setGrayScale(), getGrayScale() returns the actual grayscale value, and the other four methods return RGB values for a device-dependent color that approximates the brightness of the supplied gray. In the MIDP reference implementation, the mapping from grayscale to the returned color is a simple one: the red, green, and blue components are all set to the grayscale value. That is to say, the following code prints "127" for all three color components:

```
g.setGrayScale(127);
System.out.println("Red = " + g.getRedComponent() + ", green = " + g.
getGreenComponent() + ", blue = " + g.getBlueComponent());
```

The same might not be true for other implementations.

Drawing Lines and Arcs

The Graphics class methods that let you draw straight lines, rectangles, and arcs are very similar to those available in J2SE. There are, of course, none of the advanced features provided by Java 2D. Even some of the more basic features, such as convenience methods that let you draw polygons and polylines, are missing, although some of them can easily be simulated.

The drawing primitives work by determining the set of pixels that will be affected and setting each of them to the value of the current color attribute as set by setColor() or setGrayScale(). Because there is no support for transparency and color blending, no account is taken of the initial state of an affected pixel.

Perhaps surprisingly, no provision is made for an "exclusive-or" drawing mode, in which the new pixel value is combined with the existing one using a bitwise exclusive-or operation. This is not an issue, in practice, because MIDlets have access to a Graphics object only in the paint() method, when everything must be redrawn, whether it has moved or not. By contrast, it is possible in J2SE to get a Graphics object at any time, and, therefore, parts of the screen can be updated directly, without having to wait for the paint() method to be called.

Lines and Rectangles

The simplest shape you can draw on a Canvas is a straight line:

```
public void drawLine(int x1, int y1, int x2, int y2)
```

This method draws a line between the two pixels at (x1, y1) and (x2, y2). Usually, both these points would be within the bounds of the Canvas, but this is not a requirement. It is possible to draw a line in which one or both of the points are off the Canvas, in which case only the part of the line that crosses the Canvas is actually rendered.

The boundaries of the line include both the given endpoints. For example, the following method call actually affects 4 pixels:

```
g.drawLine(0, 0, 3, 0);
```

The pixels at both (0, 0) and (3, 0) are filled, as well as those in between, as shown in Figure 5-4.

Low-Level UI API

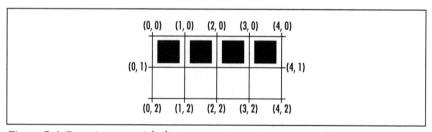

Figure 5-4: Drawing a straight line

The drawLine() method plots a single point if the start and end points are the same.

The actual pixels that are affected by the drawLine() operation depend on the Graphics stroke style. This attribute is set using the setStrokeStyle() method, which requires a single parameter that takes one of the following values:

Graphics.SOLID
> Draws a solid line in which all affected pixels are set to the current Graphics color.

Graphics.DOTTED

Draws a line in which only a subset of the pixels that would be set in `Graphics.SOLID` mode are affected.

You can see the difference between these two modes by building and running the `Chapter5` project from this book's source code examples. Launch the MIDlet called `GraphicMIDlet`, then select "Lines" from the examples list that appears. The result of running this example on the default color phone is shown in Figure 5-5.

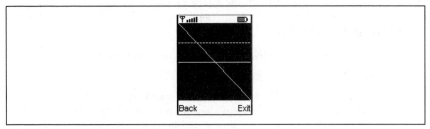

Figure 5-5: Drawing straight lines on a Canvas

The code that produced the lines in Figure 5-5 looks like this:

```
public void paint(Graphics g) {
    int width = getWidth();
    int height = getHeight();

    // Fill the background using black
    g.setColor(0);
    g.fillRect(0, 0, width, height);

    // White horizontal line
    g.setColor(0xFFFFFF);
    g.drawLine(0, height/2, width - 1, height/2);

    // Yellow dotted horizontal line
    g.setStrokeStyle(Graphics.DOTTED);
    g.setColor(0xFFFF00);
    g.drawLine(0, height/4, width - 1, height/4);

    // Solid diagonal line in brightest gray
    g.setGrayScale(255);
    g.setStrokeStyle(Graphics.SOLID);
    g.drawLine(0, 0, width - 1, height - 1);
}
```

You'll notice that the `Canvas` used here has a black background, which is due to the `fillRect()` call that is made at the start of the `paint()` method, after setting the current color to black. Because `Canvas` does not have any painting logic of its own, the MIDlet itself is responsible for filling its background. If this is not done, the `Canvas` will be transparent, which might be useful in some cases. In this case, failing to fill the background would result in the drawing operations being overlaid on top of the list from which the Lines example was selected. (The `fillRect()` method will be described shortly.)

Each invocation of drawLine() is preceded by calls to setColor() to set the appropriate color and setStrokeStyle() to select a solid or dotted line. It is not always necessary to call these methods repeatedly, because the value of a Graphics attribute is preserved over graphics operations (but not between invocations of the paint() method itself). In the case of the last line, which extends from the top left side of the canvas to the bottom right, the drawing color is set using the setGrayScale() method instead of setColor(). Passing the value 255 results in the selection of the brightest gray that the display can support, which is very likely to be white.

Drawing a rectangle is just as easy as drawing a straight line:

```
public void drawRect(int x, int y, int width, int height)
```

The point (x, y) represents the top left corner of the rectangle, and the width and height arguments obviously determine its width and height, respectively. As with straight lines, the rectangle outline touches both the start and end pixels on all sides, so that the top of the rectangle consists of a line drawn from the point (x, y) to the point (x + width − 1, y) inclusive. Whether some or all of the pixels on the rectangle boundary are set depends on whether the stroke style is SOLID or DOTTED, as shown on the left of Figure 5-6.

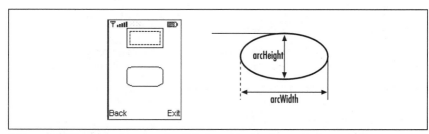

Figure 5-6: Drawing dotted and solid rectangles and rounded rectangles.

This screenshot at the left of Figure 5-6 is the result of selecting the Rectangles item from the GraphicsMIDlet, the code for which follows:

```
public void paint(Graphics g) {
    int width = getWidth();
    int height = getHeight();

    // Create a white background
    g.setColor(0xffffff);
    g.fillRect(0, 0, width, height);

    // Draw a solid rectangle
    g.setColor(0);
    g.drawRect(width/4, 0, width/2, height/4);

    // Draw a dotted rectangle inside the solid rectangle.
    g.setStrokeStyle(Graphics.DOTTED);
    g.drawRect(width/4 + 4, 4, width/2 - 8, height/4 - 8);

    // Draw a rounded rectangle
```

```
g.setStrokeStyle(Graphics.SOLID);
g.drawRoundRect(width/4, height/2, width/2, height/4, 16, 8);
}
```

Note that all rectangles are drawn with their sides parallel to those of the Canvas. The MIDP Graphics class does not provide any rotation operations that could be used to create a rectangle with its sides at an arbitrary angle to the drawing axes.

The rectangles at the top of Figure 5-6 both have sharp corners, but you can also draw a rectangle with rounded corners, as shown at the bottom of the figure. To achieve this effect, use the drawRoundRect() method, which requires two extra parameters in addition to those required to describe the rectangle itself:

```
public void drawRoundRect(int x, int y, int width, int height,
    int arcWidth, int arcHeight)
```

To understand how these extra parameters work, imagine that the rounded edges form part of an ellipse placed at the corners of the rectangle, as shown in the diagram on the right of Figure 5-6. The horizontal diameter of this ellipse is given by the arcWidth parameter and the vertical diameter by arcHeight. The rounded rectangle at the bottom of the screenshot was drawn by the following line of code:

```
g.drawRoundRect(width/4, height/2, width/2, height/4, 16, 8);
```

which results in a corner that is wider than it is tall. To get a circular corner, the arcWidth and arcHeight values should be equal.

As well as rectangular outlines, you can also draw rectangles and rounded rectangles that are filled with a solid color, using the following methods:

```
public void fillRect(int x, int y, int width, int height)
public void fillRoundRect(int x, int y, int width, int height,
    int arcWidth, int arcHeight)
```

The parameters required are the same as those for the corresponding draw methods. However, the boundaries of a drawn rectangle and a filled rectangle are not exactly the same, as shown in Figure 5-7.

The rectangle at the top of Figure 5-7 was drawn using this code:

```
g.drawRect(0, 0, 4, 2)
```

Because an outline touches the pixels at each end, this rectangle includes the points (0, 0), (4, 0), (0, 2), and (4, 2). By contrast, a filled rectangle created using the same arguments uses the width and height values to describe the exact area to be filled: 4 pixels wide and 2 pixels down, as shown at the bottom in Figure 5-7. You can see that a drawn rectangle occupies one more pixel each to the right and at the bottom than a filled rectangle.

You can see this for yourself by selecting the RectangleFills example from GraphicsMIDlet. This creates a rectangle drawn with a dotted outline and a filled rectangle, using identical arguments for each. Magnified versions of the top left and bottom right corners of these rectangles are shown in Figure 5-8. The figure clearly shows that the color fill does not reach the right side or the bottom of the drawn rectangle, but it does cover the top and left of it.

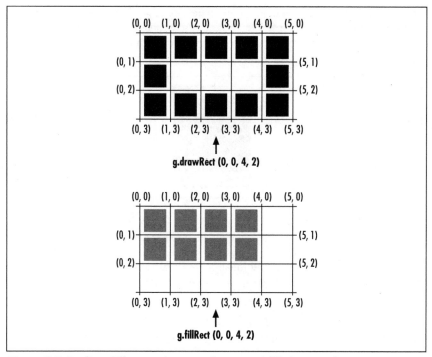

Figure 5-7: Outline differences between drawn and filled rectangles

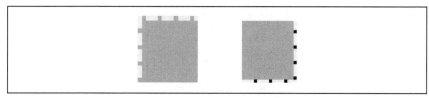

Figure 5-8: Drawn and filled rectangles

Arcs

Elliptical or circular arcs, including complete circles and ellipses, can be drawn either in outline or filled using the following methods:

```
public void drawArc(int x, int y, int width, int height, int startAngle,
    int arcAngle)
public void fillArc(int x, int y, int width, int height, int startAngle,
    int arcAngle)
```

The overall shape of the arc is determined by its bounding rectangle, specified by the x, y, width, and height arguments; if the width and height values are the same, the arc is a circle or part of a circle. The portion of the ellipse or circle to be drawn is controlled by the startAngle and arcAngle arguments, both of which are measured in degrees. The startAngle argument specifies where the arc begins; it is measured relative to the the three o'clock position on the bounding rectangle. The angle through which the arc turns from its starting position is given by the `arcAngle` argument. For both parameters, a positive value indicates a clockwise turn; a negative value indicates a counterclockwise turn. The Arcs example in the `GraphicsMIDlet` draws three arcs with different start and turning angles, as shown in Figures 5-9 and 5-10.

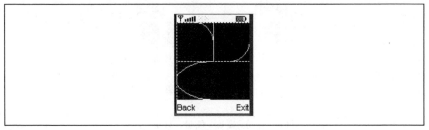

Figure 5-9: Drawing arcs

The arc in the top left corner is a counterclockwise rotation of 90° from the default starting point at the three o'clock position on the bounding box. For the sake of clarity, the bounding boxes for all the arcs are drawn also so that you can see how the arcs are positioned within them. The code that creates this arc looks like this:

```
g.drawArc(0, 0, width/2, height/2, 0, 90);
```

Since the width and height of the bounding box are equal, this arc is part of a circle. The second arc is similar, but it has a negative `arcAngle` so that it turns through 90° in a clockwise direction:

```
g.drawArc(width/2, 0, width/2, height/2, 0, -90);
```

The line drawing on the top left of Figure 5-10 shows how this arc is drawn.

Finally, the larger arc at the bottom of Figure 5-9 starts 90° clockwise from the 3 o'clock position (so that `startAngle` is –90) and sweeps through a complete clockwise half-turn:

```
g.drawArc(0, height/2, width, height/2, -90, -180)
```

In this case, the bounding box is twice as wide as it is high, so this is an elliptical arc. The angles used in this example are shown at the bottom of Figure 5-10.

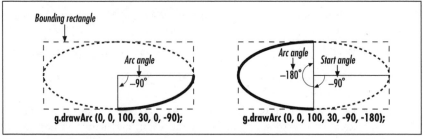

Figure 5-10: Drawing arcs

A filled arc is described in the same way as an arc outline. The pie-shaped region extending from the center of the arc to the start and end points is filled with the current `Graphics` color. Figure 5-11 shows the result of selecting the FilledArcs example from the `GraphicsMIDlet`, which fills the same arcs as those drawn in the previous example.

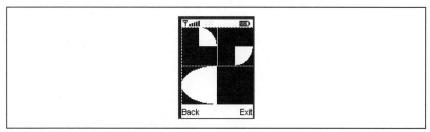

Figure 5-11: Filled arcs

Translating the Graphics Origin

The origin of the `Graphics` object that you get in the `paint()` method is initially placed at the top left of the `Canvas`. However, you can move it to any location you choose using the `translate()` method:

```
public void translate(int x, int y)
```

This method relocates the origin to the point (**x**, **y**) as measured in the coordinates that apply before this call is made. If the `paint()` method begins with the following statements:

```
g.drawLine(0, 0, 20, 0);
g.translate(10, 10);
g.drawLine(0, 0, 20, 0);
```

a line is first drawn along the top of the `Canvas` from (0, 0) to (20, 0), the origin is shifted so that (0, 0) is at the point (10, 10) relative to the top left corner of the Canvas, and finally another line is drawn. This line stretches from (0, 0) to (20, 0) in the *new* coordinate system, which is the same as (10, 10) to (30, 10) relative to the the `Canvas` itself. Figure 5-12 illustrates the effect of moving the origin.

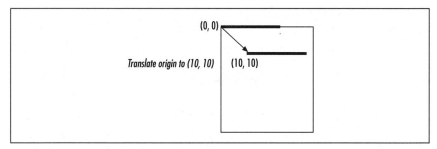

Figure 5-12: Translating the Graphics origin

Once you have moved the origin, the effect of another `translate()` call is cumulative with respect to the first. This means that, for example, the following code results in the origin being moved to (10, 10) and then back to its initial location:

```
g.translate(10, 10);
g.translater(-10, -10);
```

The following code moves to the origin to (15, 15) relative to the top left-hand corner of the Canvas:

```
g.translate(10, 10);
g.translate(5, 5);
```

The origin can be moved outside the bounds of the Canvas, if necessary. For example:

```
g.translate(-10, -10);
g.drawLine(10, 10, 30, 10);
```

The previous code moves the origin to a point that is above and to the left of the corner of the Canvas and then draws the same straight line along the top of the Canvas as the original example in this section.

Translating the origin is commonly used for the following reasons:

- To give the appearance of scrolling the screen over an image that is too large to be displayed all at once. To implement scrolling, you catch key presses or pointer actions, respond by moving the origin in the paint() method in the opposite direction from the motion requested by the user, and then paint the Canvas again. Moving the origin causes everything on the Canvas to be drawn in a different location.

- As a way to use the same code to draw a shape in different locations on the Canvas. This allows you to have a method that draws a complex shape using coordinates based at (0, 0) and then call it to draw one copy at (10, 10) and another copy at (50, 40). You do this by translating the origin first to (10, 10) and then by a further amount of (40, 30):

```
g.translate(10, 10);
drawMyShape(g);        // Draw at (10, 10)
g.translate(40, 30);
drawMyShape(g);        // Draw at (50, 40)
```

You can get the position of the origin relative to the Canvas using the following methods:

```
public int getTranslateX()
public int getTranslateY()
```

These methods let you move the origin to a specific location without needing to keep track of where it is. For example, no matter where the origin has been translated to, the following operation always moves it back to the top left corner of the Canvas:

```
g.translate(-g.getTranslateX(), -g.getTranslateY());
```

Similarly, this operation moves it to absolute coordinates (x, y) relative to the Canvas:

```
g.translate(x-g.getTranslateX(), y-g.getTranslateY());
```

A Simple Animation MIDlet

So far, all the Canvas examples have involved drawing shapes onto the screen when the platform calls the paint() method. If the content of the Canvas is static, it is sufficient to draw it only when the platform detects that the screen content has been partly or completely overwritten by an `Alert`, or when a different MIDlet screen is shown and then removed. If you want to display dynamic content, however, you can't wait for the platform to call `paint()`, because you need to repaint the `Canvas` whenever the dynamic content changes.

For example, suppose you wanted to create a simple animation that involves moving small blocks around the screen. In order to do this, you might create a class to represent each block by recording its x and y coordinates and its speeds along the x and y axes:

```
class Block {
    int x;              // X position
    int y;              // Y position
    int xSpeed;         // Speed in the X direction
    int ySpeed;         // Speed in the Y direction
}
```

The `Canvas` `paint()` method then fills its background with an appropriate color and loops over the set of blocks, drawing a filled rectangle for each, using its current coordinates to determine the location of its corresponding rectangle. Example 5-2 shows how you might implement this for a set of square blocks represented by an array of `Block` objects in an array called `blocks`.

Example 5-2: Painting Blocks onto a Canvas

```
protected void paint(Graphics g) {
    // Paint with the background color
    g.setColor(background);
    g.fillRect(0, 0, width, height);

    // Draw all of the blocks
    g.setColor(foreground);
    synchronized (this) {
        for (int i = 0, count = blocks.length; i < count; i++) {
            g.fillRect(blocks[i].x, blocks[i].y, SIZE, SIZE);
        }
    }
}
```

Each time this method is called, it paints all the blocks at their current locations. In order to create movement, you need to start a timer that periodically calls a method that updates the coordinates of each block and then causes the `Canvas` to be painted again. The problem with this is that you cannot call the `Canvas` `paint()` method directly, because there is no way to get a `Graphics` object that would allow you to draw on the screen. Fortunately, the `Canvas` class provides a method that you can call at any time to request a repaint operation:

```
public final void repaint()
```

Invoking this method does *not* result in an immediate call to `paint()`. Instead, the platform arranges for `paint()` to be invoked sometime in the near future. Using this method, you can arrange for each block to be moved to its new location and redrawn using code like that shown in Example 5-3.

Example 5-3: Moving and Redrawing Blocks

```
public synchronized void moveAllBlocks() {
    // Update the positions and speeds
    // of all of the blocks
    for (int i = 0, count = blocks.length; i < count; i++) {
        blocks[i].move();

        // Request a repaint of the screen
        repaint();
    }
}
```

This code updates the x and y coordinates of each `Block` by calling its `move()` method (which we don't show here because it is of little interest); it then invokes the `Canvas repaint()` method. Even though this code involves an invocation of `repaint()` for each block, this does not result in the same number of `paint()` calls, because the platform merges multiple `repaint()` requests into a single call to `paint()` to mimimize the amount of drawing required. The code shown above is scheduled as a `TimerTask`, which, as described in Chapter 3, is executed in a thread associated with a `Timer`. Painting, on the other hand, is performed in a system thread that also handles keyboard and pointer input events; these are discussed later in this chapter. Because both the `moveAllBlocks()` and `paint()` methods need to access the `Block` objects that hold the current locations of the blocks to be drawn, they are both synchronized to ensure thread safety.

You can see how this code works in practice by selecting the `AnimationMIDlet` from the `Chapter5` project in the Wireless Toolkit. When this MIDlet starts, it displays two `Gauges` that let you select the number of frame updates per second (from 1 to 10) and the number of blocks to display (in the range 1 to 4), as shown on the left side of Figure 5-13. Once you have set the parameters, select the Run command to start the animation.

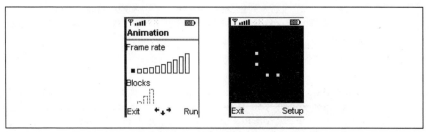

Figure 5-13: A MIDlet that performs simple animation

The Canvas showNotify() and hideNotify() Methods

The animation in this example is driven by a timer. When should this timer be started and stopped? The simplest possible approach is to start it when the `startApp()` method is called for the first time and stop it in `destroyApp()`. This might be appropriate if the `Canvas` were always visible, but that is not the case here, because the `Canvas` has a Setup command that allows the user to switch back to the configuration screen to change the frame update rate or the number of blocks to be drawn. While the configuration screen is displayed, it would be a waste of time to continue to move the blocks on the Canvas because it is not visible. The most efficient approach in cases like this is to start the timer when the Canvas becomes visible and stop it when it is hidden. You can easily implement this policy by overriding the following Canvas methods:

```
protected void showNotify()
protected void hideNotify()
```

The platform makes the following guarantees with respect to these methods:

- The showNotify() method is called just before the Canvas is made visible. Before this method is called, no invocations of paint() occur.

- The hideNotify() method is called after the Canvas has been removed from the screen. The paint() method is not called between a call to hideNotify() and the next invocation of showNotify().

As an example of how these methods are typically used, Example 5-4 shows the code that controls the animation in this example. Note that showNotify() starts the Timer for the TimerTask that moves the blocks, and hideNotify() stops it, so no time is wasted moving the blocks when the Canvas is not visible. Since the Canvas implementations of showNotify() and hideNotify() are empty, there is no need to include calls to super.showNotify() and super.hideNotify() when overriding them.

Example 5-4: Using showNotify() and hideNotify() to Control Animation

```
// Notification that the canvas has been made visible
protected void showNotify() {
    // Start the frame timer running
    startFrameTimer();
}

// Notification that the canvas is no longer visible
protected void hideNotify() {
    // Stop the frame timer
    stopFrameTimer();
}

// Starts the frame redraw timer
private void startFrameTimer() {
    timer = new Timer();

    updateTask = new TimerTask() {
        public void run() {
            moveAllBlocks();
        }
    };
    long interval = 1000/frameRate;
    timer.schedule(updateTask, interval, interval);
}

// Stops the frame redraw timer
private void stopFrameTimer() {
```

```
    timer.cancel();
}
```

The Graphics Clip

Although the previous animation example works, it is rather inefficient. The main problem lies with the way the `paint()` method interacts with the `moveAllBlocks()` method. When the frame timer expires, `moveAllBlocks()` updates the coordinates of all the blocks and then arranges for `paint()` to be called, which then redraws the whole screen. Redrawing the entire screen is, of course, highly inefficient, because most of it has not changed. In fact, when a block moves, all that you really need to do is use the background color to paint the area that it used to occupy and then redraw the block in its new location. Because you can't get hold of a `Graphics` object to do this directly within `moveAllBlocks()`, you need some way to communicate to the `paint()` method that it doesn't need to repaint everything. Fortunately, there is a simple way to do this that requires small modifications to both `moveAllBlocks()` and the `paint()` method.

In Example 5-3, `moveAllBlocks()` signals that a repaint is required by calling the `Canvas` `repaint()` method. The variant of `repaint()` that it uses signals to `paint()` that the whole screen needs to be redrawn, but there is a second version that can be used to pass more information:

```
    public void repaint(int x, int y, int width, int height)
```

This method defines a rectangle that needs to be repainted, instead of the whole screen. Using this method, `moveAllBlocks()` can be rewritten as shown in Example 5-5 to indicate that only the old and new positions of each block need to be redrawn.

Example 5-5: Using repaint( ) to Restrict the Areas to be Redrawn

```
public synchronized void moveAllBlocks() {
    // Update the positions and speeds of all of the blocks and repaint
    // only the part of the screen that they occupy
    for (int i = 0, count = blocks.length; i < count; i++) {
        // Request a repaint of the current location
        Block block = blocks[i];
        repaint(block.x, block.y, SIZE, SIZE);

        blocks[i].move();

        // Request a repaint of the new location
        repaint(block.x, block.y, SIZE, SIZE);
    }
}
```

Notice that `repaint()` is called once before the block moves, to arrange for the original location to be redrawn, and once afterwards.

The next step is to change the paint() method to take into account the information supplied to repaint(). But paint() doesn't have any parameters that describe the area to be repainted, so how is this information passed to it? The answer to this question is an attribute of the Graphics object called the *clip*. In MIDP, the clip is a rectangular subset of the drawing surface (the Canvas in this case), outside of which drawing operations are ignored.*

The effect of the clip can be seen in Figure 5-14, which shows a Canvas 40 pixels wide and 60 pixels tall, with a clip indicated by the dotted rectangle covering a subset of its surface.

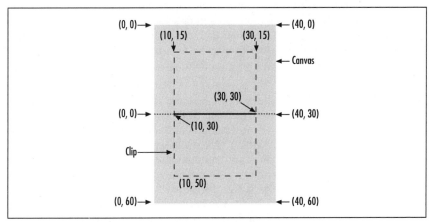

Figure 5-14: The Graphics clip

If the following line of code were to be executed in the paint() method:

```
g.drawLine(0, 30, 40, 30);
```

only the part of the line that lies within the clip is actually drawn—that is, the segment from (10, 30) to (30, 30). The parts of the line from (0, 30) to (10, 30) and from (30, 30) to (40, 30), which are dotted in Figure 5-14, are not drawn at all.

When repaint() is called with no arguments, or when the platform first displays a Canvas, the Graphics clip is set to cover the entire surface of the Canvas. However, when the other repaint() method is called, the clip is set according to its arguments. To set the clip shown in Figure 5-14, for example, the following call is made:

```
repaint(10, 15, 20, 35);
```

Now suppose that the moveAllBlocks() method moves a single square block of size 4 pixels from (0, 0) to (4, 4). In performing this operation, it executes the following pair of repaint() calls:

```
repaint(0, 0, 4, 4);      // Repaint the old location of the block
repaint(4, 4, 4, 4);      // Repaint the new location of the block
```

---

* In J2SE, the clip doesn't have to be rectangular, but that is a Java 2D feature that is not supported by MIDP.

When several repaint() calls are made, the clip is set to the smallest rectangle that covers all the areas to be redrawn. In this case, the clip covers the area from (0, 0) to (8, 8). So what effect does this have on the paint() method? Recall from Example 5-2 that the first operation performed by the paint() method is to fill the entire surface of the Canvas with its background color:

```
g.setColor(background);
g.fillRect(0, 0, width, height);
```

In the case of a device with a screen measuring 96 pixels by 100 pixels (i.e., the default color phone), this involves setting the color of 9,600 individual pixels. However, when the repaint() method sets a clipping rectangle that covers only the area occupied by the block in its old and new locations, the same fillRect() call operates only within the clip—that is, it fills only the rectangle from (0, 0) to (8, 8), a total of 64 pixels—even though its arguments still specify that all 9600 pixels should be painted. Setting the clip, then, gives a benefit even if no changes are made to the paint() method.

You can sometimes improve matters even more by taking account of the clip when implementing the paint() method. If, for example, your Canvas contains an image or a sequence of drawing operations that takes a relatively long time to draw, you don't need to do anything to keep them from being drawn when the clip is set to exclude them: all Graphics operations automatically restrict themselves to the area covered by the clip. However, making this check costs a small amount of time. If you can inspect the clip yourself and determine that an operation does not need to be performed, you may improve the performance of your MIDlet. You can get the bounds of the clip using the following methods:

```
public int getClipX()
public int getClipY()
public int getClipWidth()
public int getClipHeight()
```

Using this information, you may be able to save a small amount of time in the paint() method by explicitly restricting the fillRect() operation to the clip, as follows:

```
// Get the clipping rectangle
int clipX = g.getClipX();
int clipY = g.getClipY();
int clipWidth = g.getClipWidth();
int clipHeight = g.getClipHeight();

// Paint with the background color - only
// the area within the clipping rectangle
g.setColor(background);
g.fillRect(clipX, clipY, clipWidth, clipHeight);
```

As a general rule, when implementing a Canvas paint() method, consider taking account of the clip to skip time-consuming operations or those that involve nontrivial calculations.

Rendering Text

The Graphics class has four methods that you can use to draw text on a Canvas:

public void drawChar(char c, int x, int y, int anchor)
> Renders the single character given as the first argument. The position of the character is determined by the x, y, and anchor arguments, as described below.

public void drawChars(char[] chars, int offset, int length,
int x, int y, int anchor)
> Draws characters chars[offset] through chars[offset + length - 1] using the positioning information given by the last three arguments.

public void drawString(String str, int x, int y, int anchor)
> Renders the string str at the given location. This is the method most commonly used to draw text.

public void drawSubstring(String str, int offset, int length,
int x, int y, int anchor)
> Draws the part of the string given by the first argument that occupies the character positions offset to (offset + length - 1).

The text is drawn in the color set by the last setColor() or setGrayScale() call. Its position and style are affected by the font property of the Graphics object and the location parameters passed to the drawing method. These parameters are described in the following sections.

Fonts

The font determines the shape and size of the text it is used to render. The font attribute can be set or read using the following Graphics methods:

```
public void setFont(Font font)
public Font getFont()
```

In contrast to desktop systems, MIDP devices generally support only a very limited set of fonts, one of which is considered to be the system default font. The default font is installed automatically in the Graphics object passed to the paint() method. You can also obtain a reference to it using the following static method of the Font class:

```
public static Font getDefaultFont()
```

A font has three independent attributes that determine the appearance of rendered text:

Face
> The font face describes the overall appearance of the characters it renders. The MIDP specification defines three different font faces, each with an associated constant—defined by the Font class—that can be used to select it:

Font.FACE_MONOSPACE
> A constant-width font.

Font.FACE_PROPORTIONAL
> A proportional font.

Font.FACE_SYSTEM

The "system" font face. The MIDP specification does not define what is meant by the system font. In the case of the default color phone emulator in the Wireless Toolkit, it is the same as the proportional font.

Style

The style property determines whether text is rendered in bold, italics, or underlined. The Font class defines four values to specify the font style:

```
Font.STYLE_PLAIN
Font.STYLE_BOLD
Font.STYLE_ITALIC
Font.STYLE_UNDERLINE
```

Styles may be combined using the logical OR operator so that, for example, STYLE_BOLD | STYLE_ITALIC represents a bold italic font, and STYLE_UNDERLINED gives underlined plain text. Combining STYLE_PLAIN with any of the other style constants is allowed but has no effect, because STYLE_PLAIN has the value 0.

Size

The size argument can have one of the following values:

```
SIZE_SMALL
SIZE_MEDIUM
SIZE_LARGE
```

Unlike J2SE, MIDP does not allow a MIDlet to request a particular font size; instead, it restricts it to this narrow set of unspecific values that the platform can interpret as it chooses. This argument is not a bitmask, so combining size values is not allowed.

Font objects can be obtained by calling the following static Font method:

```
public static Font getFont(int face, int style, int size)
```

This method returns a font chosen by the platform based on the arguments supplied. The device may not have fonts that satisfy all possible combinations of these arguments, however, so the platform is permitted to substitute one that does not have all the required characteristics when it cannot provide an exact match.

Since Fonts can be obtained only from the getFont() or getDefaultFont() methods and cannot be directly instantiated, the platform can minimize the number of active Font objects (and therefore reduce memory usage and garbage collection) by returning a single instance in response to getFont() calls that specify identical attributes. As a consequence, it is possible to determine whether two fonts are the same by comparing references instead of using the equals() operator.*

Fonts have several characteristic measurements, shown in Figure 5-15, that are affected by the face, style, and size attributes. MIDP provides methods that return these measurements in the Font class, rather than having separate classes such as the J2SE FontMetrics and LineMetrics classes.

---

* Note, however, that fonts that are considered equal need not have been created with the same set of attributes.

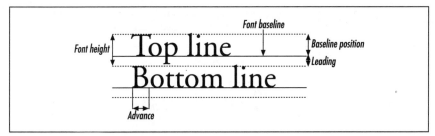

Figure 5-15: Font measurements

The *font height* is the distance that should be left between between the top of one line of text and the top of the line immediately below it to ensure no vertical overlap and satisfactory readability. The font height includes a certain amount of space, known as *leading* (pronounced *ledding*), that appears below the text itself. There is no way to get the leading value, but the font height itself can be obtained by calling the following method:

```
public int getHeight();
```

The `getBaselinePosition()` method returns the distance from the top pixel line of characters from this `Font` to the *baseline*. As shown in Figure 5-15, the baseline is the horizontal line along which text characters are placed. If you were writing longhand on a ruled page, the ruled lines would coincide with the baseline.

The following methods let you measure the *advance* (i.e., the width) of one or more text characters as rendered by a font:

```
public int charWidth(char c)
public int charsWidth(char[] c, int offset, int length)
public int stringWidth(String str)
public int substringWidth(String str, int offset, int length)
```

In a proportional font, characters have varying widths. The `charWidth()` method returns the width of the single character passed as its argument, while the other three return the total width of a string or a character array. Note that the width of a set of characters is not necessarily the same as the sum of the widths of its individual characters, because the platform may perform kerning (i.e., placing some characters closer together than their individual widths). Also, in some languages (such as Arabic), a single font character may be used to represent several characters from the string being rendered. The widths returned by all these methods include the intercharacter spacing required for readability, which appears on the right side of each character.

Text Positioning

In J2SE, you place text by supplying the coordinates of the point on the baseline at which you want rendering to start. MIDP has a more flexible scheme that lets you specify the location of one of several different anchor points on the bounding box of the text instead of restricting you to using the position of the baseline. Each text drawing method has an `anchor` argument that is constructed by combining a vertical position constant with a horizontal position constant to describe the point whose coordinates are given by the x and y method arguments. Figure 5-16 shows the vertical and horizontal text positioning values that can be used when rendering text. These values are constants defined by the Graphics class.

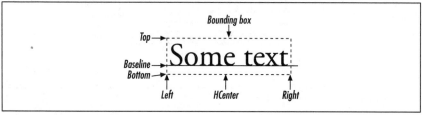

Figure 5-16: Text anchor points

The following line of code draws the string "Hello, world" with the top left corner of its bounding box at coordinates (0, 0), in the top left corner of the Canvas:

```
g.drawString("Hello, world", 0, 0, Graphics.TOP | Graphics.LEFT);
```

To right-justify the same string at the top of the Canvas, you instead write:

```
g.drawString("Hello, world", canvas.getWidth(), 0,
    Graphics.TOP | Graphics.RIGHT);
```

Because the anchor argument allows you to specify which part of the bounding box the coordinates refer to, you don't need to calculate for yourself how wide the text is in order to right-justify it, as would be necessary in J2SE. The same feature also makes it easy to center text horizontally on the screen. The following line of code achieves this by placing the center point of the top of the bounding box halfway across the top line of the Canvas:

```
g.drawString("Hello, world", canvas.getWidth()/2, 0,
    Graphics.TOP | Graphics.HCENTER);
```

 Although the Graphics class defines a constant called VCENTER, you cannot use it to vertically center text, because this operation is not supported by any of the text drawing methods. The VCENTER constraint can, however, be used when positioning an Image, as you'll see later in this chapter.

Bear in mind when positioning text that the anchor argument identifies a point on the bounding box, and the x and y coordinates specify where that point should be placed on the Canvas.* If you insist on using J2SE conventions, you could write code like the following:

```
g.drawString("Hello, world", 0, font.getBaselinePosition(),
    Graphics.BASELINE | Graphics.LEFT);
```

---

* The x and y coordinates are, of course, relative to the origin of the Graphics object. For the sake of brevity, we are equating the origin with the top left corner of a Canvas, but this need not be the case, because the Graphics origin could have been moved by calling the translate() method. As you'll see later in this chapter, a Graphics object can also be used to draw text onto a mutable Image, using the same concept of anchor points

This has the same effect as:

```
g.drawString("Hello, world", 0, 0, Graphics.TOP | Graphics.LEFT);
```

You can see more examples of text positioning by running the `GraphicsMIDlet` that we used earlier in this chapter and selecting Text from the example list. Running this example on the default color phone and the PalmOS platform produces the results shown in Figure 5-17.

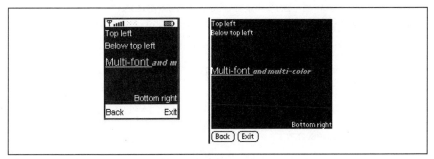

Figure 5-17: Text drawing and positioning

The two lines of text at the top left of the screen were drawn as follows:

```
// Top left of canvas
g.setColor(0xffffff);
g.drawString("Top left", 0, 0, Graphics.TOP | Graphics.LEFT);

// Draw another string one line below
Font font = g.getFont();
g.drawString("Below top left", 0, font.getHeight(),
    Graphics.TOP | Graphics.LEFT);
```

The first string is placed at the top left corner of the `Canvas` by placing the top left corner (`Graphics.TOP | Graphics.LEFT`) of its bounding box at coordinates (0, 0). The second line of text is intended to be drawn immediately below it. To do this, you use the same anchor point and x coordinate, but you increase the y coordinate by the height of the font. Refer to Figure 5-15 if necessary to see why this is the correct thing to do.

The text at the bottom right is positioned as follows:

```
// Bottom right of canvas
g.drawString("Bottom right", width, height, Graphics.BOTTOM |
    Graphics.RIGHT);
```

`width` and `height` are, respectively, the width and height of the `Canvas` in pixels. The remainder of this example, which produces the text in the middle of the `Canvas`, illustrates how to mix different fonts and colors in the same text line. Since each drawing operation uses the current font and color attributes of the `Graphics` object, you need to perform a separate operation for each font and color change. The first part of the string is drawn by the following code:

```
String str = "Multi-font ";
font = Font.getFont(Font.FACE_PROPORTIONAL, Font.STYLE_UNDERLINED,
```

```
                 Font.SIZE_LARGE);
    g.setFont(font);
    g.drawString(str, 0, height/2, Graphics.LEFT | Graphics.BASELINE);
```

This code selects a large proportional font with underlining enabled and draws the text with its baseline at the middle point of the Canvas, starting on its left side. To draw the rest of the text, you need to use the same anchor constraint, but you have to adjust the x coordinate by the amount of horizontal space taken up by the first string, which you can get using the Font stringWidth() method. Let's select a different font (bold and italic with no underlines) and change the drawing color:

```
    int x = font.stringWidth(str);
    g.setColor(0x00ff00);
    g.setFont(Font.getFont(Font.FACE_PROPORTIONAL, Font.STYLE_BOLD |
        Font.STYLE_ITALIC,

    Font.SIZE_MEDIUM));
    g.drawString("and multi-color", x, height/2, Graphics.LEFT |
        Graphics.BASELINE);
```

As you can see in Figure 5-17, if the text being rendered is too wide to fit on the screen, it is simply clipped. The low-level API does not provide automatic line wrapping; if you need this capability, you have to provide it for yourself.

Images

You have already seen that some of the components provided by the high-level user interface API allow you to display images. You can create a suitable Image object by loading it from a resource in a MIDlet suite's JAR file encoded in PNG format. This section looks at other ways to create Image objects and discuss how you can use Images with the low-level API.

Creating Images

The Image class has four static methods that can be used to create an Image:

```
    public static Image createImage(String name);
    public static Image createImage(byte[] data, int offset, int length);
    public static Image createImage(int width, int height);
    public static Image createImage(Image source);
```

The first and second methods build an Image from data stored either in a named resource within the MIDlet's JAR file (as described in "ImageItems" in Chapter 4) or as part of a byte array in memory. The image data must be in an encoding format that is both self-identifying (typically because it begins with a well-known sequence of bytes, such as "GIF" or "PNG") and supported by the platform. At the present time, the only encoding format that MIDP devices are required to support is Portable Network Graphics (PNG), which is a public domain replacement for the popular GIF format.

The first of these methods is normally used to load images that are included as part of the MIDlet installed on the device. The second is useful for creating an Image from data read into a byte array from the network or data stored in and retrieved from the device's permanent storage.* In both cases, the image created is immutable, that is, you cannot make any changes to it. Immutable images are required by high-level API components such as `ImageItem`, since they don't need to be concerned about having to redraw the image on the screen in the event of changes being made.

The third method creates a mutable image of the given width and height, in which every pixel is initialized to white. This method is used to create a buffer that you can use to create an image programmatically, using the same `Graphics` drawing methods that you would use to draw on a `Canvas`. Having created a mutable image in this way, you can use the fourth method to create an immutable copy of it so that it can be used in connection with the high-level API.

Drawing Images

Once you have an image (either mutable or immutable), you can draw it onto a `Canvas` in its `paint()` method using the following `Graphics` method:

```
public void drawImage(Image image, int x, int y, int anchor);
```

The `x`, `y`, and `anchor` arguments are used in the same way here as they are when drawing text: the `anchor` argument defines an anchor point on the bounding box of the image, and the `x` and `y` arguments specify the location relative to the origin of the `Graphics` object at which the anchor point should be placed. The legal values for the `anchor` argument are the same as those described earlier for text, except that `BASELINE` cannot be used (since images do not have the concept of a baseline), but `VCENTER` (which is not valid for text) can be used instead, to vertically center the image relative to the given location. If an image is too wide or too tall to fit on the screen when drawn at the specified location, it is clipped at boundaries of the `Canvas`. Images are never scaled to fit them into a smaller space, and there is no API that would allow a MIDlet to request that an image be scaled.

An example that illustrates image drawing can be seen by running the `Chapter5` project in the Wireless Toolkit, launching `ImageMIDlet`, and selecting Draw-Image. This example displays a `Canvas` with a `paint()` method that loads an image from the MIDlet JAR file and draws it in one of three positions, as shown in Figure 5-18.†

The implementation of the `Canvas` and its `paint()` method is shown in Example 5-6.

If you examine the `paint()` method, you'll see that there are three `drawImage()` calls that determine where the image will be drawn. The choice of which to use depends on a counter that is incremented each time the method is executed. To force the `Canvas` to repaint, use the Back command to return to the selection list on the previous screen and then reselect DrawImage.

---

* Both networking and local storage are described in Chapter 6.

† This image of the earth was taken by the astronaut crew of Apollo 8 on Christmas, 1969, and was obtained from the historical image archive of the National Aeronautical and Space Administration.

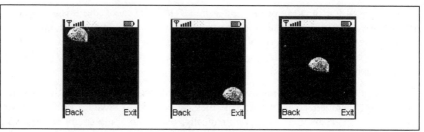

Figure 5-18: Drawing images using drawImage( )

Example 5-6: Canvas That Paints an Image in Three Different Locations

```
class DrawImageCanvas extends Canvas {
    static Image image;

    int count;

    public void paint(Graphics g) {
        int width = getWidth();
        int height = getHeight();

        // Fill the background using black
        g.setColor(0);
        g.fillRect(0, 0, width, height);

        // Load an image from the MIDlet resources
        if (image == null) {
            try {
                image = Image.createImage("/ora/ch5/resources/earth.png");
            } catch (IOException ex) {
                g.setColor(0xffffff);
                g.drawString("Failed to load image!", 0, 0, Graphics.TOP |
                    Graphics.LEFT);
                return;
            }
        }

        switch (count % 3) {
        case 0:
            // Draw the image at the top left of the screen
            g.drawImage(image, 0, 0, Graphics.TOP | Graphics.LEFT);
            break;

        case 1:
            // Draw it in the bottom right corner
            g.drawImage(image, width, height, Graphics.BOTTOM |
                Graphics.RIGHT);
            break;
        case 2:
            // Draw it in the center
            g.drawImage(image, width/2, height/2, Graphics.VCENTER |
                Graphics.HCENTER);
```

```
        }
        count++;
    }
}
```

When the MIDlet first appears, the image is drawn by this method call:

```
g.drawImage(image, 0, 0, Graphics.TOP | Graphics.LEFT);
```

which places the top left of the image at coordinate location (0, 0), as can be seen on the left of Figure 5-18. The second time, this **drawImage()** call is executed:

```
g.drawImage(image, width, height, Graphics.BOTTOM | Graphics.RIGHT);
```

Now the image appears at the bottom right of the screen. The last call is more interesting:

```
g.drawImage(image, width/2, height/2, Graphics.VCENTER |
    Graphics.HCENTER);
```

Here the **anchor** argument is **VCENTER | HCENTER**, which refers to the center of the image itself, and the **drawImage()** call places this point halfway across and halfway down the **Canvas**—in other words, the image is centered on the **Canvas**. Note that none of these examples require you to know the size of the image in order to place it properly. If you need this information, you can get it from the **Image getWidth()** and **getHeight()** methods.

Creating an Image Programmatically

If you create a mutable **Image**, you can use **Graphics** methods to draw onto it and then copy the result to the screen. This technique can be used to improve performance by drawing complex shapes that do not change or change rarely offline so that they can be quickly copied to the screen when required in the **paint()** method of the **Canvas** class. This same technique, when taken to its extreme, can also be used to implement double buffering for those devices that do not directly support it (i.e., those for which the **Canvas isDoubleBuffered()** method returns **false**).

To draw on a mutable **Image**, you first need to get a **Graphics** object using the following method:

```
public Graphics getGraphics();
```

This method throws an **IllegalStateException** if it is invoked on an immutable **Image**. The returned **Graphics** object has its coordinate origin at the top left corner of the **Image**, and a clip covers its surface. The object is initialized with the default font, the current color is black, and its stroke style is set to draw solid lines. These attributes are the same as those installed in the **Graphics** object passed to the **paint()** method. An important difference between these two, however, is that you can retain a reference to the object returned by **getGraphics()** indefinitely, and it remains valid, whereas the **Graphics** object used in the **paint()** method should not be used once **paint()** returns.

An example that uses the technique of drawing onto a mutable image can be seen by selecting the ImageGraphics example from the list offered by the

ImageMIDlet. The example creates a pattern using colored lines as shown in Figure 5-19. The code that creates this pattern is shown in Example 5-7.

Example 5-7: Drawing on a Mutable Image

```
public void paint(Graphics g) {
    int width = getWidth();
    int height = getHeight();

    // Create an Image the same size as the Canvas.
    Image image = Image.createImage(width, height);
    Graphics imageGraphics = image.getGraphics();

    // Fill the background of the image black
    imageGraphics.fillRect(0, 0, width, height);

    // Draw a pattern of lines
    int count = 10;
    int yIncrement = height/count;
    int xIncrement = width/count;
    for (int i = 0, x = xIncrement, y = 0; i < count; i++) {
        imageGraphics.setColor(0xC0 + ((128 + 10 * i) << 8) + ((128 + 10 * i)
            << 16));
        imageGraphics.drawLine(0, y, x, height);
        y += yIncrement;
        x += xIncrement;
    }

    // Add some text
    imageGraphics.setFont(Font.getFont(Font.FACE_PROPORTIONAL,
                        Font.STYLE_UNDERLINED, Font.SIZE_SMALL));
    imageGraphics.setColor(0xffff00);
    imageGraphics.drawString("Image Graphics", width/2, 0, Graphics.TOP |
        Graphics.HCENTER);

    // Copy the Image to the screen
    g.drawImage(image, 0, 0, Graphics.TOP | Graphics.LEFT);
}
```

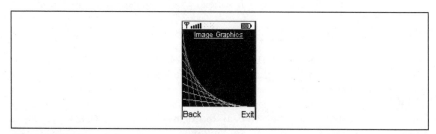

Figure 5-19: Drawing onto a mutable Image

The **paint()** method creates a blank image that is exactly the same size as the **Canvas** and uses **getGraphics()** to get a **Graphics** object that can be used to draw on it. The process of drawing the line pattern and the text that appears at the top of the image is exactly the same as would be used if they were being drawn directly onto the Canvas itself. Finally, the content of the image is copied to the Canvas itself and therefore to the screen, using the drawImage() method of the Canvas Graphics and supplying the Image object as the source:

```
g.drawImage(image, 0, 0, Graphics.TOP | Graphics.LEFT);
```

This example is a demonstration of double buffering, because the graphics are first drawn in an off-screen buffer (the Image) and then copied onto the screen. For devices that do not implement automatic double buffering, this technique can improve the appearance of a MIDlet by hiding screen updates from the user until they are complete. A possible disadvantage of this technique is that it requires more memory than direct screen updates.

Event Handling

So far, you have seen how to use the Canvas, Image, and Graphics classes to draw lines, shapes, and images onto the screen. The low-level API also provides the ability for a MIDlet to detect and respond to user input from the keypad and a pointing device, if the device has one.

Key Handling

High-level API user interface components like TextBox and TextField automatically handle interaction with the user via the keypad (or its equivalent), so that the MIDlet just has to wait for the user to indicate that input is complete and read the content of the control as a String or an array of characters. If you are using the low-level API, however, the only way to respond to keyboard input is by overriding the following methods of the Canvas class:

```
protected void keyPressed(int keyCode)
protected void keyReleased(int keyCode)
protected void keyRepeated(int keyCode)
```

The keyPressed() and keyReleased() methods are, fairly obviously, called when the user presses and releases a key. If the user holds a key down for a device-dependent time, some platforms periodically call the keyRepeated() method, passing it the same argument as that supplied to the previous keyPressed() call. Since not all devices have a repeating keyboard, a MIDlet can determine whether to expect these events by calling the Canvas hasRepeatEvents() method and adjusting its behavior appropriately.

Unlike PC keyboards, which are more or less standardized, the wide range of different devices supported by MIDP brings with it a similar range of keypads, many of which have only a very small number of keys. Examples of typical keypads can be seen in Figures 3-2 and 3-3. The low-level API assumes only that the device has the minimal set of keys required by the MIDP specification:

- The digits 0 through 9
- The star or asterisk character (*)
- The pound or hash character (#)

Low-Level UI API

The Canvas class defines constants that represent these keys, listed in Table 5-2. The MIDP platform vendor is required to ensure that these constant values are passed as the keyCode argument when keyPressed(), keyRepeated(), and keyReleased() are called whenever the keys that correspond to them are pressed or released. The actual values are, in fact, the Unicode values for the corresponding characters so that, for example, the following expression has the value true:

```
Canvas.KEY_NUM0 == '0'
```

Table 5-2: Standard Key Codes and Game Actions

Key Code/Action	Meaning	Key Code/Action	Meaning
KEY_NUM0	Number key 0	KEY_POUND	The pound key (#)
KEY_NUM1	Number key 1	UP	Game action UP
KEY_NUM2	Number key 2	DOWN	Game action DOWN
KEY_NUM3	Number key 3	LEFT	Game action LEFT
KEY_NUM4	Number key 4	RIGHT	Game action RIGHT
KEY_NUM5	Number key 5	FIRE	Game action FIRE
KEY_NUM6	Number key 6	GAME_A	Custom game action A
KEY_NUM7	Number key 7	GAME_B	Custom game action B
KEY_NUM8	Number key 8	GAME_C	Custom game action C
KEY_NUM9	Number key 9	GAME_D	Custom game action D
KEY_STAR	The star key (*)		

The example source code for this book contains a MIDlet that displays the key codes generated by the keys of a MIDP device. In the Wireless Toolkit, run the Chapter5 project and select EventsMIDlet. As you press and hold down a key, the screen displays both the numeric value of the keyCode argument passed to the keyPressed() method and the name of the Canvas constant that corresponds to it, if there is one. The screen shot on the left side of Figure 5-20 shows the result of pressing the 1 key on the keypad of the default color phone. As you can see, the key code itself has value 49, which is the Unicode value for the character 1, and it has been identified as Canvas.KEY_NUM1.

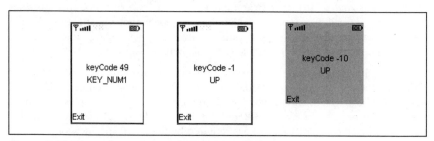

Figure 5-20: Key codes and game actions on cell phones

Portable MIDlets must rely only on the key codes (that is, the constants whose names begin with "KEY_") listed in Table 5-2. Devices with larger keyboards might be capable of returning additional key codes when other keys are pressed. For example, the RIM wireless handheld keyboard, shown in Figure 3-2, includes keys that represent alphabetic characters as well as the standard number keys. If you run the EventsMIDlet on this emulated device, you will find that the alphabetic keys also generate key codes (which also happen to be the Unicode characters that correspond to the characters on the key faces), but making use of them (or relying on their values) would introduce device-dependent assumptions into the MIDlet.

Games (and even some more serious applications) usually require movement keys and a FIRE button, and many MIDP devices have keys that are obvious candidates to be used for these functions. On the default color phone, for example, the cluster of arrow keys could be used to indicate which way to move, and the circular SELECT button at their center could be the FIRE button. On other devices, such as the RIM wireless handheld, there aren't any keys that immediately seem ideal for these functions. The Canvas class defines nine constants, shown in the "Key Code/Action" columns of Table 5-2, that can be used to identify a set of game actions in a platform-independent way, so that MIDlets do not need to be concerned about how they are mapped to keys on the keypad. Five of these values (UP, LEFT, DOWN, RIGHT, and FIRE) have obvious meanings and should be available on all MIDP devices. The remaining four (GAME_A, GAME_B, GAME_C, and GAME_D) can be used for game-specific functions. Because not all devices will necessarily be able to map keys to these functions (and those that map some of them may not provide all four), they should be used only to provide a quick and convenient way for the user to access functionality that is also accessible by more portable means, such as Commands attached to the Canvas.

Because the mapping of game actions to key codes is platform-dependent, MIDlets do not detect them by examining the keyCode argument of the keyPressed() method. In other words, the following code is incorrect:

```
if (keyCode == Canvas.FIRE) {
    // NOT CORRECT!!!
}
```

Instead, there are two Canvas methods that can be used to test whether a given key code represents a game action:

```
public int getGameAction(int keyCode)
public int getKeyCode(int gameAction)
```

The getGameAction() method converts a key code to the corresponding game action and returns 0 if the key is not mapped to an action:

```
protected void keyPressed(int keyCode) {
    if (getGameAction(keyCode) == Canvas.FIRE) {
        // FIRE action
    }
}
```

The getKeyCode() method does just the opposite: given a game action, it returns the key code for the key that is mapped to that action. This method would normally be used during initialization to get the mappings for the game actions that a MIDlet uses; this avoids method calls in the keyPressed() method. For example:

```
int fireKey = getKeyCode(Canvas.FIRE);
int upKey = getKeyCode(Canvas.UP);
int downKey = getKeyCode(Canvas.DOWN);
        .
        .
protected void keyPressed(int keyCode) {
    if (keyCode == fireKey) {
        // FIRE action
    } else if (keyCode == upKey) {
        // UP actions
    }
}
```

The advantage of using getKeyCode() in this way is that the code in the keyPressed() method will run slightly faster than if it called getGameAction() each time a key is pressed. The downside is that if the platform allows the user to change the mapping between game actions and keys, the MIDlet will no longer work as expected if any of the game actions that it uses are remapped.

The EventsMIDlet uses the getGameAction() method to check each key code passed to its keyPressed() method to determine whether it is a game action; it displays the action name if it is. By experimenting with this MIDlet on the different emulated devices in the Wireless Toolkit, you can see how device-dependent the mapping between game actions and keys is. You can see an example of this in Figure 5-20. The middle screenshot demonstrates that on the default color phone, the UP arrow key, which is mapped to the UP game action, has key code –1, whereas on the Motorola cell phone, shown on the right, the same game action is mapped from the key with key code –10.

The low-level key handling API is much more primitive than the facilities available from TextBox and TextField. In particular, the small number of standard key codes makes it impossible to provide alphabetic input in a platform-independent way. In fact, in the MIDP reference implementation, the keyboard input features used by the high-level components are actually built on the same key handling described in this section. In order to provide alphabetic and other characters, the high-level API implementation maintains internal shift state information and maps the key presses to the appropriate Unicode character values. For example, on the default color phone, the star key can be used to shift input modes. Pressing this key causes the internal state information to be changed, and a different lookup table is used to convert keycodes to characters. Furthermore, because each key has more than one legend engraved on it, more complex logic is needed to determine whether pressing the key labeled 2 should generate the code for 2 or for one of the letters A, B, or C. This process, is, of course, device-dependent since it requires knowledge of the keyboard layout, which is customized by device vendors.

If you have developed GUI applications using J2SE, you have almost certainly at some time had to develop or purchase custom components to provide functionality that isn't provided by Swing and/or AWT. Writing nontrivial custom components on the MIDP platform, however, is almost impossible. As far as the high-level API is concerned, the methods that you need to access or override to change the behavior of an existing component are all either private or package private, making them inaccessible to third-party code. There is, therefore, no base class like `Component` or `JComponent` from which you can start constructing a custom component. You can use the low-level API to develop more sophisticated user interfaces, but, as just noted, providing fully featured key input is very complex. Even if you take the trouble to implement it properly, you can't take something built for the low-level API and use it with a `Form`, so the component could not be used in the high-level API. Furthermore, there is no concept of `Container` or layout manager in MIDP, so it is not practical to build small components that you can plug into a `Canvas` without having first to reinvent much of the infrastructure provided by the high-level API. Some device vendors have solved this problem by creating their own custom components or offering toolkits that make it possible to write your own. Using these facilities will, of course, make your MIDlet nonportable to other devices.

Using the Pointer

MIDlets running on devices that have a pointing device can detect pointer state changes by overriding the following `Canvas` methods:

```
protected void pointerPressed(int x, int y)
protected void pointerDragged(int x, int y)
protected void pointerReleased(int x, int y)
```

In all cases, the x and y arguments give the position of the pointer relative to the top left corner of the `Canvas`. A MIDlet can determine whether the `pointerPressed()` and `pointerReleased()` methods will be called by using the `Canvas` `hasPointerEvents()` method; `hasPointerMotionEvents()` indicates whether `pointerDragged()` will be called.

The `EventsMIDlet` reports pointer events on devices that support them by displaying the x and y values passed to the three previous methods on the `Canvas`. If you run this MIDlet under the Wireless Toolkit and select the PalmOS device, you can click and drag the mouse on the emulator's screen to generate pointer events. If you click on the screen and drag the mouse around, you will notice the following:

- A continuous stream of events is generated as the pointer moves around, but the stream does not necessarily report every point that the pointer traverses. The faster you move the pointer, the further apart successive pairs of (x, y) values will be.

- If you drag the pointer from the top of the screen to the bottom, the y value stops increasing when you move out of the drawing area of the `Canvas`, which excludes the area allocated to `Command` buttons.

- If you drag the pointer outside the screen and even outside the emulator window, you will still get pointer events, provided that one of the coordinates is within the range of valid values for the `Canvas`. If, for example, you start from the center of the `Canvas` and drag the pointer out to the right, you will continue to receive events in which the y coordinate changes, but the x coordinate remains at its maximum value. If you then drag the pointer up, the y coordinate decreases to zero, but negative values are not returned. Starting from the center and dragging up, down, or left gives similar results. If you release the mouse (i.e., lift the pointer) when it is outside the screen area, the `pointerReleased()` method is still called, as evidenced by the fact that coordinates are no longer displayed on the screen.

Multithreading and the User Interface

If you have developed J2SE GUI applications with Swing, you know that you have to be very careful when manipulating Swing components, because, with the exception of a few special cases, they are not thread-safe. The end result of this is that, although the application may be multithreaded, any logic that affects the user interface must be executed in the event thread. The MIDP user interface components, however, are completely thread-safe, so you can create and manipulate them from any thread. This makes writing MIDlets much simpler than building Swing applications. Nevertheless, there are a few things that you need to be aware of with regard to multithreaded MIDlets. We'll cover those in this section.

Serialization of User Interface Events

Although application code can freely access user interface components from arbitrary threads, the user interface code itself arranges for all of its own event handling to be serialized. Thus, only one of the following may be happening at any given time:

- Painting of any user interface component by calling its `paint()` method

- Reporting of a key event in the `Canvas keyPressed()`, `keyRepeated()`, or `keyReleased()` methods

- Reporting of pointer events in the `pointerPressed()`, `pointerDragged()`, and `pointerReleased()` methods

This serialization is achieved by running all these methods in a single thread, which we'll refer to here as the event thread. From the MIDlet point of view, this can be a great benefit, because MIDlets that construct a user interface during initialization (which is not performed in the event thread) and then simply react to user interface events do not need to concern themselves with multithreading issues at all. All of their event handling is automatically serialized.

Note, however, that `TimerTasks` are run in the threads of their associated `Timers` and therefore are not synchronized with the event thread. Since the user interface components themselves are thread-safe, the only implications of this are that the MIDlet must be careful when modifying its internal state in methods that execute as a result of timer events. This applies especially to MIDlets that use the low-level API, where the `Canvas paint()` method might use state that is being updated in a separate thread. You saw an example of this in the `AnimationMIDlet` shown earlier in this chapter, where the section of the `paint()` code that needs to use the locations of the blocks on the screen (see Example 5-2) is synchronized so that it does not run at the same time as the section of code that moves the blocks, which is shown in Example 5-3.

Running Code in the Event Thread

Although the MIDP user interface components are thread-safe and therefore can be updated from any thread, it is sometimes useful to arrange for MIDlet code to be run in the event thread. This might come in handy if the MIDlet has a thread that obtains data from a network connection and then needs to update internal data structures that are also used by the user interface. You could handle this by applying locks around the code that performs the update and in the painting code, as we did with the `AnimationMIDlet`, or you could perform all the updates in the event thread itself, which removes the need for locking. You can implement the latter approach using the following method of the `Display` class:

```
public void callSerially(Runnable runnable);
```

The code to be executed in the event thread should be implemented in the `run()` method of the `Runnable` passed to the `callSerially()` method:

```
Display.getDisplay(midletReference).callSerially(new Runnable() {
    public void run() {
        // Code to be run in the event thread goes here
    }
});
```

The platform does not make any guarantees about when this code will be run, apart from the following:

- If there are any pending paint operations to be performed on the display, they will be completed before any code scheduled using `callSerially()` is run.

- If more than one call of `callSerially()` is made, the `run()` methods of the `Runnable` objects are executed in the same order as the `callSerially()` calls.

Since all pending paint operations are guaranteed to be complete before the code in the `run()` method is executed, you can use this mechanism to interleave code that creates the next stage of an animation with the painting operations. As an example, instead of running the frame updates for the `AnimationMIDlet` from a timer, you could instead include the following code in its `startApp()` method:

```
display.callSerially(new Runnable() {
    public void run() {
        // Move all of the blocks to their new locations.
        // This method calls repaint()
        moveAllBlocks();

        // Schedule this code to run again
        display.callSerially(this);
    }
});
```

When the `callSerially()` method is invoked for the first time, it calls `moveAllBlocks()` to place all the blocks in their new positions. Since this method calls `repaint()` internally, when it returns, there will be a pending paint operation. Finally, it uses the `callSerially()` method to cause itself to be scheduled again. However, the platform guarantees that the paint operation will be completed before code scheduled using `callSerially()`, so the painting and animation code runs alternately, like this:

1. First call to `Runnable` calls `moveAllBlocks()` (and `repaint()`) and `callSerially()`.

2. `paint()` method updates the screen.

3. On completion of `paint()`, `Runnable` is called again. This calls `moveAllBlocks()`, `repaint()`, and `callSerially()`.

4. `paint()` method updates the screen.

5. `Runnable` is called again.

And so on. This produces screen updates at the maximum rate that the platform can sustain because there is no apparent timer delay. In the MIDP reference implementation, however, calling `repaint()` does not cause an invocation of `paint()` to be scheduled immediately. There is a short delay to allow subsequent `repaint()` operations to be serviced at the same time. As a result, the previous code results in one frame update in each paint cycle, which is approximately every 30 milliseconds in the reference implementation.

Another way to produce the same effect is to create a separate thread that does nothing other than call `moveAllBlocks()` in a loop:

```
public void run() {
    while (!stopped) {
        moveAllBlocks();
    }
}
```

`stopped` is set to `true` when the MIDlet's `destroyApp()` method is called. As it stands, this code would not work well, because it would simply spin, updating the positions of all the blocks and scheduling repaints that occur in a separate thread at a much lower frequency. You really need to wait for the repaint operation to complete after each invocation of `moveAllBlocks()`, to synchonize it with the repaint cycle. The following `Canvas` method can be used to arrange this:

```
publlic void serviceRepaints()
```

`serviceRepaints()` works by blocking until all pending repaint operations on the `Canvas` have been completed. Therefore, the following code (where the `run()` method is assumed to be a method of the `Canvas` subclass in question) would implement an animation rate of one frame per paint cycle:

```
public void run() {
    while (!stopped) {
        moveAllBlocks();
        serviceRepaints();   // Block until painting done
    }
}
```

CHAPTER 6

Wireless Java: Networking and Persistent Storage

The devices that the J2ME platform is intended for are, by their nature, reliant for their usefulness on the ability to communicate with the outside world. Cell phones, of course, serve no real purpose other than to exist on a network, while PDAs would be much less useful if you could not connect them occasionally to a desktop computer to save your new customer orders or upload more appointments from your departmental calendar. As important as networking is, however, there is a certain cost to be paid for it in terms of the resources needed for the software that implements the various networking protocols in use today. Given the relatively small amount of memory and processing power available in cell phones and the smaller PDAs, compromises have to be made in order to provide networking support for the type of hardware on which profiles designed for the CLDC are run. The same constraints do not exist for the larger devices that host CDC profiles. Not surprisingly, then, these two different profile families incorporate completely different communication software architectures. This chapter looks at networking and communications in the context of the CLDC configuration and MIDP, which differs greatly from its CDC equivalent, covered in Chapter 7.

This chapter also looks at another essential feature for a mobile device: the ability to store information and access it from applications running on that device. The type of storage available, and the amount of space available, varies greatly from device to device. In order to make software written for the J2ME platform as portable as possible, MIDP includes a package that provides a simple and platform-independent mechanism for accessing whatever type of persistent storage is available on the device that the application is running on. The end of this chapter, brings together both the networking and storage threads by showing you how to create a small database of book details that resides on your cell phone or in your PDA and can also be updated from the Internet on demand.

A Networking Architecture for Small Devices

J2SE contains a low-level networking infrastructure implemented in the `java.net` package, layered on top of which are higher-level facilities such as RMI, CORBA, Jini, and the rest of the enterprise networking APIs. Since networking and communications are fundamental to any mobile device, they fall within the scope of the CLDC. Rather than specifying that mobile devices should use some or all of the `java.net` package to provide these features, the CLDC specification instead defines a completely new framework as the basis for all the external connectivity to be supplied by the profiles that depend on it. This choice was made for the following reasons:

Memory requirements

> The `java.net` package contains 21 classes, 5 interfaces, and 8 exceptions, in addition to referencing other APIs from the core packages, not all of which are guaranteed to be available in any given profile. The memory requirement for this set of classes was judged to be too great for the small footprint devices that CLDC is designed for.

Consistency

> The J2SE networking classes support both low-level socket programming and access to web servers using HTTP, which is layered above the socket interfaces. The programming model for these two modes of operation is different, however. For example, to make a socket-level connection, you need an `InetAddress` object and a port number with which you construct a `Socket`; on the other hand, to connect to a web server using HTTP, you need a `URL` from which you can then obtain a `URLConnection`. The differences are even greater when it comes to using a serial device, because you need to install an extra package and use yet another programming model. Given the diversity of devices and communication mechanisms that the CLDC might be required to support, a more uniform API was clearly required.

Implementation flexibility

> Within the `java.net` package, most of the API revolves around classes that are directly accessed by the application programmer. For example, all socket-based programs use the `Socket` class, while any application that requires HTTP obtains an instance of the `HttpURLConnection` class. In the context of J2ME, however, the mechanism by which a particular device provides these facilities might be device-specific: the HTTP implementation for a handheld with direct connectivity to the Internet is probably nothing like that for a cell phone that does not have similar connectivity. Although the J2SE networking package provides mechanisms that allow the actual classes that provide the low-level implementation details to be substituted by application code and by the J2SE platform vendor, the means by which this is achieved is different for sockets and for URL-based protocols like HTTP. Instead of using the same approach, the CLDC designers decided to use an architecture based entirely around interfaces, so that application code would not be tied to particular classes. Thus, vendors are free to provide socket and HTTP implementations that are appropriate for their specific devices.

The CLDC Generic Connection Framework (GCF) is implemented in the `javax.microedition.io` package; its class hierarchy is shown in Chapter 14.

Connection and Connector

The most basic interface in this package is `Connection`, which represents a connection of any kind. At this level, all you can do is open or close the connection. In fact, the `Connection` interface has only one method:

```
public interface Connection {
    public void close() throws IOException;
}
```

`Connection` doesn't need an `open()` method because you can't use a `Connection` to obtain a `Connection`. Instead, all `Connections` are obtained from the `Connector` class, which has three static `open()` methods that can be used for this purpose:

```
public static Connection open(String name);
public static Connection open(String name, int mode);
public static Connection open(String name, int mode, boolean timeouts);
```

The `name` parameter specifies the type of connection that is required. Its general format is:

```
scheme:address;parameters
```

The `scheme` determines the protocol or device type to be used, `address` is a protocol- or device-specific identifier for the resource to be accessed, and `parameters` provides any extra information that is required to open a connection of the required type. Although the CLDC specification defines the GCF itself, it does not require implementations to provide support for any fixed set of protocols and, therefore, does not specify any particular scheme names that might be used, although it does give examples. Sun's CLDC reference implementation includes unofficial and unsupported implementations of various schemes, the names of which are very likely to be adopted by profiles that include official support for them. Here are a few examples that show how the `name` parameter is typically constructed for a given protocol:

```
socket://www.amazon.com:80
http://www.amazon.com/index.html
comm:0;baudrate=28800;parity=even
```

At the time of writing, the only officially supported protocol is HTTP, which is specified by MIDP. Examples that use HTTP and some of the other schemes provided by the CLDC reference implementation will be shown later in this chapter.

The remaining parameters of the `open()` method specify attributes of the connection itself. The optional `mode` parameter can take one of the values `Connector.READ`, `Connector.WRITE`, or `Connector.READ_WRITE`. If you don't specify a value, `Connector.READ_WRITE` is assumed. Not all devices support both reading and writing; for example, some printers might not recognize a read mode. If you attempt to use a mode that the device does not support (which might include the default), an `IllegalArgumentException` is thrown. The optional `timeout` parameter can be used to indicate that application code can make use of timeouts on read or write operations if they are supported by the implementation. If the device or protocol implementation supports timeouts, and this parameter is `true`, an `InterruptedIOException` is thrown from any method that experiences a timeout. This is typically used to ensure that an attempt to read from a network connection does not block indefinitely. Note, however, that the length of the timeout period cannot be set by the application.

Types of Connection

The `InputConnection` and `OutputConnection` interfaces are derived directly from `Connection`. They add the ability to obtain input and output streams to access whatever underlies the connection. `InputConnection` provides two methods that provide streams for input:

```
public InputStream openInputStream() throws IOException
public DataInputStream openDataInputStream() throws IOException
```

`OutputConnection` has the corresponding methods for output streams:

```
public OutputStream openOutputStream() throws IOException
public DataOutputStream openDataOutputStream() throws IOException
```

`InputStream` and `OutputStream` provide direct, byte-level access to the underlying data stream, whereas `DataInputStream` and `DataOutputStream` allow you to work in terms of primitive Java data types such as `int`, `char`, and `String`.

Although most communications mechanisms support both input and output, these interfaces are kept separate. Thus, devices or protocols that are inherently unidirectional, at least as far as data transfer is concerned, can return a subinterface of `Connection` that either does not allow reading or does not allow writing, as appropriate. Where bidirectional, stream-based data communication is supported, the implementation can return a `StreamConnection`, which combines the methods of `InputConnection` and `OutputConnection` in a single interface:

```
public interface StreamConnection extends InputConnection,
    OutputConnection;
```

In the CLDC reference implementation, the `socket` scheme returns a `StreamConnection` from the `Connector open` method, because a socket can be used both to send and receive data.

A `StreamConnection` offers the ability to transfer a sequence of bytes from a sender to a receiver, but it leaves the interpretation of the content of the byte stream to the communicating parties. If there is a more ordered structure to the data that is being exchanged, the protocol can use the `ContentConnection` interface, which adds the following methods to those of `StreamConnection`:

```
public long getLength();
public String getType();
public String getEncoding();
```

This interface envisages the exchange of information with defined message boundaries, so that it is meaningful to have a `getLength()` method that can return the length of the next message in the input stream. The `getType()` method allows different data types to be distinguished, while the `getEncoding()` method allows the use of different schemes for encoding 16-bit Unicode character data into an 8-bit byte stream. The means by which the message boundaries, data type, and encoding are communicated from the sender to the receiver depend entirely on the underlying protocol. One protocol that can provide this information is HTTP, so it is perhaps not surprising that the `HttpConnection` interface extends `ContentConnection`. `HttpConnection` and the MIDP implementation of HTTP are described later in this chapter.

There are two more interfaces in the `javax.microedition.io` package shown in Chapter 14 that we haven't yet covered: `DatagramConnection` and `StreamConnectionNotifier`. Both these interfaces are derived directly from `Connection`, because neither of them is associated with a data stream. `DatagramConnection` is concerned with sending and receiving discrete packets of data (called datagrams) without setting up a connection between the sender and the receiver. `DatagramConnection` and the associated `Datagram` class are discussed in more detail in the later section "Datagrams." Finally, `StreamConnectionNotifier` is used when implementing a server when using sockets, which is the subject of the next section.

Sockets

Sockets are the lowest level of network communication that most programmers encounter, although real enthusiasts might choose to delve into the murky details of transport and network layers—and some even survive the experience! Because the socket API is so simple, widely known, and universally available, it is often used as the basis for distributed applications involving one or more clients talking to a single server, exchanging information using a very basic application-level protocol. In this situation, the use of a higher-level abstract such as RMI, CORBA, or one of the Java Enterprise products would not be justified. All this notwithstanding, CLDC does not require the provision of a socket interface to the network, and neither does MIDP. Part of the reason is that sockets are usually used in connection with Internet protocols such as TCP/IP, but many mobile devices do not have a direct connection to the Internet, and, therefore, the device's host software almost certainly does not include a TCP/IP protocol stack. Making sockets part of MIDP would have required manufacturers to add this software to their devices (which has an associated cost) or necessitated its inclusion in the MIDP reference implementation, which is not economically possible on many platforms because of the memory requirements. Socket support is, however, under consideration for the next version of MIDP, which is being developed under the Java Community Process as JSR 118. You can obtain information about JSR 118 from *http://www.jcp.org/jsr/detail/118.jsp*.

At the present time, therefore, applications that use sockets work on some devices, such as PDAs with modems, but not on others and thus cannot be considered portable. However, because sockets are likely to be supported in the next version of MIDP, we'll take advantage of the socket implementation in the CLDC 1.0 reference release to illustrate how sockets fit into the GCF by showing a simple application that retrieves some data from a web server.

Client Sockets

The steps required to open a socket connection to a web server and read some data from it are as follows:

Wireless Java

1. Build the appropriate name string and invoke the Connector open()
   method.

2. Get an output stream and use it to send a request message to the server.

3. Open an input stream and read the response.

4. Close both streams and the socket.

The naming scheme for sockets uses the fixed string "socket://" followed by the
server name and port, separated by a colon. Here's how you might open a socket
to a web server given the server's name and a string containing its port number
(usually 80) in variables called **server** and **port**, respectively:

```
StreamConnection socket;
try {
    String name = "socket://" + server + ":" + port;
    socket = (StreamConnection)Connector.open(name,
        Connector.READ_WRITE);
} catch (Exception ex) {
    // Handle failure to connect here...
}
```

If the address you supply is invalid, or the server is not accessible, the open()
method throws an exception. For the sake of brevity, the error handling is not
shown here. The protocol implementation for sockets returns a
StreamConnection, which means that you can send and receive data by getting a
pair of output and input streams. In this example, we're going to send a message
to the server to request a copy of its home page, which we can do as follows:

```
// Send a message to the server
String request = "GET / HTTP/1.0\n\n";
os = socket.openOutputStream();
os.write(request.getBytes());
os.close();
```

The StreamConnection openOutputStream() method returns an
OutputStream that we can use to send the HTTP message "GET / HTTP/1.0" to
the server, which is a request for the server to send its home page. Note that you
can't write the message string directly to the output stream, because it contains
Unicode characters, and the server is expecting to receive a stream of bytes. To
perform the conversion, we use the String getBytes() method, which creates
an array of bytes that represents the original String in the default encoding of the
host platform. As long as the request string contains only ASCII characters, which
is the case here, this gives the correct result, because ASCII characters are valid in
every character encoding. Writing data to the output stream does not necessarily
result in it being sent immediately to the server, because the protocol implementation is allowed to buffer unsent data. To force the message to be sent, you can use
the OutputStream flush() method or close the OutputStream.

The next step is to read the response from the server. Since we've asked for the
server's home page, we have no way of knowing in advance how much data we
have to read before we have the whole page. Because the server sends an HTTP
reply, we could look for the Content-Length header, which, if it is present, tells
us how much data to expect. In this example, however, we are simply treating the

socket connection as a byte stream, so we don't want to try to interpret the reply. The following code takes the simplest possible approach and reads up to 128 bytes from the socket, discarding anything else that might follow:

```
// Read the server's reply, up to a maximum of 128 bytes.
is = socket.openInputStream();
final int MAX_LENGTH = 128;
byte[] buf = new byte[MAX_LENGTH];
int total = 0;
while (total < MAX_LENGTH) {
    int count = is.read(buf, total, MAX_LENGTH - total);
    if (count < 0) {
        break;
    }
    total += count;
}
is.close();
String reply = new String(buf, 0, total);
```

Notice that rather than simply performing a single read for 128 bytes, this code loops around reading data in chunks until it fills its input buffer or reaches the end of the input stream (which causes the **read()** method to return –1). This is necessary because networks don't always deliver data in a single chunk, and the protocol implementation is not bound to buffer data until it has enough to satisfy the application's **read()** request. In the general case, when you ask for *N* bytes of data from an **InputStream** obtained from a network connection, you should expect to receive anything between 1 and *N* bytes.

An alternative way to achieve the same thing is to get a **DataInputStream** from the socket instead of an **InputStream**. You can then use the **readFully()** method, which blocks until its buffer is full, all the data is read, or an error occurs:

```
DataInputStream dis = socket.openDataInputStream();
final int MAX_LENGTH = 128
byte[] buf = new byte[MAX_LENGTH];
int total = dis.readFully(buf);
```

The first of these two approaches allows you to do something with the data as you receive it, but the second commits you to waiting until everything has been received. Which you choose will depend on the needs of your application.

Finally, the bytes that have been read are converted to a Unicode string using a constructor of the **String** class that accepts a byte array. As before, this relies on the returned message being encoded either in the receiver's default encoding or in ASCII. Unless you know in advance what encoding the web server used, this is the best you can do. Even if you knew the encoding, as you almost certainly would if you used HTTP to transfer the page, you still might not be able to correctly convert the incoming byte stream to Unicode, because neither CLDC nor MIDP makes any guarantees about which character conversion tables are available on any given device.

After reading all the data, both the input and output stream and the socket itself must be closed. In order to make sure that all of these resources are freed up even

Wireless Java

when an error occurs, the usual practice is to perform cleanup operations inside a `finally` block, like this:

```
StreamConnection conn = null;
InputStream is = null
OutputStream os = null;
try {
    // Code shown above
} finally {
    // Close the input stream, if we opened it
    if (is != null) {
        is.close();
        is = null;
    }
    // Repeat for the output stream and the socket.
}
```

 Ensuring that resources are properly released is of much greater importance in the J2ME environment because of the limited resources available. It is surprising how quickly you can run out of memory as a result of forgetting to close an I/O stream or a network connection. It is also good practice to get into the habit of helping the garbage collector by `nulling` references that are no longer required, as shown in the `finally` block above. Regrettably, it is also possible to find yourself short of memory even if you never leak any, as you'll see when we discuss how to analyze the content of an HTML page in the later section "HTTP Connections."

To try out the code you've just seen, start the `RunMIDlet` application from the J2ME Wireless Toolkit, point it at the *Chapter6.jad* file in the *ora\ch6* directory of this book's example code, and select the `Socket` application from the list of MIDlets. This application lets you supply the name and port address of a web server and then fetches and displays the beginning of the server's home page. In Figure 6-1, the application was pointed at O'Reilly's web server, which listens on port 80 at *www.oreilly.com*. The right side of the diagram captures the result, showing the HTTP headers preceding the O'Reilly home page.

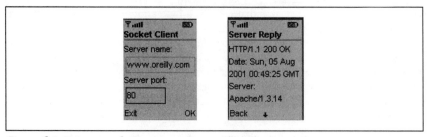

Figure 6-1: Using a socket to connect to a web server

Server Sockets

So much for client sockets, but what happens if you want to create a server and listen for incoming calls? The programming model for server sockets differs in several ways from that of client sockets. First, the name that you give to the `Connector open()` method contains the port that you want the server to listen on, but it does not specify the hostname. A server implicitly listens on the host it is running on, so there is no need to give a hostname; the protocol implementation uses this fact to distinguish a request to create a server socket from a request for a client socket. To listen on port 80, for example, you would use the following name:

```
socket://:80
```

The biggest difference with server sockets is that the `Connector open()` method doesn't return a `StreamConnection` object that you can use to send and receive data. This is because a server differs from a client in two important ways:

- When a server is started, it isn't connected to a client at all. Instead, it needs to register a port to listen on and then wait for a client to connect to that port.

- In general, a server supports many clients, either one after another or in parallel. Therefore, it needs several different sockets, one for each client that it communicates with.

Instead of returning a `StreamConnection`, the `open()` method returns a `StreamConnectionNotifier`. `StreamConnectionNotifier` is an interface, derived from `Connection`, that has only one method (in addition to the `close()` method inherited from `Connection`):

```
public StreamConnection acceptAndOpen() throws IOException
```

Once it has created its `StreamConnectionNotifier`, a server typically enters a loop in which it calls `acceptAndOpen()`. This method returns when a client connects to the server, and its return value is a `StreamConnection` object that represents the server's end of the connection. This object behaves in exactly the same way as the client's socket, so the server can use the same coding pattern as the client to send and receive data on the connection.

Because servers usually have to handle more than one client at a time, they usually create a new thread to process each connection. Thus, they avoid holding up all connections while waiting for an event on any one of them. Here is a typical coding pattern for a J2ME socket server:

```
StreamConnectionNotifier serverSocket =
    (StreamConnectionNotifier)Connector.open("socket://:8000");
for (;;) {
    // Get the next connection
    final StreamConnection socket =
        (StreamConnection)serverSocket.acceptAndOpen();

    // Handle the connection in a new thread
    Thread t = new Thread() {
        public void run() {
            OutputStream os = null;
```

Wireless Java

```
    try {
        os = socket.openOutputStream();
        // Communicate with client here . . .
    } catch (IOException ex) {
        // Handle error
    } finally {
        if (os != null) {
            try {
                os.close();
                os = null;
            } catch (IOException ex) {
            }
        }
        try {
            socket.close();
        } catch (IOException ex) {
        }
    }
};
t.start();
}
```

All you need to add to this code is the server-specific processing in the thread that
is created to handle each connection.

 At the time of writing, the reference version of MIDP recognizes client sockets, but it does not allow you to create server sockets. If you
attempt to do so, the `Connector open()` method returns `null`. You
can test J2ME socket servers if you use the CLDC reference implementation, however, because it does support them.

Datagrams

In addition to stream sockets, the CLDC reference implementation contains
support for datagrams. Datagrams and stream sockets differ in several ways:

Data stream versus message passing
A stream socket sends a continuous stream of data from a sender to a
receiver, with no provision for marking record boundaries. Datagrams are sent
in discrete packets; data sent in one packet is never delivered in the same
read as data from another packet.

Connection-oriented versus connectionless
When a stream socket is used, a connection, along which all the data flows, is
created between the sender and the receiver. As a result, there is no need to
specify where each message is going. A datagram socket does not use a
connection; each message is individually addressed, and different messages
may go to different destinations. Likewise, a datagram socket may receive
messages from any number of different sources, but a stream socket receives
data from only a single sender.

Reliability

Data sent using a stream socket is guaranteed to be delivered to the receiver, unless the intervening network fails. In that case, the receiver is notified that its connection to the sender has been lost. Furthermore, the individual bytes are delivered in the order in which they were sent, without duplication. A datagram socket makes no such promises. Messages may be lost or duplicated, or may not arrive in the order in which they were sent.

Because they do not incur the relatively large cost of setting up a connection before communication can commence, datagrams are typically used for lightweight protocols where total reliability is not required.

The CLDC datagram sockets uses the same naming scheme as stream sockets, but the protocol name is `datagram` instead of `socket`. The following code prepares a datagram listener to receive incoming datagrams addressed to port number 32767:

```
DatagramConnection receiver =
    (DatagramConnection)Connector.open("datagram://:32767");
```

On the other hand, this call creates a `Connection` that allows datagrams to be sent to port 32767 on a host called `target`:

```
DatagramConnection sender =
    (DatagramConnection)Connector.open("datagram://target:32767");
```

The object returned by these calls is a `DatagramConnection`, which is derived directly from the primitive `Connection` interface (see Chapter 14). This means that it does not have methods that return input and output streams to allow you to send and receive data—which is appropriate, because, as mentioned above, datagrams do not form a data stream of any kind.

Sending a Datagram

To send a datagram, you have to obtain a `Datagram` object, populate it with the data to be sent, and invoke the `send()` method. The `DatagramConnection` interface has four methods that you can use to get a `Datagram` object:

```
public Datagram newDatagram(int size)
public Datagram newDatagram(int size, String address)
public Datagram newDatagram(byte[] buf, int size)
public Datagram newDatagram(byte[] buf, int size, String address)
```

The first two of these methods allocate both the `Datagram` object and an associated data buffer with the given size; the last two just create a `Datagram` that points to a preallocated buffer. Notice that when you supply your own buffer, you also need to specify the buffer size. This allows you to restrict incoming data to only a portion of the actual buffer. Needless to say, the `size` parameter must not be larger than the buffer itself.

Two of these methods allow you supply an address parameter. By default, all datagrams are sent to the address that was specified in the `open()` call, but this can be overridden by supplying a different address when you create each datagram. For example:

```
DatagramConnection sender =
    (DatagramConnection)Connector.open("datagram://target:32767");
```

```
Datagram dgram = sender.newDatagram(64);
sender.send(dgram);      // Send to port 32767 on target
dgram = sender.newDatagram(64, "datagram://anotherHost:12345");
sender.send(dgram);      // Send to port 12345 on anotherHost
```

The `Datagram` interface has a number of methods that allow you to manipulate the data buffer or the destination address of the datagram. The `getData()` method returns a reference to the data buffer, which is useful if you didn't supply your own buffer when creating the datagram:

```
byte[] buffer = dgram.getData();
String message = "Hello, world\n";
byte[] dataBytes = message.getBytes();
System.arraycopy(dataBytes, 0, buffer, 0, dataBytes.length);
dgram.setLength(dataBytes.length);
sender.send(dgram);                          // Send "Hello, world\n"
```

An alternative, and probably more sensible, way to do this uses the `setData()` method to replace the `Datagram`'s data buffer with a new one:

```
byte[] dataBytes = "Hello, world\n".getBytes();
dgram.setData(dataBytes, 0, dataBytes.length);
sender.send(dgram);
```

An interesting feature of the `Datagram` interface is that it extends both `DataOutput` and `DataInput`, which means that you can use the methods of these interfaces to store Java data types in the output buffer and retrieve them at the receiving end. For example, the following code:

```
dgram.writeUTF("Hello, world\n");
dgram.writeLong(System.currentTimeMillis());
sender.send(dgram);
```

sends a datagram containing a greeting along with the current time, which the receiver can extract in a similar way:

```
String greeting = dgram.readUTF();
long time = dgram.readLong();
```

When using these methods, you need to ensure that the buffer is large enough for the data to be written into it.

Finally, you can change the destination address associated with a `Datagram` using its `setAddress()` method, where the address string is in the same format as the one passed to the `Connector open()` method:

```
dgram.setAddress("datagram://differentHost:11223");
sender.send(dgram);                  // Send to port 11223 on differentHost
```

Receiving Datagrams

To receive a datagram, you first have to allocate a `Datagram` object with a buffer large enough for the data that you expect to receive. This can be something of a difficult problem in the general case, but applications tend to exchange data with a known maximum size, which can be used when calling the `newDatagram()` method. The `DatagramConnection` interface provides two methods, `getMaximumLength()` and `getNominalLength()`, that return the theoretical maximum size and nominal size (whatever that is supposed to mean) of a datagram. However, these are not likely to be of great use, because the protocol that is usually used to send datagrams (the User Datagram Protocol, or UDP for short) can support almost 64 KB in a single message. Calling getMaximumLength() and allocating a buffer of the size that it returns is not a good idea; not only is it wasteful of space, but it is also likely to require more heap space than a typical CLDC device has available!

The following code snippet shows how to receive datagrams:

```
DatagramConnection receiver =
    (DatagramConnection)Connector.open("datagram://:32767");
byte[] buffer = new byte[256];
Datagram dgram = receiver.newDatagram(buffer, buffer.length);
for (;;) {
    dgram.setLength(buffer.length);
    receiver.receive(dgram);
    int length = dgram.getLength();
    System.out.println("Datagram received. Length is " + length);

    // Show the content of the datagram.
    for (int i = 0; i < length; i++) {
        System.out.print(buffer[i] + " ");
    }
}
```

Once this code obtains a DatagramConnection from the Connector open() method, it allocates a 256-byte buffer, gets a Datagram object pointing at the buffer, and enters a loop calling the DatagramConnection receive() method. This method blocks until a datagram is received and then reads it into the buffer, setting the Datagram length field to reflect the amount of data received; this can subsequently be retrieved using the getLength() method. Notice that at the top of the loop, the setLength() method is called to reset the length field to allow use of the whole buffer. This is necessary because receipt of a smaller datagram of, say 40 bytes, would change the length field; on the next pass of the loop, only 40 bytes of the buffer would be available to receive the next message.

 The intended result of using a buffer that is too small to receive a datagram that has been sent to it is currently not clear from the CDLC documentation. In the J2SE implementation of datagrams, any data that doesn't fit into the receive buffer is simply discarded without warning. At the time of writing, if the CDLC implementation receives a datagram that is too large for the buffer, it throws an IOException from the receive() method.

Replying to the Sender

So far, I've given the impression that datagram connections are opened either for sending or receiving, depending on the format of the address passed to the Connector open() method. In fact, this is not the case: no matter how you open the connection, you can use it to both send and receive datagrams. It is quite common for a program to listen for an incoming datagram, process it, and send a reply to the sender. A very simple example of this is the Internet daytime protocol, which is described in RFC 867 (available from *http://www.ietf.org/rfc/rfc867.txt*). To implement this protocol, you simply have to listen for incoming datagrams on port 13 and send a message back to the caller containing the time of day in any text format you choose. The content of the incoming datagram is ignored (and, in fact, there needn't be any data). This is such a simple protocol that it requires only a few lines of code:

```
Calendar cal = Calendar.getInstance();
DatagramConnection receiver =
    (DatagramConnection)Connector.open("datagram://:13");
byte[] buffer = new byte[256];
Datagram dgram = receiver.newDatagram(buffer, buffer.length);
for (;;) {
    dgram.setLength(buffer.length);

    // Wait for somebody to call...
    receiver.receive(dgram);

    // Get the time and store it in the buffer
    cal.setTime(new Date());
    String time = cal.toString();
    byte[] dataBytes = time.getBytes();
    System.arraycopy(dataBytes, 0, buffer, 0, dataBytes.length);

    // Send back the reply
    dgram.setLength(dataBytes.length);
    receiver.send(dgram);
}
```

This code allocates a 256-byte receive buffer and a `Datagram` pointing to it. When any message is received, the code gets the current time, stores it in the buffer, and sends it back to the caller. Notice that the same `Datagram` and buffer are used both to receive the caller's message and send a reply. This is useful not only for memory conservation, but also because the caller's address is stored in the `Datagram` when the message is received and is therefore already there when the reply is sent. If you need access the caller's address, you can use the `Datagram` `getAddress()` method to retrieve it.

The daytime service has been around for a very long time and is commonly available on Unix machines. You can even find this service available on the Internet. Start the `RunMIDlet` application from the J2ME Wireless Toolkit, point it at the *Chapter6.jad* file in the *ora\ch6* directory of this book's example code, and select the Time application from the list of MIDlets. This application lets you specify a hostname and then sends a datagram to port 13 at that host, to see if it is running the daytime service. If so, the application displays the time that it gets back. Such a service is provided by the U.S. Naval Observatory on a host called, appropriately, *tock.usno.navy.mil*. Figure 6-2 shows the result of sending a datagram to this host. If you don't get a response from that particular host, try *tick.usno.navy.mil* instead!

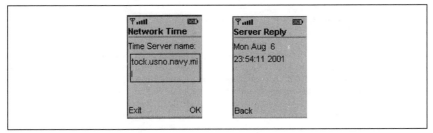

Figure 6-2: The Internet daytime service, accessed from a Java cell phone

HTTP Connections

The only communications protocol that every MIDP device is required to provide is the fairly simple Hypertext Transfer Protocol (HTTP), described in RFC 2616 (available from *http://www.ietf.org/rfc/rfc2616.txt*). HTTP makes use of stream sockets to carry messages between an HTTP client (usually a web browser) and a web server that often (but not always) returns an HTML page to the client. This works well in the desktop environment, but there are two potential problems with bringing all this to the devices for which MIDP is intended:

- Many of these devices, particularly cell phones, do not have a direct connection to the Internet and therefore almost certainly do not support sockets.

- The MIDP user interface components do not provide any support for displaying HTML, so there is no built-in browser capability in a MIDP device.

It is the responsibility of the device vendor to arrange for the device to be able to support HTTP even if it does not have a direct connection to the Internet. In most cases, this means that the device needs to connect to a gateway that can switch HTTP messages to whatever protocol is used to connect to the Internet gateway. In the wireless environment, for example, the device might use WSP (the Wireless Session Protocol) to connect to a WAP gateway that can bridge between a wireless network and the Internet. However this mapping is achieved, it must be done in such a way that the MIDP application cannot tell whether it is directly connected to the Internet.

The lack of browser support is not necessarily an issue. In many cases, applications that take advantage of MIDP HTTP support use a private message encoding scheme instead of HTML, and the client part of the application uses the MIDP GUI components to present the information that it gets from the server. Even if the application fetches an HTML page from the server, it can still scan the returned HTML for relevant information and display that information as it sees fit, therefore acting as its own microbrowser. We'll see a good example of this later in the section "An HTTP Example."

Using HTTP

As with sockets and datagrams, the first thing you need to do in order to use HTTP is call the `Connector open()` method:

```
HttpConnection conn =
    (HttpConnection)Connector.open("http://www.oreilly.com/",
    Connector.READ_WRITE);
```

The **name** parameter is the URL of the required resource. The general form of this parameter looks like this:

```
http://host:port/path?parameters#reference
```

The parts of the URL are as follows:

http

> The protocol name. The current MIDP specification requires support for HTTP Version 1.1. Higher-end or specialized devices might also provide secure HTTP, but the availability of HTTPS on any particular platform cannot be guaranteed.

host:port

> The hostname and port number of the web server. If the port is not specified, port 80 is assumed.

path

> The path of the required resource relative to the root of the web server.

parameters

> Web servers can offer dynamic content based on parameters supplied by the client; this is done by mapping the path to an executable object such as a script or Java servlet and passing it the parameters as part of its execution environment. One way to pass parameters to the web server is to append them to the URL as **name=value** pairs, separated by ampersand characters. As an example, you can get online stock quotes from Yahoo! by entering a URL like this:

> > *http://finance.yahoo.com/q?s=SUNW&d=v1*

> This URL provides two parameters (s with value SUNW and d with value v1) to the executable resource mapped to the path q at finance.yahoo.com. Another way to supply parameters is in the body of the message, an example of which will be shown in the later section "An HTTP Example."

reference

> The name associated with an <A> tag within the HTML page returned by the web server. Strictly speaking, the reference is not a true part of the URL at all, but an instruction to the browser to scroll so that the tagged location within the document is visible when it is displayed to the user. Whether and how you can include a reference in a URL depends on your application.

The object returned from the open method is of type HttpConnection, which is derived from ContentConnection, as shown in Chapter 14. This means that you can use input and output streams to transfer data, as you can with stream sockets, and the data returned from the server has an associated length, type, and encoding. These three properties are available because HTTP includes message headers that the server can set to convey this and other information to the client.

Although HTTP is predominantly used to carry HTML from web servers to web browsers, it is also possible to use it to carry other types of information such as XML, images, or even binary data. This is because one of the message headers specifies the type of the data in the message body. Furthermore, the communicating parties do not have to be a browser and a web server. The examples in this section all involve MIDlets talking to a web server, but HTTP is routinely used for other purposes, such as tunneling protocols. These allow the transmission of data that would otherwise be barred from passing through corporate firewalls, since most companies allow HTTP to transmitted through their firewalls or via a proxy server. The HTTP support in J2ME gives you access to all these possibilities.

Basic Use of HttpConnection

Using an HTTP connection is very similar to using a stream socket. Here are the basic steps that you need to perform, some of which can be omitted in many cases:

1. Construct the URL for the web page or other resource that you want to access, and call the Connector open() method to get an HttpConnection instance.

2. Set the request method. This step can often be omitted.

3. Set any request headers that you need. This is another task that you don't always need to worry about.

4. Call the openOutputStream() or openDataOutputStream() method to get a stream to write any data that needs to be sent.

5. Write the request data, if any, to the output stream and flush the stream.

6. Call the openInputStream() or openDataInputStream() method to get an input stream from which to read the response.

7. Get the response code using the getResponseCode() method. If the request was successful, read the returned data from the input stream.

8. Finally, close the input and output streams and the connection itself.

Let's clarify some of these steps by looking at an example. The earlier section "Client Sockets" showed you how to use a stream socket to fetch the home page of the O'Reilly web site. As you might expect, it is equally simple to do the same thing using an HttpConnection. Here's what the code looks like:

```
String url = "http://www.oreilly.com/";
conn = (HttpConnection)Connector.open(url, Connector.READ_WRITE);
if (conn.getResponseCode() == HttpConnection.HTTP_OK) {
    is = conn.openInputStream();
    final int MAX_LENGTH = 128;
    byte[] buf = new byte[MAX_LENGTH];
    int total = 0;
    while (total < MAX_LENGTH) {
        int count = is.read(buf, total, MAX_LENGTH - total);
        if (count < 0) {
            break;
        }
        total += count;
    }
    is.close();
    String reply = new String(buf, 0, total);
}
```

This code looks very similar to the socket code you saw earlier, but there is a striking difference. The socket code first opened an OutputStream and sent the following request to the web server before trying the read the response:

```
String request = "GET / HTTP/1.0\n\n";
```

Here, however, it isn't necessary to do that because the HttpConnection does it for you. In fact, all you have to do in this simple case is get the server's response code, check that the request succeeded, open an input stream, and read the reply. As before, only the first 128 bytes are read. If you want to read all of the data in the response message, you can use the getLength() method to retrieve the number of bytes in the message body, and then either use a loop, as shown previously, or get a DataInputStream instead of an InputStream and use its readFully() method:

```
dis = conn.openDataInputStream();
byte[] buf = new byte[conn.getLength()];
dis.readFully(buf);
```

It is important to note, however, that the HTTP reply message will not always include the header that contains the length of the reply. In this case, the setLength() method returns –1, and you will have to loop reading data from the input stream until the read() method returns –1, as shown earlier. It is important to check the server response code before trying to read any data; as we'll see later, you don't always get the data back immediately. There are cases in which you might have to make a second request. Table 6-1 shows some of the most common HTTP response codes. For a complete list, refer to RFC 2616.

Table 6-1: Common HTTP Response Codes

HttpConnection Name	Value	Meaning
HTTP_OK	200	The request succeeded.
HTTP_MOVED_PERM	301	The requested resource has been moved permanently to the URL in the Location header.
HTTP_MOVED_TEMP	302	The requested resource has been moved temporarily to the URL in the Location header.
HTTP_SEE_OTHER	303	The requested resource can be obtained by performing a GET request on the URL in the Location header.
HTTP_BAD_REQUEST	400	The request failed because it was malformed.
HTTP_FORBIDDEN	403	The request is valid, but the server is not permitted to action it, typically due to access control restrictions.
HTTP_NOT_FOUND	404	The resource corresponding to the URL supplied by the client does not exist.

To see this code in action, select the HttpClient MIDlet from the *Chapter6.jad* file in the *ora\ch6* directory of this book's example code and type a URL into the text field that appears, as shown in Figure 6-3. If you compare the result in the right-hand side of the figure with that in Figure 6-1, you'll see that what you get this time is different: here, you see the start of the web page itself, whereas in Figure 6-1 you saw the HTTP headers returned by the server; these precede the web page.

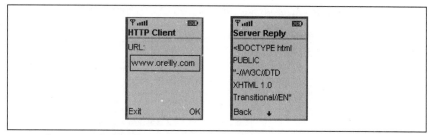

Figure 6-3: Using HTTP to retrieve an HTML page

HTTP Requests

To make proper use of the MIDP HTTP support, you need to understand a little about how HTTP requests and responses are structured and how your code interacts with them when using the `HttpConnection` interface. An HTTP request message consists of three parts:

- An HTTP request line, followed by a newline character. This part is always present.

- An optional set of request headers each on its own line, followed by a blank line.

- The message body, which contains any data that needs to accompany the request. This part is present only if it is needed.

The request line specifies the request method and the path of the resource to be retrieved, together with any query parameters and the protocol version to be used. Here is a typical request line that might be generated from the URL *http://www. oreilly.com/index.html*:

```
GET /index.html HTTP/1.1
```

The word GET corresponds to the request method, which tells the web server what it is supposed to do. HTTP 1.1 specifies seven different request methods, but MIDP does not require the implementation to provide any support for OPTIONS, PUT, TRACE, and DELETE. Only the request methods shown in Table 6-2 are guaranteed to work properly in MIDP 1.0.

Table 6-2: HTTP Request Methods Supported by MIDP 1.0

Method	Symbolic Constant	Meaning
GET	HttpConnection.GET	Requests the transfer of the resource given by the path in the request line. The path is given relative to the root of the web server's name space and may include query parameters. For the Yahoo! finance example shown earlier, the request line would look like this: `GET /q?s=SUNW&d=v1 HTTP/1.1` When GET is used, no data should be sent along with the request, but headers are permitted.

Table 6-2: HTTP Request Methods Supported by MIDP 1.0 (continued)

Method	Symbolic Constant	Meaning
HEAD	HttpConnection.HEAD	HEAD is the same as GET, but the web server returns only a response indicating whether a GET request with the same parameters would have succeeded, together with the HTTP headers that would have accompanied the data. It does not return the data itself. This can be used to obtain information such as the size of the data or the time at which the data was last modified, without having to transfer the data itself.
POST	HttpConnection.POST	It is common for HTML pages that include forms that the user fills with information to result in GET requests where the form fields are turned into parameters that are appended to the URL. The POST method is an alternative to this approach: the parameters are sent as data in the body of the request rather than in the URL. This is useful if there is a lot of query information, because some systems impose arbitrary limits on the size of the URL. It also allows the query data to be hidden from the user. An example of a POST request can be found in "An HTTP Example," later in this chapter.

The default request method for `HttpConnection` is GET. You can change this if necessary using the `setRequestMethod()` method, for example:

```
conn.setRequestMethod(HttpConnection.POST);
```

The request headers follow the request line. Each header consists of the header name (which is case-insensitive), a colon, and the header value, followed by a newline. Headers can be used to convey information to the web server, such as the encoding used for the data accompanying a POST request or specifying the amount of data that accompanies it. A POST request containg 256 bytes of data, for example, would include the following header:

```
Content-Length: 256
```

The complete set of valid headers can be found in Section 14 of RFC 2616. Table 6-3 summarizes the ones that you are likely to use most frequently.

Table 6-3: Frequently Used HTTP Headers

Name	Meaning
Connection	If this header is present and has the value `Close`, the connection will be closed once the server sends its reply message. If you do not include this header, the same connection can be used to exchange several messages.
Content-Length	Contains the number of bytes in the message, not including the headers.

Table 6-3: Frequently Used HTTP Headers (continued)

Name	Meaning
Content-Type	Describes how the data in the message body is encoded. Typically this header specifies the data type of the heading; occasionally, the character encoding is also included. The most common value for this heading is: Content-Type: text/html but you might also see something like: Content-Type: text/html; charset=ISO-8859-1 which specifies that the message contains an HTML page with characters from the ISO-8869-1 character set. The data content is described using MIME types registered by the Internet Assigned Numbers. A full list of valid MIME types can be found at *ftp://ftp.isu.edu/in-notes/iana/assignments/media-types/media-types*. This header is always sent in reply messages from a web server. Client software sometimes uses this heading in conjunction with a POST request to describe the data that it is sending to the web server.
Date	The date and time at which the message was sent. The date format is described in RFC 2616. For example: Date:Tue, 07 Aug 2001 20:14:50 GMT
Last-Modified	The date and time at which the resource returned by the server was last changed. The date is in the same format as the Date header. This may be stored by the client and used to cache the returned data. A client that caches data typically includes an If-Modified-Since header giving this time when the next request is made for this data. When this header is present, the server returns the data only if its copy is more recent.
Location	Used by a web server to redirect the client to an alternate location at which the requested resource can be found. The value of this header is an absolute URL: Location: http://www.host.com/elsewhere.html
Server	Contains text that identifies the responding server. This header is informational only: Server: Apache/1.3.14 (Unix) PHP/4.0.4
User-Agent	Contains text that identifies the client making a request. Like the Server header, this is generally used for informational purposes only. However, the MIDP specification recommends that the device profile and configuration identifier be included in this header field when communicating with a server that is supplying MIDlets to be downloaded to the device: User-Agent: Profile/MIDP-1.0 Configuration/CLDC-1.0

Wireless Java

Headers are set using the **setRequestProperty()** method, which requires the header name and the associated value as arguments. For example, the following line sets the Content-Type header:

```
conn.setRequestProperty("Content-Type",
    "application/x-www-form-urlencoded");
```

Note that you can set the request method and the headers only before any data has been sent, because this information has to be placed at the start of the byte stream sent to the server.

One final point to be aware of in connection with HTTP requests concerns the use of query parameters, either in the URL or in the message body when sent as part of a POST request. As stated earlier, query parameters are sent in the following form:

```
name1=value1&name2=value2&name3=value3
```

This looks very simple and obvious, but there is a catch: what if the value part needs to contain an ampersand or an equal sign? Simply including these characters in the value would cause confusion, because they are already used as delimiters. In fact, there are a number of characters that you can't just place in the value part of a query parameter. Instead of sending parameters as they are, you need to carry out a process known as *URL encoding* on the parameter values. The rules for URL encoding are applied to each individual character of the value:

- Uppercase and lowercase alphabetical characters in the ASCII character set (that is, a through z and A through Z) and the digits 0 through 9 are left unchanged.

- The characters . (period), - (hyphen), * (asterisk), and _ (underscore) are also left unchanged.

- Every space is changed to a plus sign (+).

- All other characters are converted to their 2-digit hexadecimal representation preceded by a percent character (%).

Since the last rule refers to using two hexadecimal digits to represent a character, it is clear that these rules were framed with standard 8-bit character encodings in mind. Java, of course, works with Unicode, so each character is 16 bits wide, requiring 4 hexadecimal digits to represent it. The correct approach to this problem is to convert each Unicode character to the corresponding bytes that would represent it in the platform's default representation (or the representation to be used on the network, which might be different). This is done by writing the value through an `OutputStreamWriter` and encoding each resulting byte as a percent sign followed by two hexadecimal digits. If you only send values that contain ASCII characters, you won't have to worry about this detail.

Say, for example, that you wanted to send a query string consisting of the following two parameters:

```
Publisher=O'Reilly
Title=Java Swing
```

After URL encoding, you would actually append the following string to the URL for a GET request or place it in the message body for a POST operation:

```
Publisher=O%27Reilly&Title=Java+Swing
```

Notice that the apostrophe has been translated to its hexadecimal equivalent, and the space in the book title has become a plus sign. The bad news about this is that, in MIDP 1.0, there is nothing equivalent to the J2SE `java.net.URLEncode` and `java.net.URLDecode` classes to do this job for you; you have to write the code yourself. In practice, you are unlikely to need the decode facility, since this is used mainly by web servers. As far as encoding is concerned, if you don't want to write the code yourself, there is a class called `EncodeURL` in the example source code for this chapter that contains the code necessary to handle URL encoding, as long as you stick to ASCII characters.

HTTP Responses

HTTP responses have an almost identical structure to HTTP requests, consisting of the following:

- A single response line, terminated by a newline.

- A set of headers, each terminated by a newline. The last header is followed by a blank line to separate it from the message body.

- The message body containing the data. The format of the data is specified in the Content-Type header.

The response line, an example of which you can see on the right side of Figure 6-1, has three parts:

- The protocol version used by the web server. This is usually HTTP/1.1, but you may come across older servers that use HTTP/1.0.

- A numeric response code that indicates the result of the request. The most common response codes are listed in Table 6-1.

- A text message that describes or qualifies the response code.

You can get the response code and response message using the HttpConnection getResponseCode() and getResponseMessage() methods. As noted earlier, you should always check that the response code is HttpConnection.HTTP_OK (which has the value 200) before interpreting the message body, since some servers send further information regarding an error in the message body.

Here is a typical set of HTTP response headers that were obtained from the O'Reilly web server:

```
date = Tue, 07 Aug 2001 20:14:50 GMT
server = Apache/1.3.14 (Unix) PHP/4.0.4
last-modified = Tue, 07 Aug 2001 17:17:13 GMT
etag = "47eb3-793f-3b702299"
accept-ranges = bytes
content-length = 31039
content-type = text/html
```

There are several ways to get the headers from a response message. You can get the value associated with any header by calling the HttpConnection getHeaderField() method, which returns a String, or null if the requested header is not present in the response:

```
String contentType = conn.getHeaderField("Content-Type");
```

Note that the header name string passed to this method and to the others in this section is not case-sensitive.

For header fields that have integer or date values, you can avoid parsing the strings yourself by using the following methods:

```
public int getHeaderFieldInt(String name, int def) throws IOException
public long getHeaderFieldDate(String name, long def) throws IOException
```

The value of the def argument is returned if the named header is not found or if it does not have a value of the required type. The getHeaderFieldDate() method returns the value in a date-valued field expressed as the number of milliseconds since January 1, 1970.

A small number of fields have dedicated methods that return the associated value:

```
public long getExpiration() throws IOException
public long getDate() throws IOException
public long getLastModified() throws IOException
```

These methods all return zero if the required information is not in the header. The getType(), getLength(), and getEncoding() methods that HttpConnection inherits from its parent interface (ContentConnection) also work by getting their return values from the header.

Finally, you can find out which headers are present in the reply using the getHeaderFieldKey() method:

```
public String getHeaderFieldKey(int index) throws IOException
```

The index starts at zero for the first header. There is no method that returns the number of available headers, so the usual approach is to loop until getHeaderFieldKey() returns null. The following code uses this method to print the names and values of all of the headers in a reply message:

```
for (int i = 0; ; i++) {
    String name = conn.getHeaderFieldKey(i);
    String value = conn.getHeaderField(i);
    if (name == null) {
        // Reached the last header
        break;
    }
    System.out.println(name + ": " + value)
}
```

Notice that this code uses an overloaded version of getHeaderField() that takes a field index instead of a header name. It could equally well have used getHeaderField(name) to get the header value.

An HTTP Example

For a MIDP application, the most likely reason to use HTTP is to fetch an HTML page from a web server and extract some information from it for display. This process almost certainly starts with the application displaying a form from which it obtains parameters that will be sent to the server along with the appropriate URL. Essentially, your application plays the role of an intelligent web browser, charged with the task of displaying only the essential parts of a web page that could not be shown in its entirety due to screen size. Because the HttpConnection is much more basic than the HTTP support in J2SE, and the environment is restrictive in terms of resources, it is a little harder to implement this kind of feature in a J2ME application that it would be with J2SE. To illustrate some of the problems that arise, let's look at what should be a relatively simple task.

In this example, we want to be able to go to *www.amazon.com*, look up a book, and find its sales ranking and the number of reader reviews that have appeared. All this information appears on a book's catalog page, but it would not be practical to display the whole page, so we want to extract the details we need and put them on the screen of the mobile device.

We first need to figure out how to get the correct catalog page for the book. For a human, the most obvious way to do this is to go to the web page and enter the book's title in the Search box. Unfortunately, instead of getting back the book's catalog page, you get a list of all the books that might match your search string, and you have to choose one. This would be very difficult for an application to handle, because it would have to interpret what it gets back and try to find the links to the real books. A more promising approach is to use the book's ISBN number, which is unique to that book. In fact, if you know a book's ISBN number, you can create a URL that you can use to make a GET request that returns the book's catalog page.

There is another, slightly more complex approach. It gets the same result, but it also allows us to show you how to extract values from a form-based interface and use them to perform an HTTP POST request. We'll use this latter approach as the basis of this example.

Obviously, we're interested mainly in the details of using `HttpConnection` to ask for the book's catalog page and how to extract the information that we need from it, so we're not going to delve into the nitty gritty of creating the user interface itself. To give you a feel for what we are aiming for, the screenshot on the left side of Figure 6-4 shows the form used to enter the ISBN; the results of the search are shown in the screenshot on the right. If you start the J2ME Wireless Toolkit MIDlet runner, you can use this application for yourself by choosing the Ranking MIDlet from *Chapter6.jad* in the directory *ora\ch6* of the examples for this book.

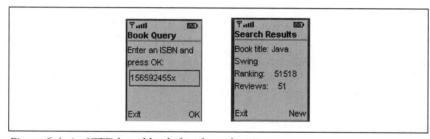

Figure 6-4: An HTTP-based book details application

This MIDlet takes the ISBN from the input form, uses it to fetch the book's catalog page, scans the HTML for the information it needs, and returns that information to be displayed by the user interface code. Given the ISBN, we need to return three pieces of information:

- The book's title
- Its current sales ranking
- The number of user reviews it has

For convenience, we'll define a class that lets us store these three properties along with the ISBN. Here's how the members of this class are defined:

```
public class BookInfo {
    int    id;                    // Used when persisting
```

```
String isbn;          // The book ISBN
String title;         // The book title
int    reviews;       // Number of reviews
int    ranking;       // Current ranking
int    lastReviews;   // Last review count
int    lastRanking;   // Last ranking
```

We've also added three other fields that we don't need in this example. They'll come in handy later in this chapter when I show you how to save this information in persistent storage on the mobile device.

This is the information we need, so how do we get it? To fetch the catalog page for a book with a given ISBN, we need to send a POST request to the following URL:

http://www.amazon.com/exec/obidos/search-handle-form/0

We also need to supply the parameters that specify the Amazon.com store to be searched and the ISBN for the book. Since we are using a POST message, these parameters go in the message body rather than in the URL itself. To look for ISBN 156592455X, for example, the message body should contain the following:

```
index=books&field-keywords=156592455X
```

(If you are wondering how you would know to do this, you simply have to examine the HTML page that contains the search box a human user would use and work out what would be sent to the web server.)

Assuming that the ISBN is valid, you'll get back the HTML for the book's catalog page. If you follow this process with a web browser and view the source of the returned page, you'll see what to do to get the needed information from the HTML. The basic technique is to scan for a fixed sequence of characters that precedes what we need and then pull out the desired bytes by reference to those fixed points. For a book catalog page, the book's title follows the string "buying info:", its sales rank is found immediately after the string "Sales Rank", and the number of reviews appears after the text "Based on". Once you've worked all this out, it should be simple to write the code to use HttpConnection to fetch the page and then scrape the desired details out of the HTML you get back. In fact, in the J2ME environment, this isn't quite as simple as you might think. Let's look at the fetching and analysis issues separately.

Fetching the HTML page

The code that fetches the HTML page for a book and creates a BookInfo class instance is implemented in a class called Fetcher. The code for the fetch() method of this class, which does all the work, is shown in Example 6-1.

Example 6-1: Fetching the HTML Page for a Book

```
private static final String BASE_URL = "http://www.amazon.com";
private static final String QUERY_URL = BASE_URL +
                          "/exec/obidos/search-handle-form/0";
private static final int MAX_REDIRECTS = 5;

public static boolean fetch(BookInfo info) throws IOException {
```

Example 6-1: Fetching the HTML Page for a Book (continued)

```
InputStream is = null;
OutputStream os = null;
HttpConnection conn = null;
int redirects = 0;
try {
    String isbn = info.getIsbn();
    String query = "index=books&field-keywords=" + isbn + "\r\n";
    String requestMethod = HttpConnection.POST;
    String name = QUERY_URL;

    while (redirects < MAX_REDIRECTS) {
        conn = (HttpConnection)Connector.open(name,
            Connector.READ_WRITE);
        // Send the ISBN number to perform the query
        conn.setRequestMethod(requestMethod);
        if (requestMethod.equals(HttpConnection.POST)) {
            conn.setRequestProperty("Content-Type",
                "application/x-www-form-urlencoded");
            os = conn.openOutputStream();
            os.write(query.getBytes());

            os.close();
            os = null;
        }
        // Read the response from the server
        is = conn.openInputStream();
        int code = conn.getResponseCode();

        // If we get a redirect, try again at the new location
        if ((code >= HttpConnection.HTTP_MOVED_PERM && code <=
                HttpConnection.HTTP_SEE_OTHER) ||
                code == HttpConnection.HTTP_TEMP_REDIRECT) {
            // Get the URL of the new location (always absolute)
            name = conn.getHeaderField("Location");
            is.close();
            conn.close();
            is = null;
            conn = null;

            if (++redirects > MAX_REDIRECTS) {
                // Too many redirects - give up.
                break;
            }

            // Choose the appropriate request method
            requestMethod = HttpConnection.POST;
            if (code == HttpConnection.HTTP_MOVED_TEMP ||
                code == HttpConnection.HTTP_SEE_OTHER) {
                requestMethod = HttpConnection.GET;
            }
            continue;
        }
```

Wireless Java

Example 6-1: Fetching the HTML Page for a Book (continued)

```
                String type = conn.getType();
                if (code == HttpConnection.HTTP_OK &&  type.equals("text/html")) {
                    info.setFromInputStream(is);
                    return true;
                }
            }
        } catch (Throwable t) {
            System.out.println(t);
        } finally {
            // Tidy up code (not shown)
        }
        return false;
}
```

As you can see, instead of simply building the URL, calling the `Connector.open()` method, sending the POST data, and reading the response, this method actually contains a loop that can make more than one request to the server. Initially, the `open()` method is called with the URL for the search form (shown earlier), the request method is set to `HttpConnection.POST`, and the data that forms the query is written to the message body, like this:

```
conn.setRequestProperty("Content-Type",
    "application/x-www-form-urlencoded");
os = conn.openOutputStream();
os.write(query.getBytes());
os.close();
os = null;
```

The query string, which contains the book ISBN, is written to the message body by obtaining an `OutputStream` and then calling its `write()` method, passing the result of converting the query string to an array of bytes in the device's local encoding. In this case, since we know the query contains only alphabetic and numeric characters, there is no need to perform URL encoding. In the general case, you would have to encode the parameter values. That is, in the following query string:

```
param1=value1&param2=value2
```

you would URL-encode `value1` and `value2`. This code also sets the Content-Type header of the outgoing request to `application/x-www-form-urlencoded`, which tells the server to interpret the message body as if it had been generated from an HTML form, which simply says that it is in `param=value` form. If you don't do this, some servers do not interpret the POST data correctly.

The next step is to open an input stream and check the response code from the server's reply message. You would hope that the server would reply with `HTTP_OK` and send the book's catalog page. However, it does not. When you submit a book search, the Amazon web server doesn't send you the page you need; instead, it sends you an HTTP redirect message that contains the URL you need to access the page directly. An HTTP redirect is a reply message where the response code is in the range 301 to 307. Redirect messages and how you are expected to respond to them are described in the HTTP 1.1 specification (RFC 2616). When you receive such a message, you need to do the following:

1. Get the URL to which you are being redirected from the `Location` header of the response. This is always an absolute URL.

2. Close the original connection and its input and output streams.

3. Use the `Connector open()` method to get an `HttpConnection` to the new URL.

4. Set the request method for the new connection. If the response code is `HTTP_MOVED_TEMP` (302) or `HTTP_SEE_OTHER` (303), use a GET instead of a POST request. For the other types, you continue to POST the original query data.

5. Send the new request, open an input stream, and check the response code again.

Theoretically, even after following one redirection you could get another one, or even several more. To accomodate this possibilty, the code in Example 6-1 makes the initial connection perform the redirection process in a loop. However, in order to avoid the consequences of a server error causing an infinite loop, it allow a maximum of five redirections. You can handle this without an arbitrary limit on the number of redirections by keeping a history of the redirection URLs and stopping only if the same one is received twice. In practice, you will rarely see more than five redirects, so the simple solution shown here will suffice.

The need for application code to follow redirects in this way is a consequence of the lightweight implementation of the `HttpConnection` interface, and it is unique to the J2ME environment. If you are familiar with using HTTP with J2SE, you will probably find this surprising, because the J2SE HTTP support handles redirection transparently, and you probably weren't even aware that it was happening.

Analyzing the HTML

Eventually, the server should return an `HTTP_OK` response code, together with the book's catalog page. Extracting the information that we need should now simply be a case of reading the reply data, converting it into a `String`, and using the `indexOf()` method to look for the strings that precede the book title, sales ranking, and review count. The code might look like this:

```
DataInputStream dis = conn.openDataInputStream();
int length = conn.getLength();  // Length from Content-Length header
byte[] buffer = new byte[length];
dis.readFully(buffer);
String reply = new String(buffer);

// Find the book's title
int index = reply.indexOf("buying info: ");
```

This code is theoretically fine, but, in practice, it is unlikely to work in all cases. In the constrained environment of most MIDP implementations, there is unlikely to be enough heap space to allow you to read the entire web page into memory and convert it into a `String` as this code requires. This is especially true in this case, because web pages returned by Amazon.com are relatively large: pages bigger than 50 KB are quite normal. A MIDP environment often has only 64 KB of heap space for the whole VM!

The only reliable way to handle this problem is to read the response byte by byte and perform the search manually (that is, without using any prewritten code from the core J2ME libraries). The details of this operation are not really relevant to our discussion of HTTP. If you're interested, you'll find the code in the `InputHelper` class in the directory *ora\ch6* of this book's example source code.

As demonstrated by this example, it is often necessary in the J2ME environment to approach a problem slightly differently than you would if you were working with J2SE, and you may have to do a little more work to achieve the same result.

Persistent Storage

Almost all MIDlets need to be able to save information so that it is retained between invocations. Examples of the types of information that might need to be stored include the following:

- Data entered by the user, such as text typed into a memo pad application.

- User configuration or preference information. For a mail application, this might be the name of the mail server to which outgoing mail should be sent or how frequently to poll for new incoming mail.

- Values that the user recently entered or uses frequently. For an application that accesses the Internet, for example, it would be helpful to keep a history of recently used URLs that the user can use as a shortcut list.

A J2SE application typically stores state in local files that are quickly and easily accessible from the hard drive or transparently accessible over a fast local area network. Mobile devices, however, do not have local disks and rarely have network connectivity that is permanently available or fast enough to support storage of frequently used information at a remote location. The MIDP specification requires all implementations to provide a persistent storage facility so that information can be preserved while a MIDlet is not running or when the device is turned off. In practice, the actual storage mechanism may vary from device to device, but the programming interface does not, which makes MIDlets that use this facility more portable than if they had been required to be aware of the device-dependent details. The MIDP storage facility is based around a class called `RecordStore` and is implemented in the `javax.microedition.rms` package.

Record Stores

A record store is a collection of records that the MIDP implementation stores in some way on its host device. Each record store is identified by a case-sensitive name consisting of 1 to 32 Unicode characters. Record store names are shared by all MIDlets in a MIDlet suite, so that the combination (record store name, MIDlet suite) uniquely identifies a record store. This has the following consequences:

- A MIDlet in a MIDlet suite has access to record stores created by itself or by any other MIDlet in the same suite. If, for example, a record store called `Scores` is created by one MIDlet, an attempt by a different MIDlet in the same suite to open a record store called `Scores` results in the same record store being accessed.

- MIDlets cannot see record stores created by MIDlets in other MIDlet suites. As a result, it is not possible for a MIDlet in suite A to open the Scores record store (or any record store) created by a MIDlet in suite B. It is not possible for a MIDlet to get any information about record stores belonging to other suites.

 Record stores are a private mechanism that allows MIDlets to retain data on a device. A consequence of the design of record stores is that it is not possible for a MIDlet to access data belonging to other MIDlet suites or, perhaps more significantly, data belonging to other non-Java applications on the same device. This latter restriction is quite significant, because it means that you cannot access things like a user's address book or appointment diary from a MIDlet. Similarly, non-Java applications cannot access data stored by MIDlets. Whether these restrictions will be addressed in a future version of the MIDP specification remains to be seen.

To create or open a record store, MIDlets use the following static RecordStore method:

```
public static RecordStore openRecordStore(String name, boolean create)
```

This method locates a record store with the given name, opens it, and returns a RecordStore object that can be used to access it. If no record store with the given name exists, and the create argument is true, a new one is created. If the create argument is false, a RecordStoreNotFoundException is thrown if the record store does not exist. The usual pattern for accessing a record store is this:

```
RecordStore scores = RecordStore.openRecordStore("Scores", true);
```

This opens the record store if it already exists and creates it if it does not. Opening and creation of record stores is handled by the same method, so if you always set the create argument to true, you do not need to be concerned about whether the record store already exists before you open it, and attempting to create a record store that has already been created by another MIDlet in the same suite is not a problem either.

When a MIDlet has finished with a record store, it should close it using the closeRecordStore() method. If a record store is opened more than once by a MIDlet, it will not actually be closed until each open instance is closed:

```
// Open the same record store twice
RecordStore scores = RecordStore.openRecordStore("Scores", true);
RecordStore scores2 = RecordStore.openRecordStore("Scores", true);

// Close the record store. This first call does not actually close it
scores.closeRecordStore();

// This call finally closes the record store
scores2.closeRecordStore();
```

In the example shown here, scores and scores2 are actually references to the same RecordStore object. Each RecordStore has a count that is incremented on each openRecordStore() call and decremented when closeRecordStore() is called. Only when this counter reaches zero is the record store itself closed. Once the record store is closed, attempts to use its RecordStore object fail with a RecordStoreNotException.

A record store can be removed by calling the static deleteRecordStore() method:

```
public static void deleteRecordStore(String name)
```

Since the name argument is automatically scoped to the current MIDlet suite, it is not possible for a MIDlet to remove a record store belonging to a MIDlet in another suite. Record stores cannot be removed while they are in use by a MIDlet. If an attempt is made to do this, a RecordStoreException is thrown. If no record store with the given name exists, a RecordStoreNotFoundException is thrown. Note that only closed record stores can be deleted, and a record store is automatically deleted when the MIDlet suite that owns it is uninstalled from the device.

A MIDlet can get the names of all the record stores owned by its MIDlet suite using the listRecordStores() method:

```
public static String[] listRecordStores()
```

If the MIDlet suite does not have any associated record stores, this method returns null rather than an empty array.

There are several other operations that can be performed at the record store level, all of which require an open RecordStore object:

```
public String getName()
public long getLastModified()
public int getVersion()
public int getSize()
public int getSizeAvailable()
```

The getName() method returns the name of the RecordStore to which it is applied. The getLastModified() method returns the time at which the last modification was made to the RecordStore, measured as the number of milliseconds from January 1, 1970 (which is the same as the values returned by the System currentTimeMillis() method). The getVersion() method returns an integer value that is changed each time a record in the record store is inserted, deleted, or modified. This method can be used by software that backs up record stores to more permanent storage by allowing it to detect quickly whether the record store has changed by comparing the current version number with that of the last archived copy.

The getSize() method returns the number of bytes that the record store occupies. The getSizeAvailable() method returns the amount by which the record store could grow given the current space available for record stores on the device. Note that both these figures include space that might be allocated to internal data structures that are used to maintain the record store itself, as well as the space occupied by record data. Therefore, if the getSizeAvailable() method returns 100, it does not follow that a 100-byte record could be created in the record store, because some space might be needed to store information to manage that record.

Records

A record store contains zero or more records, each of which is an arbitrary array of bytes with an associated integer identifier that can be used to unambiguously identify it. A record's identifier is not part of the record itself but is held separately by the implementation and assigned when the record is created. Identifiers obey the following simple rules:

- The identifier assigned to the first record created in a record store has the value 1.

- The identifier assigned to a new record is one greater than that assigned to the record created before it.

If you create a new record store and add several records to it, the identifiers assigned to these records will, therefore, be 1, 2, 3, 4, and so on. If a record is subsequently removed, its identifier is not reused; for example, if you removed the record with identifier 2 and created another new record, it would be assigned identifier 5, not 2. As a result, as records are deleted and new ones added, the set of valid identifiers no longer constitutes a contiguous sequence of numbers; instead, it is quite likely that the active identifiers will have widely different values.

A new record is created using the addRecord() method, which returns the value of the newly assigned identifier:

```
public int addRecord(byte[] data, int offset, int size)
```

The record is created from the the range of bytes from data[offset] to data[offset + size - 1]. At first sight, it may not seem very convenient to have to supply the data to be written in the form of a byte array, because most of the time you deal with objects that hold data in instance fields. A simple way to create a record from a class is to use a DataOutputStream to write the values from the class that you need to store into a ByteArrayOutputStream, which will create the appropriate array of bytes for you. Suppose, for example, that you have an object that represents a player's score in a game, and you want to save this as a record in the Scores record store for your suite of MIDlet games. The score recording class might be defined like this:

```
public class ScoreRecord {
    public String playerName;      // Player name
    public int score;              // Player's score
}
```

Here's how you would store a player's score in a record store:

```
// Create an object to be written
ScoreRecord record = new ScoreRecord();
record.playerName = "TopNotch";
record.score = 12345678;

// Create the output streams
ByteArrayOutputStream baos = new ByteArrayOutputStream();
DataOutputStream os = new DataOutputStream(baos);

// Write the values to be saved to the output streams
os.writeUTF(record.playerName);
```

```
os.writeInt(record.score);
os.close();

// Get the byte array with the saved values
byte[] data = baos.toByteArray();

// Write the record to the record store
int id = recordStore.addRecord(data, 0, data.length);
```

 You might be tempted to try to save the contents of an object by writing it to an ObjectOutputStream and feeding the output from that stream into a ByteArrayOutputStream. Unfortunately, you cannot do this because neither CLDC nor MIDP includes support for object serialization.

Using a DataOutputStream and a ByteArrayOutputStream in this way frees you from worry about how to convert Java types and primitives into a collection of bytes. It also relieves you of the responsibility of allocating the byte array. Retrieving a record from the record store and unpacking it is simply a matter of reversing the above code, using the RecordStore getRecord() method:

```
public byte[] getRecord(int recordId)
```

This method throws an InvalidRecordIDException if you pass it an identifier that does not correspond to an active record in the record store. Here is how you would retrieve a player's name and score from a record store, given the identifier of the record containing the information:

```
byte[] data = recordStore.getRecord(recordId);
DataInputStream is = new DataInputStream(new ByteArrayInputStream(data));
ScoreRecord record = new ScoreRecord();
record.playerName = is.readUTF();
record.score = is.readInt();
is.close();
```

You can update the content of an existing record by using the setRecord() method:

```
public void setRecord(int recordId, byte[] data, int offset, int size);
```

The process of modifying a record is simply a combination of the two steps shown above for reading and writing records. To add 10 to the score in a given record, for example, you would use the code just shown to read the record, change the score, and then write it back out using setRecord() instead of addRecord():

```
// Modify the score
record.score += 10;

ByteArrayOutputStream baos = new ByteArrayOutputStream();
DataOutputStream os = new DataOutputStream(baos);
os.writeUTF(record.playerName);
os.writeInt(record.score);
os.close();
```

```
byte[] data = baos.toByteArray();

// Write the record to the record store, overwriting the existing record
recordStore.setRecord(recordId, data, 0, data.length);
```

Note that there is no requirement that the new and old record sizes be the same. The implementation does whatever is needed to store the modified record content into the record store, which might involve moving other data around to accomodate an enlarged record.

A record can be deleted using the deleteRecord() method:

```
public void deleteRecord(int recordId)
```

Changes to the content of a record store are reported as events to objects that implement the RecordListener interface and register with the RecordStore using the addRecordListener() method. The RecordListener interface consists of three methods:

```
public void recordAdded(RecordStore store, int recordId);
public void recordChanged(RecordStore store, int recordId);
public void recordDeleted(RecordStore store, int recordId);
```

Each of these methods is passed a reference to the RecordStore in which the operation took place and the identifier of the record that was affected. A listener can be removed by calling the removeRecordListener() method. All listeners are automatically removed when a RecordStore is closed as a result of calling closeRecordStore(). If the store is opened more than once, the listeners are not removed until the last closeRecordStore() call is made (that is, until the record store has been closed as many times as it was opened).

There are three other record-related methods provided by the RecordStore class:

```
public int getNumRecords();
public int getRecordSize(int recordId);
public int getNextRecordID();
```

The getNumRecords() method returns the number of records in the record store. This does not, of course, include deleted records. The getRecordSize() method returns the size of a record with a given identifier. This is actually the size of the useful data in the record and does not include any implementation-dependent information that might be stored along with the MIDlet data. Finally, getNextRecordID() returns the value of the identifier that will be assigned to the next record to be created in the record store. This method is useful if you want to create a reference from one record to another (to simulate a database foreign key) or if you need to embed the identifier for a record within the record itself, because you usually don't get the identifier until after you have written the data to the record store. You'll see an example of this in "A RecordStore Example," later in this chapter. You need to be very careful when using this method, because the returned value is no longer correct once addRecord() is called. This is particularly dangerous in a multithreaded environment if a different thread can call addRecord() after getNextRecordID() is called but before addRecord() has been used to create the record in the original thread. See the section "Multithreading and Concurrent Access," later in this chapter, for a brief discussion of multithreading considerations when using record stores.

Record Enumerations

The RecordStore methods that are used to access, modify, and delete records assume that you know the identifier of the record you want to operate on. The record store uses the identifier as a key to identify a record, but it is not usually convenient for application code to remember which identifier corresponds to a piece of data. In the case of game scores, for example, you would most likely want to key on the player's name and retrieve the record for a given player. The most obvious way to do this would be to retrieve every record and compare its name field with the name of the player to be matched, using code like this:

```
for (int i = 1, limit = store.getNextRecordID(); i < limit; i++) {
    try {
        // Get the next record from the record store
        byte[] data = store.getRecord(i);
        // Get name from record (not shown)
        // If the name matches the required player name,
        // break (not shown)
    } catch (InvalidRecordIDException ex) {
        // Skip records that have been deleted
    }
}
```

The problem with this code is that it becomes less and less efficient as records are added and deleted from the record store, because, as noted earlier, the list of active record identifiers can quickly become sparse. A record store might, for example, contain three records with identifiers 1, 5001, and 10000. The code shown here would need to iterate up to 10,000 times to process all three records, with most of its execution time wasted finding out that the identifiers it is iterating through are invalid.

To avoid the need for this brute force approach, the RecordStore API includes a method called enumerateRecords() that you can use to search efficiently through all the records in the record store to get the identifier for the record that you need:

```
public RecordEnumeration enumerateRecords(RecordFilter filter,
    RecordComparator comparator, boolean keepUpdated)
```

The filter argument allows you to determine which records in the record store are included in the returned RecordEnumeration. The order of the records is controlled by the RecordComparator. The keepUpdated argument specifies whether the content of the enumeration should change to reflect modifications to the record store itself.

The following call gets a static snapshot containing all the records in the record store:

```
RecordEnumeration enum = recordStore.enumerateRecords(null, null, false);
```

The number of entries in this enumeration can be obtained using the numRecords() method. In this example, in which no filter is used, this will be the same as the number of records in the record store itself.

Using enumerateRecords() to access all the records in a record store is likely to be much more efficient than the simple-minded loop shown earlier, because the implementation can take advantage of the fact that it can directly access all the active records without having to "poll" for the existence of each record.

MIDP does not define the order of the records in this enumeration. Because records do not have any natural ordering (except, possibly, based on their identifiers), you shouldn't make any assumptions about ordering when you don't supply a RecordComparator. Before looking at how to determine an order or exclude records that are not of interest, let's look at what a RecordEnumeration is.

The RecordEnumeration interface contains a set of methods that can be used to iterate through the record identifiers that it contains. Unlike a regular Java Enumeration, a RecordEnumeration allows you to traverse either forwards or backwards and also lets you change direction at any time. The hasNextElement() and hasPreviousElement() methods allow you to find out whether the end of the enumeration has been reached, while nextRecordId() and previousRecordId() are used to fetch the actual elements of the enumeration:

```
// Traverse forwards
while (enum.hasNextElement()) {
    int id = enum.nextRecordId();

    // Do something with this record id (not shown)
}

// Traverse backwards
while (enum.hasPreviousElement()) {
    int id = enum.previousRecordId();

    // Do something with this record id (not shown)
}
```

When an enumeration is created, it is logically positioned "before" the first identifier; each time it is called, the nextRecordId() method increments the position and then returns the item at the new position. If you create an enumeration and call previousRecordId() instead of nextRecordId(), the position cursor is moved to the last element of the enumeration. Hence, the following code processes the enumeration backwards:

```
RecordEnumeration enum = recordStore.enumerateRecords(null, null, false);
while (enum.hasPreviousElement()) {
    int id = enum.previousRecordId();

    // Do something with this record id (not shown)
}
```

If you call nextRecordId() after reaching the end of the enumeration or previousRecordId() after reaching the beginning, an InvalidRecordID-Exception is thrown.

Typically, after obtaining a record identifier, you read the content of the corresponding record into memory by calling the getRecord() method. You can combine these two steps using the nextRecord() or previousRecord() methods:

```
// Traverse forwards
while (enum.hasNextElement()) {
```

```
    byte[] record = enum.nextRecord();

    // Do something with this record (not shown)
}

// Traverse backwards
while (enum.hasPreviousElement()) {
    byte[] record = enum.previousRecord();

    // Do something with this record (not shown)
}
```

These methods are convenient if you simply want read access to the records, but they are not suitable if you want to modify the data, because changes made in the returned array are not automatically reflected in the record store. Moreover, you don't have a record identifier that you could pass to setRecord() to write out the data once you have modified it in memory.

Unlike regular Enumerations, RecordEnumeration has a reset() method that allows you to restart the iteration from the beginning:

```
// Traverse forwards
while (enum.hasNextElement()) {
    byte[] record = enum.nextRecord();

    // Do something with this record (not shown)
}

enum.reset();      // Reset to initial state

// Read all the records again
while (enum.hasNextElement()) {
    byte[] record = enum.nextRecord();

    // Do something with this record (not shown)
}
```

When you call enumerateRecords() and pass false for the keepUpdated argument, you get a *static* enumeration that reflects the state of the record store at the point that the enumeration was created. Subsequent changes in the record store content (made either by the same MIDlet or by another MIDlet in the same suite) are not reflected in the enumeration. This has two consequences:

- Newly added records do not appear in the enumeration.

- If a record is deleted before its identifier has been retrieved from the enumeration, an InvalidRecordIDException is thrown if that identifier is subsequently used to retrieve the deleted record, whether by calling getRecord(enum.nextRecordId()) or enum.nextRecord().

In order to safely traverse a static enumeration if there is a possibility that records might be deleted while enumeration is being used, you need to catch and ignore InvalidRecordIDException:

```
while (enum.hasNextElement()) {
    try {
```

```
        int id = enum.nextRecordId();
        // Next line throws an exception if record "id"
        // has been deleted
        byte[] data = recordStore.getRecord(id);
    } catch (InvalidRecordIDException ex) {
        // Ignore deleted record
    }
}
```

Another way to achieve the same effect is to create a dynamically updated RecordEnumeration by setting the keepUpdated argument of enumerateRecords() to true:

```
RecordEnumeration enum = recordStore.enumerateRecords(null, null, true);
```

Now, any record that is added to or removed from the record store will also appear in or be removed from the enumeration (assuming that the record passes the enumeration's optional filter, which will be described shortly), so you don't need to take special action to ignore deleted records. The disadvantage to this approach, however, is that there is a potentially large overhead associated with rebuilding the enumeration when any change occurs in the record store.

There are three other RecordEnumeration methods that are associated with keeping enumerations consistent with changes in the record store:

```
public boolean isKeptUpdated()
public void keepUpdated(boolean keepUpdated)
public void rebuild()
```

The isKeptUpdated() method returns true if the enumeration tracks changes in the record store. The keepUpdated() method can be used to change the state of an enumeration so that it either does or does not automatically track changes; in most cases, though, you simply set this property via the enumerateRecords() method and don't change it. The rebuild() method reconstructs the enumeration from the current state of the record store. A typical way to use this method is to add a RecordListener to the RecordStore and invoke rebuild() when notification of a record addition or removal is received. In practice, application code is unlikely to use this method, because the same functionality is available from a dynamic enumeration without the need for additional code.

When you have finished using a RecordEnumeration, you should use the destroy() method to release its resources.

Record Filters and Comparators

If you don't want to iterate through all the records in a record store, you can create a RecordEnumeration containing only those records that fulfill a given criterion by supplying a filter to the enumerateRecords() method. A filter is an object that implements the RecordFilter interface, which has a single method:

```
public boolean matches(byte[] data)
```

As the enumeration is being constructed, the enumerateRecords() method reads each record from the record store and passes it to the filter's matches() method; the record is included in the final enumeration only if the matches() method returns true.

Wireless Java

Suppose that you have a record store for a suite of MIDlet games, in which each entry contains a player's name and their highest score. You want to get a list of players who have scored more than 10,000 points. Here's how you might write the `RecordFilter` implementation to achieve this:

```
RecordFilter filter = new RecordFilter() {
    public boolean matches(byte[] data) {
        try {
            DataInputStream is = new DataInputStream(
            new ByteArrayInputStream(data));
            is.readUTF();          // Skip name
            int score = is.readInt();

            // Match scores over 10000
            return score > 10000;
        } catch (IOException ex) {
            // Cannot read - no match
            return false;
        }
    }
};
```

Each record is passed to the filter as a byte array, from which the score has to be extracted using the usual combination of a `ByteArrayInputStream` and a `DataInputStream`, as outlined in the earlier section "Records." In this case, the original records were created by writing out the player name as a string and then the score as an integer; to retrieve the score, it is necessary first to skip over the player name by calling `readUTF()` on the `DataInputStream`. Once the score has been obtained, all that is necessary is to return `true` if it is greater than 10,000 or `false` if not.

Once you have a `RecordFilter`, just pass it as the first argument to the `enumerateRecords()` method. Here's how you might use this filter to extract and print the names and scores of qualifying players from an open record store:

```
// Use the filter to get an enumeration that contains only
// a subset of the records in the record store
RecordEnumeration enum = store.enumerateRecords(filter, null, false);

// Print those players whose scores match the filter
while (enum.hasNextElement()) {
    byte[] record = enum.nextRecord();
    ByteArrayInputStream bais = new ByteArrayInputStream(record);
    DataInputStream is = new DataInputStream(bais);
    System.out.println("Name: <" + is.readUTF() + ">");
    System.out.println("Score: <" + is.readInt() + ">\n");
    is.close();
}
enum.destroy();
```

You can impose an order on the records in a `RecordEnumeration` by implementing a `RecordComparator`. `RecordComparator` is another interface that has one method:

```
public int compare(byte[] first, byte[] second)
```

As the enumeration is being constructed, this method is called several times, each time with a pair of records to be compared. The details of the comparison operation depend on the structure of the records and the criteria according to which they should be sorted. The return value from this method specifies the relative position of the given records in the sorting order:

RecordComparator.EQUIVALENT

Indicates that the two records are equal as far as the sorting criterion is concerned

RecordComparator.PRECEDES

Indicates that the first record should come before the second record in the sorting order

RecordComparator.FOLLOWS

Indicates that the first record follows the second in the sorting order

The implementation of the comparator should be designed so results are consistent and independent of which record appears first in the method arguments:

- If records A and B are equivalent, compare(A, B) and compare(B, A) should both return RecordComparator.EQUIVALENT.

- If compare(A, B) and compare(B, C) both return RecordComparator. EQUIVALENT, then compare(A, C) must also return RecordComparator. EQUIVALENT.

- If record A precedes record B, compare(A, B) should return RecordComparator.PRECEDES and compare(B, A) should return RecordComparator.FOLLOWS.

Using the game scores record store as an example again, suppose we wanted to get an enumeration in which the records are returned in descending order of scores. Here's a RecordComparator that could be used to sort the records appropriately:

```
// Sort an enumeration using a RecordComparator
RecordComparator comparator = new RecordComparator() {
    public int compare(byte[] first, byte[] second) {
        try {
            DataInputStream isFirst = new DataInputStream(
                    new ByteArrayInputStream(first));
            DataInputStream isSecond = new DataInputStream(
                    new ByteArrayInputStream(second));

            // Use descending order of scores.
            String firstName = isFirst.readUTF();
            int firstScore = isFirst.readInt();
            String secondName = isSecond.readUTF();
            int secondScore = isSecond.readInt();
            if (firstScore != secondScore) {
                return firstScore > secondScore ?
                        RecordComparator.PRECEDES :
                        RecordComparator.FOLLOWS;
            }
```

```
            // When the scores are equal, sort based
            // on the player name.
            int comp = firstName.compareTo(secondName);
            if (comp == 0) {
                return RecordComparator.EQUIVALENT;
            } else if (comp < 0) {
                return RecordComparator.PRECEDES;
            } else {
                return RecordComparator.FOLLOWS;
            }

        } catch (IOException ex) {
            // Cannot read - claim that they match
            return RecordComparator.EQUIVALENT;
        }
    }
};
```

As with `RecordFilter`, the records are passed as byte arrays, so a pair of `DataInputStreams` is used to get access the the record content. The first test compares the two record scores and simply returns `FOLLOWS` or `PRECEDES`, depending on their relative values. If the scores are the same, it would be perfectly reasonable to return `EQUIVALENT`. Here, though, we choose to sort records with equal scores in ascending order based on the player's name. To do this, the names are compared using the `String compareTo()` method, and the result is interpreted to determine the appropriate return value for the compare method.

The sorted list of scores can be obtained using the following line of code:

```
RecordEnumeration enum = store.enumerateRecords(null, comparator, false);
```

The first record in this enumeration is the one with the highest score, the second the one with the next highest score, and so on.

Multithreading and Concurrent Access

The MIDP specification requires implementations to ensure that record store operations are atomic. For example, an attempt to insert two records at the same time from two separate threads (or two MIDlets in the same suite) must be serialized so that each record is safely inserted and has a separate identifier. However, there are still issues of consistency that need to be taken care of at the MIDlet level. Some examples of issues that might arise follow. Care must be taken when coding multi-threaded MIDlets or MIDlet suites that share the same record store to ensure that these conditions are properly handled.

- The `RecordStore numRecords()` method returns the number of records in the record store. Using this value as a limiting value in a loop is safe only as long as no other thread or MIDlet could add or delete records while the loop is in progress.

- Static enumerations reflect the state of the record store at the time that the enumeration is created. You can create a dynamic enumeration to ensure that the enumeration always reflects the state of the record store.

- The value returned by the getNextRecordID() method is valid only until a new record is inserted in the record store. If you need to know in advance the identifier of the next record you will write before you actually write it (perhaps because you want to include the identifier in the record itself), you must make sure that no other thread or MIDlet could write a new record first. This can be done by synchronizing on the RecordStore object as a means of gaining permission to insert a new record in a multithreaded MIDlet.

A RecordStore Example

As a practical example of the use of record stores, let's look at how to add persistence to the book-ranking application that we used in the HTTP discussion. This application allows a user to enter a book's ISBN and then fetches its title, sales ranking, and number of reviews from the *www.amazon.com* web site. By saving these details in the record store, we save the user from having to remember book ISBNs (which are not the most memorable things in the world), and it also becomes possible to compare a book's current ranking to its previous one, so that we can see how sales are going. The features that we want are these:

- When the MIDlet starts, it should retrieve the ISBNs and titles of any books it knows about and display them in a list. If the record store has not yet been created, or if it is empty, the MIDlet should display the ISBN entry screen.

- When the user selects an item from the list, the current details for the chosen book should be displayed on the screen. A command should be provided that allows the user to get the latest information from the web site, and the new details should be displayed, with an indication of how much the book's sales ranking and number of reviews have changed.

- The user should be able to enter a new ISBN to retrieve the details for a book that is not currently in the record store.

- Whenever book details are fetched for a new book, or updates are obtained for an existing book, they should be written to the record store.

- Finally, the user should be able to delete records for books that she is no longer interested in.

Modifying the MIDlet to add these features is a matter of adding a class to manage the record store, together with a set of changes to the user interface code. Because we are mainly interested in this section in the persistence aspects, we'll look only briefly at some of the modified user interface code. If you want to see the complete implementation of the GUI, you'll find it in the file *PersistentRankingMidlet.java* in this book's example source code. You can also try out the MIDlet by selecting PersistentRanking from this chapter's MIDlet suite. The first time you run this, you'll just see the same ISBN entry screen shown in Figure 6-4. When you enter an ISBN, the details for the book are fetched and displayed as before. However, this time you'll also have access to a command button labeled Back. If you press this button, you'll see that your chosen book has been entered into a list, as shown on the left in Figure 6-5.

When you next start this MIDlet, the stored book list is displayed so that you can update the state of any book that it contains. When you select an entry from the list, the information that is stored for it is shown, along with a command button

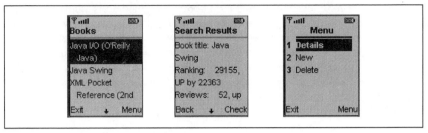

Figure 6-5: A book-ranking application

labeled Check. If you press this button, updated information is obtained from the web site and the change in sales ranking and number of reviews appears, as shown in the middle of Figure 6-5. There are also commands available to allow you to create an entry for a new book and delete an existing entry. On a typical cell phone, these commands would be presented on a separate menu, as shown on the right side of Figure 6-5.

Now let's look at some of the implementation details. In order to keep the persistence issues separate from the user interface, we encapsulate access to the record store in a class called `BookStore` that works in terms of the `BookInfo` objects that were created for the original application. The `BookStore` class provides the following features:

- Returns the number of books in the `BookStore`.

- Returns a list of all the books in the `BookStore` in the form of a `RecordEnumeration`. The books are sorted alphabetically by title.

- Stores the content of a `BookInfo` object in the record store, creating a new record or updating an existing one as necessary.

- Gets the details for a book with a given record identifier or ISBN from the record store and returns the corresponding `BookInfo` object.

The most fundamental aspects of the `BookStore` class are the way in which it manages the underlying record store and how it stores the `BookInfo` objects. Example 6-2 shows the methods of the `BookStore` class that manage the `RecordStore` itself.

Example 6-2: Managing a RecordStore

```
// A class that implements a persistent store
// of books, keyed by ISBN.
public class BookStore implements RecordComparator, RecordFilter {
    // The name of the record store used to hold books
    private static final String STORE_NAME = "BookStore";

    // The record store itself
    private RecordStore store;

    // Creates a bookstore and opens it
    public BookStore() {
        try {
            store = RecordStore.openRecordStore(STORE_NAME, true);
```

Example 6-2: Managing a RecordStore (continued)

```
        } catch (RecordStoreException ex) {
            System.err.println(ex);
        }
    }

    // Closes the bookstore
    public void close() throws RecordStoreException {
        if (store != null) {
            store.closeRecordStore();
        }
    }

    // Gets the number of books in the book store
    public int getBookCount() throws RecordStoreException {
        if (store != null) {
            return store.getNumRecords();
        }
        return 0;
    }

    // Adds a listener to the book store
    public void addRecordListener(RecordListener l) {
        if (store != null) {
            store.addRecordListener(l);
        }
    }

    // Removes a listener from the book store
    public void removeRecordListener(RecordListener l) {
        if (store != null) {
            store.removeRecordListener(l);
        }
    }

    // More code (not shown)

}
```

This code makes direct use of RecordStore interfaces to manage the underlying record store. The constructor uses the openRecordStore() method to open a record store called BookStore. This call creates the record store if it does not exist. Similarly, the close() method closes the record store by calling the closeRecordStore() method, and the getBookCount() method obtains the number of books by calling numRecords(). The addRecordListener() and removeRecordListener() methods delegate directly to the RecordStore methods of the same name. These methods allow users of the BookStore class to be notified when book details are added, removed, or modified. In this MIDlet, this facility is used by the user interface code to keep the list of books shown on the left side of Figure 6-5 up to date.

Saving and retrieving BookInfo objects is also straightforward, requiring only the use of the appropriate input and output streams, as shown in Example 6-3. The

Wireless Java

deleteBook() method, which deletes the entry for a book, given its BookInfo object, is also shown here.

Example 6-3: Saving and Retrieving BookInfo Objects

```
// Writes a record into a byte array.
private byte[] toByteArray(BookInfo bookInfo) throws IOException {
    ByteArrayOutputStream baos = new ByteArrayOutputStream();
    DataOutputStream os = new DataOutputStream(baos);

    os.writeUTF(bookInfo.isbn);
    os.writeUTF(bookInfo.title == null ? "" : bookInfo.title);
    os.writeInt(bookInfo.ranking);
    os.writeInt(bookInfo.reviews);
    os.writeInt(bookInfo.lastRanking);
    os.writeInt(bookInfo.lastReviews);

    return baos.toByteArray();
}

// Gets a BookInfo from a store record
// given its record identifier
public BookInfo getBookInfo(int id) throws RecordStoreException,, IOException
{
    byte[] bytes = store.getRecord(id);
    DataInputStream is = new DataInputStream(new
        ByteArrayInputStream(bytes));

    String isbn = is.readUTF();
    BookInfo info = new BookInfo(isbn);
    info.id = id;
    info.title = is.readUTF();
    info.ranking = is.readInt();
    info.reviews = is.readInt();
    info.lastRanking = is.readInt();
    info.lastReviews = is.readInt();

    return info;
}

// Deletes the entry for a book from the store
public void deleteBook(BookInfo bookInfo) throws RecordStoreException {
    if (store != null) {
        store.deleteRecord(bookInfo.id);
    }
}
```

RecordStore methods use record identifiers to denote individual records whereas, for the most part, application code would prefer to deal exclusively with a BookInfo object or an ISBN and not be concerned about the implementation details of the storage mechanism. This is, of course, one of the reasons why the original design of the BookInfo class included a field to hold the RecordStore identifier for the book's stored record. As a result, the deleteBook() method can use a BookInfo object to identify the book to be deleted. The getBookInfo()

method, however, uses a record identifier to identify the book. This is because it is useful to be able to get a RecordEnumeration containing all or a subset of the books and then retrieve the corresponding records. A RecordEnumeration contains a record identifier, so there is a need for a public method that accepts such a value as its argument.

The remaining methods in the BookStore class satisfy the requirements of the book-ranking MIDlet. When the MIDlet starts, it needs to get a list of all of the books in the BookStore so that it can populate a list for display to the user. For convenience, this list is displayed in alphabetical order by title. This functionality can obviously be provided by RecordEnumeration:

```
public RecordEnumeration getBooks() throws RecordStoreException {
    if (store != null) {
        return store.enumerateRecord(null, this, false);
    }
}
```

The alphabetical sorting is performed by a RecordComparator, which, to avoid introducing extra classes, is provided by BookStore itself (which is why the second argument of the enumerateRecord() call is this):

```
// RecordComparator implementation
public int compare(byte[] book1, byte[] book2) {
    try {
        DataInputStream stream1 =
            new DataInputStream(new ByteArrayInputStream(book1));
        DataInputStream stream2 =
            new DataInputStream(new ByteArrayInputStream(book2));

        // Match based on the ISBN, but sort based on the title.
        String isbn1 = stream1.readUTF();
        String isbn2 = stream2.readUTF();
        if (isbn1.equals(isbn2)) {
            return RecordComparator.EQUIVALENT;
        }
        String title1 = stream1.readUTF();
        String title2 = stream2.readUTF();
        int result = title1.compareTo(title2);
        if (result == 0) {
            return RecordComparator.EQUIVALENT;
        }
        return result < 0 ? RecordComparator.PRECEDES :
                            RecordComparator.FOLLOWS;
    } catch (IOException ex) {
        return RecordComparator.EQUIVALENT;
    }
}
```

To determine whether the two records are equal, the ISBNs are compared. If they do not match, the titles are compared, and PRECEDES, EQUIVALENT, or FOLLOWS is returned, depending on the outcome. The MIDlet user interface code builds the book list by using the getBooks() method to get a sorted list of books, then calling getBookInfo() with each record identifier returned in the RecordEnumerator, as follows:

Wireless Java

```
RecordEnumeration enum = bookStore.getBooks();
while (enum.hasNextElement()) {
    int id = enum.nextRecordId();
    BookInfo info = bookStore.getBookInfo(id);
    bookInfoList.addElement(info);
}
enum.destroy();
```

When the user selects an item from the list, its details need to be displayed. Since the list contains each book's `BookInfo` object, the information is immediately available. If the user asks for new information to be retrieved from the web site, however, the stored information will ultimately need to be updated. Similarly, if the user enters an ISBN for a new book, and that book's details are retrieved, a new record needs to be created. The `BookStore` class provides a method called `saveBookInfo()` to satisfy this requirement:

```
// Adds an entry to the store or modifies the existing
// entry if a matching ISBN exists.
public void saveBookInfo(BookInfo bookInfo) throws IOException,
RecordStoreException {
    if (store != null) {
        searchISBN = bookInfo.getIsbn();
        RecordEnumeration enum = store.enumerateRecords(this, null,
            false);
        if (enum.numRecords() > 0) {
            // A matching record exists. Set the id
            // of the BookInfo to match the existing record
            bookInfo.id = enum.nextRecordId();
            byte[] bytes = toByteArray(bookInfo);
            store.setRecord(bookInfo.id, bytes, 0, bytes.length);
        } else {
            // Create a new record
            bookInfo.id = store.getNextRecordID();
            byte[] bytes = toByteArray(bookInfo);
            store.addRecord(bytes, 0, bytes.length);
        }

        // Finally, destroy the RecordEnumeration
        enum.destroy();
    }
}
```

If the book already has an entry in the record store, the `setRecord()` method is used to update it. If it does not, `addRecord()` must be used to create a new record. As we have already seen, the quickest way to determine whether a record exists in a record store is to use a `RecordEnumeration` and search it for the required record. Here, we use a variant of that technique: it supplies a filter that allows through only a book with a given ISBN, stored in the `searchISBN` instance variable. The filter implementation (which, like the `RecordComparator`, is provided directly by the `BookStore` class) is very simple:

```
// RecordFilter implementation
public boolean matches(byte[] book) {
    if (searchISBN != null) {
        try {
```

```
        DataInputStream stream =
            new DataInputStream(new ByteArrayInputStream(book));

        // Match based on the ISBN.
        return searchISBN.equals(stream.readUTF());
      } catch (IOException ex) {
        System.err.println(ex);
      }
    }

    // Default is not to match
    return false;
  }
```

If the returned enumeration is not empty, we know that the book is already in the record store, so the setRecord() method is used to update it, after calling the toByteArray() method shown in Example 6-3 to convert the BookInfo object to a byte array for storage. If a new record is needed, addRecord() must be used instead. In this case, however, we haven't yet assigned a record store identifier to the record, so we use the RecordStore getNextRecordID() method to get the identifier under which the record will be stored. We save that in the BookInfo object before calling toByteArray() and addRecord().

Finally, for completeness, although it is not used by the book ranking MIDlet, BookStore also provides a method that searches for a book given its ISBN. This method uses the same technique that SaveBookInfo() does of creating a filtered RecordEnumeration to locate the record for the book. Because this search also uses the book ISBN, the same RecordFilter implementation is used:

```
public BookInfo getBookInfo(String isbn) throws RecordStoreException,
IOException {
    BookInfo bookInfo = null;
    searchISBN = isbn;

    // Look for a book with the given ISBN
    RecordEnumeration enum = store.enumerateRecords(this, null, false);

    // If found, get its identifier and fetch its BookInfo object
    if (enum.numRecords() > 0) {
        int id = enum.nextRecordId();
        bookInfo = getBookInfo(id);
    }

    // Release the enumeration
    enum.destroy();

    return bookInfo;
}
```

This completes our examination of MIDP's networking and storage capabilities. The example in this chapter demonstrates not only how powerful the provided facilities can be, but also how simple it is to use them to create a useful application using a relatively small amount of code. At the same time, you have seen that it is important to be aware of the limited resources available on these platforms—particularly memory—and to adjust your coding style accordingly.

CHAPTER 7

The Connected Device Configuration and Its Profiles

The Connected Limited Device Configuration (CLDC) and the Mobile Information Device Profile (MIDP) bring a usable, if restricted, Java programming capability to a very large number of small devices. There is a wide gulf between the cell phones and small PDAs that the CLDC profiles address and the desktop world of J2SE, and between these two extremes lie a range of other devices. Among these are consumer electronic devices such as set-top boxes, two-way pagers, and larger PDAs that, while not needing to support the complete J2SE environment, are nevertheless not well served by CLDC and MIDP and have the resources to host a more capable Java platform. The Connected Device Configuration (CDC) is the J2ME configuration that is aimed at this class of device. This chapter provides an overview of CDC and the current state set of profiles that are defined for it, many of which are, as yet, not fully specified.

The CDC

The CDC is targeted at devices that have a minimum of 2 MB of memory available to be used by the Java VM and its class libraries. As with CLDC, most devices probably have the VM and the core class libraries in ROM or Flash memory, but they also require RAM for application classes (unless the application is embedded and hence also included in the ROM) and the Java heap.

CDC devices typically have a 32-bit processor and a network connection, which may be intermittent or permanent, often directly to the Internet or a TCP/IP-based intranet. This contrasts to the CLDC environment, which is often hosted by slower 16-bit processors, and which has only a relatively low-bandwidth, nonpermanent connection to a network that cannot be assumed to support TCP/IP.

Like CLDC, the CDC specification requires a VM and a set of class libraries represent the minimal subset of the Java 2 platform required for all devices to which this configuration is targeted. The CDC specification was prepared under the Java Community Process as JSR 36, which can be downloaded from *http://jcp.org/jsr/*

detail/36.jsp. Devices built to target specific applications or markets require additional software facilities that are provided by CDC's associated profiles, which will be described later in this chapter. Figure 7-1 shows the relationship between CDC and the profiles that are currently defined for it; they are described in the later section "CDC Profiles."

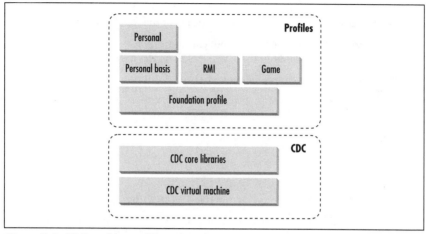

Figure 7-1: CDC and its profiles

The CDC Virtual Machine

Because CDC devices are much more capable than those targeted by CLDC, they can support a full Java VM. In fact, any VM provided as part of a CDC implementation must provide all the features described in the second edition of the Java Virtual Machine specification. Sun provides a reference implementation of CDC, downloadable from *http://java.sun.com/products/cdc/*, that is based on the CVM,[*] a virtual machine that supports all the features of the full J2SE VM, but which operates with a smaller memory footprint and has a garbage collector that is designed to work in a limited-memory environment.

The CDC reference implementation contains the source code for the CVM and the core CDC Java class libraries. If you download it, you will find that you have to build it for yourself, because class files and executables are not included. The reference implementation can be compiled for Linux (strictly speaking, only Red Hat Linux Version 6.2 is supported) and VxWorks, a real-time operating system. However, CVM is designed to be highly portable, and the download includes documentation that covers the details of the porting layer for those who need to implement it for a different platform. Perhaps somewhat surprisingly, Sun does not provide a version of CVM for PocketPC platforms such as the Compaq iPAQ range of PDAs, which would be an ideal host for a Java 2 programming environment.

---

[*] Although the initials "CVM" were originally short for "Compact Virtual Machine," this description was thought to be likely to lead to confusion with KVM, which is also "compact." As a result, CVM is now called just CVM.

Third party support for these devices is almost certain to appear, however, when the GUI-based profiles become available.*

CVM uses the same ROMizing feature used by KVM to reduce VM startup time and minimize memory usage by building a prelinked set of Java classes directly into the VM. The reference implementation produces a CVM prelinked with most of the core CDC classes and, optionally, some the classes in the Foundation Profile. See "Preloading Java Classes" in Chapter 2 for details of the ROMizing mechanism.

Since CVM is a full virtual machine, the VM and the core libraries include many features that are not available in the KVM, including the following:

- Floating-point byte codes and data types
- Native code execution using the Java Native Interface
- Weak references
- Reflection
- Object serialization
- Developer-defined class loaders
- Java Virtual Machine Debugging Interface (JVMDI) support

The availability of JVMDI means that it is possible to connect a debugger to the CVM without the use of the debug proxy agent required by the KVM. The CDC platform also incorporates the full Java 2 security model and byte-code verification, which means that the off-device preverification process used by KVM is unnecessary.

Despite the fact that the CVM has all the features of the J2SE VM as defined by the JVM specification, it is *not* the same as the J2SE Version 1.3 virtual machine. In particular, it does not have hotspot technology or even a just-in-time (JIT) compiler. CVM is strictly a byte-code interpreter, albeit an optimized one.

Running Java Code with the CVM

Before you can use the CVM, you will need to download the source code and compile it. There are two downloads available from Sun from which you can build the VM. From *http://java.sun.com/products/cdc/* you can get the CDC reference implementation, while the Foundation Profile can be downloaded from *http://java. sun.com/products/foundation/*. Both of these downloads contain the same source code, which includes the CVM and the CDC core libraries and the libraries for the Foundation Profile. The only difference between them is that the first contains the CDC documentation, while the second has the documentation for the Foundation Profile, which is a superset of CDC as far as the class libraries are concerned.

---

* There are actually two Java platforms already in existence for the Compaq iPAQ: PersonalJava and Savaje. The former is Sun's implementation of Java 1.1.8 for small devices. The long-term aim is to replace PersonalJava with the Java 2–based Personal Profile, running atop CDC, as described later in this chapter. Savaje is an entirely different approach that replaces the PocketPC host operating system with a native Java 2 platform that includes all of Java 2 Version 1.3, to produce a Java-only PDA.

You can build the reference implementations on either VxWorks or Linux. The documentation supplied with the download includes build instructions for both platforms; the rest of this chapter assumes you are using Linux. Although the documentation specifies that the target platform is Red Hat 6.2, it is possible to build and run the CVM on other Linux distributions, provided you have installed the correct releases of the C compiler and the *make* command. Although the build process is not described here (because it is very simple and adequately covered in the product documentation), it is worth noting that there are several options you can choose when building the VM that determine what is produced. In order build a VM that can be used for development and debugging with both the CDC core libraries and the Foundation Profile, the following command should be used:

```
make CVM_DEBUG=true CVM_JVMDI=true J2ME_CLASSLIB=foundation
```

The arguments you can supply to the *make* command to control the build process are listed in the build instructions. The three options used here have the following effects:

CVM_DEBUG=true
> Builds the CVM with debugging enabled. All the core and Foundation Profile Java classes are compiled with the –g option, so that they contain debugging information required by debuggers.

CVM_JVMDI=true
> Enables the CVM JVMDI support. This option must be set to true if you intend to use a debugger with the CVM.

J2ME_CLASSLIB=foundation
> Builds both the CDC and Foundation Profile classes. If this option is not specified or has the value cdc, only the CDC core libraries are built.

The build process produces three files that you will need to use when running CVM application. The pathnames given here use the shell variable *CDC* as shorthand for the directory in which the downloaded source code was unpacked:

$CDC/build/linux/bin/cvm
> The CVM executable

$CDC/build/linux/lib/cdc.jar or $CDC/build/linux/lib/foundation.jar
> Java class libraries for CDC or the Foundation Profile, respectively; only one of these files will be created, depending on the value of the *J2ME_CLASSLIB* option supplied to the *make* command

$CDC/build/linux/btclasses.zip
> The CDC boot classes

The CVM is built with the majority of the classes in the CDC core libraries preloaded (and many of the Foundation Profile classes, if you have chosen to compile them). The classes that are not preloaded are included in *cdc.jar* or *foundation.jar*, depending on your build choice.

In order to run a CDC application, you first need to compile the source code. CDC does not include its own compilation system, so you'll need to have J2SE Version 1.3 (or higher) installed to perform the compilation. As was the case with CLDC, if you use the classes that the J2SE compiler links to by default, you won't find out until runtime if you inadvertently used J2SE classes that are not part of CDC or the profile that you are targeting. Also, you won't be able to use classes that are specific to J2ME (such as those in the `javax.microedition` package hierarchy). In order to force the compiler to use the correct classes, you need to use the *–bootclasspath* option. As an example, if you have installed this book's source code in the directory pointed to by the environment variable *EXAMPLES,* you could use the following shell commands to compile the file *CVMProperties.java*:

```
cd $EXAMPLES/src/ora/ch7
javac -bootclasspath $CDC/build/linux/lib/foundation.jar:$CDC/build/
    linux/btclasses.zip CVMProperties.java
```

Notice that the list of archive files supplied with the *–bootclasspath* option includes not only *foundation.jar,* but also *btclasses.zip.* The reason for this is that *foundation.jar* includes only those classes that are *not* prelinked into the VM; the prelinked classes are stored in *btclasses.zip* instead. The reason that the prelinked classes are not included in *foundation.jar* (or in *cdc.jar*) is that they don't need to be there at runtime (because they are already preloaded in the VM). Including them would both increase the total memory requirement and incur a performance overhead due to the increased times required to search a larger JAR file for classes that have not been included in the ROMized image of the VM.

In order to run this example, make sure that your *PATH* environment variable includes the directory *$CDC/build/linux/bin* and type the command:

```
cvm  -Xbootclasspath:$CDC/build/linux/lib/foundation.jar -Djava.class.
    path=$EXAMPLES/src  ora.ch7.CVMProperties
```

CVM provides a small set of command-line options, some of which are covered in this section. You'll find a complete description of all the available options in Chapter 8.

In this example, most of the classes that the VM needs are preloaded. However, it is still necessary to supply the location of *foundation.jar* (or *cdc.jar*) using the *–Xbootclasspath* option, because the VM loads a small number of classes from this file in order to access the local filesystem. This is necessary here in order to open the JAR file and to load the example class file. Note, however, that there is no need to use *btclasses.zip* here, because the classes that it contains are part of the *cvm* executable. In the special (but not very likely) case in which your working directory is *$CDC/build/linux/bin,* you won't need to use the *–Xbootclasspath* option, because CVM will look for a file called *../lib/foundation.jar* by default.

The `java.class.path` system property specifies the application classpath and so is set here to point to the example source code directory. Unlike the J2SE virtual machine, CVM does not automatically set this property from the *CLASSPATH* environment variable.

This simple example lists all the system properties that are set during CVM startup. Since CDC fully supports the J2SE `Properties` class and the `System` `getProperties()` method, most of the properties that you may be familiar with from J2SE are also available to CDC applications. Table 7-1 shows the values of some of these properties as printed by this example.

Table 7-1: CVM System Properties

Property Name	Value
java.runtime.name	Java (TM) 2, Micro Edition
java.vm.name	CVM
java.vm.specification.name	Java Virtual Machine Specification
java.specification.name	Java Platform API Specification
java.specification.version	1.3
java.version	J2ME Foundation 1.0

Debugging Java Code in the CVM

CVM supports the JVMDI, so you can connect a JPDA debugger to it without involving a separate debug proxy of the type used by KVM. However, before you can start debugging, you need to do two things:

1. Build the CVM with the *CVM_DEBUG* and *CVM_JVMDI* options to the *make* command set to true.

2. Build the library libjdwp, which contains the native code that implements the Java Debug Wire Protocol (JDWP). This protocol allows debuggers to connect to the VM over a socket or using shared memory.*

You can build libjdwp using the following commands:

```
cd $CDC/ext/jpda/build/linux
make
```

This creates the library and writes it to the file *$CDC/jdk_build/linux/lib/i386/libjdwp.so*.

Starting CVM for debugging requires quite a long command line:

```
cvm -Xdebug  -Xrunjdwp:transport=dt_socket,server=y,address=5000
-Xbootclasspath:$CDC/build/linux/lib/foundation.jar -Dsun.boot.library.
path=$CDC/jdk_build/linux/lib/i386 -Djava.class.path=$EXAMPLES/src  ora.
ch7.CVMProperties
```

The options used here are as follows:

−Xdebug

> Starts the VM in debug mode. When this option is used, the VM suspends operation before entering the main() method of the initial application class.

−Xrunjdwp

> Tells the VM to use JDWP for debugging. This option requires several parameters, separated from it by a colon and from each other by commas, that specify how the debugger will connect to the VM. In this case, the parameters supplied are as follows:

> *transport=dt_socket*

> > Specifies that the debugger will connect over a socket.

---

* JDWP and the role that it plays in Java-level debugging is described in the section "The JPDA" in Chapter 2.

CDC and Profiles

server=y

Tells JDWP to take on the server role. The debugger itself acts as the client.

address=5000

Specifies the port number that the server should use to listen for a connection from the debugger client.

–Xbootclasspath

Specifies the location of VM's boot classes, in this case the set of core and Foundation Profile classes that have not been prelinked into the VM.

–Dsun.boot.library.path

Gives the directory in which the JWDP implementation library (*libjdwp.so* for Linux) can be found.

–Djava.class.path

Specifies the locations to be searched for application classes.

Once the CVM has started, it will suspend and wait for a debugger to connect to it on the port specified in the *–Xrunjdwp* argument. If you have an IDE that supports remote JPDA debugging (such as Forte for Java), you can use it to perform source- level debugging using the same technique as shown in "Debugging a KVM Application" in Chapter 2. Alternatively, you can use the command-line tool *jdb*, which is part of the J2SE SDK. To connect using *jdb*, you need to specify the socket address on which the VM is listening and the location at which the source code for the application's classes can be found:

```
jdb -attach localhost:5000 -sourcepath $EXAMPLES/src
```

Here, *jdb* and the CVM are assumed to be on the same machine, but this need not be the case. Following connection, you need to use the *step* command to force the VM to enter the **main()** method. From here, you can use *jdb* commands to set breakpoints, list the source code around the line currently being executed, inspect and modify objects and fields, and so on. The *jdb* command is described in detail in *Java in a Nutshell* by David Flanagan (O'Reilly).

By default, when you use the *–Xdebug* argument, the JVMDI support in the VM starts at the same time as the VM itself and suspends execution until a debugger connects to it. However, you can choose to have JVMDI defer its initialization until an exception of a named type or an uncaught exception is thrown. The latter case is often the type of error that you would like to use a debugger to investigate, but starting the VM in debug usually causes it to execute byte codes more slowly. Using this feature, you can run the VM at full speed until the exception occurs.

The options that control the point at which the debugging features initialize is part of the *–Xrunjdwp* argument. The following command:

```
cvm  -Xdebug  -Xrunjdwp:transport=dt_
socket,server=y,address=5000,onuncaught=y  -Xbootclasspath:$CDC/build/
linux/lib/foundation.jar -Dsun.boot.library.path=$CDC/jdk_build/linux/
lib/i386 -Djava.class.path=$EXAMPLES/src  ora.ch7.CVMException
```

adds the *onuncaught* option with value y, which delays initialization of the JVMDI until an uncaught exception occurs. The class ora.ch7.CVMException used here waits for 10 seconds, then deliberately causes a NullPointerException that it does not catch, at which point the debug facilities initialize and the VM is suspended. You can now start *jdb* to analyze the problem.

Alternatively, if you simply want to start debugging when a NullPointerException occurs, use the *onthrow* option, which requires the class name of the exception to wait for:

```
cvm -Xdebug -Xrunjdwp:transport=dt_
socket,server=y,address=5000,onthrow=java.lang.NullPointerException
-Xbootclasspath:$CDC/build/linux/lib/foundation.jar -Dsun.boot.library.
path=$CDC/jdk_build/linux/lib/i386 -Djava.class.path=$EXAMPLES/src
ora.ch7.CVMException
```

Finally, you can use the *launch* option to cause a command to be executed when the VM debug facilities initialize. This option requires the name of the command, which should be either an absolute path or the name of an executable on your search path (i.e., included in the *PATH* variable for Linux). When it is started, the program receives the transport name and address used by the debugger as arguments—that is, it is effectively run with arguments like this:

```
name dt_socket 5000
```

One way to make use of this is to create a script that starts *jdb* when the condition that starts the JVMDI support occurs, like this:

```
#!/bin/sh
jdb -attach localhost:$2 -sourcepath $EXAMPLES/src
```

If you put these lines into a file called *startdbg.sh* (in a directory included in your *PATH* variable) and make it executable (using a command like chmod +x startdbg.sh), the following command:

```
cvm -Xdebug -Xrunjdwp:transport=dt_
socket,server=y,address=5000,onthrow=java.lang.
NullPointerException,launch=startdbg.sh -Xbootclasspath:$CDC/build/
linux/lib/foundation.jar -Dsun.boot.library.path=$CDC/jdk_build/linux/
lib/i386 -Djava.class.path=$EXAMPLES/src ora.ch7.CVMException
```

runs the VM until a NullPointerException occurs, at which point it initializes the JVMDI code, suspends bytecode execution, and runs your script. This results in *jdb* starting and connecting to the VM, using the port number that is passed as the second argument to the script.

CDC Class Libraries

The CDC specification includes a minimal set of core Java classes that provide the common functionality required by every CDC platform. According to the specification, the core libraries represent little more than the minimum needed to support a Java VM. They include classes from the following packages:

```
java.io
java.lang
java.lang.ref
java.lang.reflect
java.math
java.net
```

CDC and Profiles

```
java.security
java.security.cert
java.text
java.util
java.util.jar
java.util.zip
javax.microedition.io
```

Unlike CLDC, a class included in CDC is unchanged from its J2SE counterpart, unless it has deprecated APIs. Because there is no legacy CDC application code to support, there is no requirement for backward compatibility, and, therefore, the opportunity has been taken to remove APIs that are deprecated in J2SE Version 1.3, whenever there is an alternative available. In general, however, working with CDC or a CDC-based profile is much closer to using a full J2SE Version 1.3 platform than CLDC, so there is much less to relearn.

The following paragraphs briefly cover the differences between the CDC packages and their J2SE counterparts. You'll find a complete list of the classes from these packages that are included in CDC in Chapter 10.

The java.io package
Most of the J2SE classes in this package are included in CDC, with the exception of some of the less commonly used Reader and Writer subclasses, as well as LineNumberInputStream and StringBufferInputStream, both of which are deprecated in J2SE.

The java.lang package
In this package, only the Compiler class and UnknownException have been omitted.

The java.lang.ref package
Complete.

The java.lang.reflect package
Complete.

The java.math package
This package contains only two classes in J2SE. The CDC version includes BigInteger but excludes BigDecimal.

The java.net package
CDC provides the classes necessary to support datagrams (i.e., the UDP protocol), but it does not support sockets (i.e., TCP) or HTTP and therefore omits classes that relate to these two features. URL-based operations can be used, provided they do not rely on HTTP or sockets. This means, for example, that file and jar-based URLs are allowed, but http URLs are not.

The java.security package
Only those parts of the java.security package that deal with handling fine-grain security for Java classes is included, together with minimal support for creating and checking message digests.

The java.security.cert package

Contains only the `Certificate` class and two certificate-related exception classes. This package is of limited use because it does not include any concrete certificate implementations (such as `X509Certificate`).

The java.text package

The CDC `java.text` package provides support for locale-specific formatting, parsing of numbers and dates, and formatting of error messages. Classes that support advanced locale-sensitive collation and attributed character strings are omitted.

The java.util package

This useful package is almost complete in CDC. The only omissions are classes that relate to event handling (such as `Observer` and `EventObject`) and timers. Unlike CLDC, CDC includes both the JDK 1.1 and Java 2 collection frameworks.

The java.util.jar package

This package is complete, apart from the `JarOutputStream` class, which means that it is possible to read but not create a JAR file. This distinction is possible because, although the VM has to be able to load Java classes and other resources from a JAR file, it never needs to write to one.

The java.util.zip package

This package contains the classes that are necessary for the VM to read from a compressed or uncompressed ZIP file, but it omits the classes that allow writing or provide streams that handle compression and decompression of data for the benefit of applications. Compressed ZIP files are supported by virtue of the inclusion of the `Inflater` class.

The javax.microedition.io package

This package is provided for upward compatibility with applications written for CLDC. It contains the classes and interfaces that make up the Generic Connection Framework and includes support for datagrams. Interestingly, the `StreamConnection` and `StreamConnectionNotifier` classes, which are intended for support of TCP-based sockets, are included, even though the `java.net` package excludes socket support, and a CDC implementation is not required to allow socket communication. Furthermore, in the reference implementation, it is possible to connect using a GCF socket URL. The `HttpConnection` class is, however, not included.

CDC Profiles

At the time of writing, CDC has only one profile, the Foundation Profile, for which a reference implementation is available. Another, the RMI profile, has been specified, but an implementation has not yet been released. Three others are still in the process of being specified. This section provides an overview of the Foundation Profile and touches briefly on the remaining profiles, which are currently of little practical use because there are no implementations available.

CDC and Profiles

The Foundation Profile

Most of the CDC profiles are based on the Foundation Profile, which adds to the minimal facilities of the CDC core libraries in much the same way that MIDP extends CLDC. This profile fills many of the gaps in the basic CDC class libraries by supplying most of the omitted classes from the packages that CDC supports; it also adds many of the other J2SE packages that are not included by CDC. The most important omissions from the Foundation Profile are the user interface classes, which are not required on all devices and which are instead provided by the Personal Basis and Personal profiles that are layered on top of the Foundation Profile. The specification of this profile can be obtained from *http://jcp.org/jsr/detail/46.jsp.*

The packages in the Foundation Profile include all the classes from their J2SE counterparts. The following packages are provided:

```
java.io (but not LineNumberInputStream and
    StringBufferInputStream, which are deprecated in J2SE)
java.lang
java.lang.ref
java.lang.reflect
java.math
java.net
java.security
java.security.acl
java.security.cert
java.security.interfaces
java.security.spec
java.text
java.util
java.util.jar
java.util.zip
```

The Foundation Profile also supports all of the `javax.microedition.io` package, including HTTP connections.

The RMI Profile

The RMI profile adds a subset of the J2SE Remote Method Invocation facility on top of the Foundation Profile. Since CDC devices are typically used in the role of the RMI client, only the client RMI functionality is included in this profile. At the time of writing, the RMI profile is available only in the form of a specification. There is, as yet, no reference implementation.

The RMI packages and classes provided by this profile are listed in Chapter 10. The specification can be downloaded from *http://jcp.org/jsr/detail/66.jsp.*

Other CDC Profiles

Unlike MIDP, the Foundation Profile does not have any support for a user interface of any kind. This is entirely appropriate for some devices, such as set-top boxes, where only a very primitive style of interaction with the user occurs, and the overhead of GUI classes is not required. For applications that require a user interface, CDC provides the Personal Basis and Personal profiles, which together are intended to provide a Java 2–based replacement for Sun's PersonalJava platform, which is derived from JDK 1.1.8. At the time of writing, the specifications for these profiles are still being developed. You can check the current state of this work at *http://jcp.org/jsr/detail/129.jsp* for the Personal Basis profile and *http://jcp. org/jsr/detail/62.jsp* for the Personal profile.

The Game Profile, which is aimed at providing a platform for writing game software, is currently in the process of being defined as JSR 134. As shown in Figure 7-1, at the time of writing there is some uncertaintly as to whether this profile will be based on CDC itself or assume the presence of the Foundation Profile. The current state of this specification can be found at *http://jcp.org/jsr/ detail/134.jsp*.

CDC and Profiles

CHAPTER 8

J2ME Command-Line Tools

J2ME developers have a range of visual environments to choose from when developing and debugging applications. Some of these have already been mentioned or will be covered in Chapter 9. In some cases, however, it is necessary to come to grips with the lower-level tools that lie behind these development environments. This chapter provides reference material for some of the command-line tools that developers are most likely to need to use.

cvm: The Connected Device Configuration Virtual Machine

Availability

CDC Reference Implementation, Foundation Profile Reference Implementation

Synopsis

```
cvm [options] [properties] classfile [args]
```

Description

CVM is a virtual machine that meets the requirements of the Connected Device Configuration specification. It provides all of the features required by the second edition of the Java Virtual Machine Specification and incorporates a garbage collector that is optimized for a small memory environment. In order to reduce startup time and memory overhead, the CVM usually has the core Java classes prelinked with it at build time using a process called ROMizing, which is also used by the CLDC virtual machine (KVM) and described in "Preloading Java Classes" in Chapter 2.

CVM is provided in source code form as part of the CDC and Foundation Profile reference implementations, which are supported on Linux and VxWorks.

Options

–version

> Displays version information and exits. Typical output from this command looks like this:

```
java version "J2ME Foundation 1.0"
Java(TM) 2, Micro Edition (build 1.0fcs-ar)
CVM (build .0fcs-ar, native threads)
```

–showversion

> Prints the same information as *–version* but does not exit afterwards. This option can be used to output version information before running an application.

–fullversion

> Despite its name, this option displays less information than *–version*. Typical output is the following:

```
java full version "1.0fcs-ar"
```

> The VM exits after processing this option.

–Xbootclasspath:list
–Xbootclasspath=list

> Sets the list of directories, JAR files, or ZIP files in which the VM looks to load boot classes that are not part of its preloaded set. List entries should be separated by a colon on the Linux platform or a semicolon for VxWorks.

–Xbootclasspath/p:list
–Xbootclasspath/p=list

> Prepends a given list of directories, JAR files, or ZIP files to the existing boot class path. List entries should be separated by a colon on the Linux platform or a semicolon for VxWorks.

–Xbootclasspath/a:list
–Xbootclasspath/a=list

> Appends a given list of directories, JAR files, or ZIP files to the existing boot class path. List entries should be separated by a colon on the Linux platform or a semicolon for VxWorks.

–Xsssize

> Sets the native language thread stack size to *size* bytes. To specify a size in kilobytes or megabytes, the letters *k*, *K*, *m*, or *M* may be appended. Note that no space is allowed between the characters *–Xss* and the specified size, so *–Xss1m* is valid, but *–Xss 1m* is not.

–Xmssize

> Sets the size of the Java heap. The *size* value is specified in the same way as it is for the *–Xss* option. The actual value used may be rounded to a size that is more convenient for the VM.

–Xgc:gc_specific_options

> Specifies options for the garbage collector. The set of valid options depends on the garbage collector implementation in use.

*Command-
Line Tools*

–Xverify:type

Specifies the scope of class verification. If *type* is not specified or has the value *all*, then all classes are verified as they are loaded. To verify only classes loaded remotely, use *remote*, and, to disable class verification, specify *none*. If this option is omitted, only remotely loaded classes are verified.

–Xdebug

Enables the VM support for JPDA debugging. This option is used in conjunction with *–Xrunjdwp* and may be used only if the VM was built with JVMDI support enabled. See the later section "Debugging" for further details.

–Xrunname:options

Loads the native code library specified by *name* into the VM. This argument may appear more than once to cause several libraries to be loaded. The *name* string is converted to the name of a library in a platform-dependent way. For Linux, this follows the pattern *lib*name*.so*, while for VxWorks the pattern is *lib*name*.o*. If the VM is built with debugging enabled, however, the patterns become *lib*name*_g.so* and *lib*name*_g.o* respectively. No spaces may appear between *–Xrun* and the library name. To load *libjdwp.so* (or *libjdwp.o*), therefore, the argument *–Xrunjdwp* is supplied. The system properties sun.boot. library.path and java.library.path determine the locations that are searched for the library.

The library name may optionally be followed by a set of options, separated from the name by a colon. The format and meaning of the options string is determined by the library. If the library contains a function called JVM_onLoad(), it is called during the loading process with the options string as one of its arguments. See the later section "Debugging" for an example of the use of this feature.

–Xtrace:value

Turns on low-level tracing in the virtual machine. The *value* argument determines exactly what is traced, by adding values from the following table. This option is available only if the VM was compiled with debugging enabled.

Value	What Is Traced
0x0000001	Byte-code execution
0x0000002	Method execution
0x0000004	Internal state of the interpreter loop on method calls and returns
0x0000008	Fast path of Java synchronization
0x0000010	Slow path of Java synchronization
0x0000020	Mutex locking and unlocking operations
0x0000040	Consistent state transitions
0x0000080	Beginning and end of garbage collection
0x0000100	Garbage collector root scans
0x0000200	Garbage collector heap object scans
0x0000400	Object allocation
0x0000800	Garbage collector internal details
0x0001000	Transition between garbage collector safe and unsafe states
0x0002000	Execution of class static initializers

Value	What Is Traced
0x0004000	Java exception handling
0x0008000	Heap initialization and destruction, global state initialization and safe exits
0x0010000	Read and write barriers for the garbage collector
0x0020000	Generation of garbage collection maps for Java stacks
0x0040000	Class loading
0x0080000	Lookup of classes in VM internal tables
0x0100000	Type system operations
0x0200000	Java class verification
0x0400000	Weak reference handling
0x0800000	Class unloading
0x1000000	Class linking

Properties

Arguments of the following form:

```
-Dname=value
```

can be used to set the value of a property in the system properties table called name to value. Java code can retrieve the property value using code of the form:

```
String value = System.getProperty("name");
```

Several properties have specific meanings to the virtual machine and the core class libraries. In particular, the following properties influence the loading of Java classes and native code libraries:

java.class.path

Interpreted as a list of directories, JAR files, and ZIP files from which application classes are loaded. Entries in the list should be separated using colons on the Linux platform and semicolons for VxWorks. This property is the CVM equivalent of the J2SE *CLASSPATH* environment variable, but it must be set explicitly because CVM does not read *CLASSPATH*. See the later section "Examples" for an example of the use of this property.

sun.boot.class.path

This property plays the same role as `java.class.path` but determines the location of system (or boot) classes. This property can more conveniently be set using one of the *–Xbootclasspath* options.

java.library.path

A colon- (Linux) or semicolon-separated (VxWorks) list of directories to be searched for native code libraries used with JNI. This path is intended to be used for native libraries belonging to application classes.

sun.boot.class.path

Specifies the library search path for boot classes. This is the system-level equivalent of `java.library.path`.

Debugging

If the CVM is built with JVMDI support enabled, Java source-level debugging can be performed by connecting a JPDA debugger, provided that the VM is started with the *–Xdebug* and *–Xrunjdwp* options, the latter required to load the library that contains the JDWP implementation. The *–Xrunjdwp* option requires additional parameters that the library uses to configure itself. The overall format of this argument is:

```
-Xrunjdwp:parameter=value[,parameter=value....]
```

The valid parameters and their meanings are as follows:

transport=type

Specifies the type of transport that the VM should use to communicate with the debugger. At the time of writing, only sockets are supported, requiring the type to be specified as *dt_socket.*

address=value

The transport address on which the VM should listen for a connection from a debugger. The format of the accompanying value depends on the value of the transport parameter. For the *dt_socket* transport, the value is a TCP/IP port number.

server=y | n

Specifies whether the JDWP library should adopt the server (value *y*) or client (value *n*) role. In order to receive a connection from a JPDA debugger, the value *y* should be used.

suspend=y | n

If this option has the value *y*, which is the default, the VM suspends execution during initialization of the JVMDI debugging code until a debugger connects. Normally, this is at VM startup, but the initialization of the debugging facilities can be deferred until an exception occurs if the *onuncaught* or *onthrow* options are used.

strict=y | n

Specifies whether the CVM debugging support adheres strictly to the JVMDI specification. By default, this option has value *n*. This option is not likely to be of general use.

onuncaught=y | n

By default, the debugger initializes during VM startup. If this option has value *y*, however, the debugger delays initialization until an uncaught exception is thrown. This avoids the overhead of the debugger until the point of failure.

onthrow=value

This option is similar to onuncaught, except that it delays debugger initialization until a specific exception is thrown (whether it is caught or not). The *value* argument gives the class name of the exception. The debugger initializes when an exception of this exact class is thrown. To initialize when a NullPointerException is thrown, for example, use:

```
onthrow=java.lang.NullPointerException
```

stdalloc=y | n

If this option has value *y*, the standard C-library memory allocation methods are used. Otherwise, the VM uses its own memory allocation package, which is the default.

launch=value

Causes an executable whose name is specified by the *value* parameter to be run when the debugger initializes. The executable is passed two parameters: the name of the transport over which the debugger is communicating (e.g., *dt_socket*) and the transport address. The *value* parameter should be an absolute path name or the name of an executable that is on the VM's search path.

Examples

cvm −Xbootclasspath:../lib/foundation.jar −Djava.class.path=/home/user/project myPkg.myClass

Loads and runs a Java application beginning with the `main()` method of the class `myPkg.myClass`. The core classes that are not built into the VM are loaded from *../lib/foundation.jar,* and application classes can be found below the directory */home/user/project.*

cvm −Xbootclasspath:../lib/foundation.jar −Djava.class.path=/home/user/project −Djava.library.path=/home/user/nativecode/lib myPkg.myClass

Runs the same application, but allows loading of native libraries from the directory */home/user/nativecode/lib.*

See Also

* The *Java 2 Platform, Micro Edition Connected Device Configuration (CDC) 1.0 Porting Guide* in the CDC or Foundation Profile reference implementation downloads

* "Debugging Java Code in the CVM" in Chapter 7 for an example that shows how to enable JPDA debugging

kdp: The KVM Debug Proxy

Availability

CLDC Reference Implementation

Synopsis

```
java kdp.KVMDebugProxy [options]
```

Description

kdp is a Java application that acts as a proxy between a JPDA-conformant debugger and a virtual machine such as the KVM. While fully featured VMs, such as those supplied with J2SE, have their own built-in implementation of the JDWP that allows them to be directly connected to a debugger, the resource constraints that apply to a typical CLDC VM do not allow a complete implementation of

Command-Line Tools

JDWP. The Java debug proxy interposes itself between a debugger and the VM to offload some of the implementation details from the VM.

kdp usually runs on a desktop system so as not to consume any resources on the target platform; it communicates with the KVM over a socket connection, using a cut-down version of JDWP called KDWP (the KVM Debug Wire Protocol).

Options

–classpath path
> Lists the locations of copies of the class files that will be loaded in the VM being debugged. Locations, which may be directory names or JAR filenames, are separated by the platform's path separator (i.e., a semicolon for the Windows platform or colon for Unix). This option is required only if the *–p* option is used.

–cp path
> A synonym for *–classpath*.

–l localport
> The port number on which the debug proxy listens for a connection from a JPDA-conformant debugger.

–p
> If this argument is present, the debug proxy handles operations that involve classes locally instead of passing them to the target VM. This argument is normally supplied when debugging with the KVM to offload the overhead of storing class-related information from the VM to the debug proxy. The *–cp* or *–classpath* option must also be supplied so that the proxy can load copies of the classes being used by the VM itself.

–r host port
> The name or IP address of the host on which the VM being debugged is running, and the port at which it is listening for a connection from the debug proxy. This port number is set using the KVM's *–port* argument.

–v verbosity
> Enables the output of debug trace information and controls the level of debugging. The *verbosity* argument can take the values 1 through 9, where a higher value corresponds to more detailed debugging.

Examples

To start the debug proxy and connect to a KVM listening on port 2000 of the same machine, load class files from the classpath defined by the environment variable *CP*, and listen for a connection from a debugger on port 3000:

```
java kdp.KVMDebugProxy -l 3000 -p -r localhost 2000 -cp %CP%
```

See Also

*   *kvm*

*   The *KVM Debug Wire Protocol Specification* in the CLDC reference implementation download

kvm: The Kilobyte Virtual Machine

Availability

CLDC Reference Implementation

Synopsis

```
kvm [options] classfile [args]
```

Description

The *kvm* command is a reference implementation of a Java virtual machine that meets the requirements of the CLDC specification. KVM can load classes from a directory structure in a local file system or from a set of JAR files. In order to reduce memory footprint and application startup time, it is usually built with a copy of the core Java libraries preloaded, using a technique known as ROMizing.

The *kvm* command provided with the CLDC reference implementation does not provide support for Java-level debugging. However, a second version, *kvm_g*, is provided. This version can provide this capability in conjunction with the KVM debug proxy (*kdp*), together with a set of additional command-line options that can be used to request debug trace information to be written to the standard output stream. It is also possible to build a version of the KVM that includes an implementation of a Java application manager (JAM) that can be used to load applications over a network and install them in local filestore. This feature is usually not used, however, since most systems prefer to incorporate more sophisticated application manager software of the type provided by the *emulator* and *midp* commands.

Options

The following options are available in all versions of the KVM:

−version
> Prints the version number of the CLDC reference implementation, and exits.

−classpath path
> Lists the locations of the class files to be loaded into the VM. Locations, which may be directory names or JAR filenames, are separated by the platform's path separator (i.e., a semicolon for the Windows platform or colon for Unix). The class path can also be set from the *CLASSPATH* environment variable.

−heapsize size
> Sets the size of the Java heap, overriding the implementation-dependent default value. The *size* parameter may be an absolute value in bytes (such as 131072) or an abbreviated value like 512k or 2M. It must not be less than 32K or larger than 64M.

−help
> Prints a synopsis of the command and a list of the available options and exits.

The following additional options are available when the KVM is built to include JPDA debugging support:

–debugger

> Enables JDPA debugging in the VM.

–port number

> Sets the port number on which to listen for connections from the KVM debug proxy. Port number 2800 is used if this option is not supplied.

–suspend

> Causes the VM to suspend execution of the Java application until requested to resume by a remote debugger. This is the default action when the *–debugger* argument is supplied.

–nosuspend

> When the *–debugger* argument is used, application execution is not suspended to wait for a debugger to connect.

The following additional options are provided when debug tracing is built into the VM:

–traceall

> Enables all debug tracing. Equivalent to specifying all of the remaining options.

–traceallocation

> Enables tracing of memory allocation, including the size of each allocated block and the amount of free memory remaining.

–tracebytecodes

> Enables tracing of each bytecode instruction as it is executed. The output includes the instruction name, the operand values, and the method that it is part of.

–traceclassloading

> Traces loading and initialization of Java classes.

–traceclassloadingverbose

> Traces loading and initialization of Java classes, supplying more detailed information than *–traceclassloading*.

–tracedebugger

> Traces debugging operations.

–traceevents

> Enables tracing of events (such as pen movements) received from the host platform. Only the event type is traced.

–traceexceptions

> Writes trace information when any exception is thrown.

–traceframes

> Traces pushing and popping of stack frames as methods are called or returned.

–tracegc

> Traces when garbage collection starts and ends and the number of bytes freed during each garbage collection phase.

–tracegcverbose

Produces the same output as *–tracegc* but also logs objects that the garbage collector is inspecting.

–tracemethods

Traces entry to and exit from every method, logging the class name and method name.

–tracemethodsverbose

Traces entry to and exit from every method, logging the type of call (virtual, static, special, interface, etc.), the class name, the method name, and the method signature.

–tracemonitors

Traces monitor activity. Monitors are used to control synchronized methods or blocks of code.

–tracenetworking

Traces networking activity.

–tracestackchunks

Traces the creation of new stacks (when a new thread is started) and pushing and popping of execution frames on the stack (like *–traceframes*).

–tracestackmaps

Traces stack map activities. Stack maps are used to record live references on the stack for use when garbage collecting.

–tracethreading

Traces threading activity, such as:

> Thread creation
> Thread startup
> Thread switching
> Thread termination
> Thread suspension
> Thread resumption

–traceverifier

Traces the activity of the runtime byte-code verifier.

If the KVM JAM feature is compiled into the VM, the following options can also be used:

–jam

Enables the use of the KVM Java application manager. When this option is used, the *classfile* argument must be supplied and should be the URL of a descriptor file that describes the application to be loaded and executed. The format of this file is described in the *KVM Porting Guide*, which is part of the CLDC reference implementation download.

–appsdir directory

Sets the local directory in which applications loaded by the JAM are installed.

–repeat

Repeats loading and execution of the application whose class file is named on the command line, until interrupted by the user.

Command-
Line Tools

Examples

kvm –classpath myApp.jar com.myco.MyApp
> Loads and runs the class `com.myco.MyApp`, searching for classes in the JAR file *myApp.jar.*

kvm_g –traceall –classpath myApp.jar com.myco.MyApp
> Loads and runs the class `com.myco.MyApp`, searching for classes in the JAR file *myApp.jar* and turning on all trace logging. This produces a lot of output.

kvm_g –debugger –port 2850 –classpath myApp.jar com.myco.MyApp
> Loads the class `com.myco.MyApp`, searching for classes in the JAR file *myApp. jar* and suspends execution waiting for a debugger to connect via port 2850 and resume execution.

See Also

• The *KVM Porting Guide* in the CLDC reference implementation download

midp: The MID Profile Execution Environment

Availability

MIDP Reference Implementation

Synopsis

```
midp [options]
midp [options] [-Xdescriptor filename] class
midp [options] -Xdescriptor   filename
midp [options] -autotest descriptor_URL [MIDlet_name]
midp [options] -transient descriptor_URL [MIDlet_name]
midp [options] -install [-force] descriptor_URL
midp [options] -run (suite number | storage name) [MIDlet_name]
midp [options] -remove (suite number | storage name | all)
midp [options] -list
midp [options] -storageNames
```

Description

midp is an executable program that contains a KVM implementation, classes required by MIDP Version 1.0, and an implementation of an Application Management Software subsystem. It is, therefore, a complete environment for testing the execution and installation of MIDlets.

MIDlet Management and Storage

A MIDlet consists of one or more class files and associated resources stored in a JAR file. Several MIDlets may be combined into a MIDlet suite. All the MIDlets that make up a given suite are packaged in the same JAR file and are managed as a single unit: they are installed together in the simulated nonvolatile device storage maintained by the midp command and removed together. Furthermore, they all execute in the same instance of the Java VM.

MIDlets may be loaded from a local filesystem for testing purposes, but, in the real world, they will almost always be installed over a network or via a local connection to an associated host system, such as a desktop computer. Because the JAR file that contains a MIDlet suite may be large, each suite has an associated Java Archive Descriptor file (JAD) that is small enough to download quickly, but which contains enough information about the suite to allow the user to decide whether to install it. The Application Management Software (AMS) of a MIDP device (such as a cell phone) typically first downloads the JAD file, whose location is specified by its URL. If the user decides to install the MIDlet suite, the AMS downloads the JAR file, which can be located by using one of the attributes in the JAD. The MIDlet suite is then stored on the device, and subsequently, the MIDlets it contains can be loaded from the locally installed copy.

The various synopses of the *midp* command reflect the ways in which a MIDlet can be run and the set of management functions that the AMS supports.

Execution without permanent installation

For testing purposes, it is possible to execute a MIDlet or load a MIDlet suite and allow a MIDlet to be selected from it without permanently installing it in the simulated nonvolatile memory of the emulated device. The simplest way to run a specific MIDlet is to use the variant of *midp* that requires the name of the MIDlet class. For example:

```
midp -classpath . ora.ch4.FormExampleMIDlet
```

This form of the command is useful for testing MIDlets that have not yet been packaged into a JAR file for deployment. If the MIDlet needs to be able to access application properties stored in a JAD file, the *–Xdescriptor* argument can provide the location of the JAD file to be used, which must be the name of a file on the local system:

```
midp -classpath . -Xdescriptor ora\ch4\Chapter4.jad ora.ch4.
FormExampleMIDlet
```

To launch a MIDlet suite and allow the user to select a MIDlet to execute, supply the name of the suite's JAD file, but omit the MIDlet class name:

```
midp -classpath .  -Xdescriptor ora\ch4\Chapter4.jad
```

This variant of *midp* requires that the MIDlet suite be packaged into a JAR file that is referenced from the MIDlet-Jar-URL attribute of the application descriptor. It is also possible to install a MIDlet suite temporarily, select and execute a MIDlet from it, and uninstall it automatically using the –*transient* or –*autotest* options. For example:

```
midp -transient http://www.midlethost.acme.com/suite.jad CalendarMIDlet
midp -transient http://www.midlethost.acme.com/suite.jad
midp -autotest http://www.midlethost.acme.com/suite.jad CalendarMIDlet
```

The –*transient* option performs a single install/execute/remove cycle, whereas –*autotest* repeats this set of operations until it is interrupted, which is useful for automated testing of MIDlets, particularly those that do not require user input. If a MIDlet name is not supplied on the command line, a menu of all of the MIDlets in the suite referenced by the JAD file is displayed to allow the user to choose which should be executed.

MIDlet suite management

The Application Management Software (AMS) built into the *midp* command can be driven from the command line or its graphical user interface. The following command launches a cell phone emulator and displays a menu that allows the user to enter the AMS to install a MIDlet suite over the network:

```
midp
```

Alternatively, the information required to fetch and permanently install a MIDlet suite can be provided on the command line, avoiding the need for interaction with the graphical AMS:

```
midp -install http://www.midlethost.acme.com/suite.jad
midp -install -force http://www.midlethost.acme.com/suite.jad
```

The –*force* option can be used to force reinstallation of an already installed MIDlet suite without removing it first. The *midp* command supports download of a MIDlet suite from a network server using an implementation of OTA provisioning (see "Over-the-Air Provisioning" in Chapter 3), where HTTP is used as the underlying communications mechanism.

A list of installed MIDlet suites can be obtained by using the –*list* option:

```
midp -list
```

This command prints summary information for each MIDlet suite, an example of which follows:

```
[1]
  Name: Chapter4
  Vendor: J2ME in a Nutshell
  Version: 1.0
  Storage name: #J2#M#E%0020in%0020a%0020#Nutshell_#Chapter4_
  Size: 23K
  Installed From: http://hostname/path/Chapter4.jad
  MIDlets:
    [list of MIDlets in the suite]
```

Each MIDlet suite is assigned a suite number (1 in the example above) and a storage name, the format of which depends on the implementation. The *midp* command creates the storage name using the rule vendorName_suiteName_, but precedes uppercase letters with a # symbol and converts nonalphabetic, nonnumeric characters to their Unicode values preceded by a % symbol. This allows the name to be stored without loss in a storage system that supports only 8-bit characters, and even on systems that cannot distinguish upper- and lowercase characters. A list of the storage names of all installed MIDlet suites can be obtained as follows:

```
midp -storageNames
```

Once a MIDlet suite is installed, you start the emulator so that it displays a menu of the MIDlets within the suite and allows one to be chosen for execution. You do this by using the *–run* option together with the suite's storage number or storage name:

```
midp -run 1
midp -run #J2#M#E%0020in%0020a%0020#Nutshell_#Chapter4_
```

Similarly, you can use the suite number or storage name to remove an installed MIDlet suite:

```
midp -remove 1
midp -remove #J2#M#E%0020in%0020a%0020#Nutshell_#Chapter4_
```

Options

The *midp* command has three optional arguments:

–classpath path
> Lists the locations of MIDlet class files. This option is useful when running MIDlets developed and installed locally and not yet packaged for network installation. Locations, which may be directory names or JAR file names, are separated by the platform's path separator (i.e., a semicolon for the Windows platform, colon for Unix).

–help
> Prints a message displaying the available options and command usage and exits.

–version
> Displays the supported versions of CLDC and MIDP and the version number of the executable and exits.

In addition to these arguments, any of the options provided by KVM (see the earlier section "kvm: The Kilobyte Virtual Machine") may also be used, including the debugging options if the *midp* executable has been built with debugging enabled.

See Also

- *kvm*
- *emulator*

Command-
Line Tools

emulator: The J2ME Wireless Toolkit Emulator

Availability

J2ME Wireless Toolkit

Synopsis

```
emulator [options] [classname]
```

Description

The *emulator* command provides the execution environment and application management software for the J2ME Wireless Toolkit. Its functionality and command-line interface are both very similar to those of *midp*, but it supports the use of device skins together with a configuration file, so different devices can be emulated without the need to modify any code. Although the emulator can be used from the command line, it is most frequently accessed indirectly via the KToolBar interface provided by the Wireless Toolkit.

Options

The operation of the *emulator* command is determined by the options supplied to it. There are three different modes of operation:

- Displaying information using the *–help*, *–version*, and *–Xquery* options. Here, the *classname* argument is not required, and the command exits after printing the required information.

- Running a MIDlet from the local system or by loading from a network server, but without installing it. This mode of operation uses the *–classpath* option together with a class name or the *–Xdescriptor* option, which may or may not be accompanied by a class name.

- Using the emulator's application management software to install, run, list, or delete MIDlet suites. This mode of operation uses the *–Xjam* option.

The following list describes *emulator* options:

–classpath path
> Lists the locations in which MIDlet class files can be found. This option is useful when running MIDlets developed and installed locally and not yet packaged for network installation. Locations, which may be directory names or JAR filenames, are separated by the platform's path separator (i.e., a semicolon for the Windows platform, colon for Unix).

–cp path
> A synonym for *–classpath*.

–help
> Displays the valid command arguments and exits.

–version
> Prints the version numbers of the J2ME Wireless Toolkit and the embedded CLDC and MIDP implementations, then exits.

–Xdebug

Prepares the emulator for runtime debugging. This option must be used in conjunction with *–Xrunjdwp.*

–Xdevice:name

Runs the emulation using the named device. Selecting a difference device affects the quantity of memory and the input and display capabilities available to MIDlets, and it also causes a different skin to be used for the benefit of the user. The following *name* values are recognized by default:

DefaultColorPhone
> A cell phone with a color display

DefaultGrayPhone
> A cell phone with a grayscale display

MinimumPhone
> A basic telephone with a two-color display

Motorola_i85s
> The Motorola i85s cell phone

PalmOS_Device
> A PalmOS pseudo-device

RIMJavaHandheld
> The Research In Motion wireless handheld

–Xdescriptor:fileName

Loads a MIDlet suite given the location of a JAD file and allows the user to select a MIDlet to be executed. If the optional *classname* argument is supplied, it is assumed to be a MIDlet in that MIDlet suite to be executed. The fileName argument may be a URL or a local filename.

–Xheapsize:size

Sets the size of the Java heap, overriding the implementation-dependent default value. The *size* parameter may be an absolute value in bytes (such as 131072) or an abbreviated value like 512k or 2M.

–Xjam:command

Starts the emulator and performs the operation indicated by the command argument using its application management software. The legal operations are described in the next section.

–Xquery

Lists the properties of all the devices that the emulator can emulate, including the device description and details of its screen and input capabilities. See the later section "Examples" for some example output.

–Xrunjdwp:options

When used in conjunction with *–Xdebug*, this argument sets the transport type and transport address at which the VM listens for a connection from a remote debugger. The *options* value is specified as follows:

```
transport=<transport>,address=<address>,server=<y/n>
```

where *transport* must currently take the value *dt_socket*, and *address* has the form *host:port*. The server argument should always be *y*.

–Xverbose:options

Switches on verbose output of trace information according to *options*, which can either take the value `all` or be a comma-separated list of one or more of the following:

allocation	bytecodes	class
classverbose	events	exceptions
frames	gc	gcverbose
methods	methodsverbose	monitors
networking	stackchunks	stackmaps
threading	verifier	

Application Management Commands

You can control the emulator's application management software by using the *–Xjam* argument, followed by a colon and one of the commands from Table 8-1. The *–Xjam* argument may also be used on its own to start the emulator and run the graphical interface to the AMS, as described in "The Wireless Toolkit Application Management Software" in Chapter 3.

Table 8-1: Wireless Toolkit Emulator AMS Control Commands

Command	Description
force	When used in conjuction with *install*, forces installation even if the MIDlet suite is already installed.
install=descriptor_URL	Installs the MIDlet suite whose JAD is at the given location.
list	Lists information regarding the installed MIDlet suites, including the suite number and storage name. The format of this data is described in the earlier section "MIDlet suite management."
remove=storage_name	Removes the MIDlet suite with the given storage name.
remove=suite_number	Removes the MIDlet suite with the given suite number.
remove=all	Removes all installed MIDlet suites.
run=storage_name	Displays a menu allowing the user to select a MIDlet from the installed suite with the given storage name, then executes the MIDlet.
storageNames	Lists the storage names of all installed MIDlet suites. Storage names are described in the earlier section "MIDlet suite management."
transient=descriptor_URL	Temporarily installs a MIDlet suite, allows the user to select and run a MIDlet, and then removes the MIDlet suite. If the suite is already installed, the installation step is skipped, but the removal is still performed.

Examples

emulator –cp dir1;dir2;dir3 ora.ch5.AttributesMIDlet

Executes the MIDlet `ora.ch5.AttributesMIDlet`, loading its classes from the supplied classpath.

emulator –Xdebug –Xrunjdwp:transport=dt-socket,address=2000,server=y –cp dir1;dir2;dir3 ora.ch5.AttributesMIDlet

Executes the MIDlet `ora.ch5.AttributesMIDlet`, loading its classes from the supplied classpath and preparing the VM for debugging.

emulator –Xdescriptor:http://servername/path/suite.jad

Loads the MIDlet suite whose JAD file is at the given URL and allows the user to select a MIDlet to be executed.

emulator –Xdescriptor:http://servername/path/suite.jad ora.ch5.AttributesMIDlet

Loads the MIDlet suite whose JAD file is at the given URL and runs the MIDlet from the suite whose class file is `ora.ch5.AttributesMIDlet`.

emulator –Xquery

Prints information for all the devices supported by the emulator. The following is typical output for a single device:

```
# Properties for device DefaultGrayPhone
DefaultGrayPhone.description: DefaultGrayPhone
DefaultGrayPhone.screen.width: 96
DefaultGrayPhone.screen.height: 128
DefaultGrayPhone.screen.isColor: false
DefaultGrayPhone.screen.isTouch: false
DefaultGrayPhone.screen.width: 96
DefaultGrayPhone.screen.bitDepth: 8
```

emulator –Xjam:install=http://servername//path/suite.jad

Installs a MIDlet suite over the network given the location of its JAD file. If the MIDlet suite is already installed, this command fails.

emulator –Xjam:install=http://servername//path/suite.jad –Xjam:force

Installs the given MIDlet suite, forcing it to overwrite any copy of the MIDlet suite that is already installed.

*emulator –Xjam:run=#J2#M#E%0020in%0020a%0020#Nutshell_#Chapter5_*

Displays a menu listing all the MIDlets in the suite with the given storage name, and allows the user to select one to be executed.

emulator –Xjam:storageNames

Lists the storage names of all installed MIDlet suites.

emulator –Xjam:remove=1

Removes the installed MIDlet suite with suite number 1.

See Also

* *midp*

preverify: The KVM Class Preverifier

Availability

CLDC Reference Implementation, MIDP Reference Implementation, Wireless Toolkit

Synopsis

```
preverify [options] classnames | dirnames | JARnames
```

Command-Line Tools

Description

The class preverifier for classes to be loaded into a CLDC-conformant virtual machine, such as the KVM. All classes must be preverified before use to ensure that they are valid and do not attempt to circumvent Java programming language rules in such a way as to cause a potential security breach.

The *preverify* command processes a set of input class files and writes them to an output location, which must be different from the input location. The set of class files to be processed can be specified using any combination of the following:

- A set of class names, in which each class is located relative to the class path given by the *–classpath* argument or via the *CLASSPATH* environment variable
- A JAR file or ZIP file containing Java class files
- A directory that is recursively searched for class files, JAR files, or ZIP files

The output from this process is written to the directory specified by the *–d* argument or to a directory called *output* if the *–d* argument is omitted. JAR or ZIP file contents are written to a JAR or ZIP file with the same name in the output directory.

Options

@filename

Supplies the name of a file from which command-line arguments are read. The file must contain only a single line consisting of legal program arguments, which are processed as the file is read. Directory and class names included in this file must be enclosed in double quotes and may contain whitespace.

–classpath path

Lists the locations of class files. Locations, which may be directory names or JAR file names, are separated by the platform's path separator (i.e., a semicolon for the Windows platform or colon for Unix). The *–classpath* option should specify the location of the core libraries as well as that of the classes to be preverified, unless this information can be obtained from the *CLASSPATH* environment variable.

–cldc

If present, this argument causes the preverifier to check that class files do not attempt to use VM features that are not part of the CLDC specification; that is, they may not use native methods, floating point operations, or object finalization. It is equivalent to supplying all of the *–nofinalize*, *–nofp*, and *–nonative* arguments.

–d outputdirname

Supplies the name of the directory to which the preverified classes will be written, defaulting to *output* if this argument is not supplied. If the *preverify* command reads any ZIP or JAR files, the processed versions will also be written to this directory.

–nofinalize

If present, this argument causes the preverifier to ensure that classes do not attempt to make use of object finalization. If this argument is omitted, and the

–cldc option is not supplied, use of object finalization causes an error at runtime.

–nofp

If present, this argument causes the preverifier to ensure that classes do not attempt to use floating point operations. If this argument is omitted, and the *–cldc* option is not supplied, use of floating point operations causes an error at runtime.

–nonative

If present, this argument causes the preverifier to ensure that classes do not declare native methods. If this argument is omitted and the *–cldc* option is not supplied, use of native methods may cause an error at runtime. Note, however, that applications specifically written for a customized version of the KVM may use native methods, as described in "Interfacing with Native Code" in Chapter 2. In such cases, use of this argument would not be appropriate.

–verbose

Causes debug information to be written to the standard error stream.

–verify-verbose

Causes detailed debug information for the class verification process to be written to the standard error stream. This option can result in large amounts of output.

Examples

To preverify a single class called `ora.ch2.KVMProperties` at location *tmpclasses\ora\ch2\KVMProperties.class* relative to the current directory, where the core library classes are located in the directory *c:\j2me\j2me_cldc\bin\common\api\lclasses*, and writing the verified class to a file called *output\ora\ch2\KVMProperties.class*:

```
preverify -classpath c:\j2me\j2me_cldc\bin\common\api\lclasses;tmpclasses
ora.ch2.KVMProperties
```

To preverify all the classes in *tmpclasses\native.jar*, writing the output to *native.jar* in the current directory and ensuring that floating point operations and object finalization are not used:

```
preverify -classpath c:\j2me\j2me_cldc\bin\common\api\lclasses -nofp -
nofinalize -d . tmpclasses\native.jar
```

To preverify all the classes in the directory *tmpclasses* and all of its subdirectories, writing the output to an identical directory hierarchy in the current directory:

```
preverify -classpath c:\j2me\j2me_cldc\bin\common\api\lclasses -d .
tmpclasses
```

See Also

- *kvm*

- The *KVM Porting Guide* in the CLDC reference implementation download

Command-Line Tools

MakeMIDPApp: JAD to PRC Conversion Tool

Availability

MIDP for PalmOS

Synopsis

```
java   -cp   Converter.jar   com.sun.midp.palm.database.MakeMIDPApp
[options] jarfile
```

Description

The *MakeMIDPApp* command converts a MIDlet suite in the form of a JAR and a
JAD file into a form suitable for installation on a PalmOS device. *MakeMIDPApp* is
a Java language utility found in the file *%INSTALL_DIR%\Converter\Converter.jar*,
where *%INSTALL_DIR%* is the installation directory of the MIDP for PalmOS
product, of which it is a part.

Options

–help

> Prints a synopsis of the command and the options that it recognizes.

–v

> Provides verbose output. If you use this option twice (i.e., *–v –v*), slightly
> more output is produced.

–jad file

> Supplies the Java Archive Descriptor (JAD) for the MIDlet suite. This argu-
> ment is optional, but if you don't supply it, any application properties held in
> the JAD file that are not also in the manifest file of the JAR will not be acces-
> sible at runtime. See "A Simple MIDlet" in Chapter 3 for a discussion of
> application properties.

–name name

> Gives the name to be associated with the MIDlet suite when it is displayed on
> the PalmOS device's application launcher screen. The name may contain
> spaces, provided that quotes are used to separate it from other arguments.
> Names longer than nine characters are not guranteed to be displayed in full. If
> this argument is not supplied, the MIDlet suite name from the manifest file or
> the JAD file (if supplied) is used instead.

–longname name

> Supplies a name of up to 31 characters that will be used to describe the
> MIDlet where there is room for a slightly longer name, such as in the list of
> MIDlets that can be displayed from the developer preferences dialog (which is
> accessible from the Options menu of the MIDlet while it is running). Quotes
> should be used to delimit the name if it contains spaces.

–icon file

Specifies an icon to be used for the MIDlet suite when it appears on the device's launcher screen in "icon" mode. A default icon is used if this argument is supplied. The icon may be in one of three image formats:

BMP

Windows bitmap format

PBM

Portable bitmap format

BIN

PalmOS bitmap format

Compressed or color Windows bitmaps are not supported. For best results, the image should be a 32-pixel square bitmap, in which the 5 leftmost and rightmost columns and the last 10 rows should be white. If the image size is incorrect, it will be adjusted to the right size, which may result in a loss of quality.

–smallicon file

Specifies an icon to be used for the MIDlet suite when it appears on the device's launcher screen in "list" mode. A default icon is used if this argument is supplied. The image bitmap should be 15 pixels wide and 9 pixels high.

–creator id

Assigns a four-character PalmOS creator ID to the MIDlet suite. If you intend to assign a creator ID to a commercial product, you should register it at *http://www.palm.com/devzone/*. The creator ID is assigned to the RMS storage that the MIDlet suite creates and also appears in the list of installed MIDlet suites available from the developer preferences dialog. If you don't supply a creator ID, one will be assigned for you. In this case, you must also supply the arguments *–type Data*.

–type type

Specifies the type of output file to create. The *type* argument is case sensitive and may take the values *appl* (which is the default) or *Data*. If you do not use the *–creator* argument to assign an explicit creator ID, the type must be given as *Data*. MIDlet suites created with type *Data* cannot be beamed between PalmOS devices.

–outfile file

The name of the file to which the converted MIDlet suite should be written. Output file names conventionally use the suffix *.prc*.

–o file

Synonym for *–outfile*.

Examples

java –cp Converter.jar com.sun.midp.palm.database.MakeMIDPApp –icon myIcon. bmp –smallicon myListIcon.bmp –jad Chapter3.jad –o Chapter3.prc –type Data Chapter3.jar

Converts the MIDlet suite packaged in the file *Chapter3.jar* and its associated attributes from the file *Chapter3.jad* into a form suitable for loading onto a

PalmOS device. The output is written to a file called *Chapter3.prc*. The icons to be displayed on the device's launcher screen are held in the files *myIcon.bmp* (for icon mode) and *myListIcon.bmp* (for list mode), respectively. Since an explicit creator ID is not being assigned, the type is given as *Data*.

java –cp Converter.jar com.sun.midp.palm.database.MakeMIDPApp –jad Chapter3.
jad –o Chapter3.prc –creator ORA3 –name "Ch 3" –longname "J2ME Chapter 3"
Chapter3.jar

Converts the MIDlet suite packaged in the file *Chapter3.jar* and its associated attributes from the file *Chapter3.jad* into a form suitable for loading onto a PalmOS device. The output is written to a file called *Chapter3.prc*. On the launcher screen, the MIDlet suite will be displayed with the default icons and with the name "Ch 3". In contexts where a longer name is used, the text "J2ME Chapter 3" will appear. A creator ID of *ORA3* is associated with this MIDlet suite, so the *–type* argument does not need to be supplied.

Be aware that not all combinations of creator ID and type result in a MIDlet suite that can be executed on a PalmOS device. The following list, in which XXXX represents any four-character creator ID, summarizes the various combinations of these arguments and the results that are obtained:

–creator XXXX –type appl

Always results in an executable MIDlet suite. MIDlets can be beamed to another PalmOS device.

–creator XXXX –type Data

The MIDlet suite can be installed but is not executable and cannot be beamed.

–type Data

The MIDlet suite is executable but cannot be beamed.

MEKeyTool: Public Key Certificate Management Tool

Availability

MIDP Reference Implementation, Wireless Toolkit

Synopsis

```
java -jar MEKeyTool.jar -help

java -jar MEKeyTool.jar -list [-MEkeystore filename]

java -jar MEKeyTool.jar -import [-MEkeystore filename] [-keystore
filename] [-storepass password] -alias keyAlias [-domain domain]

java -jar MEKeyTool.jar -delete [-MEKeystore filename] -owner
ownerName
```

Description

MEKeyTool is a Java language utility used to manage a keystore that holds public key certificates required to use the support for secure networking (HTTPS) provided by the MIDP reference implementation and the J2ME Wireless Toolkit. *MEKeyTool* is shipped in the form of a JAR file called *MEKeyTool.jar* in the directory *%INSTALL_DIR%\bin*, where *%INSTALL_DIR%* is the directory in which the J2ME Wireless Toolkit is installed. It is also provided in source code form as part of the MIDP reference implementation.

When used with the J2ME Wireless Toolkit, *MEKeyTool* maintains a certificate keystore (it is referred to here as the *ME keystore*), that is held, by default, in a file called *%INSTALL_DIR%\appdb_main.ks*. All operations implicitly apply to this keystore, unless you supply an alternative using the *–MEkeystore* option. *MEKeyTool* can list the content of the keystore, import a certificate from a J2SE keystore, or delete a certificate from the keystore. In order to make proper use of *MEKeyTool*, you need to be familiar with the J2SE keystore and the *keytool* command that is used to manage it, both of which are covered in *Java in a Nutshell* by David Flanagan (O'Reilly).

Options

–MEKeystore filename

> Specifies the location of the ME keystore. By default, the keystore is held in the file *appdb_main.ks* below the installation directory of the wireless toolkit.

–keystore filename

> Gives the location of the J2SE keystore. J2SE ships with a set of certificates for root certification authorities which can be used to populate the ME keystore. This keystore is located at *%JAVA_HOME%\jre\lib\security\cacerts*.

–storepass filename

> The password used to protect the J2SE keystore. By default, the password for the default J2SE keystore is *changeit*, but this may be changed using the J2SE *keytool* command.

–alias aliasName

> Identifies the certificate from the J2SE keystore that is to be exported. You can get a list of the certificates in a J2SE keystore, which shows the alias for each certificate, by using the J2SE *keytool* command with the *–list* option:

```
keytool -list -keystore C:\jdk1.3.1\jre\lib\security\lib\cacerts
    -storepass changeit
```

> A typical line of output from this command looks like this:

```
Certificate fingerprint (MD5):
18:87:5C:CB:F8:20:5D:24:4A:BF:19:C7:13:0E:FD:B4
verisignserverca, Mon Jun 29 18:07:34 BST 1998, trustedCertEntry,
```

> The *aliasName* that you would use to import this certificate into the ME keystore is *verisignserverca*.

–owner ownerName

> Specifies the owner name of a key to be deleted from the ME keystore. Owner names are rather cumbersome, as the following extract from the keystore shows:

```
Key 1
    Owner: OU=Class 2 Public Primary Certification
Authority;O=VeriSign, Inc.;C=US
```

```
Valid from Mon Jan 29 00:00:00 GMT 1996 to Wed Jan 07 23:59:59 GMT
2004
    Domain: untrusted
```

Here, the owner is the string "OU=Class 2 Public Primary Certification Authority;O=VeriSign, Inc.;C=US".

–domain domainName

This option can be used to associate a security domain with the key when it is imported into the ME keystore. This option does not need to be used when installing certificates for use with the HTTPS support in the MIDP reference implementation.

Examples

MEKeyTool accesses its default keystore using the relative filename *appdb_main. ks*. To avoid having to use the *–MEkeystore* option to specify an explicit pathname, it is usually most convenient to make the J2ME wireless toolkit installation directory your working directory before using *MEKeyTool*. The examples in this section assume that this has been done.

To import into the default ME keystore a certificate with alias *versignserverca* from the J2SE keystore in the file *c:\jdk1.3.1\jre\lib\security\cacerts*:

```
set JCE=c:\jdk1.3.1\jre\lib\security\cacerts
java -jar bin\MEKeyTool.jar -import -keystore %JCE% -storepass changeit
verisignserverca
```

To list the entire content of the default ME keystore:

```
java -jar bin\MEKeyTool.jar -list
```

The following is typical output from the previous command:

```
Key 1
  Owner: OU=Secure Server Certification Authority;O=RSA Data Security,
Inc.;C=US
  Valid from Wed Nov 09 00:00:00 GMT 1994 to Thu Jan 07 23:59:59 GMT 2010
  Domain: untrusted
Key 2
  Owner: OU=Class 3 Public Primary Certification Authority;O=VeriSign,
Inc.;C=US
  Valid from Mon Jan 29 00:00:00 GMT 1996 to Wed Jan 07 23:59:59 GMT 2004
  Domain: untrusted
```

To delete from the default keystore the second key in the output shown above:

```
java -jar bin\MEKeyTool.jar -delete -owner "OU=Class 3 Public Primary
Certification Authority;O=VeriSign, Inc.;C=US"
```

See Also

*   The description of the **keytool** command in O'Reilly's *Java in a Nutshell*

CHAPTER 9

J2ME Programming Environments

Java developers who worked with the JDK 1.0 and 1.1 no doubt recall how much time it took for the first production quality integrated development environments to come to market. Most developers at that time had little choice but to create their code with their favorite editor and compile it using the command-line tools included with the JDK.[*] Debugging was even more of a nightmare, because the only tool available, *jdb*, was low-powered and not very robust. In the last few years, and especially since the release of the Java 2 platform, J2SE IDEs have matured to the point that you can now place your trust in them for routine development tasks. Most of them even have wizards that build JAR files for you or extract your Javadoc documentation.

Happily for J2ME developers, it has not been necessary to wait such a long time for reasonable development software to appear. Sun has made available the J2ME Wireless Toolkit, which can be used alone or integrated into some of the leading IDEs on the market. Several cell phone manufacturers provide their own development environments, which can be used to develop and test MIDlets on their devices. This chapter looks in some detail at the J2ME Wireless Toolkit and at Forte for Java, which provides a seamless environment for developing MIDlet suites, based on its ability to be tightly integrated with the Wireless Toolkit. The chapter also lists some other third-party IDEs that provide support for J2ME, together with the URLs from which they can be downloaded. Many of these IDEs, including the Wireless Toolkit and Forte for Java, are either free or have no-cost or

---

[*] In fact, many serious developers still work this way, feeling that there is no need to use a full-blown development environment. This is a view that I have a great deal of respect for, having trod this path myself for many years. It is only quite recently that I have found that the advantages of using an IDE can sometimes outweigh the disadvantages, but no doubt there will always be those who prefer to work with notepad, *vi* or *emacs*, and *javac*. The good news for them is that Sun includes the command-line tools that they require either in the JDK or with the J2ME reference releases and the Wireless Toolkit. The most important of these tools are covered in Chapter 8.

low-cost entry-level editions that make them a convenient way to build J2ME applications.

The J2ME Wireless Toolkit

The J2ME Wireless Toolkit is based on Sun's reference implementation of the MIDP 1.0 and CLDC 1.0 specifications. It includes a graphical user interface that allows you to build and run MIDlet suites, together with some additional features, such as support for OTA provisioning and HTTPS, that are not currently part of the official MIDP specification. We have already used the Wireless Toolkit in this book, and you'll find an introduction that shows you how to use it to create a new project and build a MIDlet suite in Chapter 3. In this section, you'll find a brief recap of its major features, followed by a more detailed examination of those aspects of the Wireless Toolkit that have not been mentioned in earlier chapters.

J2ME Wireless Toolkit Overview

When you install the J2ME Wireless Toolkit, you get several command-line and GUI utilities:

KToolBar

KToolBar is the main user interface component of the Wireless Toolkit. You can use it to create and manage projects, compile, package, and run MIDlet suites, and select the emulated device to be used. The basic operation of KToolBar is summarized in the next section.

Run MIDP Application

This utility pops up a dialog that allows you to browse your computer's filesystem for a MIDlet suite packaged in a JAR with an associated JAD file and run it using the currently selcted default device. It is useful if you want to demonstrate a MIDlet without starting the full toolkit.

Default device selection

The default device selection utility lets you select the device that will be used when you run a MIDlet suite using the Run MIDP Application utility or by double-clicking on the icon representing a JAD file.

Preferences

This utility opens a dialog box that lets you change customizable features of the emulators that the Wireless Toolkit uses to run MIDlet suites. The same dialog can also be accessed directly from KToolBar.

Utilities

The Utilities application opens a dialog that provides two features:

— For PalmOS devices, it allows you to convert a MIDlet suite to *.prc* format, which is required to install the suite on a PalmOS device or the PalmOS emulator. See the later section "MIDP for PalmOS" for more information on deploying MIDlets onto PalmOS devices.

— For other devices, it provides the ability to remove the files that are used to emulate RMS storage on your system. See "Persistent Storage" in Chapter 6 for a discussion of RMS storage.

The same dialog can be accessed directly from KToolBar.

Command-line tools

All of the graphical utilities that are part of the toolkit are installed as command-line tools in the *bin* directory of the toolkit installation. In addition to these, the toolkit provides the *emulator* command, which can be used to execute MIDlet suites from the command line (see "emulator: The J2ME Wireless Toolkit Emulator" in Chapter 8), and MEKeyTool, which manages the certificates and keys required by the Wireless Toolkit HTTPS support, a feature that is described in "Secure Networking," later in this chapter.

Developing MIDlet Suites with the Wireless Toolkit

The Wireless Toolkit is based around projects, where a project contains all the source files and resources for a MIDlet suite. When you start the KToolBar application, you can choose either to open an existing project or to create a new one (see Figure 3-7). If you create a new project, you are prompted to supply a project name, which will be used to create a new directory hierarchy to contain all of the project's files. By default, this directory will be created under *%INSTALL_DIR%\apps\project_name*, where *INSTALL_DIR* is the directory in which the Wireless Toolkit is installed. The project's files are organized within these directories as follows:

bin

The toolkit uses this directory to store the manifest file for the JAR into which the MIDlet is packaged, the JAD file used to describe the MIDlet suite, and the MIDlet suite's JAR file itself. Note that the JAR file is not created by the usual build and testing process; it is built only if you request that the suite be packaged.

classes

Contains the compiled class files for the MIDlet suite after they have been preverifed.

lib

This directory can be used to hold JAR and ZIP files containing classes that are not part of the project you want to be incorporated when compiling, running, and packaging the MIDlet suite. The content of these libraries is extracted and included in the JAR created when the MIDlet suite is packaged.

Files stored in this directory are used only in connection with its containing project. You can arrange for libraries to be available to all projects by placing their JAR or ZIP files in the toolkit's own *lib* directory (*%INSTALL_DIR%\lib*).

res

This directory should be used to store resource files, such as images, that MIDlets in the MIDlet suite will need to access at runtime.

src

This is where you place the source code for your MIDlets. The usual mapping between package name and directories should be used, so that, for example, the source files for a MIDlet in a package called `ora.ch3` should be placed in the directory *src\ora\ch3*. Note that the Wireless Toolkit is not a full-fledged IDE and does not provide the ability to edit source files. You will need to use your own editor or that of a third-party IDE to create and edit MIDlet source files. For greater convenience, you can also integrate the Wireless Toolkit with certain IDEs, including Forte for Java and Borland JBuilder—see "J2ME and Forte For Java," later in this chapter, for further information.

tmpclasses

This is a working directory that the Wireless Toolkit creates when required. It uses this directory to store compiled class files before they are preverified and copied into the *classes* directory.

tmplib

This directory is used to hold copies of the JAR and ZIP files read from the project *lib* directory, in which the class files have been converted to their corresponding preverified forms.

You can specify the names of the MIDlets included in a MIDlet suite, along with their MIDlet class files and associated icons, by pressing the Settings button in the KToolBar main window. Similarly, you can compile all of the MIDlet class files using the Compile button. These processes are described in detail in "Building a MIDlet with the Wireless Toolkit" in Chapter 3.

Once you have compiled your MIDlets, there are several ways to test them. The simplest way is simply to use the Run button on the KToolBar window, which uses the device selected in the Device combo box to run the project's MIDlet suite using the class files in the *classes* directory, the resources in the *res* directory, and any library classes in the *tmplib* directory. Alternatively, you can arrange for the Wireless Toolkit to package the project contents into a JAR file by using the Package command on the Project menu, which places the resulting JAR file in the project *bin* directory. From here, you can run it using the Run MIDP Application utility or, from the command line, using the *emulator* or *midp* commands (see Chapter 8 for a full description of these commands). In order to minimize the size of the JAR file, the packaged version of the project is built without debugging information, whereas the classes created when you run the project within the KToolBar environment include debug information.

Debugging MIDlets with the Wireless Toolkit

The Wireless Toolkit does not incorporate its own debugger, but you can use it to set up a debugging session between a MIDlet running in one of the Toolkit's emulated devices and a third-party debugger that supports remote debugging using the Java Platform Debugging Architecture (JPDA). Most commercial IDEs provide support for JPDA, although some of them do not include remote debugging in their entry-level products. (Borland JBuilder is an example of this: it supports remote debugging only in the Professional and Enterprise editions.)

The KVM does not directly support the JPDA architecture, but the Wireless Toolkit incorporates a debug proxy agent that can be used together with the KVM to provide support for remote debugging.* To debug a MIDlet, first open its project in the KToolBar, choose the device that you want to run it on, and then select Debug from the Project menu. This opens a dialog (see Figure 9-1) that invites you

---

* Details of the debug proxy agent and the JPDA as it relates to the KVM can be found in "KVM Debugging" in Chapter 2.

to supply the port number on which the debug proxy will wait for a connection from the JPDA debugger. Choose a suitable port (the default value of 5000 should be fine in most cases), and press the Debug button to start the emulator and the debug proxy. At this point, the device emulator window appears, but the MIDlet does not start executing because the KVM is suspended waiting for the debugger to connect.

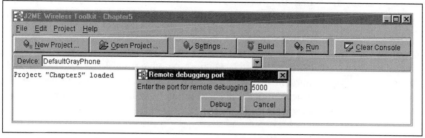

Figure 9-1: Using the Wireless Toolkit to debug a MIDlet

The next step is to open the IDE and start the remote debugger. Here, we'll use Forte for Java as the IDE, but the steps to be followed are similar for other development environments. Once you have started the IDE, you need to point it at the source file or source files for the MIDlet that you want to debug and place a breakpoint. Using Forte for Java, you do this by mounting the project's *src* directory as a filesystem in the Explorer window and opening the MIDlet source for editing; then select a line of code and press Ctrl+F8, or use the editor's context menu and select the Add/Remove Breakpoint menu item, as shown in Figure 9-2.

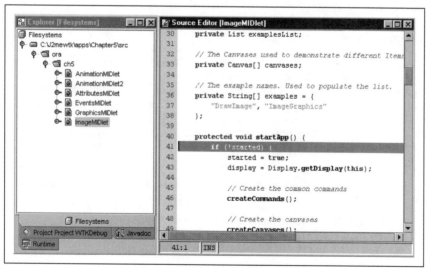

Figure 9-2: Setting a breakpoint using Forte for Java

Once you've set a breakpoint, start the debugger by opening the Debug menu and selecting Attach to VM. Because you need to connect using sockets, make sure that the connector shown uses sockets, type the port number supplied to the Wireless Toolkit (typically 5000) into the port number box (and the name of the host on which the Wireless Toolkit is running, if it is not the same as the system running Forte), and press OK.

Once the debugger connects to the debug proxy, the device emulator will resume execution* and the usual MIDlet selection menu appears. Select a MIDlet and start using it as usual. When the breakpoint is reached, the emulator is suspended again, and you can use the debugger's facilities to inspect and modify data in the usual way.

A somewhat simpler way to debug MIDlets is to integrate the Wireless Toolkit with your IDE instead of using it directly. At the time of writing, this is possible with two of the most popular third-party IDEs: Forte for Java (see "J2ME and Forte For Java," later in this chapter) and Borland JBuilder. It is likely that other IDEs will also support the integration of the Wireless Toolkit in the near future.

Wireless Toolkit Localization Features

The MIDP specification requires a device to support only a single locale and a single character encoding at a time. In the real world, MIDP device manufacturers are likely to customize a device for the locale in which it is being used. For example, a cell phone intended for use in Japan or by a Japanese-speaking person will be configured with Japanese fonts and Japanese character sets. From the point of view of the application developer, it is useful to be able to develop and test MIDlets on devices that are customized for different locales. The J2ME Wireless Toolkit enables this by allowing the fonts and available encodings for emulated devices to be changed to any of those supported by the J2SE platform on which the emulator is running.

Changing fonts

The MIDP specification requires application code to specify the characteristics of a font in strictly logical terms by using a combination of three attributes—face, style and size—as described in "Fonts" in Chapter 5. As a typical example, an application might request a 12-point, proportional, bold font or a 14-point, system, italic font. The MIDP implementation must map this logical request to the closest font that it has available. The Wireless Toolkit emulator does this by reference to a set of font definitions that map logical font descriptions to actual J2SE platform fonts.

The font definitions applicable to a device are contained in its properties file, which is supplied by the Wireless Toolkit and held in a directory specific to that device.† For the default color phone, for example, the properties file is called:

%INSTALL_DIR%\wtklib\devices\DefaultColorPhone
DefaultColorPhone.properties

---

* Execution resumes automatically when the Forte for Java debugger is used. Some debuggers might need to be explicitly told to resume the debugged process.

† The device properties file actually defines all the configurable characteristics of an emulated device. For detailed information on all of these characteristics, refer to the J2ME Wireless Toolkit's *Basic Customization Guide*.

The properties file for the emulated Motorola i85s cell phone can be found at:

%INSTALL_DIR%\wtklib\devices\Motorola_i85s\Motorola_i85s.properties

%INSTALL_DIR% is the directory in which the J2ME Wireless Toolkit is installed.

Within the properties file, the fonts are defined by associating a property name, constructed from the parts of the logical font definition used by application code, with a property value that specifies the actual J2SE font to be used when the font given by the property name is requested.

The property name has the following general form:

```
font.face.style.size
```

The components of the name are the following:

- *face* is derived from the font face value specified by the application and must be one of monospaced, proportional, or system.

- *style* is derived from the font styles specified by the application, excluding underlining (which is handled separately). The legal combinations of font styles are mapped to the following possible values in the properties file: plain, bold, italic, and bold.italic.

- *size* is the font size requested by the application and must be one of small, medium, or large.

The property value associated with each of these properties can be one of two things:

- The name of a font available on the host platform described using the usual J2SE font naming conventions, referred to as a system font definition.

- The name of a properties file that describes a font in terms of its metrics and a bitmap image containing representations of the font glyphs, referred to as a bitmap font definition.

The creation and use of bitmap fonts is beyond the scope of this book. If you need to use a bitmap font, you should refer to the *Basic Customization Guide* included with the J2ME Wireless Toolkit download for further information.

System fonts are described in terms of font name, style, and size, using the following format:

```
fontName-style-pointsize
```

SansSerif-plain-9 or Monospaced-bolditalic-14 are examples of system fonts.

Using these definitions, the following is a typical extract from a device properties file, which provides the mappings for the system font face:

```
font.system.plain.small: SansSerif-plain-9
font.system.plain.medium: SansSerif-plain-11
font.system.plain.large: SansSerif-plain-14

font.system.bold.small: SansSerif-bold-9
font.system.bold.medium: SansSerif-bold-11
font.system.bold.large: SansSerif-bold-14
```

Programming
Environments

```
font.system.italic.small: SansSerif-italic-9
font.system.italic.medium: SansSerif-italic-11
font.system.italic.large: SansSerif-italic-14

font.system.bold.italic.small: SansSerif-bolditalic-9
font.system.bold.italic.medium: SansSerif-bolditalic-11
font.system.bold.italic.large: SansSerif-bolditalic-14
```

As a result of these definitions, the font requested using the following line of code would actually be realized using a 9-point, bold, sans-serif font.:

```
Font font = Font.getFont(Font.FACE_SYSTEM, Font.STYLE_BOLD, Font.SIZES_
SMALL);
```

It is also necessary to define a default font, which is installed into a `Graphics` object when no other font is requested, and a font to be used for the text that appears on soft buttons in the user interface. These fonts are defined as the values of the `font.default` and `font.softButton` properties:

```
font.default=SansSerif-plain-10
font.softButton=SansSerif-plain-11
```

Changing the font associated with an application font definition is simply a matter of modifying the property value associated with it in the device properties file. If you would prefer to use the Comic Sans MS font as the system font for the default color phone, for example, you would replace `SansSerif` in the block of properties shown above by `Comic Sans MS`, as the following extract shows:

```
font.system.plain.small:Comic Sans MS-plain-9
font.system.plain.medium: Comic Sans MS-plain-11
font.system.plain.large: Comic Sans MS-plain-14
    .
    .
    .
font.system.bold.italic.large: Comic Sans MS-bolditalic-14
```

You need to restart the Wireless Toolkit for the font change to take effect.

Changing the available character encodings

The set of character encodings available to an emulated device can be configured in its properties file by associating the appropriate values with two properties:

`microedition.encoding`
> Specifies the default encoding, as returned by `System.getProperty("microedition.encoding")`.

`microedition.encoding.supported`
> A comma-separated list defining the complete set of supported encodings. All the encodings in this list must be available in the J2SE platform on which the Wireless Toolkit is running.

The following extract from a device property file sets the default encoding for the device to ISO-8859-5 and makes four other encodings available to applications running on the device:

```
microedition.encoding = ISO-8859-5
microedition.encoding.supported =
    ISO-8859-1, ISO-8859-2, UTF-8, UTF-16, ISO-8859-5
```

Note that ISO-8859-1 is always available, even if it is not included in the list of supported encodings.

There is currently no way for a MIDlet to programmatically obtain the list of supported encodings. However, including an encoding in the microedition. encoding.supported list makes it possible to use that encoding with constructor and method calls that require an encoding name. For example, the following code results in an UnsupportedEncodingException unless ISO-8859-5 is in the list of supported encodings:

```
byte[] bytes = new byte[32];
String str = new String(bytes, "ISO-8859-5");
```

Secure Networking

Although it is not a requirement of the MIDP specification, the MIDP reference implementation includes support for HTTPS. HTTPS creates a secure environment for e-commerce and other applications by exchanging HTTP messages over secure sockets rather than their vanilla (and insecure) counterparts. Since the Wireless Toolkit is based on the reference implementation, it inherits the HTTPS support and also provides a command-line tool that allows you to install the public key certificates you will need in order to use HTTPS.

SSL, HTTPS, and certificates

Network traffic exchanged over the Internet (and potentially over insufficiently secure intranets) using vanilla sockets is insecure for at least three reasons:

- Unauthorized parties can receive and read data in transit and extract potentially useful information from it, such as credit-card numbers or commercial secrets.

- Because the data passes through routers that are not under the control of the sender, it is possible for modifications to be made that appear to the receiver to have come from the sender. This is, obviously, undesirable for many reasons.

- There is no way for a communicating party to be sure that they are connected to the other party that they think they are connected to.

SSL and its successor, TLS, were designed to solve all three of these problems. HTTPS is the same as HTTP, except that it is transmitted using SSL rather than ordinary sockets and, therefore, inherits the security supplied by SSL. Although a thorough discussion of general network security and the details of SSL are beyond the scope of this book, it is worth looking briefly at the mechanisms that SSL uses to secure a network connection.

SSL addresses the three security issues listed above as follows:

- Data that is exchanged between the communicating parties is encrypted using a symmetric encryption algorithm, which requires both the sender and the receiver to know the encryption key. Encrypting the data prevents unauthorized snooping, unless the snooper manages to work out what the key is. In order to minimize the chances of this happening, the key is randomly chosen for each communication session, so that discovering the key for one session—most likely by analyzing captured data offline—will be of no use, because the next session will use a different key.

- Simply encrypting data does not keep a third party from modifying it, because random data could be inserted, or data could be deleted or modified. In order to make it possible to detect such changes (even though they cannot be prevented), a secure message digest is sent with each package of data. The message digest is computed from the data content using an algorithm that is designed to make it extremely unlikely that any change to the data would result in its new content having the same digest value. When data is received, the receiver calculates the digest and compares it to the value computed and supplied by the sender. If they do not match, the message must have been tampered with.

- Finally, there is the matter of authenticating the communicating parties. This is done during connection establishment by using *public key certificates*. Simply put, a public key certificate uniquely identifies its owner. In most cases, the server sends its certificate to the client so that the client can be sure that it is talking to the correct counterparty. Optionally, the server may also require the client to authenticate itself by sending its own certificate. This is not usually done, however, because the client provides a credit card number that acts as its identity, or simply because the server doesn't need to trust the client.[*]

Public key certificates are extremely important to SSL. A company or individual obtains a certificate by applying to a certification authority or *root CA* (such as Thawte or Verisign). After applying vetting procedures, the CA issues the certificate in electronic form. The certificate is actually one end of a certificate chain that may have two or more entries. A certificate obtained directly from a CA might have only two entries: the certificate itself and the certificate of the CA that issued it. In some cases, commercial organizations find it convenient to be able to issue certificates directly to their own customers; to do so, they become intermediate certification authorities by registering themselves with a root CA and obtaining an intermediate CA certificate. Certificates issued by such a CA have a chain of at least three entries: the issued certificate itself, the certificate of the intermediate CA, and the certificate of the root CA.

In effect, each certificate is vouched for by the one above it in the certificate chain. For example, if you apply to a root CA and obtain a certificate, your certificate is authenticated by the fact that it comes with a copy of the root CA's certificate. To prevent forgeries, the root CA applies to your certificate a cryptographic signature that only it could generate. When you present your certificate to a third party, they can check this signature. If it is found to be correct, then the third party knows that the certificate was issued by the owner of the certificate above it in the certificate chain. When there are multiple certificates in the chain, each one can be checked against the one above it.

At the end of this process, the certificate chain has either been rejected or is known to be consistent. However, it is still not known to be valid. If I wanted to

---

[*] The SSL implementation in the Wireless Toolkit does not currently support client authentication.

forge a certificate chain, I could create a certificate and sign it with another certificate that claims to have been issued by a root CA, but which I also created. The receiver of such a certificate chain would not be able to detect that it is a forgery simply by checking the cryptographic signatures, because they would be correct. The solution to this problem is for the certificates of the root CAs and intermediate CAs involved in the path to be held on the client so that they can be compared to those received in any certificate chain. When a client is sent a certificate claiming to have been issued by Verisign, not only can the client check cryptographic signatures to verify internal consistency, but it can also compare the certificate in the path that claims to be from Verisign with its own copy of that certificate. If they match, the client finally can be sure that the whole certificate chain is valid. When an SSL connection is being established, the client verifies the server's certificate by checking its cryptographic signature and comparing the CA certificates in its certificate chain with the ones that it holds locally. If they do not match, or if the chain includes CA certificates that the client does not have its own copies of, the client can reject the connection as untrusted.

Browsers that support HTTPS come with a database of root CA and intermediate CA certificates. To see an example, start Internet Explorer and select Tools → Internet Options → Content → Certificates → Trusted Root Certification Authorities. You'll see the set of CA certificates that Internet Explorer knows about. Figure 9-3 shows a typical set of certificates; a similar list is held by other browsers such as Netscape Navigator.

If you use Internet Explorer to open a secure web page, such as *https://www.microsoft.com*, you can view the server certificate that is used to authenticate the SSL connection by right-clicking on the page in the browser, selecting Properties and then Certificate, and finally activating the Certification Path tab of the dialog that appears, as shown in Figure 9-4. As you can see, Microsoft's certificate is vouched for by Verisign's secure server CA certificate.

Using HTTPS with the J2ME Wireless Toolkit

From the application point of view, using HTTPS is almost identical to using HTTP. The only differences are that you specify the protocol in the `Connector open()` call as `https` instead of `http` and the default port number (which you don't need to supply) is 443 instead of 80. Once the connection has been established, you use exactly the same code to inspect the HTTP header values and exchange data; all the connection setup details and the encryption and decryption of data are handled for you automatically. The only difference you will notice is that the connection process takes much longer because of the need to transfer the server certificate chain and establish the encryption key to be used when transferring data.

To see how HTTPS works in practice, start the J2ME Wireless Toolkit and open the `Chapter6` project from this book's source code, build the project (if you have not already done so), and run it. From the list of MIDlets, choose HTTP; this runs the same HTTP example that you saw in Chapter 6, whose opening screen is shown in Figure 6-3. In the textbox, type the URL *https://www.verisign.com* and press OK. What you would expect to see, after a short delay, is the first part of the HTML for Verisign's home page, but what you'll almost certainly see instead is a screen

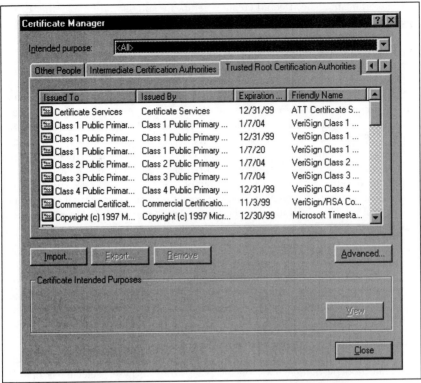

Figure 9-3: Certification Authority Certificates stored by Internet Explorer

reporting an I/O error. If you look in the Wireless Toolkit console, there will be an error message, probably one saying "not a CA" or "no trusted keystore given." So what went wrong here?

During connection setup, the certficate chain sent by the server has to be verified. As described earlier, not only must the cryptographic signatures be verified, but the CA certificates must also be checked to see if they are valid. To do this, the SSL implementation has to compare them to reference copies stored locally. Therein lies the problem: where are the local copies of the certificates held? The MIDP reference implementation holds CA certificates in a keystore. When running under the control of the Wireless Toolkit, this keystore is located at *%INSTALL_DIR%\appdb_main.ks*, where *%INSTALL_DIR%* is the directory in which the J2ME Wireless Toolkit is installed. When you first install the Wireless Toolkit, however, there are no certificates in this file. To add them, you need to use a command-line utility called MEKeyTool, which allows you to import certificates that are already installed in a J2SE keystore. J2SE ships with a keystore in the file *%JAVA_HOME%\ jre\lib\security\cacerts* that contains root CA certificates for the most common used certification authorities. You can inspect the content of this file using the *keytool* command, which can be found in the directory *%JAVA_HOME%\bin*, and which is discussed in detail in *Java in a Nutshell*. The following command shows

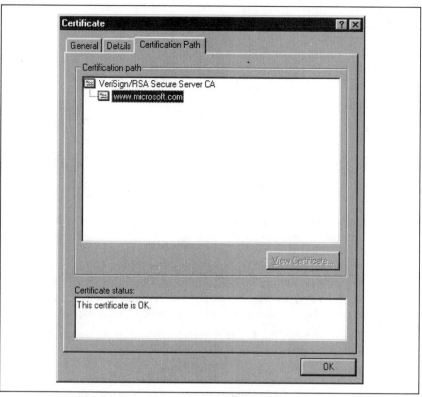

Figure 9-4: A certificate chain from a secure web site

all of the certificates in this keystore, which is protected by a password (set initially to *changeit*):

```
keytool -list -keystore %JAVA_HOME%\jre\lib\security\cacerts -storepass
changeit
```

The following is typical output:

```
Keystore type: jks
Keystore provider: SUN

Your keystore contains 10 entries:

thawtepersonalfreemailca, Fri Feb 12 20:12:16 GMT 1999, trustedCertEntry,
Certificate fingerprint (MD5):
1E:74:C3:86:3C:0C:35:C5:3E:C2:7F:EF:3C:AA:3C:D9
thawtepersonalbasicca, Fri Feb 12 20:11:01 GMT 1999, trustedCertEntry,
Certificate fingerprint (MD5):
E6:0B:D2:C9:CA:2D:88:DB:1A:71:0E:4B:78:EB:02:41
verisignclass3ca, Mon Jun 29 18:05:51 BST 1998, trustedCertEntry,
Certificate fingerprint (MD5):
78:2A:02:DF:DB:2E:14:D5:A7:5F:0A:DF:B6:8E:9C:5D
thawtepersonalpremiumca, Fri Feb 12 20:13:21 GMT 1999, trustedCertEntry,
```

```
Certificate fingerprint (MD5):
3A:B2:DE:22:9A:20:93:49:F9:ED:C8:D2:8A:E7:68:0D
thawteserverca, Fri Feb 12 20:14:33 GMT 1999, trustedCertEntry,
Certificate fingerprint (MD5):
C5:70:C4:A2:ED:53:78:0C:C8:10:53:81:64:CB:D0:1D
verisignclass4ca, Mon Jun 29 18:06:57 BST 1998, trustedCertEntry,
Certificate fingerprint (MD5):
1B:D1:AD:17:8B:7F:22:13:24:F5:26:E2:5D:4E:B9:10
verisignclass1ca, Mon Jun 29 18:06:17 BST 1998, trustedCertEntry,
Certificate fingerprint (MD5):
51:86:E8:1F:BC:B1:C3:71:B5:18:10:DB:5F:DC:F6:20
verisignserverca, Mon Jun 29 18:07:34 BST 1998, trustedCertEntry,
Certificate fingerprint (MD5):
74:7B:82:03:43:F0:00:9E:6B:B3:EC:47:BF:85:A5:93
thawtepremiumserverca, Fri Feb 12 20:15:26 GMT 1999, trustedCertEntry,
Certificate fingerprint (MD5):
06:9F:69:79:16:66:90:02:1B:8C:8C:A2:C3:07:6F:3A
verisignclass2ca, Mon Jun 29 18:06:39 BST 1998, trustedCertEntry,
Certificate fingerprint (MD5):
EC:40:7D:2B:76:52:67:05:2C:EA:F2:3A:4F:65:F0:D8
```

Each entry begins with an alias that can refer to the certificate. The first certificate shown above, for example, has the alias *thawtepersonalfreemailca*. As you can see, all these certificates are issued either by Thawte, Inc., or Verisign, Inc.

To import a certificate into the keystore used by the SSL implementation (the *ME keystore*), open a command window and make the Wireless Toolkit installation directory (e.g., *c:\j2mewtk*) your current directory, and then use the *MEKeyTool* command to copy the certificate from the J2SE keystore, using the alias to identify the certifcate you want. (The *MEKeyTool* command is documented in detail in Chapter 8.) As an example, the following set of commands imports the certificate with alias *verisignserverca*, where the shell variable JCE is initialized to point to the J2SE keystore for convenience:

```
cd c:\j2mewtk
set JCE=c:\jdk1.3.1\jre\lib\security\cacerts
java -jar bin\MEKeyTool.jar -import -keystore %JCE%
    -storepass changeit verisignserverca
```

Repeat this command for each certificate in the J2SE keystore, so your ME keystore is equipped to handle certificate chains where the certificate was issued directly by Verisign or Thawte. Then restart the Wireless Toolkit, run the HttpClient MIDlet again, and try connecting to *https://www.verisign.com* once more. It should work this time, because the required certificate is in the keystore.

Failures due to problems with certificate chains are commonly seen when testing with HTTPS, at least until you get all the certificates you require in your certificate keystore. These errors cause an IOException to be thrown during connection establishment. If you print the message from this exception, the one that you'll most commonly see has the form:

```
(x) bad certificate [details of certificate]
```

where x is a number that identifies the problem with the certificate, and [details of certificate] is a short description of the server certificate. The numeric identifier is the most useful part of this message; the possible values are shown in Table 9-1.*

Table 9-1: Certificate Problems

Code	Meaning
1	Certificates are valid only for a period of time determined by the certificate issuer. This error occurs when a certificate whose validity period has expired is received.
2	The period of certificate validity has not yet started.
3	The signature of at least one certificate in the chain is not valid.
4	The signature of a certificate in the chain was created using an algorithm that is not recognized by the MIDP SSL implementation.
5	A certificate in the chain was issued by an authority that is not recognized. This is usually caused by the fact that the CA's certificate is not in the ME keystore.
6	A certificate contains the name of the server from which it was sent, but that is not the server to which the client connected. This check is intended to prevent one server masquerading as another by copying its certificate chain and claiming it as its own.
7	The certificate chain exceeds the maximum length supported by the implementation.
8	A certificate in the chain does not contain a signature.
9	A certificate in the exchange has one or more critical extensions that are unrecognized. An extension is an optional part of a certificate. However, if the extension is marked as critical, the receiver must act on it. When a critical extension is not recognized by the receiver, it must report an error and consider the certificate to be invalid.
10	The certificate has an inappropriate keyUsage or extendedKeyUsage extension.
11	A certificate in the chain was not issued by the next certificate above it in the chain. This is like receiving a Verisign certificate chained to a Thawte root CA certificate.
12	One of the certificates in the chain belonging to root or intermediate CA has expired.

Unfortunately, there is little that you can do to work around most of these errors, because the SSL implementation does not allow you to ask the user if they would like to ignore a problem and continue anyway.

If the problem is due to a missing certificate that is not in the J2SE keystore, you can obtain a copy of the certificate by opening the same web page in your browser and examining the certificate chain, as shown in Figure 9-4. Select the certificate that you need from the chain and click View Certificate. In the dialog that appears, click Copy to File . . . and then select an export format, such as "DER encoded binary X.509 (.CER)", to store the certificate in a file. Next, import the certificate into your J2SE keystore:

```
keytool -import -keystore %JCE% -storepass changeit -alias CERTALIAS -
file filename.cer
```

---

* The information in this table is not part of the official Wireless Toolkit documentation; it was, in fact, obtained from the source code of the MIDP reference implementation. It is, therefore, possible that new error codes will be added in the future.

filename.cer is the name of the file to which you exported the certificate, and `CERTALIAS` should be replaced by a short and meaningful description of the certificate (such as `verisgnclass1ca`). The final step is to copy the certificate from the J2SE keystore to the ME keystore:

```
java -jar bin\MEKeyTool.jar -import -keystore %JCE% -storepass changeit -
alias CERTALIAS
```

Although the HTTPS support in the MIDP reference implementation and Wireless Toolkit and the certificate handling provided by MEKeyTool are useful for testing access to secure servers, the way in which certificates are handled for real devices is the concern of the device manufacturer and will probably be very different from the mechanism used here. This area is being addressed for a future version of the MIDP specification.

MIDP for PalmOS

MIDP for PalmOS is an implementation of MIDP 1.0 and CLDC 1.0 for devices running PalmOS Version 3.5 or higher. It is developed by Sun Microsystems and available for free download from *http://java.sun.com/products/midp4palm/index.html.*

MIDP for PalmOS can be installed on a real device, or, for ease of development, you can use it together with the PalmOS Emulator (POSE) on your PC to develop and debug MIDlets using the J2ME Wireless Toolkit or one of the other IDEs that support J2ME.

MIDP for PalmOS is delivered with documentation that describes in detail how to install and configure it. Rather than repeat what is in the official documentation, in this section, we briefly cover the most important aspects of installation and configuration. Then we look at some of the features that are relevant from the development and debugging point of view.

The PalmOS Emulator (POSE)

When you are creating MIDlets, you'll find it much easier and quicker to use an emulated PalmOS device than a real one. Once you are confident that the MIDlet is working, you can then deploy it to the real device for final testing. The PalmOS emulator is a free product that can be downloaded from *http://www.palmos.com/dev/tech/tools/emulator/.* Once you have downloaded and installed it, you need to upload a ROM image. If you have a real PalmOS device, you can transfer the contents of its ROM to the emulator by placing it in its cradle and following the instructions in the documentation that comes with the emulator.* If you do not have a PalmOS device, then you need to register with Palm Computing and download a ROM image from their site. Note that the registration process includes offline authorization and takes some time. Visit *http://www.palmos.com/dev/* for details on how to obtain a downloadable ROM image.

---

* Note that older versions of POSE support transfer of the ROM image only if the device is connected to its host system via a serial cradle. If you have a USB cradle, you will need to get the most recent release of the emulator.

MIDP for PalmOS Installation and Configuration

.MIDP for PalmOS is delivered in the form of two ZIP files, one containing the product itself, the other the documentation. When you expand the ZIP files, you will find a directory called *PRCfiles* that contains the files that need to be installed on your PalmOS device or in the emulator:

MIDP.prc

> This file contains the MIDP for PalmOS implementation, including the KVM and the core and MIDP libraries. When you install this file, it creates an icon labeled JavaHQ that can be used to set global preferences. This is the file that an end user would install if they wanted to run MIDP applications on their PalmOS device.

Developer.prc

> This is an additional file that is intended for use by developers only. When it is installed, it adds its own icon, called Developer, that allows you to enable extra options in the JavaHQ application that select features that are useful for debugging.

Both these files should be installed on your PalmOS device in the same way as any other application, using the Install feature of the PalmOS desktop and performing a HotSync operation. You should also install them in the PalmOS emulator by right-clicking on the emulator window, selecting Install → Other, and browsing the filesystem until you find the files. Once you have successfully installed the files, there are several steps you need to take, both on the real device and the emulator, to complete the setup:

- Click on the Developer icon. This displays a screen that allows you to enable debugging options for the JavaHQ application. Click on Show and return to the home screen.

- Click on the JavaHQ icon and select Preferences. The current global settings are displayed, as shown in Figure 9-5 (although the settings that you see may not be the same). Global settings are valid for all applications.

The Colors setting is initially set to a value that depends on the capabilities of the real or emulated PalmOS device in use. You can change it in order to see how your MIDlet would behave on a device with lesser capabilities.

Drawing Speed lets you choose between smooth or fast animation.

The App Memory setting determines the size of the heap that will be available to the Java VM. The initial setting depends on the amount of memory available in the emulated device, subject to a maximum of 64 KB. Although you can decrease this value to simulate operation in a smaller device, you cannot increase it beyond its initial setting.

If you plan to use networking, you should enable it. MIDP for PalmOS supports HTTP (but not HTTPS) and also has an unsupported implementation of client sockets (but not server sockets). If you do not have direct access to the Internet, you need to configure an HTTP proxy.

If you are configuring the emulator and have enabled networking, you need to make sure that all network access is directed to the TCP/IP stack of the system on which the emulator is running. To do this, right-click on the emulator

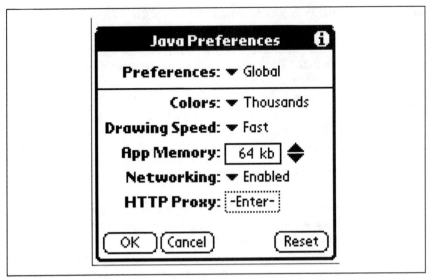

Figure 9-5: The JavaHQ Global Preferences screen

window and select Settings → Properties. In the dialog that appears, check the box labeled "Redirect NetLib calls to host TCP/IP."

Note that networking must be enabled if you want to debug MIDlets in the PalmOS emulator using the J2ME Wireless Toolkit, because the debug proxy connects to the VM using TCP/IP. The procedure for debugging with POSE is the same as it is for any other emulator. Refer to the earlier section "Debugging MIDlets with the Wireless Toolkit" if you are going to use the Wireless Toolkit; refer to "J2ME and Forte For Java," later in this chapter, for an example involving integrated debugging with another development environment.

- From the Preferences combo box at the top of the screen, select Developer. The screen that appears (Figure 9-6) contains the options provided by *Developer.prc.*

The Heap Status option, if set to Show, causes the amount of heap space allocated to the Java VM to be displayed when it starts up.

The Save Output option is probably the most useful for developers. If you set it to Yes, another button labeled Output appears between Cancel and Reset, and the standard output and standard error streams of the Java VM are saved during MIDlet execution and can be viewed on demand. You can view this saved output while a MIDlet is executing; refer to "Application menus and preferences," earlier in this chapter, for further information.

If you are using the PalmOS emulator, this output is also directed to files that you can inspect once you close down the emulator, thus allowing you to check trace output or read exception stack traces generated during MIDlet execution. These files are called *STDOUT.txt* and *STDERR.txt*, and they reside in the emulator's installation directory. When this option is set to Yes, another button labeled Output appears between Cancel and Reset that allows you to view the same output on the screen.

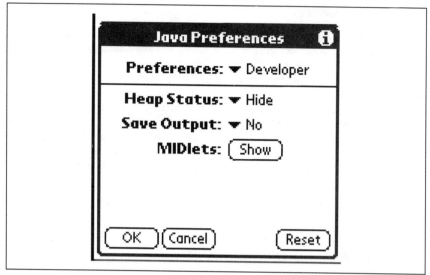

Figure 9-6: JavaHQ Developer Preferences

The MIDlets button does not change the setting of an option. When you press it, it shows a list of up to 100 MIDlet suites that are currently installed on the device, together with their assigned creator IDs. Only MIDlets whose creator IDs are of the form VM*nn* will be shown; IDs of this form are automatically assigned by MIDP for PalmOS. If you assign your own creator ID to a MIDlet suite and it is not of this form, it will not appear in this list. See "MIDlet suite conversion," in the next section, for information on how to assign a creator ID.

In addition to these global and developer preferences, MIDP for PalmOS provides application preferences that must be set individually for each MIDlet suite. These settings are discussed in the next section.

Using MIDlet Suites with MIDP for PalmOS

MIDP for PalmOS is simply an implementation of the MIDP 1.0 and CLDC 1.0 specifications. From the developers point of view, therefore, in most respects there is no real difference between developing MIDlets for PalmOS devices or for cell phones. Most importantly, the API seen by a MIDlet running under MIDP for PalmOS is exactly the same as that seen when it is executing on a cell phone. There are, however, some differences that you need to be aware of in the areas of MIDlet suite installation and management and display and input devices.

If you are planning to use POSE for MIDlet development, you can use it as a standalone program and install MIDlet suites into it as you would any other PalmOS applications (converting them first, as described in the next section). Alternatively, you can use POSE as just another emulated device for the J2ME wireless emulator, which takes care of the installation process for you. Both these cases are covered in the next section, which also describes how to work with a real PalmOS device.

MIDlet suite conversion

The MIDP specification requires that a MIDlet suite be packaged in a single JAR file for delivery to a device, and devices must, at a minimum, be able to install MIDlet suites packaged in this way. However, it does contain a caveat indicating that it is acceptable for some preprocessing of the JAR to be performed before it is actually installed, in order to create a delivery package suitable for devices that have their own storage mechanisms. PalmOS devices expect to receive installable applications in the form of PRC files. Since MIDP for PalmOS uses the standard installation mechanism, it is necessary to convert any MIDlet suite to be used with a PalmOS device from a JAR file to the corresponding PRC file. Fortunately, a tool is provided to carry out this conversion. This tool can be used in three different ways:

- Directly, as a command-line utility with all necessary information provided to it as arguments
- Directly, via its own GUI interface
- Indirectly, through the J2ME Wireless Toolkit or another compatible IDE

Of these choices, the last two are the most convenient, since they don't require much work on the part of the developer. The disadvantage of these two options is that you don't have any control over the details of the conversion process. In most cases, this is not an issue, because the defaults are usually acceptable. If you use the command-line interface, however, you have complete control over the conversion process.

Using the converter with the J2ME Wireless Toolkit

This is the simplest way to prepare a MIDlet suite to run with the PalmOS emulator. All that is necessary is to open a project and select PalmOS_Device as the target device, then press the Run button. The MIDlet suite is automatically converted into a *.prc* file and loaded into the emulator.

Using the converter GUI

If you want more control over the conversion process, you can initiate the conversion process using the converter tool's graphical interface with the following command:

```
java -jar %INSTALL_DIR%\Converter\Converter.jar
```

where *%INSTALL_DIR%* is the installation directory of the MIDP for PalmOS product. The user interface, shown on the left side of Figure 9-7, allows you to select the JAD/JAR file combination to be converted and determine where the output should be written. The Preferences item on the File menu lets you specify whether the *.prc* file should be written to the same directory as the JAD file (the default), or to another directory of your choice, as shown on the right side of Figure 9-7. The Convert menu item (or toolbar button) opens a file selection dialog that lets you browse to locate the JAD file for the MIDlet suite to be converted. The JAR file is located using the MIDlet-Jar-URL attribute in the JAD file.

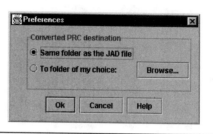

Figure 9-7: The PRC Converter Tool user interface

Using the converter command-line interface

If you want maximum control over the creation of the *.prc* file, you need to use the conversion tool's command-line interface, provided by the class com.sun.midp.palm.database.MakeMIDPApp, which can be found in *Converter.jar.*

```
java -cp %INST_DIR%\Converter\Converter.jar
    com.sun.midp.palm.database.MakeMIDPApp [options] jarfile
```

%INST_DIR% is the directory in which MIDP for PalmOS is installed, and *jarfile* is the name of the JAR file to be converted. You will find full details of this command and its associated options in "MakeMIDPApp: JAD to PRC Conversion Tool" in Chapter 8. Among the more useful possibilities offered by this command is the ability to choose the icons that are displayed for your MIDlet suite on the device's launcher screen.

Installing and running MIDlet suites on a PalmOS device

There are three ways to install and run a MIDlet suite. The first, and probably the most commonly used, is to open a project in the J2ME Wireless Toolkit, select PalmOS_Device as the target emulator, and press the Run button. This carries out the *.prc* file conversion and installation in a single step and initiates the execution of the MIDlet suite. Note that the first time you attempt to use the PalmOS_Device, a dialog box appears, prompting you to supply the location of the PalmOS emulator file. Since this method always performs the *.prc* conversion process, you can't use it to install and run files that you have converted using the GUI or command-line interface to the converter.

The second way to use a *.prc* file, which is applicable if you perform the conversion yourself, is to start the emulator and use its popup menu to install the *.prc* file. The popup menu is accessed by right-clicking on the emulator window. When you select the Install option, a menu appears; it contains the paths of *.prc* files you have recently installed, together with a menu item that lets you browse for a new *.prc*

file. Once you have installed your MIDlet suite, it appears in the device's launcher window, as shown in Figure 9-8, where the MIDlet suite containing the example code for Chapter 6 of this book has been installed. The left side of the figure shows the device launcher in list mode; the right side uses icon mode. You can choose the icons used to represent your MIDlet suite in both of these modes if you use the command-line version of the converter tool.

Figure 9-8: MIDlet suites installed in the PalmOS Emulator

The third and final way to use your *prc* file is to install it on a real PalmOS device using the Install feature of the Palm desktop to select the *prc* file (or whatever equivalent functionality your device uses for application installation) and then perform a HotSync operation. The result should be the same as performing an installation in the emulator.

In all three cases, to run the MIDlet suite, you simply tap on its icon and then choose a MIDlet from the menu that appears. Note that, unlike the cell phone version of the AMS in the reference implementation and the Wireless Toolkit, you won't see a MIDlet list for a MIDlet suite that contains only one MIDlet; in this case, tapping the MIDlet icon starts the MIDlet without further user intervention.

Application menus and preferences

Every MIDlet that uses the high-level user interface is provided with a menu bar. The menu bar contains a mixture of menu items created from the Command objects assigned to each screen by the MIDlet (as described in "Command placement on a PalmOS device" in Chapter 4) and commands that are installed by MIDP for PalmOS.* The Go menu, for example, includes a menu item that lets you beam a MIDlet suite from one PalmOS device to another, as shown at the top of Figure 9-9.

This menu item is always present, but it works only if the MIDlet suite was built in such a way as to allow beaming. Beaming is allowed by default, but you can disallow it if you use the command-line version of the *prc* conversion utility and specify the output file type as *Data* instead of *appl.* See "MakeMIDPApp: JAD to PRC Conversion Tool" in Chapter 8 for further information. Note that you cannot beam MIDlet suites using the Beam command on the App menu on the

---

* Menu bars are not provided on Canvases.

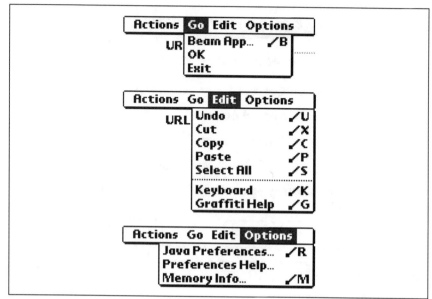

Figure 9-9: JavaHQ application menus

application launcher main page, and you can only beam entire MIDlet suites, not individual MIDlets.

The Edit menu, shown on the right of Figure 9-9, contains standard commands for working with text input. The most useful menu for the developer is Options, which contains three menu items, as shown at the bottom of Figure 9-9. The middle one, Preferences Help, just displays a help screen that explains the use of preferenecs, but the other two are more useful.

The Java Preferences menu displays a screen that gives access to all of the preferences supported by MIDP for PalmOS. Initially, this screen displays the global preferences, as shown in Figure 9-5. If *Developer.prc* is installed, you can also access the developer preferences, shown in Figure 9-6, from here. This is useful, because it lets you look at any messages that have been sent to the `System.out` and `System.err` streams even while the MIDlet is executing, provided that you have set the Save Output preference setting to Yes. Finally, this screen also provides access to preferences that apply only to the executing MIDlet suite, as shown in Figure 9-10. These preferences, which are discussed further in the next section, can only be set from these screen; they are related to the way in which the screen and the limited number of input devices available on most PalmOS platforms are used.

The Memory Info menu item displays a screen that shows memory usage information for both the PalmOS device as a whole and the Java VM itself, an example of which is shown in Figure 9-11. From the point of view of a MIDlet developer, the most interesting value on this screen is *javafreeheap*, which shows how much space is left for the allocation of Java objects and execution stack frames. The other value, *permanent*, is the amount of space allocated for internal use by the VM.

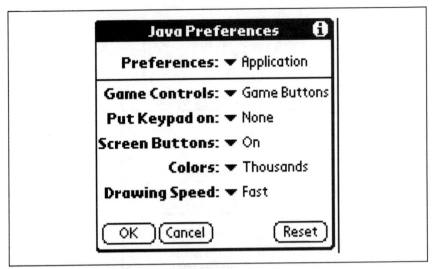

Figure 9-10: JavaHQ application preferences

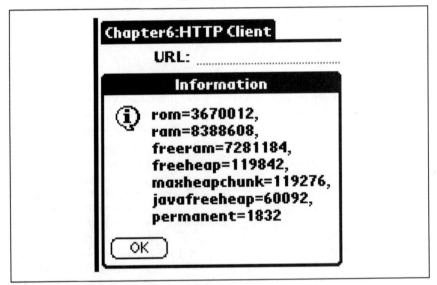

Figure 9-11: JavaHQ memory usage information

Display and input devices

The application preferences dialog provides several settings that determine whether or not input is performed via real buttons on the PalmOS device or emulated controls drawn on the display. Using emulated controls has the effect of reducing the screen area available to MIDlets; because this choice is made by the user, you should develop and test your MIDlets with this possibility in mind. The following sections briefly describe these settings and the effect they have.

Game controls

By default, the game actions described in Chapter 5 (LEFT, RIGHT, UP, DOWN, FIRE) are mapped to keys on the PalmOS device or the emulator. Figure 9-12 shows these buttons and the actions they correspond to on a typical device. There are, however, two alternative ways to map the game actions, both of which involve using the device screen. These alternative modes are selected through the Game Controls setting on the application preference screen:

Joystick
> This mode includes four arrow keys and a fire button drawn in a rectangular area on one side of the screen, as shown on the left of Figure 9-13.

Full keypad
> This mode uses slightly more screen space but includes not only the directional arrows and fire button, but also the letters A through D, representing the four customizable game actions, and a cell phone–style numeric keypad, as shown on the right of Figure 9-13. This mode is useful for MIDlets that were developed for cell phones, which rely heavily on the numeric keypad for input.

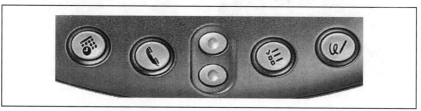

Figure 9-12: Game Buttons on a typical PalmOS device

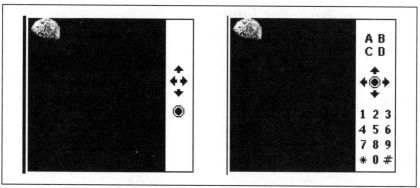

Figure 9-13: Alternate game button configurations: joystick (left), full keypad (right)

Keypad

The Keypad setting is used only if Game Buttons is set to display a joystick or a full keypad on the screen. The setting determines whether the joystick or keypad is displayed on the right or left side of the screen. The default is to display the joystick or keypad on the right.

Soft buttons

This setting determines whether Commands added to Canvases are represented with soft buttons at the bottom of the screen, as, for example, the Setup button is on the left of Figure 9-14, which uses the default value of this option. When Soft Buttons is set to off, as shown on the right of Figure 9-14, the button no longer appears, and the MIDlet has access to the full screen area. When soft buttons are disabled, the functions that they provide can be accessed from the menu. The menu is not visible by default when the current Displayable is a canvas, but it can be displayed using a device-dependent button, which, in the case of Palm devices, is a soft button in the Graffiti area.

This option does not affect screens built with the high-level user interface API.

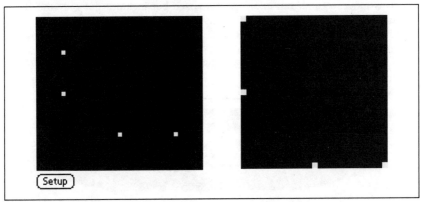

Figure 9-14: A Canvas with and without soft buttons in MIDP for PalmOS

J2ME and Forte For Java

Sun's Forte for Java IDE can be used to develop and debug MIDlets through its tight integration with the J2ME Wireless Toolkit. The Community Edition of Forte for Java is free and can be downloaded from *http://www.sun.com/forte/ffj/*. Once you have installed it, you need to install (or reinstall) the Wireless Toolkit in order to integrate its features into the IDE. During the Wireless Toolkit installation, a dialog appears, offering two different types of setup: standalone or integrated. To use the features of the Wireless Toolkit from within Forte for Java, you must select integrated setup.

Once you have completed the setup, the extra features that let you create MIDlet suites and MIDlets and run and debug them in the emulators supported by the Wireless Toolkit appear in the IDE's menu system. The rest of this section assumes that you are reasonably familiar with Forte for Java and concentrate on demonstrating some of the J2ME-related functionality without going into much detail on the IDE itself.

Creating a Project and Importing Source Code

Like most IDEs, Forte for Java is based around projects. In order to create and compile source code, you first need to create a project, which you can do by

---

selecting Project → Project Manager → New . . . and supplying a name for your project. A project has an associated set of filesystems that represent the directories and JAR or ZIP files that the IDE tools work with. All the class libraries and source code that you want to work with must be mounted as filesystems before you can compile or test anything. In order to begin development of a MIDlet suite, you need to do the following:

- Mount the class files for the CLDC and MIDP class libraries.

- Mount the directory or directories containing the CLDC and MIDP source code if you need to perform source-level debugging that includes stepping through or setting breakpoints in system-level code.

- Mount the directory or directories containing your own source code, or create them if they do not exist.

Filesystems are mounted in the Explorer window. To mount a directory or a JAR or ZIP file, right-click on the Filesystems node, select the appropriate command from the popup menu, and navigate to the directory or file in the file chooser that appears. The class files for the CLDC and MIDP class libraries, for example, can be found in *%INSTALL_DIR%\lib\midpapi.zip*, where *%INSTALL_DIR%* is the installation directory of the J2ME Wireless Toolkit. To include the MIDP and CLDC source code, you'll need to download and install the CLDC and MIDP reference implementations. Referring to the installation directories for these two products as *%CLDC_DIR%* and *%MIDP_DIR%*, respectively, the directories to be mounted to make all of their Java-level source code available are:

%MIDP_DIR%\src\share\classes
%CLDC_DIR%\api\src

Finally, you need to mount the directory containing your source code, if you have any. In this section, we'll be using this book's example source code for demonstration purposes. To make this code accessible to the IDE, you should mount the directory *src*, which is found in the directory in which you installed the book's source code. Figure 9-15 shows the Explorer window after all these filesystems have been mounted.

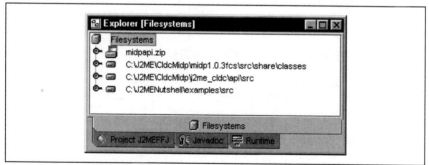

Figure 9-15: Mounting filesystems for MIDlet development in Forte for Java

If you don't have any existing source code, you should first create the directory beneath which you intend to store it, and then mount that directory in the

Explorer window. If you are developing MIDlets, the first thing you'll need to do is create a new package and a new MIDlet suite.

To create a new package, right-click on the directory in the Explorer window that will contain your source code, select New Package from the popup menu, and type the full package name in the dialog box that appears. This creates the directories that match the package hierarchy and displays them in the Explorer window. If, for example, you supply the package name myCo.myPackage, the directory *myCo\myPackage* is created below your source code directory.

To create the MIDlet suite, right-click the node for the directory created for your package (i.e., *myCo\myPackage*) and select New from the popup menu. This opens another menu containing an item labeled MIDP that gives access to all of the MIDP-related items that you can create within the IDE, as shown in Figure 9-16. Select the item labeled MIDletSuite, and, in the dialog that appears next, supply the name of your MIDlet suite and press Next. The next dialog that appears allows you to create the first MIDlet in the new MIDlet suite. In the MIDlet Name field, type the name of the MIDlet as you want it to appear when the list of MIDlets in the suite is displayed to the user at runtime. Type the name of its implementation class (which will be derived from javax.microedition. midlet.MIDlet) in the Class Name field, leaving out the package prefix (that is, supply the class name TestMIDlet, not myCo.myPackage.TestMIDlet). When you press Finish, the IDE creates a file to represent the MIDlet suite and the Java source file for the MIDlet itself. You can create additional MIDlets in the same suite by right-clicking the directory node, opening the same menus, and selecting MIDletClass instead of MIDletSuite.

Compiling MIDlet Source Code

Compiling MIDlet source code is extremely simple. To see how it's done, open the node in the Explorer window that contains this book's example source code, open the *ora* node beneath it, and, finally, the *ch4* subnode. This node contains the example source code for Chapter 4. To compile all of the source files in the ora. ch4 package, right-click on the *ch4* node and select Compile All from the popup menu. To compile a single source file, right-click on the node for the file and select Compile—that's all there is to it. The CLDC and MIDP classes used by the compiler are those that are mounted from *midpapi.zip* in the project's filesystem.

The Compile commands check whether anything needs to be done by comparing the modification time of the source code to that of the corresponding class files, then compiling only those source files that are newer than their class files. If you want to force a recompilation regardless of the relative ages of the source and class files, you can use the Build command instead.

Creating the MIDlet JAR and JAD Files

Before you can test a MIDlet, you need to package its MIDlet suite in a JAR and create the JAD file. To do this, double-click on the node that represents the MIDlet suite itself, which, in this case, is labeled Chapter4, as shown in Figure 9-17. This opens a dialog box with two tabs that let you specify the attributes for the MIDlets in the suite and select the files to be included in the JAR.

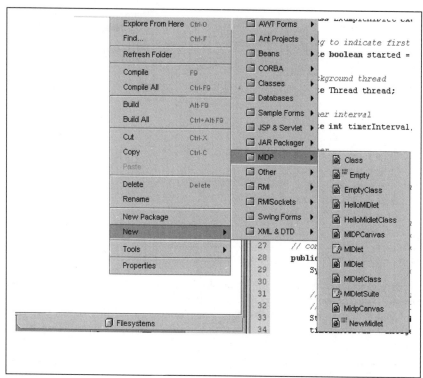

Figure 9-16: MIDP-related items provided by Forte for Java

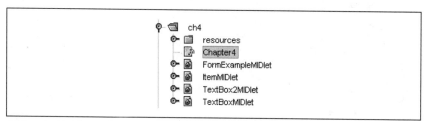

Figure 9-17: The node representing a MIDlet suite

The Descriptor tab, shown in Figure 9-18, lets you set the attributes that will appear in the JAD file and the JAR's manifest file. Initially, only a single MIDlet appears in this dialog. To add a new MIDlet, type MIDlet-2 in the input field at the bottom of the dialog and press the New Tag button. You can use the same technique to create application properties that MIDlets can retrieve using the getAppProperty() method. The attribute values can be edited by clicking in the appropriate row in the column headed Value. The names and values of the standard attributes can be found in "MIDlet Packaging" in Chapter 3.

Unlike the J2ME Wireless Toolkit, Forte for Java does not automatically determine the set of files to be included in the JAR. Instead, you have to specify them in the Content tab, shown in Figure 9-19. The left side of this tab shows the content of

Programming Environments

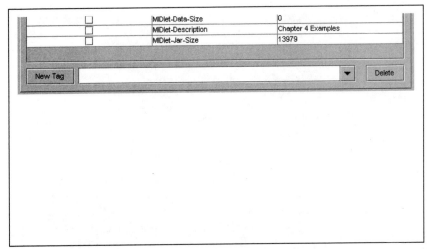

Figure 9-18: Specifying the attributes of MIDlets in a MIDlet suite

the Explorer window, while the right side lists the files selected for inclusion. Usually, you choose to include all of the MIDlet suite class files and any resource files that it needs, which includes images and other external files referenced from within the code and any images referred to from the MIDlet-n attributes in the JAD file.

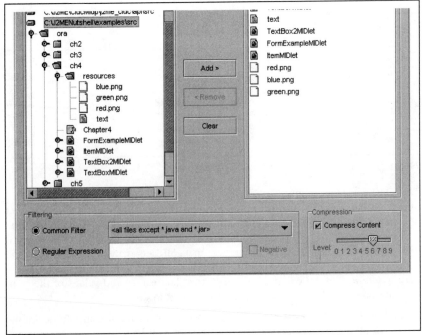

Figure 9-19: Specifying which files should be included in a MIDlet suite JAR

Once you have completed both tabs of this dialog and closed it, you can build the JAR by right-clicking on the MIDlet suite node in the Explorer window and selecting Update JAR. This command preverifies all the class files, constructs the JAD file and the JAR, and places them in the same directory as the MIDlet source code.

Running MIDlets

Once a JAR file has been built, you can use the IDE to load it into any of the device emulators supported by the J2ME Wireless Toolkit. To select the emulator you want to use, right-click the MIDlet suite node, choose Emulator → Select Device, and select the emulator from the dialog that appears. The Emulator menu also contains menu items that allow you to access the Preferences and Utilities facilities of the J2ME Wireless Toolkit that were mentioned earlier in this chapter. Having selected the emulator, right-click the MIDlet suite node again and select Execute. This starts the selected device, loads the MIDlet suite, and starts execution. Output written by MIDlets to the standard output or standard error streams will be routed to Forte for Java's Output window.

 If you right-click on the node for a MIDlet source file, you'll see a menu item labeled Execute. It is tempting to use this to try to run a single MIDlet, but it doesn't work. This command is intended to run the main() method of a Java class and therefore is not suitable for testing MIDlets.

Note that, to use the PalmOS_Device emulator, you need to have the PalmOS emulator installed and configured. When using this emulator, the standard output and standard error streams are not connected to the Output window, but their content can be saved in a file or viewed on the device. Refer to "Using MIDlet Suites with MIDP for PalmOS," earlier in this chapter, for further information on running MIDlets in the PalmOS emulator.

Debugging MIDlets

Debugging a MIDlet with Forte for Java is a very simple process that requires the following steps:

1. Open one of the MIDlet's source files in the Editor window by double-clicking on its node in the Explorer window. Click on any line where you would like to place a breakpoint, then press Ctrl+F8, or right-click and select Toggle Breakpoint from the popup menu. The selected line will be highlighted in red.

2. Select the MIDlet suite node in the Explorer window.

3. On the Forte for Java main menu, select Debug → Start. This runs the MIDlet suite under the debugger in the currently selected emulator device.

4. When the breakpoint is reached, execution is suspended, and the corresponding source line is highlighted in blue.

At this point, you can use all the debugging features of the IDE to inspect and change values, look at the stack frames of all active threads, and so on.

This process is essentially the same as that described in the earlier section "Debugging MIDlets with the Wireless Toolkit," where the J2ME Wireless Toolkit itself was used to build and run MIDlet suites, and Forte for Java was simply used as a convenient JPDA debugger. Using Forte directly is quicker and easier, because there is no need to start the Wireless Toolkit separately.

 It is essential that you select the MIDlet suite node in the Explorer window before starting the debugger. If you forget to do this, Forte will try to run your MIDlet suite as a Java application and fail, because it won't be able to find a `main()` method.

Other Integrated Development Environments

The J2ME Wireless Toolkit and Forte for Java are not the only development environments that you can use to develop J2ME applications. Several of the IDEs that are commonly used for J2SE and J2EE development now have support for J2ME. Some of the cell phone vendors that have Java-based products in the market place have created IDE add-ins that you can use to develop software for their devices. The following list describes some of these products, together with information on where to get them. Unless otherwise noted, these products are supported only on the Windows platform.

Borland JBuilder MobileSet
 JBuilder MobileSet is an add-in for JBuilder 5 or JBuilder 6. It allows JBuilder to integrate mobile device development kits from third parties in much the same way as the J2ME Wireless Toolkit can be integrated into Forte for Java. In order to use it, you must do the following:

 1. Install JBuilder itself, which can be downloaded from *http://www.borland.co.uk/jbuilder/*.

 2. Install JBuilder MobileSet from *http://www.borland.co.uk/jbuilder/mobileset/*.

 3. Download and install an appropriate adapter for a third-party wireless development kit. At the present time, Borland provides two such adapters, both of which can be downloaded from *http://www.borland.co.uk/jbuilder/mobileset/*. One of them allows JBuilder to integrate the J2ME Wireless Toolkit, while the other is for the Nokia Developer's Suite.

Nokia Developer's Suite
 The Nokia Developer Suite is an add-in that provides an emulator for Nokia's Java-enabled phones. It can be used with JBuilder or Forte for Java Version 3. 0 and can be downloaded from *http://americas.forum.nokia.com/java/*.

Metroworks CodeWarrior

Metroworks CodeWarrior is a popular IDE that has built-in support for MIDlet development and a cell-phone emulator. It runs on either Windows or MacOS and can be obtained from *http://www.metroworks.com/desktop/java/*.

Zucotto Whiteboard SDK

Another IDE with support for CLDC and MIDP development, the Zucotto Whiteboard SDK can be obtained from *http://www.zucotto.com/whiteboard/index.html*. It is supported on the Windows platform only.

Visual Age for Java, Microedition

Visual Age for Java, Microedition, is a version of IBM's Java development environment intended for developers building solutions for small and embedded devices. It is based on IBM's own J9 virtual machine, which is highly portable and available on a range of platforms, rather than on Sun's KVM. The Windows port of the J9 VM includes an implementation of CLDC and MIDP; it can be downloaded from *http://www.embedded.oti.com*.

Siemens Mobility Toolkit

The Siemens Mobility Toolkit is an add-in for Forte for Java that includes a version of CLDC and MIDP and an emulator for the Siemens SL45i Java-enabled cell phone. The Siemens MIDP includes proprietary extensions that allow greater access to the capabilities of the phone than MIDP itself does. To obtain this development kit, go to *http://www.siemens-mobile.de/mobile/*, and follow the links to Developer Portal and then Wireless Java, where you will need to register before gaining access to the download area.

Programming Environments

PART II

API Quick Reference

Part II is the real heart of this book: quick-reference material for the Java 2 Micro Edition platform APIs. Please read the following section, "How to Use This Quick Reference," to learn how to get the most out of this material.

How to Use This Quick Reference

The quick-reference section that follows packs a lot of information into a small space. This introduction explains how to get the most out of that information. It describes how the quick reference is organized and how to read the individual quick-reference entries.

Finding a Quick-Reference Entry

The quick reference is organized into chapters, each of which documents a single package of the Java platform or a group of related packages. Packages are listed alphabetically within and between chapters, so you never really need to know which chapter documents which package: you can simply search alphabetically, as you might do in a dictionary. The documentation for each package begins with a quick-reference entry for the package itself. This entry includes a short overview of the package and a listing of the classes and interfaces included in the package. In this listing of package contents, classes and interfaces are first grouped by general category (interfaces, classes, and exceptions, for example). Within each category, they are grouped by class hierarchy, with indentation to indicate the level of the hierarchy. Finally, classes and interfaces at the same hierarchy level are listed alphabetically.

Each package overview is followed by individual quick-reference entries for the classes and interfaces defined in the package. All the entries in this reference are organized alphabetically by class *and* package name, so related classes are grouped near each other. This means that to look up a quick-reference entry for a particular class, you must also know the name of the package that contains that class. Usually, the package name is obvious from the context, and you should have no trouble looking up the quick-reference entry you want. Use the tabs on the outside edge of the book and the dictionary-style headers on the upper corner of each page to help you quickly find the package and class you need.

Occasionally, you may need to look up a class for which you do not already know the package. In this case, refer to Chapter 25. This index allows you to look up a class by class name and find out what package it is part of.

Reading a Quick-Reference Entry

The quick-reference entries for classes and interfaces contain quite a bit of information. The sections that follow describe the structure of a quick-reference entry, explaining what information is available, where it is found, and what it means. While reading the descriptions that follow, you may find it helpful to flip through the reference section itself to find examples of the features being described.

Class Name, Package Name, Availability, and Flags

Each quick-reference entry begins with a four-part title that specifies the name, package name, and availability of the class, and may also specify various additional flags that describe the class. The class name appears in bold at the upper left of the title. The package name appears, in smaller print, in the lower left, below the class name.

The upper-right portion of the title indicates the availability of the class; it specifies the earliest release that contained the class. If a class was introduced in Java 1.1, for example, this portion of the title reads "Java 1.1". The availability section of the title is also used to indicate whether a class has been deprecated, and, if so, in what release. For example, it might read "Java 1.1; Deprecated in Java 1.2".

In the lower-right corner of the title you may find a list of flags that describe the class. The possible flags and their meanings are as follows:

checked
> The class is a checked exception, which means that it extends `java.lang.Exception`, but not `java.lang.RuntimeException`. In other words, it must be declared in the `throws` clause of any method that may throw it.

cloneable
> The class, or a superclass, implements `java.lang.Cloneable`.

collection
> The class, or a superclass, implements `java.util.Collection` or `java.util.Map`.

comparable
> The class, or a superclass, implements `java.lang.Comparable`.

error
> The class extends `java.lang.Error`.

event
> The class extends `java.util.EventObject`.

event adapter
> The class, or a superclass, implements `java.util.EventListener`, and the class name ends with "Adapter".

event listener
> The class, or a superclass, implements `java.util.EventListener`.

runnable

The class, or a superclass, implements `java.lang.Runnable`.

unchecked

The class is an unchecked exception, which means it extends `java.lang.`
`RuntimeException` and therefore does not need to be declared in the
`throws` clause of a method that may throw it.

Description

The title of each quick-reference entry is followed by a short description of the
most important features of the class or interface. This description may be
anywhere from a couple of sentences to several paragraphs long.

Hierarchy

If a class or interface has a nontrivial class hierarchy, the "Description" section is
followed by a figure that illustrates the hierarchy and helps you understand the
class in the context of that hierarchy. The name of each class or interface in the
diagram appears in a box; classes appear in rectangles (except for abstract classes,
which appear in skewed rectangles or parallelograms). Interfaces appear in
rounded rectangles, in which the corners have been replaced by arcs. The current
class—the one that is the subject of the diagram—appears in a box that is bolder
than the others. The boxes are connected by lines: solid lines indicate an
"extends" relationship, and dotted lines indicate an "implements" relationship. The
superclass-to-subclass hierarchy reads from left to right in the top row (or only
row) of boxes in the figure. Interfaces are usually positioned beneath the classes
that implement them, although in simple cases an interface is sometimes positioned on the same line as the class that implements it, resulting in a more
compact figure. Note that the hierarchy figure shows only the superclasses of a
class. If a class has subclasses, those are listed in the cross-reference section at the
end of the quick-reference entry for the class.

Synopsis

The most important part of every quick-reference entry is the class synopsis, which
follows the title and description. The synopsis for a class looks a lot like the
source code for the class, except that the method bodies are omitted and some
additional annotations are added. If you know Java syntax, you know how to read
the class synopsis.

The first line of the synopsis contains information about the class itself. It begins
with a list of class modifiers, such as **public**, **abstract**, and **final**. These modifiers are followed by the **class** or **interface** keyword and then by the name of
the class. The class name may be followed by an **extends** clause that specifies the
superclass and an **implements** clause that specifies any interfaces the class
implements.

The class definition line is followed by a list of the fields and methods that the
class defines. Once again, if you understand basic Java syntax, you should have no
trouble making sense of these lines. The listing for each member includes the

modifiers, type, and name of the member. For methods, the synopsis also includes the type and name of each method parameter and an optional **throws** clause that lists the exceptions the method can throw. The member names are in boldface, so it is easy to scan the list of members looking for the one you want. The names of method parameters are in italics to indicate that they are not to be used literally. The member listings are printed on alternating gray and white backgrounds to keep them visually separate.

Member availability and flags

Each member listing is a single line that defines the API for that member. These listings use Java syntax, so their meaning is immediately clear to any Java programmer. There is some auxiliary information associated with each member synopsis, however, that requires explanation.

Recall that each quick-reference entry begins with a title section that includes the release in which the class was first defined. When a member is introduced into a class after the initial release of the class, the version in which the member was introduced appears, in small print, to the left of the member synopsis. For example, if a class was first introduced in Java 1.1, but had a new method added in Java 1.2 the title contains the string "Java 1.1", and the listing for the new member is preceded by the number "1.2". Furthermore, if a member has been deprecated, that fact is indicated with a hash mark (#) to the left of the member synopsis.

The area to the right of the member synopsis is used to display a variety of flags that provide additional information about the member. Some of these flags indicate additional specification details that do not appear in the member API itself. Other flags contain implementation-specific information. This information can be quite useful in understanding the class and in debugging your code, but be aware that it may differ between implementations. The implementation-specific flags displayed in this book are based on Sun's Linux implementation of Java.

The following flags may be displayed to the right of a member synopsis:

native
> An implementation-specific flag that indicates that a method is implemented in native code. Although **native** is a Java keyword and can appear in method signatures, it is part of the method implementation, not part of its specification. Therefore, this information is included with the member flags, rather than as part of the member listing. This flag is useful as a hint about the expected performance of a method.

synchronized
> An implementation-specific flag that indicates that a method implementation is declared **synchronized**, meaning that it obtains a lock on the object or class before executing. Like the **native** keyword, the **synchronized** keyword is part of the method implementation, not part of the specification, so it appears as a flag, not in the method synopsis itself. This flag is a useful hint that the method is probably implemented in a thread-safe manner.

> Whether or not a method is thread-safe is part of the method specification, and this information *should* appear (although it often does not) in the method

documentation. There are a number of different ways to make a method thread-safe, however, and declaring the method with the synchronized keyword is only one possible implementation. In other words, a method that does not bear the synchronized flag can still be thread-safe.

Overrides:

This flag indicates that a method overrides a method in one of its superclasses. The flag is followed by the name of the superclass that the method overrides. This is a specification detail, not an implementation detail. As we'll see in the next section, overriding methods are usually grouped together in their own section of the class synopsis. The Overrides: flag is only used when an overriding method is not grouped in that way.

Implements:

This flag indicates that a method implements a method in an interface. The flag is followed by the name of the interface that is implemented. This is a specification detail, not an implementation detail. As we'll see in the next section, methods that implement an interface are usually grouped into a special section of the class synopsis. The Implements: flag is only used for methods that are not grouped in this way.

empty

This flag indicates that the implementation of the method has an empty body. This can be a hint to the programmer that the method may need to be overridden in a subclass.

constant

An implementation-specific flag that indicates that a method has a trivial implementation. Only methods with a void return type can be truly empty. Any method declared to return a value must have at least a return statement. The "constant" flag indicates that the method implementation is empty except for a return statement that returns a constant value. Such a method might have a body like return null; or return false;. Like the "empty" flag, this flag may indicate that a method needs to be overridden.

default:

This flag is used with property accessor methods that read the value of a property (i.e., methods whose names begins with "get" and take no arguments). The flag is followed by the default value of the property. Strictly speaking, default property values are a specification detail. In practice, however, these defaults are not always documented, and care should be taken, because the default values may change between implementations.

Not all property accessors have a "default:" flag. A default value is determined by dynamically loading the class in question, instantiating it using a no-argument constructor, and then calling the method to find out what it returns. This technique can be used only on classes that can be dynamically loaded and instantiated and that have no-argument constructors, so default values are shown for those classes only. Furthermore, note that when a class is instantiated using a different constructor, the default values for its properties may be different.

For static final fields, this flag is followed by the constant value of the field. Only constants of primitive and String types and constants with the value null are displayed. Some constant values are specification details, while others are implementation details. The reason that symbolic constants are defined, however, is so you can write code that does not rely directly upon the constant value. Use this flag to help you understand the class, but do not rely upon the constant values in your own programs.

Functional grouping of members

Within a class synopsis, the members are not listed in strict alphabetical order. Instead, they are broken down into functional groups and listed alphabetically within each group. Constructors, methods, fields, and inner classes are all listed separately. Instance methods are kept separate from static (class) methods. Constants are separated from non-constant fields. Public members are listed separately from protected members. Grouping members by category breaks a class down into smaller, more comprehensible segments, making the class easier to understand. This grouping also makes it easier for you to find a desired member.

Functional groups are separated from each other in a class synopsis with Java comments, such as "// Public Constructors", "// Inner Classes", and "// Methods Implementing DataInput". The various functional categories are as follows (in the order in which they appear in a class synopsis):

Constructors
Displays the constructors for the class. Public constructors and protected constructors are displayed separately in subgroupings. If a class defines no constructor at all, the Java compiler adds a default no-argument constructor that is displayed here. If a class defines only private constructors, it cannot be instantiated, so a special, empty grouping entitled "No Constructor" indicates this fact. Constructors are listed first because the first thing you do with most classes is instantiate them by calling a constructor.

Constants
Displays all of the constants (i.e., fields that are declared static and final) defined by the class. Public and protected constants are displayed in separate subgroups. Constants are listed here, near the top of the class synopsis, because constant values are often used throughout the class as legal values for method parameters and return values.

Inner classes
Groups all of the inner classes and interfaces defined by the class or interface. For each inner class, there is a single-line synopsis. Each inner class also has its own quick-reference entry that includes a full class synopsis for the inner class. Like constants, inner classes are listed near the top of the class synopsis because they are often used by a number of other members of the class.

Static methods
Lists the static methods (class methods) of the class, broken down into subgroups for public static methods and protected static methods.

Event listener registration methods

Lists the public instance methods that register and deregister event listener objects with the class. The names of these methods begin with the words "add" and "remove" and end in "Listener". These methods are always passed a java.util.EventListener object. The methods are typically defined in pairs, so the pairs are listed together. The methods are listed alphabetically by event name rather than by method name.

Property accessor methods

Lists the public instance methods that set or query the value of a property or attribute of the class. The names of these methods begin with the words "set", "get", and "is", and their signatures follow the patterns set out in the Java-Beans specification. Although the naming conventions and method signature patterns are defined for JavaBeans, classes and interfaces throughout the Java platform define property accessor methods that follow these conventions and patterns. Looking at a class in terms of the properties it defines can be a powerful tool for understanding the class, so property methods are grouped together in this section. Property accessor methods are listed alphabetically by property name, not by method name. This means that the "set", "get", and "is" methods for a property all appear together.

Public instance methods

Contains all of the public instance methods that are not grouped elsewhere.

Implementing methods

Groups the methods that implement the same interface. There is one subgroup for each interface implemented by the class. Methods that are defined by the same interface are almost always related to each other, so this is a useful functional grouping of methods.

Note that if an interface method is also an event registration method or a property accessor method, it is listed both in this group and in the event or property group. This situation does not arise often, but when it does, all of the functional groupings are important and useful enough to warrant the duplicate listing. When an interface method is listed in the event or property group, it displays an "Implements:" flag that specifies the name of the inter-face of which it is part.

Overriding methods

Groups the methods that override methods of a superclass broken down into subgroups by superclass. This is typically a useful grouping, because it helps to make it clear how a class modifies the default behavior of its superclasses. In practice, it is also often true that methods that override the same super-class are functionally related to each other.

Sometimes a method that overrides a superclass is also a property accessor method or (more rarely) an event registration method. When this happens, the method is grouped with the property or event methods and displays a flag that indicates which superclass it overrides. The method is not listed with other overriding methods, however. Note that this is different from interface methods, which, because they are more strongly functionally related, may have duplicate listings in both groups.

Protected instance methods
Contains all of the protected instance methods that are not grouped elsewhere.

Fields
Lists all the non-constant fields of the class, breaking them down into subgroups for public and protected static fields and public and protected instance fields. Many classes do not define any publicly accessible fields. For those that do, many object-oriented programmers prefer not to use those fields directly, but instead to use accessor methods when such methods are available.

Deprecated members
Deprecated methods and deprecated fields are grouped at the very bottom of the class synopsis. Use of these members is strongly discouraged.

Cross-References

The synopsis section of a quick-reference entry is followed by a number of optional cross-reference sections that indicate other, related classes and methods that may be of interest. These sections are the following:

Subclasses
This section lists the subclasses of this class, if there are any.

Implementations
This section lists classes that implement this interface.

Passed To
This section lists all of the methods and constructors that are passed an object of this type as an argument. This is useful when you have an object of a given type and want to figure out what you can do with it.

Returned By
This section lists all of the methods (but not constructors) that return an object of this type. This is useful when you know that you want to work with an object of this type, but don't know how to obtain one.

Thrown By
For checked exception classes, this section lists all of the methods and constructors that throw exceptions of this type. This material helps you figure out when a given exception or error may be thrown. Note, however, that this section is based on the exception types listed in the throws clauses of methods and constructors. Subclasses of RuntimeException and Error do not have to be listed in throws clauses, so it is not possible to generate a complete cross reference of methods that throw these types of unchecked exceptions.

Type Of
This section lists all of the fields and constants that are of this type, which can help you figure out how to obtain an object of this type.

A Note About Class Names

Throughout the quick reference, you'll notice that classes are sometimes referred to by class name alone and at other times referred to by class name and package name. If package names were always used, the class synopses would become long and hard to read. On the other hand, if package names were never used, it would sometimes be difficult to know what class was being referred to. The rules for including or omitting the package name are complex. They can be summarized approximately as follows, however:

- If the class name alone is ambiguous, the package name is always used.

- If the class is part of the `java.lang` package or is a very commonly used class, the package name is omitted.

- If the class being referred to is part of the current package (and has a quick-reference entry in the current chapter), the package name is omitted.

CHAPTER 10

J2ME Packages and Classes

There are two types of packages and classes in the J2ME platform:

- Those that are inherited from the J2SE platform
- Those that are specific to J2ME and have no counterpart in J2SE

Most of J2ME falls into the first category. Depending on the configuration and profile you are using, you can use a different subset of J2SE packages and a subset of those packages that are part of J2ME itself, as shown in Table 10-1. Some J2SE packages, particularly those associated with the user interface, are not currently part of any J2ME profile. These classes are listed in Table 10-2.

Even when a package is available, it is not necessarily the case that all of its classes are included in the J2ME implementation. The remaining sections of this chapter list all classes in the J2SE packages included in at least one J2ME profile and show, for each configuration and profile, the classes applicable to it.* In some cases, you'll see that a J2SE class is not available at all in J2ME. Classes are usually omitted because of resource limitations, but there has also been an effort to remove classes that are deprecated in Java 2 Version 1.3; where this is the case, it is indicated in the tables.

J2ME Packages

The following table shows the packages that make up J2ME and the configurations and profiles in which they are available. For example, the ✓ appearing on the top row of the "CLDC 1.0" column indicates that the java.io package is available in the CLDC configuration.

---

* Since all of the J2ME profiles are based on Java 2 Version 1.3, the tables in this chapter show the packages and classes from that version.

Table 10-1: J2ME Package List

Package	CLDC 1.0	MID Profile 1.0	CDC 1.0	Foundation Profile 1.0	RMI Profile 1.0
java.io	✓	✓	✓	✓	✓
java.lang	✓	✓	✓	✓	✓
java.lang.ref			✓	✓	✓
java.lang.reflect			✓	✓	✓
java.math			✓	✓	✓
java.net			✓	✓	✓
java.rmi					✓
java.rmi.activation					✓
java.rmi.dgc					✓
java.rmi.registry					✓
java.rmi.server					✓
java.security			✓	✓	✓
java.security.acl				✓	✓
java.security.cert			✓	✓	✓
java.security.interfaces				✓	✓
java.security.spec				✓	✓
java.text			✓	✓	✓
java.util	✓	✓	✓	✓	✓
java.util.jar			✓	✓	✓
java.util.zip			✓	✓	✓
javax.microedition.io	✓	✓	✓	✓	✓
javax.microedition.lcdui		✓			
javax.microedition.midlet		✓			
javax.microedition.rms		✓			

Note that the presence of a package does not mean that all classes in that J2SE package are available in J2ME. Class availability is covered in later sections of this chapter.

J2SE Packages Not Present in J2ME

The J2SE packages listed in the following table are not included in any J2ME configuration or profile. Since all J2ME configurations and profiles are based on Java 2 Version 1.3, this list does not include classes available in later J2SE platform releases.

Table 10-2: J2SE Packages Not Included in J2ME

java.applet	javax.swing
java.awt	javax.swing.border
java.awt.color	javax.swing.colorchooser
java.awt.datatransfer	javax.swing.event
java.awt.dnd	javax.swing.filechooser
java.awt.event	javax.swing.plaf
java.awt.font	javax.swing.plaf.basic
java.awt.geom	javax.swing.plaf.metal
java.awt.im	javax.swing.plaf.multi
java.awt.im.spi	javax.swing.table
java.awt.image	javax.swing.text
java.awt.image.renderable	javax.swing.text.html
java.awt.print	javax.swing.text.html.parser
java.beans	javax.swing.text.rtf
java.beans.beancontext	javax.swing.tree
java.sql	javax.swing.undo
javax.accessibility	javax.transaction
javax.naming	org.omg.CORBA
javax.naming.directory	org.omg.CORBA_2_3
javax.naming.event	org.omg.CORBA_2_3.portable
javax.naming.ldap	org.omg.CORBA.DynAnyPackage
javax.naming.spi	org.omg.CORBA.ORBPackage
javax.rmi	org.omg.CORBA.portable
javax.rmi.CORBA	org.omg.CORBA.TypeCodePackage
javax.sound.midi	org.omg.CosNaming
javax.sound.midi.spi	org.omg.CosNaming.NamingContextPackage
javax.sound.sampled	org.omg.SendingContext
javax.sound.sampled.spi	org.omg.stub.java.rmi

J2ME Package Contents

This section contains tables that indicate which classes are available in each of the J2ME packages, itemized by configuration or profile. The presence of a ✓ symbol in a cell indicates that the class corresponding to its row is available in the configuration or profile corresponding to its column.

The java.io Package

Table 10-3: Classes in the J2ME java.io Package

Class	CLDC 1.0	MID Profile 1.0	CDC 1.0	Foundation Profile 1.0	RMI Profile 1.0
BufferedInputStream			✓	✓	✓
BufferedOutputStream			✓	✓	✓

Table 10-3: Classes in the J2ME java.io Package (continued)

Class	CLDC 1.0	MID Profile 1.0	CDC 1.0	Foundation Profile 1.0	RMI Profile 1.0
BufferedReader				✓	✓	✓
BufferedWriter				✓	✓	✓
ByteArrayInputStream	✓	✓	✓	✓	✓
ByteArrayOutputStream	✓	✓	✓	✓	✓
CharArrayReader				✓	✓
CharArrayWriter				✓	✓
CharConversionException			✓	✓	✓
DataInput	✓	✓	✓	✓	✓
DataInputStream	✓	✓	✓	✓	✓
DataOutput	✓	✓	✓	✓	✓
DataOutputStream	✓	✓	✓	✓	✓
EOFException	✓	✓	✓	✓	✓
Externalizable			✓	✓	✓
File			✓	✓	✓
FileDescriptor			✓	✓	✓
FileFilter			✓	✓	✓
FilenameFilter			✓	✓	✓
FileInputStream			✓	✓	✓
FileNotFoundException			✓	✓	✓
FileOutputStream			✓	✓	✓
FilePermission			✓	✓	✓
FileReader			✓	✓	✓
FileWriter			✓	✓	✓
FilterInputStream			✓	✓	✓
FilterOutputStream			✓	✓	✓
FilterReader				✓	✓
FilterWriter				✓	✓
InputStream	✓	✓	✓	✓	✓
InputStreamReader	✓	✓	✓	✓	✓
InterruptedIOException	✓	✓	✓	✓	✓
InvalidClassException			✓	✓	✓
InvalidObjectException			✓	✓	✓
IOException	✓	✓	✓	✓	✓
LineNumberInputStream			Deprecated		
LineNumberReader				✓	✓
NotActiveException			✓	✓	✓

Packages and Classes

Table 10-3: Classes in the J2ME java.io Package (continued)

Class	CLDC 1.0	MID Profile 1.0	CDC 1.0	Foundation Profile 1.0	RMI Profile 1.0
NotSerializableException			✓	✓	✓
ObjectInput			✓	✓	✓
ObjectInputStream			✓	✓	✓
ObjectInputStream.GetField			✓	✓	✓
ObjectInputValidation			✓	✓	✓
ObjectOutput			✓	✓	✓
ObjectOutputStream			✓	✓	✓
ObjectOutputStream.PutField			✓	✓	✓
ObjectStreamClass			✓	✓	✓
ObjectStreamConstants			✓	✓	✓
ObjectStreamException			✓	✓	✓
ObjectStreamField			✓	✓	✓
OptionalDataException			✓	✓	✓
OutputStream	✓	✓	✓	✓	✓
OutputStreamWriter	✓	✓	✓	✓	✓
PipedInputStream			✓	✓	✓
PipedOutputStream			✓	✓	✓
PipedReader				✓	✓
PipedWriter				✓	✓
PrintStream	✓	✓	✓	✓	✓
PrintWriter			✓	✓	✓
PushbackInputStream			✓	✓	✓
PushbackReader				✓	✓
RandomAccessFile				✓	✓
Reader	✓	✓	✓	✓	✓
SequenceInputStream				✓	✓
Serializable			✓	✓	✓
SerializablePermission			✓	✓	✓
StreamCorruptedException			✓	✓	✓
StreamTokenizer			✓	✓	✓
StringBufferInputStream			Deprecated		
StringReader				✓	✓
StringWriter				✓	✓
SyncFailedException			✓	✓	✓
UnsupportedEncodingException	✓	✓	✓	✓	✓
UTFDataFormatException	✓	✓	✓	✓	✓

Table 10-3: Classes in the J2ME java.io Package (continued)

Class	CLDC 1.0	MID Profile 1.0	CDC 1.0	Foundation Profile 1.0	RMI Profile 1.0
Writer	✓	✓	✓	✓	✓
WriteAbortedException			✓	✓	✓

The java.lang Package

Table 10-4: Classes in the J2ME java.lang Package

Class	CLDC 1.0	MID Profile 1.0	CDC 1.0	Foundation Profile 1.0	RMI Profile 1.0
AbstractMethodError			✓	✓	✓
ArithmeticException	✓	✓	✓	✓	✓
ArrayIndexOutOfBoundsException	✓	✓	✓	✓	✓
ArrayStoreException	✓	✓	✓	✓	✓
Boolean	✓	✓	✓	✓	✓
Byte	✓	✓	✓	✓	✓
Character	✓	✓	✓	✓	✓
Character.Subset			✓	✓	✓
Character.UnicodeBlock			✓	✓	✓
Class	✓	✓	✓	✓	✓
ClassCastException	✓	✓	✓	✓	✓
ClassCircularityError			✓	✓	✓
ClassFormatError			✓	✓	✓
ClassLoader			✓	✓	✓
ClassNotFoundException	✓	✓	✓	✓	✓
Cloneable			✓	✓	✓
CloneNotSupportedException			✓	✓	✓
Comparable			✓	✓	✓
Compiler				✓	✓
Double			✓	✓	✓
Error	✓	✓	✓	✓	✓

Table 10-4: Classes in the J2ME java.lang Package (continued)

Class	CLDC 1.0	MID Profile 1.0	CDC 1.0	Foundation Profile 1.0	RMI Profile 1.0
Exception	✓	✓	✓	✓	✓
ExceptionInInitializerError			✓	✓	✓
Float			✓	✓	✓
IllegalAccessError			✓	✓	✓
IllegalAccessException	✓	✓	✓	✓	✓
IllegalArgumentException	✓	✓	✓	✓	✓
IllegalMonitorStateException	✓	✓	✓	✓	✓
IllegalStateException			✓	✓	✓
IllegalThreadStateException	✓	✓	✓	✓	✓
IncompatibleClassChangeError			✓	✓	✓
IndexOutOfBoundsException	✓	✓	✓	✓	✓
InheritableThreadLocal			✓	✓	✓
InstantiationError	✓	✓	✓	✓	✓
InstantiationException			✓	✓	✓
Integer	✓	✓	✓	✓	✓
InternalError			✓	✓	✓
InterruptedException	✓	✓	✓	✓	✓
LinkageError			✓	✓	✓
Long	✓	✓	✓	✓	✓
Math	✓	✓	✓	✓	✓
NegativeArraySizeException	✓	✓	✓	✓	✓
NoClassDefFoundError			✓	✓	✓
NoSuchFieldError			✓	✓	✓
NoSuchFieldException			✓	✓	✓
NoSuchMethodError			✓	✓	✓
NoSuchMethodException			✓	✓	✓
NullPointerException	✓	✓	✓	✓	✓
Number			✓	✓	✓
NumberFormatException	✓	✓	✓	✓	✓
Object	✓	✓	✓	✓	✓
OutOfMemoryError	✓	✓	✓	✓	✓
Package			✓	✓	✓
Process			✓	✓	✓
Runnable	✓	✓	✓	✓	✓
Runtime	✓	✓	✓	✓	✓
RuntimeException	✓	✓	✓	✓	✓

Table 10-4: Classes in the J2ME java.lang Package (continued)

Class	CLDC 1.0	MID Profile 1.0	CDC 1.0	Foundation Profile 1.0	RMI Profile 1.0
RuntimePermission			✓	✓	✓
SecurityException	✓	✓	✓	✓	✓
SecurityManager			✓	✓	✓
Short	✓	✓	✓	✓	✓
StackOverflowError			✓	✓	✓
StrictMath			✓	✓	✓
String	✓	✓	✓	✓	✓
StringBuffer	✓	✓	✓	✓	✓
StringIndexOutOfBoundsException	✓	✓	✓	✓	✓
System	✓	✓	✓	✓	✓
Thread	✓	✓	✓	✓	✓
ThreadDeath			✓	✓	✓
ThreadGroup			✓	✓	✓
ThreadLocal			✓	✓	✓
Throwable	✓	✓	✓	✓	✓
UnknownError				✓	✓
UnsatisfiedLinkError			✓	✓	✓
UnsupportedClassVersionError			✓	✓	✓
UnsupportedOperationException			✓	✓	✓
VerifyError			✓	✓	✓
VirtualMachineError	✓	✓	✓	✓	✓
Void			✓	✓	✓

The java.lang.ref Package

Table 10-5: Classes in the J2ME java.lang.ref Package

Class	CLDC 1.0	MID Profile 1.0	CDC 1.0	Foundation Profile 1.0	RMI Profile 1.0
PhantomReference			✓	✓	✓
Reference			✓	✓	✓

Table 10-5: Classes in the J2ME java.lang.ref Package (continued)

Class	CLDC 1.0	MID Profile 1.0	CDC 1.0	Foundation Profile 1.0	RMI Profile 1.0
ReferenceQueue			✓	✓	✓
SoftReference			✓	✓	✓
WeakReference			✓	✓	✓

The java.lang.reflect Package

Table 10-6: Classes in the J2ME java.lang.reflect Package

Class	CLDC 1.0	MID Profile 1.0	CDC 1.0	Foundation Profile 1.0	RMI Profile 1.0
AccessibleObject			✓	✓	✓
Array			✓	✓	✓
Constructor			✓	✓	✓
Field			✓	✓	✓
InvocationHandler			✓	✓	✓
InvocationTargetException			✓	✓	✓
Member			✓	✓	✓
Method			✓	✓	✓
Modifier			✓	✓	✓
Proxy			✓	✓	✓
ReflectPermission			✓	✓	✓
UndeclaredThrowableException			✓	✓	✓

The java.math Package

Table 10-7: Classes in the J2ME java.math Package

Class	CLDC 1.0	MID Profile 1.0	CDC 1.0	Foundation Profile 1.0	RMI Profile 1.0
BigDecimal					
BigInteger			✓	✓	✓

The java.net Package

Table 10-8: Classes in the J2ME java.net Package

Class	CLDC 1.0	MID Profile 1.0	CDC 1.0	Foundation Profile 1.0	RMI Profile 1.0
Authenticator				✓	✓
BindException			✓	✓	✓
ConnectException				✓	✓
ContentHandler			✓	✓	✓
ContentHandlerFactory			✓	✓	✓
DatagramPacket			✓	✓	✓
DatagramSocket			✓	✓	✓
DatagramSocketImpl			✓	✓	✓
DatagramSocketImplFactory			✓	✓	✓
FileNameMap			✓	✓	✓
HttpURLConnection				✓	✓
InetAddress			✓	✓	✓
JarURLConnection			✓	✓	✓
MalformedURLException			✓	✓	✓
MulticastSocket				✓	✓
NetPermission			✓	✓	✓
NoRouteToHostException				✓	✓
PasswordAuthentication				✓	✓
ProtocolException			✓	✓	✓
ServerSocket				✓	✓

Table 10-8: Classes in the J2ME java.net Package (continued)

Class	CLDC 1.0	MID Profile 1.0	CDC 1.0	Foundation Profile 1.0	RMI Profile 1.0
Socket				✓	✓
SocketException			✓	✓	✓
SocketImpl				✓	✓
SocketImplFactory				✓	✓
SocketOptions			✓	✓	✓
SocketPermission			✓	✓	✓
UnknownHostException			✓	✓	✓
UnknownServiceException			✓	✓	✓
URL			✓	✓	✓
URLClassLoader			✓	✓	✓
URLConnection			✓	✓	✓
URLDecoder				✓	✓
URLEncoder				✓	✓
URLStreamHandler			✓	✓	✓
URLStreamHandlerFactory			✓	✓	✓

The java.rmi Package

Table 10-9: Classes in the J2ME java.rmi Package

Class	CLDC 1.0	MID Profile 1.0	CDC 1.0	Foundation Profile 1.0	RMI Profile 1.0
AccessException					✓
AlreadyBoundException					✓
ConnectException					✓
ConnectIOException					✓
MarshalException					✓
MarshalledObject					✓
Naming					✓
NoSuchObjectException					✓
NotBoundException					✓

Table 10-9: Classes in the J2ME java.rmi Package (continued)

Class	CLDC 1.0	MID Profile 1.0	CDC 1.0	Foundation Profile 1.0	RMI Profile 1.0
Remote					✓
RemoteException					✓
RMISecurityException					
RMISecurityManager					✓
ServerError					✓
ServerException					✓
ServerRuntimeException					
StubNotFoundException					✓
UnexpectedException					✓
UnknownHostException					✓
UnmarshalException					✓

The java.rmi.activation Package

Table 10-10: Classes in the J2ME java.rmi.activation Package

Class	CLDC 1.0	MID Profile 1.0	CDC 1.0	Foundation Profile 1.0	RMI Profile 1.0
Activatable					
ActivateFailedException					✓
ActivationDesc					
ActivationException					✓
ActivationGroup					
ActivationGroupDesc					
ActivationGroupDesc. CommandEnvironment					
ActivationGroupID					
ActivationID					✓
ActivationInstantiator					
ActivationMonitor					
ActivationSystem					

Table 10-10: Classes in the J2ME java.rmi.activation Package (continued)

Class	CLDC 1.0	MID Profile 1.0	CDC 1.0	Foundation Profile 1.0	RMI Profile 1.0
Activator					✓
UnknownGroupException					
UnknownObjectException					✓

The CDC RMI profile contains only a small subset of the J2SE `java.rmi.activation` package, because it provides only the client-side functionality. The server side is assumed to be hosted in a J2SE or J2EE environment.

The java.rmi.dgc Package

Table 10-11: Classes in the J2ME java.rmi.dgc Package

Class	CLDC 1.0	MID Profile 1.0	CDC 1.0	Foundation Profile 1.0	RMI Profile 1.0
DGC					✓
Lease					✓
VMID					✓

The java.rmi.registry Package

Table 10-12: Classes in the J2ME java.rmi.registry Package

Class	CLDC 1.0	MID Profile 1.0	CDC 1.0	Foundation Profile 1.0	RMI Profile 1.0
LocateRegistry					✓
Registry					✓
RegistryHandler				Deprecated	

The java.rmi.server Package

Table 10-13: Classes in the java.rmi.server Package

Class	CLDC 1.0	MID Profile 1.0	CDC 1.0	Foundation Profile 1.0	RMI Profile 1.0
ExportException					✓
LoaderHandler			Deprecated		
LogStream			Deprecated		
ObjID					✓
Operation					✓
RemoteCall					✓
RemoteObject					✓
RemoteRef					✓
RemoteServer					✓
RemoteStub					✓
RMIClassLoader					✓
RMIClientSocketFactory					✓
RMIFailureHandler					✓
RMIServerSocketFactory					✓
RMISocketFactory					✓
ServerCloneException					✓
ServerNotActiveException					✓
ServerRef					
Skeleton			Deprecated		
SkeletonMismatchException			Deprecated		
SkeletonNotFoundException			Deprecated		
SocketSecurityException					✓
UID					✓
UnicastRemoteObject					✓
Unreferenced					✓

The java.security Package

Table 10-14: Classes in the J2ME java.security Package

Class	CLDC 1.0	MID Profile 1.0	CDC 1.0	Foundation Profile 1.0	RMI Profile 1.0
AccessControlContext			✓	✓	✓
AccessControlException			✓	✓	✓
AccessController			✓	✓	✓
AlgorithmParameterGenerator				✓	✓
AlgorithmParameterGeneratorSpi				✓	✓
AlgorithmParameters				✓	✓
AlgorithmParametersSpi				✓	✓
AllPermission			✓	✓	✓
BasicPermission			✓	✓	✓
Certificate				✓	✓
CodeSource			✓	✓	✓
DigestException			✓	✓	✓
DigestInputStream				✓	✓
DigestOutputStream			✓	✓	✓
DomainCombiner			✓	✓	✓
GeneralSecurityException			✓	✓	✓
Guard			✓	✓	✓
GuardedObject			✓	✓	✓
Identity				✓	✓
IdentityScope				✓	✓
InvalidAlgorithmParameterException				✓	✓
InvalidKeyException			✓	✓	✓
InvalidParameterException			✓	✓	✓
Key			✓	✓	✓
KeyException			✓	✓	✓
KeyFactory				✓	✓
KeyFactorySpi				✓	✓
KeyManagementException				✓	✓
KeyPair				✓	✓
KeyPairGenerator				✓	✓
KeyPairGeneratorSpi				✓	✓
KeyStore				✓	✓
KeyStoreException				✓	✓
KeyStoreSpi				✓	✓

Table 10-14: Classes in the J2ME java.security Package (continued)

Class	CLDC 1.0	MID Profile 1.0	CDC 1.0	Foundation Profile 1.0	RMI Profile 1.0
MessageDigest			✓	✓	✓
MessageDigestSpi			✓	✓	✓
NoSuchAlgorithmException			✓	✓	✓
NoSuchProviderException			✓	✓	✓
Permission			✓	✓	✓
PermissionCollection			✓	✓	✓
Permissions			✓	✓	✓
Policy			✓	✓	✓
Principal				✓	✓
PrivateKey				✓	✓
PrivilegedAction			✓	✓	✓
PrivilegedActionException			✓	✓	✓
PrivilegedExceptionAction			✓	✓	✓
ProtectionDomain			✓	✓	✓
Provider			✓	✓	✓
ProviderException			✓	✓	✓
PublicKey			✓	✓	✓
SecureClassLoader			✓	✓	✓
SecureRandom				✓	✓
SecureRandomSpi				✓	✓
Security			✓	✓	✓
SecurityPermission			✓	✓	✓
Signature				✓	✓
SignatureException			✓	✓	✓
SignatureSpi				✓	✓
SignedObject				✓	✓
Signer				✓	✓
UnrecoverableKeyException				✓	✓
UnresolvedPermission			✓	✓	✓

The java.security.acl Package

Table 10-15: Classes in the J2ME java.security.acl Package

Class	CLDC 1.0	MID Profile 1.0	CDC 1.0	Foundation Profile 1.0	RMI Profile 1.0
Acl				✓	✓
AclEntry				✓	✓
AclNotFoundException				✓	✓
Group				✓	✓
LastOwnerException				✓	✓
NotOwnerException				✓	✓
Owner				✓	✓
Permission				✓	✓

The java.security.cert Package

Table 10-16: Classes in the J2ME java.security.cert Package

Class	CLDC 1.0	MID Profile 1.0	CDC 1.0	Foundation Profile 1.0	RMI Profile 1.0
Certificate			✓	✓	✓
Certificate.CertificateRep			✓	✓	✓
CertificateEncodingException			✓	✓	✓
CertificateException			✓	✓	✓
CertificateExpiredException				✓	✓
CertificateFactory				✓	✓
CertificateFactorySpi				✓	✓
CertificateNotYetValidException				✓	✓
CertificateParsingException				✓	✓
CRL				✓	✓
CRLException				✓	✓
X509Certificate				✓	✓

Table 10-16: Classes in the J2ME java.security.cert Package (continued)

Class	CLDC 1.0	MID Profile 1.0	CDC 1.0	Foundation Profile 1.0	RMI Profile 1.0
X509CRL				✓	✓
X509CRLEntry				✓	✓
X509Extension				✓	✓

The java.security.interfaces Package

Table 10-17: Classes in tn the J2ME java.security.interfaces Package

Class	CLDC 1.0	MID Profile 1.0	CDC 1.0	Foundation Profile 1.0	RMI Profile 1.0
DSAKey				✓	✓
DSAKeyPairGenerator				✓	✓
DSAParams				✓	✓
DSAPrivateKey				✓	✓
DSAPublicKey				✓	✓
RSAKey				✓	✓
RSAPrivateCrtKey				✓	✓
RSAPrivateKey				✓	✓
RSAPublicKey				✓	✓

The java.security.spec Package

Table 10-18: Classes in the J2ME java.security.spec Package

Class	CLDC 1.0	MID Profile 1.0	CDC 1.0	Foundation Profile 1.0	RMI Profile 1.0
AlgorithmParameterSpec				✓	✓
DSAParameterSpec				✓	✓
DSAPrivateKeySpec				✓	✓
DSAPublicKeySpec				✓	✓
EncodedKeySpec				✓	✓
InvalidKeySpecException				✓	✓
InvalidParameterSpecException				✓	✓
KeySpec				✓	✓
PKCS8EncodedKeySpec				✓	✓
RSAKeyGenParameterSpec				✓	✓
RSAPrivateCrtKeySpec				✓	✓
RSAPrivateKeySpec				✓	✓
RSAPublicKeySpec				✓	✓
X509EncodedKeySpec				✓	✓

The java.text Package

Table 10-19: Classes in the J2ME java.text Package

Class	CLDC 1.0	MID Profile 1.0	CDC 1.0	Foundation Profile 1.0	RMI Profile 1.0
Annotation				✓	✓
AttributedCharacterIterator				✓	✓
AttributedCharacterIterator.Attribute				✓	✓
AttributedString				✓	✓
BreakIterator				✓	✓
CharacterIterator				✓	✓
ChoiceFormat			✓	✓	✓
CollationElementIterator				✓	✓

Table 10-19: Classes in the J2ME java.text Package (continued)

Class	CLDC 1.0	MID Profile 1.0	CDC 1.0	Foundation Profile 1.0	RMI Profile 1.0
CollationKey				✓	✓
Collator				✓	✓
DateFormat			✓	✓	✓
DateFormatSymbols			✓	✓	✓
DecimalFormat			✓	✓	✓
DecimalFormatSymbols			✓	✓	✓
FieldPosition			✓	✓	✓
Format			✓	✓	✓
MessageFormat			✓	✓	✓
NumberFormat			✓	✓	✓
ParseException			✓	✓	✓
ParsePosition			✓	✓	✓
RuleBasedCollator				✓	✓
SimpleDateFormat			✓	✓	✓
StringCharacterIterator				✓	✓

The java.util Package

Table 10-20: Classes in the J2ME java.util Package

Class	CLDC 1.0	MID Profile 1.0	CDC 1.0	Foundation Profile 1.0	RMI Profile 1.0
AbstractCollection			✓	✓	✓
AbstractList			✓	✓	✓
AbstractMap			✓	✓	✓
AbstractSequentialList			✓	✓	✓
AbstractSet			✓	✓	✓
ArrayList			✓	✓	✓
Arrays			✓	✓	✓
BitSet			✓	✓	✓
Calendar	✓	✓	✓	✓	✓

Table 10-20: Classes in the J2ME java.util Package (continued)

Class	CLDC 1.0	MID Profile 1.0	CDC 1.0	Foundation Profile 1.0	RMI Profile 1.0
Collection			✓	✓	✓
Collections			✓	✓	✓
Comparator			✓	✓	✓
ConcurrentModificationException			✓	✓	✓
Date	✓	✓	✓	✓	✓
Dictionary			✓	✓	✓
EmptyStackException	✓	✓	✓	✓	✓
Enumeration	✓	✓	✓	✓	✓
EventListener				✓	✓
EventObject				✓	✓
GregorianCalendar			✓	✓	✓
HashMap			✓	✓	✓
HashSet			✓	✓	✓
Hashtable	✓	✓	✓	✓	✓
Iterator			✓	✓	✓
LinkedList			✓	✓	✓
List			✓	✓	✓
ListIterator			✓	✓	✓
ListResourceBundle			✓	✓	✓
Locale			✓	✓	✓
Map			✓	✓	✓
Map.Entry			✓	✓	✓
MissingResourceException			✓	✓	✓
NoSuchElementException	✓	✓	✓	✓	✓
Observable				✓	✓
Observer				✓	✓
Properties			✓	✓	✓
PropertyPermission			✓	✓	✓
PropertyResourceBundle			✓	✓	✓
Random	✓	✓	✓	✓	✓
ResourceBundle			✓	✓	✓
Set			✓	✓	✓
SimpleTimeZone			✓	✓	✓
SortedMap			✓	✓	✓
SortedSet			✓	✓	✓
Stack	✓	✓	✓	✓	✓

Table 10-20: Classes in the J2ME java.util Package (continued)

Class	CLDC 1.0	MID Profile 1.0	CDC 1.0	Foundation Profile 1.0	RMI Profile 1.0
StringTokenizer			✓	✓	✓
Timer		✓		✓	✓
TimerTask		✓		✓	✓
TimeZone	✓	✓	✓	✓	✓
TooManyListenersException				✓	✓
TreeMap			✓	✓	✓
TreeSet			✓	✓	✓
Vector	✓	✓	✓	✓	✓
WeakHashMap			✓	✓	✓

The java.util.jar Package

Table 10-21: Classes in the J2ME java.util.jar Package

Class	CLDC 1.0	MID Profile 1.0	CDC 1.0	Foundation Profile 1.0	RMI Profile 1.0
Attributes			✓	✓	✓
Attributes.Name			✓	✓	✓
JarEntry			✓	✓	✓
JarException			✓	✓	✓
JarFile			✓	✓	✓
JarInputStream			✓	✓	✓
JarOutputStream				✓	✓
Manifest			✓	✓	✓

Packages and Classes

The java.util.zip Package

Table 10-22: Classes in the J2ME java.util.zip Package

Class	CLDC 1.0	MID Profile 1.0	CDC 1.0	Foundation Profile 1.0	RMI Profile 1.0
Adler32				✓	✓
CheckedInputStream				✓	✓
CheckedOutputStream				✓	✓
Checksum			✓	✓	✓
CRC32			✓	✓	✓
DataFormatException			✓	✓	✓
Deflater				✓	✓
DeflaterOutputStream				✓	✓
GZIPInputStream				✓	✓
GZIPOutputStream				✓	✓
Inflater			✓	✓	✓
InflaterInputStream			✓	✓	✓
ZipEntry			✓	✓	✓
ZipFile			✓	✓	✓
ZipException			✓	✓	✓
ZipInputStream			✓	✓	✓
ZipOutputStream				✓	✓

The javax.microedition.io Package

Table 10-23: Classes in the J2ME javax.microedition.io Package

Class	CLDC 1.0	MID Profile 1.0	CDC 1.0	Foundation Profile 1.0	RMI Profile 1.0
Connection	✓	✓	✓	✓	✓
Connector	✓	✓	✓	✓	✓
ConnectionNotFoundException	✓	✓	✓	✓	✓
ContentConnection	✓	✓	✓	✓	✓
Datagram	✓	✓	✓	✓	✓

Class	CLDC 1.0	MID Profile 1.0	CDC 1.0	Foundation Profile 1.0	RMI Profile 1.0
DatagramConnection	✓	✓	✓	✓	✓
HttpConnection		✓		✓	✓
InputConnection	✓	✓	✓	✓	✓
OutputConnection	✓	✓	✓	✓	✓
StreamConnection	✓	✓	✓	✓	✓
StreamConnectionNotifier	✓	✓	✓	✓	✓

The javax.microedition.lcdui Package

Table 10-24: Classes in the J2ME javax.microedition.lcdui Package

Class	CLDC 1.0	MID Profile 1.0	CDC 1.0	Foundation Profile 1.0	RMI Profile 1.0
Alert		✓			
AlertType		✓			
Canvas		✓			
Choice		✓			
ChoiceGroup		✓			
Command		✓			
CommandListener		✓			
DateField		✓			
Display		✓			
Displayable		✓			
Font		✓			
Form		✓			
Gauge		✓			
Graphics		✓			
Image		✓			
ImageItem		✓			
Item		✓			
ItemStateListener		✓			

Class	CLDC 1.0	MID Profile 1.0	CDC 1.0	Foundation Profile 1.0	RMI Profile 1.0
List		✓			
Screen		✓			
StringItem		✓			
TextBox		✓			
TextField		✓			
Ticker		✓			

The javax.microedition.midlet Package

Table 10-25: Classes in the J2ME javax.microedition.midlet Package

Class	CLDC 1.0	MID Profile 1.0	CDC 1.0	Foundation Profile 1.0	RMI Profile 1.0
MIDlet		✓			
MIDletStateChangeException		✓			

The javax.microedition.rms Package

Table 10-26: Classes in the javax.microedition.rms Package

Class	CLDC 1.0	MID Profile 1.0	CDC 1.0	Foundation Profile 1.0	RMI Profile 1.0
InvalidRecordIDException		✓			
RecordComparator		✓			
RecordEnumeration		✓			
RecordFilter		✓			

Table 10-26: Classes in the javax.microedition.rms Package (continued)

Class	CLDC 1.0	MID Profile 1.0	CDC 1.0	Foundation Profile 1.0	RMI Profile 1.0
RecordListener		✓			
RecordStore		✓			
RecordStoreException		✓			
RecordStoreFullException		✓			
RecordStoreNotFoundException		✓			
RecordStoreNotOpenException		✓			

CHAPTER 11

java.io

Package java.io

This package, whose class hierarchy is shown in Figure 11-1, contains interfaces and classes used to access input and output sources and treat them either as a sequence of 8-bit bytes or 16-bit characters.

The CLDC version of this package contains only the basic classes and interfaces from its J2SE counterpart that provide 8-bit input and output, together with support for Unicode conversion using the InputStreamReader and OutputStreamWriter classes. Most of the concrete input and output stream and reader/writer classes available in J2SE are not provided. In addition, some abstract classes (such as FilterInputStream) are also omitted so that derived classes in CLDC are reparented directly to InputStream or OutputStream.

ByteArrayInputStream

java.io

This is a subclass of InputStream that returns data from an array of bytes passed into one of its constructors. It is useful when you have data stored in a byte array and wish to read it as if it were coming from a file, pipe, or socket. A good example of this is provided by MIDlet RecordStores, which hold their content in byte arrays. MIDlets typically read these records by creating a ByteArrayInputStream from the content of a record and then wrap it with a DataInputStream to recover strings and Java data types without assuming the format used to store them.

This class supports the mark() and reset() operations of InputStream. Once constructed, the byte array from which this stream gets its data cannot be switched. However, because the data is not copied by the stream, the contents of the array can be modified and then re-read following a reset(). Note that such an approach is only practical if the original byte array is large enough to hold any desired modifications.

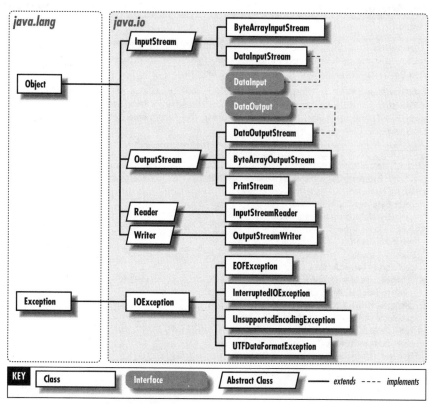

Figure 11-1: The java.io hierarchy

```
Object — InputStream — ByteArrayInputStream

public class ByteArrayInputStream extends InputStream {
// Public Constructors
    public ByteArrayInputStream(byte[ ] buf);
    public ByteArrayInputStream(byte[ ] buf, int offset, int length);
// Public Methods Overriding InputStream
    public int available();                                        synchronized
    public void close() throws IOException;                  synchronized empty
    public void mark(int readAheadLimit);
    public boolean markSupported();                                  constant
    public int read();                                            synchronized
    public int read(byte[ ] b, int off, int len);                 synchronized
    public void reset();                                          synchronized
    public long skip(long n);                                     synchronized
// Protected Instance Fields
    protected byte[ ] buf;
    protected int count;
    protected int mark;
    protected int pos;
}
```

ByteArrayOutputStream   CLDC 1.0, MIDP 1.0

java.io

This subclass of OutputStream stores data written to it in a buffer which can later be retrieved using its toByteArray() method. When the stream is created, the buffer is empty. It is then expanded as data is written to the stream.

ByteArrayOutputStream is often used in J2ME in conjunction with a DataOutputStream to allow strings and Java primitives types to be stored in a byte array. This byte array is written to persistent storage on a device using the RecordStore APIs in the javax.microedition.rms package.

```
Object — OutputStream — ByteArrayOutputStream
```

```
public class ByteArrayOutputStream extends OutputStream {
// Public Constructors
    public ByteArrayOutputStream();
    public ByteArrayOutputStream(int size);
// Public Instance Methods
    public void reset();                                                    synchronized
    public int size();
    public byte[ ] toByteArray();                                           synchronized
// Public Methods Overriding OutputStream
    public void close() throws IOException;                                 synchronized
    public void write(int b);                                              synchronized
    public void write(byte[ ] b, int off, int len);                        synchronized
// Public Methods Overriding Object
    public String toString();
// Protected Instance Fields
    protected byte[ ] buf;
    protected int count;
}
```

DataInput   CLDC 1.0, MIDP 1.0

java.io

This interface is implemented by classes that can read strings and Java primitive types from a platform-independent binary encoding created by a class implementing the DataOutput interface.

The class provides methods for reading primitives of type boolean, byte, char, int, long and short. There is also provision for reading an *unsigned short*, which is a 16-bit value that is returned in a Java int without sign extension.

Strings are held in a slightly modified form of UTF-8, which results in Unicode characters with values in the range 0-127 inclusive being encoded as a single byte. This is an optimization for the most common characters in Western locales. The readUTF() returns a String from a sequence of bytes held in this form.

The readFully() methods read a stream of bytes into a buffer, blocking until either a specified number of bytes has been read or an end-of-file is reached. This is a convenience method that repeatedly reads from the underlying input stream until the end condition is met; it removes the need for application code to include this loop.

```
public interface DataInput {
// Public Instance Methods
    public abstract boolean readBoolean() throws IOException;
    public abstract byte readByte() throws IOException;
```

```
    public abstract char readChar() throws IOException;
    public abstract void readFully(byte[ ] b) throws IOException;
    public abstract void readFully(byte[ ] b, int off, int len) throws IOException;
    public abstract int readInt() throws IOException;
    public abstract long readLong() throws IOException;
    public abstract short readShort() throws IOException;
    public abstract int readUnsignedByte() throws IOException;
    public abstract int readUnsignedShort() throws IOException;
    public abstract String readUTF() throws IOException;
    public abstract int skipBytes(int n) throws IOException;
}
```

Implementations: DataInputStream, javax.microedition.io.Datagram

Passed To: DataInputStream.readUTF()

DataInputStream

CLDC 1.0, MIDP 1.0

java.io

This subclass of InputStream implements the methods of the DataInput interface, reading encoded data as a sequence of bytes from another InputStream. Instances of this class can not only be created directly, but can also be obtained from various other methods, such as the openDataInputStream method of javax.microedition.io.Connector. In this case, the openDataInputStream method returns a stream to read data from a network connection or some other type of data source accessed using the CLDC Generic Connection Framework.

Note that the CLDC version of this class is derived from InputStream and not FilterInput-Stream as in J2SE. This is because CLDC does not have a FilterInputStream class.

```
Object ─┤InputStream├─ DataInputStream
                  ┊
                DataInput
```

```
public class DataInputStream extends InputStream implements DataInput {
// Public Constructors
    public DataInputStream(InputStream in);
// Public Class Methods
    public static final String readUTF(DataInput in) throws IOException;
// Methods Implementing DataInput
    public final boolean readBoolean() throws IOException;
    public final byte readByte() throws IOException;
    public final char readChar() throws IOException;
    public final void readFully(byte[ ] b) throws IOException;
    public final void readFully(byte[ ] b, int off, int len) throws IOException;
    public final int readInt() throws IOException;
    public final long readLong() throws IOException;
    public final short readShort() throws IOException;
    public final int readUnsignedByte() throws IOException;
    public final int readUnsignedShort() throws IOException;
    public final String readUTF() throws IOException;
    public final int skipBytes(int n) throws IOException;
// Public Methods Overriding InputStream
    public int available() throws IOException;
    public void close() throws IOException;
    public void mark(int readlimit);                                          synchronized
    public boolean markSupported();
```

```
    public int read() throws IOException;
    public final int read(byte[ ] b) throws IOException;
    public final int read(byte[ ] b, int off, int len) throws IOException;
    public void reset() throws IOException;                                          synchronized
    public long skip(long n) throws IOException;
// Protected Instance Fields
    protected InputStream in;
}
```

Returned By: javax.microedition.io.Connector.openDataInputStream(),
javax.microedition.io.InputConnection.openDataInputStream()

DataOutput   CLDC 1.0, MIDP 1.0

java.io

This interface is implemented by classes that write strings and Java primitive types to a
platform-independent binary encoding that can be read by a class implementing the
DataInput interface.

Methods are provided for writing a single byte or an array of bytes as well as primitives
of type boolean, char, int, long and short.

The writeChars() method writes the content of a String as an array of 16-bit characters. In
many cases, it is more efficient to output a String by using the writeUtf() method. This
method encodes the characters in the String using a slightly modified form of UTF-8,
which results in Unicode characters with values in the range 0-127 inclusive being
encoded as a single byte. This is an optimization for the most common characters in
Western locales.

```
public interface DataOutput {
// Public Instance Methods
    public abstract void write(byte[ ] b) throws IOException;
    public abstract void write(int b) throws IOException;
    public abstract void write(byte[ ] b, int off, int len) throws IOException;
    public abstract void writeBoolean(boolean v) throws IOException;
    public abstract void writeByte(int v) throws IOException;
    public abstract void writeChar(int v) throws IOException;
    public abstract void writeChars(String s) throws IOException;
    public abstract void writeInt(int v) throws IOException;
    public abstract void writeLong(long v) throws IOException;
    public abstract void writeShort(int v) throws IOException;
    public abstract void writeUTF(String str) throws IOException;
}
```

Implementations: DataOutputStream, javax.microedition.io.Datagram

DataOutputStream   CLDC 1.0, MIDP 1.0

java.io

This is a subclass of OutputStream that implements the methods of the DataOutput interface, writing encoded data as a sequence of bytes to another OutputStream. Instances of
this class can be created directly. In addition, they can also be obtained from various
other sources, such as the openDataOutputStream method of the javax.microedition.io.Connec-
tor. This example returns a stream to write data to a network connection or some other
type of data source accessed using the CLDC Generic Connection Framework.

Note that the CLDC version of this class is derived from OutputStream and not FilterOutput-Stream, as it is in J2SE. This is because the CLDC does not have a FilterOutputStream class.

```
Object ├ OutputStream ├ DataOutputStream
                        DataOutput
```

```
public class DataOutputStream extends OutputStream implements DataOutput {
// Public Constructors
    public DataOutputStream(OutputStream out);
// Methods Implementing DataOutput
    public void write(int b) throws IOException;
    public void write(byte[ ] b, int off, int len) throws IOException;
    public final void writeBoolean(boolean v) throws IOException;
    public final void writeByte(int v) throws IOException;
    public final void writeChar(int v) throws IOException;
    public final void writeChars(String s) throws IOException;
    public final void writeInt(int v) throws IOException;
    public final void writeLong(long v) throws IOException;
    public final void writeShort(int v) throws IOException;
    public final void writeUTF(String str) throws IOException;
// Public Methods Overriding OutputStream
    public void close() throws IOException;
    public void flush() throws IOException;
// Protected Instance Fields
    protected OutputStream out;
}
```

Returned By: javax.microedition.io.Connector.openDataOutputStream(),
javax.microedition.io.OutputConnection.openDataOutputStream()

EOFException   CLDC 1.0, MIDP 1.0

java.io   *checked*

An exception that signals that all available data on an input stream or a reader has been consumed. This class is identical to its J2SE equivalent, apart from its inability to be serialized.

```
Object ├ Throwable ├ Exception ├ IOException ├ EOFException
```

```
public class EOFException extends IOException {
// Public Constructors
    public EOFException();
    public EOFException(String s);
}
```

InputStream   CLDC 1.0, MIDP 1.0

java.io

This is an abstract class that defines the methods used to read data from an input source in the form of a stream of bytes.

The no-argument read() method returns a single byte from the stream in the low-order 8 bits of an int, blocking until a byte is available to be read. If no more data is available from the stream, -1 is returned. There are also two other variants of read() that read a sequence of bytes into a buffer and return the number of bytes actually read, or -1 if end-of-file has been reached. These methods also block until data is available; however, they only guarantee to return a single byte—they do not block until the buffer is full. If you need this functionality, wrap the InputStream with a DataInputStream and use the readFully() method.

The available() method can be used to determine how much data is available to be read without blocking; this method is useful when the input source is a network connection which typically does not have all of its data immediately available. The skip() skips over a given number of bytes in the input stream; this method returns the number of bytes that it actually skipped, which may be fewer than the number requested if end-of-file was reached before or during the operation.

The mark() and reset() methods provide the capability for application code to mark a position in the input stream, which may be returned to later. The argument passed to the mark() method specifies the maximum number of bytes that application code will read beyond the mark before invoking the reset() and therefore represents the maximum buffering that the stream will need to use to save the data if it cannot be re-read on demand from the underlying data source. Not all InputStream subclasses support this functionality; markSupported() can be used to discover whether this facility is available.

The close() method closes the InputStream and releases any resources associated with it. An IOException may be thrown if an attempt is made to use a closed input stream (although not all InputStream subclasses do this).

It is important to note that an InputStream is *byte*-oriented and not character-oriented and therefore cannot safely be used on its own to read character data by widening a sequence of bytes into a sequence of chars. Instead, character data should be handled using the readUTF() or readChar() methods of DataInputStream or by using an InputStreamReader with the appropriate encoding for the data in the input stream.

```
public abstract class InputStream {
// Public Constructors
    public InputStream();
// Public Instance Methods
    public int available() throws IOException;                         constant
    public void close() throws IOException;                              empty
    public void mark(int readlimit);                         synchronized empty
    public boolean markSupported();                                    constant
    public abstract int read() throws IOException;
    public int read(byte[ ] b) throws IOException;
    public int read(byte[ ] b, int off, int len) throws IOException;
    public void reset() throws IOException;                        synchronized
    public long skip(long n) throws IOException;
}
```

Subclasses: ByteArrayInputStream, DataInputStream

Passed To: DataInputStream.DataInputStream(), InputStreamReader.InputStreamReader()

Returned By: Class.getResourceAsStream(), javax.microedition.io.Connector.openInputStream(), javax.microedition.io.InputConnection.openInputStream()

Type Of: DataInputStream.in

InputStreamReader   CLDC 1.0, MIDP 1.0

java.io

InputStreamReader is a subclass of Reader that reads bytes from an underlying 8-bit input stream and converts them to Unicode characters. The mapping of the bytes from the InputStream to the characters returned by the InputStreamReader is performed using the encoding specified in the constructor, or the default encoding of the host platform if the single-argument constructor is used. Note that InputStreamReader supports the mark() and reset() methods only if the underlying InputStream does.

CLDC devices typically support only their own default encoding. Hence, it is unlikely that many alternative encodings will be available. The CLDC specification does not provide any mechanism that would allow application code to determine the available encodings at runtime apart from the default encoding, which can be obtained from the system property microedition.encoding. The CLDC version of this class does not include the getEncoding() method from J2SE, which returns the name of the encoding used by an InputStreamReader.

Object — Reader — InputStreamReader

```
public class InputStreamReader extends Reader {
// Public Constructors
    public InputStreamReader(InputStream is);
    public InputStreamReader(InputStream is, String enc) throws UnsupportedEncodingException;
// Public Methods Overriding Reader
    public void close() throws IOException;
    public void mark(int readAheadLimit) throws IOException;
    public boolean markSupported();
    public int read() throws IOException;
    public int read(char[] cbuf, int off, int len) throws IOException;
    public boolean ready() throws IOException;
    public void reset() throws IOException;
    public long skip(long n) throws IOException;
}
```

InterruptedIOException

CLDC 1.0, MIDP 1.0

java.io

checked

This is an exception that is thrown when an I/O operation is interrupted, usually as a result of a timeout. The bytesTransferred() method can be used to find out how much data, if any, was transferred before the interruption occurred. This class is the same as its J2SE equivalent, apart from its inability to be serialized.

Object — Throwable — Exception — IOException — InterruptedIOException

```
public class InterruptedIOException extends IOException {
// Public Constructors
    public InterruptedIOException();
    public InterruptedIOException(String s);
// Public Instance Fields
    public int bytesTransferred;
}
```

IOException

CLDC 1.0, MIDP 1.0

java.io

checked

This exception signals that an error has occurred during an I/O operation. Some I/O failures are reported using a more specific exception derived from this class. IOException is not derived from java.lang.RuntimeException and therefore it must be caught and handled by application code. This class is the same as its J2SE equivalent, apart from its inability to be serialized.

Object — Throwable — Exception — IOException

```
public class IOException extends Exception {
// Public Constructors
```

```
    public IOException();
    public IOException(String s);
}
```

Subclasses: EOFException, InterruptedIOException, UnsupportedEncodingException,
UTFDataFormatException, javax.microedition.io.ConnectionNotFoundException

Thrown By: Too many methods to list.

OutputStream

java.io

OutputStream is an abstract class that defines methods used to write a stream of bytes to
an output source. The write() methods write either a single byte or an array of bytes to
the output stream. Any error encountered when writing the data results in an IOException. Note that some subclasses may buffer data internally instead of writing directly to
the underlying storage mechanism. Application code may use the flush() to force any
buffered data to be written out. Buffered data is automatically flushed when the stream
is closed by the close() method.

Like InputStream, OutputStream is *byte*-oriented and not character-oriented and cannot
safely be used to write character data by storing the bottom 8 bits of each character in a
byte and writing out the resulting byte array. Character data should be handled using
the writeUTF() or writeChars() methods of DataOutputStream or by using an OutputStreamWriter
with the appropriate encoding for the data being written.

```
public abstract class OutputStream {
// Public Constructors
    public OutputStream();
// Public Instance Methods
    public void close() throws IOException;                              empty
    public void flush() throws IOException;                             empty
    public abstract void write(int b) throws IOException;
    public void write(byte[] b) throws IOException;
    public void write(byte[] b, int off, int len) throws IOException;
}
```

Subclasses: ByteArrayOutputStream, DataOutputStream, PrintStream

Passed To: DataOutputStream.DataOutputStream(), OutputStreamWriter.OutputStreamWriter(),
PrintStream.PrintStream()

Returned By: javax.microedition.io.Connector.openOutputStream(),
javax.microedition.io.OutputConnection.openOutputStream()

Type Of: DataOutputStream.out

OutputStreamWriter

java.io

This is a subclass of Writer that writes its output into an 8-bit output stream. The mapping from the 16-bit Unicode characters passed into this class to the bytes required by
the underlying output stream is performed according to the encoding whose name is
passed to the constructor, or the default encoding of the host platform if the single-argument constructor is used.

CLDC devices typically support only their own default encoding. Therefore, it is
unlikely that many alternative encodings will be available. The CLDC specification does
not provide any mechanism that would allow application code to determine the available encodings at run time, apart from the default encoding which can be obtained

from the system property microedition.encoding. Note that the CLDC version of this class does not include the getEncoding() method from J2SE, which returns the name of the encoding used by an OutputStreamWriter.

Object — Writer — OutputStreamWriter

```
public class OutputStreamWriter extends Writer {
// Public Constructors
    public OutputStreamWriter(OutputStream os);
    public OutputStreamWriter(OutputStream os, String enc) throws UnsupportedEncodingException;
// Public Methods Overriding Writer
    public void close() throws IOException;
    public void flush() throws IOException;
    public void write(int c) throws IOException;
    public void write(char[ ] cbuf, int off, int len) throws IOException;
    public void write(String str, int off, int len) throws IOException;
}
```

PrintStream

CLDC 1.0, MIDP 1.0

java.io

PrintStream is an OutputStream subclass that contains methods that convert Java primitive types and objects into a printable format before writing them to an underlying Output-Stream.

The overloaded variations of the print() method handle primitives of type boolean, char, char[], int, long, String and Object. The string representation of an Object is obtained from its toString() method. The println() methods behave in the same way as print(), but follow their output with a newline character.

The System.out and System.err variables hold instances of PrintStream. Because streams of this type are often used when inserting debugging or tracing code where it would be inconvenient to catch exceptions, the print() and println() methods do not throw an IOException if an error is detected. Instead, they set an internal error state that can be checked by calling the checkError() method.

Object — OutputStream — PrintStream

```
public class PrintStream extends OutputStream {
// Public Constructors
    public PrintStream(OutputStream out);
// Public Instance Methods
    public boolean checkError();
    public void print(long l);
    public void print(int i);
    public void print(char[ ] s);
    public void print(Object obj);
    public void print(String s);
    public void print(char c);
    public void print(boolean b);
    public void println();
    public void println(long x);
    public void println(int x);
    public void println(Object x);
    public void println(String x);
    public void println(char[ ] x);
    public void println(char x);
```

```
    public void println(boolean x);
// Public Methods Overriding OutputStream
    public void close();
    public void flush();
    public void write(int b);
    public void write(byte[ ] buf, int off, int len);
// Protected Instance Methods
    protected void setError();
}
```

Type Of: System.{err, out}

Reader

java.io

Reader is an abstract class that defines the methods implemented by subclasses that provide character input. A Reader differs from an InputStream in that it works in terms of 16-bit Unicode characters rather than 8-bit bytes. An 8-bit InputStream can be converted to a sequence of Unicode characters by wrapping it with an instance of the InputStream-Reader class, which is the only concrete subclass of Reader provided in the CLDC java.io package.

Most of the methods provided by Reader are the same as those available from Input-Stream, except that the fundamental unit of transfer is a char rather than a byte. The read() methods copy data from the data source into a character array, or return a single character held in the least significant 16 bits of an int. The skip() method skips over the given number of chars in the input source, or until end-of-file is reached. The mark(), reset() and markSupported() methods behave the same as an InputStream, except that the limit value passed to the mark() method is expressed in characters, not bytes.

Reader does not have an available() method that returns the amount of data waiting to be read without blocking. Instead, it has a ready() method that simply returns true if there is some data to be read, and false if there is not.

```
public abstract class Reader {
// Protected Constructors
    protected Reader();
    protected Reader(Object lock);
// Public Instance Methods
    public abstract void close() throws IOException;
    public void mark(int readAheadLimit) throws IOException;
    public boolean markSupported();                                          constant
    public int read() throws IOException;
    public int read(char[ ] cbuf) throws IOException;
    public abstract int read(char[ ] cbuf, int off, int len) throws IOException;
    public boolean ready() throws IOException;                               constant
    public void reset() throws IOException;
    public long skip(long n) throws IOException;
// Protected Instance Fields
    protected Object lock;
}
```

Subclasses: InputStreamReader

UnsupportedEncodingException

java.io

This exception signals that an attempt has been made to create an InputStreamReader or an OutputStreamWriter using an encoding that the platform does not support. This class is the same as its J2SE equivalent, apart from its inability to be serialized.

Object — Throwable — Exception — IOException — UnsupportedEncodingException

```
public class UnsupportedEncodingException extends IOException {
// Public Constructors
   public UnsupportedEncodingException();
   public UnsupportedEncodingException(String s);
}
```

Thrown By: InputStreamReader.InputStreamReader(), OutputStreamWriter.OutputStreamWriter(), String.{getBytes(), String()}

UTFDataFormatException

java.io

This exception signals that an incorrect sequence of bytes has been found when reading a byte stream encoded in UTF-8. The UTF-8 encoding allows 16-bit Unicode characters to be sent in an 8-bit stream, where characters with values in the range 0-127, which are the most commonly used in Western locales, occupy only a single byte. This class is the same as its J2SE equivalent, apart from its inability to be serialized.

Object — Throwable — Exception — IOException — UTFDataFormatException

```
public class UTFDataFormatException extends IOException {
// Public Constructors
   public UTFDataFormatException();
   public UTFDataFormatException(String s);
}
```

Writer

java.io

Writer is an abstract class that defines the methods implemented by subclasses that provide character output. A Writer differs from an OutputStream in that it works in terms of 16-bit Unicode characters rather than 8-bit bytes. A sequence of Unicode characters can be safely converted to an 8-bit data stream by wrapping an output stream with an instance of the OutputStreamWriter class, which is the only concrete subclass of Writer provided in the CLDC java.io package.

Most of the methods provided by Writer are the same as those available from OutputStream, except that the fundamental unit of transfer is a char rather than a byte. The write() methods copy Unicode characters instead of bytes to the underlying storage. Writer also provides overloaded variants of write() that write out some or all of a String. Because some implementations may buffer data internally, Writer provides a flush() to force buffered data to be written. Buffered data is always written out when the close() method is called.

```
public abstract class Writer {
// Protected Constructors
   protected Writer();
   protected Writer(Object lock);
```

```
// Public Instance Methods
    public abstract void close() throws IOException;
    public abstract void flush() throws IOException;
    public void write(String str) throws IOException;
    public void write(char[ ] cbuf) throws IOException;
    public void write(int c) throws IOException;
    public void write(String str, int off, int len) throws IOException;
    public abstract void write(char[ ] cbuf, int off, int len) throws IOException;
// Protected Instance Fields
    protected Object lock;
}
```

Subclasses: OutputStreamWriter

CHAPTER 12

java.lang

The java.lang package, whose class hierarchy is shown in Figure 12-1, contains the classes that form the core of the Java language API. The CLDC version of this package contains just under half of the classes and interfaces of its J2SE counterpart. The major omissions are:

- Most of the Error classes, which are not required because the CLDC VM does not support them. Some of the J2SE Exception classes are also omitted.

- The Float and Double types, omitted because the VM does not provide floating point operations.

- Various other classes such as ClassLoader, SecurityManager and StrictMath which are not needed because the associated functionality is not part of the CLDC specification.

The most fundamental classes in this package are Object, Class and Throwable.

Object is the base class for all Java objects. The CLDC Object class provides most of the methods of its J2SE counterpart, with the notable exceptions of clone() and finalize(), which are omitted because neither cloning nor finalization is supported in the CLDC Java virtual machine.

Class contains the information used to manage a class in the Java virtual machine. The CLDC version of this class does not contain the methods from the J2SE version that are related to reflection, again because reflection is not provided by the CLDC virtual machine.

Throwable is the base class for all Java exceptions. Throwable has two subclasses, Exception and Error, that are the roots of separate class hierarchies of recoverable and non-recoverable errors, respectively. The set of Errors supported by the CLDC Java VM is much smaller than that in J2SE, because the VM considers most of the error conditions that are reported by J2SE to be fatal and hence does not need to be able to report them to Java code.

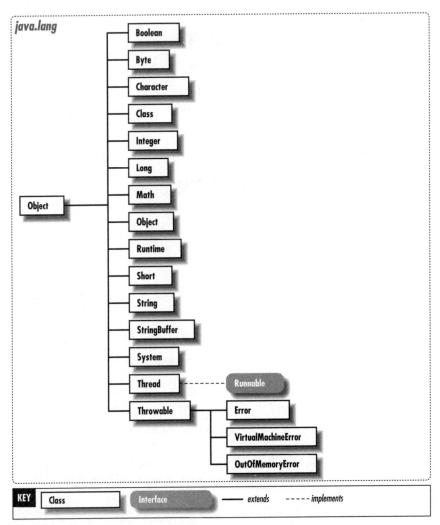

Figure 12-1: The java.lang hierarchy

ArithmeticException

java.lang   *unchecked*

This exception signals an attempt to divide by zero or use the modulus operator (%) to determine the remainder on division by zero. This class is the same as its J2SE equivalent, apart from its inability to be serialized.

Object — Throwable — Exception — RuntimeException — ArithmeticException

```
public class ArithmeticException extends RuntimeException {
// Public Constructors
    public ArithmeticException();
    public ArithmeticException(String s);
```

}

ArrayIndexOutOfBoundsException

java.lang

This exception signals an attempt to access an element of an array using an index that is negative or greater than or equal to the number of elements in the array (recall that arrays are zero-based in Java). This class is the same as its J2SE equivalent, apart from its inability to be serialized.

Object ─ Throwable ─ Exception ─ RuntimeException ─ IndexOutOfBoundsException ─ ArrayIndexOutOfBoundsException

```
public class ArrayIndexOutOfBoundsException extends IndexOutOfBoundsException {
// Public Constructors
    public ArrayIndexOutOfBoundsException();
    public ArrayIndexOutOfBoundsException(String s);
    public ArrayIndexOutOfBoundsException(int index);
}
```

ArrayStoreException

java.lang

This exception signals an attempt to store an object in an array entry that is not the same type as the array, a subclass of that type, or in the case of an array of interface types, is not an object that implements that interface. This class is the same as its J2SE equivalent, apart from its inability to be serialized.

Object ─ Throwable ─ Exception ─ RuntimeException ─ ArrayStoreException

```
public class ArrayStoreException extends RuntimeException {
// Public Constructors
    public ArrayStoreException();
    public ArrayStoreException(String s);
}
```

Boolean

java.lang

Boolean provides an object wrapper for a Java boolean primitive. The constructor initializes the wrapper with the value true or false, after which the object becomes immutable. For convenience, the static variables Boolean.TRUE and Boolean.FALSE refer to predefined instances of this class with the values true and false, respectively, and should normally be used instead of constructing a new instance.

The booleanValue() method can be used to retrieve the boolean value of a Boolean object. In addition, the toString() method will return the string "true" or "false" as appropriate.

```
public final class Boolean {
// Public Constructors
    public Boolean(boolean value);
// Public Instance Methods
    public boolean booleanValue();
// Public Methods Overriding Object
    public boolean equals(Object obj);
    public int hashCode();
    public String toString();
```

}

Byte CLDC 1.0, MIDP 1.0

java.lang

Byte provides an object wrapper for a Java byte primitive value. The constructor initializes the wrapper with a byte value, after which the object becomes immutable. The value associated with a Byte object can be retrieved using the byteValue() method.

The static parseByte() converts a numeric value held in a string into a primitive byte. The single-argument variant of this method assumes that the string is encoded in base 10; the two-argument variant can be used to specify a different number base if necessary. A NumberFormatException is thrown if the string does not represent a valid number in the given number base.

The static variables Byte.MIN_VALUE and Byte.MAX_VALUE are *byte* (not Byte) values that represent the smallest and largest values, respectively, that can be held in a byte primitive.

Note that this class is derived from Object and not Number, as the CLDC does not provide a Number class as the J2SE does.

```
public final class Byte {
// Public Constructors
    public Byte(byte value);
// Public Constants
    public static final byte MAX_VALUE;                                          =127
    public static final byte MIN_VALUE;                                          =-128
// Public Class Methods
    public static byte parseByte(String s) throws NumberFormatException;
    public static byte parseByte(String s, int radix) throws NumberFormatException;
// Public Instance Methods
    public byte byteValue();
// Public Methods Overriding Object
    public boolean equals(Object obj);
    public int hashCode();
    public String toString();
}
```

Character CLDC 1.0, MIDP 1.0

java.lang

Character provides an object wrapper for a Java char primitive. The constructor initializes the wrapper with a char value, after which the object is immutable. The value associated with a Character object can be retrieved using the charValue() method.

The Character class contains several static methods that are useful for handling characters without making any assumptions about the locale in which an application is executing. The digit() method returns the integer value of a character provided that it represents a digit in a given number base, or -1 if it does not. Use the isDigit() method to test whether a given character represents a numeric digit in a given number base. The isUpperCase() and isLowerCase() methods return true if the primitive char passed to them is an upper-case or lower-case letter, respectively, while toUpperCase() and toLowerCase() convert a char to upper- or lower-case and return the result, or the original char if it has no upper- or lower-case equivalent.

The static variables Character.MIN_VALUE and Character.MAX_VALUE are *char* (not Character) values that represent the smallest and largest values that can be held in a char primitive.

```
public final class Character {
// Public Constructors
    public Character(char value);
// Public Constants
    public static final int MAX_RADIX;                                      =36
    public static final char MAX_VALUE;                          ='[bsol ]uFFFF'
    public static final int MIN_RADIX;                                       =2
    public static final char MIN_VALUE;                                     =' '
// Public Class Methods
    public static int digit(char ch, int radix);
    public static boolean isDigit(char ch);
    public static boolean isLowerCase(char ch);
    public static boolean isUpperCase(char ch);
    public static char toLowerCase(char ch);
    public static char toUpperCase(char ch);
// Public Instance Methods
    public char charValue();
// Public Methods Overriding Object
    public boolean equals(Object obj);
    public int hashCode();
    public String toString();
}
```

Class

java.lang

This class contains information representing a Java class or interface. Only one instance of this object exists for each class loaded within the Java virtual machine, no matter how many instances of that class are created. The Class object for a class can be obtained by using the getClass() method of any instance of that class, or by calling the static Class forName() method and supplying the fully-qualified class name. For example, the expression Class.forName("java.lang.Class") would return a Class object for Class itself.

A Class object can be used to discover various attributes of a class. The getName() method returns the fully-qualified name of the class (e.g., java.lang.Class). The isArray() method returns true if the class represents an array, such as the one returned by the expression new Object[0].getClass(). The isInterface() returns true if the Class object to which it is applied represents an interface.

The isAssignableFrom() and isInstance() methods can be used to determine the relationship between one class or interface and another. The isInstance() method returns true if the object passed as its argument is of the same class as the Class object, or an instance of a subclass. If the Class object represents an interface, then the object passed as the argument to isInstance() must implement that interface or one of its subinterfaces.

The isAssignableFrom() method also takes a Class object as its argument and returns true if that object could be assigned to a varable of the type of Class to which it is applied.

The newInstance() method constructs a new instance of the Class to which it is applied using its no-argument constructor. An exception will occur if the class does not have a no-argument constructor, if the caller does not have access to that constructor, or if the class is abstract or represents an interface.

The getResourceAsStream() method returns an InputStream that can be used to read the content of a resource whose name is supplied as its argument. This method is typically used to access images or text files that are included in the same JAR file as a MIDlet or a package Java application. The resource name must be either an absolute name beginning with the "/" character (e.g., "/com/acme/MIDlets/resources/icon.png"), or a name that is resolved relative to the package of the Class object, such as "resources/icon.png". The latter would correspond to the same resource if the Class object on which it is invoked is for a class or interface in the com.acme.MIDlets package.

```
public final class Class {
// No Constructor
// Public Class Methods
    public static Class forName(String className) throws ClassNotFoundException;          native
// Public Instance Methods
    public String getName();                                                             native
    public java.io.InputStream getResourceAsStream(String name);
    public boolean isArray();                                                            native
    public boolean isAssignableFrom(Class cls);                                          native
    public boolean isInstance(Object obj);                                               native
    public boolean isInterface();                                                        native
    public Object newInstance() throws InstantiationException, IllegalAccessException;    native
// Public Methods Overriding Object
    public String toString();
}
```

Passed To: Class.isAssignableFrom()

Returned By: Class.forName(), Object.getClass()

ClassCastException   CLDC 1.0, MIDP 1.0

java.lang   *unchecked*

This exception signals an attempt to cast an object to a type that it is not an instance of, or an attempt to cast an object to an interface that it does not implement. This class is the same as its J2SE equivalent, apart from its inability to be serialized.

```
Object ─ Throwable ─ Exception ─ RuntimeException ─ ClassCastException
```

```
public class ClassCastException extends RuntimeException {
// Public Constructors
    public ClassCastException();
    public ClassCastException(String s);
}
```

ClassNotFoundException   CLDC 1.0, MIDP 1.0

java.lang   *checked*

This exception signals that the class named by the argument of the Class forName() method was not found. This class is the same as its J2SE equivalent, apart from its inability to be serialized.

```
Object ─ Throwable ─ Exception ─ ClassNotFoundException
```

```
public class ClassNotFoundException extends Exception {
// Public Constructors
    public ClassNotFoundException();
    public ClassNotFoundException(String s);
}
```

Thrown By: Class.forName()

Error

java.lang

Error is a subclass of Throwable. It is the base class for exceptions that are not likely to be recoverable by application code, but also do not represent programming errors (and hence are not derived from RuntimeException). Methods that might throw Errors are not required to indicate that fact by including a throws declaration. In the same manner, code that calls such a method is not required to catch the Error.

The number of Error subclasses defined by CLDC is much less than the number that exist in J2SE, primarily because the cause of most errors on this platform is device-specific and therefore not susceptible to common handling by platform-independent code. Errors that are reported as such in J2SE are often regarded as terminal conditions that should halt the execution of the virtual machine in CLDC.

This class is the same as its J2SE equivalent, apart from its inability to be serialized.

```
Object — Throwable — Error
```

```
public class Error extends Throwable {
// Public Constructors
    public Error();
    public Error(String s);
}
```

Subclasses: VirtualMachineError

Exception

java.lang

Exception is the base class for Java language exceptions. Exceptions represent non-fatal error conditions that applications may be able to recover from. Exception is derived from the Throwable class, which is also the parent of Error. However, exceptions derived from Error differ from those derived from Exception in that they represent conditions from which application code would not usually be expected to recover.

Methods that throw Exceptions are required to include a throws clause in their declarations, except under one condition: methods are not obliged to declare any exceptions that derive from the RuntimeException class. These types of exceptions typically indicate a programming error that cannot be recovered from.

This class is the same as its J2SE equivalent, apart from its inability to be serialized.

```
Object — Throwable — Exception
```

```
public class Exception extends Throwable {
// Public Constructors
    public Exception();
    public Exception(String s);
}
```

Subclasses: java.io.IOException, ClassNotFoundException, IllegalAccessException, InstantiationException, InterruptedException, RuntimeException, javax.microedition.midlet.MIDletStateChangeException, javax.microedition.rms.RecordStoreException

IllegalAccessException

java.lang

This exception signals that a class has attempted to perform an operation on an object which it does not have access. This typically occurs when an attempt is made to create an instance of a class using the Class newInstance() method and the executing code does not have access to the no-argument constructor, even though it has access to the class itself. This class is the same as its J2SE equivalent, apart from its inability to be serialized.

```
Object ─ Throwable ─ Exception ─ IllegalAccessException
```

```
public class IllegalAccessException extends Exception {
// Public Constructors
    public IllegalAccessException();
    public IllegalAccessException(String s);
}
```

Thrown By: Class.newInstance()

IllegalArgumentException

CLDC 1.0, MIDP 1.0

java.lang

unchecked

This exception signals that a method has been passed an argument whose value does not meet certain conditions. This exception is often thrown to signal that a null reference has been passed to a method that expects a non-null argument. This class is the same as its J2SE equivalent, apart from its inability to be serialized.

```
Object ─ Throwable ─ Exception ─ RuntimeException ─ IllegalArgumentException
```

```
public class IllegalArgumentException extends RuntimeException {
// Public Constructors
    public IllegalArgumentException();
    public IllegalArgumentException(String s);
}
```

Subclasses: IllegalThreadStateException, NumberFormatException

IllegalMonitorStateException

CLDC 1.0, MIDP 1.0

java.lang

unchecked

This is an exception that signals one of the following conditions:

- A thread has called the Object wait() method on a object for which it does not hold the monitor.

- A thread has called the Object notify() or notifyAll() method on a object for which it does not hold the monitor.

The *monitor* for an object obj is acquired either by synchronizing on that object using the synchronized (obj) expression, or by entering a non-static method of that object's class that is declared using the synchronized keyword.

This class is the same as its J2SE equivalent, apart from its inability to be serialized.

```
Object ─ Throwable ─ Exception ─ RuntimeException ─ IllegalMonitorStateException
```

```
public class IllegalMonitorStateException extends RuntimeException {
// Public Constructors
    public IllegalMonitorStateException();
    public IllegalMonitorStateException(String s);
}
```

IllegalStateException

java.lang   *unchecked*

This exception is thrown to indicate that a method has been invoked under inappropriate circumstances. For example, a method may throw this exception to indicate that it expected the caller to first set the parameters that it requires to complete its operation. This class is the same as its J2SE equivalent, apart from its inability to be serialized.

Object — Throwable — Exception — RuntimeException — IllegalStateException

```
public class IllegalStateException extends RuntimeException {
// Public Constructors
    public IllegalStateException();
    public IllegalStateException(String s);
}
```

IllegalThreadStateException

java.lang   *unchecked*

This exception is thrown when an operation is performed on a Thread that is not in the proper state. In J2SE, there are several circumstances in which this exception is thrown. In CLDC, however, most of these are not possible because the Thread operations that throw this exception simply do not exist. The only cause for this exception in CLDC is calling the start() method on a Thread that has already been started. This class is the same as its J2SE equivalent, apart from its inability to be serialized.

Object — Throwable — Exception — RuntimeException — IllegalArgumentException — IllegalThreadStateException

```
public class IllegalThreadStateException extends IllegalArgumentException {
// Public Constructors
    public IllegalThreadStateException();
    public IllegalThreadStateException(String s);
}
```

IndexOutOfBoundsException

java.lang   *unchecked*

This exception indicates that an operation used an index value that was invalid for the given data. J2SE provides two subclasses of IndexOutOfBoundsException that are commonly used with arrays and strings: ArrayIndexOutOfBoundsException and StringIndexOutOfBoundsException. This class is the same as its J2SE equivalent, apart from its inability to be serialized.

Object — Throwable — Exception — RuntimeException — IndexOutOfBoundsException

```
public class IndexOutOfBoundsException extends RuntimeException {
// Public Constructors
    public IndexOutOfBoundsException();
    public IndexOutOfBoundsException(String s);
}
```

Subclasses: ArrayIndexOutOfBoundsException, StringIndexOutOfBoundsException

InstantiationException

java.lang

This exception is thrown when the Class newInstance() method is used to either create an instance of a class that represents an array, or cannot be instantiated because it is an interface or is declared to be abstract. This class is the same as its J2SE equivalent, apart from its inability to be serialized.

```
Object ├ Throwable ├ Exception ├ InstantiationException
```

```
public class InstantiationException extends Exception {
// Public Constructors
    public InstantiationException();
    public InstantiationException(String s);
}
```

Thrown By: Class.newInstance()

Integer

java.lang

Integer provides an object wrapper for a Java int primitive value. The constructor initializes the wrapper with an int value, after which the object is immutable. The value associated with an Integer object can be retrieved as a byte, short, int or long using the byteValue(), shortValue(), intValue() and longValue() methods, respectively. If the value is too large to fit into a byte or short, the high-order bits of the integer are truncated.

The static parseInt() converts a numeric value held in a String into a primitive int. The single-argument variant of this method assumes that the string is encoded in base 10; the two-argument variant can be used to specify a different number base if necessary. A NumberFormatException is thrown if the String does not represent a valid number in the given number base. There are also two static valueOf methods that parse a string and return an Integer object— one assumes that the String is a base 10 number, the other accepts a number base argument.

The zero-argument toString() method returns a String representation of the value of the Integer encoded as a base 10 number. There is also a static variant of this method that prints the value of a given int as a base 10 number, as well as a two-argument variant that prints a value using digits from the number base supplied as its second argument. The static toHexString(), toOctalString and toBinaryString() methods return a String that represents the value of a given int as a number in base 16, 8 and 2 respectively.

The static variables Integer.MIN_VALUE and Integer.MAX_VALUE are *int* (not Integer) values that represent the smallest and largest values that can be held in a int primitive.

Note that this class is derived from Object and not Number, as the CLDC does not provide the Number class.

```
public final class Integer {
// Public Constructors
    public Integer(int value);
// Public Constants
    public static final int MAX_VALUE;                                      =2147483647
    public static final int MIN_VALUE;                                     =-2147483648
// Public Class Methods
    public static int parseInt(String s) throws NumberFormatException;
    public static int parseInt(String s, int radix) throws NumberFormatException;
    public static String toBinaryString(int i);
```

```
    public static String toHexString(int i);
    public static String toOctalString(int i);
    public static String toString(int i);
    public static String toString(int i, int radix);
    public static Integer valueOf(String s) throws NumberFormatException;
    public static Integer valueOf(String s, int radix) throws NumberFormatException;
// Public Instance Methods
    public byte byteValue();
    public int intValue();
    public long longValue();
    public short shortValue();
// Public Methods Overriding Object
    public boolean equals(Object obj);
    public int hashCode();
    public String toString();
}
```

Returned By: Integer.valueOf()

InterruptedException

CLDC 1.0, MIDP 1.0

java.lang

checked

In J2SE, this exception is thrown when one thread uses the interrupt() method to interrupt another thread that is blocked due to the Thread sleep() or join() methods. In CLDC, however, the Thread interrupt() method does not exist, so this exception will not actually be thrown in these cases. However, for reasons of compatibility, this exception is still declared to be thrown from the Object wait() and the Thread sleep() and join() methods.

The actual use of this exception is in the implementation of the socket support for the Generic Connection Framework, which is not a required part of the specification and is not visible to application code.

This class is the same as its J2SE equivalent, apart from its inability to be serialized.

```
Object ├ Throwable ├ Exception ├ InterruptedException
```

```
public class InterruptedException extends Exception {
// Public Constructors
    public InterruptedException();
    public InterruptedException(String s);
}
```

Thrown By: Object.wait(), Thread.{join(), sleep()}

Long

CLDC 1.0, MIDP 1.0

java.lang

Long provides an object wrapper for a Java long primitive. The constructor initializes the wrapper with a long value, after which the object is immutable. The value associated with a Long object can be retrieved using the longValue() method.

The static parseLong() converts a numeric value held in a String into a primitive long. The single-argument variant of this method assumes that the String is encoded in base 10; the two-argument variant can be used to specify a different number base if necessary. A NumberFormatException is thrown if the String does not represent a valid number in the given number base.

The zero-argument toString() method returns a String representation of the value of the Long encoded as a base 10 number. There is also a static variant of this method that prints the value of a given long as a base 10 number, as well as a two-argument variant that prints a value using digits from the number base supplied as its second argument.

The static variables Long.MIN_VALUE and Long.MAX_VALUE are *long* (not Long) values representing the smallest and largest values, respectively, that can be held in a long primitive.

Note that this class is derived from Object and not Number, as it is in the J2SE. This is because the CLDC does not provide the Number class.

```
public final class Long {
// Public Constructors
    public Long(long value);
// Public Constants
    public static final long MAX_VALUE;                                        =9223372036854775807
    public static final long MIN_VALUE;                                       =-9223372036854775808
// Public Class Methods
    public static long parseLong(String s) throws NumberFormatException;
    public static long parseLong(String s, int radix) throws NumberFormatException;
    public static String toString(long i);
    public static String toString(long i, int radix);
// Public Instance Methods
    public long longValue();
// Public Methods Overriding Object
    public boolean equals(Object obj);
    public int hashCode();
    public String toString();
}
```

Math   CLDC 1.0, MIDP 1.0

java.lang

The CLDC Math class is an extremely small subset of its J2SE counterpart, providing utility methods that work with int and long values. Most of the J2SE methods cannot be included because a CLDC VM does not provide for floating point arithmetic.

The abs() methods return the absolute value of an int or long pased as its argument. The max() method returns the larger of two ints or longs, while min() returns the smaller.

```
public final class Math {
// No Constructor
// Public Class Methods
    public static int abs(int a);                                                     strictfp
    public static long abs(long a);                                                   strictfp
    public static int max(int a, int b);                                              strictfp
    public static long max(long a, long b);                                           strictfp
    public static int min(int a, int b);                                              strictfp
    public static long min(long a, long b);                                           strictfp
}
```

NegativeArraySizeException   CLDC 1.0, MIDP 1.0

java.lang   *unchecked*

This exception signals that an attempt has been made to create an array with a negative number of elements. This class is the same as its J2SE equivalent, apart from its inability to be serialized.

Object ─ Throwable ─ Exception ─ RuntimeException ─ NegativeArraySizeException

```
public class NegativeArraySizeException extends RuntimeException {
// Public Constructors
    public NegativeArraySizeException();
    public NegativeArraySizeException(String s);
}
```

NullPointerException

java.lang   *unchecked*

This exception is thrown when an application attempts to use a null object reference.
This class is the same as its J2SE equivalent, apart from its inability to be serialized.

```
Object ⊢ Throwable ⊢ Exception ⊢ RuntimeException ⊢ NullPointerException
```

```
public class NullPointerException extends RuntimeException {
// Public Constructors
    public NullPointerException();
    public NullPointerException(String s);
}
```

NumberFormatException

java.lang   *unchecked*

This exception signals that an attempt has been made to convert a String to a numeric
type when the String contains a sequence of characters that does not form a valid number. This class is the same as its J2SE equivalent, apart from its inability to be serialized.

```
Object ⊢ Throwable ⊢ Exception ⊢ RuntimeException ⊢ IllegalArgumentException ⊢ NumberFormatException
```

```
public class NumberFormatException extends IllegalArgumentException {
// Public Constructors
    public NumberFormatException();
    public NumberFormatException(String s);
}
```

Thrown By: Byte.parseByte(), Integer.{parseInt(), valueOf()}, Long.parseLong(), Short.parseShort()

Object

java.lang

This class that represent a Java object. Object is an ancestor of every Java class. Therefore, a variable of type Object can be safely assigned a reference to any Java object,
array, or interface type without casting. In addition, the methods of this class can be
invoked on all objects, arrays, and interface types.

The equals() method determines whether the current object is equal to the object passed
in. The default case defines two objects as equivalent if they are the same object
instance. However, most subclasses override this method and use it to test for byte-to-
byte equivalence, instead of testing for the same object instance.

getClass() returns a Class object representing the object's class or interface. hashCode()
returns a hash code that can be used as a non-unique hashing key for the object. Note
that invoking this method on different objects that are equivalent according to equals()
must result in the same value being returned. Also, it is important to point out that two
different objects may return the same hash code. Subclasses may override this method
to return a hash code more suitable to particular object types. The value returned by

the Object implementation of this method can always be obtained by calling the System.identityHashCode() method.

The wait() method provides a way for a thread to wait for a specific condition to be met. notify() and notifyAll() allow another thread to signal that either one waiter or all waiters should re-evaluate whether that condition has been met. A thread that wishes to wait should first obtain the monitor of an object. This can be done either by entering an instance method of that object that is declared to be synchronized, or by entering a synchronized block on that object and invoking one of its wait() methods. Depending on the variant of wait() that is used, the calling thread will be suspended until another thread notifies the condition or until a given time interval expires. To notify a condition on an object, a thread must obtain the object's monitor and invoke the object's notify() or notifyAll() method. If notify() is used, one thread waiting on the object is resumed and returns from its wait(). If notifyAll() is used, it resumes all waiting threads.

Note that the CLDC Object class does not include the J2SE clone() and finalize methods. This is because cloning and finalization are not supported by a CLDC virtual machine.

```
public class Object {
// Public Constructors
    public Object();                                                           empty
// Public Instance Methods
    public boolean equals(Object obj);
    public final Class getClass();                                             native
    public int hashCode();                                                     native
    public final void notify();                                                native
    public final void notifyAll();                                             native
    public String toString();
    public final void wait() throws InterruptedException;
    public final void wait(long timeout) throws InterruptedException;          native
    public final void wait(long timeout, int nanos) throws InterruptedException;
}
```

Subclasses: Too many classes to list.

Passed To: Too many methods to list.

Returned By: Class.newInstance(), java.util.Enumeration.nextElement(), java.util.Hashtable.{get(), put(), remove()}, java.util.Stack.{peek(), pop(), push()}, java.util.Vector.{elementAt(), firstElement(), lastElement()}

Type Of: java.io.Reader.lock, java.io.Writer.lock, java.util.Vector.elementData

OutOfMemoryError   CLDC 1.0, MIDP 1.0

java.lang   *error*

An OutOfMemoryError is thrown when an allocation of memory has been attempted, either in Java code or native code, and both the VM and the garbage collector cannot satisfy the request. This class is the same as its J2SE equivalent, apart from its inability to be serialized.

```
Object — Throwable — Error — VirtualMachineError — OutOfMemoryError
```

```
public class OutOfMemoryError extends VirtualMachineError {
// Public Constructors
    public OutOfMemoryError();
    public OutOfMemoryError(String s);
}
```

Runnable

java.lang

This interface is implemented by a class containing code that is to be run either in a thread of its own or with a TimerTask. The code to be scheduled should be implemented in the run() method.

```
public interface Runnable {
// Public Instance Methods
    public abstract void run();
}
```

Implementations: Thread, java.util.TimerTask

Passed To: Thread.Thread(), javax.microedition.lcdui.Display.callSerially()

Runtime

java.lang

The Runtime class contains methods and variables that provide access to low-level facilities provided by the Java virtual machine. In order to access these facilities, application code must first use the static getRuntime() method to obtain an instance of the Runtime class. The CLDC version of this class contains only a small subset of the functionality of its J2SE counterpart.

The exit() method causes the virtual machine to terminate. A CLDC application is permitted to use this method. However, a MIDlet will receive a SecurityException if it attempts to do so.

The gc() method hints to the garbage collector that it should attempt to reclaim unreferenced memory. Garbage collectors implemented in small-footprint virtual machines (e,g, the KVM) are typically quite agressive at cleaning up unused memory, so the programmer should not have to call this method very often. The totalMemory() method returns the total amount of memory, in bytes, occupied by the Java virtual machine. In some environments, demand for more memory can cause this value to increase as the VM uses extra system resources. The freeMemory() method returns a value that indicates approximately how much of the total memory occupied by the Java VM is free for allocation to new objects.

```
public class Runtime {
// No Constructor
// Public Class Methods
    public static Runtime getRuntime();
// Public Instance Methods
    public void exit(int status);
    public long freeMemory();                                         native
    public void gc();                                                 native
    public long totalMemory();                                        native
}
```

Returned By: Runtime.getRuntime()

RuntimeException

java.lang

A base class for Exception subclasses that need not be be declared in the throws clause of a method definition and, consequently, application code need not catch. Exceptions of this type are generally caused by programming errors and need to be addressed during application development, rather than attempting recovery at run time. This class is the same as its J2SE equivalent, apart from its inability to be serialized.

```
Object — Throwable — Exception — RuntimeException
```

```
public class RuntimeException extends Exception {
// Public Constructors
   public RuntimeException();
   public RuntimeException(String s);
}
```

Subclasses: ArithmeticException, ArrayStoreException, ClassCastException, IllegalArgumentException, IllegalMonitorStateException, IllegalStateException, IndexOutOfBoundsException, NegativeArraySizeException, NullPointerException, SecurityException, java.util.EmptyStackException, java.util.NoSuchElementException

SecurityException
java.lang

CLDC 1.0, MIDP 1.0

unchecked

This exception signals that a run time security check has been violated. This class is the same as its J2SE equivalent, apart from its inability to be serialized.

```
Object — Throwable — Exception — RuntimeException — SecurityException
```

```
public class SecurityException extends RuntimeException {
// Public Constructors
   public SecurityException();
   public SecurityException(String s);
}
```

Short
java.lang

CLDC 1.0, MIDP 1.0

Short provides an object wrapper for a Java short primitive. The constructor initializes the wrapper with a short value, after which the object becomes immutable. The value associated with a Short object can be retrieved using the shortValue() method.

The static parseShort() converts a numeric value held in a String into a primitive short. The single-argument variant of this method assumes that the String is encoded in base 10; the two-argument variant can be used to specify a different number base if necessary. A NumberFormatException is thrown if the String does not represent a valid number in the given number base.

The static variables Short.MIN_VALUE and Short.MAX_VALUE are *short* (not Short) values that represent the smallest and largest values, respectively, that can be held in a short primitive.

Note that this class is derived from Object and not Number. This is because CLDC does not provide the Number class.

```
public final class Short {
// Public Constructors
   public Short(short value);
// Public Constants
   public static final short MAX_VALUE;                              =32767
   public static final short MIN_VALUE;                              =-32768
// Public Class Methods
   public static short parseShort(String s) throws NumberFormatException;
```

```
      public static short parseShort(String s, int radix) throws NumberFormatException;
// Public Instance Methods
      public short shortValue();
// Public Methods Overriding Object
      public boolean equals(Object obj);
      public int hashCode();
      public String toString();
}
```

String

java.lang

This class represents a immutable character string. Operations on String objects that change their content actually place their results in other String objects. When concatenating strings or changing the values of characters within a string, it is more efficient to use a StringBuffer instead.

The CLDC String class is similar to its J2SE equivalent, but lacks the following methods: compareToIgnoreCase(), copyValueOf(), equalsIgnoreCase() and intern(). It also does not contain the variants of lastIndexOf() that accept a String- valued argument, or the valueOf() methods for types float and double.

A String can be constructed as a copy of another String, from the content of a StringBuffer, or from an array of characters or bytes. When constructing a String from bytes, the appropriate character encoding must be used; if an encoding is not specified, the platform's default encoding is assumed. A String can also be created by applying the static valueOf() methods to a boolean, a char, an array of characters (char[]), an int, a long or an arbitrary Java Object. With an Object, the String is created using the return value of the object's toString() method.

The toCharArray() method returns an array of chars initialized with the content of the String. The getChars() method is similar, but requires the caller to allocate the destination array and can be used to extract a subset of the string. The getBytes() methods copy a subset of the String into a pre-allocated byte array, using either a specified encoding or the platform's default encoding. The charAt() method can be used to retrieve the value of a single character whose location is specified by a zero-based index. The length of the String, in characters, can be obtained using the length() method.

There are several methods that can be used to compare strings or search the content of a string. The compareTo() method performs a comparison of one string with another; it returns 0 if they are equal, or a negative or positive value depending on whether the source string is lexicographically less than or greater than the string passed as an argument. The startsWith() and endsWith() method determine whether a string starts or ends with a sequence of characters represented by a second string, while the regionMatches() method determines whether a region of the string matches a given region (of the same length) of another string.

The indexOf() method looks for either an individual character or a substring. It returns the offset at which the match was found, or -1 if there was no match, and the search may start either at the beginning of the String or from any specified index within it. The lastIndexOf() method is similar but returns the index of the last match for a given character, searching back either from the end of the string or from a given offset. Note that unlike indexOf(), there is no variant of lastIndexOf() that accepts a string-valued argument.

The replace() method returns a new String object in which all occurrences of one character have been replaced by a second character. The substring() methods return a new String created from a given range of characters from the String to which it is applied. The toUpperCase() and toLowerCase() methods create a new String in which the characters of the original have been converted to upper- or lower-case respectively (characters that are not case-dependent are left unchanged.) The trim() method returns a new String formed by removing all leading and trailing white space from the String to which it is applied.

```java
public final class String {
// Public Constructors
    public String();
    public String(byte[ ] bytes);
    public String(String value);
    public String(char[ ] value);
    public String(StringBuffer buffer);
    public String(byte[ ] bytes, String enc) throws java.io.UnsupportedEncodingException;
    public String(byte[ ] bytes, int off, int len);
    public String(char[ ] value, int offset, int count);
    public String(byte[ ] bytes, int off, int len, String enc) throws java.io.UnsupportedEncodingException;
// Public Class Methods
    public static String valueOf(char c);
    public static String valueOf(int i);
    public static String valueOf(long l);
    public static String valueOf(boolean b);
    public static String valueOf(Object obj);
    public static String valueOf(char[ ] data);
    public static String valueOf(char[ ] data, int offset, int count);
// Public Instance Methods
    public char charAt(int index);                                                          native
    public int compareTo(String anotherString);
    public String concat(String str);
    public boolean endsWith(String suffix);
    public byte[ ] getBytes();
    public byte[ ] getBytes(String enc) throws java.io.UnsupportedEncodingException;
    public void getChars(int srcBegin, int srcEnd, char[ ] dst, int dstBegin);
    public int indexOf(int ch);                                                             native
    public int indexOf(String str);
    public int indexOf(int ch, int fromIndex);                                              native
    public int indexOf(String str, int fromIndex);
    public int lastIndexOf(int ch);
    public int lastIndexOf(int ch, int fromIndex);
    public int length();
    public boolean regionMatches(boolean ignoreCase, int toffset, String other, int ooffset, int len);
    public String replace(char oldChar, char newChar);
    public boolean startsWith(String prefix);
    public boolean startsWith(String prefix, int toffset);
    public String substring(int beginIndex);
    public String substring(int beginIndex, int endIndex);
    public char[ ] toCharArray();
    public String toLowerCase();
    public String toUpperCase();
    public String trim();
// Public Methods Overriding Object
    public boolean equals(Object anObject);                                                 native
    public int hashCode();
    public String toString();
}
```

Passed To: Too many methods to list.

Returned By: Too many methods to list.

Type Of: javax.microedition.io.HttpConnection.{GET, HEAD, POST}

StringBuffer

java.lang

A StringBuffer is an array of characters that can be expanded or contracted as necessary. StringBuffers are typically used to construct an array of characters that is then converted into an immutable String.

The characters that make up the content of a StringBuffer are held in an internal array. The number of entries in the array is referred to as the *capacity* of the StringBuffer, while the actual number of characters in use is referred to as its size. A StringBuffer is constructed with a specific initial capacity (the default is 16 characters). It can also be constructed from the content of a String, in which case an appropriate initial capacity is determined. When the size approaches the capacity, a new character array is allocated and the existing characters are copied into it. Note that this can be a costly operation that may have to be repeated if the StringBuffer's size grows continuously. If possible, the StringBuffer should be created with sufficient capacity to hold all of the characters that it will contain.

Following construction, the ensureCapacity() method is used to ensure that the internal array can hold at least the number of characters specified without needing to be expanded any further. capacity() returns the current capacity of the StringBuffer, while length() returns its actual size. The actual number of characters in use can be changed by calling the setLength() method. If the new length is smaller than the old length, the characters at the end are lost. If it is larger, null characters are appended.

A common use of a StringBuffer is to concatenate several Strings. This can be achieved by using one of the overloaded append() methods, which accept arguments of type boolean, char, char[], int, long, Object and String. These methods convert the target data value to character form and add its content to the end of the internal array. Each of these methods returns a reference to the StringBuffer itself, so that the programmer can chain commands together (e.g., sb.append("x = ").append(x)). The toString() method is used to convert the characters in a StringBuffer into an immutable String.

It is also possible to insert content into a StringBuffer using one of the insert() methods, which has the same variants as the append() methods. These methods insert characters before the position given by the specified index, shifting all characters that follow to higher indices. As with append(), these methods also return a reference to the StringBuffer to allow command chaining. The value of a single character can be changed using the setCharAt() method; this method supplies the new character value and the index of the character to replace. Characters can be removed from the StringBuffer using the delete() and deleteCharAt() methods. Finally, the content of the internal array can be reversed efficiently by calling reverse().

Apart from toString(), there are two ways to extract characters from a StringBuffer. To get the value of a single character, invoke the charAt() method with the index of the required character in the internal array. To get a range of characters in the form of a String, use one of the two variants of substring().

```
public final class StringBuffer {
// Public Constructors
    public StringBuffer();
    public StringBuffer(String str);
```

java.lang

```
    public StringBuffer(int length);
// Public Instance Methods
    public StringBuffer append(char[ ] str);                                        synchronized
    public StringBuffer append(String str);                                  native synchronized
    public StringBuffer append(Object obj);                                        synchronized
    public StringBuffer append(boolean b);
    public StringBuffer append(long l);
    public StringBuffer append(int i);                                                    native
    public StringBuffer append(char c);                                            synchronized
    public StringBuffer append(char[ ] str, int offset, int len);                  synchronized
    public int capacity();
    public char charAt(int index);                                                 synchronized
    public StringBuffer delete(int start, int end);                                synchronized
    public StringBuffer deleteCharAt(int index);                                   synchronized
    public void ensureCapacity(int minimumCapacity);                               synchronized
    public void getChars(int srcBegin, int srcEnd, char[ ] dst, int dstBegin);     synchronized
    public StringBuffer insert(int offset, int i);
    public StringBuffer insert(int offset, Object obj);                            synchronized
    public StringBuffer insert(int offset, long l);
    public StringBuffer insert(int offset, boolean b);
    public StringBuffer insert(int offset, char c);                                synchronized
    public StringBuffer insert(int offset, char[ ] str);                           synchronized
    public StringBuffer insert(int offset, String str);                           synchronized
    public int length();
    public StringBuffer reverse();                                                 synchronized
    public void setCharAt(int index, char ch);                                     synchronized
    public void setLength(int newLength);                                          synchronized
// Public Methods Overriding Object
    public String toString();                                                            native
}
```

Passed To: String.String()

Returned By: Too many methods to list.

StringIndexOutOfBoundsException   CLDC 1.0, MIDP 1.0

java.lang   *unchecked*

This exception is thrown when an operation is attempted on a String or StringBuffer object involving an index that is either negative or too large. This class is the same as its J2SE equivalent, apart from its inability to be serialized.

| Object |—| Throwable |—| Exception |—| RuntimeException |—| IndexOutOfBoundsException |—| StringIndexOutOfBoundsException |

```
public class StringIndexOutOfBoundsException extends IndexOutOfBoundsException {
// Public Constructors
    public StringIndexOutOfBoundsException();
    public StringIndexOutOfBoundsException(int index);
    public StringIndexOutOfBoundsException(String s);
}
```

System   CLDC 1.0, MIDP 1.0

java.lang

The System class contains static methods and variables that provide access to low-level facilities. The CLDC version of this class contains only a small subset of the functionality of its J2SE counterpart.

The public static variables out and err are PrintStream objects that can be used for standard output and error output. With J2ME, these streams are useful when running code in an emulated environment, where they typically result in the creation of log files. Note that there is no in variable as there is no standard input stream for a CLDC device.

The currentTimeMillis() method returns the current time as a millisecond offset from 0:00 UTC on January 1st, 1970. This is the same representation used by the java.util.Date and java.util.Calendar classes.

The exit() method causes the virtual machine to terminate. A CLDC application is permitted to invoke this method. However, a MIDlet will receive a SecurityException if it attempts to do so. The gc() method hints to the garbage collector that it should attempt to reclaim unreferenced memory. Note that the garbage collectors implemented in the small-footprint virtual machines (such as the KVM) are aggressive at cleaning up unused memory, so this method should not need to called very often.

The identityHashCode() method returns a system-defined hash code for the object passed as its argument. This method returns the same value as the hashCode() method in the Object class would for the same object. It is provided as a convenience because many classes override the hashCode() method to return a different hash code.

The arraycopy() method provides an efficient means of copying a portion of an array of objects into a separate array. The source and destination arrays may be the same. In addition, the source and target ranges may overlap. The getProperty() method returns the value of a named system property. CLDC does not provide any means to retrieve the complete list of available properties. Instead, an application must know beforehand the names of the properties that it accesses. The properties defined by CLDC are listed in Chapter 2; those for MIDP are listed in Chapter 3.

```
public final class System {
// No Constructor
// Public Constants
    public static final java.io.PrintStream err;
    public static final java.io.PrintStream out;
// Public Class Methods
    public static void arraycopy(Object src, int src_position, Object dst, int dst_position, int length);     native
    public static long currentTimeMillis();                                                                   native
    public static void exit(int status);
    public static void gc();
    public static String getProperty(String key);
    public static int identityHashCode(Object x);                                                             native
}
```

Thread

java.lang

runnable

A class that represents a thread of execution in the Java virtual machine. Each thread has its own call stack and its own copy of local variables created by the Java methods that it executes.

An application may create a new thread of execution by instantiating a subclass of Thread and overriding the run() method, or by implementing a Runnable interface and passing its reference to the Thread constructor. A new thread is created in an inactive state. To begin execution, its start() method must be invoked. The total number of threads in existence can be obtained by calling the static activeCount() method.

Once a thread is running, it continues to do so until the run() of the Thread subclass terminates, or the Runnable returns control to its caller. Note that even though its thread of execution has ended, a Thread object continues to exist until all references to it have been released and the object is removed by the garbage collector. The isAlive() method can be used to determine whether a Thread object still has an active thread of execution.

Unlike J2SE, the CLDC Thread class does not provide the stop(), suspend() and resume() methods. However, there are two Thread methods that allow a thread to suspend its own execution. The static sleep() method suspends the thread for a fixed period of time specified in milliseconds. The thread will be scheduled for resumption when the delay period expires, but may not resume immediately if another thread is currently running. The join() method forces the current thread to block until the passed-in Thread thread terminates. Both sleep() and join() can throw an InterruptedException in the event of an interruption. (In practice, this is not likely to happen because the CLDC Thread does not include the J2SE interrupt() method.) The yield() method allows a thread to temporarily yield control to other threads that are waiting to run.

Each thread has an execution priority that may be used when determining which thread should be chosen for execution. The setPriority() can be used to set a thread's priority and the getPriority() method used to retrieve it. Three standard priority levels (MIN_PRIORITY, NORM_PRIORITY and MAX_PRIORITY) are defined. Only priorities in the range of MIN_PRIORITY to MAX_PRIORITY inclusive are valid. Threads with higher priority that are ready to run are chosen in preference over those with lower priority. The algorithm used to choose between threads that have the same priority is not defined and therefore may be platform- and VM-dependent.

The static currentThread() is used to obtain a reference to the Thread that is currently executing. This method can be used to allow a thread to perform operations on itself.

```
Object ├─ Thread ┤┈ Runnable

public class Thread implements Runnable {
// Public Constructors
    public Thread();
    public Thread(Runnable target);
// Public Constants
    public static final int MAX_PRIORITY;                                      =10
    public static final int MIN_PRIORITY;                                       =1
    public static final int NORM_PRIORITY;                                      =5
// Public Class Methods
    public static int activeCount();                                        native
    public static Thread currentThread();                                   native
    public static void sleep(long millis) throws InterruptedException;      native
    public static void yield();                                             native
// Public Instance Methods
    public final int getPriority();                                      default:5
    public final boolean isAlive();                            native default:false
    public final void join() throws InterruptedException;
    public final void setPriority(int newPriority);
    public void start();                                     native synchronized
// Methods Implementing Runnable
    public void run();
// Public Methods Overriding Object
    public String toString();
}
```

Returned By: Thread.currentThread()

Throwable

java.lang

Throwable is the base class from which all Java exception types are derived. Throwable objects may be constructed with an associated message that provides diagnostic information relating to the cause of the exception. The message, if it is set, can be retrieved using the getMessage() method.

Throwable has two subclasses that are base classes for different types of exceptions. The Error class and its subclasses describe errors that application code is not expected to recover from. J2SE has a large number of error subclasses; however, the CLDC supports only two of them. The Exception class is the base class for exceptions that an application can recover from. Application code is required to declare any Exceptions that it throws. It must also catch those exceptions thrown by methods that it invokes, apart from RuntimeException and its subclasses.

A Throwable contains a stack backtrace that contains the method call stack at the point at which the exception was thrown. The stack trace may be printed using the printStackTrace() method. Unlike J2SE, the CLDC Throwable class does not include a stack trace when it is created and does not provide a fillInStackTrace() method to force the stack trace to be written to it on demand. The CLDC reference implementation virtual machine fills in the stack trace only when the exception is thrown.

```
public class Throwable {
// Public Constructors
    public Throwable();
    public Throwable(String message);
// Public Instance Methods
    public String getMessage();                                default:null
    public void printStackTrace();
// Public Methods Overriding Object
    public String toString();
}
```

Subclasses: Error, Exception

VirtualMachineError

java.lang

error

This is an error that indicates that a fatal condition has been detected with the Java virtual machine. In CLDC, this error is never thrown. Instead, it is used only as the parent class of OutOfMemoryError. This class is the same as its J2SE equivalent, apart from its inability to be serialized.

```
Object — Throwable — Error — VirtualMachineError
```

```
public abstract class VirtualMachineError extends Error {
// Public Constructors
    public VirtualMachineError();
    public VirtualMachineError(String s);
}
```

Subclasses: OutOfMemoryError

CHAPTER 13

java.util

The java.util package, whose class hierarchy is shown in Figure 13-1, contains several utility classes that are of general use, but not central enough to the Java language to be included in the java.lang package.

The Java 2 version 1.3 java.util package contains 54 classes and interfaces. By contrast, the CLDC version contains only 10 classes; MIDP adds another two for timer handling. As a result, these platforms have drastically reduced support for collections and internationalization. The CDC platform provides a much more complete implementation of this package, leaving out only 7 classes, and the Foundation Profile requires that all of the J2SE classes and interfaces be present. As with the other packages in this reference section, we won't address the CDC and Foundation Profile versions here because the classes they contain are identical to those in J2SE. See *Java in a Nutshell* (O'Reilly) for more information.

The collection classes in this package are a subset of those available with JDK 1.1. All vestiges of the Java 2 collections framework have been removed. One consequence of this is that some classes have been reparented. Vector, for example, is derived from Object in CLDC rather than from AbstractList, as it is in J2SE. Other notable changes are the removal of the Properties class as well as the Dictionary class, the latter being the parent of Hashtable. In CLDC, Hashtable remains, but it is derived from Object instead.

CLDC retains the J2SE Calendar and Date classes, but with reduced functionality. See the descriptions of these classes in this chapter for more detailed information.

The removal of the Cloneable, Comparable and Serializable interfaces from the CLDC java.lang package means that some of the classes in the java.util can no longer implement these interfaces. In practice, this will have little effect since most of the facilities that use these interfaces have also been removed. A possible minor annoyance is that it is no longer possible to compare two Date objects using the compareTo() method as in J2SE.

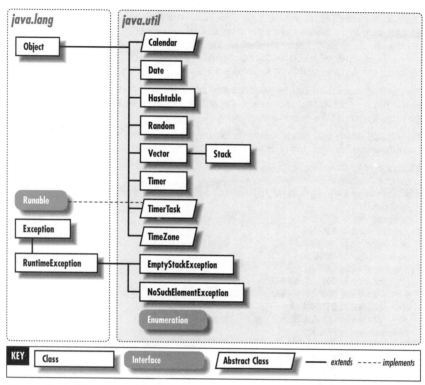

Figure 13-1: The java.util hierarchy

Calendar

CLDC 1.0, MIDP 1.0

java.util

Calendar is an abstract base class for platform-dependent classes that convert between date and time offsets. Since the rules for converting between an absolute UTC time and a date may depend on local conventions, application code does not directly instantiate a subclass of Calendar. Instead, it uses one of the static getInstance() methods, which returns an object that can handle dates using rules appropriate to the device's default locale. This arrangement allows an application running in a device in a western locale to obtain a Calendar that uses the rules of the Gregorian calendar, while allowing the same application to work with other calendars (such as Japanese Gregorian) in other locales.

The proper conversion of a point in time measured in UTC depends on the time zone in which a device is being used. The Calendar object returned by the zero-argument variant of getInstance() performs the proper conversions for the default time zone of the device it is running on. To create a Calendar for a different time zone, obtain a TimeZone object for that time zone and use the variant of getInstance() that accepts a TimeZone argument. Alternatively, any Calendar offset can be set to work in a different time zone by calling the setTimeZone() method.

The date and time associated with a Calendar object can be set from a Date object using the setTime() method, or to an absolute time using the setTimeInMillis() method, which requires a millisecond offset from 0:00 UTC on January 1st, 1970. Once the time has been set, the get() method can be used to get various fields of the associated date. The date or time field that is required is specified using one of the constants defined by the Calendar. For example, to get the year associated with a given date, use the expression get(Calendar.YEAR). Constants are also defined that correspond to days of the week and months of the year. To test whether a date falls on a Thursday, use the expression (cal.get(Calendar.DAY_OF_WEEK) == Calendar.THURSDAY), or to check whether the date falls in May, use (cal.get(Calendar.MONTH) == Calendar.MAY).

The reverse conversion can be performed by using the set() method to change the individual fields of a Calendar and calling the getTime() or getTimeInMillis() method to obtain the corresponding Date or millisecond time offset.

The equals(), after() and before() methods can be used to compare the date and time in a Calendar to another object, which must also be of type Calendar.

public abstract class **Calendar** {	
// Protected Constructors	
protected **Calendar**( );	
// Public Constants	
public static final int **AM**;	=0
public static final int **AM_PM**;	=9
public static final int **APRIL**;	=3
public static final int **AUGUST**;	=7
public static final int **DATE**;	=5
public static final int **DAY_OF_MONTH**;	=5
public static final int **DAY_OF_WEEK**;	=7
public static final int **DECEMBER**;	=11
public static final int **FEBRUARY**;	=1
public static final int **FRIDAY**;	=6
public static final int **HOUR**;	=10
public static final int **HOUR_OF_DAY**;	=11
public static final int **JANUARY**;	=0
public static final int **JULY**;	=6
public static final int **JUNE**;	=5
public static final int **MARCH**;	=2
public static final int **MAY**;	=4
public static final int **MILLISECOND**;	=14
public static final int **MINUTE**;	=12
public static final int **MONDAY**;	=2
public static final int **MONTH**;	=2
public static final int **NOVEMBER**;	=10
public static final int **OCTOBER**;	=9
public static final int **PM**;	=1
public static final int **SATURDAY**;	=7
public static final int **SECOND**;	=13
public static final int **SEPTEMBER**;	=8
public static final int **SUNDAY**;	=1
public static final int **THURSDAY**;	=5
public static final int **TUESDAY**;	=3
public static final int **WEDNESDAY**;	=4
public static final int **YEAR**;	=1
// Public Class Methods	
public static Calendar **getInstance**( );	*synchronized*
public static Calendar **getInstance**(TimeZone *zone*);	*synchronized*
// Public Instance Methods	
public boolean **after**(Object *when*);	
public boolean **before**(Object *when*);	
public final int **get**(int *field*);	

```
    public final Date getTime();
    public TimeZone getTimeZone();
    public final void set(int field, int value);
    public final void setTime(Date date);
    public void setTimeZone(TimeZone value);
// Public Methods Overriding Object
    public boolean equals(Object obj);
// Protected Instance Methods
    protected long getTimeInMillis();
    protected void setTimeInMillis(long millis);
}
```

Returned By: Calendar.getInstance()

Date   CLDC 1.0, MIDP 1.0
java.util

The Date class represents a date and time held internally as a millisecond offset from 0:00 UTC on January 1st, 1970. The default constructor creates a Date that represents the date and time at the time of its creation. A Date object for an arbitrary time can be created by passing the appropriate offset to the Date(long offset) constructor. Negative offsets can be used to represent dates in 1969 and earlier years. The time associated with a Date can be changed using the setTime() method and the time offset for a Date can be obtained using getTime().

The CLDC version of Date is much simpler than the J2SE implementation. Deprecated APIs and constructors have been removed, as have methods that allow two Date objects to be compared. A consequence of this is that it is no longer possible to convert between a Date object and the corresponding parts of a date, such as year, month, day, etc. The Calendar class must be used to perform these conversions instead.

Note that a Date object always contains a time offset measured relative to UTC. To work in other time zones, an appropriate TimeZone object must be obtained and used together with an instance of the Calendar class.

```
public class Date {
// Public Constructors
    public Date();
    public Date(long date);
// Public Instance Methods
    public long getTime();                                   default:1010205995686
    public void setTime(long time);
// Public Methods Overriding Object
    public boolean equals(Object obj);
    public int hashCode();
}
```

Passed To: Calendar.setTime(), Timer.{schedule(), scheduleAtFixedRate()}, javax.microedition.lcdui.DateField.setDate()

Returned By: Calendar.getTime(), javax.microedition.lcdui.DateField.getDate()

EmptyStackException

CLDC 1.0, MIDP 1.0

java.util

unchecked

This is an exception that is thrown to signal that an attempt has been made to remove or peek at the top element of an empty Stack. This class is the same as its J2SE equivalent, apart from its inability to be serialized.

Object — Throwable — Exception — RuntimeException — EmptyStackException

```
public class EmptyStackException extends RuntimeException {
// Public Constructors
    public EmptyStackException();
}
```

Enumeration

CLDC 1.0, MIDP 1.0

java.util

Enumeration is an interface that provides methods to access an underlying sequence of objects that can be traversed in an implementation-defined order. An Enumeration is often used to traverse the elements of a Vector as an alternative to directly accessing each element by its index.

The hasMoreElements() method returns false if the Enumeration is empty or has already returned its last element. The first call to nextElement() returns the first element in the Enumeration, if it is not empty. Each subsequent invocation of this method returns the following element. Calling this method after the last element has been returned results in a NoSuchElementException. The hasMoreElements() is typically called before each use of nextElement() to check whether the end of the sequence has been reached. Note that the values of an Enumeration can be iterated through only once; there is no way to reset it to the beginning.

```
public interface Enumeration {
// Public Instance Methods
    public abstract boolean hasMoreElements();
    public abstract Object nextElement();
}
```

Returned By: Hashtable.{elements(), keys()}, Vector.elements()

Hashtable

CLDC 1.0, MIDP 1.0

java.util

Hashtable is a collection class in which objects (referred to as *values*) are stored with associated keys. An entry is added to the Hashtable using the put() method, which takes a key and a value. Both the key and the value can be arbitrary Java objects, but neither may be null. Only one instance of each key may appear in the Hashtable; an attempt to store a second value with the same key will replace the first value. Key equality is determined by using the equals() method.

The value associated with a key can be obtained by passing the key to the get() method. If there is no value in the Hashtable with the supplied key, then null is returned. The contains() method can be used to determine whether an entry with a given key exists. The containsKey() method returns true if at least one entry with the supplied *value* is found in the table. Since only keys are required to be unique, it is possible for the same value (or values that are equal according to their equals() methods) to appear in the table more than once.

The size() method returns the number of entries in the Hashtable. However, to determine whether the Hashtable is empty, it is often more convienent to use the isEmpty() method.

To remove an entry from the Hashtable, pass its key to the remove() method. If an entry with the given key was found in the table, the remove() method returns its value, implementing a read-and-clear operation. All of the entries in the Hashtable can be deleted by calling the clear() method.

To create a loop that accesses all of the values in the Hashtable, use the elements() method, This method returns an Enumeration with one entry for each value in the table. The order in which the values are returned is not defined. To obtain an Enumeration that iterates over all of the keys in the table, use the keys() method.

```
public class Hashtable {
// Public Constructors
    public Hashtable();
    public Hashtable(int initialCapacity);
// Public Instance Methods
    public void clear();                                          synchronized
    public boolean contains(Object value);                       synchronized
    public boolean containsKey(Object key);                      synchronized
    public Enumeration elements();                               synchronized
    public Object get(Object key);                              synchronized
    public boolean isEmpty();                                    default:true
    public Enumeration keys();                                   synchronized
    public Object put(Object key, Object value);                synchronized
    public Object remove(Object key);                            synchronized
    public int size();
// Public Methods Overriding Object
    public String toString();                                    synchronized
// Protected Instance Methods
    protected void rehash();
}
```

NoSuchElementException

CLDC 1.0, MIDP 1.0

java.util

unchecked

This exception is thrown to signal that an attempt has been made to access an element of a collection or an enumeration that does not exist. This class is the same as its J2SE equivalent, apart from its inability to be serialized.

```
Object ─ Throwable ─ Exception ─ RuntimeException ─ NoSuchElementException
```

```
public class NoSuchElementException extends RuntimeException {
// Public Constructors
    public NoSuchElementException();
    public NoSuchElementException(String s);
}
```

Random

CLDC 1.0, MIDP 1.0

java.util

This class generates pseudo-random numbers based on an initial seed value. The algorithm used is deterministic in that two instances of this class, initialized with the same seed and subject to the same method calls in the same order, will return identical sequences of numbers. Subclasses can implement a different random number generation algorithm by overriding the protected next() method to return a pseudo-random number with the specified number of bits.

The nextInt() and nextLong() methods return the next pseudo-random integer and long values, respectively, from the random number sequence of this generator. The default algorithm generates numbers that are approximately evenly distributed over the total range of values for the return type, which implies that there is an almost equal chance that any given bit in the random value will be 0 or 1.

The setSeed() can be used to set a new seed value from which subsequent random numbers will be generated. The seed can also be supplied when an instance of this class is created. A Random object constructed with its default constructor is seeded with the current time, expressed as the number of milliseconds since Jan 1st, 1970.

The CLDC implementation of this class does not include the J2SE methods for random floating point numbers (the CLDC VM does not support floating point values), nor does it offer the ability to obtain random boolean values and random-valued byte arrays.

```
public class Random {
// Public Constructors
    public Random();
    public Random(long seed);
// Public Instance Methods
    public int nextInt();
    public long nextLong();
    public void setSeed(long seed);                              synchronized
// Protected Instance Methods
    protected int next(int bits);                                synchronized
}
```

Stack
CLDC 1.0, MIDP 1.0

java.util

A class that represent a last-in, first-out push down stack. Items on the stack can be arbitrary Java objects. The push() method is used to add another item to the top of the stack. The uppermost item on the stack can be removed using the pop() method, which returns the item to the caller. The peek() method returns the uppermost object without removing it from the stack. If either peek() or pop() is called when the stack is empty, an EmptyStackException is thrown. This situation can be detected in advance by checking the empty() method, which returns true when there are no items on the stack.

The search() method can be used to determine whether a given object is in the stack. If the object is found, its distance from the top of the stack is returned, where the top-most object is considered to be at distance 1. If the object is not found in the stack, -1 is returned. The Stack class does not provide any methods that allow direct access to any item other than the topmost element . However, the methods of its Vector superclass can be used to access and remove any item on the stack. (This practice is not recommended, however, since it breaks the encapsulation of the data within the stack.)

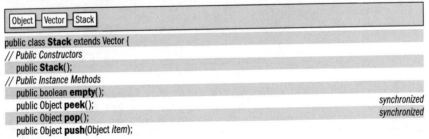

```
public class Stack extends Vector {
// Public Constructors
    public Stack();
// Public Instance Methods
    public boolean empty();
    public Object peek();                                        synchronized
    public Object pop();                                         synchronized
    public Object push(Object item);
```

```
     public int search(Object o);                                    synchronized
}
```

Timer

java.util

A class that allows code to be scheduled for execution in the future. A Timer creates a dedicated thread which it uses to execute code in one or more TimerTask objects. These objects are passed to it using its schedule() and scheduleAtFixedRate() methods.

To schedule a task to be run once, use one of the two-argument variants of schedule(), passing it either the delay in milliseconds until its only execution, or a Date object holding the required execution time.

The three-argument schedule() methods arrange for the task to be run at a given initial time, or after an initial delay and then subsequently executed with a fixed delay between the *start* times. If task execution is delayed for any reason, the next execution of the same task will also be delayed. Over time, these delays can increase, so this mode of operation is acceptable when the total number of times that the task is run in a given period is not critical (e.g., polling a mail server for undelivered mail).

When it is important that tasks be executed with a given average frequency, such as graphics animation, the scheduleAtFixedRate() method should be used instead. This method does not schedule each execution relative to the start time of the previous one. Instead, it attempts to compensate for delays by scheduling the task more often in order to maintain the desired long-term execution frequency. This might mean that the task will occasionally run more often than an identical task scheduled using the schedule() method. Consequently, successive executions might be separated by a smaller time interval than the delay specified in the scheduleAtFixedRate() call.

Since all of the TimerTasks associated with a Timer execute in the same thread, a delay caused by one task may result in other tasks not being executed in a timely manner. In a J2SE system, delays of this type may be avoided by assigning tasks to more than one Timer. A CLDC system, however, may not have native thread support in its operating system. Hence, such a strategy may not achieve the desired effect.

The cancel() method can be used to cancel all pending task executions and terminate the thread associated with the Timer. A task that is executing when this method is invoked will be allowed to complete.

```
public class Timer {
// Public Constructors
    public Timer();
// Public Instance Methods
    public void cancel();
    public void schedule(TimerTask task, Date time);
    public void schedule(TimerTask task, long delay);
    public void schedule(TimerTask task, Date firstTime, long period);
    public void schedule(TimerTask task, long delay, long period);
    public void scheduleAtFixedRate(TimerTask task, Date firstTime, long period);
    public void scheduleAtFixedRate(TimerTask task, long delay, long period);
}
```

TimerTask

java.util

runnable

An abstract class that should be subclassed to provide a unit of work. The TimerTask can then be scheduled for execution through the use of the Timer object. Subclasses should place code to be executed by the Timer in the run() method and use either the schedule() or scheduleAtFixedRate() method to arrange for it to be scheduled.

Once a task has been scheduled, future execution can be canceled by calling the cancel() method. If the task is executing when this method is called, however, it will be allowed to complete. A task will not be scheduled for execution again once the cancel() method returns.

The scheduledExecutionTime() method can be used to get the time at which the task was most recently scheduled for execution, as a millisecond offset from 0:00 UTC on January 1st, 1970.

```
Object ├ TimerTask ┤ Runnable

public abstract class TimerTask implements Runnable {
// Protected Constructors
    protected TimerTask();
// Public Instance Methods
    public boolean cancel();
    public long scheduledExecutionTime();
// Methods Implementing Runnable
    public abstract void run();
}
```

Passed To: Timer.{schedule(), scheduleAtFixedRate()}

TimeZone   CLDC 1.0, MIDP 1.0

java.util

A TimeZone object holds information for a specific time zone, such as its offset from GMT and whether it observes daylight savings. The getDefault() method returns the default TimeZone for the device. A list of the time zones that a device supports can be obtained using the static getAvailableIDs() method. A TimeZone object for a specific time zone can be obtained by calling the getTimeZone() method, passing the time zone's identifier, which must be one of the strings returned by the getAvailableIDs() method. Note that CLDC devices are only required to support their default time zone. Therefore, it may not be possible for application code to obtain a TimeZone object for any other time zone.

A TimeZone object contains a fixed time offset from GMT. This value, which is expressed in milliseconds, can be obtained by calling the getRawOffset() method. This value does not take into account daylight savings time. If a time zone uses daylight savings time, which can be determined from the useDaylightTime() method, the actual offset on any given date depends on whether daylight savings time is in force. The offset from GMT adjusted for daylight savings can be obtained from the getOffset() method, which returns the offset in force at a specified date and time.

```
public abstract class TimeZone {
// Public Constructors
    public TimeZone();
// Public Class Methods
    public static String[] getAvailableIDs();
    public static TimeZone getDefault();                                synchronized
    public static TimeZone getTimeZone(String ID);                      synchronized
// Public Instance Methods
    public String getID();                                              constant
    public abstract int getOffset(int era, int year, int month, int day, int dayOfWeek, int millis);
    public abstract int getRawOffset();
```

```
    public abstract boolean useDaylightTime( );
}
```

Passed To: Calendar.{getInstance(), setTimeZone()}, javax.microedition.lcdui.DateField.DateField()

Returned By: Calendar.getTimeZone(), TimeZone.{getDefault(), getTimeZone()}

Vector   CLDC 1.0, MIDP 1.0
java.util

Vector is a collection class that behaves like a variable-length array of objects. A Vector can contain an arbitrary number of Java objects, accessed with an integer position index. The first entry is index 0. Since an entry in a Vector is distinguished only by its index, the same object can appear any number of times in the same Vector.

Entries can be appended to the end of the Vector using the addElement() method. Entries can be inserted at a given index using the insertElementAt() method. The insertElementAt() method causes all elements at that location and higher to be shifted up by one position. An element at a given index can be replaced using the setElementAt() method.

Elements can be removed from a Vector by index or by value. The removeElementAt() method removes the element with the given index, while removeElement(Object obj) removes the element with the lowest index that is equivalent to the object passed in. Both of these methods cause the indices of all elements that follow the removed element to be reduced by 1. The removeAllElements() removes all entries from the Vector.

There are several ways to access the elements in a Vector. The elementAt() returns the element at the specified index. The convenience methods firstElement() and lastElement() return the first and last elements (which will be the same if the Vector has only one element). The elements() method returns an Enumeration that iterates over all of the elements in the Vector in order of increasing index. Finally, the contents of the Vector can be copied into a pre-allocated array (which must be large enough to hold it) using the copyInto() method. In many cases, it is quicker to use this method than it is to use the Enumeration returned by the elements(). However, the possible performance gain must be weighed against the memory required for the array if the Vector is large.

The number of elements in a Vector can be obtained from the size() method. To determine whether a Vector is empty, use the isEmpty() method. The size of a Vector can be explicitly set using the setSize() method. If the value passed to this method is smaller than the current size, elements with indices greater than or equal to the new size are removed. If the new size is larger than the existing size, then slots with indices greater than or equal to the old size are filled with null.

A Vector manages its elements using an internal array that is larger than the number of elements that it contains. The size of this array is referred to as the Vector's *capacity* and can be retrieved using the capacity() method. As elements are added, the Vector increases its capacity by allocating a new internal array with additional entries and copying the element list from the old array to the new one. The initial capacity and the amount that it increases when necessary can be supplied to the constructor. Since the process of increasing an array's capacity is expensive, it is a good idea to set the initial capacity so that it is large enough to hold all of the elements that it may contain in its lifetime, if this is known in advance. The same effect can be obtained at run time by calling the ensureCapacity() method, supplying the expected number of Vector elements. The size of the internal array can be reduced to the number required to actually hold its content using the trimToSize() method.

Vector provides methods that allow its content to be searched for a given object. The contains() method returns true if the Vector holds an element that is equivalent to its argument. To find the index of an element that matches a given object, use indexOf(), which has two variants. The first searches from the start of the Vector, while the second searches from a specified starting index. The lastIndexOf() methods are similar, but return the index of the *last* matching element. Each of these methods return -1 if no match is found.

```
public class Vector {
// Public Constructors
    public Vector();
    public Vector(int initialCapacity);
    public Vector(int initialCapacity, int capacityIncrement);
// Public Instance Methods
    public void addElement(Object obj);                          synchronized
    public int capacity();
    public boolean contains(Object elem);
    public void copyInto(Object[ ] anArray);                     synchronized
    public Object elementAt(int index);                          synchronized
    public Enumeration elements();                               synchronized
    public void ensureCapacity(int minCapacity);                synchronized
    public Object firstElement();                                synchronized
    public int indexOf(Object elem);
    public int indexOf(Object elem, int index);                  synchronized
    public void insertElementAt(Object obj, int index);          synchronized
    public boolean isEmpty();                                     default:true
    public Object lastElement();                                  synchronized
    public int lastIndexOf(Object elem);
    public int lastIndexOf(Object elem, int index);              synchronized
    public void removeAllElements();                             synchronized
    public boolean removeElement(Object obj);                    synchronized
    public void removeElementAt(int index);                      synchronized
    public void setElementAt(Object obj, int index);             synchronized
    public void setSize(int newSize);                            synchronized
    public int size();
    public void trimToSize();                                     synchronized
// Public Methods Overriding Object
    public String toString();                                     synchronized
// Protected Instance Fields
    protected int capacityIncrement;
    protected int elementCount;
    protected Object[ ] elementData;
}
```

Subclasses: Stack

CHAPTER 14

javax.microedition.io

Package javax.microedition.io   **CLDC 1.0, MIDP 1.0, CDC 1.0**

This package contains the interfaces and classes that form the Generic Connection Framework. This framework provides a simpler and more uniform interface for accessing external devices, such as networks and serial communication ports, than the corresponding classes in J2SE.

The key elements of this package are the Connector class and the Connection interface. The Connector class contains static methods that create specialized connections (i.e. objects that implement the Connection interface) to various types of device or network protocol. The Connector open() method accepts a name argument that describes the connection target; it then returns an instance of a class that implements a sub-interface of Connection suitable for the specified protocol or device. Note that the actual classes that are returned are not part of the public API, but the interfaces that they implement (e.g., HttpConnection) are all contained in this package.

The Generic Connection Framework is part of the CLDC specification. Although it defines the framework and most of the interfaces in this package, it does not require the implementation of any specific protocols. The HttpConnection interface is introduced by the MID profile rather than being part of CLDC. MIDP requires only that the HTTP protocol be supported, although device vendors are free to implements sockets, datagrams and other protocols according to the requirements of their devices.

Although intended for CLDC and its associated profiles, this package is also included in the Connected Device Configuration (CDC) and the Foundation Profile, for reasons of compatibility.

Figure 14-1 shows the class hierarchy of this package. See Chapter 6 for more details about the Generic Connection Framework.

java.micro-edition.io

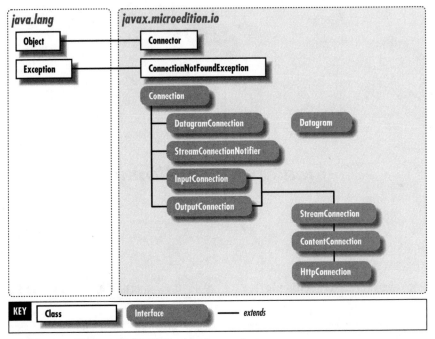

Figure 14-1: The java.microedition.io hierarchy

Connection

javax.microedition.io

Connection is a base interface that represents a generic connection to a device or remote object accessed over a network. This interface defines only a close() method. A class that implements this interface is obtained from the open() method of the Connector class. These connections are already in the open state, so there is no open() method in the Connection interface.

```
public interface Connection {
// Public Instance Methods
    public abstract void close() throws java.io.IOException;
}
```

Implementations: DatagramConnection, InputConnection, OutputConnection, StreamConnectionNotifier

Returned By: Connector.open()

ConnectionNotFoundException

javax.microedition.io

checked

This exception reports an error related to the Generic Connection Framework. It is thrown when the Connector open() method is invoked requesting a protocol that is not supported by the implementation.

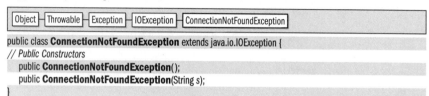

```
public class ConnectionNotFoundException extends java.io.IOException {
// Public Constructors
    public ConnectionNotFoundException();
    public ConnectionNotFoundException(String s);
}
```

Connector

javax.microedition.io

The Connector class is a factory that creates Connection objects, which encapsulate a protocol connection with another target device. Note that the communications mechanism that each device supports is implementation-dependent. The CLDC specification does not require any protocols to be supported, and MIDP 1.0 requires only HTTP.

The three open() methods create and return a Connection to an entity that is defined by the name argument. The legal values of the name argument and their precise interpretations are implementation-dependent. However, they always take the form of a URL. The most common forms of this argument are:

http://host:port/path

> Creates an HTTP connection to a server at port number port on the given host, to access the resource named by path. Some implementations may also support secure communications using HTTPS, which would use https: as the protocol selector.

socket://host:port

> Creates a socket connection to a server at port number port on the given host.

socket://:port

> Creates a server socket to receive connections addressed to port port on the local host.

datagram://host:port

> Creates a connection to send datagrams to port port on the given host.

datagram://:port

> Creates a connection to receive datagrams addressed to port port on the local host.

comm://port;params

> Opens a serial port on the local host. The params argument may supply optional parameters such as the required baud rate.

file://path

> Opens a file in the filestore of the host system.

If the value of the name argument is not recognized or support for the underlying communication mechanism is not provided, the method throws a ConnectionNotFoundException.

java.micro-edition.io

The mode takes the values READ, WRITE or READ_WRITE and specifies the type of access required to the connection. Some connection types may place restrictions on the values of this argument that they accept. For example, a connection to a printer may not allow read access. If this argument is not specified, the value READ_WRITE is assumed.

A timeout argument can be also supplied to the method. By default, this parameter has the value false. When timeouts are requested and supported, a connection timeout causes this method to throw an InterruptedIOException.

The type of object returned by the open() method is implementation-dependent. This object, however, always implements an interface derived from Connection that is appropriate for the device or communication protocol being used. For example, if the name argument indicates an HTTP connection, then the returned object will implement the HttpConnection interface. Similarly, sockets return either a StreamConnection or StreamConnectionNotifier object. Datagrams return a DatagramConnection.

The openInputStream(), openOutputStream(), openDataInputStream() and openDataOutputStream() methods return I/O streams without returning the underlying Connection object to the caller. The name argument is interpreted in the same way as if it were passed to the open() method. These methods succeed only if the name argument is valid and supported on the local system, and the underlying communication mechanism allows reading or writing (depending on whether an input or output stream is requested).

```
public class Connector {
// No Constructor
// Public Constants
    public static final int READ;                                                   =1
    public static final int READ_WRITE;                                             =3
    public static final int WRITE;                                                  =2
// Public Class Methods
    public static Connection open(String name) throws java.io.IOException;
    public static Connection open(String name, int mode) throws java.io.IOException;
    public static Connection open(String name, int mode, boolean timeouts) throws java.io.IOException;
    public static java.io.DataInputStream openDataInputStream(String name) throws java.io.IOException;
    public static java.io.DataOutputStream openDataOutputStream(String name) throws java.io.IOException;
    public static java.io.InputStream openInputStream(String name) throws java.io.IOException;
    public static java.io.OutputStream openOutputStream(String name) throws java.io.IOException;
}
```

ContentConnection   CLDC 1.0, MIDP 1.0, CDC 1.0

javax.microedition.io

ContentConnection is a StreamConnection whose data is some kind of identifiable object. The type of object depends on the communicating entities and must either be known in advance or be identifiable from the value returned by the getType() method. A ContentConnection may convey one object, or a sequence of objects.

The getType() method returns a String that identifies the type of the data in the input stream. In most cases, the object type will be identified by its MIME type, but any arbitrary string that has meaning to both the sender and the receiver can be used. When the connection between sender and receiver is implemented using HTTP, the type is conveyed in the HTTP Content-Type header field.

The getLength() method returns the number of bytes that make up the object's representation in the data stream. This method may return -1 if the protocol used to carry the data does not include a mechanism for conveying the length of the object. In this case, the receiver should continue to read data until an end-of-file indication is received or some characteristic of the data indicates that a complete object has been read. Where a stream may carry several objects in succession, the value returned by this method may be used to mark the boundary between them. When the connection between sender and receiver is implemented using HTTP, the length is conveyed in the HTTP Content-Length header field.

The getEncoding() method returns a String that indicates the character set in which the bytes are encoded. This method is useful when the data consists of a sequence of bytes that represent strings that need to be converted into Unicode by the receiver, rather than binary data that needs no conversion. When the connection between sender and receiver is implemented using HTTP, the length is conveyed in the HTTP Content-Encoding header field.

```
                                    ┌──────────────────┐ ┌──────────────────┐
                                    │ StreamConnection ├─┤ ContentConnection │
                                    └──────────────────┘ └──────────────────┘
┌────────────┐  ┌─────────────────┐ ┌────────────┐ ┌──────────────────┐
│ Connection ├──┤ InputConnection │ │ Connection ├─┤ OutputConnection │
└────────────┘  └─────────────────┘ └────────────┘ └──────────────────┘
```

public interface **ContentConnection** extends StreamConnection {
// *Public Instance Methods*
    public abstract String **getEncoding**();
    public abstract long **getLength**();
    public abstract String **getType**();
}

Implementations: HttpConnection

Datagram

CLDC 1.0, MIDP 1.0, CDC 1.0

javax.microedition.io

A Datagram represents a message to be sent from a sender to a receiver. A Datagram consists of an arbitrary sequence of bytes together with an address. Datagram objects are created using the newDatagram() method of the DatagramConnection class.

When preparing a Datagram for transmission, the data content must be set using the setData() method, which requires the data to be supplied in the form of an array of bytes, where the offset and len arguments specify the portion of the array that is to be used to form the message body. The maximum permitted length of a Datagram can be obtained from the DatagramConnection object. The data length associated with the Datagram can be changed using the setLength() method, but it cannot be increased beyond the end of the buffer supplied by the setData method. The reset() method is used to set the offset and length values to zero. This method is often used when creating the message body using the DataOutput interface methods.

A Datagram must have a destination address, which is set using one of the two setAddress() methods. One variant allows the address to be copied from another Datagram, which is a convenient when creating a response to a received Datagram. The other variant accepts a string of the form datagram://host:port, where host is the host name or IP address of the destination and port is the destination's port number. A Datagram without a destination address to be sent using a DatagramConnection in *client* mode (see the description of DatagramConnection for more information) will use the DatagramConnection's address. If the Datagram address is set, however, it temporarily overrides the address associated with the DatagramConnection.

When a Datagram is received, the address of the sender can be obtained by calling the getAddress() method. This returns a String encoded in the form datagram://host:port. The message content is obtained by calling the getData(), getLength(), and getOffset() methods. The first of these methods returns an array of bytes, while the other two return the offset of the first byte that contains the message data and the length of that data. (In other words, the first valid data byte is given by dgram.getData()[dgram.getOffset()] and the last valid byte by dgram.getData()[dgram.getOffset() + dgram.getLength() - 1].

For convenience when creating or reading the body of a message, Datagram implements both the DataInput and DataOutput interfaces. This is primarily a convience when reading or writing to the message body. For example, one way to create a datagram is to use the setData() method to supply the output buffer, passing the offset and length arguments as zero, and then call methods of the DataOutput interface (such as writeInt() or writeUTF()) to store data in the buffer. When these methods are used, the length of the outgoing Datagram is automatically set to match that of the data written to the buffer. The same Datagram can be used to create more than one message by calling the reset() method to empty the buffer after the Datagram has been sent.

Similarly, on receiving a Datagram, the DataInput methods (such as readInt() and readUTF()) can be used to extract fields from the message body. These methods automatically update the offset value so that subsequent methods read from the next available byte in the buffer. Note that the reset() method should never be called in this case, as it would have the effect of making the received message appear to be empty.

```
public interface Datagram extends java.io.DataInput, java.io.DataOutput {
// Public Instance Methods
    public abstract String getAddress( );
    public abstract byte[ ] getData( );
    public abstract int getLength( );
    public abstract int getOffset( );
    public abstract void reset( );
    public abstract void setAddress(Datagram reference);
    public abstract void setAddress(String addr) throws java.io.IOException;
    public abstract void setData(byte[ ] buffer, int offset, int len);
    public abstract void setLength(int len);
}
```

Passed To: Datagram.setAddress(), DatagramConnection.{receive(), send()}

Returned By: DatagramConnection.newDatagram()

DatagramConnection
CLDC 1.0, MIDP 1.0, CDC 1.0

javax.microedition.io

DatagramConnection is a Connection that is used to send Datagram objects to one or more receivers. A datagram is a sequence of bytes that is delivered together in the form of a message. Datagrams are not guaranteed to be delivered. In addition, the order of delivery of successive datagrams does not always match the order in which they were sent. Since a DatagramConnection deals in discrete messages, it does not have any associated input or output streams.

A DatagramConnection receiver is obtained by calling the Connector open() method with a name argument of the form datagram://:port, where port is the port number to which senders should address messages. DatagramConnections created in this way can also be used to send Datagrams, often as responses. A DatagramConnection created in this way is said to be in *server* mode.

A DatagramConnection sender is obtained by supplying a name argument of the form datagram://host:port. This type of DatagramConnection is said to be in *client* mode. The difference between server and client modes is that the port number for server mode is known in advance (and must be known by senders so that they can address messages). In client mode, the port number is dynamically allocated, and it may be different each time the client executes. The client port number will appear in the messages received by the server and can be used to address the reply message. There is currently no direct way for a client to find out the port number that has been allocated to it.

Once a DatagramConnection has been obtained, Datagrams can be created by calling one of the newDatagram() methods. There are four variants of this method that either specify or omit the data and the address. If either one is not specified with newDatagram(), they can be supplied later using the setData() and setAddress() methods provided by the Datagram interface.

To send a Datagram, use the send() method. Note that the send() method requires that the destination address in the Datagram has been set. The receive() retrieves a message addressed to the specified DatagramConnection, stores it in the Datagram passed to it, and returns the number of bytes copied. If the buffer associated with the Datagram is not large enough to receive the entire message, the excess bytes are discarded and no error is reported. The address field of the Datagram should represent the host and port number of the message sender.

```
Connection ─ DatagramConnection
```

```
public interface DatagramConnection extends Connection {
// Public Instance Methods
    public abstract int getMaximumLength() throws java.io.IOException;
    public abstract int getNominalLength() throws java.io.IOException;
    public abstract Datagram newDatagram(int size) throws java.io.IOException;
    public abstract Datagram newDatagram(byte[ ] buf, int size) throws java.io.IOException;
    public abstract Datagram newDatagram(int size, String addr) throws java.io.IOException;
    public abstract Datagram newDatagram(byte[ ] buf, int size, String addr) throws java.io.IOException;
    public abstract void receive(Datagram dgram) throws java.io.IOException;
    public abstract void send(Datagram dgram) throws java.io.IOException;
}
```

HttpConnection

CLDC 1.0, MIDP 1.0, Foundation 1.0

javax.microedition.io

HttpConnection is a ContentConnection that uses HTTP 1.1 as its underlying protocol. An instance of HttpConnection is obtained by invoking the Connector open() with a name argument of the form http://host:port/path. Some implementations may also support a secure connection using HTTPS.

The usual sequence of events when using an HttpConnection is to first call setRequest-Method() to set the request method type to either GET (the default), HEAD or POST. Next, add any optional HTTP headers using the setRequestProperty() method. Finally, if this is a POST request, write any data to be sent to an output stream obtained from the openOutputStream() or openDataOutputStream() methods (inherited from ContentConnection).

The getResponseCode() method can be called to retrieve the server's response, which will indicate whether the request was successful (HTTP_OK). Some response codes, such as HTTP_MOVED_TEMP or HTTP_UNAUTHORIZED, require the application to take further action before the request can be performed. The getResponseMessage() method returns any message sent by the server to further explain or qualify the response code.

HTTP headers sent by the server can be retrieved in several ways. The getHeaderField-Key() and getHeaderField() methods can be used to access all of the headers in the request by supplying a zero-based index. These methods return null when the last header has been reached. Given the name of a header, its value can either be retrieved in string form using an overloaded form of getHeaderField() that accepts the header name, or decoded as a Java int or Date object using the getHeaderFieldInt() and getHeaderFieldDate methods. Finally, some fields can be obtained using convenience methods such as get-Date() and getExpiration().

The reply data can be read from an InputStream obtained from the openInputStream() or openDataInputStream() methods. The getType() and getEncoding() methods can be used to get the MIME type and character encoding of the data, respectively. Both of these methods may return null, in which case the application will need to make suitable default assumptions. The number of bytes available to be read can be obtained from the getLength() method, which returns the value of the Content-Length header. If this header was not included by the server, the application must repeatedly read the input stream until an end-of-file condition is returned.

```
                              StreamConnection ┄ ContentConnection ┄ HttpConnection

  Connection ┄ InputConnection    Connection ┄ OutputConnection

public interface HttpConnection extends ContentConnection {
// Public Constants
    public static final String GET;                                = [quot ] GET [quot ]
    public static final String HEAD;                               = [quot ] HEAD [quot ]
    public static final int HTTP_ACCEPTED;                         =202
    public static final int HTTP_BAD_GATEWAY;                      =502
    public static final int HTTP_BAD_METHOD;                       =405
    public static final int HTTP_BAD_REQUEST;                      =400
    public static final int HTTP_CLIENT_TIMEOUT;                   =408
    public static final int HTTP_CONFLICT;                         =409
    public static final int HTTP_CREATED;                          =201
    public static final int HTTP_ENTITY_TOO_LARGE;                 =413
    public static final int HTTP_EXPECT_FAILED;                    =417
    public static final int HTTP_FORBIDDEN;                        =403
    public static final int HTTP_GATEWAY_TIMEOUT;                  =504
    public static final int HTTP_GONE;                             =410
    public static final int HTTP_INTERNAL_ERROR;                   =500
    public static final int HTTP_LENGTH_REQUIRED;                  =411
    public static final int HTTP_MOVED_PERM;                       =301
    public static final int HTTP_MOVED_TEMP;                       =302
    public static final int HTTP_MULT_CHOICE;                      =300
    public static final int HTTP_NO_CONTENT;                       =204
    public static final int HTTP_NOT_ACCEPTABLE;                   =406
    public static final int HTTP_NOT_AUTHORITATIVE;                =203
    public static final int HTTP_NOT_FOUND;                        =404
    public static final int HTTP_NOT_IMPLEMENTED;                  =501
    public static final int HTTP_NOT_MODIFIED;                     =304
    public static final int HTTP_OK;                               =200
    public static final int HTTP_PARTIAL;                          =206
    public static final int HTTP_PAYMENT_REQUIRED;                 =402
    public static final int HTTP_PRECON_FAILED;                    =412
    public static final int HTTP_PROXY_AUTH;                       =407
    public static final int HTTP_REQ_TOO_LONG;                     =414
    public static final int HTTP_RESET;                            =205
    public static final int HTTP_SEE_OTHER;                        =303
    public static final int HTTP_TEMP_REDIRECT;                    =307
    public static final int HTTP_UNAUTHORIZED;                     =401
    public static final int HTTP_UNAVAILABLE;                      =503
    public static final int HTTP_UNSUPPORTED_RANGE;                =416
    public static final int HTTP_UNSUPPORTED_TYPE;                 =415
    public static final int HTTP_USE_PROXY;                        =305
```

```
    public static final int HTTP_VERSION;                                =505
    public static final String POST;                            = [quot  ] POST [quot  ]
// Property Accessor Methods (by property name)
    public abstract long getDate() throws java.io.IOException;
    public abstract long getExpiration() throws java.io.IOException;
    public abstract String getFile();
    public abstract String getHost();
    public abstract long getLastModified() throws java.io.IOException;
    public abstract int getPort();
    public abstract String getProtocol();
    public abstract String getQuery();
    public abstract String getRef();
    public abstract String getRequestMethod();
    public abstract void setRequestMethod(String method) throws java.io.IOException;
    public abstract int getResponseCode() throws java.io.IOException;
    public abstract String getResponseMessage() throws java.io.IOException;
    public abstract String getURL();
// Public Instance Methods
    public abstract String getHeaderField(int n) throws java.io.IOException;
    public abstract String getHeaderField(String name) throws java.io.IOException;
    public abstract long getHeaderFieldDate(String name, long def) throws java.io.IOException;
    public abstract int getHeaderFieldInt(String name, int def) throws java.io.IOException;
    public abstract String getHeaderFieldKey(int n) throws java.io.IOException;
    public abstract String getRequestProperty(String key);
    public abstract void setRequestProperty(String key, String value) throws java.io.IOException;
}
```

InputConnection   CLDC 1.0, MIDP 1.0, CDC 1.0

javax.microedition.io

InputConnection is an interface implemented by connections that can provide an input
stream from the data source. Most connections allow input, but in exceptional cases,
such as a connection to a printer, this might not be the case.

The openInputStream() method obtains an input stream that can be used to read an
ordered sequence of bytes from the data source, while openDataInputStream() returns a
stream that can also be used to decode Java primitive data types written to the connection using a DataOutputStream.

The result of calling these methods more than once is not defined by the specification.
Sun's reference implementations treat a second call as an error and throw an IOException.
The openInputStream() and openDataInputStream() methods will also throw an IOException if
the InputConnection was obtained from a Connector open() call which specified a mode of
Connector.WRITE.

```
  ┌──────────────┐   ┌─────────────────┐
  │  Connection  │···│ InputConnection │
  └──────────────┘   └─────────────────┘
```

```
public interface InputConnection extends Connection {
// Public Instance Methods
    public abstract java.io.DataInputStream openDataInputStream() throws java.io.IOException;
    public abstract java.io.InputStream openInputStream() throws java.io.IOException;
}
```

Implementations: StreamConnection

OutputConnection   CLDC 1.0, MIDP 1.0, CDC 1.0

javax.microedition.io

OutputConnection is an interface implemented by connections that can provide an output stream to the data source.

The openOutputStream() obtains an output stream that can be used to write an ordered sequence of bytes from the data source, while openDataOutputStream returns a stream that can be used to write Java primitive data types to the connection in a platform-independent format. Data written using the latter method can be retrieved on the other side using a DataInputStream.

The result of calling these methods more than once is not defined by the specification. Sun's reference implementations treat a second call as an error and throw an IOException. The openOutputStream() and openDataOutputStream() methods will also throw an IOException if the OutputConnection was obtained from a Connector open() call which specified a mode of Connector.READ.

Connection ┈ OutputConnection

```
public interface OutputConnection extends Connection {
// Public Instance Methods
    public abstract java.io.DataOutputStream openDataOutputStream() throws java.io.IOException;
    public abstract java.io.OutputStream openOutputStream() throws java.io.IOException;
}
```

Implementations: StreamConnection

StreamConnection   CLDC 1.0, MIDP 1.0, CDC 1.0

javax.microedition.io

StreamConnection is an interface that combines the methods of InputConnection and OutputConnection, allowing a connection that is capable of both input and output. Although there is no method that explicitly returns a StreamConnection, most invocations of Connector open() will return an object that implements this interface, as most connection types support both input and output.

Even though a StreamConnection is capable of allowing both input and output, it is an error to obtain an input stream from a StreamConnection that was obtained using the Connector open() method with Connector.WRITE, or to obtain an output stream if Connector.READ mode was used.

StreamConnection

Connection ┈ InputConnection   Connection ┈ OutputConnection

```
public interface StreamConnection extends InputConnection, OutputConnection {
}
```

Implementations: ContentConnection

Returned By: StreamConnectionNotifier.acceptAndOpen()

StreamConnectionNotifier   CLDC 1.0, MIDP 1.0, CDC 1.0

javax.microedition.io

StreamConnectionNotifier is a type of Connection returned when the application invokes the Connector open() method with the name argument of the form socket://:port. This creates a server socket, which listens for connections from clients and creates a StreamConnection for each connection received.

Connections can be retrieved by calling the acceptAndOpen() method, which blocks until a connection is available. Application code will normally loop through calling this method and creating a new thread to service each connection. Invoking the StreamConnectionNotifier close() method causes acceptAndOpen() to throw an IOException, which can be used to break out of such a loop.

Connection -- StreamConnectionNotifier

```
public interface StreamConnectionNotifier extends Connection {
// Public Instance Methods
    public abstract StreamConnection acceptAndOpen() throws java.io.IOException;
}
```

CHAPTER 15

javax.microedition.lcdui

This package, whose class hierarchy is shown in Figure 15-1, contains the user interface classes for the Mobile Information Device Profile.

Each MIDlet is associated with an instance of the Display class, which represents the MIDlet's view of the screen. At any given time, at most one MIDlet has access to the actual screen and the keyboard and pointer, if the device has them. This MIDlet is said to be in the *foreground*. While a MIDlet is in the foreground, the content of its Display object will be visible to the user and any changes to it will be seen some time after they are made.

A Display shows an object derived from the abstract class Displayable, of which there are two types: Screen and Canvas. Screen is a base class for a set of form-based screens that are part of the the *high-level* user interface API, while Canvas is a drawing surface for the *low-level* API.

The high-level API provides a set of components, derived from the Item class, that allow the construction of simple user interfaces containing text fields, check boxes, radio buttons and lists. Since the range of devices for which MIDP is intended has a wide variety of input and output capabilities, these classes deliberately provide a programming interface that hides the details of the platform itself and very little customization of the appearance of these components is possible. In particular, it is not possible to change the colors or fonts used to render these components.

Items are arranged on a Screen subclass called a Form, which is somewhat like the AWT Frame class. The layout of Items within a Form cannot be directly controlled by the application and may vary from device to device, subject to certain rules that are described in the reference material for the Form class.

The ListBox and TextBox classes are full-screen lists and text entry components that, like Form, are derived from Screen. All of these components have the ability to display a title and a *ticker*, a scrolling text string that works in the same way as a stock price ticker. The same capabilities are also inherited by the Alert class, which behave like a dialog and is usually used to display error, warning and informational messages.

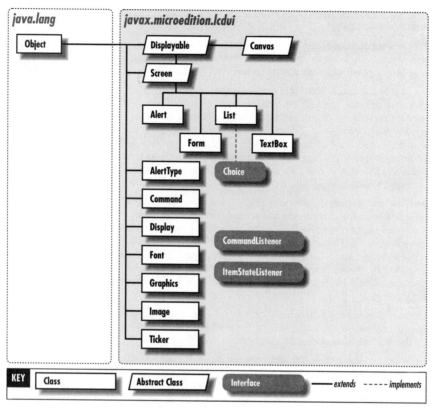

Figure 15–1: The java.microedition.lcdui hierarchy

The low-level API allows the developer to access the screen at the pixel level, but does not provide any GUI components other than the Canvas class, which the developer must subclass to provide painting logic and to handle keyboard and pointer input events.

Both the low-level Canvas class and the Screens of the high-level API can be associated with one or more Commands. Commands are usually represented in the user interface in the form of buttons, but may also appear in the menu system, if the device has one. When the user activates a Command, an event is generated to which application code can respond by performing some action. Several standard Commands, such as OK, EXIT and CANCEL, are defined.

Both the high- and low-level APIs allow the display of images, with a fidelity that depends on the capabilities of the screen. MIDP 1.0 supports images encoded in Portable Network Graphics (PNG) format, via the Image and ImageItem classes.

User interface operations that are initiated by the device itself, such as event notification and screen repainting operations, take place in a dedicated thread and therefore application code that executes in response to these events should be written in such a way that it executes quickly and delegates time-consuming operations to a separate thread. All of the user interface classes are thread-safe, so it is safe to call their methods in arbitrary threads.

Alert

javax.microedition.lcdui

Alert is a subclass of Screen that behaves somewhat like a dialog. There are several standard Alert styles that can be used; the style is specified using an AlertType object which may be supplied when the Alert is constructed or using the setType() method.

An Alert has a title, a message, and an image. These attributes may be set at construction time or using the setTitle(), setString() and setImage() methods. An Alert with no image may be created by calling setImage() with argument null. The way in which the Alert is rendered is platform-dependent. A device is not required to display an image and, even if it does, need not display the image suggested by the application. However, if the platform displays an image at all, changing the AlertType results in a different image being drawn on the Alert. An image explicitly supplied at construction time or using setImage() would override the default one associated with the AlertType.

An Alert will usually be displayed for a fixed length of time, after which it will be removed from the display and the screen previously on view will be restored. The display time may be specified using the setTimeout() method, which requires an argument in milliseconds. The special value Alert.FOREVER may be used to create an Alert that remains visible until the user explicitly dismisses it using a control (usually a button) provided by the platform for that purpose. The default time for which an Alert will be displayed (if no explicit timeout is provided) can be obtained using the getDefaultTimeout() method.

Devices that have sound capability may play a sound when displaying an Alert. The sound may be a default supplied by the platform, or a specific sound that is determined by the AlertType associated with the Alert.

Unlike other Displayables, an Alert may not have application-supplied Commands or CommandListeners and an attempt to call methods that set these attributes will result in an IllegalStateException.

```
Object ├─┤ Displayable ├─┤ Screen ├─┤ Alert
```

```
public class Alert extends Screen {
// Public Constructors
    public Alert(String title);
    public Alert(String title, String alertText, Image alertImage, AlertType alertType);
// Public Constants
    public static final int FOREVER;                                          =-2
// Property Accessor Methods (by property name)
    public int getDefaultTimeout();
    public Image getImage();
    public void setImage(Image img);
    public String getString();
    public void setString(String str);
    public int getTimeout();
    public void setTimeout(int time);
    public AlertType getType();
    public void setType(AlertType type);
// Public Methods Overriding Displayable
    public void addCommand(Command cmd);
    public void setCommandListener(CommandListener l);
}
```

Passed To: Display.setCurrent()

AlertType

javax.microedition.lcdui

This is a class that provides a set of type-safe constants that are used to specify the type of an Alert. The AlertType provides a hint to the platform as to how it should render the Alert and typically causes an appropriate icon to be included along with the application-supplied message. On devices that have a sound capability, a sound (which might be type-dependent) may also be played when the alert is displayed.

The playSound() method may be used to play the sound associated with the AlertType, even when no Alert is displayed. Since not all devices will be able to play sounds, the playSound() method returns a boolean indicating whether a sound was produced, to allow the application to use an alternate mechanism to attract the user's attention if sound is not available.

```
public class AlertType {
// Protected Constructors
    protected AlertType();
// Public Constants
    public static final AlertType ALARM;
    public static final AlertType CONFIRMATION;
    public static final AlertType ERROR;
    public static final AlertType INFO;
    public static final AlertType WARNING;
// Public Instance Methods
    public boolean playSound(Display display);
}
```

Passed To: Alert.{Alert(), setType()}

Returned By: Alert.getType()

Type Of: AlertType.{ALARM, CONFIRMATION, ERROR, INFO, WARNING}

Canvas

javax.microedition.lcdui

Canvas is a Displayable that serves as the most fundamental class of the low-level user interface API. A Canvas can be thought of as a blank sheet of paper that covers the accessible area of a device's screen. In order to use the Canvas class, a MIDlet must subclass it to provide drawing and event handling logic. When such a subclass is installed as a MIDlet's current screen (using the Display.setCurrent() method) and the MIDlet is in the foreground, the paint() method will be called as necessary to cause the content of the Canvas to be drawn onto the screen. Similarly, events from the keyboard or a pointing device, if there is one, will be notified to the Canvas and can be handled appropriately by the MIDlet.

The abstract paint() method must be implemented to draw the content of the canvas onto the screen, using the Graphics object supplied as its argument. The clipping rectangle in this Graphics object may only cover a subset of the entire Canvas if only part of the screen needs to be repainted. In general, the paint() method should query the clipping rectangle and only perform graphics operations that would affect this part of the screen, where this can be economically determined.

A device may or may not double-buffer its screen to provide smoother updates and eliminate flashing caused by partial updates that are visible to the user. The process of double-buffering is transparent to the paint() method, but a MIDlet can determine whether double-buffering is being used by calling isDoubleBuffered(). If this method returns false, a MIDlet may choose to implement its own double-buffering by allocating an Image with the same dimensions as the Canvas (or its clipping rectangle), getting a Graphics object for the image using its getGraphics() method, painting into the image and then copying it to the screen using the Graphics.drawImage() method. The size of the Canvas can be obtained by calling the getWidth() and getHeight() methods. Note that the Canvas may be smaller than the screen because the device may reserve some space for command buttons and soft keypads.

Painting operations are always performed in a thread that is dedicated to servicing the user interface. MIDlet code in any thread can request that part or all of the screen be repainted by calling one of the Canvas repaint() methods, which will cause the paint() method to be called in turn at some time in the future. Multiple calls to repaint() may be coalesced into a single paint() call to minimize painting overhead. Code that needs to flush all pending repaint operations may call the serviceRepaints() method, which blocks until all such operations have been completed.

The showNotify() and hideNotify() methods may be overridden to receive notification when the Canvas becomes visible to the user or is hidden. These methods may, for example, be used by a MIDlet that performs background calculations to update the contents of a Canvas to temporarily suppress them while the Canvas is not visible.

The keyPressed(), keyReleased() and keyRepeated() methods can be overridden to handle events from the keyboard or keypad, if the device has one. Some devices that do not have a physical keypad may provide an on-screen emulation that will result in the generation of the same events. On some platforms, holding a key down for a short period will cause it to repeat and call the keyRepeated(). A MIDlet can determine whether these events are supported by calling the hasRepeatEvents() method.

The argument passed to the key handling methods is an integer key code. Some key codes are standardized over all platforms, while others are not. For portability, a MIDlet should only directly test the values of the standard key codes, which correspond to the digits 0 through 9 and the star and pound keys found in cell phone keypads. The values of these key codes are available as numeric constants, such as KEY_NUM0 and KEY_STAR. Support is also provided for *game actions*, which are mapped to platform-dependent keys or buttons. Each game action has a corresponding numeric constant, such as LEFT, RIGHT, FIRE or GAME_A that should be used by application code instead of hard-coding non-portable key code values. The game action for a key code can be obtained by calling the getGameAction() method so that, for example, the expression (getGameAction(keyCode) == Canvas.LEFT) can be used to check whether the key that corresponds to LEFT has been pressed (or released). An alternative is to use the getKeyCode() method to get the key code for a game action, as in the expression (getKeyCode(Canvas.LEFT) == keyCode).

There is no portable way to handle keys that are not numeric and do not map to a game action. In particular, proper handling of text input, including shift states, is difficult and is better handled by using high-level components such as TextField on separate screens.

On devices that have a pointing device, the pointerPressed(), pointerDragged() and pointerReleased() methods can be overridden to react to pointer actions. All of these methods receive the coordinates of the pointer relative to the top left-hand corner of the Canvas at the time that the event occurred. The hasPointerEvents() method can be used to determine whether pressed and release events will be notified, and hasPointerMotionEvents() indicates whether pointer drag events are available.

```
Object ─ Displayable ─ Canvas
```

public abstract class **Canvas** extends Displayable {
// Protected Constructors

```
    protected Canvas( );
// Public Constants
    public static final int DOWN;                                            =6
    public static final int FIRE;                                            =8
    public static final int GAME_A;                                          =9
    public static final int GAME_B;                                          =10
    public static final int GAME_C;                                          =11
    public static final int GAME_D;                                          =12
    public static final int KEY_NUM0;                                        =48
    public static final int KEY_NUM1;                                        =49
    public static final int KEY_NUM2;                                        =50
    public static final int KEY_NUM3;                                        =51
    public static final int KEY_NUM4;                                        =52
    public static final int KEY_NUM5;                                        =53
    public static final int KEY_NUM6;                                        =54
    public static final int KEY_NUM7;                                        =55
    public static final int KEY_NUM8;                                        =56
    public static final int KEY_NUM9;                                        =57
    public static final int KEY_POUND;                                       =35
    public static final int KEY_STAR;                                        =42
    public static final int LEFT;                                            =2
    public static final int RIGHT;                                           =5
    public static final int UP;                                              =1
// Property Accessor Methods (by property name)
    public boolean isDoubleBuffered( );
    public int getHeight( );
    public int getWidth( );
// Public Instance Methods
    public int getGameAction(int keyCode);
    public int getKeyCode(int gameAction);
    public String getKeyName(int keyCode);
    public boolean hasPointerEvents( );
    public boolean hasPointerMotionEvents( );
    public boolean hasRepeatEvents( );
    public final void repaint( );
    public final void repaint(int x, int y, int width, int height);
    public final void serviceRepaints( );
// Protected Instance Methods
    protected void hideNotify( );                                        empty
    protected void keyPressed(int keyCode);                              empty
    protected void keyReleased(int keyCode);                             empty
    protected void keyRepeated(int keyCode);                             empty
    protected abstract void paint(Graphics g);
    protected void pointerDragged(int x, int y);                         empty
    protected void pointerPressed(int x, int y);                         empty
    protected void pointerReleased(int x, int y);                        empty
    protected void showNotify( );                                        empty
}
```

Choice

MIDP 1.0

javax.microedition.lcdui

Choice is an interface that contains the methods common to user interface components that allow the user to choose from several possible alternatives. This interface is implemented by the full-screen List control and by ChoiceGroup, which is an Item.

A Choice can operate in one of three different modes:

EXCLUSIVE

> Only one alternative can be selected. If the user selects one item from the set of offered alternatives, any item already selected is deselected. In this mode, the control behaves as (and is usually rendered to look like) a set of radio buttons.

MULTIPLE

> Any number of alternatives can be selected. Selecting one item from the list has no effect on the selected state of other entries. In this, the control behaves like a collection of check boxes.

IMPLICIT

> This mode is available only with the List control. It allows only one item to be selected at any given time and is typically used to create a menu. The difference between this mode and EXCLUSIVE, apart from the visual differences, lies in the way in which selection changes are notified to application code. See the description of the List control for details.

Each entry in a Choice consists of one or both of an image provided in the form of an Image object and a text string. The image, if provided, is rendered in addition to any icon, such as a check box or radio button, supplied by the control itself. The number of entries can be obtained by calling the size() method. An entry is distinguished by its index, where the first entry has index 0 and the last has index size() - 1. New entries can be added to the end of the list using the append() method, or inserted before an existing entry with a given index by calling insert(). The set() method replaces the text and image associated with an entry at a specified index and the delete() method removes an entry.

The platform will provide some means for the user to navigate the entries in the Choice. Usually, one entry will be considered to have the input focus and will be highlighted in some way to distinguish it from the other entries. The platform will also supply a mechanism for the user to toggle the selected state of the highlighted entry. It is important to realize that selection and highlighting are different, in that highlighting is used only for the convenience of the user, whereas selection changes the state of the control. Changing the selection may cause a notification to be delivered to a listener. The specifics of event notification depend on the control itself and are described in the reference entries for the ChoiceGroup and List controls.

There are three methods that application code can use to access the selected state of entries in the Choice. The getSelectedIndex() method returns the index of the selected entry, or -1 if no entry is selected. In MULTIPLE mode, this method always returns -1 because more than one entry could be selected. The isSelected() method returns true if the entry with a given index is selected, false if it is not. Finally, the getSelectedFlags() method returns the selected state of each entry in an array of booleans that must be allocated by the caller and must have at least as many entries as there are entries in the Choice. The entry at index n in the array is returned with value true if the entry at index n in the Choice is selected, false if it is not. The return value of this method is the total number of selected entries.

There are two methods that allow the selection in the Choice to be programmatically changed. The setSelectedIndex() method sets the selected state of an entry with a given index according to the boolean value supplied as its second argument. In MULTIPLE mode, this method simply changes the selected state of the given entry and has no effect on other entries. In EXCLUSIVE and IMPLICIT modes, this method has an effect only if the boolean argument is true. In both modes, the given entry is selected and any previously selected entry is deselected. The setSelectedFlags() method sets the state of every element in the Choice from the corresponding entry in an array of boolean values supplied as its argument. In EXCLUSIVE and IMPLICIT modes, only one entry in the array can have value true. If this is not the case, then the first entry in the Choice will be selected and all other entries will be deselected.

Programmatic changes to the selection do not generate notifications to listeners.

```
public interface Choice {
// Public Constants
    public static final int EXCLUSIVE;                                          =1
    public static final int IMPLICIT;                                           =3
    public static final int MULTIPLE;                                           =2
// Public Instance Methods
    public abstract int append(String stringElement, Image imageElement);
    public abstract void delete(int elementNum);
    public abstract Image getImage(int elementNum);
    public abstract int getSelectedFlags(boolean[ ] selectedArray_return);
    public abstract int getSelectedIndex();
    public abstract String getString(int elementNum);
    public abstract void insert(int elementNum, String stringElement, Image imageElement);
    public abstract boolean isSelected(int elementNum);
    public abstract void set(int elementNum, String stringElement, Image imageElement);
    public abstract void setSelectedFlags(boolean[ ] selectedArray);
    public abstract void setSelectedIndex(int elementNum, boolean selected);
    public abstract int size( );
}
```

Implementations: ChoiceGroup, List

ChoiceGroup   MIDP 1.0

javax.microedition.lcdui

This class is an Item that presents a list of alternatives to the user and allows one or more of them to be selected. Most of the methods of the ChoiceGroup class are implementations of those specified by the Choice interface, which it implements, and are described in the reference entry for Choice.

A ChoiceGroup can be constructed in either Choice.EXCLUSIVE mode, when it behaves as a group of radio buttons, or in Choice.MULTIPLE mode when it acts like a collection of check boxes. ChoiceGroup does not implement the Choice.IMPLICIT mode.

At any given time, one entry in the ChoiceGroup control has the input focus. The user can move the focus to any entry in the list using keys on the keypad or the pointer, depending on the platform. The entry with the input focus will be highlighted in some way to distinguish it from the other entries. The user can change the selected state of the focused entry. When the selection is changed in this way, the ItemStateListener for the Form containing the ChoiceGroup is notified. Note, however, that changing the entry that has the input focus has no effect on the selection and is not notified to the listener.

```
Object — Item — ChoiceGroup
                     Choice
```

```
public class ChoiceGroup extends Item implements Choice {
// Public Constructors
    public ChoiceGroup(String label, int choiceType);
    public ChoiceGroup(String label, int choiceType, String[ ] stringElements, Image[ ] imageElements);
// Methods Implementing Choice
    public int append(String stringElement, Image imageElement);
    public void delete(int index);
    public Image getImage(int i);
```

```
    public int getSelectedFlags(boolean[ ] selectedArray_return);
    public int getSelectedIndex( );
    public String getString(int i);
    public void insert(int index, String stringElement, Image imageElement);
    public boolean isSelected(int index);
    public void set(int index, String stringElement, Image imageElement);
    public void setSelectedFlags(boolean[ ] selectedArray);
    public void setSelectedIndex(int index, boolean selected);
    public int size( );
// Public Methods Overriding Item
    public void setLabel(String label);
}
```

Command   MIDP 1.0

javax.microedition.lcdui

Command is a class that represents an operation that the may be represented in the user interface. Commands may be added to any Displayable with the exception of Alerts and are rendered in a platform-dependent way, often using buttons or as entries in a menu system. When the user activates the user interface control associated with a Command, the CommandListener associated with the Displayable is notified.

A Command has three attributes that are set at construction time. Once set, the values of these attributes can be obtained using the getLabel(), getCommandType() and getPriority() methods, but cannot be changed:

Label
  The command name that the user will see in the user interface.

Type
  A constant value that indicates the semantic intent of the command.

Priority
  An integer value that gives the priority of this command relative to others of the same type. Lower values indicate higher priority.

The *type* is used to indicate to the platform whether the command is one of the standard types that it knows about and might provide special display handling for, or an application-private command. The standard types, whose meanings should be obvious from their names, are BACK, CANCEL, EXIT, HELP, OK and STOP. Application-private commands are assigned types of ITEM or SCREEN.

The type usually determines where the platform will display the command. Where there is more than one command with the same type, the priority value is used to determine the relative prominence of each of those competing commands. If a device has a policy of attaching commands of type SCREEN to its two soft buttons, for example, and a Displayable has three such commands, the device might assign the command with lowest numerical priority value to one of the buttons and then create a menu to hold the other two commands and attach the menu to the other soft button. It is important to note that the application can only hint to the implementation as to how it would like it commands to be displayed - no direct control is possible, and different results will be obtained on different platforms.

Unlike a Swing Action, a Command does not contain the implementation of the action to be carried when it is activated - it is simply a value that a CommandListener can use to determine which operation the user wants to perform.

```
public class Command {
// Public Constructors
    public Command(String label, int commandType, int priority);
// Public Constants
    public static final int BACK;                                    =2
    public static final int CANCEL;                                  =3
    public static final int EXIT;                                    =7
    public static final int HELP;                                    =5
    public static final int ITEM;                                    =8
    public static final int OK;                                      =4
    public static final int SCREEN;                                  =1
    public static final int STOP;                                    =6
// Public Instance Methods
    public int getCommandType();
    public String getLabel();
    public int getPriority();
}
```

Passed To: Alert.addCommand(), CommandListener.commandAction(), Displayable.{addCommand(), removeCommand()}

Type Of: List.SELECT_COMMAND

CommandListener   MIDP 1.0
javax.microedition.lcdui

An interface implemented by objects that want to be notified when the user activates a Command associated with a Displayable. A Displayable can have a single CommandListener, set using its setCommandListener() method.

When any Command on a Displayable is activated, its CommandListener's commandAction() method is called. In order to allow a single listener to handle the actions associated with more than one Command, this method receives a reference to both the Command itself and the Displayable that this instance of the Command is associated with. The commandAction() method is typically invoked in the context of the thread that is responsible for managing the user interface and therefore any delay caused by this method may cause the user interface to appear to be unresponsive.

```
public interface CommandListener {
// Public Instance Methods
    public abstract void commandAction(Command c, Displayable d);
}
```

Passed To: Alert.setCommandListener(), Displayable.setCommandListener()

DateField   MIDP 1.0
javax.microedition.lcdui

This class is an Item that displays and allows the user to edit the value of a date, a time or both date and time, held internally as a java.util.Date object. Like all Items, DateField can have a label that is displayed near to it to indicate its function.

The *input mode*, which can be one of DATE, TIME, or DATE_TIME, determines which parts of the Date object associated with the DateField are displayed for editing. It can be set at construction time or by calling the setInputMode() method.

By default, the DateField is initialized with a null date and time value. An explicit date and time can be set using the setDate() method, which requires a Date object containing the new value. If the DateField is in DATE, the time portion of the Date object is ignored. If it is in TIME mode, the date portion *must* be set to Jan 1st, 1970.

The date is displayed according to the default time zone for the device. A different time zone can be specified by passing a suitable TimeZone object to the constructor. However, the MIDP specification does not provide full support for time zones and therefore some restrictions on the available time zones might be encountered on some devices.

When the user interacts with the DateField and changes its value, the ItemStateListener for the Form on which the control appears is notified. The new date and time can be retrieved using the getDate() method.

```
Object — Item — DateField
```

```
public class DateField extends Item {
// Public Constructors
    public DateField(String label, int mode);
    public DateField(String label, int mode, java.util.TimeZone timeZone);
// Public Constants
    public static final int DATE;                                          =1
    public static final int DATE_TIME;                                     =3
    public static final int TIME;                                          =2
// Public Instance Methods
    public java.util.Date getDate();
    public int getInputMode();
    public void setDate(java.util.Date date);
    public void setInputMode(int mode);
// Public Methods Overriding Item
    public void setLabel(String label);
}
```

Display   MIDP 1.0

javax.microedition.lcdui

This class represents a MIDlet's view of the screen of the device on which it is running. Every MIDlet has access to a single instance of this class, which it may obtain a reference to by calling the static getDisplay() method once its startApp() method has been entered for the first time. Subsequent calls will return the same instance, which remains valid until the MIDlet's destroyApp() method completes, or until the MIDlet calls notifyDestroyed(). When a MIDlet is in the foreground, the Display object becomes associated with the screen; when the MIDlet is not in the foreground, operations performed on the Display have no effect until the MIDlet gains the foreground.

A Display object shows the content of the Displayable passed to its setCurrent() method. MIDlets usually use the single-argument variant of this method to switch from one screen to another. When displaying an Alert, if the single-argument variant is used, the Displayable that was originally displayed will be restored when the Alert is dismissed. If it is appropriate to display a different screen when the Alert is dismissed, the two-argument variant may be used and the new Displayable supplied as its second argument.

The getCurrent() method returns a reference to the Displayable that the Display object is currently showing to the user if it is in the foreground, or would show to the user if it is in the background. It is important to note when using getCurrent() that the setCurrent() method does not necessarily take effect immediately - an implementation is permitted to defer changing the screen to a time convenient for itself. This means that it is not safe to assume that the value returned by the getCurrent() method is the Displayable passed to the last invocation of setCurrent().

Another possible side effect of this feature is that calling setCurrent() to display a screen and then blocking to wait for some condition set by the logic implemented in the event handlers for that screen may result in an application hang if setCurrent() is called in the thread used to manage the user interface, because the new screen may not be displayed until the method that called setCurrent() returns

The isColor() and numColors() methods can be used to discover the capabilities of the screen. If isColor() returns true, then the number returned by numColors() is the number of different colors that the screen is able to display. If, however, isColor() returns false, then numColors() indicates the number of available shades of gray. A typical, two-color cell phone for example, would return false to isColor() and 2 from numColors().

The callSerially() method can be used to arrange for a segment of code, implemented in the run() method of a Runnable, to be executed in the thread used to manage the user interface. This method might be used to defer the execution of such code until all pending repaint operations have been completed, or so that code that needs to operate on data that is relied upon by painting logic does not have to be made thread-safe.

```
public class Display {
// No Constructor
// Public Class Methods
    public static Display getDisplay(javax.microedition.midlet.MIDlet c);
// Public Instance Methods
    public void callSerially(Runnable r);
    public Displayable getCurrent();
    public boolean isColor();
    public int numColors();
    public void setCurrent(Displayable next);
    public void setCurrent(Alert alert, Displayable nextDisplayable);
}
```

Passed To: AlertType.playSound()

Returned By: Display.getDisplay()

Displayable   MIDP 1.0
javax.microedition.lcdui

Displayable is an abstract base class for objects that can be shown by a Display.

The addCommand() method provides the ability to associate one or more Commands with the displayable object. The way in which these Commands are represented in the user interface is platform-dependent, but would normally involve one or both of a button and a menu item. A Command may be removed using the removeCommand() method.

The setCommandListener() allows a single CommandListener to be registered to be notified when a Command is activated. If this method is called when a listener is already registered, the original listener is removed and will not receive further event notifications. Calling this method with argument null removes any registered listener.

The isShown() method can be used to determine whether the Displayable is currently visible. This method returns true when the owning MIDlet is in the foreground and the Displayable is the object currently displayed by its Display.

```
public abstract class Displayable {
// No Constructor
// Public Instance Methods
    public void addCommand(Command cmd);
    public boolean isShown();
    public void removeCommand(Command cmd);
```

```
    public void setCommandListener(CommandListener l);
}
```

Subclasses: Canvas, Screen

Passed To: CommandListener.commandAction(), Display.setCurrent()

Returned By: Display.getCurrent()

Font   MIDP 1.0

javax.microedition.lcdui

This class represents a font that can be used to render text in the low-level API. A device has a default font that can be obtained from the static getDefaultFont() method. Other fonts, if there are any, can be obtained from the getFont() method, which requires three attributes:

Font face
> An integer value that describes the type of font based on its appearance. The legal values are FACE_MONOSPACE, FACE_PROPORTIONAL and FACE_SYSTEM, which corresponds to a platform-dependent system font.

Font style
> Selects a style of the given font face. Legal values are STYLE_PLAIN, STYLE_ITALIC, STYLE_BOLD and STYLE_UNDERLINE. STYLE_ITALIC and STYLE_BOLD may be used together to request a bold, italic font. STYLE_UNDERLINE may be combined with any of the other styles.

Font size
> The relative size of the font, chosen from SIZE_SMALL, SIZE_MEDIUM and SIZE_LARGE.

Since the capabilities of MIDP devices vary widely, the application is only able to select a font based on this narrow set of logical attributes. The getFont() method returns the font from the set available to it that most closely matches the arguments supplied to it. Some devices may be able to closely match a wide range of requested fonts, while others might only be able to accurately represent a very small number. In order to minimize memory usage, the same Font instance will be returned by this method whenever the arguments supplied to it resolve to the same device font. This is possible because Font objects are immutable.

The Font object has methods that allow certain font attributes to be retrieved, including isBold(), isItalic() and isUnderlined(), which return the component parts of the font style. Note that the values returned by these methods represent the font actually selected and may not match those supplied to getFont(). The selected font size and face can also be retrieved using the getSize() and getFace() methods.

Several methods of the Font class perform functions that are supplied by the FontMetrics and LineMetrics classes in J2SE. The charWidth(), charsWidth(), stringWidth() and substringWidth() methods measure the horizontal size of a string or set of characters when rendered by the Font object on which they are called. The getHeight() method returns the height of a standard line in the font, including interline spacing, while getBaselinePosition() returns the distance from the top of the font to its baseline, both of these being measured in pixels. These methods can be used when manually placing text using the methods of the Graphics class.

```
public final class Font {
// No Constructor
// Public Constants
```

```
public static final int FACE_MONOSPACE;                                    =32
public static final int FACE_PROPORTIONAL;                                 =64
public static final int FACE_SYSTEM;                                        =0
public static final int SIZE_LARGE;                                        =16
public static final int SIZE_MEDIUM;                                        =0
public static final int SIZE_SMALL;                                         =8
public static final int STYLE_BOLD;                                         =1
public static final int STYLE_ITALIC;                                       =2
public static final int STYLE_PLAIN;                                        =0
public static final int STYLE_UNDERLINED;                                   =4
// Public Class Methods
   public static Font getDefaultFont();
   public static Font getFont(int face, int style, int size);
// Property Accessor Methods (by property name)
   public int getBaselinePosition();
   public boolean isBold();
   public int getFace();
   public int getHeight();
   public boolean isItalic();
   public boolean isPlain();
   public int getSize();
   public int getStyle();
   public boolean isUnderlined();
// Public Instance Methods
   public int charsWidth(char[] ch, int offset, int length);             native
   public int charWidth(char ch);                                        native
   public int stringWidth(String str);                                   native
   public int substringWidth(String str, int offset, int len);           native
}
```

Passed To: Graphics.setFont()

Returned By: Font.{getDefaultFont(), getFont()}, Graphics.getFont()

Form MIDP 1.0

javax.microedition.lcdui

Form is a subclass of Screen that is used to build form-like screens using Items. It inherits from its superclass the ability to have a title, a ticker and to have associated Commands and a CommandListener.

Items are usually added to a Form using the append(Item item) method, which adds the Item to the end of an internal list maintained by the Form. There are also two overloaded versions of this method that accept arguments of type String and Image. These methods are simply wrappers that add respectively a StringItem and an ImageItem to the form, with an empty label. It is also possible to insert an Item in between those already added by calling the insert() method, which requires the index of the Item before which the new one is to be added. The set() method can be used to replace an Item at a given index with a new one. Finally, the delete() method removes the Item at the supplied index. The total number of Items on a Form can be obtained from the size() method.

When rendered on the screen, Items appear on the Form from top to bottom in the order in which they appear in the Form's internal list. With the exception of StringItem and ImageItem, each Item is rendered on a line of its own. When the Item is too wide to fit the screen, it may be shortened or, in the case of a StringItem, the text will overflow onto following lines as necessary. A Form is always as wide as the display area available to it, but its height may exceed the total viewable area of the screen. When this is the

javax.micro- edition.lcdui

case, the implementation will provide some means (such as a scrollbar) to allow the user to move the viewable area over the entire vertical extent of the Form. Horizontal scrolling is not required and is never provided.

When an Item has an associated label, it will normally be placed close to the rest of the Item and may be displayed in such as way as to distinguish itself. In the PalmOS implementation, for example, Items are arranged in two columns with the label in the left-hand column rendered in bold and the rest of the Item in the right-hand column.

Successive StringItems and ImageItems that do *not* have associated labels are laid out horizontally whenever possible. If there is insufficient room, the text of a StringItem is broken at white space if possible and the balance appears on succeeding lines. An image that is too wide for the space allocated to its ImageItem is displayed on the next line and is truncated on the right if it is too wide for the device's screen. When these Items have labels, a line break will occur before the label in the usual way.

The setItemStateListener() method allows application code to register a single ItemStateListener to receive notification of state changes in any of the Items on the Form. Calling this method when there is already a listener registered replaces that listener with the new one, while invoking it with a null argument completely removes any existing listener.

```
Object ├ Displayable ├ Screen ├ Form

public class Form extends Screen {
// Public Constructors
    public Form(String title);
    public Form(String title, Item[ ] items);
// Public Instance Methods
    public int append(String str);
    public int append(Image image);
    public int append(Item item);
    public void delete(int index);
    public Item get(int index);
    public void insert(int index, Item item);
    public void set(int index, Item item);
    public void setItemStateListener(ItemStateListener iListener);
    public int size( );
}
```

Gauge   MIDP 1.0

javax.microedition.lcdui

This class is an Item that can be used as either a progress bar or a slider. The Gauge displays a fixed range of integer values together with the *current* value. The maximum value of the range and the initial value are set when the Gauge is constructed and may subsequently be changed using the setMaxValue() and setValue() methods. The minimum value is always implicitly zero.

In normal operation, the current value would probably start at zero and be updated by application code by calling the setValue() method to reflect the progress of an ongoing operation. In this mode, the Gauge operates as a progress bar and its value cannot be changed by the user. To prevent the user changing the value, the Gauge should be made *non-interactive*, which can be done by setting the interactive constructor argument to false. Note that this attribute cannot be changed once the Gauge has been constructed, although its value can be obtained by calling isInteractive().

To use the Gauge as a slider, it should be made interactive. In this mode, the user can change the current value within the permitted range using a device-dependent gesture.

As the value changes, the Gauge notifies the ItemStateListener for the Form on which it is displayed, which can retrieve the new value using the getValue() method.

Owing to display limitations, it may not be possible for every possible value in the allowed range to be displayed and therefore the user may have to adjust the Gauge value several times before a change in its appearance is seen. For this reason, it is recommended that the current value also be displayed in another control, such as a StringItem, so that the user can see the result of every adjustment.

```
Object — Item — Gauge

public class Gauge extends Item {
// Public Constructors
    public Gauge(String label, boolean interactive, int maxValue, int initialValue);
// Public Instance Methods
    public int getMaxValue();
    public int getValue();
    public boolean isInteractive();
    public void setMaxValue(int maxValue);
    public void setValue(int value);
// Public Methods Overriding Item
    public void setLabel(String label);
}
```

Graphics

MIDP 1.0

javax.microedition.lcdui

The Graphics class provides drawing and fill operations that can be used to paint the content of a Canvas or a mutable Image. A Graphics object for a Canvas is passed to its paint() method and is valid only within that method. A Graphics object for an Image can be obtained from its getGraphics() method and remains valid as long as the Image is referenced.

All operations on a Graphics object use a coordinate reference system measured in pixels, in which the origin is initially at the top-left hand corner of the Canvas or Image. Values of the x coordinate increase when moving to the right, while y value increase downwards. The coordinate origin may be moved by calling the translate() method, supplying the coordinates of the new origin relative to the current origin. Negative coordinate values are valid and, depending on the location of the origin, may or may not correspond to points on the drawing surface. It is permissible to move the origin to a location that is outside the drawing area.

A Graphics object has an associated clipping rectangle which bounds the area within which graphics operations will be performed. The clipping rectangle for an Image is initially set to cover the entire image, while that for a Canvas is set by the platform to cover the part of the Canvas that needs to be repainted. Operations performed on a Graphics object will not change pixels that lie outside clipping rectangle, even if their scope would include those pixels. Thus, setting the clipping rectangle can be used as a means of protecting areas that should not be changed. The bounds of the clipping rectangle, relative to the current origin, can be obtained from the getClipX(), getClipY(), getClipWidth() and getClipHeight() methods. The clipping rectangle can be changed using the setClip() method which sets an entirely new clip, and clipRect() intersect the current clip with the rectangular area specified by its arguments to produce smaller clipping area.

All drawing and filling operations make use of the currently selected color. When a Graphics object is created, its drawing color is black. The drawing color can be changed by calling the setColor() or setGrayScale() methods. Colors are represented as 24-bit RGB values held in an integer where the least significant 8 bits encode the blue value, the

javax.micro-edition.lcdui

next 8 bits hold the green value and the next 8 hold the red value. Using this scheme, the values 0xFF0000 and 0x7F0000 represent shades of red, whereas 0xFF represents blue. There are two variants of the setColor() method that allow the specification of the individual red, green and blue components, or of all of the components in a single integer. On devices that only support gray scale, the setGrayScale() method can be used to set a gray level in the range 0 to 255 inclusive, where 0 represents black and 255 is white.

The drawArc(), drawLine(), drawRect() and drawRoundRect() methods draw outline shapes in the current color using coordinates that are specified by their arguments. The pixels that are affected by these methods depend on the *stroke style*, which can be set using the setStrokeStyle() method to DOTTED or SOLID. By default, solid lines are drawn. Each drawing primitive, apart from drawLine(), has a corresponding fill operation that fills the shape with the current drawing color instead of drawing the outline. The fillRect() method, for example, can be used to create a solid, filled rectangular shape. The stroke style is not relevant for fill operations.

Text may be drawn onto a Canvas or an Image by using the drawChar(), drawChars(), drawString() and drawSubstring() methods, which specify the characters to be drawn and the location of an *anchor point* that determines where the text will be placed. To understand how the anchor point works, it is necessary to consider the text as being tightly wrapped in a rectangle. The anchor point specifies a point on the boundary of the rectangle and the drawing primitive gives the coordinates at which the anchor point will be placed, relative to the origin. For example, if the anchor point is specified as (TOP | LEFT) and the location is (40, 50), then the top-left of the bounding rectangle of the text will be placed at coordinates (40, 50) relative to the origin. On the other hand, if the anchor is (TOP | HCENTER), then the top of the bounding rectangle will be at y coordinate 50, and the text will be horizontally centered around x = 40. Use of the anchor point in this way makes it possible to center or right-align text without having to compute the width of the text using the text measurement methods of the Font class. Note, however, that vertical centering is not supported, even though there is a Graphics.VCENTER constant. This constant can, however, be used to vertically center an Image, as described below.

Text is always drawn using the current font, which may be set using the setFont() method, using a font obtained from the Font getFont() or getDefaultFont() methods. When it is created, a Graphics object is initialized to use the system default font.

An Image can be drawn onto the drawing surface of a Canvas or another Image by using the drawImage() method. By default, this method draws the whole image with its top left corner at a given coordinate location. However, it is possible to copy only a subset of the Image by setting the clipping rectangle of the Graphics object to bound the exact area of the target onto which the Image section should be copied. Neither the stroke style nor the drawing color is relevant to the drawImage method, since all pixels are copied from the source image. The coordinate location for the drawImage() method includes the specification of an anchor point, which is used in the same way as it is when drawing text, with the exception that vertical centering is also allowed. The bounding box used when determining the location of anchor points is the rectangle formed by the outer edge of the Image.

```
public class Graphics {
// No Constructor
// Public Constants
    public static final int BASELINE;                              =64
    public static final int BOTTOM;                                =32
    public static final int DOTTED;                                =1
    public static final int HCENTER;                               =1
    public static final int LEFT;                                  =4
```

```
    public static final int RIGHT;                                                         =8
    public static final int SOLID;                                                         =0
    public static final int TOP;                                                           =16
    public static final int VCENTER;                                                       =2
// Property Accessor Methods (by property name)
    public int getBlueComponent();
    public int getClipHeight();
    public int getClipWidth();
    public int getClipX();
    public int getClipY();
    public int getColor();
    public void setColor(int RGB);
    public void setColor(int red, int green, int blue);
    public Font getFont();
    public void setFont(Font font);
    public int getGrayScale();
    public void setGrayScale(int value);
    public int getGreenComponent();
    public int getRedComponent();
    public int getStrokeStyle();
    public void setStrokeStyle(int style);
    public int getTranslateX();
    public int getTranslateY();
// Public Instance Methods
    public void clipRect(int x, int y, int width, int height);
    public void drawArc(int x, int y, int width, int height, int startAngle, int arcAngle);    native
    public void drawChar(char character, int x, int y, int anchor);                            native
    public void drawChars(char[ ] data, int offset, int length, int x, int y, int anchor);     native
    public void drawImage(Image img, int x, int y, int anchor);                                native
    public void drawLine(int x1, int y1, int x2, int y2);                                      native
    public void drawRect(int x, int y, int width, int height);                                 native
    public void drawRoundRect(int x, int y, int width, int height, int arcWidth, int arcHeight); native
    public void drawString(String str, int x, int y, int anchor);                             native
    public void drawSubstring(String str, int offset, int len, int x, int y, int anchor);      native
    public void fillArc(int x, int y, int width, int height, int startAngle, int arcAngle);    native
    public void fillRect(int x, int y, int width, int height);                                 native
    public void fillRoundRect(int x, int y, int width, int height, int arcWidth, int arcHeight); native
    public void setClip(int x, int y, int width, int height);
    public void translate(int x, int y);
}
```

Passed To: Canvas.paint()

Returned By: Image.getGraphics()

Image

MIDP 1.0

javax.microedition.lcdui

A class that represents a memory-resident image that can be drawn onto the screen. Images are used in both the high- and low-level user interface APIs. In the high-level API, Images can be used with Alerts, ChoiceGroups, ImageItems and Lists. In the low-level API, an Image can be drawn onto any part of a Canvas object from within its paint() method.

An Image may be either *mutable* or *immutable*. Images used in the high-level API must be immutable; either type may be used with the low-level API. Given an arbitrary Image, the isMutable() method can be used to determine whether it is mutable or not.

The dimensions of an Image can be obtained by calling its getWidth() and getHeight() methods.

There are are four static createImage() methods can be used to create an Image. The createImage(byte[] data, int offset, int length) method creates an immutable image from data held in a portion of a given byte array. The data must be encoded in a format that is supported by the implementation. The only format that the MIDP specification requires a device to support is Portable Network Graphics (PNG). The image data can be obtained from any source, such as over a network or from a record in a RecordStore on the device. The createImage(String fileName) method uses the content of a file addressable using the resource name fileName as the image data and creates an immutable image from it. fileName is usually the absolute path name of a file within the MIDlet suite's JAR file, such as /ora/ch4/resources/red.png. The createImage(int width, int height) method returns a blank, mutable image with the supplied dimensions, that the application can use as the target of drawing operations by obtaining a Graphics object using its getGraphics() method. Finally, the createImage(Image source) creates an immutable copy of an existing image. This method can be used, for example, to create an immutable copy of a mutable image so that it can be used with the high-level API.

```
public class Image {
// No Constructor
// Public Class Methods
    public static Image createImage(String name) throws java.io.IOException;
    public static Image createImage(Image image);
    public static Image createImage(int width, int height);
    public static Image createImage(byte[ ] imagedata, int imageoffset, int imagelength);
// Public Instance Methods
    public Graphics getGraphics();
    public int getHeight();
    public int getWidth();
    public boolean isMutable();                                              constant
}
```

Passed To: Too many methods to list.

Returned By: Alert.getImage(), Choice.getImage(), ChoiceGroup.getImage(), Image.createImage(), ImageItem.getImage(), List.getImage()

ImageItem   MIDP 1.0

javax.microedition.lcdui

This class is a subclass of Item that displays an Image as well as the optional label provided by Item. The image to be displayed is supplied as an instance of the Image class and must be immutable. It is also possible to supply an alternate text string that is displayed in place of the image if the platform does not support images. These attributes are usually set at construction time, but may be changed later using the setImage() and setAltText() methods.

By default, an ImageItem that has a null or empty label is placed on the same line as any preceding StringItem or ImageItem, provided that there is room to accomodate the image. If there is insufficient room, then a line break will occur. The application may request that a different layout policy be applied by supplying an explicit layout argument to the constructor or using the setLayout() method.

The layout value consists of an optional alignment value together with an optional request for line breaks. The alignment value must be one (and only one) of the following:

LAYOUT_DEFAULT
   Applies the default layout policy described above

LAYOUT_LEFT
   Left justifies the image within the space allocated to it.

LAYOUT_RIGHT
   Right justifies the image within the space allocated to it.

LAYOUT_CENTER
   Centers the image within the space allocated to it.

A line break can be requested before and/or after the ImageItem by including the values LAYOUT_NEWLINE_BEFORE and LAYOUT_NEWLINE_AFTER in the layout value. The value (LAY-OUT_CENTER | LAYOUT_NEWLINE_BEFORE | LAYOUT_NEWLINE_AFTER), for example, centers the image on a line of its own. LAYOUT_NEWLINE_BEFORE is redundant if the ImageItem includes a non-empty label, because a label always forces a line break. Similarly, LAY-OUT_NEWLINE_AFTER is redundant if the next Item would force a line break.

```
┌────────┬──────┬───────────┐
│ Object ┤ Item ┤ ImageItem │
└────────┴──────┴───────────┘
public class ImageItem extends Item {
// Public Constructors
   public ImageItem(String label, Image img, int layout, String altText);
// Public Constants
   public static final int LAYOUT_CENTER;                              =3
   public static final int LAYOUT_DEFAULT;                             =0
   public static final int LAYOUT_LEFT;                                =1
   public static final int LAYOUT_NEWLINE_AFTER;                     =512
   public static final int LAYOUT_NEWLINE_BEFORE;                    =256
   public static final int LAYOUT_RIGHT;                               =2
// Public Instance Methods
   public String getAltText();
   public Image getImage();
   public int getLayout();
   public void setAltText(String altText);
   public void setImage(Image img);
   public void setLayout(int layout);
// Public Methods Overriding Item
   public void setLabel(String label);
}
```

Item   MIDP 1.0

javax.microedition.lcdui

This class is the base class for the high-level API user interface components that can be added to a Form. An Item has a label that is displayed near to and closely associated with the component itself. The label can be set using the setLabel() method and its value retrieved using getLabel(). The implementation is recommended to arrange for the label and the component to either both be visible or both be invisible when they are affected by the scrolling of the Form that they are part of.

On some platforms, some components, such as TextFields, may display a full-screen edi-tor that hides the original Form while the user is interacting with them. When this is the case, the label may be displayed as part of the editor as a reminder to the user of the meaning of the value being entered.

Even though, in implementation terms, Item is very much like the AWT Component class, in MIDP 1.0 it is not possible to subclass it to create custom high-level components.

```
public abstract class Item {
// No Constructor
// Public Instance Methods
    public String getLabel();
    public void setLabel(String label);
}
```

Subclasses: ChoiceGroup, DateField, Gauge, ImageItem, StringItem, TextField

Passed To: Form.{append(), Form(), insert(), set()}, ItemStateListener.itemStateChanged()

Returned By: Form.get()

ItemStateListener   MIDP 1.0

javax.microedition.lcdui

An interface implemented by objects that want to be notified when the state of an Item is changed as the result of user action. Each Form can have a single ItemStateListener that is registered by calling its setItemStateListener() method. Programmatic changes to the state of an Item are never notified to the ItemStateListener.

The ItemStateListener's itemStateChanged() method is called when the user makes a notifiable change in the state of any Items on the Form. The circumstances that result in notification depend on the nature of the Item. A text field, for example, will typically not notify every character entered or deleted, but will delay notification until the user moves the input focus elsewhere. A ChoiceGroup, on the other hand, will notify the Form's ItemStateListener whenever the user changes its selection state.

```
public interface ItemStateListener {
// Public Instance Methods
    public abstract void itemStateChanged(Item item);
}
```

Passed To: Form.setItemStateListener()

List   MIDP 1.0

javax.microedition.lcdui

List presents a list of alternatives to the user and allows one or more of them to be selected. Most of the methods of the List class are implementations of those specified by the Choice interface, which it implements, and are described in the reference entry for Choice. Since List is derived from Screen, it occupies the entire screen of the device and, unlike ChoiceGroup, cannot appear together with other controls.

A List can be constructed in Choice.EXCLUSIVE mode, when it behaves as a group of radio buttons, in Choice.MULTIPLE mode when it acts like a collection of check boxes or in Choice.IMPLICIT mode, which is usually used to create a full-screen menu. Both IMPLICIT and EXCLUSIVE modes allow only one entry in the LIST to be selected at any given time. The difference between these modes is the way they handle event notification as described below.

At any given time, one entry in the List control has the input focus. The user can move the focus to any entry in the list using keys on the keypad or the pointer, depending on the platform. The entry with the input focus will be highlighted in some way to distinguish it from the other entries and its state can be toggled between selected and unselected using a platform-dependent gesture.

Unlike ChoiceGroup, a List is not associated with an ItemStateListener because it is not an Item. How the application is made aware of selection changes depends on the mode.

In MULTIPLE and EXCLUSIVE modes, selection changes are not notified by the control. Instead, the application should attach a Command to the List that the user can activate to instruct application code to retrieve and act upon the current selected state of the List entries. In IMPLICIT mode, only one entry can be selected at any given time. Changing the selected entry results in the commandAction() method of the CommandListener attached to the List being called, with the Displayable argument referencing the List and the Command set to the special value List.SELECT_COMMAND. This arrangement makes it possible to use an IMPLICIT List that behaves like a menu without having to attach an application-defined Command to it. Note that changing the *highlighted* entry or changing the selection programmatically does not cause an event to be generated.

```
Object ─ Displayable ─ Screen ─ List
                                 │
                              Choice
```

```
public class List extends Screen implements Choice {
// Public Constructors
    public List(String title, int listType);
    public List(String title, int listType, String[ ] stringElements, Image[ ] imageElements);
// Public Constants
    public static final Command SELECT_COMMAND;
// Methods Implementing Choice
    public int append(String stringElement, Image imageElement);
    public void delete(int index);
    public Image getImage(int index);
    public int getSelectedFlags(boolean[ ] selectedArray_return);
    public int getSelectedIndex();
    public String getString(int index);
    public void insert(int index, String stringElement, Image imageElement);
    public boolean isSelected(int index);
    public void set(int index, String stringElement, Image imageElement);
    public void setSelectedFlags(boolean[ ] selectedArray);
    public void setSelectedIndex(int index, boolean selected);
    public int size();
}
```

Screen

MIDP 1.0

javax.microedition.lcdui

This class is an abstract class derived from Displayable that is the base from which the screen classes used in the high-level API (Alert, Form, List and TextBox) are derived. This class adds two features to those provided by its superclass:

A title

An optional string that is typically displayed at the top of the screen and describes the function of the screen. The title is set using the setTitle() method and may be retrieved using getTitle().

A ticker

An optional scrolling string that is usually placed above the screen, alongside, above or below the title, depending on the implementation. The ticker is an

javax.micro-edition.lcdui

instance of the Ticker class that may be installed using the setTicker(). The same ticker may be associated with more than one Screen.

Object ├ Displayable ├ Screen

public abstract class **Screen** extends Displayable {
// No Constructor
// Public Instance Methods
    public Ticker **getTicker**();
    public String **getTitle**();
    public void **setTicker**(Ticker ticker);
    public void **setTitle**(String s);
}

Subclasses: Alert, Form, List, TextBox

StringItem   MIDP 1.0

javax.microedition.lcdui

StringItem is a subclass of Item that displays a string as well as the label associated with its superclass. The string to be displayed can be set using the setText() and retrieved using getText(). In normal use, the label would remain unchanged and would describe the meaning of the text, which would vary depending on context. Typical usage might be to set the label to Address: and display an address using the text part of the StringItem.

The platform may choose to render the label and the text differently so as to highlight the distinction between them, but is not obliged to do so. The MIDP for PalmOS implementation, for example, uses a bold font for the label.

Placing a StringItem with a null or empty label on a Form does not cause a line break, so that successive StringItems (or ImageItems) that do not have labels may appear together on the same line if there is room. Newline characters may be embedded anywhere within the label or the text to force a line break to occur. Where a line break is required because there is insufficient space, the implementation will normally break at whitespace, where possible.

Object ├ Item ├ StringItem

public class **StringItem** extends Item {
// Public Constructors
    public **StringItem**(String label, String text);
// Public Instance Methods
    public String **getText**();
    public void **setText**(String text);
// Public Methods Overriding Item
    public void **setLabel**(String label);
}

TextBox   MIDP 1.0

javax.microedition.lcdui

TextBox is a full-screen text editing component that has almost the same programming interface as TextField. Apart from the fact that a TextBox is visually represented as a multi-line control and occupies the whole screen whereas TextField usually appears as a single line in a Form, the only real difference between these two controls is the fact that TextBox does not notify content changes to a listener. Application code should add a Command to the TextBox to allow the user to request that its content be processed.

```
Object ─ Displayable ─ Screen ─ TextBox

public class TextBox extends Screen {
// Public Constructors
    public TextBox(String title, String text, int maxSize, int constraints);
// Public Instance Methods
    public void delete(int offset, int length);
    public int getCaretPosition();
    public int getChars(char[ ] data);
    public int getConstraints();
    public int getMaxSize();
    public String getString();
    public void insert(String src, int position);
    public void insert(char[ ] data, int offset, int length, int position);
    public void setChars(char[ ] data, int offset, int length);
    public void setConstraints(int constraints);
    public int setMaxSize(int maxSize);
    public void setString(String text);
    public int size();
}
```

TextField   MIDP 1.0

javax.microedition.lcdui

TextField is an Item that may be placed on a Form to display and allow the editing of a text string. The initial content of a TextField is set at construction time or by using the set-String() method and the possibly modified value can be retrieved at any time by calling getString(). A TextField may initially appear as a single-line control in the user interface, but multi-line input is permitted and some devices may provide a separate full-screen editor that can be invoked by user action to make it easier for the user to edit the field content.

Two types of constraint may be applied to the string displayed by a TextField - a length constraint and a content constraint.

The maximum size of the text that may appear in the field is set at construction time and can subsequently be changed using setMaxSize(). The implementation may impose a fixed upper limit on all TextFields, which overrides the value requested by application code. The actual maximum size can be obtained from the getMaxSize() method. The maximum size is applied whenever the content of the field is changed, whether programmatically or by the user.

A content constraint can be applied either at construction time or using the setConstraints() method to limit the type of data that the field may contain. When a constraint is in place, the TextField ensures that each character entered is consistent with the constraint and will reject characters that are not permitted. Constraints are applied both during editing and when the content of the field is changed programmatically. The following constraints are defined by the MIDP specification; not all of these are implemented by all devices:

ANY

Represents the absence of any constraint, allowing the field to contain any characters

EMAILADDR
> Constrains the input to be an e-mail address

NUMERIC
> Requires the field to contain a valid number.

PASSWORD
> Does not constrain the characters that can be entered, but specifies that they should not be echoed.

PHONENUMBER
> Specifies that the field will contain a phone number. The device may apply checks to ensure that the value entered conforms with one or more well-known formats for telephone numbers.

URL
> Specifies that the field should contain a Uniform Resource Locator (URL).

In some cases, the presence of a content constraint also causes the field to format the field content to reflect the data type. In the case of PHONENUMBER, for example, the field may insert parentheses and other characters that give the value entered the appearance of a telephone number. Characters that are added in this way are visible to the user, but are not part of the content of the field. If, for example, the user enters the digits 1234567890 into a field with this constraint applied, they may be displayed in the form (123) 456-7890, but the getString() method would return the value 1234567890.

There are several ways to change the content of a TextField. The setString() method over-writes the whole field content with the string passed as its argument and setChars() does the same, except that the new value is given as a portion of an array of characters. In both cases, using a null reference for the new data causes the field to be emptied. The insert methods cause a string or a set of characters to be inserted before a given location in the field, given by its index. The index should be 0 to insert characters before the first character of the field and the value returned by the size() method to add characters at the end. A range of characters can be removed from the field using the delete() method. Any insertion and removal operation will fail and throw an IllegalArgumentException if the modified content would violate the field's content or length constraints.

The content of a TextField can be retrieved in the form of a string using the getString() or as a character array using getChars(). The latter method is preferred for password fields, because the content of the returned array can be cleared once the password has been verified, to minimize the possibility of accidental disclosure of the password. This cannot be done when the password is extracted in string form, because Strings are immutable.

Changes in the content of a TextField are notified to the ItemStateListener of the Form that it is contained in. An implementation is not obliged to notify every change in the field content made while focus remains in the field , but must do so at the latest when the user moves the input focus elsewhere.

```
┌────────┬──────┬───────────┐
│ Object ├─ Item ├─ TextField │
└────────┴──────┴───────────┘
```

```
public class TextField extends Item {
// Public Constructors
    public TextField(String label, String text, int maxSize, int constraints);
// Public Constants
    public static final int ANY;                              =0
    public static final int CONSTRAINT_MASK;              =65535
    public static final int EMAILADDR;                        =1
```

```
    public static final int NUMERIC;                                              =2
    public static final int PASSWORD;                                         =65536
    public static final int PHONENUMBER;                                          =3
    public static final int URL;                                                  =4
// Public Instance Methods
    public void delete(int offset, int length);
    public int getCaretPosition();
    public int getChars(char[ ] data);
    public int getConstraints();
    public int getMaxSize();
    public String getString();
    public void Insert(String src, int position);
    public void Insert(char[ ] data, int offset, int length, int position);
    public void setChars(char[ ] data, int offset, int length);
    public void setConstraints(int constraints);
    public int setMaxSize(int maxSize);
    public void setString(String text);
    public int size();
// Public Methods Overriding Item
    public void setLabel(String label);
}
```

Ticker   MIDP 1.0

javax.microedition.lcdui

A high-level API class that displays a scrolling text message on a Screen. The ticker is typically displayed at the top of the screen adjacent to the screen title, if there is one. The ticker is associated with a Screen by calling its setTicker(). The same ticker instance may be associated with more than one screen so that the same information can remain displayed as the user navigates through the application.

The text to be displayed by the ticker is set using the setString method. The rate at which the text is scrolled and the scrolling direction are platform-dependent and cannot be controlled by the application. It is not possible to halt the scrolling effect, but the ticker can be removed from a screen by calling its setTicker() method with argument null.

```
public class Ticker {
// Public Constructors
    public Ticker(String str);
// Public Instance Methods
    public String getString();
    public void setString(String str);
}
```

Passed To: Screen.setTicker()

Returned By: Screen.getTicker()

CHAPTER 16

javax.microedition.midlet

This package contains only two classes: MIDlet and MIDletStateChangeException. The MIDlet class is the base class for all MIDlets, which are the Mobile Information Device Profile's equivalent of Java applets. Like applets, MIDlets have a small number of methods that must be overridden so that MIDlets can respond to state changes. These state changes are caused by interactions with the user or with other MIDlets. Under certain circumstances, a MIDlet can report a problem during a state change by throwing a MIDletStateChangeException, which may or may not stop the state change from being completed.

Figure 16-1 shows the class hierarchy of this package. See Chapter 3, "The Mobile Information Device Profile and MIDlets," for more details about MIDlets.

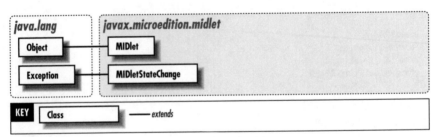

Figure 16–1: The javax.microedition.midlet hierarchy

MIDlet   **MIDP 1.0**

javax.microedition.midlet

This class is the abstract base class from which all MIDlet classes are derived. MIDlets run on devices that support the Mobile Information Device Profile (MIDP), under the control of device-dependent application management software (AMS) that creates, schedules, and destroys them.

MIDlets are grouped together into suites. MIDlet suites are always installed, managed, and removed as a single unit. All MIDlets from the same suite execute within a single Java virtual machine instance, enabling them to share data using static variables declared in their class implementations. MIDlets can also share information by using RecordStores, which can be accessed using the APIs defined in the javax.microedition.rms package. Partitioning MIDlets so that only those from the same suite execute in the same VM ensures that potentially malicious MIDlets from one suite cannot read or modify information belonging to another. RecordStores are similarly protected by ensuring that they are private to the MIDlet suite whose MIDlets create them.

Of all the MIDlets that are currently executing on a device, only one of them is considered to be in the *foreground*. The foreground MIDlet is unique in that it has access to the device's screen, keypad, and pointer (if the device supports them). Updates to the screen made by the foreground MIDlet will be seen by the user—possibly after a short delay— whereas those made in a MIDlet that is in the background will not affect the display until that MIDlet comes to the foreground again. The selection of the foreground MIDlet is made by the AMS scheduler. A MIDlet may influence the choice of the foreground MIDlet by calling its resumeRequest() method to indicate that it would like to move to the foreground. The scheduler may ignore this request or it may assign the MIDlet to the foreground at some future time. Similarly, a MIDlet uses the notify-Paused() method to give up the foreground. Since both of these methods are public, a MIDlet may invoke them on an instance of a different MIDlet from the same suite, provided that it can obtain a reference to it. In addition, the resumeRequest() method can be called by a MIDlet to have a second MIDlet perform a task on its behalf. The first MIDlet must then rely on the second one to resume it once the assigned task has been completed.

To implement a MIDlet, create a MIDlet subclass that provides implementations of the methods startApp(), pauseApp() and destroyApp(). These methods are declared to be abstract in the base class and are invoked by the scheduler at well-defined points in the MIDlet's life cycle. A MIDlet's constructor is called as soon as it is created. Its startApp() method is invoked when the MIDlet is moved to the foreground, which may (or may not) be shortly after its construction. Since this method can be called several times during its lifecycle, a MIDlet often contains an instance variable that it uses to detect the first invocation of startApp() so that it can perform initialization of resources that are not required until it has access to the screen. A MIDlet's startApp() method can indicate to the scheduler that it does not wish to be moved to the foreground by throwing a MIDlet-StateChangeException, perhaps because it is currently performing a background activity. This typically leaves the MIDlet in a state from which another attempt can be made to resume it later. If the MIDlet encounters an error from which it cannot recover, it may throw a different exception (which must be derived from RuntimeException), or it may call the notifyDestroy() method.

The pauseApp() method is called to notify the MIDlet that it is no longer in the foreground. A MIDlet typically uses this method to free any resources that it only needs while it has access to the screen. These resources can then be reallocated when the MIDlet regains the foreground using the startApp() method. A paused MIDlet may continue to do useful work in other threads, but should consume as little resources as possible if it chooses to do so.

The destroyApp() method is called to notify the MIDlet that it is being terminated. This method has a boolean argument. If this argument has the value true (which will always be the case when it is called from the scheduler) the termination is unconditional and the MIDlet must release any resources it is holding and return. The MIDlet will lose the foreground and will not be scheduled again after it returns from the destroyApp() method. The destroyApp() method may also be called by the MIDlet itself (or by another MIDlet in the same suite) with a false argument; this notifies the MIDlet that it has the option of terminating. If the MIDlet is in a state in which it is convenient to stop, it should behave as described above; the code that called destroyApp() must then call notify-Destroyed() to tell the scheduler that the MIDlet is in the destroyed state. However, if the MIDlet does not wish to stop, it may signal this fact to the caller by throwing a MIDlet-StateChangeException.

The notifyDestroyed() method tells the scheduler that the MIDlet has voluntarily terminated. Before calling this method, the MIDlet should release its resources, as the scheduler does not invoke its destroyApp() method to give it an opportunity to do so. MIDlets that call notifyDestroyed() usually precede the call with an invocation of destroyApp() to achieve this.

A MIDlet can retrieve the values of properties set in either its application descriptor file (JAD) or in the manifest file of the JAR in which it is packaged using the getAppProperty() method. If the same property is defined in both the manifest and the JAD, the value in the JAD is returned. Property values are read-only and are shared by all of the MIDlets in a MIDlet suite. They are typically used to customize a MIDlet's behavior without requiring recompilation.

```
public abstract class MIDlet {
// Protected Constructors
    protected MIDlet();
// Public Instance Methods
    public final String getAppProperty(String key);
    public final void notifyDestroyed();
    public final void notifyPaused();
    public final void resumeRequest();
// Protected Instance Methods
    protected abstract void destroyApp(boolean unconditional) throws MIDletStateChangeException;
    protected abstract void pauseApp();
    protected abstract void startApp() throws MIDletStateChangeException;
}
```

Passed To: javax.microedition.lcdui.Display.getDisplay()

MIDletStateChangeException

javax.microedition.midlet

checked

This exception signals that a MIDlet state change failed. This exception may be thrown from the MIDlet's startApp() method to indicate that it currently does not wish begin or resume execution, but may be able to do so at a later time. It may also be thrown from destroyApp() if that method was called with a false argument and the MIDlet does not wish to terminate.

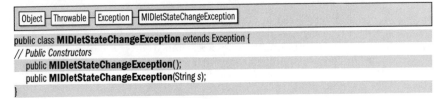

```
public class MIDletStateChangeException extends Exception {
// Public Constructors
    public MIDletStateChangeException();
    public MIDletStateChangeException(String s);
}
```

Thrown By: MIDlet.{destroyApp(), startApp()}

CHAPTER 17

javax.microedition.rms

Package javax.microedition.rms

MIDP 1.0

This package, whose class hierarchy is shown in Figure 17-1, allows MIDlets to store information on a device that will persist even when the MIDlet is not running. How the information is stored is device-specific and is not intended to be visible to MIDlets.

The key class in this package is RecordStore, which represents a collection of records. Each record in the record store is an array of bytes with an associated identifier. This identifier can be used to retrieve the record, modify it, or delete it. MIDlets in the same MIDlet suite can share record stores, but may not access (or even know of the existence of) record stores in other suites. All record stores belonging to a suite are automatically removed if the suite is removed from the device.

Records in a record store can be traversed by creating a RecordEnumeration. The enumeration may contain all of the records, or a subset filtered according to some MIDlet-defined criterion. The order in which the records appear in the enumeration can also be controlled through the use of a RecordComparator.

InvalidRecordIDException

MIDP 1.0

javax.microedition.rms

checked

This exception signals that a RecordStore operation has been attempted using an invalid record ID. A record ID is invalid if it does not correspond to a record in the RecordStore. Zero is always an invalid ID, as are all negative integers.

Object — Throwable — Exception — RecordStoreException — InvalidRecordIDException

```
public class InvalidRecordIDException extends RecordStoreException {
// Public Constructors
    public InvalidRecordIDException();
    public InvalidRecordIDException(String message);
}
```

Thrown By: RecordEnumeration.{nextRecord(), nextRecordId(), previousRecord(), previousRecordId()}, RecordStore.{deleteRecord(), getRecord(), getRecordSize(), setRecord()}

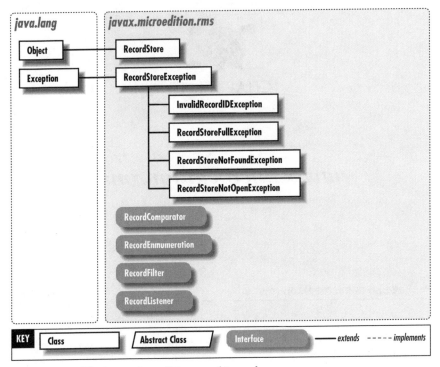

Figure 17-1: The java.microedition.rms hierarchy

RecordComparator

javax.microedition.rms

This is an interface used when creating a RecordEnumeration that determines the order in which records are returned. The interface consists of the single method compare(), which is passed a pair of byte-array records, rec1 and rec2. The method returns one of the following integer values to indicate their relative ordering:

PRECEDES
    Indicates that rec1 should appear before rec2

EQUIVALENT
    Indicates that rec1 and rec2 are equivalent according to the sorting criterion applied by this comparator. Note that this does not imply that the records are equal, although equal records would result in this value being returned.

FOLLOWS
    Indicates that rec1 should appear after rec2

A typical implementation of this method wraps each of the records with a ByteArrayInput-Stream and a DataInputStream so that the contents of the records can be accessed as a set of fields. To construct a filter that sorts based on the natural sorting order of the first field in the record, which is assumed to be a String, the record in the byte arrays rec1 and rec2 is converted to DataInputStreams like this:

```
DataInputStream dis1 = new DataInputStream(new ByteArrayInputStream(rec1));

DataInputStream dis2 = new DataInputStream(new ByteArrayInputStream(rec2));
```

At this point, the field to be compared is extracted from each record using the DataInput-Stream readUTF() method, and the comparison is performed:

```
int res = dis1.readUTF().compareTo(dis2.readUTF());
```

The return value from the method should be PRECEDES if res is negative, EQUIVALENT if res is zero and FOLLOWS otherwise.

```
public interface RecordComparator {
// Public Constants
    public static final int EQUIVALENT;                                    =0
    public static final int FOLLOWS;                                       =1
    public static final int PRECEDES;                                      =-1
// Public Instance Methods
    public abstract int compare(byte[ ] rec1, byte[ ] rec2);
}
```

Passed To: RecordStore.enumerateRecords()

RecordEnumeration   MIDP 1.0
javax.microedition.rms

RecordEnumeration is an interface that provides method to enumerate, or iterate, through a set of records in a RecordStore. The RecordEnumeration may be constructed so that only a subset of the records appear. In addition, it may also specify the order in which the records are presented. Once the enumeration has been constructed, records may be traversed either forwards or backwards, and the traversal direction may be changed at any time.

A RecordEnumeration is obtained by calling the RecordStore enumerateRecords() method, which accepts three parameters that determine the content and ordering of the enumeration:

filter

> A RecordFilter that selects which records will appear in the enumeration. If this argument is null, the enumeration will include all of the records.

comparator

> A RecordComparator that determines the order in which the records appear in the enumeration. If this parameter is null, the record order is undefined.

keepUpdated

> If this parameter has the value false, the set of records that appears in the enumeration, as well as their order, is determined once and is thereafter fixed, even if the underlying RecordStore content changes. If this parameter is true, changes in the RecordStore will be immediately visible in the enumeration. Note that setting this parameter to true can be very expensive as each change to the RecordStore requires a potentially time-consuming operation to rebuild the enumeration.

Once an enumeration has been created, the numRecords() method can be used to check the number of records that it will return. If the enumeration is dynamically updated, the number of records in the enumeration may vary and the value returned by this method may be unreliable. The isKeptUpdated() method may be used to determine whether the enumeration is updated in this way. The keepUpdated() method can be used to convert a static enumeration to one that is dynamically updated, or vice versa. An alternative to creating a dynamically updated enumeration is to call the rebuild() method, which recreates the enumeration to reflect the current state of the RecordStore and resets it so that it is pointing to the first record.

An enumeration may be traversed in the forward direction using the nextRecordId() or nextRecord() methods, which return the identifier of the next record or the record itself, respectively. The hasNextElement() method can be used to determine when there are no more records to be retrieved. If nextRecordId() or nextRecord() methods are called when the last record in the enumeration has already been returned, an InvalidRecordIDException is thrown.

The enumeration may be traversed in the opposite direction using the previousRecordId() and previousRecord() methods. The hasPreviousElement() can be used to determine whether an invocation of either of these methods would return a record or throw an InvalidRecordIDException. It is possible to change the direction of traversal by mixing the use of nextRecord() and previousRecord(). It is also possible to reset the enumeration to its initial state using the reset() method.

There is a possibility that records in the RecordStore might be deleted by another thread in the MIDlet or by another MIDlet in the same suite. If this is the case, the nextRecord() or previousRecord() methods will throw an InvalidRecordIDException when they reach a record that has been deleted. It is safe to catch this exception and continue to the next record. This only happens if the enumeration is not dynamically updated. In the same manner, the nextRecordId() and previousRecordId() methods may return record identifiers for records that have been deleted. If an attempt is made to read such a record, an InvalidRecordIDException is thrown. Note that this issue exists even for dynamically updated enumerations, because the record could be removed after its identifier is returned but before it is read from the RecordStore. Consequently, application code should always be prepared to receive an InvalidRecordIDException and simply advance to the next record if the cause is not the enumeration's end.

When the application has no further use for a RecordEnumeration, it must call the destroy() method to release its resources. Once done, any further attempts to use the enumeration results in an IllegalStateException. Also, if the RecordStore that the enumeration is associated with is closed, nextRecord() and previousRecord() will fail with a RecordStoreNotOpenException.

```
public interface RecordEnumeration {
// Public Instance Methods
    public abstract void destroy();
    public abstract boolean hasNextElement();
    public abstract boolean hasPreviousElement();
    public abstract boolean isKeptUpdated();
    public abstract void keepUpdated(boolean keepUpdated);
    public abstract byte[ ] nextRecord() throws InvalidRecordIDException, RecordStoreNotOpenException,
        RecordStoreException;
    public abstract int nextRecordId() throws InvalidRecordIDException;
    public abstract int numRecords();
    public abstract byte[ ] previousRecord() throws InvalidRecordIDException, RecordStoreNotOpenException,
        RecordStoreException;
    public abstract int previousRecordId() throws InvalidRecordIDException;
    public abstract void rebuild();
    public abstract void reset();
}
```

Returned By: RecordStore.enumerateRecords()

RecordFilter

javax.microedition.rms

This interface selects which RecordStore records should be included in a RecordEnumeration. It consists of a single method, matches(), which examines the contents of a record and returns true if the record should be included, or false if it should not.

A typical implementation of this method wraps the incoming record with a ByteArrayInputStream and a DataInputStream so that the contents of the record can be accessed as a set of fields. For example, to construct a filter that would include only records whose first field (assumed to be a String) starts with the letter S, first create a DataInputStream from the candidate:

```
DataInputStream dis = new DataInputStream(new ByteArrayInputStream(candidate));
```

Then, extract the field to be compared using the DataInputStream readUTF() method and test its first character:

```
return dis.readUTF().startsWith("S");
```

```
public interface RecordFilter {
// Public Instance Methods
    public abstract boolean matches(byte[ ] candidate);
}
```

Passed To: RecordStore.enumerateRecords()

RecordListener

javax.microedition.rms

This interface is implemented by classes that wish to be notified of changes to the content of one or more RecordStores. A listener is registered by calling the addRecordListener() method of a RecordStore and removed using the removeRecordListener() method.

This interface has three methods. The recordAdded() method is called when a new record is added to a RecordStore. recordDeleted() is called when a new record is removed from a RecordStore. Finally, recordChanged() is called when the content of an existing record is modified. Each of these methods are passed a reference to the RecordStore and the ID of the affected record. This allows a single listener to monitor more than one RecordStore. Note that in the case of recordDeleted(), the record ID will already be invalid by the time this method is invoked, so it is not possible to retrieve the contents of the deleted record.

```
public interface RecordListener {
// Public Instance Methods
    public abstract void recordAdded(RecordStore recordStore, int recordId);
    public abstract void recordChanged(RecordStore recordStore, int recordId);
    public abstract void recordDeleted(RecordStore recordStore, int recordId);
}
```

Passed To: RecordStore.{addRecordListener(), removeRecordListener()}

RecordStore

javax.microedition.rms

A RecordStore provides persistent storage for a collection of records. The means by which the records are stored is device-dependent. A RecordStore may be implemented using a native feature of the host operating system; therefore the data that it contains might be visible or subject to modification by native applications. The programming interface provided by the RecordStore class is intended to be simple enough that it can be implemented across a variety of different platforms. A RecordStore does not expose the details of the underlying storage mechanism.

A RecordStore is identified by its name, which is a string of up to 32 Unicode characters. RecordStores can be shared by all MIDlets in the same MIDlet suite; hence, the name must be unique within the MIDlet suite. RecordStores belonging to one suite are not visible to MIDlets in other suites as the MIDlet suite itself is implicitly part of the RecordStore name. As a result, MIDlets in different suites can create stores with the same name without conflict.

The static openRecordStore() method opens an existing RecordStore given its name. The createIfNecessary argument should be set to true to create the RecordStore if it does not already exist. The openRecordStore() method may be called several times within the same MIDlet and will always return the same RecordStore instance given the same name. When a MIDlet no longer needs to access a RecordStore, it should call the closeRecord-Store() method. Note that the number of times a store is opened by a MIDlet is counted and the store is not actually closed until the number of closeRecordStore() calls matches the number of opens.

There are two other static methods that operate at the RecordStore level. The listRecord-Stores() method returns the names of all of the record stores belonging to the MIDlet suite in the form of a string array. The deleteRecordStore() method deletes a named RecordStore. This operation succeeds only if the record store is not currently open. A RecordStore is automatically deleted when the MIDlet suite that owns it is uninstalled from the host device.

A RecordStore consists of a set of records, each of which is simply an array of bytes with an associated record identifier. The record identifier is a unique, positive integer value assigned by the RecordStore implementation when the record is created. The first record to be created in a record store is assigned the identifier 1, and subsequent records are assigned an identifier that is one greater then that assigned to the record created before it. If a record is deleted, its identifier is *not* reused, even if it is the most recently created record. The getNextRecordID() can be used to get the value of the next identifier to be assigned. The value returned should be used carefully, however, because it will become invalid if another thread in the same MIDlet or another MIDlet creates a new record. Although RecordStore operations are thread-safe, it is the MIDlet's responsibility to ensure that the required level of consistency is maintained when multiple operations must be performed without other changes being made. One way to achieve this is to code multi-step operations in a block that is synchronized on the RecordStore reference.

While the RecordStore is open, you can use the getNumRecords(), getSize() and getSizeAvail-able() methods to get the total number of records in the record store, the number of bytes that the record store occupies and the approximate number of bytes by which the record store may grow before reachings its size limit, respectively. Since the record store implementation uses some space for its management information, the value returned by the getSize() method may be larger than the total size of the existing records and the value returned by getSizeAvailable() will be larger than the remaining space available for the storage of records.

A new record can be added to the record store using the addRecord() method, which is given the record content in the form of a range of bytes from a byte array and returns the identifier assigned to the record. Records are usually created by wrapping a ByteAr-rayOutputStream with a DataOutputStream and then writing Java primitive types and strings to the record using DataOutputStream methods. When the record is complete, the ByteAr-rayOutputStream toByteArray() can be used to get the byte array to be passed to addRecord().

The content of an existing record can be obtained using the getRecord() methods, which require the record identifier and, optionally, a preallocated buffer into which the record will be read. The size of a record can be obtained by calling the getRecordSize() method.

Once a record has been retrieved, its content can be modified and the updated version written back to the record store using the **setRecord()** method. This method can also be used to set the content of an existing record from a byte array containing arbitrary content that was not initialized by calling **getRecord()**. The setRecord() method always overwrites a complete record and may increase or decrease the record size. It is not possible to update only part of a record other than by reading it into memory, modifying the affected portion and writing the result back in its entirety.

Records can be deleted using the **deleteRecord()** method. Once a record has been deleted, its record identifier becomes permanently invalid.

To scan the records in a record store, the **enumerateRecords()** method should be used to get a RecordEnumeration. The arguments passed to this method allow for the returned enumeration to present the records in a specified order and to include only records that meet a given criterion. See the description of the RecordEnumeration interface for further information.

The record store has an associated version number that is incremented whenever a record is added, deleted or changed. The time of the last modification is also recorded. The version number and last modification time can be obtained using the **getVersion()** and **getLastModified()** methods, respectively. The modification time is returned in the same form as the system time returned by the System currentTimeMillis() method.

A more immediate way to discover changes in the record store is to register a RecordListener using the **addRecordListener()** methods. Listeners are notified each time a record is added, removed or changed. A listener can be removed using the **removeRecordListener()** method; all listeners are automatically deregistered when the record store is closed.

```
public class RecordStore {
// No Constructor
// Public Class Methods
    public static void deleteRecordStore(String recordStoreName) throws RecordStoreException,
        RecordStoreNotFoundException;
    public static String[ ] listRecordStores();
    public static RecordStore openRecordStore(String recordStoreName, boolean createIfNecessary)
        throws RecordStoreException, RecordStoreFullException, RecordStoreNotFoundException;
// Event Registration Methods (by event name)
    public void addRecordListener(RecordListener listener);
    public void removeRecordListener(RecordListener listener);
// Property Accessor Methods (by property name)
    public long getLastModified() throws RecordStoreNotOpenException;
    public String getName() throws RecordStoreNotOpenException;
    public int getNextRecordID() throws RecordStoreNotOpenException, RecordStoreException;
    public int getNumRecords() throws RecordStoreNotOpenException;
    public int getSize() throws RecordStoreNotOpenException;
    public int getSizeAvailable() throws RecordStoreNotOpenException;
    public int getVersion() throws RecordStoreNotOpenException;
// Public Instance Methods
    public int addRecord(byte[ ] data, int offset, int numBytes) throws RecordStoreNotOpenException,
        RecordStoreException, RecordStoreFullException;
    public void closeRecordStore() throws RecordStoreNotOpenException, RecordStoreException;
    public void deleteRecord(int recordId) throws RecordStoreNotOpenException, InvalidRecordIDException,
        RecordStoreException;
    public RecordEnumeration enumerateRecords(RecordFilter filter, RecordComparator comparator,
                                boolean keepUpdated) throws RecordStoreNotOpenException;
    public byte[ ] getRecord(int recordId) throws RecordStoreNotOpenException, InvalidRecordIDException,
        RecordStoreException;
    public int getRecord(int recordId, byte[ ] buffer, int offset) throws RecordStoreNotOpenException,
        InvalidRecordIDException, RecordStoreException;
```

```
public int getRecordSize(int recordId) throws RecordStoreNotOpenException, InvalidRecordIDException,
    RecordStoreException;
public void setRecord(int recordId, byte[ ] newData, int offset, int numBytes) throws RecordStoreNotOpenException
    , InvalidRecordIDException, RecordStoreException, RecordStoreFullException;
}
```

Passed To: RecordListener.{recordAdded(), recordChanged(), recordDeleted()}

Returned By: RecordStore.openRecordStore()

RecordStoreException   MIDP 1.0

javax.microedition.rms   *checked*

This is the base class for all exceptions thrown by RecordStore operations. This class is also used as a generic exception that is thrown when none of the more specific exceptions are appropriate. The getMessage() method is used to obtain further information on the problem that caused the exception.

```
Object ├─ Throwable ├─ Exception ├─ RecordStoreException
```

```
public class RecordStoreException extends Exception {
// Public Constructors
    public RecordStoreException();
    public RecordStoreException(String message);
}
```

Subclasses: InvalidRecordIDException, RecordStoreFullException, RecordStoreNotFoundException, RecordStoreNotOpenException

Thrown By: RecordEnumeration.{nextRecord(), previousRecord()}, RecordStore.{addRecord(), closeRecordStore(), deleteRecord(), deleteRecordStore(), getNextRecordID(), getRecord(), getRecordSize(), openRecordStore(), setRecord()}

RecordStoreFullException   MIDP 1.0

javax.microedition.rms   *checked*

This exception signals that the RecordStore operation could not be performed because there is insufficient space available. Note that a RecordStore implementation may require its own private space in the RecordStore, so that there may be insufficient space for an operation to be performed even when it appears that there is enough space.

```
Object ├─ Throwable ├─ Exception ├─ RecordStoreException ├─ RecordStoreFullException
```

```
public class RecordStoreFullException extends RecordStoreException {
// Public Constructors
    public RecordStoreFullException();
    public RecordStoreFullException(String message);
}
```

Thrown By: RecordStore.{addRecord(), openRecordStore(), setRecord()}

RecordStoreNotFoundException

MIDP 1.0

javax.microedition.rms

checked

This exception signals that a RecordStore to be opened or deleted could not be found. One common cause of this error is trying to access a RecordStore in another MIDlet suite, which is not allowed.

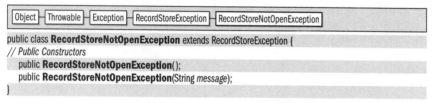

Object ├ Throwable ├ Exception ├ RecordStoreException ├ RecordStoreNotFoundException

public class **RecordStoreNotFoundException** extends RecordStoreException {
// *Public Constructors*
   public **RecordStoreNotFoundException**();
   public **RecordStoreNotFoundException**(String *message*);
}

Thrown By: RecordStore.{deleteRecordStore(), openRecordStore()}

RecordStoreNotOpenException

MIDP 1.0

javax.microedition.rms

checked

This exception signals that an operation was attempted on a RecordStore that has already been closed using the closeRecordStore() method.

Object ├ Throwable ├ Exception ├ RecordStoreException ├ RecordStoreNotOpenException

public class **RecordStoreNotOpenException** extends RecordStoreException {
// *Public Constructors*
   public **RecordStoreNotOpenException**();
   public **RecordStoreNotOpenException**(String *message*);
}

Thrown By: Too many methods to list.

CHAPTER 18

Class, Method, and Field Index

The following index allows you to look up a class or interface and find what package it is defined in. It also allows you to look up a method or field and find what class it is defined in. Use it when you want to look up a class but don't know its package, or when you want to look up a method but don't know its class.

charValue(): Character
charWidth(): Font
checkError(): PrintStream
Choice: javax.microedition.lcdui
ChoiceGroup: javax.microedition.lcdui
Class: java.lang
ClassCastException: java.lang
ClassNotFoundException: java.lang
clear(): Hashtable
clipRect(): Graphics
close(): ByteArrayInputStream, ByteArrayOutput-
Stream, Connection, DataInputStream, DataOut-
putStream, InputStream, InputStreamReader,
OutputStream, OutputStreamWriter, PrintStream,
Reader, Writer
closeRecordStore(): RecordStore
Command: javax.microedition.lcdui
commandAction(): CommandListener
CommandListener: javax.microedition.lcdui
compare(): RecordComparator
compareTo(): String
concat(): String
CONFIRMATION: AlertType
Connection: javax.microedition.io
ConnectionNotFoundException: javax.microedition.io
Connector: javax.microedition.io
CONSTRAINT_MASK: TextField
contains(): Hashtable, Vector
containsKey(): Hashtable
ContentConnection: javax.microedition.io
copyInto(): Vector
count: ByteArrayInputStream, ByteArrayOutputStream
createImage(): Image
currentThread(): Thread
currentTimeMillis(): System

D

Datagram: javax.microedition.io
DatagramConnection: javax.microedition.io
DataInput: java.io
DataInputStream: java.io
DataOutput: java.io
DataOutputStream: java.io
Date: java.util
DATE: Calendar, DateField
DATE_TIME: DateField
DateField: javax.microedition.lcdui
DAY_OF_MONTH: Calendar
DAY_OF_WEEK: Calendar

DECEMBER: Calendar
delete(): Choice, ChoiceGroup, Form, List, String-
Buffer, TextBox, TextField
deleteCharAt(): StringBuffer
deleteRecord(): RecordStore
deleteRecordStore(): RecordStore
destroy(): RecordEnumeration
destroyApp(): MIDlet
digit(): Character
Display: javax.microedition.lcdui
Displayable: javax.microedition.lcdui
DOTTED: Graphics
DOWN: Canvas
drawArc(): Graphics
drawChar(): Graphics
drawChars(): Graphics
drawImage(): Graphics
drawLine(): Graphics
drawRect(): Graphics
drawRoundRect(): Graphics
drawString(): Graphics
drawSubstring(): Graphics

E

elementAt(): Vector
elementCount: Vector
elementData: Vector
elements(): Hashtable, Vector
EMAILADDR: TextField
empty(): Stack
EmptyStackException: java.util
endsWith(): String
ensureCapacity(): StringBuffer, Vector
enumerateRecords(): RecordStore
Enumeration: java.util
EOFException: java.io
equals(): Boolean, Byte, Calendar, Character, Date,
Integer, Long, Object, Short, String
EQUIVALENT: RecordComparator
err: System
ERROR: AlertType
Error: java.lang
Exception: java.lang
EXCLUSIVE: Choice
EXIT: Command
exit(): Runtime, System

F

FACE_MONOSPACE: Font
FACE_PROPORTIONAL: Font
FACE_SYSTEM: Font
FEBRUARY: Calendar
fillArc(): Graphics
fillRect(): Graphics
fillRoundRect(): Graphics
FIRE: Canvas
firstElement(): Vector
flush(): DataOutputStream, OutputStream, Output-
    StreamWriter, PrintStream, Writer
FOLLOWS: RecordComparator
Font: javax.microedition.lcdui
FOREVER: Alert
Form: javax.microedition.lcdui
forName(): Class
freeMemory(): Runtime
FRIDAY: Calendar

G

GAME_A: Canvas
GAME_B: Canvas
GAME_C: Canvas
GAME_D: Canvas
Gauge: javax.microedition.lcdui
gc(): Runtime, System
GET: HttpConnection
get(): Calendar, Form, Hashtable
getAddress(): Datagram
getAltText(): ImageItem
getAppProperty(): MIDlet
getAvailableIDs(): TimeZone
getBaselinePosition(): Font
getBlueComponent(): Graphics
getBytes(): String
getCaretPosition(): TextBox, TextField
getChars(): String, StringBuffer, TextBox, TextField
getClass(): Object
getClipHeight(): Graphics
getClipWidth(): Graphics
getClipX(): Graphics
getClipY(): Graphics
getColor(): Graphics
getCommandType(): Command
getConstraints(): TextBox, TextField
getCurrent(): Display
getData(): Datagram

getDate(): DateField, HttpConnection
getDefault(): TimeZone
getDefaultFont(): Font
getDefaultTimeout(): Alert
getDisplay(): Display
getEncoding(): ContentConnection
getExpiration(): HttpConnection
getFace(): Font
getFile(): HttpConnection
getFont(): Font, Graphics
getGameAction(): Canvas
getGraphics(): Image
getGrayScale(): Graphics
getGreenComponent(): Graphics
getHeaderField(): HttpConnection
getHeaderFieldDate(): HttpConnection
getHeaderFieldInt(): HttpConnection
getHeaderFieldKey(): HttpConnection
getHeight(): Canvas, Font, Image
getHost(): HttpConnection
getID(): TimeZone
getImage(): Alert, Choice, ChoiceGroup, ImageItem,
    List
getInputMode(): DateField
getInstance(): Calendar
getKeyCode(): Canvas
getKeyName(): Canvas
getLabel(): Command, Item
getLastModified(): HttpConnection, RecordStore
getLayout(): ImageItem
getLength(): ContentConnection, Datagram
getMaximumLength(): DatagramConnection
getMaxSize(): TextBox, TextField
getMaxValue(): Gauge
getMessage(): Throwable
getName(): Class, RecordStore
getNextRecordID(): RecordStore
getNominalLength(): DatagramConnection
getNumRecords(): RecordStore
getOffset(): Datagram, TimeZone
getPort(): HttpConnection
getPriority(): Command, Thread
getProperty(): System
getProtocol(): HttpConnection
getQuery(): HttpConnection
getRawOffset(): TimeZone
getRecord(): RecordStore
getRecordSize(): RecordStore
getRedComponent(): Graphics
getRef(): HttpConnection

---

getRequestMethod(): HttpConnection
getRequestProperty(): HttpConnection
getResourceAsStream(): Class
getResponseCode(): HttpConnection
getResponseMessage(): HttpConnection
getRuntime(): Runtime
getSelectedFlags(): Choice, ChoiceGroup, List
getSelectedIndex(): Choice, ChoiceGroup, List
getSize(): Font, RecordStore
getSizeAvailable(): RecordStore
getString(): Alert, Choice, ChoiceGroup, List, TextBox,
    TextField, Ticker
getStrokeStyle(): Graphics
getStyle(): Font
getText(): StringItem
getTicker(): Screen
getTime(): Calendar, Date
getTimeInMillis(): Calendar
getTimeout(): Alert
getTimeZone(): Calendar, TimeZone
getTitle(): Screen
getTranslateX(): Graphics
getTranslateY(): Graphics
getType(): Alert, ContentConnection
getURL(): HttpConnection
getValue(): Gauge
getVersion(): RecordStore
getWidth(): Canvas, Image
Graphics: javax.microedition.lcdui

H

hashCode(): Boolean, Byte, Character, Date, Integer,
    Long, Object, Short, String
Hashtable: java.util
hasMoreElements(): Enumeration
hasNextElement(): RecordEnumeration
hasPointerEvents(): Canvas
hasPointerMotionEvents(): Canvas
hasPreviousElement(): RecordEnumeration
hasRepeatEvents(): Canvas
HCENTER: Graphics
HEAD: HttpConnection
HELP: Command
hideNotify(): Canvas
HOUR: Calendar
HOUR_OF_DAY: Calendar
HTTP_ACCEPTED: HttpConnection
HTTP_BAD_GATEWAY: HttpConnection
HTTP_BAD_METHOD: HttpConnection

HTTP_BAD_REQUEST: HttpConnection
HTTP_CLIENT_TIMEOUT: HttpConnection
HTTP_CONFLICT: HttpConnection
HTTP_CREATED: HttpConnection
HTTP_ENTITY_TOO_LARGE: HttpConnection
HTTP_EXPECT_FAILED: HttpConnection
HTTP_FORBIDDEN: HttpConnection
HTTP_GATEWAY_TIMEOUT: HttpConnection
HTTP_GONE: HttpConnection
HTTP_INTERNAL_ERROR: HttpConnection
HTTP_LENGTH_REQUIRED: HttpConnection
HTTP_MOVED_PERM: HttpConnection
HTTP_MOVED_TEMP: HttpConnection
HTTP_MULT_CHOICE: HttpConnection
HTTP_NO_CONTENT: HttpConnection
HTTP_NOT_ACCEPTABLE: HttpConnection
HTTP_NOT_AUTHORITATIVE: HttpConnection
HTTP_NOT_FOUND: HttpConnection
HTTP_NOT_IMPLEMENTED: HttpConnection
HTTP_NOT_MODIFIED: HttpConnection
HTTP_OK: HttpConnection
HTTP_PARTIAL: HttpConnection
HTTP_PAYMENT_REQUIRED: HttpConnection
HTTP_PRECON_FAILED: HttpConnection
HTTP_PROXY_AUTH: HttpConnection
HTTP_REQ_TOO_LONG: HttpConnection
HTTP_RESET: HttpConnection
HTTP_SEE_OTHER: HttpConnection
HTTP_TEMP_REDIRECT: HttpConnection
HTTP_UNAUTHORIZED: HttpConnection
HTTP_UNAVAILABLE: HttpConnection
HTTP_UNSUPPORTED_RANGE: HttpConnection
HTTP_UNSUPPORTED_TYPE: HttpConnection
HTTP_USE_PROXY: HttpConnection
HTTP_VERSION: HttpConnection
HttpConnection: javax.microedition.io

I

identityHashCode(): System
IllegalAccessException: java.lang
IllegalArgumentException: java.lang
IllegalMonitorStateException: java.lang
IllegalStateException: java.lang
IllegalThreadStateException: java.lang
Image: javax.microedition.lcdui
ImageItem: javax.microedition.lcdui
IMPLICIT: Choice
in: DataInputStream
indexOf(): String, Vector

IndexOutOfBoundsException: java.lang
INFO: AlertType
InputConnection: javax.microedition.io
InputStream: java.io
InputStreamReader: java.io
insert(): Choice, ChoiceGroup, Form, List, StringBuffer, TextBox, TextField
insertElementAt(): Vector
InstantiationException: java.lang
Integer: java.lang
InterruptedException: java.lang
InterruptedIOException: java.io
intValue(): Integer
InvalidRecordIDException: javax.microedition.rms
IOException: java.io
isAlive(): Thread
isArray(): Class
isAssignableFrom(): Class
isBold(): Font
isColor(): Display
isDigit(): Character
isDoubleBuffered(): Canvas
isEmpty(): Hashtable, Vector
isInstance(): Class
isInteractive(): Gauge
isInterface(): Class
isItalic(): Font
isKeptUpdated(): RecordEnumeration
isLowerCase(): Character
isMutable(): Image
isPlain(): Font
isSelected(): Choice, ChoiceGroup, List
isShown(): Displayable
isUnderlined(): Font
isUpperCase(): Character
Item: javax.microedition.lcdui
ITEM: Command
itemStateChanged(): ItemStateListener
ItemStateListener: javax.microedition.lcdui

J

JANUARY: Calendar
join(): Thread
JULY: Calendar
JUNE: Calendar

K

keepUpdated(): RecordEnumeration
KEY_NUM0: Canvas
KEY_NUM1: Canvas
KEY_NUM2: Canvas
KEY_NUM3: Canvas
KEY_NUM4: Canvas
KEY_NUM5: Canvas
KEY_NUM6: Canvas
KEY_NUM7: Canvas
KEY_NUM8: Canvas
KEY_NUM9: Canvas
KEY_POUND: Canvas
KEY_STAR: Canvas
keyPressed(): Canvas
keyReleased(): Canvas
keyRepeated(): Canvas
keys(): Hashtable

L

lastElement(): Vector
lastIndexOf(): String, Vector
LAYOUT_CENTER: ImageItem
LAYOUT_DEFAULT: ImageItem
LAYOUT_LEFT: ImageItem
LAYOUT_NEWLINE_AFTER: ImageItem
LAYOUT_NEWLINE_BEFORE: ImageItem
LAYOUT_RIGHT: ImageItem
LEFT: Canvas, Graphics
length(): String, StringBuffer
List: javax.microedition.lcdui
listRecordStores(): RecordStore
lock: Reader, Writer
Long: java.lang
longValue(): Integer, Long

M

MARCH: Calendar
mark: ByteArrayInputStream
mark(): ByteArrayInputStream, DataInputStream, InputStream, InputStreamReader, Reader
markSupported(): ByteArrayInputStream, DataInputStream, InputStream, InputStreamReader, Reader
matches(): RecordFilter
Math: java.lang
max(): Math
MAX_PRIORITY: Thread

MAX_RADIX: Character
MAX_VALUE: Byte, Character, Integer, Long, Short
MAY: Calendar
MIDlet: javax.microedition.midlet
MIDletStateChangeException: javax.microedition.midlet
MILLISECOND: Calendar
min(): Math
MIN_PRIORITY: Thread
MIN_RADIX: Character
MIN_VALUE: Byte, Character, Integer, Long, Short
MINUTE: Calendar
MONDAY: Calendar
MONTH: Calendar
MULTIPLE: Choice

N

NegativeArraySizeException: java.lang
newDatagram(): DatagramConnection
newInstance(): Class
next(): Random
nextElement(): Enumeration
nextInt(): Random
nextLong(): Random
nextRecord(): RecordEnumeration
nextRecordId(): RecordEnumeration
NORM_PRIORITY: Thread
NoSuchElementException: java.util
notify(): Object
notifyAll(): Object
notifyDestroyed(): MIDlet
notifyPaused(): MIDlet
NOVEMBER: Calendar
NullPointerException: java.lang
NumberFormatException: java.lang
numColors(): Display
NUMERIC: TextField
numRecords(): RecordEnumeration

O

Object: java.lang
OCTOBER: Calendar
OK: Command
open(): Connector
openDataInputStream(): Connector, InputConnection
openDataOutputStream(): Connector, OutputConnection
openInputStream(): Connector, InputConnection

openOutputStream(): Connector, OutputConnection
openRecordStore(): RecordStore
out: DataOutputStream, System
OutOfMemoryError: java.lang
OutputConnection: javax.microedition.io
OutputStream: java.io
OutputStreamWriter: java.io

P

paint(): Canvas
parseByte(): Byte
parseInt(): Integer
parseLong(): Long
parseShort(): Short
PASSWORD: TextField
pauseApp(): MIDlet
peek(): Stack
PHONENUMBER: TextField
playSound(): AlertType
PM: Calendar
pointerDragged(): Canvas
pointerPressed(): Canvas
pointerReleased(): Canvas
pop(): Stack
pos: ByteArrayInputStream
POST: HttpConnection
PRECEDES: RecordComparator
previousRecord(): RecordEnumeration
previousRecordId(): RecordEnumeration
print(): PrintStream
println(): PrintStream
printStackTrace(): Throwable
PrintStream: java.io
push(): Stack
put(): Hashtable

R

Random: java.util
READ: Connector
read(): ByteArrayInputStream, DataInputStream, InputStream, InputStreamReader, Reader
READ_WRITE: Connector
readBoolean(): DataInput, DataInputStream
readByte(): DataInput, DataInputStream
readChar(): DataInput, DataInputStream
Reader: java.io
readFully(): DataInput, DataInputStream
readInt(): DataInput, DataInputStream

readLong(): DataInput, DataInputStream
readShort(): DataInput, DataInputStream
readUnsignedByte(): DataInput, DataInputStream
readUnsignedShort(): DataInput, DataInputStream
readUTF(): DataInput, DataInputStream
ready(): InputStreamReader, Reader
rebuild(): RecordEnumeration
receive(): DatagramConnection
recordAdded(): RecordListener
recordChanged(): RecordListener
RecordComparator: javax.microedition.rms
recordDeleted(): RecordListener
RecordEnumeration: javax.microedition.rms
RecordFilter: javax.microedition.rms
RecordListener: javax.microedition.rms
RecordStore: javax.microedition.rms
RecordStoreException: javax.microedition.rms
RecordStoreFullException: javax.microedition.rms
RecordStoreNotFoundException: javax.microedition.rms
RecordStoreNotOpenException: javax.microedition.rms
regionMatches(): String
rehash(): Hashtable
remove(): Hashtable
removeAllElements(): Vector
removeCommand(): Displayable
removeElement(): Vector
removeElementAt(): Vector
removeRecordListener(): RecordStore
repaint(): Canvas
replace(): String
reset(): ByteArrayInputStream, ByteArrayOutputStream, Datagram, DataInputStream, InputStream, InputStreamReader, Reader, RecordEnumeration
resumeRequest(): MIDlet
reverse(): StringBuffer
RIGHT: Canvas, Graphics
run(): Runnable, Thread, TimerTask
Runnable: java.lang
Runtime: java.lang
RuntimeException: java.lang

S

SATURDAY: Calendar
schedule(): Timer
scheduleAtFixedRate(): Timer
scheduledExecutionTime(): TimerTask
SCREEN: Command
Screen: javax.microedition.lcdui
search(): Stack
SECOND: Calendar
SecurityException: java.lang
SELECT_COMMAND: List
send(): DatagramConnection
SEPTEMBER: Calendar
serviceRepaints(): Canvas
set(): Calendar, Choice, ChoiceGroup, Form, List
setAddress(): Datagram
setAltText(): ImageItem
setCharAt(): StringBuffer
setChars(): TextBox, TextField
setClip(): Graphics
setColor(): Graphics
setCommandListener(): Alert, Displayable
setConstraints(): TextBox, TextField
setCurrent(): Display
setData(): Datagram
setDate(): DateField
setElementAt(): Vector
setError(): PrintStream
setFont(): Graphics
setGrayScale(): Graphics
setImage(): Alert, ImageItem
setInputMode(): DateField
setItemStateListener(): Form
setLabel(): ChoiceGroup, DateField, Gauge, ImageItem, Item, StringItem, TextField
setLayout(): ImageItem
setLength(): Datagram, StringBuffer
setMaxSize(): TextBox, TextField
setMaxValue(): Gauge
setPriority(): Thread
setRecord(): RecordStore
setRequestMethod(): HttpConnection
setRequestProperty(): HttpConnection
setSeed(): Random
setSelectedFlags(): Choice, ChoiceGroup, List
setSelectedIndex(): Choice, ChoiceGroup, List
setSize(): Vector
setString(): Alert, TextBox, TextField, Ticker
setStrokeStyle(): Graphics

setText(): StringItem
setTicker(): Screen
setTime(): Calendar, Date
setTimeInMillis(): Calendar
setTimeout(): Alert
setTimeZone(): Calendar
setTitle(): Screen
setType(): Alert
setValue(): Gauge
Short: java.lang
shortValue(): Integer, Short
showNotify(): Canvas
size(): ByteArrayOutputStream, Choice, ChoiceGroup, Form, Hashtable, List, TextBox, TextField, Vector
SIZE_LARGE: Font
SIZE_MEDIUM: Font
SIZE_SMALL: Font
skip(): ByteArrayInputStream, DataInputStream, InputStream, InputStreamReader, Reader
skipBytes(): DataInput, DataInputStream
sleep(): Thread
SOLID: Graphics
Stack: java.util
start(): Thread
startApp(): MIDlet
startsWith(): String
STOP: Command
StreamConnection: javax.microedition.io
StreamConnectionNotifier: javax.microedition.io
String: java.lang
StringBuffer: java.lang
StringIndexOutOfBoundsException: java.lang
StringItem: javax.microedition.lcdui
stringWidth(): Font
STYLE_BOLD: Font
STYLE_ITALIC: Font
STYLE_PLAIN: Font
STYLE_UNDERLINED: Font
substring(): String
substringWidth(): Font
SUNDAY: Calendar
System: java.lang

T

TextBox: javax.microedition.lcdui
TextField: javax.microedition.lcdui
Thread: java.lang
Throwable: java.lang
THURSDAY: Calendar

Ticker: javax.microedition.lcdui
TIME: DateField
Timer: java.util
TimerTask: java.util
TimeZone: java.util
toBinaryString(): Integer
toByteArray(): ByteArrayOutputStream
toCharArray(): String
toHexString(): Integer
toLowerCase(): Character, String
toOctalString(): Integer
TOP: Graphics
toString(): Boolean, Byte, ByteArrayOutputStream, Character, Class, Hashtable, Integer, Long, Object, Short, String, StringBuffer, Thread, Throwable, Vector
totalMemory(): Runtime
toUpperCase(): Character, String
translate(): Graphics
trim(): String
trimToSize(): Vector
TUESDAY: Calendar

U

UnsupportedEncodingException: java.io
UP: Canvas
URL: TextField
useDaylightTime(): TimeZone
UTFDataFormatException: java.io

V

valueOf(): Integer, String
VCENTER: Graphics
Vector: java.util
VirtualMachineError: java.lang

W

wait(): Object
WARNING: AlertType
WEDNESDAY: Calendar
WRITE: Connector
write(): ByteArrayOutputStream, DataOutput, DataOutputStream, OutputStream, OutputStreamWriter, PrintStream, Writer
writeBoolean(): DataOutput, DataOutputStream

writeByte(): DataOutput, DataOutputStream
writeChar(): DataOutput, DataOutputStream
writeChars(): DataOutput, DataOutputStream
writeInt(): DataOutput, DataOutputStream
writeLong(): DataOutput, DataOutputStream
Writer: java.io
writeShort(): DataOutput, DataOutputStream
writeUTF(): DataOutput, DataOutputStream

Y

YEAR: Calendar
yield(): Thread

Index

We'd like to hear your suggestions for improving our indexes. Send email to *index@oreilly.com*.

About the Author

Kim Topley is a freelance Java developer with his own consulting company based near London, England. By day, he develops Java applications for a variety of prominent companies in the financial marketplace; he spends most evenings and weekends either keeping abreast of the latest developments in the Java world or writing about aspects of Java that he finds topical or interesting. Out of these long evenings (and nights) have come two other books, *Core Java Foundation Classes* and *Core Swing: Advanced Programming* (both published by Prentice Hall). Prior to being caught up in the Java phenomenon, Kim was a Unix kernel developer and, even further back, created microcode for mainframe computers. Kim has a B.A. degree in mathematics from the University of Cambridge, England.

When he's not working, Kim enjoys playing golf (badly, unfortunately), traveling abroad with his family, and flying Microsoft Flight Simulator with his son Andrew, contesting periodic flight challenges to prove who is the better pilot. He is currently in second place, and extremely proud of it.

Colophon

Our look is the result of reader comments, our own experimentation, and feedback from distribution channels. Distinctive covers complement our distinctive approach to technical topics, breathing personality and life into potentially dry subjects.

The animal on the cover of *J2ME in a Nutshell* is a galago. Galagos are prosimian primates, "pre-monkeys" that existed before monkeys, apes, and humans evolved. These small (10–35 cm long, not including their tail, which ranges from 20 to nearly 50 cm long), nocturnal animals live in Africa, spending much of their time in trees and eating mostly bugs, fruit, and the occasional small bird. Their big ears, featured prominently on the cover, can be bent almost completely back, either one at a time or both together, something the galagos apparently like to do quite frequently.

Leanne Soylemez was the production editor and copyeditor for *J2ME in a Nutshell*. Mary Anne Weeks Mayo was the proofreader, and Matt Hutchinson and Jane Ellin provided quality control. John Bickelhaupt wrote the index.

Ellie Volckhausen designed the cover of this book, based on a series design by Edie Freedman. The cover image is from *Animal Creation*. Emma Colby produced the cover layout with QuarkXPress 4.1 using Adobe's ITC Garamond font.

Melanie Wang and David Futato designed the interior layout based on a series design by Nancy Priest. Neil Walls cleaned up the original FrameMaker files for Part I. The print version of Part II was generated from XML using a basic macro set developed by Steve Talbott from the GNU troff -gs macros and adapted to the book design by Lenny Muellner; Norm Walsh wrote the Perl filter that translates XML source into those macros. The text and heading fonts are ITC Garamond Light and Garamond Book. The illustrations that appear in the book were produced by Robert Romano and Jessamyn Read using Macromedia FreeHand 9 and Adobe Photoshop 6. This colophon was written by Leanne Soylemez.

More Titles from O'Reilly

Java

Learning Wireless Java

By Qusay Mahmoud
1st Edition January 2002
262 pages, ISBN 0-596-00243-2

Wireless Java is a solid introduction to working with the Mobile Information Device Profile (MIDP), which contains the APIs designed specifically for writing applications that need to run on wireless and embedded devices. It includes reference material on the core and javax.microedition classes, as well as on the classes specific to the various wireless platforms the J2ME supports.

Java Security, 2nd Edition

By Scott Oaks
2nd Edition May 2001
618 pages, ISBN 0-596-00157-6

The second edition focuses on the platform features of Java that provide security—the class loader, bytecode verifier, and security manager—and recent additions to Java that enhance this security model: digital signatures, security providers, and the access controller. The book covers in depth the security model of Java 2, version 1.3, including the two new security APIs: JAAS and JSSE.

Database Programming with JDBC and Java, 2nd Edition

By George Reese
2nd Edition August 2000
352 pages, ISBN 1-56592-616-1

This book describes the standard Java interfaces that make portable object-oriented access to relational databases possible, and offers a robust model for writing applications that are easy to maintain. The second edition has been completely updated for JDBC 2.0, and includes reference listings for JDBC and the most important RMI classes. The book begins with a quick overview of SQL for developers who may be asked to handle a database for the first time, and goes on to explain how to issue database queries and updates through SQL and JDBC.

Java Threads, 2nd Edition

By Scott Oaks & Henry Wong
2nd Edition January 1999
336 pages, ISBN 1-56592-418-5

Revised and expanded to cover Java 2, *Java Threads*, 2nd Edition, shows you how to take full advantage of Java's thread facilities: where to use threads to increase efficiency, how to use them effectively, and how to avoid common mistakes. It thoroughly covers the Thread and ThreadGroup classes, the Runnable interface, and the language's synchronized operator. The book pays special attention to threading issues with Swing, as well as problems like deadlock, race condition, and starvation to help you write code without hidden bugs.

Java Network Programming, 2nd Edition

By Elliotte Rusty Harold
2nd Edition August 2000
760 pages, ISBN 1-56592-870-9

Java Network Programming, 2nd Edition, is a complete introduction to developing network programs (both applets and applications) using Java, covering everything from networking fundamentals to remote method invocation (RMI). It includes chapters on TCP and UDP sockets, multicasting protocol and content handlers, and servlets. This second edition also includes coverage of Java 1.1, 1.2 and 1.3. New chapters cover multithreaded network programming, I/O, HTML parsing and display, the Java Mail API, the Java Secure Sockets Extension, and more.

Java Programming with Oracle JDBC

By Donald Bales
1st Edition January 2002
496 pages, ISBN 0-596-00088-X

Here is the professional's guide to leveraging Java's JDBC in an Oracle environment. Readers learn the all-important mysteries of establishing database corrections; issuing SQL queries and getting results back; and advanced topics such as streaming large objects, calling PL/SQL procedures, and working with Oracle9*i*'s object-oriented features.

O'REILLY®

TO ORDER: **800-998-9938** • **order@oreilly.com** • **www.oreilly.com**
ONLINE EDITIONS OF MOST O'REILLY TITLES ARE AVAILABLE BY SUBSCRIPTION AT **safari.oreilly.com**
ALSO AVAILABLE AT MOST RETAIL AND ONLINE BOOKSTORES

Java

Creating Effective JavaHelp

By Kevin Lewis
1st Edition June 2000
188 pages, ISBN 1-56592-719-2

JavaHelp is an online help system developed in the Java programming language. *Creating Effective JavaHelp* covers the main features and options of JavaHelp and shows how to create a basic JavaHelp system, prepare help topics, and deploy the help system in an application. Written for all levels of Java developers and technical writers, the book takes a chapter-by-chapter approach to building concepts, to impart a complete understanding of how to create usable JavaHelp systems and integrate them into Java applications and applets.

Java Performance Tuning

By Jack Shirazi
1st Edition September 2000
440 pages, ISBN 0-596-00015-4

Java Performance Tuning contains step-by-step instructions on all aspects of the performance tuning process, right from such early considerations as setting goals, measuring performance, and choosing a compiler. Extensive examples for tuning many parts of an application are described in detail, and any pitfalls are identified. The book also provides performance tuning checklists that enable developers to make their tuning as comprehensive as possible.

Java RMI

By William Grosso
1st Edition November 2001
576 pages, ISBN 1-56592-452-5

Enterprise Java developers, especially those working with Enterprise JavaBeans, and Jini, need to understand RMI technology in order to write today's complex, distributed applications. O'Reilly's *Java RMI* thoroughly explores and explains this powerful but often overlooked technology. Included is a wealth of real-world examples that developers can implement and customize.

Learning Java

By Pat Niemeyer & Jonathan Knudsen
1st Edition, May 2000
726 pages, Includes CD-ROM
ISBN 1-56592-718-4

For programmers either just migrating to Java or already working steadily in the forefront of Java development, *Learning Java* gives a clear, systematic overview of the Java 2 Standard Edition. It covers the essentials of hot topics like Swing and JFC; describes new tools for signing applets; and shows how to write networked clients and servers, servlets, JavaBeans, and state-of-the-art user interfaces. Includes a CD-ROM containing the Java 2 SDK, version 1.3.

Java Internationalization

By Andy Deitsch & David Czarnecki
1st Edition March 2001
451 pages, ISBN 0-596-00019-7

Java Internationalization shows how to write software that is truly multilingual, using Java's very sophisticated Unicode internationalization facilities. Java Internationalization brings Java developers up to speed for the new generation of software development: writing software that is no longer limited by language boundaries.

Java Cookbook

By Ian Darwin
1st Edition June 2001
882 pages, ISBN 0-59600-170-3

This book offers Java developers short, focused pieces of code that are easy to incorporate into other programs. The idea is to focus on things that are useful, tricky, or both. The book's code segments cover all of the dominant APIs and many specialized APIs and should serve as a great "jumping-off place" for Java developers who want to get started in areas outside their specialization.

O'REILLY®

TO ORDER: **800-998-9938** • **order@oreilly.com** • **www.oreilly.com**
ONLINE EDITIONS OF MOST O'REILLY TITLES ARE AVAILABLE BY SUBSCRIPTION AT **safari.oreilly.com**
ALSO AVAILABLE AT MOST RETAIL AND ONLINE BOOKSTORES

Java

Java Servlet Programming, 2nd Edition

By Jason Hunter with William Crawford
2nd Edition April 2001
780 pages, ISBN 0-596-00040-5

The second edition of this popular book has been completely updated to add the new features of the Java Servlet API Version 2.2, and new chapters on servlet security and advanced communication. In addition to complete coverage of the 2.2 specification, we have included bonus material on the new 2.3 version of the specification.

Java & XML, 2nd Edition

By Brett McLaughlin
2nd Edition September 2001
528 pages, ISBN 0-596-000197-5

New chapters on Advanced SAX, Advanced DOM, SOAP, and data binding, as well as new examples throughout, bring the second edition of *Java & XML* thoroughly up to date. Except for a concise introduction to XML basics, the book focuses entirely on using XML from Java applications. It's a worthy companion for Java developers working with XML or involved in messaging, web services, or the new peer-to-peer movement.

JavaServer Pages

By Hans Bergsten
1st Edition December 2000
572 pages, ISBN 1-56592-746-X

JavaServer Pages shows how to develop Java-based web applications without having to be a hardcore programmer. The author provides an overview of JSP concepts and illuminates how JSP fits into the larger picture of web applications. There are chapters for web authors on generating dynamic content, handling session information, and accessing databases, as well as material for Java programmers on creating Java components and custom JSP tags for web authors to use in JSP pages.

Java and XSLT

By Eric M. Burke
1st Edition September 2001
528 pages, ISBN 0-596-00143-6

Learn how to use XSL transformations in Java programs ranging from stand-alone applications to servlets. *Java and XSLT* introduces XSLT and then shows you how to apply transformations in real-world situations, such as developing a discussion forum, transforming documents from one form to another, and generating content for wireless devices.

Enterprise JavaBeans, 3rd Edition

By Richard Monson-Haefel
3rd Edition September 2001
592 pages, ISBN 0-596-00226-2

Enterprise JavaBeans has been thoroughly updated for the new EJB Specification. Important changes in Version 2.0 include a completely new CMP (container-managed persistence) model that allows for much more complex business function modeling; local interfaces that will significantly improve performance of EJB applications; and the "message driven bean," an entirely new kind of Java bean based on asynchronous messaging and the Java Message Service.

Java Message Service

By Richard Monson-Haefel &
David Chappell
1st Edition December 2000
238 pages, ISBN 0-596-00068-5

This book is a thorough introduction to Java Message Service (JMS) from Sun Microsystems. It shows how to build applications using the point-to-point and publish-and-subscribe models; use features like transactions and durable subscriptions to make applications reliable; and use messaging within Enterprise JavaBeans. It also introduces a new EJB type, the MessageDrivenBean, that is part of EJB 2.0, and discusses integration of messaging into J2EE.

O'REILLY®

TO ORDER: *800-998-9938* • *order@oreilly.com* • *www.oreilly.com*
ONLINE EDITIONS OF MOST O'REILLY TITLES ARE AVAILABLE BY SUBSCRIPTION AT **safari.oreilly.com**
ALSO AVAILABLE AT MOST RETAIL AND ONLINE BOOKSTORES

How to stay in touch with O'Reilly

1. Visit Our Award-Winning Web Site

http://www.oreilly.com/

★ "Top 100 Sites on the Web" —PC Magazine
★ CIO Magazine's Web Business 50 Awards

Our web site contains a library of comprehensive product information (including book excerpts and tables of contents), downloadable software, background articles, interviews with technology leaders, links to relevant sites, book cover art, and more. File us in your bookmarks or favorites!

2. Join Our Email Mailing Lists

Sign up to get email announcements of new books and conferences, special offers, and O'Reilly Network technology newsletters at:
elists.oreilly.com.
It's easy to customize your free elists subscription so you'll get exactly the O'Reilly news you want.

3. Get Examples from Our Books

To find example files for a book, go to:
http://www.oreilly.com/catalog
select the book, and follow the "Examples" link.

4. Contact Us via Email

order@oreilly.com
For answers to problems regarding your order or our products. To place a book order online visit:
http://www.oreilly.com/order_new/

catalog@oreilly.com
To request a copy of our latest catalog.

booktech@oreilly.com
For book content technical questions or corrections.

proposals@oreilly.com
To submit new book proposals to our editors and product managers.

international@oreilly.com
For information about our international distributors or translation queries. For a list of our distributors outside of North America check out:
http://international.oreilly.com/distributors.html

5. Work with Us

Check out our web site for current employment opportunites:
http://jobs.oreilly.com/

6. Register your book

Register your book at:
http://register.oreilly.com

O'Reilly & Associates, Inc.
1005 Gravenstein Hwy North
Sebastopol, CA 95472 USA
TEL   707-827-7000 or 800-998-9938
        (6am to 5pm PST)
FAX   707-829-0104

O'REILLY®

TO ORDER: **800-998-9938** • order@oreilly.com • www.oreilly.com
ONLINE EDITIONS OF MOST O'REILLY TITLES ARE AVAILABLE BY SUBSCRIPTION AT **safari.oreilly.com**
ALSO AVAILABLE AT MOST RETAIL AND ONLINE BOOKSTORES

International Distributors

http://international.oreilly.com/distributors.html • international@oreilly.com

UK, EUROPE, MIDDLE EAST, AND AFRICA (EXCEPT FRANCE, GERMANY, AUSTRIA, SWITZERLAND, LUXEMBOURG, AND LIECHTENSTEIN)

INQUIRIES
O'Reilly UK Limited
4 Castle Street
Farnham
Surrey, GU9 7HS
United Kingdom
Telephone: 44-1252-711776
Fax: 44-1252-734211
Email: information@oreilly.co.uk

ORDERS
Wiley Distribution Services Ltd.
1 Oldlands Way
Bognor Regis
West Sussex PO22 9SA
United Kingdom
Telephone: 44-1243-843294
UK Freephone: 0800-243207
Fax: 44-1243-843302 (Europe/EU orders)
or 44-1243-843274 (Middle East/Africa)
Email: cs-books@wiley.co.uk

FRANCE

INQUIRIES & ORDERS
Éditions O'Reilly
18 rue Séguier
75006 Paris, France
Tel: 33-1-40-51-71-89
Fax: 33-1-40-51-72-26
Email: france@oreilly.fr

GERMANY, SWITZERLAND, AUSTRIA, LUXEMBOURG, AND LIECHTENSTEIN

INQUIRIES & ORDERS
O'Reilly Verlag
Balthasarstr. 81
D-50670 Köln, Germany
Telephone: 49-221-973160-91
Fax: 49-221-973160-8
Email: anfragen@oreilly.de (inquiries)
Email: order@oreilly.de (orders)

CANADA
(FRENCH LANGUAGE BOOKS)
Les Éditions Flammarion ltée
375, Avenue Laurier Ouest
Montréal, QC H2V 2K3 Canada
Tel: 1-514-277-8807
Fax: 1-514-278-2085
Email: info@flammarion.qc.ca

HONG KONG
City Discount Subscription Service, Ltd.
Unit A, 6th Floor, Yan's Tower
27 Wong Chuk Hang Road
Aberdeen, Hong Kong
Tel: 852-2580-3539
Fax: 852-2580-6463
Email: citydis@ppn.com.hk

KOREA
Hanbit Media, Inc.
Chungmu Bldg. 210
Yonnam-dong 568-33
Mapo-gu
Seoul, Korea
Tel: 822-325-0397
Fax: 822-325-9697
Email: hant93@chollian.dacom.co.kr

PHILIPPINES
Global Publishing
G/F Benavides Garden
1186 Benavides Street
Manila, Philippines
Tel: 632-254-8949/632-252-2582
Fax: 632-734-5060/632-252-2733
Email: globalp@pacific.net.ph

TAIWAN
O'Reilly Taiwan
1st Floor, No. 21, Lane 295
Section 1, Fu-Shing South Road
Taipei, 106 Taiwan
Tel: 886-2-27099669
Fax: 886-2-27038802
Email: mori@oreilly.com

INDIA
Shroff Publishers & Distributors PVT. LTD.
C-103, MIDC, TTC Pawane
Navi Mumbai 400 701
India
Tel: (91-22) 763 4290, 763 4293
Fax: (91-22) 768 3337
Email: spdorders@shroffpublishers.com

CHINA
O'Reilly Beijing
SIGMA Building, Suite B809
No. 49 Zhichun Road
Haidian District
Beijing, China PR 100080
Tel: 86-10-8809-7475
Fax: 86-10-8809-7463
Email: beijing@oreilly.com

JAPAN
O'Reilly Japan, Inc.
Yotsuya Y's Building
7 Banch 6, Honshio-cho
Shinjuku-ku
Tokyo 160-0003 Japan
Tel: 81-3-3356-5227
Fax: 81-3-3356-5261
Email: japan@oreilly.com

SINGAPORE, INDONESIA, MALAYSIA, AND THAILAND
TransQuest Publishers Pte Ltd
30 Old Toh Tuck Road #05-02
Sembawang Kimtrans Logistics Centre
Singapore 597654
Tel: 65-4623112
Fax: 65-4625761
Email: wendiw@transquest.com.sg

AUSTRALIA
Woodslane Pty., Ltd.
7/5 Vuko Place
Warriewood NSW 2102
Australia
Tel: 61-2-9970-5111
Fax: 61-2-9970-5002
Email: info@woodslane.com.au

NEW ZEALAND
Woodslane New Zealand, Ltd.
21 Cooks Street (P.O. Box 575)
Waganui, New Zealand
Tel: 64-6-347-6543
Fax: 64-6-345-4840
Email: info@woodslane.com.au

ARGENTINA
Distribuidora Cuspide
Suipacha 764
1008 Buenos Aires
Argentina
Phone: 54-11-4322-8868
Fax: 54-11-4322-3456
Email: libros@cuspide.com

ALL OTHER COUNTRIES
O'Reilly & Associates, Inc.
1005 Gravenstein Hwy North,
Sebastopol, CA 95472 USA
Tel: 707-827-7000
Fax: 707-829-0104
Email: order@oreilly.com

O'REILLY®

TO ORDER: **800-998-9938** • order@oreilly.com • www.oreilly.com
ONLINE EDITIONS OF MOST O'REILLY TITLES ARE AVAILABLE BY SUBSCRIPTION AT **safari.oreilly.com**
ALSO AVAILABLE AT MOST RETAIL AND ONLINE BOOKSTORES